The Psychoanalytic Study
of the Child

VOLUME XI

The Psychoanalytic Study

of the Child

VOLUME XI

INTERNATIONAL UNIVERSITIES PRESS, INC.
New York   New York

Second Printing, 1962

Manufactured in the United States of America

CONTENTS

Theoretical Contributions

Normal and Pathological Development

Clinical Contributions

Applied Psychoanalysis

THEORETICAL CONTRIBUTIONS

EXPERIENCES OF AWE IN CHILDHOOD[1]

PHYLLIS GREENACRE, M.D. (New York)[2]

I

The present paper is a continuation and an expansion of a paper published in 1953. That paper was concerned chiefly with the difference between awe and envy, especially awe and envy of the phallus, and the effect of the interplay between these two emotional states on girls. This leads to further questions regarding the presence of such states in boys and their sequelae in later life. These then will be the main foci of this contribution. But I wish also to present some additional considerations regarding the experience of awe—awe which is not manifestly or consciously centered on the phallus. I must add, however, that the link back to the phallus is certainly often present.

The term *awe* has been used, at different times, with many different shades of meaning, accenting one or another facet in this complex state: "terror or dread"; "dread mingled with veneration, as of the Divine Being"; "solemn and reverential wonder tinged with latent fear inspired by what is sublime and majestic in nature"; "anger, fierceness and rage."[3] There is usually an overtone of strangeness or unfamiliarity or great and overpowering size in any awe-inspiring situation.

The first experiences of awe can occur only after the child is sufficiently developed to realize himself fairly well as a separately functioning being, no longer confused between the I and the other, whether the other be animate or inanimate object. There may be a reflection of himself and his inner feelings in the outer world, or the sensing of something from the outside may stir some very specific bodily and psychic emotional response in him—but the near fusion is past. In looking over the records of my clinical work, I am impressed with the fact that experiences of awe are first reported from the age of four or five, rarely earlier—that rather crucial experiences seem to occur sometimes at six or seven and again at adolescence.

[1] Read as the Brill Memorial Lecture at the New York Academy of Medicine, March 20, 1956.
[2] From the New York Hospital and the Department of Psychiatry, Cornell University Medical College, New York.
[3] See *Oxford English Dictionary*.

Since specific illustations are needed and since for many reasons it seems desirable not to call extensively and explicitly on the material furnished by my patients, I shall rely, for descriptions of childhood states of awe, on accounts which have already been published by others. For this purpose I have selected five examples: three of these are from auto-biographical accounts of rather gifted men, one from a work of fiction, in which the account must be regarded as some projection from the author himself; while the fifth is from a biography of a woman who lived so long ago that one must accept the story as a precipitate, formed from the individual experience but molded by and meeting the inner needs of the countless biographers through whom the story has been passed.

Albert Schweitzer (1955), writing with delightful simplicity of his Alsatian childhood, describes his first recollection of all as a most terri-fyingly awful one of seeing the devil each Sunday morning as he sat in his father's church listening to and thrilled by the sound of the organ. All week he looked forward to the experience, as it appears that there was some pleasure in it too. Each Sunday he saw with terror the face of the devil appear in a metal frame beside the organ, while the positive elements of the experience were reflected in his feeling toward the organ music itself and especially toward the father whose preaching invariably announced the disappearance of the devil. This recollection is told with all the vividness of a screen memory. Its significance is further brought out by the next anecdotal recollections. The little boy developed himself a fear of growing horns, a fear which was painfully emphasized by the teasing sexton. To quote from Schweitzer's own account:

> The terror of my childhood was the Sacristan and gravedigger. . . . Every Sunday morning when he had rung the bells and come to the manse to learn the numbers of the hymns to be sung and to get the needed things for baptisms, he would make a grab at my forehead and say, "Yes, the horns are really growing!" These horns were my bugbear. I had, as a matter of fact, two rather prominent lumps on my forehead and these had filled me with most unpleasant thoughts ever since in the Bible I had seen a picture of Moses with horns. How the Sacristan had learnt of my worry I do not know, but he knew of it and fanned its flame. When he was at the door on Sundays wiping his feet before he rang the bell, I longed to run away, but he had me in his power, as a snake has the fascinated rabbit. I could do nothing but simply go to meet him, feel his hand on my forehead and listen submissively to the fatal declaration.

The little boy was reassured when his father told him that Moses was the only man who had horns. Similarly he had been relieved of his church-devil terror when he came to realize that the face of the devil peering at him from the frame beside the organ was that of the organist reflected in a mirror which was fastened near the organ in a position to let the player see when the father preacher was at the altar and when he went up to the pulpit.

Still another incident, told by Schweitzer, belongs integrally with the two already given. It relates to his feeling of embarrassment at having unwittingly shown off. Even before his school years, when he had begun to have music lessons from his father, he did not play much from notes, but was delighted to improvise and to reproduce songs and hymn tunes with an accompaniment of his own invention. In the singing lesson, however, the woman teacher continually played the hymn tunes with one finger and no accompaniment.

> I asked why she did not play it properly with the harmony. Then in my enthusiasm I sat down at the harmonium and played it straight away to her out of my head, but with harmony in several parts. Then she became very friendly with me, and used to look at me in a new and unusual way, but went on herself always picking out the tunes with one finger only. Then it occurred to me that I could do something which she could not, and I was ashamed at having made a show before her of my ability which I had till then taken as something which I possessed as a matter of course.

It is probably further significant that this embarrassing superiority of ability was sensed in regard to a female teacher. The terror of his earlier awe and fascination was now quieted by the realization of his own power, probably first shared with and then venturing beyond his father.

Indeed, Schweitzer verifies this with a further anecdote regarding his new-found critical perspective and enlarged horizons. After an unusually wet summer, probably when he was six or seven, he surprised his father with the remark, "Why, it must have been raining here now for nearly forty days and forty nights but the water has not yet got up to the houses, much less to the tops of mountains!" His father adroitly saved face by explaining that at the time of the beginning of the world it did not rain just drops, but buckets full of water. This seemed to assuage his dissatisfaction, but one senses a compromise. For soon in school when the teacher told the story of the Flood without explaining the difference in rain then and now, young Albert aggressively interrupted her, supplied the missing information, and reproached her for her inexactness, but was soon entered again into a season of skeptical questioning of the Bible stories which began to seem improbable and full of flaws.

A somewhat similar picture of childhood awe, from a fictional source, brings out clearly the responsive body feelings of hyperanimation when the terror part of the awe is overcome. The account is of a very young child in church with his grandfather. He is bored. He is not comfortable. The people look solemn and gloomy. He is a little afraid, and he becomes fidgety, digging at the straw of the chair seat to make a hole if possible.

> Suddenly there is a deluge of sound; the organ is played. A thrill goes down his spine. He turns and stands with his chin resting on the back of his chair, and he looks very wise. He does not understand this noise; he does not know the meaning of it; it is dazzling, bewildering, and he can hear nothing clearly. But it is good. It is as though he were no longer sitting there on an uncomfortable chair in a tiresome old house. He is suspended in mid-air like a bird; and when the flood of sound rushes from one end of the church to the other, filling the arches, reverberating from wall to wall, he is carried with it, flying and skimming hither and thither, with nothing to do but abandon himself to it. He is free, he is happy. The sun shines. . . . He falls asleep. . . . His grandfather is displeased with him He behaves ill at Mass.

Later he has become a magician.

> He walks with great strides through the fields, looking at the sky and waving his arms. He commanded the clouds. He wished them to go to the right but they went to the left. Then he would abuse them out of the corner of his eye, and his heart would beat as he looked to see if there were not at least a little one which would obey him. But they went on calmly moving to the left. Then he would stamp his foot and threaten them with his stick, and angrily order them to go to the left, and this time, in truth, they obeyed him. He was happy and proud of his power.

I quote from Romain Rolland's *Jean Christophe*. It will be remembered that the little boy's father and grandfather were both musicians.

The three other clinical examples of awe in childhood have been taken, one from the life of St. Catherine of Siena, one from the autobiographical account of Edmund Gosse, and one from the autobiography of Herbert Read: Italy in the fourteenth century compared with England in the nineteenth.

Catherine's first vision occurred at the age of five. The child is described as gay, overactive, tempestuous and charming; already nicknamed Euphrosyne, the child of Joy. I quote the story as given by Mrs. Aubrey Richardson (n.d.).

> Coming back with her brother, Stefano, a boy probably only a year or two older than herself, from the house of their married sister, Bonaventure, the children crossed the valley that separated the hill upon which the towering transept of the magnificent Duomo dominates the city, from that crowned by the gaunt vast church of San

Domenico. Gazing upward as she turned to climb the street that led to . . . her home, the child of quick and contemplative imagination saw above the sky-obscuring church roof, a group of wondrous personages who could but be associated for her with the church and with the Heavens. Our Lord was in the vesture imposed upon the mind of tiny Catherine as the most sacred and awe-inspiring garb imaginable. He wore the robes and the tiara of the Pope of Rome. With the Savior were St. Peter, St. Paul, and St. John the Evangelist backed by a crowd of white robed figures. The flash of the sudden picture upon the sensitive mind of the child . . . stunned all thought in her. She gazed in ecstasy, holding the vision in view by the wrapt intensity of her delight in it.

And from the account of Mrs. Augusta Theodosia Drame, the child

continued to stand and gaze, wholly absorbed and as it were united spiritually with that most glorious Lord whom she there beheld, so that she forgot not only whither she was going, but her own self also, and remained there motionless, giving no heed to men or beasts that passed that way; and so she would have remained even longer had no one called her away. But at last her brother, Stephen, who had gone on his way . . . turned back, and seeing her thus standing still in the midst of the road and gazing into the air, called her name aloud, but she gave him no answer and seemed not so much as to hear him. Then he drew near, still calling her, until at last coming up to the spot where she stood he took her by the hand, saying, "What are you doing? Why are you staying here?" . . . Roused as it were out of a deep sleep, . . . she cast down her eyes, and looking at him for a moment, "Oh did you but see the sight I saw," she said, "never would you have disturbed me." Then she once more raised her eyes, thinking again to have seen the lovely vision; but all had vanished; and full of grief she began to weep bitterly, supposing that she had through her own fault, by turning away her looks, deserved to lose that precious favor.

Having returned home, she said nothing to father or mother of what she had seen, but from that day there grew up in her a certain carefulness of soul, a fear and remorse of conscience and dread of committing sin as far as was possible to one of her age. And ever as she grew in years there increased in her this anxiety and she bethought her what means she might take to offend God less, and was always seeking to be alone, and to steal away somewhere out of her parents' sight that she might say her prayers in secret.

Whether or not Catherine's vision of awe and magnificence was, as Mrs. Richardson implies, a vivid impression of an evening sunset, perhaps an afterimage projected onto the buildings which then obscured the sky; whether indeed it was really an individual experience at all, or perhaps a kernel of individual experience accepted and elaborated by those to whom it was communicated until it emerged as an appealing religious fairy tale—we need not be concerned just now with the precise ratio of objectivity and subjectivity. That it was enormously subjectively stirring not only to one but to many, and that it was accepted as occurring at the age of five—these are matters of special interest.

The early memories from Edmund Gosse's childhood are in sharp contrast to that of the little Catherine on the Italian hillside. Gosse relates them in *Father and Son* (1934), which, he says, is the record of a struggle between two temperaments, two consciences, and almost two epochs—a struggle which ended inevitably in disruption. He was the only child of rather elderly parents who married late. Both enjoyed a moderate contemporary distinction, the father as a zoologist and the mother as a writer of religious verse. Both had had more colorful early years, which contrasted somewhat with the puritanical austerity of their middle years —the father as a zoological explorer in the South Seas, the mother as the only daughter of rich, extravagant, and careless landowners, with an estate on the slope of Mount Snowden in North Wales. Both must how-ever have been severely compulsive, for duty took the place of spon-taneous affection, any show of which was considered unsuitable. They were members of a singularly strict Puritanical sect in the south of England, known as the Brethren or the Plymouth Brethren.

At the time of the birth of this first child and son, the father wrote in his journal: "*E* delivered of a son. Received green swallow from Jamaica." The mother kept a secret journal in which she wrote of her secret devotion to her baby, even preferring his company to that of the "Saints," i.e., the Puritan Brethren.

Edmund Gosse's early awe experiences were expressed in a negative form, with defiance, with debunking—the strength of which indicated the intensity of the hidden emotion which must have preceded, but could under the circumstances not be accepted and felt openly. His very first memory, the date of which was not clear, probably concerned an event in his third or more probably his fourth year. He remarks that he did not talk well yet, but that he was inordinately slow in talking any-way. He sat alone in his baby chair, at a table which was prepared for a number of people. A leg of mutton had been brought in and left upon the table. Two low windows opened onto a garden. Suddenly, noiselessly, an animal head appeared at the window, and then a very large long grey animal (probably a grey hound) leaped quietly into the room, seized the leg of mutton and disappeared again out of the window.

This memory remained the typically distinct isolated screen memory of infancy and it stayed with him, unspoken, as it was originally experienced, until his adult life. Then he mentioned it to some older cousins, who greeted it mirthfully with the response, "That then was what became of the mutton! It was not you, who, as your Uncle A pretended, ate it up in the twinkling of an eye, bone and all!" What is most interesting here is not only the memory itself, the overly distinct impression of the enormous, lithe, and sinuously moving animal apparition and the equally sudden disappearance of both animal and roast, but what was forgotten by him and almost certainly joked about in front of the little child at the time and afterward—viz., the awful suspicion that he had himself taken the leg of mutton and devoured it at a single gulp.

There follow then a series of memories, all discrete, vivid, realistic, and yet screening; and all directed at the father. Against the background of the outbreak of the Crimean War, the little boy, then aged four, was given a stiff soldier "dressed smartly in a red tunic." He admitted it to the company of his two other lady dolls, limp and rather undistinguished specimens, and played indiscriminately with them all. But a maid servant reproached the child: "What, playing with a soldier, when you have got two lady dolls to play with!" After this he played the more with his soldier to make up for the maid's insult. This memory led directly to another of about the same time, that of seeing in their own breakfast room "an amazing figure, a very tall young man as stiff as the doll, in a gorgeous scarlet tunic." His mother sat across the room with her Bible in front of her. Of this he remarks:

> She promptly told me to run away and play, but I had seen a great sight. This guardsman was in the act of leaving for the Crimea—. He was killed in battle, and this added an extraordinary lustre to my dream of him.[4] I see him still in my mind's eye, large, stiff, and unspeakably brilliant, seated as near as possible to our parlor door. This apparition gave reality to my subsequent conversations with the soldier doll.

Again there is a memory of the father standing with his back to the light, reading with excitement from the newspaper concerning the Battle of the Alma—breaking off so that he and the mother might sink to their knees in prayer when they were assured of the decisive victory. The debunking had begun, for the critical child felt a belittlement of the father in this, the father who had previously referred to himself as a citizen of no earthly state and claimed to put his heavenly citizenship

[4] His adventures, his conversion, and his death were later told in a tract written by the mother, called "The Guardsman of the Alma." Half a million copies were circulated and must have contributed much to the aura around the mother.

above all earthly claims. The little boy was developing. As he says in later years,

> In consequence of hearing so much about an omniscient God . . . who was always with us . . . I had come to think of Him, not without awe, but with absolute confidence . . . My mother always deferred to my father and in his absence spoke of him as all wise. I confused him in some sense with God; at all events, I believed that my father knew everything and saw everything.

Then there came another clear memory, a shock as of a thunderbolt when the child realized that what the father said was not true. The mother too detected the inaccuracy and the father accepted the correction. It was all simple. But God had been destroyed. He had yielded to his wife. The shock was not caused by any suspicion that he was deliberately lying, but only by "the awful proof" that he was not omniscient. The boy continued to put both father and God to his own tests; he put a chair on a table and prayed to it to see if God would really punish him, as his father had told him idolatry, which meant prayer to the stone or wood, was evil and brought down God's wrath.

There was emerging in this what Edmund Gosse, the adult, referred to as "a consciousness of self, as a force and as a companion"; a self-realization which was further solidified by a second shock. The father had built a rockery for ferns and mosses, and was preparing to construct a fountain from a piece of lead pipe. The rebelliously investigative child, seeing a workman's tool at hand, tried to see if the tool would make a hole in the pipe. It did, and the event was soon forgotten, to be remembered later when the fountain, constructed, would not function, but, leaking at its base, ruined the rockery. The father's anger was directed toward a workman, who was presumed to have done the mischief. The real culprit was not detected, neither was he devastated—the act was his conquest of his father. Yet its conflict was never really solved, a fact to which the whole of the book bore testimony. Nor could it be solved in so direct a way, for it was obvious that much of the father had been taken in and made part of the boy himself, and the inner struggle could not be silenced by an outer victory.

But the description of the duality of the subjective state is interesting:

> But of all the thoughts that rushed upon my savage and undeveloped little brain at this crisis, the most curious was that I had found a companion and a confidant in myself. There was a secret in this world and it belonged to me and to a *somebody* who lived in the same body with me. There were two of us, and we could talk to one another. It is difficult to define impressions so rudimentary but it is

certain that it was in this dual form that the sense of my individuality now suddenly descended upon me, and it is certain that it was a great solace to me to find a sympathizer in my own breast.

The period that followed this is so well-described and so characteristic of developments, some of which I shall emphasize later in this paper, that at the expense of boring with quotation, I shall use Gosse himself further as a clinical example. Following the emergence of his confidential self in the little Edmund, the child and parents seemed to draw unwittingly apart, both sides involved in separate and antagonistic pursuits. The little boy repaired to the attic, where he busied himself in magic plays of various sorts, all attempts to aggrandize himself and assert his power, supplemented by scantily veiled oedipal fantasies of rescuing his mother from distress. He believed that if he could only discover the proper word to say or the proper passes to make, he might induce the gorgeous birds and butterflies in his father's illustrated manuals to come to life, fly out of the books, leaving holes behind them. He thought that in chapel he might be able to boom forth with a sound equal to a dozen singers, if he could only find the right formula. He hoped, too, to liberate, with the proper magic key, one of the two selves within him, who might then fly up during prayers and sit aloof on the cornice looking down at his other self and his parents still praying. He counted numbers in endless series and with demands for complete perfection to achieve his magic, but did not achieve it. Still unaware of his guilt feelings, he developed magic formulas demanding running pins into himself and otherwise hurting himself. And finally so great was his rage that it burst forth in a wild frenzy from which he sought comfort, which he could not accept, from this same father.

The last example is taken from the autobiography of Herbert Read (1940). He regards early childhood as years of singular innocence. Although he grants that "the child may have a natural craving for horrors," still he regards himself as unaffected by the bloody scenes of slaughter, birth of animals and lewdness of farm hands—dramatic events experienced, he believes, with the "complete passivity of innocence." "Pity and even terror are emotions which develop when we are no longer innocent." It is clear from Read's account that innocence ends somewhere around the age of five, for by six he was suffering terrors which he later believed to be nightmares, though they were related in memory with an extraordinary sense of pressing reality. Just about the time of the turn from innocence to experience (Read's autobiography is called *Annals of Innocence and Experience*), there was an incident when he saw his usually temperate, thoughtful, and wise father go into a state of rage because a stupid farm hand overworked a pregnant mare and caused a miscarriage. The physical event as well as the father's reaction was observed by the boy. This memory which is recorded as a "terrible scene" is followed by accounts of the Machine God—namely, the visit of the threshing machine to the farm. Now follow at the age of six, his two hyperreal experiences, which he was convinced were dreams though he could never quite believe this. They were experiences of the greatest horror. Again quotation seems best:

> I "appeared" to walk down the cart track that led along the topside of two or three fields toward Peacock's farms. I climbed onto the gate . . . I was terrified by the sudden onrush of a large steamroller, travelling northwards. It was distinguished from ordinary steamrollers which I had no doubt seen at work on the roads, by the fact that the boiler rested on an enormous bellows, and as the engine rolled onwards, these bellows worked up and down and so seemed to throw up through the chimney a fiery column of smoke, steam and sparks. This apparition which came to me perhaps in my seventh year (i.e., at the age of six) remains in my mind today distinct in every detail.

> I do not believe that I was more than usually subject to nightmares (if such this was), but one is also remembered by me with peculiar vividness, though it is difficult to describe. I am laid as in a bed on a bank of clouds. The sky darkens, grows bluish black. Then the darkness seems to take visible shape, to separate into long bolsters, or objects which I would now compare to airships. These then point themselves toward me and approach me, magnifying themselves enormously as they get nearer. I awake with a shriek, quivering with terror. My mother comes quickly to comfort me, perhaps to take me back with her to sleep away the sudden terror.

Elsewhere in his account of himself, Read gives a picture of his reaction to the violin, in a way which reminds us of Schweitzer and Jean Christophe with the organ; and of a growing faith in himself and his inner disposition, more complete and freer of conflict, but suggestively similar to Gosse's "consciousness of self as a force and a companion."[5]

[5] One could cite many other examples. The recent autobiography of C. S. Lewis (1955), entitled *Surprised by Joy*, gives one of the most interesting descriptions of ecstatic Moses-like awe—which he compares to Milton's "Enormous bliss"—giving the full and ancient meaning to the word *enormous* (i.e., monstrous). He described this occurrence as a memory of a memory. As he stood beside a flowering currant bush on a summer day there suddenly arose in him without warning, as if from the depths of not years but of centuries, the memory of an earlier morning in the Old House where his brother had brought his toy garden into the garden. The evoking of this memory produced a sensation of desire—which went almost before he knew what he desired, and the world was turned commonplace again. The experience had taken only a moment of time, but in a certain sense everything else that ever happened later was insignificant in comparison.

II

It will be noted that in these clinical examples, the experience of awe in early chidhood was closely associated with relationship to the father, even in the manifest content. In all instances there was a religious atmosphere. In the cases of the four boys, a father or grandfather was present either in the original awe or wonderment experience, or in associated memories immediately connected with it. In the case of the little Catherine, the brother was present, but the awful vision was of the Heavenly Father direct. From the case material of patients, it seems that this difference between the sexes in the experince of awe or extreme wonder is fairly typical: namely, that in males the route to the father may be generally more easily traceable than in girls, in whom the whole experience may be felt either as a shock or in a more detached and diffusely exalted way (Greenacre, 1947). We are grateful to the literary ladies and gentlemen for giving us these detailed accounts, but must rely now more on our own clinical studies for the rest of this paper.

Surely the memories cited are for the most part typical screen memories. It is evident too that the awe, extreme wonder or terror has come in response to experience involving the show of masculine strength, power, glory, virility, or of the phallus itself. In the case of Read, however, there is an additional element, in that the sight of the distressed parturient mare probably combined with the effect of the enraged father to give the peculiarly terrifying aspect to the Machine God and of the threatening gigantic airplanes. The vicissitudes of phallic awe in boys will form the basis of the rest of this paper. The related problem of masculine awe of pregnancy, so apparent also in the worship of the Virgin Mary, cannot now be dealt with at all. One other special limitation of the material of this paper should be mentioned. Perhaps it is an inconsistency that all of the examples of early awe here cited have been reported by extraor-

---

An experience very similar to Lewis' is reported by Walter Pater (1895), writing of himself in the third person:

"As he walked one evening, a garden gate, usually closed, stood open; and lo! a great red hawthorn in full flower, embossing heavily the bleached and twisted trunk and branches. . . [He] was now allowed to fill his arms with the flowers,—flowers enough for all the old blue china pots along the chimney piece. . . The beauty of the thing struck home to him feverishly; and in dreams all night he loitered along a magic roadway of crimson flowers, which seemed to open ruddily in thick fresh masses . . . and fill all the hollows in the banks on either side. . . A touch of regret or desire mingled all night with the remembered presence of the red flowers, and their perfume in the darkness about him; and the longing for some undivined entire possession of them was the beginning of a revelation to him. . . a kind of tyranny of the senses over him."

dinarily gifted people, whereas the rest of the paper will deal with material from a psychoanalytic consulting room, where certainly there are many bright and even moderately talented patients, but not many Saint Catherines or Schweitzers. It is impressive to me, however, how much the descriptions given resemble those of my patients and how much they actually have in common. Even so, it seems that potential genius may give differences in overtones and textures sometimes perceptible quite early and sometimes only discernible much later. It is possible that some portion of what is utilized in the developmental unfolding of the very gifted person may become more firmly precipitated in the neurosis of the less favored one.

It has already been noted that the first remembrances of awe are placed at the age of four or five, i.e., during the phallic-oedipal period. This was true also among my patients. This seems natural indeed since at this period not only is the entire body enlivened, but there is simultaneously a marked rise in the genital thrust and in the focal sensitivity of the genital organs. The motor play seems increasingly activated by and patterned after the genital pressure. Moreover, the very selectivity of perceptive responses to the outer world is increasingly similarly determined. The whole body is invigorated to feats of jumping, leaping, and dreams of flying; and the choice of toys and even the awareness of shapes and forms in the surroundings reflect the inner body feelings.[6] Both projective

[6] A beautiful description of the invigoration of the phallic phase, combined probably with that of the period at fifteen to eighteen months, when the child has just learned to walk and is also undergoing a marked flowering of sensory stimulation, is given by Pierre Loti (1890).

"One evening stands out as clearly in my mind as if it were last night—the one when I all of a sudden found out how to run and jump: and how carried away I was by the exquisiteness of this new idea, so much so that I could not stand up straight.

"This would be about the beginning of my second winter, during the hour of gloom when night is falling. . . A servant came and threw an armful of twigs on the dying embers in the fireplace and straightway a gay and beautiful set of flames illuminated everything. . . And these flames danced, changed their shapes, intermingled; leaping and rioting more and more. . . Oh, then I stood straight up, astounded, in ecstasy. . . and moved nearer these flames and. . . began to walk around, turning quicker and quicker until I felt a sudden elasticity in my legs and invented a new and entertaining way of behaving. . . Thence forward I knew how to jump and run. . . But furthermore, when I ran, I was thinking. . . very hard and differently from usual. . . A clearness and vividness shot through that brain of mine, whose ideas lay still amid the mists of dawn." (He next describes the awareness of difference between animate and inanimate objects, of the chairs from the people who habitually sat in them.) ". . . and it may be, there and then began a consciousness of affections for aunts and grandmothers. . . whom I wanted to see sitting around me as usual." (This is then followed by an account of developing panics regarding open doors and the dark which continued throughout childhood.)

While Loti places this at the beginning of the second year, it must be remembered

and introjective attitudes may be under the genital dominance. This seems usually greater in boys than in girls—perhaps because of stronger phallic feelings than those experienced in the clitoris by the girl; but probably also because of the reinforcement of these subjective feelings by the greater visual and tactile participation of the male genitals in the total body image and functioning.

It is understandable then that the little boy of four or so may be more alert and responsive to the sight of the adult male organ than he has been earlier. Certainly in most households the child sees his father in the bath or in the bathroom at some time. He has some opportunity thus to reinforce his sense of his own body and of himself. This does not always lead to awe or even to extreme wonder, but rather it is assimilated into his growth and development—through his ambitiously interested response. If, however, he sees the father or some other adult male in a state of tumescent excitement, the effect is more complicated. This may be in part due to the fact that such a situation is most apt to arise under conditions which do not permit of the same friendly intimacy as the bathroom. The child feels alienated and separate and is impressed by the general as well as the local body excitement, although the fascination seems most often to be with the phallus itself. It substantiates the strange magical responses which the child is experiencing in himself.

There is a set of circumstances which, among my cases, has seemed the source of some further susceptibility to phallic awe reactions in the child. Especially in boys who are the youngest children or greatly petted by the mother, there is an increase in the secondary gain of remaining the baby—with the emphasis on being little and cute. This is most marked when there is a considerable gap between this youngest boy child and the older children, or if the boy is both the youngest child and the only boy in the family. Such boys may remain in intimate contact with the mothers—even to the point of some identification. The discrepancy between the body and early self-image of the child and that of the father, especially as perceived in the phallic-oedipal periods, is unusually intensified and accentuates the feeling in the child of having only a *very* little penis. The child is then at a disadvantage in the oedipal struggle and may fall back further into a more complete feminine identification, but retain the longing for the power of the paternal phallus. Particularly in those cases where the father is physically strong and sexually active but is not very successful in other respects in life and the

---

that this is the time of learning to walk. Jumping is not achieved nor awareness of the thoughts, until the age of three to four, the height of the phallic phase. But these two periods of learning to walk and of learning to jump are closely related.

mother is felt as the dominant person in the household, the competitiveness with the father may become very much focused on the genital itself,
and some attempt is made to bolster the situation by endowing the mother
with an illusory penis, much as in the prefetishistic development. But
this is an unsatisfactory compromise bound to ultimate failure. Often it is
very incompletely believed at best.

If the father has become a weak figure, the child reacts with an
increase in the devaluation as part of the oedipal struggle but loses also
his own masculine ideal in this and suffers accordingly. There is then in
many instances, a hunt for a new father ideal, to reinstate the lost image
of the father from the earlier time. This may develop in the direction of
the family romance or it may lead to the precipitation of disturbing
homosexual seduction at the hands of an older boy or man—usually in
the postoedipal period, or early latency. The fantasy wish of the child
is to acquire, visually and orally, the large phallus of the father. When
this is acted out to the extent of an actual homosexual contact, the
experience is generally repressed, but fragments and derivatives of it
remain in symptoms, attitudes and screen memories and reappear in
dreams of awe, with a peculiar religious quality. For example, one patient
had from the beginning of his analysis, a recurrently persistent hallucination of considerable strength that he had a hair in his mouth—later this
shifted to a less intense but troublesome feeling of a hair in his eye,
with itching behind the eye. Another patient developed somnambulistic
behavior in childhood, during which he wandered from his room in a
school dormitory toward that of an older boy, and was discovered kneel-
ing as though in worship of an electric light on the stairway.

In both of these patients, as in several others, the search for the
strong father has been deflected onto a brother or brothers sufficiently
older to have passed puberty, while the younger child was only six or
seven. The younger one was admitted then to masturbatory exhibitions
on the part of the brother and his friends and developed an attitude of
intense admiring envy, to the point of enthrallment, with an accompanying fantasy of possession of the larger more effective ejaculating organ,
very similar indeed to the envy of the little girl who develops and clings
to the possession of an illusory phallus in competition with the boy, whose
organ seems more effective for pleasure than her own. In the setting of a
generally rather sturdy sense of reality, the illusory phallus of great size
has ultimately to be given up. At best it has existed side by side with the
realization of possessing a smaller organ.

In some patients the tendency to retain two self-images seemingly
influenced, though not created, by the two phallic images, lasted through-

out their lives, up to the time of analysis. The successful utilization of cute, precocious, charming or playful baby attitudes was one of the larger obstacles in their developing and claiming anything approximating their own potential abilities in adult life. It also goes, almost without saying, that such instability or variability in the phallic part of the body image predisposes to disturbances of potency and sometimes of fundamental sexual orientation. In some, too, under the pressure of increased castration anxiety at puberty, the illusion of size, ability and strength of phallic prowess becomes allocated to and fixated in competitive fantasies of having great wealth, great fame, great athletic ability, or some other prowess. The fantasy of inheriting great wealth showed, on analysis, a clear link back to the original oedipal struggle and the wish to kill and rob the father. These fantasies, essentially of the Walter Mitty type, might become the habitual way of solace and self-pacification in the face of almost any anxiety. The development permitted then a reversal of the illusory big phallus conviction to the earlier one of having too small an organ, or in some further displacement, the conviction that some other part of the body was inadequate or undeveloped.

Two other sequelae of these and similar early events are especially noteworthy: first, certain urinary symptoms; and second, additional related character traits. While the most telling way of presenting these would be through detailed clinical case reports, both time and discretion make this less feasible.

Urinary problems of one sort or another appear in a fair proportion of male patients suffering from phallic awe. Perhaps the nature and development of these can best be indicated by describing the extreme situation—that of confusion between urination and ejaculation to the point of inability to distinguish between the two, even during intercourse. A minor degree of latent confusion is common enough, evident in the feeling of the patient who awakens from a wet dream believing that he has urinated in bed, only to find that he has had an emission. Or under other circumstances, the patient may have had a dream of urinating and finds on awakening that the urine is indeed seminal fluid. Still a conscious uncertainty of what has occurred during intercourse stands out as something extraordinary, or even bizarre, especially against the background of a generally secure sense of reality. It then has the appearance of a body illusion which, in its tenacity, approaches the form of a delusion.

A couple of hours from one such patient, hours which condense much of what has been less personally presented, may here be helpful. The patient began the hour with the remark that he had drunk a little at

dinner on the preceding evening—not excessively at all, but still a little
more than was his habit—a strong scotch and soda and some wine with
the meal. He had awakened early with a sense of incipient diarrhea,
which had, however, not materialized. During the hour he was still in
this expectant state. He then reported the following dream.

> I was in a group of people. I asked someone about Dr. Robbin
> (a man who was professor in the college I attended). This was not
> so much because I wanted to know about him, as that I wanted others
> to know that I knew him,—to impress them with the fact.
> Next I was flying with Dr. R. and was going to land on an island.
> He was obviously nervous and regretful of having flown. His wife,
> much younger than he, was waiting for him. She had started out at
> the same time we had, but had come much more quickly, having
> arrived by train and subway. I had the feeling, "What if the plane
> had fallen?" And then, "Nothing would happen except the people
> would have gotten wet."

He then continued the hour remarking that he had bit his cold sore (a
labial herpes) during the night, and found in the morning that it was
puffy and swollen. His wife had complained of a sore throat and he
thought her face looked puffy and swollen also. On the night before he
had dined with an old classmate who had prospered greatly and had
talked of his summer place on an island and of his yacht. He had thought
enviously of how well off his former classmate was, especially as the latter
had married such a beautiful actress wife. He next thought of how his
mother blamed his father for the fact that she had not been at her
mother's bedside when she died. The grandmother had been in a frail
condition and the mother had made two or three visits, but "nothing
had happened"—i.e., the old lady did not die, and the mother had returned home. Then one day a bird, either a robin or a swallow, had
flown down the chimney. The mother knew this was a bad omen and
wished to go to her mother. But the father had dissuaded her. Soon they
learned that the omen had proved true, for the grandmother had died.

The patient's thoughts next went to getting money through the death
of others, inheriting money. He thought of another college friend, whose
father had amassed a considerable fortune by possibly shady but pretentious business deals. The son had seemed possibly like the father in
temperament, but was more troubled. He had gone to an analyst for a
time, then stopped and entered a monastery. But after a few months he
withdrew from this also, and was now in California prospering in exactly
the same sort of business as that in which his father had made a fortune.

As for the flight over water, this was like Northern Italy or like
Miami. In the dream, the landing was in a comfortable resort area. Dr.
R. was a man who knew a lot about primitive plant and animal forms,
such as lived in the water. He also knew much about spores which resisted drying up and had written impressive articles in highly technical
language on these subjects. The patient thought this subject of the spores
and the primitive animal life somehow related to his feeling about his

incipient diarrhea, and next recalled that his wife expected her period the next day. Both he and his wife were disappointed in not having a second child, and especially so on the preceding evening when he realized that the other young couples had larger families. He thought that Dr. R. had no children at all. *His* wife was younger, an intellectual woman, who went back to her profession after some years of marriage. He had been feeling very angry at his cold sore. He would like to just erase it, to obliterate it, to rub it out. Only at this pont he remarked that he had awakened with an urge to urinate and had had a slight erection. But he also had an uncomfortable feeling that his penis was small, long and narrow—a very uncomfortable feeling of smallness. Now he recalled that his mother would be flying south the next day. This recalled to him a period at seven, spent in the south, when there had been a time of nocturnal enuresis. He had been rather fat and sluggish. Also he had exhibited himself urinating where little girls could see him. What he did not mention during this hour but had on the day before was that he was expecting his older brother to arrive presently on a business trip. This was the brother who in group masturbatory play had excited his extreme envy, such that he had pretended with self-deluding force that his urination was really an ejacultion.

A second hour some few weeks later brings again the substitution of urination for ejaculation and the confusion about it. At this time the patient entered the analytic room with the statement that he had been having a strange feeling of unreality about the analysis and about me. Who was I anyway? And what was his relationship to me? It was as though everything was only an illusion. The day before he had been aware of sharp twinges of anxiety when he thought of situations in the past when his pretentiousness had not come off well. He wondered why he had found it such a temptation to pretend. He had also developed an itching behind his left eye. He then reported a dream.

> I was riding down the highway with a man of forty-five, a rough laboring man. He had on his lap (i.e., covering his genital area) a book labeled "Shooting Guns"—I knew that this man's son was a crack shot and just by way of keeping up my end of the conversation, I remarked that someone I knew was an especially good shot also.

He then interrupted his dream to say that he had intercourse the night before, which had been most satisfying, quite excellent, in fact. He built up to an orgasm, that is to a pitch of movement and excitement, then rather relaxed and had a pleasant anticipation of the ejaculation before it occurred. It was rather a slow, gentle ejaculation, but very pleasant, though mixed with pain. "Then I was not sure whether it was actually an ejaculation or urination." (His description had already so much impressed me as resembling his earlier description of awaking in childhood with the need to urinate and then allowing himself the pleasure of a slow warm bed wetting that I was not surprised when he reported his dilemma.[7] He then returned to his dream.

[7] See also Abraham (1917).

Some birds were flying by. I thought I did not want to be tested for my ability to shoot.

The man in the dream was associated with his father, who was a man of big and impressive stature but had been unable to make a living, and with me about whose financial position he had been puzzled. He realized then that he had suddenly forgotten my address and had actually substituted a zero for the number one in it. This too seemed strange, since he came to my office every day for many months. He next thought again of a college friend who had come from a modest background, had married a rich girl and now had a town house, a country estate, and occupied a more advanced position in business than he quite merited. He felt envious. This man had everything hunky-dory. But would it collapse; were there flaws in it?—The material of these two hours needs no further specific interpretation. In general it speaks for itself. This patient was one who had earlier been even more generally unclear as to whether he urinated or ejaculated.

All of the patients whom I have analyzed who had such pronounced urinary symptoms had had actual childhood experiences of comparing themselves with postpubery boys or older men whom they saw masturbating. They had been literally spellbound by this and repeated it in fantasy associated with masturbation and with feats of urinary prowess which they passed off on themselves as being ejaculation. It was when this use of pretense became deflected into fantasy competitiveness of other sorts that the invasion of the total character was most severe.

Even in their serious or leading interests these people rarely trust their own judgment, but tend to hunt for a model to copy, although in their fantasies they continue to surpass all others. They are apt to be bitterly envious when reality does not support these latent fantasies. There tends, too, to be an emphasis on form, technique, and appearance, and the achievement of recognition by these rather than on content or substance.

There is another group of patients who show character involvements to be compared somewhat with those whom I have just described. Pretentious and competitive people, also, they tend to exalt themselves in talk, and they impress one as being even less solid in their performances. The quality of self-delusion is not as strong, their pretentions are not as focused, nor do they so nearly approach the dignity of values as in the last group. There is a subjective and rather diffused feeling of being impostrous. The imposter attitude, however, is not represented in action in any dramatic or daring way—that is, imposterdom is not achieved beyond a rather ordinary degree of transparent boastfulness. What is conspicuous, however, is the real need to be superficial in performance, even when there is the ability and the training to be more substantial. The superficiality is accompanied by a repeated overselling of the self and repeated unmaskings. The neurotic drive to produce illusions rather than substance is painfully recognized but yielded to by the individual himself and is exceedingly uncomfortable. Such individuals seem sometimes to fear committing themselves to a sustained or well-developed interest, as though this in itself would be risky and lead to being caught. If they do succeed, it is likely to be by attaching themselves to some well-established and respected person. A secondary distressing development is the inevitable rationalizing support of shifting grievances, which sometimes give a paranoid cast to the character, which, however, is not deep or progressive. Although these character traits may occur in women as well as in men, they are more striking and perhaps less socially acceptable in the latter.

Not many cases of this kind have come to me, but those which I have seen have shared certain characteristics. It is apparent even from the external behavior that the whole character structure bears the imprint of illusion—but peculiarly enough, illusion with some degree of insight, which checks the development of a true charlatanism. Indeed, this illusory quality in the development has begun early, preceding the phallic-oedipal phase. These men have been precocious infants—not babied or made cute, but pushed ahead, aggrandized, and worshiped by their mothers. As might be expected, they were the children of ambitious, driving, dominating and usually intellectual mothers who, dissatisfied with rather weak or unimpressive husbands, demanded too much of the child, even in the earliest years. They were little kings, even before the oedipal phase and did not suffer adequate dethronement then. Particularly if the father was absent or ill, the child suffered little check from the ordinary oedipal fear of the father. The child might not suffer even an ordinary amount of phallic awe or fear in circumstances where it would be expected, because his own omnipotence was still so great that nothing could compare with him. He was, in a sense, in awe of himself and his own abilities. The fantasies of magic, and especially of the magic power of thought flourished then in the extreme in the latency period—fascination with body mechanisms in general and especially the own genitourinary performances. In those patients whom I have seen, there has come a time' then of humiliation, brought about by their grandiose images of themselves. In the competition of school life, the first severe reality checks were imposed—not in the school room so often as on the playground where ridicule was severe and sometimes excruciatingly painful. The unchecked expansiveness of the subjective feelings of the phallic phase development had added its part to the earlier exaggerated infantile omnipotence. Then there was a collapse in the face of the more concretistic performances and ridicule of other boys, followed by a new defense of even more far-reaching, but guarded illusions.

What is interesting here is that the body-phallus identification which so much influences the self-image is based then not on an exaggerated conception of the phallus, but rather on an exaggerated illusory female phallus, with which the mother is endowed. It seems important to emphasize that in these cases, as in many others, the illusory character of the maternal phallus is thoroughly sensed, even though the illusion is persistently held on to. This identification of the self with the female phallus has been forecast early by the mother's handling of her son as though he were her phallus, and is not wholly dependent on the severity of his castration problems. It is most striking that these men develop a quality of intellectualism which is based on a displacement from this illusory phallus to the thinking. This, in turn, is reinforced by a defense against the magic quality of the early fantasying, resulting in a peculiarly sterile, compulsive type of impressive fact gathering, with a real fear of sustained intellectual functioning. One might decribe this as a kind of intellectual transvestitism.

In the course of analyzing patients who have fairly well-focused phallic awe problems, the analyst is confronted with the reproduction of the awe reaction in the transference whenever the memory of experiences inducing the original reactions approaches consciousness. This is not always readily recognized. It may take various forms, according to the secondary defenses upon which the patient further depends. Usually it is ushered in with some degree of feeling of unreality, haziness, doubt, and diffuse resistance. The second of the analytic hours already quoted is very characteristic; the hour beginning with the patient's announcement that he has a strange feeling of unreality about the analysis and about me, and his question whether everything was an illusion. This feeling of unreality seems inherent in awe itself, which is a response to something which goes beyond understanding, but it is frequently covered by feelings of stupidity, triviality, and sometimes by rather silly humor and clowning. In other patients where the visual-oral elements are particularly strong, fascination itself may be reproduced with tubular vision or a blurring of vision. Very often there is a substitution of early primal scene experiences which have already been analyzed. This material is now reoffered in place of the more direct phallic awe. The aggression aroused is intense but often expressed itself in stubborn, passive and furtive

ways, which make analysis particularly difficult and the need for a sound
"working through" imperative.

To return to the consideration of experiences of awe in the childhood
of gifted people, some examples of which were given in the first part of
this paper, these do not differ in content from similar experiences reported by my patients, except in the richness of their coloring and
elaboration. From a rather incomplete review of published autobiographies, I would think that such experiences are not uncommon among
artists, poets and prophets. One suspects that these gifted individuals,
with a wider, more varied, and intense sensory response, may vibrate
with awe to more situations in the environment and that the whole reaction may not be as restricted to the phallic sensations and reciprocal
awarenesses as is true among neurotic individuals of lesser inborn talent.
This does not mean, however, that the rise of sensation in the phallic
phase is not the center of such reactions. The autobiographical stories
of later childhood and like events do not seem to portray the same degree
of later humiliation and increasing defense. One must be extremely
guarded in assaying this, however, as only a careful scrutiny of the works
of these gifted ones may give the clues to such situations, which at best
are usually deeply repressed and their elements projected backward, en-
hancing the brightness of the original screen memory. It is possible also
that the gift of heightened sensation, perceptivity and expressiveness
permits a better toleration of these early childhood experiences and saves
the gifted child oft times from that humiliation of deflated pretentiousness which is a haunting nuclear disturbance of the neurotic patient.

To summarize, awe reactions in childhood begin most frequently at
the age of four or five years, definitely associated with the expansive ex-
hilarated feelings of the phallic phase. Such reactions are described in
screen memories and are apparently fairly frequent, both in literary
autobiographies and in psychoanalytic practice. Penis awe occurs in boys
as well as in girls, but does not then involve the same degree of stunning
shock reaction, and is less intense. This is due to the fact that there is
less discrepancy between the body-self image of the boy and the image
of the man than can be true in the girl. The greatest impression is made
when the man's phallus is seen in a state of sexual excitement. Whether
the reaction is one of fascination focused almost exclusively on the organ
or whether it involves a reaction to the total man depends chiefly on the
setting of the occurrence and the intrinsic relation to the man himself.

The awe reaction entails fear and intense admiration, with some
degree of exalted envy. Where the focusing is chiefly on the organ and
does not involve admiration of the man, especially of the father, the re-

action is extremely complicating to the oedipal relationship and further
sets up persistent attempts to possess such an organ, leading then sometimes
to repetitive receptive homosexual activities, and/or the development of
stubborn competitive fantasies, with expansively pretentious but passive
attitudes in reality performances. In some cases, there is a fixation of the
envy on the ejaculatory process itself. A self-delusion beginning in early
latency that the urination actually is a seminal ejaculation may develop.
Urethral erotism is marked and disturbances of potency follow.

The two contrasting images of the phallus frequently persist into
adult life. The inner psychic situation leads to the persistence of a small
penis complex. This reaction to the phallus is often duplicated in the
total self-image and influences the character development. A review of
this clinical material indicates the influence of the conditions of the
phallic phase in the development of the sense of body-self, so important
in the vicissitudes of later character formations. One of the most interesting parts of the awe reaction is its association with inspiration, with
creativity, and with religious feelings. These are frequent and deserve
special study.

BIBLIOGRAPHY

Abraham, K. (1917), Ejaculatio Praecox. *Selected Papers on Psycho-Analysis*. London:
    Hogarth Press, 1927, p. 281.
Drame, A. T. (n.d.), Saint Catherine of Siena and Her Time. Quoted by A. Richardson,
    p. 23.
Gosse, E. (1934), *Father and Son*. New York: Oxford University Press, pp. 15-16, 27-42.
Greenacre, P. (1947), Vision, Headache and the Halo. In: *Trauma, Growth and Per-
    sonality*. New York: Norton, 1952.
—— (1953), Penis Awe and Its Relation to Penis Envy. In: *Drives, Affects, Behavior*,
    ed. R. M. Loewenstein. New York: International Universities Press.
Lewis, C. S. (1955), *Surprised by Joy*. London: Geoffrey Bles, p. 22.
Loti, P. (1890), *Le roman d'un enfant*. Paris: Calmann Levy.
Pater, W. (1895), The Child in the House. *Miscellaneous Studies*. London: Macmillan.
Read, H. (1940), *Annals of Innocence and Experience*. London: Faber & Faber, p. 36.
Richardson, A. (n.d.), *The Mystic Bride*. London: T. Werner Laurie, pp. 18-19.
Rolland, R. (1910-1913), *Jean Christophe*, 3 Vols. New York: Henry Holt.
Schweitzer, A. (1955), *Memories of Childhood and Youth*. New York: Macmillan.

NOTES ON THE REALITY PRINCIPLE

HEINZ HARTMANN, M.D. (New York)[1]

If we are to study the processes and the problems which the concept "reality principle" is meant to cover, there is still no better point of departure than Freud's paper on the "Two Principles of Mental Functioning," first published in 1911. This work is important and interesting in another respect also. It deals specifically with a number of ego functions, such as consciousness, thinking, attention, judgment, action—and does so *avant la lettre*, if I may say so, before ego psychology had become an integrated part of psychoanalysis; that is to say, his studies of ego functions had not yet appeared in the framework of the set of propositions which we call ego psychology today. At the time Freud used the terms pleasure ego and reality ego, and what was later to become the distinction of ego and id was still represented as an opposition of ego drives and sexual drives. One of the many essential contributions of the paper was the observation that while the ego drives are ready to yield to the influence of the reality principle, the sexual drives remain much longer under the dominance of the pleasure principle, a fact that is significant for mental development in general and for neurosis in particular.

The idea that pleasure and unpleasure are dominant forces in motivating human behavior had, of course, not escaped the attention of earlier thinkers; it goes far back in the history of philosophy and has been strongly emphasized especially by a school of British philosophers. Bentham, to quote at least one of them, said that nature has put man under the control of two sovereign masters, pain and pleasure. We find also in the pre-Freudian literature references to a development toward a more adaptive state of affairs. Freud has never claimed property rights in this respect; on the contrary, in discussing the pleasure principle, he said that "priority and originality are not among the aims that psychoanalytic work sets itself" (1920). Originality was not the aim of his work, although it was, in the case of Freud, invariably its outcome. It was with

[1] Presented at the Freud Centenary Sessions of the Hampstead Child-Therapy Clinic, London, May 4th, 1956.

Freud's pleasure and reality principles in a way as with his concepts of the unconscious mental processes. While the terms had been used before, the decisive achievements of finding a method to study these processes, of filling the terms with specific psychological meaning, and of assigning them their place in a coherent structure, are Freud's.

If the infant finds himself in a situation of need, and if attempts toward hallucinatory gratification have proved disappointing, he will turn toward reality; and the repetition of such situations will gradually teach him better to know reality and to strive for those real changes that make gratification possible. This is what Freud says in the "Two Principles." It gives us a solid basis and point of departure for the following considerations. In the case described, the first step, the turning toward reality in search of gratification, simply follows the pleasure principle. Both the cognition and the purposive change of reality involved in the process we attribute to functions of the ego. But the reality principle, according to Freud, means also that uncertain pleasure is renounced, with the purpose of ascertaining, in a new way, that an assured pleasure will come later. This clearly presupposes two other ego functions of the greatest importance, postponement and anticipation. Thus the question arises (Hartmann, 1939a): how far does the development of ego functions enter as an independent variable into the processes described by Freud? It is true, we are wont to say that the "demands of reality" are responsible for them. But this is, of course, a metaphorical way of putting the case; it is correct only if we presuppose the existence of something in the individual that speaks out for reality—a tendency toward self-preservation which, in the mental life of man, we attribute mostly to the ego and to its precursors. The question whether the ego plays a primary role in the institution of the reality principle will be answered differently, according to whether we view the ego as an agent active from the beginning, though only in a limited way (as Freud did in later writings), or as something traceable only to the impact of the interaction of reality and drives (as he did earlier). Freud's formulations of the reality principle vary. In quite a few passages he simply states that the institution of the reality principle is due to the influence of the external world on the individual. And often he describes the reality principle just as one form of regulating mental processes and achieving mastery of part of them. In these definitions it is not traced to the activity of specific mental functions or groups of functions. But I can also quote some passages in which he explicitly describes the influence of the ego on its emergence. In *Beyond the Pleasure Principle* (1920) we read that the substitution of the pleasure principle by the reality principle is due to the "self-preserving instincts of the ego";

in *The Problem of Lay Analysis* (1926b) he says that the ego replaces the pleasure principle, which before then had been the only dominating force, by the reality principle. In the *New Introductory Lectures* (1932) we find a similar statement. These latter descriptions seem to me to be more in line with what we know about the facts, and more in line also with Freud's later formulations on the role of the ego.

There is another aspect to this same question, one closely related, though, to that just discussed. Freud distinguishes three principles of regulation which he calls pleasure principle, Nirvana principle, and reality principle, respectively. They are described as tendencies which in a general way aim at regulating the excitations in the mental apparatus, in modifying them as to quantity, quality, or rhythm. The first two, the pleasure and the Nirvana principles, easily fit this definition; their regulating activities are concerned with the whole mental apparatus. Here again, the reality principle stands apart. It originates in one mental system only; also, its power over the mental apparatus extends no further than the power of this system. The reality principle seems to represent the modifications imposed by the ego on the functions of the two other principles and is therefore not quite on the same plane as the others (Hartmann, 1948). It is, indeed, an ego principle; that is, the concept of the tendencies we ascribe to the reality principle is identical with that of a group of ego functions (though not of the ego as a whole). It seems advantageous to keep this in mind when speaking of the reality principle.

In our literature, two meanings are currently attached to the term reality principle. Used in one sense, it indicates a tendency to take into account in an adaptive way, in perception, thinking and action, whatever we consider the "real" features of an object or a situation. But in another, maybe we could say, narrower sense, we refer primarily to the case in which it represents a tendency to wrest our activities from the immediate need for discharge inherent in the pleasure principle. It is in this sense that we speak of the reality principle as the natural opponent, or at least modifier, of the pleasure principle. This poses a problem. One cannot state in a general way that reality-syntonic behavior curtails pleasure. This would be a quite illegitimate generalization, and not only because— as Freud repeatedly emphasized and I have just quoted—behavior under the guidance of the reality principle is aimed at gaining, in a new way, assured pleasure at a later stage, while giving up momentary pleasure. In this case, its timing determines whether or not discharge is reality-syntonic. But beyond this consideration of expected or assured gains, there is also the fact that the activities of the functions that constitute the reality principle can be pleasurable in themselves. I remind you at this point of the pleasurable potentialities of sublimated activities. Organized thought or action, in which postponement is of the essence, can become a source of pleasure. While this, at first sight, seems to complicate things, there is no way denying it; indeed, it becomes perfectly clear if we think of the reality principle in terms of ego functions. If I have emphasized here the double meaning of the term reality principle, it was in order to forestall possible misunderstandings; failure to note the double meaning has occasionally led to a misrepresentation of Freud's thinking on the subject. In opposing reality principle and pleasure principle, he certainly did not mean to negate the pleasures we derive from the world outside; and he repeatedly commented on the advantages the ego provides for instinctual gratifications, aside from its different role as an opponent of the drives.

Freud emphasized, as I reminded you before, the importance of situations of frustration in the development of the reality principle.[2] The assumption that in the hypothetical case of continuous and full gratification the objectivating and anticipating functions would be badly impaired is, indeed, quite convincing. But we should also consider here the thought first expressed, I think, by Anna Freud (1936), that the postponement or control of discharge is one of the essential features of the human ego from its beginnings; it is probably an essential feature already of its forerunners, before the ego as a system of personality has been fully established. We should also consider what is, I think, a necessary assumption (Hartmann, 1952), that the child is born with a certain degree of

2 Recently, two interesting papers, replete with thoughts pertinent to this point, were published by Loewald (1951) and by Székely (1951). It is emphasized that Freud's concept of reality is bound up with the figure of the father, and that in Freud's mind the castration threat is the clearest representations of the demands of reality. But, on the other hand, the concept of reality is also connected with the role of the mother. It is not possible to discuss here in detail the contributions of these authors. I just want to note the obvious truth that the child's attitudes toward reality and conceptions of reality pass through several stages of relations to the objects which leave their imprints on them. I fully agree to the importance, also in this respect, of those stages the authors put in the center of their presentations, though I do not propose to include these aspects in this paper. Both mother and father play a dominant role in the vicissitudes of the child's relations to reality. But I think that the concepts both of reality and of the reality principle as presented by Freud are of a far more general nature. The child's concepts of reality can be followed through the vicissitudes of object relations and conflicts. But "the reality concept of psychoanalysis" cannot be defined by these. Nor would such an attempt at defining our concepts be of any advantage in dealing with other psychological processes of a general nature. In this context it may be instructive to remember how Freud rejected what he called the "sexualization" of the concept of repression, the attempt (suggested to him by Wilhelm Fliess and Adler) to limit this concept to the opposition of two specific groups of instinctual tendencies, masculine and feminine (Freud, 1919).

preadaptiveness; that is to say, the apparatus of perception, memory, mobility, etc., which help us to deal with reality are, in a primitive form, already present at birth; later they will mature and develop in constant interaction, of course, with experience; you know that the very system to which we attribute these functions, the ego, is also our organ of learning. What I have said is to the point here, because it means that some preparedness for dealing with reality precedes those experiences Freud referred to in the passage quoted.

Another point, related to the foregoing, though not identical with it, is the question of the occurrence of the first "positive" attitudes of the infant to the world outside. It is a complex problem, to which both Spitz and Erikson have given considerable thought. In a remarkable paper by Charlotte Buehler (1954), which follows in part analytic reasoning, great emphasis is put on "primary positive responses" to reality alongside the primary negative ones—and this both on observational and theoretical grounds. There is no reason to deny these findings and the assumption that later on, when the differentiation of self and object has taken place, the positive object relations also draw on these primordial experiences is plausible enough. However, while the child does not have to learn everything the hard way, for many important functions this situation proves unavoidable. And there is certainly nothing to invalidate any of Freud's statements on the impact of situations of deprivation on the evolution of the reality principle. While Freud has not discussed all the implications of his theory, we find here and there in his work contributions to some facets of the problem, as, e.g., in his paper on "Instincts and Their Vicissitudes" (1915).

Sooner or later, though not every step has been clarified thus far, the child unlearns and outgrows the distortions inherent in the purified pleasure position described in that essay. The impact of all stages of child development—the typical conflicts, the sequence of danger situations, and the ways they are dealt with—can be traced in this process. The problem has been most extensively studied as to the development of object relations. Perception, objectivation, anticipation, intentionality, neutralization of energy—all participate on the side of the ego in this process. One may well ask why this whole development of the reality principle (or the corresponding ego functions) shows such a high degree of complexity in man, a complexity to which there is hardly a parallel elsewhere, except, perhaps, for some other higher mammals. No doubt, one reason is that in the human the pleasure principle is a less reliable guide to self-preservation. Also, self-preservation is mainly taken care of by the slowly developing ego with its considerable learning capacity. But pleasure conditions for the ego on the one hand and the id on the other differ significantly, while the instincts of the animals represent at the same time what we would call in man ego functions and functions of the drives. Also, probably as a result of the differentiation of the human mind into systems of functioning, the id is here much farther removed from reality than are the instincts of animals (Hartmann, 1948).

But let us return to the meaning of the relationships of the reality and pleasure principles in individual development. It is here, in the study of ontogenesis, that the mainsprings of psychoanalytic knowledge lie, and most of what we say analytically about the differences of man and lower animals, or about the special characteristics of the human mind and related questions, is ultimately traceable to what we know about ontogenesis. The reality principle includes postponement of gratification and a temporary toleration of unpleasure. Another source of unpleasurable experiences, and an essential one, "is to be found in the conflicts and divisions that take place in the mental apparatus" (Freud, 1920) in the course of development. That is, what would have been a pleasurable experience under other conditions—namely, without the differentiation into ego, id, superego—may now be felt as unpleasure. This is a process clearly distinguishable from the one we discussed earlier. In the case of postponement of satisfaction and temporary tolerance of unpleasure, the pleasant or unpleasant nature of the elements involved is a "given thing." But the second case we could state only in a general way by saying that the conditions themselves, on which the pleasurable or unpleasurable characters of a situation rest, have been changed. There is no other way of accounting for this than, again, to attribute it to the development of the ego (to which, however, we must add here the development of the superego). These developmental changes in the pleasure conditions, consecutive to ego (and superego) development might, in so far as maturation participates in them, be compared to the changes of pleasure conditions induced by the sequence of libidinal phases. In the statement which I just quoted from Freud, he finds an explanation of the reasons why structural differentiation can induce a state of affairs in which earlier sources of pleasure, in the course of development, lose their pleasure qualities. If we look at it from a point at which structuralization has actually taken place, we have the right to draw from this finding two conclusions. The reality principle, in the narrower sense, imposes restrictions on the pleasure principle, if only to secure a future pleasure gain. But the aspect of structure formation under scrutiny now has changed also the conditions for pleasure gain;

it has not only limited them, but also newly defined what is and what is not pleasurable (or less unpleasurable). This is the more remarkable as we are impressed by the tenacity with which man so often clings to the sources of experienced pleasure. But there is no denying that a reassessment of pleasure values does take place, a differentiation according to their various sources, which one may well describe as a modification of the pleasure principle, or perhaps as a partial domestication of the pleasure principle—different from the reality principle in the stricter sense. Not only the reality-tuned functions of the ego but also its organizing function play a role in it. Obviously, this change in pleasure-unpleasure conditions grows parallel with other developmental changes.[3] One may say that this aspect of the pleasure principle develops a bias in favor of the ego and superego or, better, it comes partly under their control. However, what I have said certainly does not apply to the id, where we find only instinctual tendencies seeking discharge, but does appear to be valid for the interactions of the systems. If you remember what, for the case of repression, Freud says about the ego setting the power of the pleasure principle in motion (1932) or his statement that the essential point in turning "a possibility of pleasure into a source of unpleasure" is "that pleasure and unpleasure being conscious feelings, are attached to the ego" (1920), then it seems to me, you will be not very far from the interpretation I have just given you. This seems an interesting development indeed, particularly if we consider what we think of the discharge value of the primary as against that of the secondary processes. It may seem difficult to account for this in metapsychological terms. It would be especially hard on the basis of Freud's earlier theory which established a direct coordination of the feelings of the pleasure-unpleasure series with the lowering or heightening of the stimulus tension in the mind. Later, he said that this view could not be correct. He thought rather that pleasure and unpleasure could be referred to peculiarities like "something rhythmic, the periodical duration of the changes, the risings and fallings of the volume of stimuli" (1924). This problem is one of the most obscure among those psychoanalysis has to deal with. But I think it is at least not inconceivable that changes in the relations of the factors Freud mentions here with pleasure and unpleasure go on parallel with mental development. At any rate, whether we chose to interpret it metapsychologically in this or in a different way, we can say that the pleasure principle itself has a history too, besides the

[3] The hypothesis that certain activities or organs owe their exceptional pleasure potentialities to the important biological functions they serve, is familiar in analysis from phylogenetic propositions (Ferenczi, 1924); see also Hartmann (1939a).

limitations imposed on its manifestations by the reality principle in the narrower sense of the term. To avoid a possible misunderstanding I may repeat: it is, of course, not the essential characteristics of the pleasure-unpleasure principle, by which we define it (that is the striving for pleasure and avoiding of unpleasure) that change in the course of development; what does change are the conditions of pleasure and unpleasure.

The second reflexion relevant at this point brings us back to another aspect of the reality principle. I said earlier that in man the pleasure principle is not a very reliable guide to self-preservation. There are, though, exceptions to this rule; the avoidance of pain (*Schmerz*), e.g., retains its biological significance. As a very important exception we might also consider what we are discussing just now. In those situations in which pleasure in one system (id) would induce unpleasure in another one (ego), the child learns to use the danger signal (a dose of unpleasure) to mobilize the pleasure principle and in this way to protect himself (Freud, 1926a). He will not only use this mechanism against danger from within but also against danger from without. The process is directly guided by the pleasure principle; it is really the pleasure principle that gives this move its power. What interests us in this connection is that through a special device an aspect of the pleasure principle itself (avoidance of unpleasure) is made to serve one of the most essential functions we make use of in our dealings with reality. It is a definite step in development to be distinguished from what I called the reality principle in its narrower sense (the so-called modification of the pleasure principle, meaning postponement of discharge, temporary tolerance of unpleasure)—and I may refer you here to what I said, partly with this case in mind, of the necessity of keeping apart the two concepts of the reality principle. Genetically, of course, the use of the pleasure principle we are discussing now is also dependent on the development of the ego, as is the reality principle in the narrower sense.

Over and over again we see how our understanding of these problems depends on our insight into the evolution of the ego, but also that this insight has not yet made sufficient progress to allow us more than highly hypothetical answers to a number of questions. Summarizing this first part of my paper, I may say: We assume that at birth (and actually before) certain dispositions for future ego functions exist, whose growth will later influence the pleasure and reality principles in a variety of ways. Freud assumes that the tendency to pleasure gain is there from the beginning and that at an early stage it predominates over the tendency to avoid unpleasure. Both together, however, cannot fully account for the institution of the reality principle, in the sense of postponement of dis-

charge and toleration of unpleasure; we have to assume that the development of ego functions enters the process as an independent variable. At
this point, objectivation and anticipation begin to play a decisive role.
What one could call the pleasure-unpleasure balance (that is, the sum
total of pleasurable and unpleasurable elements in a situation, an activity,
and so on) will now include, beyond the consideration of the present,
also the consideration of the future.[4] The question of whether the accent
is on pleasure gain or on avoidance of unpleasure remains relevant for
the "acceptance of the reality principle" as a factor variable not only
developmentally but also individually. According to this, quantitatively
identical pleasure-unpleasure balances may produce different reactions.
The foresight we spoke about includes judgments on the relations of
cause and effect, both as to what happens in outer reality and in the
child's mind. Structure later induces, as a new element, a change in the
pleasure conditions, as described above. At this point the direct use by the
ego of the pleasure principle for the mastery of outer and inner reality
becomes important in a specific way. And, as a further step, in the case
of the danger signal, an unpleasant feeling is intentionally reproduced
by the ego for that very purpose.

This summary is, of course, strikingly sketchy. It is far from rendering
even that knowledge of which we feel reasonably sure. May I, then, at
least add that the pleasure-unpleasure balance is decisively changed as a
consequence of the fact that the child renouncing an instinctual desire
expects, and often gets, a recompense in the form of love or approval by
the parents. There is also the pleasure the child derives from participating
in the world of the grownups. Here we have, then, a substitution of one
form of gratification (through the object) for another one. We also know
that once the superego has been established, the child will often feel
pride in foregoing a pleasure (Freud, 1939). This is certainly a strong
motivation for accepting certain demands made by the reality principle.
As I have said, I think that the gradual development of the pleasure
potentialities provided by the ego works in the same direction—not only
in so far as it provides us with ways in which to achieve instinctual
satisfaction, but equally because of the pleasurable feelings so often
connected with sublimation. Of course, the pleasure principle does not
stop at the door of the ego; it is simply that the psychology of discharge

4 Once a certain level of differentiation and integration has been reached, it becomes
inadequate in an increasing number of cases to describe an experience (actual or
expected) as simply "pleasant" or "unpleasant." What we are confronted with is rather a
series of pleasant elements, weighed against a series of unpleasant elements. It is to
account for this fact and to warn of oversimplification that I use the term "pleasure-
unpleasure balance."

has been much better studied as to the instinctual drives than as to the secondary processes.

The reality principle includes both knowledge of reality and acting in regard to it. Biologically speaking, it is part of what we usually term adaptation. As you know, Freud called the two ways by which a more suitable relation to reality can be achieved alloplastic and autoplastic behavior respectively, according to whether the individual effects a change in the outside world or in himself. Incidentally, I may add that we could consider a third case (Hartmann, 1939a), in which neither the outside world nor the individual is really changed; instead their relationship is changed: I am thinking of the search for and finding of a more appropriate environment. This process, too, plays a considerable role in the development of the species and also of the individual, very clearly in the case of man.

But in this context I want to make only one point, referring to the relations of the knowledge and action aspects of the reality principle. First of all, we should consider that, in a general way, maximal utilization of one partial function of those that serve adaptation is not always compatible with the optimal functioning of the whole system (Hartmann, 1939b). Also, we should be mindful of the fact that if we state, let's say, that a certain thought is reality-syntonic in a given situation, this may refer to either one of two meanings. It may mean that the thought is true in the sense that it corresponds to reality. On the other hand, it may also mean that its use, in a given reality situation, leads to a successful mastery of this situation. That in a large sector of human behavior there is no simple correlation between the degree of objective insight and the degree of adaptiveness of the corresponding action is not in need of being proved. Objective knowledge of and practical orientation in reality do not necessarily coincide. We all know that action in line with "common sense," which is practically oriented, can be more efficient. But it is hard to state in general terms where it will be efficient and where, on the other hand, the kind of thinking we call scientific is called for. The French, very aptly, distinguish *savoir-faire, savoir-vivre,* and *savoir tout court.* If we sometimes tend to forget these differences, it is probably because in our analytic work the relation between truth-finding and an effective therapeutic change is a particularly close one. This therapeutic value of insight in analysis we can take for granted and I do not propose to discuss it here. It is rather in a broader psychological framework that the distinction I have in mind becomes significant.

Developmentally speaking, a degree of avoidance of outer reality, of restrictions of insight, or of denials can often be harmless in the child and even, in certain situations, useful, which, as Anna Freud (1936) has explained, in the adult would lead to far more serious consequences. As to inner reality, there is no doubt that withdrawal from insight, the restriction of inner reality testing, that follow the typical repressions occur also in normal development. It appears that later, though less incisive, techniques of compromise in the grownup, which neglect some aspects of reality but nevertheless remain adaptive, are partly built on the early models. Of course, we are very familiar with the cases in which such compromises miscarry; but in this context, dealing with general psychology rather than with pathology, my point is just the opposite: that they often do not. Minor refusals to acknowledge part of reality without a consequent impairment of reality-syntonic action are pretty much ubiquitous. They may even serve a more reality-syntonic behavior, in the second sense, a subject to which we will presently turn. These phenomena may be situational and are often more or less mobile. They may also become parts of automatized patterns. These are, in a way, defensive maneuvers, but hardly always defense mechanisms, in the stricter sense in which we use the word as an analytic term. I think we should say that, in these phenomena, what is not conscious avoidance is very often, though by no means always, preconscious rather than unconscious; it is kept from consciousness by that censorship which, according to Freud, works between the conscious and the preconscious mind.

But allow me to turn back once more to problems of development. We take man's unique learning capacity for granted, but we are impressed again by the complex steps, the detours, by, one might say, the devious means necessary to achieve "acceptance of reality." It has been said that in man "there is a long way from pleasure-principle to self-preservation" (Freud), and this may be one reason why so much of adaptive behavior has to be wrung from the pleasure principle. We may now add that this is not the only cause of those complexities. We have to face the fact that what is adaptive in one respect may interfere with adaptation in another. We just touched upon the question in speaking of the relations between objective knowledge of and action vis-à-vis reality. An equilibrium between the various adaptive trends will finally, more or less successfully, be established by experience and by the integrative, or synthetic, or organizing function of the ego, which works on several levels and correlates aspects of mental functioning with each other and with outer reality. However, what I want to emphasize next is that there exist similar discrepancies even in regard to the forms of "knowledge of reality" itself; also that from the beginning the very ways in which the

child acquires knowledge of reality are fraught with instigations to distort it.

The main early sources of learning about reality are in the child's
relations to his own body and to the objects. Identification and object
relations will for a decisive period of time dominate this process and will,
even later, never become quite irrelevant to it.[5] Both the development
of ego functions and the constitution of constant objects represent a
moving away from what Freud calls primary narcissism, and are closely
interrelated. They probably already presuppose the use of a mode of
energy different from the instinctual one. In contact and communication
with the object, the child learns to demarcate his "self" and to realize the
first vestiges of objectivity. The transition from "egocentric" thinking to
recognizing the relativity of qualities depends on insight into the relativity
of the "me" (Piaget, 1937; Rapaport, 1951). Much careful and interesting
work on the subject has been done recently, inside and outside of analysis,
which I am sorry not to be able to discuss in this connection.

The protracted helplessness of the human child causes a situation
in which "the value attached to the object . . . is enormously increased"
(Freud, 1926a). One may well say that in man the human objects are by
far the most important sector of reality. The dependence upon the
object, as is well known, becomes an essential factor in the human child's
learning about reality. It is responsible also for typical or individual
distortions of the picture of reality which the child develops. Thus the
same factor acts in both directions (on either side, of course, it is combined with others). Its "not-objective" imprints will differ in different
sectors of the child's thinking. We may expect them to be comparatively
insignificant in the area of perception, though even here the higher
processes by which sensory data are integrated are accessible to subjective
modification. They are certainly clear in concept formation, in habits of
thought and of emotion. Language, one of the most characteristic achievements of man, and one the child largely owes to the objects, might be one
of the most general examples because it opens a decisive avenue to
objective knowledge, but at the same time preserves forms of thinking that
are often neither realistic nor logical. One aspect of this, the taking over
of "stereotypes" by the child, has been discussed by Sullivan (1953). It is,
of course, not possible to present in this paper the manifold practical
problems raised by this double-faceted impact of socialization on the
child's learning about reality.

[5] See also de Saussure (1950), and Axelrad and Maury (1951).

A "realistic" object can be of great assistance to the child in dis-criminating fantasy and reality; it will help him to meet real dangers on their own grounds, as Anna Freud has said recently. When Freud speaks about reality testing he usually means the capacity to distinguish between ideas and perceptions. In a broader sense, reality testing also refers to the ability to discern subjective and objective elements in our judgments on reality. The former we expect to function rather reliably in normal adult persons; the learning of the latter is an unending process. It is here that the criteria are, in most people, rather poorly defined and the temptations to tamper with objective judgment are considerable. There are, of course, many well-known reasons for this, but I propose to limit myself to the one point under discussion only. I mentioned the well-known fact that pleasure premia are in store for the child who conforms to the demands of reality and of socialization; but they are equally avail-able if this conforming means the acceptance by the child of erroneous and biased views which the parents hold of reality.

What I said on the essentially helpful, but also prejudicial, impact of the objects on learning about the outside world is true also in regard to the child's inner world, and self-deceptions are the inevitable result. The ways in which the data of inner reality are organized or integrated, the image of his own self, and its evaluation, are codetermined by these powers, in their role of models or of prohibiting agents. This does not start with, but finds its clearest expression in, the formation of the super-ego, which of course includes, among other and partly opposite results, also some degree of narrowing or distortion of the child's knowledge of inner reality. We should not omit that the superego may occasionally influence even the testing of outer reality (Freud, 1936). On the other hand, the superego may add to the motivation for objectivity, at least in so far as the characters of objectivity, intellectual honesty, truthfulness, etc., are included in its demands. Actually, these are rather widely em-phasized, even in otherwise divergent value systems.

There is, then, interference with objective cognizance of the world not only through the action of instinctual needs; it may be handicapped also by ego (and superego) functions, even such as in other circumstances can lead to adjustment. And, more specifically, there is the case we are discussing here, namely, the taking over by the individual of the picture of reality accepted and taught by the love objects, but also, in a broader sense, of the picture commonly accepted in the culture to which he belongs. The child learns his approach to reality in constant relation to the adult's approach to it. It adjusts to a world which is not only to a considerable extent man-made, but also man-thought. As a consequence, two different criteria of reality develop, and in the world of every individual both play a role.

Without entering into the philosopher's discussions of what constitutes reality, a few words about how we use the term in analysis may be to the point here. The criteria chiefly used by Freud are those of science, or, more correctly, those that find their clearest expression in science. Science strives for validation of its statements on reality, it accepts as "objective" what is verifiable by certain methods. Intersubjectivity plays a role in scientific validation. But "conventional" or "socialized knowledge" of reality, means, in contradistinction to scientific knowledge, often not so much what allows intersubjective validation, but rather what is intersubjectively accepted, to a considerable extent without validation, or attempt at validation. For the child, this means accepted by the objects closest to him.[6] What the mother, according to objective standards, is "neurotically" afraid of can (but in this second sense only) mean "real" danger for the child. Incidentally, there is in this socializing of reality-knowledge also a tradition-forming element, besides the one recognized in the superego.[7]

In our clinical evaluation of "realistic" behavior we commonly use both concepts of knowledge; in theoretical discussions we mostly refer to the concept of "objective knowledge." How the relations between the two concepts of reality-knowledge or, maybe we should say, how the criteria of "truth"[8] about reality evolve, I cannot discuss here in detail. In his stages of rebelliousness the growing individual also rebels against the commonly accepted view of reality. His tendency toward objective knowledge may also muster the help of instinctual drives. However, after having become autonomous, it may reach a considerable amount of stability. In certain situations the resistance against group contamination can be considered an indication of ego strength (Redl and Wineman,

[6] In enlarging upon Piaget's concept of "realism" in the child, we could speak of "social realism": opinions of the objects are taken for objective. For the same problem (and also for the difference of "reality testing" and "sense of reality") see Weiss (1950).

[7] I would like to mention in this connection also another aspect that often leads to distortions of objective thinking. The child is constantly confronted with value judgments which cannot be validated objectively but which are presented to him as statements of fact. "This is good" and "that is bad" are often presented to him in the same way as "this is red" and "that is green." Such presentations also become part of "socialized reality," which may well be one of the reasons why many adults (some great philosophers among them) cannot accept the logical difference between a moral imperative and a factual statement.

[8] Gide speaks about *vérités de constatation* and *vérités de convention*.

1951).[8a] Actually, many factors would have to be considered if we were to study the various types of independent as contrasted with the various types of conforming behavior. My main point here is only that the preponderance of one adaptive ego function may mean the weakness of another one, equally adaptive in itself. The scientific conception of knowledge of reality will never entirely eliminate the other conception except in the case of the scientist, and, even here, only as long as he does scientific work. It is not to be forgotten that much of our "knowledge" of reality is of the socially accepted kind, with most of our actions based on it. "Objective" knowledge does not, of course, have to contradict the accepted picture of reality; but it often does. Perhaps the best example of this second case is psychoanalysis, which put objective knowledge into a field where only socially accepted knowledge had existed, and thus interfered with conventional thought in a particularly sensitive area. What Einstein (1950) said about the desirable freedom of thought "from the restrictions of authoritarian and other social prejudices as well as from unphilosophical routinizing and habit in general," is to the point here and closely corresponds to Freud's thinking. It is clear that not every judgment of or dealing with our fellow men calls for the same level of objective thinking. What one usually calls *Menschenkenntnis* belongs to a greater part to the level of common sense. However, it is one of the most characteristic features of psychoanalytic work that it transcends the conventional level of our thinking on man, not only occasionally, but essentially. In this field, the usefulness of an approach on the common-sense level seems rather limited. It is, I believe, empirically true that adherents of a great variety of philosophies, of political and religious denominations, may be competent psychoanalysts; and it would be quite unrealistic to expect that the analyst cannot share some of the prejudices of his culture, his nation, his social class, or his age group. But it is probable that too strong a bent toward general conformism, or conformism beyond a certain threshold, can create a disposition unfavorable to his professional work. At any rate, he can, strictly speaking, be an analyst only in so far as he is able, in the thinking and acting which constitute his work, to detach himself from the socialized knowledge of man and to move on the level of what Freud calls reality.

There are, then, two pictures of reality opposed to the concept of "objective" reality, which Freud mostly used: the one, as we know, corresponds to what we usually, in a simplifying way, call magical thinking;

[8a] I need hardly remind you that, on the other hand, the inability to conform is very often of a pathological nature.

the other, to a view in which not validation but intersubjective acceptance is used as a criterion of reality. Though the two undoubtedly
overlap to some degree, nevertheless their structural and economical
differences are very significant. I think the distinction proves useful also
for the understanding of certain aspects of pathology. To give you a
simple example: if somebody tells you the prophet Elias has ascended
into Heaven, this will not lead you to any doubts as to his mental health,
though you may not share his opinion. If he says the same of his neighbor, you can make the diagnosis of a psychosis. This means that of the
two reality concepts which are opposed to the concept of objective reality, one may be pathognomonic while the other is not. It has often been
said that the incorrigibility of an idea which is not substantiated by objective criteria marks it as a delusion. But this idealizes the critical faculty
of man. Everybody has his share of erroneous and incorrigible ideas. It
would seem that for an understanding of why we consider an idea pathological, the distinction between "conventional" or just socially accepted
"knowledge" and objective knowledge can be helpful.

I spoke of various functions serving the reality principle, such as cognition and action—both obviously adaptive but also occasionally in contradiction with each other. I added that even for knowledge itself at least two
different concepts are developmentally significant. These complexities
of the reality principle are more easily understood if we think of them
in terms of a variety of partly independent ego functions, of their syner-
gisms and antagonisms, and of various states of intrasystemic equilibria.
This necessity for considering the specific functions which determine our
relations to reality in addition to the more global concept of the reality
principle becomes clearest, of course, where these functions are at least
partly opposed to each other. Thus, to make my point I had to emphasize this aspect; I do not overlook or underrate the more familiar situations in which they work together in the service of adaptation.

Taking as my point of departure the discussion of objective versus
conventional knowledge, I suggest that we take one more step toward
clarifying our thinking on reality, a step which will again land us in a
kind of dichotomy; this dichotomy, too, can on principle be accounted
for in psychological terms. The problem I have in mind has not been
much discussed in analysis,[9] but I think it belongs in the context of my
presentation.

Scientific thinking, the purest form of objective thinking, gives us a

[9] See, however, Winnicott (1953).

knowledge of reality which is formally but often also materially different
from everyday knowledge. I discussed the case of conventional knowledge, but there is still another aspect to this difference. As an attitude,
objective thinking presupposes a certain degree of detachment from
immediate experience. Freud describes thinking in general as a trial
activity with small amounts of cathexis. That is, trial is interiorized.
Thinking is a detour activity which requires first some detachment from
the outer world, in order better to understand, predict, and master it.
This detour is necessary for the efficiency of objectivation. Objective
thinking is the more essential in man, because his drives are much further
removed from adaptive aims than are the instincts of lower animals. I
spoke of detachment from immediate experience. This world of immediate experience, which is what we commonly mean in speaking of
"the world we live in," is not easy to define. Not speaking scientifically,
most people would call it the "real" world.

This poses a number of interesting problems. However, what interests us here is only one aspect, namely the relation of this world to
what I said before about "reality." On the one hand, it is obviously not
what we call an "autistic" world. On the other hand, the world of exact
science certainly does not simply coincide with that "world" we are
considering now. For one thing, the latter contains the element of
quality, of color, sound, touch, and taste, while the world of strict science
does not. The biological meaning of quality has been accounted for in
various ways. Freud seems to have been interested in the problem (and,
in connection with it, in the function of consciousness) in his early work.
He wrote about it in the "Project" (1895) and in *The Interpretation of
Dreams* (1900), where he said that qualities direct cathexis, that they act
as regulators. Of course, quality is only one of the differences between
the scientific concept of the world and its everyday meaning. Specific
factors of coherence and organization have entered our everyday perceptual picture of reality, and this is true also of our thinking about
reality. That is, data are assimilated in a way which gives us knowledge
of the outside but which also tries to give them a meaningful place with
respect to our mental functioning. This is based on the structure of our
mental apparatus (it certainly has a physiological aspect too), on conscious, preconscious, and unconscious previous experience, and on present mental activity also. If we speak of assimilating a part of reality, or
of making it our own, this does not refer only to the knowledge of objective data; it also refers to their cathexis and integration. The difference
in cathexis of objective data and those that are also in a more personal
sense part of "our world," I cannot discuss here. At any rate, the eco-

nomic and dynamic status of knowledge is changed by this process of
assimilation which introduces it into the interplay of our psychic tendencies. This world we are discussing now, different from the world of
science, is clearly an important aspect of our relations with reality and
it is, particularly as a developmental problem, a very much worth-while
subject also of scientific study. The absence of, or rather restrictions on
the capacity to build this world, we know as pathological phenomena.
Most frequently in schizophrenics it is seen that reality becomes meaningless, reduced to "pure environment," that they are deprived of the
processes which normally give it a place in one's personal world. In this
case, we speak of a withdrawal of cathexis from reality (or rather from the
presentations of reality), which is certainly a correct description, though
probably incomplete. Beyond this, it is likely that specific functions of
the ego, which normally account for our world being meaningful also in
a personal way, are impaired in the schizophrenic. Also, in so far as the
world is personally meaningful for him, the meanings have often changed
as compared to his earlier, normal stage.

What is commonly called "reality" outside science is formed, then,
also by the nature of our mental apparatus in general and by our
history. A constant process of taking in—assimilation—and putting
out is going on in our minds. This brings us face to face with a familiar problem, rather well understood psychologically in some aspects
—although other aspects raise questions which concern physiology, and
a third group constitute one of the central issues of epistemology. In a
thoughtful paper on the "Sense of Reality," Zilboorg (1941) states the
question: what is "external" and what is "externalized"? He also remarks
that "the ego's actual manipulation of reality has hardly been taken into
consideration," which was more true at the time of writing than it is
today, though even now this aspect of our studies is still in its beginnings.
We know projection as a pathogenic mechanism, but it is, of course, also
part of normal functioning. In the grownup, a workable equilibrium is
normally established between what we here call "our world" and the
objective knowledge of reality. It is workable if the ego is strong enough
not to be impinged upon in its essential functions by the id, and strong
enough also not to exhaust itself in its struggles against the drives—
that is, if those of its functions which serve reality and synthesis have
reached a certain degree of autonomy. Reality testing can then function
not only in the narrower sense—the distinction between perception and
idea, which is normally established rather early in life—but also in the
broader sense we mentioned before. However, it does not, of course,
always reach out into strictly "objective" knowledge but mostly balances

one element of the "world of immediate experience," in the somewhat hazy sense we use the word here, against others.

Thus we have actually two organized systems of orientation, the world of science and the world of a more immediate experience. The principles inherent in these organized systems differ; both are "selective," though in a different way. There is also, as I have just said, overlapping. The cues to our actions are widely found in the world of immediate experience. There is no doubt that the evolving of this world, though it falls short of exactly reproducing or corresponding to "objective reality," is helpful toward developing our relations to it. By assimilating it, we learn to handle it. The transformation, or molding, of data into this more or less coherent world fulfills, then, a necessary function. Here again, we see a compromise formation between two ways of dealing with reality, each one of which is in itself adaptive. The coherence of this "world" is dependent, among others, on the ego's capacities for integration, which in dealing with outer reality at the same time consider the state of the mental systems. This is a contribution of the synthetic function to our approach to outer and inner reality. Nunberg (1931) relates the development of causal thinking to the synthetic function. I may add that causal thinking is only one, though an essential, aspect of the processes I have in mind here.

Part of what I have said can also be presented in different language by stating that the relation between stimuli from without and our response to them is commonly a rather complex process. The stimulus can, of course, be complex in itself, but there is also the fact that individuals will react differently to different stimuli. There is usually no one-to-one reaction. The basis of the reaction includes the structure of the mental apparatus, intersystemic as well as intrasystemic relations, and is formed by earlier experience. The nature of this integrated response determines also whether a situation is "meaningful" for us or not. In this sense, Freud (1926a) speaks, e.g., of the fact that "external [reality] danger must have undergone internalization if it is to become significant for the ego; its relation to a situation of helplessness which has been lived through must be recognized." Dealing with similar problems, though from a different point of view, and exemplifying them by the problem of pain, Buytendijk (1955) said recently in an interesting paper, which is representative of a definite trend in contemporary thinking, that "one's world . . . is no system of objective correlations, but a system of meanings and thus of values." He regrets that the possibility that something acts through its meaning is an annoyance to the scientifically oriented physician. I do not think the possibility is annoying to the

scientifically oriented psychoanalyst, though the analyst will tend to look
at it from a different angle. First, while we realize that both values and
meanings enter "one's world," we would keep "value" and "meaning" con-
ceptually apart. And, beyond this, meanings, in our sense, that is, regarded
in the framework of our thinking, are considered as psychological facts;
they refer to mental tendencies involved in a situation; they refer to the
sign or the symbol characters with which we invest our experiences. That
an attitude to reality is "subjective" does not mean, to us, that the
psychological factors accounting for this "subjectivity" cannot be studied
objectively. This reorientation as to the problems of "subjectivity" and
"objectivity" is actually an essential feature of psychoanalysis, which has
subjected that "world" we spoke of in relevant aspects to objectifying
thinking. In the process of analysis itself, the patient's relations to inner
and outer reality are restructured, distortions are undone, and a more
"objective" picture is substituted for them. Particularly with respect to
childhood material, the resulting picture is far more "objective" and also
coherent than the one the child could form at the time the experience
took place. In regard to this, analysis means increased knowledge of
reality, outer and inner, in the strict, objective sense. Also, psychoanalysis
tends to eliminate "quality" from its basic concepts (Hartmann, 1927).
But in the course of analysis, these objective insights are also integrated,
though to an individually varying degree, into the patient's "world," in
the sense we use this term here.

In the foregoing, I have repeatedly referred to inner as against outer
reality. I have now to make clear that inner reality is not quite the same
thing which Freud had in mind in speaking of "psychic reality," a concept he used in his explanation that fantasy activities can have the same
motivating power as realistic behavior, and that in parts of our mental
apparatus reality testing does not exist. In speaking here of "inner reality," I am referring to the fact that in a sense all mental functions,
tendencies, contents are "real"; fantasy activity also is real, though not
realistic. That is, to recognize that a fantasy is, as a mental act, real does
not mean that its contents reproduce reality.[10]

Problems of acceptance, of distortion, of denial occur in relation to
inner as well as outer reality. How the attitude toward the one affects
the attitude toward the other is a fascinating object of study. Developmentally, the problem has been extensively investigated by M. Klein
(1932), who emphasizes that the relation to inner reality has already
become important at the time when the reality principle is instituted;

[10] See also Dorsey (1943).

by Winnicott (1953), who refers to an intermediate area of experience, in which both inner and outer reality participate; and recently by Frumkes (1953), among others. To speak only of one later developmental phase, it seems certain that after a given age the child learns, in his successful dealings with external reality, to include in his plans of action the consideration also of his own mental processes (Hartmann, 1947). He learns to anticipate the interaction of inner with outer reality. This has been well described as an aspect of action by Parsons and Shils (1951): "In accordance with a value standard and/or an expectation, the actor through effort manipulates his own resources, including his own body, voice, etc., in order to facilitate the direct or indirect approximation to a certain cathected goal—object or state." What has been called "attitudes on a realistic basis" includes certainly also some knowledge of and consideration of one's own person. About the distorted pictures of inner reality, about typical and individual self-deception, we have learned more from analytic work than from any other source. To account for it, it seems reasonable to speak of a testing of the within, in addition to the testing of the without—that is, to distinguish inner reality testing from outer reality testing. Impediments of inner reality testing are so common that, as to certain functions and contents of the mind, we do not expect much objectivity even in a normal person, except in the course of the psychoanalytic process. These impediments will, of course, sometimes also alter the picture of outer reality, as a consequence of repression, for instance. But in the neurotic, interference with the testing of inner reality is in the foreground. The basic properties of outer reality testing, we know, break down in psychoses only.

This was the last point I wanted to present to you today. My paper dealt with problems of general psychology, not specifically with the theory of neurosis. This is in line with Freud's approach in the paper I took as my point of departure. You may well feel that I have introduced a bewildering number of differentiations and complexities into a basically simple question. I shall be glad if at least some of you agree that these complexities are not arbitrarily introduced but are features of the problems under consideration today. Once one gets used to the manifold aspects of "reality" and "reality principle," this variety no longer appears bewildering. It seems to correspond rather neatly to the variety of those ego functions and their interactions which led Freud long since to speak of the ego as a "representative" of reality. I also think that their differential consideration proves helpful in practice in evaluating the different modes of reality-syntonic behavior.

BIBLIOGRAPHY

Axelrad, S. and Maury, L. M. (1951), Identification as a Mechanism of Adaptation. In: *Psychoanalysis and Culture*, ed. G. B. Wilbur and W. Muensterberger. New York: International Universities Press.

Buehler, C. (1954), The Reality Principle. *Am. J. Psychother.*, VIII.

Buytendijk, F. J. J. (1955), Über den Schmerz. *Psyche*, IX.

de Saussure, R. (1950), Present Trends in Psychoanalysis. *Congrès International de Psychiatrie, Paris 1950*, V.

Dorsey, J. (1943), Some Considerations on Psychic Reality. *Int. J. Psa.*, XXIV.

Einstein, A. (1950), *Out of My Later Years*. New York: Philosophical Library.

Ferenczi, S. (1924), *Thalassa: Theory of Genitality*. New York: Psychoanalytic Quarterly, Inc.

Freud, A. (1936),*The Ego and the Mechanisms of Defence*. New York: International Universities Press, 1946.

Freud, S. (1895), Project for a Scientific Psychology. In: *Origins of Psychoanalysis*. New York: Basic Books, 1954.

—— (1900), The Interpretation of Dreams. *Standard Edition*, V. London: Hogarth Press, 1953.

—— (1911), Formulations regarding the Two Principles in Mental Functioning. *Collected Papers*, IV. London: Hogarth Press, 1925.

—— (1915), Instincts and Their Vicissitudes. *Collected Papers*, IV. London: Hogarth Press, 1925.

—— (1919), "A Child Is Being Beaten." *Standard Edition*, XVII. London: Hogarth Press, 1955.

—— (1920), Beyond the Pleasure Principle. *Standard Edition*, XVIII. London: Hogarth Press, 1955.

—— (1924), The Economic Problem in Masochism. *Collected Papers*, II. London: Hogarth Press, 1924.

—— (1926a), *The Problem of Anxiety*. New York: Norton, 1936.

—— (1926b), *The Problem of Lay Analysis*. New York: Brentano, 1927.

—— (1932), *New Introductory Lectures on Psychoanalysis*. New York: Norton, 1933.

—— (1936), A Disturbance of Memory on the Acropolis. *Collected Papers*, V. London: Hogarth Press, 1950.

—— (1939), *Moses and Monotheism*. New York: Knopf.

Frumkes, G. (1953), Impairment of the Sense of Reality as Manifested in Psychoneurosis and Everyday Life. *Int. J. Psa.*, XXXIV.

Hartmann, H. (1927), *Die Grundlagen der Psychoanalyse*. Leipzig: Thieme.

—— (1939a), Ichpsychologie und Anpassungsproblem. *Int. Ztschr. Psa. & Imago*, XXIV. Transl. in part in: *Organization and Pathology of Thought*, ed. D. Rapaport. New York: Columbia University Press, 1951.

—— (1939b), Psychoanalysis and the Concept of Health. *Int. J. Psa.*, XX.

—— (1947), On Rational and Irrational Action. *Psychoanalysis and the Social Sciences*, I. New York: International Universities Press.

—— (1948), Comments on the Psychoanalytic Theory of Instinctual Drives. *Psa. Quart.*, XVII.

—— (1952), The Mutual Influences in the Development of Ego and Id. *This Annual*, VII.

Klein, M. (1932), *The Psycho-Analysis of Children*. London: Hogarth Press.

Loewald, H. W. (1951), Ego and Reality. *Int. J. Psa.*, XXXII.

Nunberg, H. (1931), The Synthetic Function of the Ego. *Int. J. Psa.*, XII.

Parsons, T. and Shils, E. (1951), *Toward a General Theory of Action*. Cambridge: Harvard University Press.

Piaget, J. (1937), Primary Factors Determining Intellectual Evolution from Childhood to Adult Life. In: *Factors Determining Human Behavior*. Cambridge: Harvard University Press.

Rapaport, D. (ed. 1951), *Organization and Pathology of Thought*. New York: Columbia University Press.

Redl, F. and Wineman, D. (1951), *Children Who Hate*. Glencoe, Ill.: Free Press.

Sullivan, H. S. (1953), *The Interpersonal Theory of Psychiatry*. New York: Norton.

Székely, L. (1951), Die Realität in der Auffassung Freuds. *Theoria*, XVII.

Weiss, E. (1950), Reality and Reality Testing. *Samiksa*, IV.

Winnicott, D. W. (1953), Transitional Objects and Transitional Phenomena. *Int. J. Psa.*, XXXIV.

Zilboorg, G. (1941), The Sense of Reality. *Psa. Quart.*, X.

THE RECOVERY OF CHILDHOOD MEMORIES IN PSYCHOANALYSIS[1]

ERNST KRIS, Ph.D. (New York)[2]

INTRODUCTION

This presentation might be compared to the visit to a familiar scene, repeated after a lapse of time. I propose to pass over a wide and well-mapped-out area and to stop at certain points in order to see in what way our reactions to the scenery may have changed. Though I do not set a definite date for our last visit, I have a period of a quarter of a century in mind. During these years we have been exposed to the impact of new observations and to more numerous, more varied and (possibly through the advantages of cooperative teamwork) better recorded therapeutic experiences. Few, if any, parts of psychoanalysis as a body of knowledge have not profited by these developments. Though neither in theory nor in clinical or therapeutic practice it can be stated with general (or possibly even wide) agreement in which specific respects changes of assumptions or reformulation of hypotheses are required, it seems that the progress of which I speak allows in several instances for fruitful perspectives where alternative hypotheses have been proposed, some as part of broader controversies.

The area of this survey is firmly established in psychoanalysis: the recovery of childhood memories by analytic patients. The advance in ego psychology and the more detailed understanding of childhood conflicts seem to have an immediate bearing on our study. I shall deal with these influences in the two major sections of this paper.

Where any advance in our understanding, in our experience or in our clinical practice can be reported, we tend to become aware of new uncertainties and limitations in our knowledge. We are forced to realize that some of our general assumptions need to be elaborated and some to be modified. Tentative suggestions of this order will be offered in a third concluding section.

[1] Paper presented to the Midwinter Meeting of the American Psychoanalytic Association, New York, on December 4, 1955.
[2] From The Child Study Center, Yale University School of Medicine.

At no point can it be attempted to pursue all of the ramifications of the problems on which I shall have to touch. My aim is to characterize these aspects as well as possible and to illustrate them by examples. If in the end even these aspects turn out to appear familiar, this would confirm the impression that at this time the progress in psychoanalysis tends to manifest itself by a gradual, sometimes imperceptible shading of our views and procedures, as a process of sifting, of constant adjustment of theory and practice—on the whole as a process of learning adapted to the uniquely complex adventure in which psychoanalysis as a science is engaged.

As I mentioned, I shall be mainly concerned with the question how the recovery of childhood memories is brought about and with the dynamic context in which it occurs. This discussion implies certain impressions on the therapeutic effectiveness of the recovery of memories. It is well known that in this respect our views have undergone important modifications, since the model of hysteria has lost its paramount importance in psychoanalytic thinking. In a subtle way this model has overshadowed psychoanalytic discussions, even after it had lost its value as prototype, i.e., after the introduction of the structural approach in Freud's work. Since we no longer view repression as the only mechanism of defense, the tendency to measure results of psychoanalytic treatments in terms of "new" memories recovered is—as Glover (1928, 1940) suggested some twenty years ago—outdated. And yet this tendency seems to linger on, as part of an unwarranted simplification in our thinking. But while it is comparatively easy to state what we no longer hold true, to say what we believe to be true, is a much more difficult matter. At the end of the paper I shall briefly try to make explicit what I will have implied in its course.

Ego Psychology, Reconstruction and Recall

The bend to link present to past experience reflects the very structure of man's mental apparatus. It is part and parcel of many types of introspection and, in higher civilizations, part of the tradition of contemplative and speculative thinking. The study of the interaction between past and present stood at the beginning of psychoanalytic work and has remained alive throughout its development. An interaction it is. Not only does the present experience rest on the past, but the present supplies the incentive for the viewing of the past; the present selects, colors and modifies. Memory, at least autobiographical or personal memory, i.e., the least autonomous area of memory function, is dynamic and telescopic.[3]

The central role of the interrelation of past and present in psychoanalytic work needs hardly to be justified. The psychoanalytic situation with its stress on partial and controlled regression— the request for free association being only the most obvious instance—is so designed that the borders between past and present tend to be blurred. The psychoanalytic situation encourages frequent and imperceptible transitions from reporting to remembering—even the yesterday is part of the past—and from repetition to recall. Certain extreme variations in these transitions and interactions pose well-known problems in therapeutic technique of which the apparently simplest one is here taken as starting point. Both the patient's dwelling on the past and his persistent adherence to the present can function as resistance. In Freud's technical writings there is a notable rule of the thumb,[4] which advises the analyst to turn his attention to the past when the patient insists on the present and to look for present material when the patient dwells in his past. However, it seems that this aspect of resistance can be infinitely more complex, and that its understanding can in itself provide important material for the course of analytic work. I select an example from the beginning of my clinical experience, which illustrates a layering of resistance that suggests a more general formulation. It occurred in the analysis of a young female psychologist whose interest in psychoanalysis had been stimulated by reading of analytic literature, which, at the time and in her eastern European academic environment, was considered as somewhat extravagantly progressive and not part of science in the proper sense. The young woman, who under another name had gained distinction in literary work, came to analysis with a detailed history of the startling involvements through which a sense of adventure had carried her during a period of a few years. The havoc caused in her homeland by the first World War, with its aftermath of revolution and economic crisis, had affected the life of her student years. A member of the aristocracy had been her teacher and lover, and she was anxious to trace back the pattern of this relationship to her childhood, to the peaceful years of the early century. Death had been a familiar specter in her early years. Her mother died when she was three, and in later years of childhood death had separated her from

---

3 I here summarize views best formulated in the study of screen memories, where Freud's (1899, 1901) own initial approach has been elaborated by Fenichel (1927), Glover (1929), and more recently by Katan (1939), Reider (1953), and particularly by Greenacre (1949). For the relation of the present to the past in reconstruction see particularly Loewenstein (1951), Kanzer (1953), and Ekstein (1954). For a discussion of autonomy in memory function see Rapaport (1951) and Kris (1956).

4 See also Sharpe (1927).

some of those to whom she felt most closely attached. Peculiar circumstances fortified the impression of an intimate linkage of sexual love
and separation by death. Attempts to focus on these, at first dim, connections filled many months, in which recollections played a dominant
role. I was at the time much less sensitized to the analysis of resistances
than we all are now, and followed the patient for some time on her way
into the past, until three features imposed themselves on my attention.
They represented three aspects of resistance: the talk of the past served
to counterbalance the drab present, in which the patient was forced to
live. She spoke about her current difficulties, but was constantly trying
to avoid the impact they exercised, both as humiliating reverses of her
fortunes and as challenging predicaments, which one had to meet and
conquer. The memories she produced were in themselves likely to bring
back pleasurable tensions with varied and rapidly changing adventures,
which had long become part of her fantasy life and crystallized in sadomasochistic masturbation fantasies of prepuberty. But while the tensions
of the present were threatening, she was master of those she conjured in
recollection.

A second aspect of the wealth of "memories" was the repetition of a
rivalrous relation to her brother in the transference. The productions
of childhood memories became part of a competitive venture in analysis,
part of a race for "reconstructing" early traumatic experiences. Self-
analysis became the nucleus of the analytic experience and the analytic
hour a mere supplement. The fraternal rival was raised into the position
of a noble but seducible teacher, whose interest might be gained by his
pupil's stupendous progress.

The third aspect of resistance was more deeply rooted, and though
its appearance had struck me first, its meaning became only gradually
clear. I had at the time just become familiar with the work of Proust and
was suddenly struck by the similarity between the patient's reminiscing
mood and the delight and almost sensual pleasure which remembrance
gains in Proust's writings. I was first inclined to connect the libidinization with the content of her recollections, but I soon learned to distinguish between this factor and the libidinization of the function of
reminiscing itself. This investment seemed ultimately to be derived from
the desire to be close to those she had lost early in life.

Needless to say that only viewed in the context of the shifting aspects
of the transference situation the layers of multiple determination could
be reorganized into a pattern of development; and only the pattern of
development allowed to replace the dwelling in the past by insight into
the life history and by changes in the self-representation. These steps,

however, could be achieved only as gradually the material which had
been revealed in a Proustean mood reappeared dynamically linked to
current conflict situations, of which only the transference conflict has
been mentioned in this digest. This then seems to throw light on the
manifestation and function of resistance in this case. Neither the
avoidance of reality conflicts nor the competitive character of the
transference, nor the libidinization of remembering—none of these
elements (or their combination) suffices to characterize the dynamics
of resistance involved. The resistance had broken the link between
present and past and thus the analytic process had been interrupted.
I suggest that many manifestations of resistance could well be described
from this angle. It seems that during certain presumably later stages
of analytic work this interruption is the hallmark of resistance whatever the defense mechanism utilized.[5] Best known is the group of cases
(sometimes seen in reanalysis) in which reconstructive work and the biographical connections established remain either insufficiently invested,
and only intellectually perceived or isolated in other ways. Sometimes
reconstructive work may thus acquire the function of a screen behind
which relevant conflicts remain sheltered. However, the changes in analytic technique which have come about during the last twenty years reduce the danger that such separation of the past from the present should
establish itself. To repeat what has been said on previous occasions
(Kris, 1951): the change to which I refer has not come about in a jolt or
in the course of a few years. It has gradually crystallized, starting from
first suggestions in Freud's technical papers, supported by his formulations on personality structure and on the nature of defense, elaborated
in the work of others—as far as defenses are concerned particularly by
Anna Freud (1936)—and consolidated in many years of clinical work,
initially under the guidance of textbooks and teaching manuals, of
which Fenichel's (1941) treatise on technique surely deserves separate
mention.

The more systematic and more careful exploration of the psychic
surface, the greater consistency in a preparatory phase in which attention
is focused on the structure of defense, seems to reduce the degree to
which every one of the patient's reactions is directly dependent on the
analyst's interventions (Loewenstein, 1951). These interventions, it seems,
have a more limited purpose. With only slight exaggeration, one might
say that the analyst watches a reorganization of forces in the patient's
behavior and guides this reorganization by his interpretations. This inter-

---

[5] Among these mechanisms, "acting out" and "regression" play a particular part,
since both tend to lead to the substitution of repeating for remembering.

action results in what we usually mean by "the analytic process." In the course of this process the past emerges into the present, and a readiness, a "need" for reconstructive interpretations may be noticed.

One of the oldest and most tenacious controversies in psychoanalysis rests on the fact that this readiness, this pressure exercised by the structure of the material, can be overlooked by the analyst. When more than forty years ago Jung found that Freud exaggerated the role of the past, when much later Horney found psychoanalysis "too genetic," they seem to have underrated the self-propelled elements in the patient's participation in the analytic process.[6]

But also among writers on analytic technique there were a few who felt that only the analysis of resistance and discharge in acting out was decisive (e.g., Kaiser, 1934). To others such "purism" seems paradoxical. I take it that the guiding principle of analytic technique is firmly rooted in the idea that interpretation works on the border between unconscious and preconscious processes, and designates what with this help can become conscious. As far as the recall of the past is concerned, the interpretation may then be linked to the process of recognition. We suggest a connection of thoughts, feelings or events which might have taken place in the past and, if this interpretation, or this reconstruction, has some validity and the material has entered the preconscious, the patient "recognizes" the picture drawn as familiar. At a previous time, i.e., before the readiness had come about, he would have reacted differently.[7] It is well known (but remains a matter of considerable clinical interest) that the reaction to recognition need not lead to positive verbalization and certainly not to (immediate) recall. The range of reactions may vary, from outright negation to gradual acceptance, from reinforcement of defense and reanimation of symptoms to relief and the feeling of liberation—a series of reactions, on the whole still intriguing, to which Freud (1938) has late in life devoted his attention. These reactions remind us once more of the fact that the communication with the patient is never exclusively regulated by the secondary process. Our interpretations may stimulate linkages between various strata of the mind which reawaken the flow of primary process connections.[8] Hence short-term predictions of specific reactions to an interpretation are in analytic work hazardous. The recovery of childhood memories is frequently one of the alternative or subsequent reactions to a specific interpretation or to preceding

[6] For the dynamics of these elements, particularly in relation to recollecting, see Nunberg (1932), pp. 348-352.

[7] See also below, p. 64.

[8] See Hartmann (1951) who speaks of the multiple appeal of interpretations.

analytic work in general. The more restrained and gradual the interventions of the analyst are, the more they tend to fit into the flow of the
analytic process (thus avoiding the danger that the search for memories
becomes an intellectualized epiphenomenon), the more frequently memories seem to appear as if they had always been a part of the patient's
recollections. While I shall later return to this point, I am here interested in the relation of various types of interpretations to the process
of memory recovery. It is a process which interpretations set into motion
but which in many instances seems to proceed on its own impetus.

An illustration, familiar in all essential features, is now offered as
concrete basis for our further discussions. It concerns an episode in the
treatment of a forty-year-old member of a respected family of British
merchants, who returned to analysis after two unsuccessful attempts with
other analysts. The episode here reported occurred toward the end of the
fourth year of his analysis. It seemed at first hardly connected with the
patient's central complaint. This complaint had two major aspects. A
widely diversified sexual life with many and attractive lady friends,
facilitated by his social position, had followed a youthful failure in
marriage; but the pleasure in these associations was limited by guilt
toward his partners. None, he knew, would be able to retain his attention.

His passing attachments had one feature in common: the ladies,
almost all of them somewhat lower in social status, would respond to him
with feelings of devotion, and this devotion would stimulate a depressive
reaction in him. He had to rescue them from the mortification which his
future desertion would inflict upon them. This distilled presentation of a
complex pattern which could only be established after several years of
detailed scrutiny points to one of the unconscious determinants of the
cycle. He himself is conqueror and victim, in part identified with the
rejected partner, and he anticipates his own sadistic act by masochistic
suffering. The whole sequence proved ultimately a reflection of the contrasting wishes of "eating" and of "being eaten up."

I shall not enter into further vicissitudes of this one group of symptoms but limit myself to mentioning that the mechanism of identification
had played a decisive part in his life. As if under fateful command, he
had assumed shortcomings and pitfalls in the character and career of a
successful father, who had achieved considerable recognition in a profession which he had pursued without having been trained for it. Due to
this early failure, the father had been excluded from social and professional associations to which he would have been entitled by the position
of his family and his own later achievements.

None of these limitations operated in the patient's life. His socio-scholastic career—to coin a term adapted to the conditions under which he was brought up—was impeccable. He had gone to the right public school, and had been at one of the great universities. And yet he had joined none of the clubs to which he was expected to belong, but had sought association with one or two clubs in which members seemed to gather who, as a rule, had no access to the social set of which he was a part. He thus artificially created for himself the marginal position, to which his father had been relegated. I might add that the choice of myself as analyst was determined by the same propensity: for an Englishman of his class it meant a conspicuous effort to turn to a foreigner of my kind.

The character of the precarious and marginal was apparent in other features. He suffered from a difficulty to recall things, which affected less his work than his social contacts. He could frequently not recall the nature or topic of a last conversation with one of his acquaintances. But even in his business activity a sense of anxious tension maintained itself. He lived under the impression that a "bad memory" would prevent him from the full use of favorable opportunities.

At first it seemed that his memory problem mirrored the father's behavior. Immersed in the pressure of work, he appeared to the little boy preoccupied, distracted, and only half interested in the child's attempt to gain his attention. Gradually other determinants became apparent. We were able to establish a link between his bad memory and certain experiences concerning his genitals. Throughout the later years of his puberty he had been dissatisfied with his penis. In his early sexual exploits a feeling of "local inhibition" had prevailed. On slight provocation a physician whom he had met in the Navy arranged for a circumcision. After it he felt as if liberated; the penis, he thought, had grown.

The episode of the analysis to which I refer and which covered a period of several months centered around two sets of experiences: the feeling of (memory) inferiority became heightened when the role which envy played in his life became meaningful to him. This envy centered at first on a sister, one year older, who since latency years had been the father's pet. She was recognizable as the prototype of many of his lady friends, but supplied also traits to his own personality. However, he had not identified himself with the radiant child, but with the suffering adolescent of later years. Envy also extended to his male competitors, mainly to members of the distinguished club which he had failed to join, and appeared in violent outbursts in which he would imagine how, in debates, he would destroy his adversaries by sarcastic remarks. If ever there was a doubt about the psychological meaning of sarcasm, this man's behavior and fantasies would eliminate it: the Greek root of the word means tearing apart with one's teeth.

Here we were on familiar ground. Memories of early rages, when he was kept waiting for food, fused with his mother's report on outbursts of the toddler, seemed not to fit to the restrained gentleman of his later years, whose fastidiousness in eating was marked: meat had to be well done, sinews and gristles had to be carefully eliminated, so that eating was either a matter of indifference or an almost surgical procedure— once more one of the traits, borrowed from his father and carefully integrated into the general restraint of his manners. Material from dreams, unambiguous in their context and symbolic character, had long ago made clear that oral-aggressive tendencies had early predominated in his instinctual life. In his previous analyses this had been energetically stressed. In the period of analysis about which I report one of the leading themes had been the gradual realization that lethargy and paralysis appeared frequently when envy had been unsuccessfully suppressed. At this point the insight seemed to be near that various feelings of discomfort which pained the patient were equivalents of anxiety. The way which was to lead from the one point to the other seemed winding and extended. The emphasis shifted to the discovery of defects. His sarcasm was fed by a careful inspection of the opponent and what he feared was the opponent's retaliatory criticism, in the course of which his own defects— mainly his wanting memory—would be discovered. It is at this point that in association to a dream the recollection of a childhood scene appeared in which his father inspected the patient's penis. The penis had been slightly inflamed and the foreskin had to be pushed away. It was on the mother's suggestion that this inspection had to be performed. Circumstances of a special kind permitted the dating of the episode. It must have occurred when the patient was four years of age, and all details seemed to fit into the picture we had gained. The slight adhesions of the foreskin (which justified twenty years later the circumcision) had been irritated by the masturbatory activity of the little boy—the masturbatory activity, we add, which had caused "intellectual impairment." In his association to the scene the patient who in his life and work had little contact with Jews reported suddenly and, as it were, abruptly that he had heard that certain "rabbis" who perform circumcisions on Jewish infants tend to bite off the foreskin. The interpretation was offered that as a child he had had the wish to bite off the father's penis and that he feared that his own genital would be bitten off by the father. The patient's reaction, however, was unexpected. He focused on one point: my remarks had implied that he had revealed a new piece of information, whereas he was convinced that he had not only always known about the scene of the inspection of the penis, but also that he had told me about it. Briefly, the *déjà raconté* experience (Freud, 1913) appeared in the context of a memory rivalry.[9] Soon the connections became more meaningful. The feeling of memory insufficiency was suddenly experienced as pressure of the skull cap upon the brain, which was visualized as if it were compressed and hemmed in by this outer surrounding. The analogy with the glans penis and the quest for circumcision was unmistakable. I cannot report on other inter-connections in the material but must limit myself to mentioning some which are directly related to the further piece of analytic material which I propose to report. The idea of circumcision was overdetermined: the foreskin, represented at the same time a protection of the penis against attack, the protecting female and the patient's own femininity (Nunberg, 1947). As female he had been in vain competing with the sister for the father's love, after a period in which during a prolonged absence of the father he had felt extremely close to his mother and sexually attracted to her. The turning to the father, after his return culminated in a classical though transient obsessional-compulsive episode between seven and eight in which a ritual had to be adopted, to protect the members of his family during the night. At the same time his intellectual interest had grown and found many outlets. While the prehistory of the patient's obsessional neurosis cannot be reported in detail, one episode which arose during this time of analysis must still be mentioned. In association to a dream in which a bird, whose name he could not recall, played a dominant part, he reported that during the years eight and nine he had been an eager student of the encyclopedia. While somewhat later the encyclopedia had attracted his sexual curiosity—particularly illustrations that showed ex-posed breasts—at this earlier age his interest had centered on an innocuous problem, on birds of prey. He studied their ecology, their behavior and learned to distinguish ever rarer species. But already at that time he was tortured by the difficulty to remember their Latin names.

I interrupt here the report. The choice of birds of prey as special objects of interest seemed overdetermined in several ways. It continued in sublimated form the older comparative preoccupation with the nature and sizes of male genitals. Moreover, beaks represented the fusion between phallic and oral-aggressive impulses whose derivations overshadowed his sexual life. These were also the years when he had first been forced to wear glasses, as his mother did, and the traditionally stressed sharpness of vision of birds of prey added a further incentive for exploration. In this attempt at sublimation the feeling of memory defect, i.e., the displace-

9 For the dynamics of *déjà raconté*, see now Siegman (1955).

ment of the feeling of defectiveness to the brain, made its appearance.
This sign of intellectual inhibition entered his life at the time when his
sister had found access to the father's interest by her intellectual exploits.
The failure in sublimation was thus related to the envy of the sister,
was self-punitive and a derivative of the conflict between the wish for
and the fear of castration.

The sequence of material here reported suggests a number of generalizations on the relation of interpretation to the appearance of
memories in the context of analytic work. In a schematic form we may
distinguish various levels on which interpretations had been of influence.
The atmosphere of prolonged analytic work had activated the patient's
interest in his childhood in a general way. There had been times when
this interest appeared as resistance, when he would repeat certain crucial
screen memories on which he had worked in his previous analyses. This
resistance, however, had not been operative at the time. Both the memory
of the inspection of the penis by the father and of his interest in birds
of prey had never been mentioned previously, at least not during his
contact with me. The general activation of interest in his childhood may
have facilitated the associative connection with the past, but this associative connection emerged in the context of the current conflict situation
in which the role of envy had become an experience to him. Previous
analytic interpretation may have facilitated the appearance of the association that rabbis perform circumcision by biting, with its obvious
transference implications. But once more there had been no reference to
oral material in the recent or even more distant course of the analysis.
The material appeared since a previously repressed fantasy could at this
time become conscious. The interpretations concerning the rivalry in his
club life had established an understanding for the dynamic of aggressive
rivalry in his mind. A situation was thus created in which impulses, long
in abeyance, became more accessible and in which derivatives of repressed
wishes could reach the preconscious. Interpretation, then, did not produce recall, but rather it established dynamic conditions under which
recall became possible, conditions more similar to those which existed
when the recalled scenes and events occurred.

The detailed analysis of current conflict situations and the recall
of the past are therefore not accidentally but essentially interrelated, cannot exist without each other. Hence the impression that when the influence of instinctual forces and unconscious fantasies on current conflicts
are analyzed, the reappearance of childhood material may follow spontaneously. We may thus schematically distinguish between the "dynamic
interpretation" mainly concerned with conflicts in the current situation

and "genetic interpretations" of various kinds (Hartmann and Kris, 1945). The continuum represented by these genetic interpretations may be characterized by an artificial but possibly useful device: by characterizing extremes. One extreme would be represented by genetic interpretations pointing to archaic impulses, as they become accessible in current material. These impulses represent continuations of preverbal and nonverbal ideations, imbedded in unconscious fantasies with later experiences.[10] The other extreme would be represented by interpretations which try to establish a historical context between the various pieces of the patient's material. Next to numerous inferences drawn from all sources available in analysis, the inventory of always-remembered memory pictures (screen memories) and the recovered memories often foreshadowed in dreams are part of these interpretations, into which ultimately all interpretative work might be integrated. I believe that Freud (1937) had this integration in mind when he said that ultimately interpretations are constructions (or reconstructions). The historical context into which these interpretations are fitted establishes a biographical picture. Even in the ideal case it is a biographical picture of a special kind, one which would not satisfy any requirements of ordinary biography. The nature and dynamic character of this biographical picture may become clearer if we approach our subject from another side.

Problems of Genetic Interpretation

The discovery of the importance of ontogeny, first in the etiology of mental disorders and then in the development of personality, was one of Freud's most momentous steps and certainly the one least prepared by traditional views within the orbit of science. In no other area of psychoanalysis has the progress in knowledge been as continuous as in the understanding of the nature and vicissitudes of infancy and childhood. During the last thirty years the progress has gained in momentum, as if through the added interest in preoedipal development a barrier had suddenly been removed. The extraordinary richness of new insight, as it keeps accumulating, sems to defy any attempt at comprehensive classification. No such classification is intended when I here focus on a continuum characterized by its extremes, by the stress on *endopsychic* and the stress on *environmental* factors.

The dichotomy between these two approaches has its roots in Freud's early work. Shortly after he had become aware of the extreme importance

[10] The term "unconscious fantasy" is here not used in the sense defined by some authors who call "the original primary mental activity, which usually remains unconscious . . . unconscious fantasy" (Riviere, 1952, p. 14).

of childhood experiences for the etiology of neuroses, he formulated a set of hypotheses which were "environmentalist" to the extreme: a seduction during childhood was viewed as cause of neurotic illness. Freud's assumptions went further. He thought that perversion in the seducer produced hysteria in the seduced. This hypothesis, which postulated a high incidence of adult (parental) perversion, enabled Freud to recognize first the improbability and shortly thereafter the incorrectness of his views. He himself described the crisis in his life and the emergence of new insight which evolved from the initial failure (Freud, 1887-1902). Since the reports of his patients did not describe real events but fantasies, the study of fantasy life became essential. The study of these fantasies led to the discovery of the oedipus complex and to that of the various manifestations of infantile sexuality.

While the seduction hypothesis had maximized attention on concrete experiences to which the child was exposed, the later orientation was implicitly based on the supposition that relatively minimal external stimulation would produce the reactions observed; and these reactions, the working of the mental apparatus rather than concrete environmental conditions, were investigated in detail.

It is not my intention to trace the role of these alternative approaches in Freud's work. But it may be well to remind us of the changes his genetic constructions underwent in his clinical work. Detailed evidence seems available only for a period of fifteen years (1900-1915), and it seems appropriate to compare the cases of Dora and the "Wolf-man" in this respect. The difference is not one which can be solely accounted for by the different duration of treatment. It is a difference in essence. In Dora's case (1905), Freud's interest was focused on some general connections between her symptoms and her infantile experiences. In the case of the "Wolf-man" (1918), a history of crucial conflicts is given, in which all then available knowledge on dynamic and genetic questions is combined. The "Wolf-man's" development is not only seen as centered around phases of psychosexual development and their vicissitudes, but specific events were set in relation to each other. A dynamic biographical structure emerged which leads from event to event. But in the analysis of the "Wolf-man," Freud made also decisive advances in the understanding of repressed early fantasies of a preverbal stage of development and laid the foundation to the idea, which has since become one of the cornerstones upon which much of our work rests. We take it for granted that the impact of such preverbal imprints may determine the modes of later reactions to environmental stimuli. The question whether at the age of one and a half years the patient had witnessed parental intercourse

or whether we are faced with a primal scene fantasy was one which occupied Freud's thinking for some time.[11] Out of this dichotomy arose
Freud's formulations on psychic reality which have proved their value,
and these formulations gave the search for unconscious fantasies of a
preverbal period their standing in analysis.

The advances in our understanding of such early unconscious fantasies through Melanie Klein's contribution are well known. Much of her
earlier work has become widely accepted and many fantasy formations
to which she first drew attention have become familiar configurations in
clinical study. The points of controversy have at the same time sharpened
in other respects. It is less the stress on endopsychic factors—somewhat
modified in her latest contributions—than the disregard of maturational
processes which constitutes the difference between her approach and that
of others.[12]

Much less frequently is it being stressed that in our notion of environmental conditions an increase in knowledge has occurred, which has
deeply affected our theoretical assumptions and our clinical work. We
are no longer satisfied to view the development of the child in terms of
his psychosexual maturation only; we find that the development of ego
functions and object relations, to use convenient headings, are of equal
and intrinsic importance. Indeed, the history of the "Wolf-man's" infantile neurosis would appear in a different light, if observed today—
by Freud.

The progress to which I refer has come from many sources. Contributions from psychoanalytic work with adults, with children, combined
therapies of mother and child in child guidance and treatment centers,
and finally the impact of analytic views on the study of child development have all had their share.

It is at this point that I want to state an impression, or even advance
a thesis. This increase in our knowledge, I believe, permits us to understand in greater detail the ways in which interpretations aimed at demon-
strating in the patient's behavior the survival of deeply repressed largely
preverbal impulses can be enriched and supplemented by the recovery
of memories.[13] Since our reconstructions tend to encompass more details

---

[11] It is a problem which already twenty years earlier, in the "Project for a Scientific
Psychology" (1895) had captured his imagination (Freud, 1887-1902).

[12] See in this connection particularly Lewin's succinct comments (1950).

[13] In terms of the controversy between the "British School of Psychoanalysis"
(Glover, 1928, 1945; Bibring, 1947; Zetzel, 1956; and others) this concerns not the question of the "existence" or "importance" of certain unconscious fantasies, but the
criteria that decide at which point they become accessible in analytic material—a question which in turn is related to the "time" of their formation.

and have become more specific, we are better equipped to learn how various levels of genetic interpretations "dovetail." It is one of the areas in analytic work in which the observation in the analytic situation once more discloses its stimulating potentialities as investigative procedure.

I first turn to findings to which child analysis has made the decisive contribution: to the importance of the early relationship of parent and child and more specifically the reaction of the child to peculiarities of the parent's personality. In our analytic work with adult patients we are only rarely able to include this factor. In my experience we succeed only in the course of long and on the whole successful analytic treatments, since interpretations which take the nature of the parents' personality into account obviously require particular caution and a wealth of affirmative impressions, such as in this instance only the prolonged analysis of reactions in the transference situation can provide. Only this caution can protect us against the distorting element of memory which is hardly ever deeper ingrained than in the changing facets which characterize the report of adult patients on their parents.[14]

And yet, when we succeed in encompassing such details of a "traumatic situation" in our reconstructive work, we gain an essential and sometimes possibly crucial supplement. In the analysis of an on the whole successful but inhibited man of forty whose dominant symptoms were uneasiness in a number of specific situations, the attempt to reach an understanding of the origin of scoptophilic impulses played a significant part. These impulses had not invaded his adult sexual life, but were intertwined with attempts to master and control the human environment. The obvious relation to the displacement of oral impulses, the wish to incorporate with his eyes, was important both in his relation to currently significant objects and to their infantile imagines, particularly in his relevant but sharply circumscribed feminine identifications. But such elements of understanding were finally supplemented by one of a peculiar nature, dimly connected with memory images. One component of his scoptophilic propensities led into a specific phase in his childhood relationship to a mother who, as "beloved stranger," had later played a dominant part throughout his life. Behind this contradictory image in which closeness and distance were strangely intertwined, there emerged the reflection of a period when the mother, under the impact of a period

14 Global and stereotypical characterizations such as those given in anamnestic interviews prove almost regularly to dissolve under the analytic microscope. For a clinical illustration, see Kris (1956); for one frequently neglected root of the changing images of the mother in the variations of her own reactions to the growing child, see Coleman, Kris, and Provence (1953).

of depression, found it difficult to relate to her child, by other means than by her facial expression, which the boy learned to decipher.

Puzzled by the nature of these recovered circumstances I discussed several years ago the type of reconstructive assumptions here involved with Miss Freud. To my astonishment, she mentioned that she had observed a "searching look" and an emphasis on visual contact with people in the treatment of children of mothers with various intensities of depression, and subsequent observations in the Hampstead Clinic for Child Therapy confirmed this finding.

One might at this point speculate as to antecedents of this reaction. We have recently been reminded of the fact that in the nursing situation the child's look is frequently centered on the mother's face, and that the ability to react to the human face as a configuration of forms is part of the child's early endowment (Spitz, 1955). May we not assume that oral and visual incorporation grows out of the same situational set-up, and normally merge? The searching look, in the last analysis, connected with the notion of the breast, would in the material of the adult patient appear colored and overshadowed by oral needs. We continue our speculation in assuming that if the nursing situation offers markedly less than the needed gratification, if there is—to speak in analytic shorthand— a breast but no maternal smile, then the two pathways of object relation, oral and visual incorporation, may become separated.

The child that feeds well may still be searching with his eyes as if the visual hunger remained forever pressing. The searching eye of toddlers in institutions is an unforgettable impression, even for the casual visitor.[15] Moreover, it seems that the historical setting in which extreme (i.e., perverse) voyeurism (or exhibitionism) originates, might well confirm (or at least not contradict) the assumption of an early (and possibly specific) deficit in the nursing situation. In the case which I reported above, no such extreme disturbance had developed. As far as I could see from the analytic material, the mother's depression had not been of a severe kind, nor did it occur during the earliest infancy of the patient, but probably only after he was three years old (or alternatively it had gained importance only during the early phases of the patient's phallic development). The child's reaction had soon become part of an effort to sublimate the instinctual forces involved—an attempt which was only in part successful. The recovery of the memory concerned with the patient's relation to his mother contributed essentially to an understanding of this

---

15 I am indebted to R. Coleman and S. Provence for reports on their work on institutionalized children. For an observation of the searching look as distress signal in a two-year-old, see my own observations (Kris, 1951b).

inhibition in sublimation, and thus to the analysis of the situation in which the symptom had established itself.

Another illustration refers to a traumatic situation, the impact of which has only during the last decade been fully appreciated—the separation of mother and child. In the setting of Freud's theory the traumatic character of separation had been anticipated. When he developed in 1926 one of his most grandiose constructs, the sequence of crucial danger situations in the child's life, there was no awareness among analysts— and I here can bear witness as a contemporary—to what typical concrete situations this would apply. Nobody realized that the fear of losing the object and the object's love were formulae to be implemented by material which now seems to us self-evident beyond any discussion. We have become aware of the meaning which separation from the mother plays at various points in the child's development and will not hesitate to use it in our reconstructions, i.e., in establishing the frame into which we fit the material which reaches us during the analytic process by the very extended set of avenues, on which the patient communicates with us.

The early and fully repressed development of a negative oedipus complex in the life history of a patient could be traced back into his childhood years. But only when the need to relinquish one allegiance and to turn to the opposite one had been understood as a dominant pattern in his life, could the vicissitudes of his adult existence be traced back to a peculiar constellation of events, which threw light on its genesis. Before the recovery of the memories which I shall report, we knew that his mother had disappointed him. We assumed that he had reacted to the birth of a sister at the age of three and a half with a violent rageful revival of oral-aggressive impulses, presumably as to a repetition of "the weaning trauma." Slight but recurrent laryngial spasms, allegedly on an allergic basis, and a compulsive symptom regulating inbreathing and outbreathing as part of retention and expulsion of objects during latency, seemed well to fit to this assumption. But the way which led from these symptoms and discharge pathways to his characterological problems seemed obscure until a group of recovered memories appeared. The three-and-a-half-year-old had been suddenly separated from his mother. She, who had been wholly and warmly devoted to her first child, went to the hospital to give birth to a little girl. During the absence of the mother the boy developed a febrile illness which proved to be diphtheria. The mother accelerated her return from the hospital, but she either came the day when the patient had to be hospitalized, or even after he had been taken away. In the child's mind there survived the impression of a long-lasting separation. But it remained unclear who had gone and who was left. He turned to his father until further traumatic experiences drove him back to the mother's spell, but retained in life a need to change allegiances, to shift from one side of the controversy to the other, until, only in analysis, he found the way to compromise. The evaluation of the significance of the recollection had become possible only by our general knowledge of the impact of separation on children. Without that knowledge the memory might have suggested various causal relationships. One might have stressed the sibling rivalry as a central theme, or the idea that the absence of the mother had been experienced as retaliation for libidinous or aggressive desires, and a number of other possible interconnections. Though these and several other interpretations went through my mind and some were used, as it were as subsidiary themes, the central avenue remained the active repetition of the passive experience of separation. Only gradually another line of interpretation was added, one which had suggested itself before the recollection appeared, but which at the time seemed not sufficiently connected with the pattern of joining and relinquishing allegiances. I had thought at the time that these interpretations would at best strengthen skepticism and resistance: I refer to interpretations which pointed to the connection of oral incorporation and expulsion of objects which covered both his somatic symptoms and his pattern of life. After the recollection the way seemed open to this expansion of our area of understanding.[16]

This instance is not meant to illustrate that the "deep" interpretation of the archaic impulse group, i.e., the propensity to incorporate and expel, should necessarily follow the memory recovery. Any such suggestion would seem to me pedantic and unwarranted since it overlooks the nature of communication between analyst and patient. Interpretations and inferences on opposing tendencies in object relations, on specific manifestations of ambivalence, on importance of oral experiences in specific current situations had naturally been part of the preceding analytic work. How far such interpretations are being carried at each given point remains obviously a matter of choice and is in the context of this presentation of secondary interest, provided that one outcome is avoided. The deep interpretation should not supply the patient with an empty "id vernacular" which can easily be used for resistance, and thus help to maintain repression. In the illustration offered this repression would presumably have been directed against the memory recovery. The recovery of memory, however, is only one of the reactions which might be barred by resistance. The much more general reactions concern the

16 For a fuller case report, see Kris (1956).

conviction that the patient must gain. The more archaic the material is that appears in the analytic process, the more will its derivatives be spread over wide areas of behavior. The broader the basis from which the specific reconstruction of early experiences and archaic impulses is reached, the greater the chance of reawakening their full impact.[17]

The area where the most effective link between reconstruction and experience can be established is subject to great variations according to factors in the patient's personality and illness which I am at a loss to specify. To mention contrasting examples: I remember one instance in which the aggressive and teasing interplay between mother and child during early feeding was mainly reconstructed from the consistency and gradual sharpening of verbalizations in the transference situation—a reconstruction accidentally and spontaneously confirmed by an early observer, who had been in the house when the mother breast fed the patient. In another instance, the discussion of the long-suppressed dissatisfaction in life was during later stages of analysis accompanied by burning sensations in the oral cavity and the palate. Interpretations of the traumatic experience in the suppression of rage, focused in earlier remembered instances from the period of toilet training, could thus plausibly be extended into the nursing situation. In both these instances, however, the patient's conviction could only arise by the felt or experienced link between past and present. Through the lifting of anticathectic energies which makes the conviction possible (Lewin, 1950), the reconstructive effort gains new impetus. In the instance of our patient with the separation experience, the continued course of the analysis led to a more specific insight into what was incorporated and what expelled and the variations of patterns which can be studied when an unconscious fantasy is followed on its secret progression throughout a patient's life.

We assume that the fantasy whose reflections and reverberations we thus study retains reactions to and imprints of a traumatic situation— hence the following question now presents itself: What properties of this situation can reconstructive work in psychoanalysis hope to recapture? It is a question which, hardly posed, reminds us of intriguing limitations in our knowledge. Almost to our surprise we find ourselves unable to answer questions which, we feel, are bound to be of considerable clinical relevance. Thus it seems that we are not always, and only rarely with the desirable sharpness, able to distinguish between the effects of two kinds of traumatic situations: between the effects of a single experience, when reality powerfully and often suddenly impinges on the child's life—the

[17] For a somewhat different emphasis, see Lampl-de Groot (1951).

shock trauma, as I should like to call it—and the effect of long-lasting situations, which may cause traumatic effects by the accumulation of frustrating tensions—the strain trauma, as I would like to say. It is well known and has not long ago been emphasized by Anna Freud (1950) that what the analytic patient reports as an event which had taken place once appears in the life of the growing child as a more or less typical experience, which may have been repeated many times. Her suggestion, then, is that analysts tend to be misled by the telescopic character of memory. On the other hand, the single dramatic shock, e.g., seduction at an early age, appears usually not with sharp outline;[18] the experience is overlaid with its aftermath, the guilt, terror and thrill elaborated in fantasy, and the defense against these fantasies. We are misled if we believe that we are, except in rare instances, able to find the "events" of the afternoon on the staircase when the seduction happened: we are dealing with the whole period in which the seduction played a role— and in some instances this period may be an extended one. The problem is further complicated by the fact that the further course of life seems to determine which experience may gain significance as a traumatic one. In order to illustrate the complexity of these processes I choose an example which concerns not an actual but a prospective analytic patient. I should like to report on a brief sequence of experiences of a child and her dog, which were observed over a period of several months. The data I offer stem from a longitudinal study at Yale University, Child Study Center, in which a team of pediatricians, social workers, nursery school teachers, and psychoanalysts attempt to follow the development of non-selected and hence presumably normal children from birth on.[19]

Dorothy satisfies in all respects the criteria of normal development. The well-developed and determined two-year-old was, as first-born, in the center of her parents' attention. The marriage went through stormy episodes, and the child learned early to find her way between the struggling parents, to keep the mother closely attached to herself—she frequently slept in her bed—and the father in the position of an interested suitor. There were definite areas in which she sided with her father. He was an outdoor person, a lover of animals, and Dorothy shared his interest and, except for a short period when she was twelve to fourteen months old, did not follow her mother into her phobic tendencies. These tendencies included an old dog phobia, reduced to a violent dislike of dogs.

18 For an example of this kind, see recently Rosen (1955).
19 The study is supported by a Grant of the Commonwealth Foundation in New York City.

When Dorothy was two years old a brother was born. Though the mother accorded to the newborn much attention, the ties to her daughter were not loosened. Four months later, shortly after the family had moved to a new home, the father brought a small dog and a cat home. Dorothy became very attached to the dog. She was constantly involved with him and her body showed at the time innumerable scratches which were due to the dog's outbursts in response to her teasing love play. The dog's attacks were not limited to Dorothy: he chewed the cat's tail, so that the father had to cut off the tail. During the same period—i.e., when Dorothy was twenty-six to twenty-nine months old—the relation of the parents to each other was a particularly stormy one, with frequent fights, in which Dorothy was using and sharpening her technique of both understandingly adapting to an environment in which she had a pivotal position and of manipulating the situation with some determination. Those who observed the child in the nursery school during these months were struck by two features. Dorothy showed extraordinary understanding for emotional needs in the people around her. She was always aware of the needs of other children, and capable of poignant verbalizations. At the same time she showed an unusual determination—already earlier manifested—which seemed to spring from a substructure of stubbornness disguised by the engaging surface.

It is during this period (October) that her paternal grandfather died. Dorothy was then twenty-nine months old. Two months later the puppy was run over by a car and had to be buried. The family reacted strongly to the accident, the father with agitation, the mother with guilt, since she had not kept the dog leashed. In Dorothy's mind the death of grandfather and dog were soon condensed. Immediately after the dog's death she had spoken about it in the nursery school (early December). But late in January the death and separation had gained for her a greater significance. For some time I had been particularly interested in Dorothy, and functioned in the nursery school as an assistant teacher. From September on, that is from Dorothy's entry into the school, I had been in regular touch with both her and her mother, so that the child seemed particularly attached to me. From mid-December to late in January I was kept away by one thing and another, and when Dorothy saw me again her reaction clearly indicated that she had missed me; she greeted me with the words: "My dog has gone away, where Nonny is, very far." It is significant that she had substituted the pet name of the maternal grandmother, whom she saw daily, for that of the paternal grandfather, but equally indicative that she had equated separation from me with the thought that I might have died.

The attachment to the dog had not vanished in spite of the fact that shortly after its accident the father had introduced a new and different pet, a parakeet with whom Dorothy engaged in excited games, in this instance supported and aided by her mother. But the father must have realized that the child's mind was still occupied with the dead dog. Early in February a stray dog greeted by Dorothy with great pleasure joined the family for a few days. After his disappearance the father brought home a new dog which had been given to him by a man whose wife had to be hospitalized (for hysterectomy). Dorothy welcomed the dog with great excitement. Four days after its arrival she was heard to communicate to one of the teachers part of the fantasy context which surrounded the new pet: *"My doggie died, my Mommy has a new baby—in the hospital."* She thus responded to the new dog with reinforced longing for the old one and with a fantasy taking her back to the time when her brother was born. A stimulus for the reminiscent thought may well be the fact that the former owner of the dog, whom Dorothy did not know personally, was in the hospital. The memory of separation, the fear of death and the fear of her own death wishes were thus condensed—and the fact that the new dog was to her a child from father was denied by the double reference: she, Dorothy, had lost the dog, and mother had the baby.

This interpretation was firmly supported by a large number of data, and particularly by the mother's reaction. Her resentment turned against the new dog, which father and daughter shared, and she declared spontaneously that the fact that Dorothy did not share her own apprehension of dogs made her feel jealous, and made her realize that father and daughter were "ganging up against her." It was a genuine outburst, uncontaminated by psychological indoctrination, which had not penetrated to the educational and economic stratum of the family.

Let me conclude by reporting that when the new dog's leg was hurt in an accident and he had to be left for a short period with the veterinarian, Dorothy developed her first acute fear of her otherwise beloved pediatrician, whom she had known since birth. But once more the sequence of events was confusing. A few weeks before the dog's accident, mother's menstrual pad had for the first time attracted Dorothy's attention. She was then thirty-two months of age.

May I engage your interest in an experiment in thought: let us imagine how after twenty years the recollection of the material here reported in considerable simplification may appear in Dorothy's analysis. The network of overdeterminations seems almost infinite: the wish for a child from father, the death wish against the mother, the fear about both sexual and destructive impulses, and finally the fear of castration which seems age adequately added and superimposed, are likely to baffle the future analyst's imagination.

In Dorothy's case we can follow the development of the transformation to which the memory of the experiences with the pet was exposed one step further. During her fourth and fifth year of life Dorothy was seen in play-therapy sessions, from four years and four months on regularly, three times a week by a young analyst under experienced supervision.[20] Early in this contact material concerning Dorothy's interest in dogs had appeared. It gained momentum when her dog, which had grown too big, had to be given away by the father and replaced by a smaller dog. Dorothy recalled on this occasion the death of her first dog. She could not verbalize and re-experience her affect fully. However, in describing her feeling, she said that "she felt like putting her head into a bucket with water." Whatever the source of the metaphor, it clearly expressed the painful affect in ascribing the tears to external influence. The thoughts originally associated with the death of the dog were not recalled, but the fear of Nonny's death, who had lately suffered from high blood pressure, reappeared. Even clearer and more significant was a second connection. The death of the dog appeared no longer closely connected to the loss of the fantasy child from father, but as connected to the loss of a penis, dimly linked to disappointment in the mother. In Dorothy's current conflict the rivalry with her brother stood at that time in the foreground.

This simple example illustrates some steps in the elaboration of reactions to an early experience. The transformation, which occurred between the ages of two and a half and four and a half, might have many intermediary stages, which we did not recapture. It seems likely that the transformation we observe is itself only preparatory to a further (gradual?) repression of the whole set of memories which, we suspect, might occur early in latency. But the complexity of the steps we observe makes us once more aware of the nature of reconstructive work in analysis. In one sense one may say it is a hopeless task. Indeed it is, if it were our intention to reconstruct what had happened in Dorothy's life in the period of five months, during which the vicissitudes with her pet occurred. But reconstructive work in analysis cannot aim at such a goal: its purpose is more limited and yet much vaster. The material of actual occurrences, of things as they happen, is constantly subjected to the selective scrutiny of memory under the guide of the inner constellation.

[20] The exploratory treatment was conducted by Dr. S. Perlswig under supervision by Dr. S. Ritvo.

What we here call selection is itself a complex process. Not only were the events loaded with meaning when they occurred; each later stage of the conflict pattern may endow part of these events or of their elaboration with added meaning. But these processes are repeated throughout many years of childhood and adolescence and finally integrated into the structure of the personality. They are molded, as it were, into patterns, and it is with these patterns rather than with the events that the analyst deals.

Let me illustrate this point by some amplification of an example previously offered. It concerns the little boy who succumbed to diphtheria while the mother was away for her delivery and whom we met as a man with shifting allegiances. This pattern of behavior did not result from the infantile experience, but from the interaction of this infantile experience with later events. The years after the illness were years of extreme marital discord. The parents were involved in almost incessant nightly fighting in which, in more than one instance, the little boy felt the impulse to protect his mother against the violence of an attacker to whom he felt dedicated. This period was followed by years of separation, when the father had deserted the family with another woman, until, during the later years of latency, the family was reunited once more. This is the way in which even the single dramatic experience is built into the sequence of time, and merges into the course of the life history out of which, by reconstructive work, some episodes can be regained; it will be those episodes which have become dynamically operative, because they became, when they occurred, or later in life, at one of its crucial crossroads, invested with greatest "meaning." The memories of such events seem then to become nodal points. Hence the defense against the revival of certain memories becomes essential: anticathectic investment is directed against the re-emergence of the derivatives of instinctual forces and the affects attached to the memory image.

Genetic interpretations aim at these investments rather than at the "original events": hence the well-known fact that the reconstruction of childhood events may well be, and I believe regularly is, concerned with some thought processes and feelings, which did not necessarily "exist" at the time the "event" took place. They may either never have reached consciousness or may have emerged at a later time, during "the chain of events" to which the original experience became attached.[21] Through reconstructive interpretations they tend to become part of the selected

---

[21] See Kris (1950b), where the topic is discussed in some detail. When Freud formulated this principle for the first time (1917), he was obviously already under the impact of the analysis of the "Wolf-man."

set of experiences constituting the biographical picture which in favorable cases emerges in the course of analytic therapy.

CONCLUSIONS

This seems to be the point at which we may turn finally or at least explicitly to some general aspects which this survey suggests. The recovery of childhood memories is part of the struggle between the ego and the id, and of another struggle, a rear-guard struggle, as it were, which takes place "within" the ego itself.

In most instances the recovery of childhood memories is—as we said—an inconspicuous affair and at least initially not necessarily connected with any deeply moving experiences. The patient may have mentioned the particular recollection in an aside, as something he had always remembered. When the importance of the memory has gradually become acceptable to him, he may show some disappointment which seems most marked in training analyses. The analysand had expected a startling revelation and seems to resent that what he considers a familiar reminiscence is now being advanced to key position in the biographical reconstruction of his childhood. Almost thirty years ago Glover (1928) seems to have expected that with the change in our views on the function of repression, this attitude would lose in poignancy, an expectation which my own experience does not confirm. While the hunger for dramatic revelations still persists, sometimes as expression of passive desires, dramatic memory recoveries have probably become even rarer since interpretations tend to be better planned, more cohesive, and since surprise is being considered a reaction, though germane to the inquisitive mind of the analyst, yet one which he does not intentionally elicit in his patients. We do not as a rule want to catch patients by surprise, we do not want to shock them into reactions or recall.

It seems therefore necessary to distinguish between memories which suddenly emerge from repression and memories which had been preconsciously available before they entered the patient's communication in analysis. They had, however, not been sufficiently invested, stood outside of circumscribed mental contexts, and could not be mobilized without further instigation. In practice a sharp distinction between these two cases is only rarely possible. In theory the difference may lie in the reaction to recognition. The formula "what can be mobilized in recognition must have been preconscious" seems valid.[22]

---

[22] I here quote from a previous publication: "When recall is not yet possible, recognition may already be accomplished. The vicissitudes of the relationship between

The distinction between the two cases is made difficult by the fact that a constant flow of derivatives from repressed material enters the preconscious ego, particularly during the analytic process; these derivatives, we say, move into the reach of interpretations. Of the variety of such transitions only one has been particularly studied by Freud (1913), the phenomenon of *déjà raconté*, of which an instance was here reported. Our patient's recollection of the inspection of the penis by his father had, we assume, gradually become available to the preconscious, was possibly for some time uninvested or cut off from other connections, and could then, on further instigation by analytic work, become part of a trend of thought, i.e., part of the integrative function of the ego, and thus appear in the patient's associations.

This description is based on the assumption of the regular or frequent interaction of repression and other mechanisms of defense.[23] Freud suggested that other defense mechanisms may have to operate, where, for one reason another, repression failed to eliminate the dangerous impulse, drive representation or associated notion. Some of these mechanisms are more archaic than repression, of simpler construction, but not necessarily less effective or less powerful as sources of resistance. Their "strength," to

---

recognition and recall are particularly familiar in reconstructions of infantile experiences. While few, if any, case histories go to the length to which Freud went when, in the case of the Wolf-man, he studied the reactions of the patient to various alternative reconstructions (1918), it seems to be the general experience that in many instances reconstructions must be varied and modified until they are correct. These various steps may all be described in terms of stages in the interaction of recognition and recall.

"The suggestion that historical interpretations in analysis stimulate memory to recognition leading to recall is in accord with experimental findings. These experiments show how recognition improves recall or guarantees retention. The theoretical, psychoanalytic explanation of the relationship between recognition and recall is that the synthetic function of the ego, establishing a context, is in the case of recognition facilitated by the help of perception (in our example, the analyst's interpretation). Recall then fills a gap, fits into a pattern. . . . The complexity of the interdependent factors during the psychoanalytic process is such that we can surely not assume that any one single operation is responsible for major dynamic changes; thus any release from repression depends on the strength of defenses used for the purposes of countercathexis which, in turn, depends on the ego's capacity to cope with the prevailing intensity of conflict. It seems therefore reasonable to assume that facilitation of the ego's integrative or synthetic function by recognition is one of the dynamic factors leading to recall.

"The relation of recognition to recall of the repressed can be tentatively described in these terms: since the 'original' situation has been recognized, previously not sufficiently invested id derivatives can be integrated into the pattern indicated by the reconstruction; this in turn strengthens the ego's position, permits a reduction of countercathexes and the gradual infiltration of further material—a result in the end not dissimilar to sudden recall, in cases in which the interpretation has led to the spectacular revival of repressed traumata" (Kris, 1950b, pp. 309-310).

[23] For the following, see also Gero (1951, 1953) and Gero and Rubinfine (1955).

continue in metaphorical terms, is difficult to assess, since in neurotic illness they tend to be sheltered by the main line of fortifications, behind
the wall that we call repression. Freud's general assumption (1926) applied
to the problem of memory recovery. "The forgetting of impressions,
scenes, events," he wrote in 1914, "nearly always reduces itself to *dissociation* of them." The word "dissociation" here clearly stands for
"isolation," a mechanism studied by Freud in his later work. Isolation
excludes certain experiences from associative connections (which are
said to be "interrupted" or "suppressed"), and can therefore not be
"reproduced" in ordinary thought process (Freud, 1926, p. 76).

At this point a slight readjustment of current assumptions seems required, one, foreshadowed already by Fenichel's treatment of the subject
(1946) and by the use of the term "isolation" in current clinical understanding. Some degree of isolation is part of normal mental life and
of all or almost all pathological configurations of defense. Isolation as
resistance during the analytic process, then, can be studied not only in
obsessional neuroses but in every analytic treatment at one time and in
one form. The isolation of memories in the preconscious would be only
one instance in point.

The interaction between repression and isolation constitutes a parallel
to the classical instance, in which the appearance in consciousness of the
formerly repressed (or isolated) thought is unsuccessfully warded off by a
derivative of the former anticathexis; the thought appears in negative
form. Repression has been substituted by negation as a reflection—in this
instance, a feeble one. In other, less well-described instances, the memory,
when it first appears, remains vague. A doubt may arise as to whether
or not the event that had been remembered has actually occurred. I
assume that in this instance repression is supplemented and followed by
an attempt to use denial.[24] Much less often is it possible to study in the
recovery of memories the interaction of repression and projection, and
instances I can recall seem to be particularly complex. In the simplest
of these cases the memory is attributed to the analyst as one of his
constructions.

The dynamics of memory recovery might be said to reflect, in some
not too direct and not too regular sense, the functional distribution of
various defenses in each personality and particularly the interaction between repression and the more archaic methods, which with some individuals have remained part of their central equipment for the solution of
conflicts. Though a wealth of clinical material is available on the inter-

[24] Alternatively one might think of "undoing"—but there are reasons, too complex
to discuss here, which make me prefer the assumption of the working of denial.

action of various defenses in the great nosological pictures, only one group of afflictions has been studied in great detail from this angle: I refer to Lewin's (1950) classical study of elations. Through the homology between the interaction of repression with other mechanisms in memory recovery and in the structure of neuroses in general, the study of the former has strengthened two clinical impressions of possibly wider significance. The interaction of repression and isolation, which we here considered as part of the normal process of recovery of the repressed, has a particular significance in obsessional neuroses, where isolation seems omnipresent and specifically directed against the affect charge. (Hence the tempting danger of intellectualization in the treatment of obsessional characters.) However, it seems that not only the function of isolation but also that of repression can be particularly excessive. A certain proliferation of anti-cathectic energies, one may speculate, could well be related to the premature ego development, so frequently detected in the development of obsessional neurotics and obsessional characters and to the interconnected need to invest large amounts of aggressive energy into anticathectic function. From the archaic equipment, of which, as Freud stresses, isolation is a part (in its derivation from the motor sphere of "do not touch"), particularly projection seems either to survive or, in the course of regression, to have acquired renewed power. One might assume that hysterias would offer an opposite picture—apart from the specific instance of phobias—but since hysteria as a clinical entity seems at this stage ever more amorphous, it is best to state that wherever clearly hysterical symptomatology plays a central part, repression is dominant, sometimes like an iron curtain, which, once one knows the mechanism, can be easily lifted, though it seemed immovable before. Though the subsidiary mechanisms seem highly variable, it is my impression that at least in a group of cases in which also typical conversion symptoms tend to occur, particularly one mechanism of the archaic equipment plays often a subsidiary and perhaps in some instances an altogether important role: I refer to denial.

It cannot be attempted to continue such a survey. Suffice it to say that the interaction of numerous archaic mechanisms can be studied in the transition from cases with clearer neurotic to those with clearer psychotic pictures, where for instance particularly the combination of projection and denial in paranoid psychoses might be prototypical. The function of this interaction was recently indicated by Waelder (1951). However, in this connection it seems relevant to stress that the access to the understanding of some psychotic afflictions seems open only if one assumes that the hypertrophy of a large variety of archaic mechanisms

8

ERNST KRIS

of defense is at least sometimes concomitant with a dysfunction of repression. Memory phenomena studied in some psychotic children (Mahler and Elkisch, 1953), the memory hypertrophy in some schizophrenic processes with adults, and the stream of reminiscences with which some borderline patients overwhelm the analytic process—all are well-known instances in point.[25]

We have briefly mentioned these phenomena, since a conclusion pertinent to the subject of this paper presents itself. The closer we approach the area where repression has lost its power as central defense, the less can the transition from past to present become one of the indicators of progress in analytic work and the less significant is the recovery of memories and the emergence of a biographical picture. The core of its therapeutic effectiveness rests in the dynamics of the lifting of anticathexes. The interpretation establishes the situation in which the lifting becomes possible. Then derivatives of repressed impulse groups enter the preconscious, the investment of the subsidiary defenses are lessened, and the released energies now at the disposal of the ego can be used for its integrative function. Thus memories enter the stream of thought, first in associative connections from which they had been excluded (Nunberg, 1931), then they take their place in the picture of the personal past, at which reconstructive work aims. The full investment of the causal connections established by the insight into the personal history protects in turn the preconsciously available memories against disappearance from the realm of the ego. Without that protection they can easily once more become part of the id by repression and by other mechanism, which will draw them back into the whirl of the primary process. Such vicissitudes of remembering and—to coin a term fashioned in "Through the Looking Glass"—of "unremembering" are part and parcel of almost every analysis.

Memory recovery is thus part of a circular process. While it has been traditionally stressed that the lifting of repression (or, as we would say, of anticathexes) strengthen the ego, it is equally true that increasing strength of the ego facilitates further reduction of anticathectic energies.[26] The emergence of insight, related as it is to the integrative functions of the ego, has its place in the center of these transactional events.

Reconstructive work offers insight into causal connections on various

---

[25] For a recent clinical example, see for instance Kramer (1955). For the vivid description of the "unnaturally strong" memory of a famous patient, see a letter of Charles Lamb (Feb. 14, 1834, to Miss Freyer) in which he describes the "reminiscences" of his sister Mary, the matricidal psychotic with whom he had shared his life.

[26] Alexander (1948) and Alexander and French (1946) recently have stressed this point, and view recall only as a manifestation of increased ego strength.

levels. To take the best documented area of examples: the existence of traits or symptoms, which remain enigmatic when seen in the context of present behavior, may become meaningful once the veil that covers the past has been lifted.[27] To refer to one of our illustrations: the co-existence of the feeling of memory defect and the difficulties in object choice of our patients seemed isolated and unconnected. The recovered past established various interconnections and the memory concerning the preoccupation with birds of prey during latency brought an attitude and experiences into the analytic discussion, in which the investment of certain thoughts and ideas became particularly clear, as if a nodal point in a complex texture had been exposed. A similar insight into the genetic interconnection between two sets of symptoms, between upper respiratory complaints and the compulsion to change allegiances, appeared in another illustration where the recovered episode of the separation from the mother and the question of who was deserted and who the deserter played a decisive role.

In speaking of insight, the reaction of the analyst should be distinguished from that of the patient. The recovered memories strengthen the analyst's conviction, fortify him against doubt and may help him to gear his subsequent interpretations more closely to such points in which the past seems to live on in the present.

In the patient himself the development of insight is once more a highly complex process and one subject to many vicissitudes. The intellectual and emotional acceptance should be sharply distinguished. To put it in the briefest formula: not only memories are screened and repressed; the same is true of the affective experience. I borrow the term of screen affects from Lewin's presentation of these issues (1950), to which I have nothing to add. To transform insight from an intellectual into a total experience is one of the essential parts of "working through." Hence the similarity between the patient's work in analysis and the process of grief and mourning. In fact, it seems that a repressed unconscious fantasy can be treated like a possession or a love object. One can sometimes actually observe how certain memories acquire such meanings. They may be treated as treasured possessions invested with energies derived from anal experience[28] and may alternatively or concomitantly represent a part of the self, which is unwillingly relinquished to scrutiny.

Lewin (1939) has convincingly described how the sense of the real is added to that of insight when the sense of certitude is established by the reawakening of the past as a revival of infantile omniscience. When anti-

27 See Hartmann and Kris (1945).
28 For a discussion of this point, see Kris (1956).

cathexes are fully lifted, when autonomous ego functions are fully invested the sense of conviction may be seen as essential progress in the individual's mental organization (Kris, 1950b). While the dynamics of the process of assimilation of insight are thus clearly outlined, individual variations as to the course of this process and as to its final result are great, and there is at this time hardly evidence available which would allow for generalizations.

In favorable, or one might as well say, optimal cases—they naturally need not be the cases in which analytic work produces the most dramatic therapeutic changes—some historical reconstructions or even the total biographical picture becomes part of the patient's changed self-representation, and the patient remains aware of the relation of these changes to the analytic material. Part of this awareness concerns the preanalytic distortion of his past by defensive operations. After analysis the once recognized lines that connect past and present form a pattern which the patient is able to experience as familiar, and which in exceptional cases he may even be able to expand. These are, however, on the whole not too frequent results, and I see no reason why one should necessarily aim at such an outcome of analytic work, except possibly in training analyses. At least some analysts successfully pursue the arduous task of self-analysis, either as concomitant part of their work or at times of personal crises. In this connection a wide area of awareness of their past has proved of value. But even here detailed information is at this time hardly available. The other extreme is represented by patients whose recollection of what has occurred in their analysis is blurred; and yet some of these seem to have no reason to complain about results. However, I would postulate that with many of these patients at one time during the course of treatment, particularly during the latter phase of the working through process, the effect of reconstructive work was operative. This period was apparently only a transient one, lasting for some time, until the acquired insight became warded off once more.[29]

At the present stage of our knowledge one may well find it difficult and futile to indicate clinical or structural conditions which favor one outcome or the other. But it is by no means a question which needs to remain outside the area of investigation. Material may be derived from several sources, from second analyses in general, particularly if analytic work with the same patient is resumed after several years of interruption.

[29] This clearly does not take the interaction of various other therapeutically operative factors into account, which constitute psychoanalytic treatment. Some of these other factors bring the "corrective experience" about, the role of which has been stressed by Alexander.

Moreover, empirical research in psychoanalysis could well expand its limits, and particularly if conducted by teams of investigators, it may in some instances help to replace opinion by decision. One might think of systematic analytic catamneses—utopian as such a suggestion may still seem at this time. In such investigations the question might be studied how after analysis the insight in his personal history has remained operative in each patient's experience or to what extent it has become blurred, and in what detailed way both outcomes are related to therapeutic results in general and particularly to significant changes in the patient's self-representation. It is in this area where I expected for some time a high positive correlation between the continued investment of the personal analytic biography and the effects of treatment. But when I examined the basis of this expectation, I found only in one instance stringent evidence at my disposal, due to an unintentional experiment in psychoanalytic catamnesis, which had remained fixed in my mind.

Some years ago I prepared an extensive case history of a patient, of which I finally used a fragment for publication. At the time when I intended to publish the whole report I decided to let the patient read it, whose analysis had been concluded five years earlier. The patient reported a feeling of full and intense familiarity and indicated which interpretations had seemed to him particularly crucial at the time. In one instance he definitely stressed that the awareness of a deep emotional reaction, of "a shattering experience," as he put it, had remained alive in his mind, though the intensity of his reactions had at the time not fully been noticeable in what he had told me. In this instance the lasting effect of analysis had, in fact, closely related to the area of self-representation. The patient had been liberated from the pressure of guilt feelings and fantastic ambitions, which, before his analysis, he had re-enacted in life.

Approac. .ng our topic from several sides we have become aware of the centr. . function of the ego in the recovery of memory, and in the assimilation of both the recovered memories and the analytic biography. The reconstructive approach in psychoanalysis is linked to the idea that changes in the structure of defense as part of therapy are indicated. Not in all types of illness are they indicated, nor in all stages of one and the same process. Our theory can specify which of the functions of the ego has to be investigated, in order to make the decision as to the indication of psychoanalytic therapy reliable: it is the capacity of neutralization of instinctual energy. The energy quanta, to continue in theoretical terms, set free by the analytic exploration of defense and repressed ideations, should ideally be discharged in social function of the indi-

86   ERNST KRIS

vidual, to repeat a well-known Freudian statement, in the capacity for
work and love. In both these connections the discharge presupposes various degrees of neutralization.[30]

One of the relationships in which the importance of the capacity to
neutralize plays its part is the analytic situation itself. It is one in which
the adjustment to changing levels of behavior, to regression and progression, to self-oblivion and re-emergent self-observation, plays its part. It
is a situation in which in the relationship to the analyst, the patient is
required to learn and to experience the double discernment of the present liberated from the shadow of the past, and the past, liberated from
defensive distortions.

BIBLIOGRAPHY

Alexander, A. (1948), Fundamentals of Psychoanalysis. New York: Norton.
—— and French, T. (1946), Psychoanalytic Therapy. New York: Ronald Press.
Bibring, E. (1947), The So-called English School of Psychoanalysis. Psa. Quart., XVI.
Coleman, R. W.; Kris, E.; Provence, S. (1953), The Study of Variations of Early Paren-
tal Attitudes. This Annual, VIII.
Ekstein, R. (1954), The Space Child's Time Machine: On "Reconstruction" in the
Psychotherapeutic Treatment of a Schizophrenic Child. J. Orthopsychiat., XXIV.
Fenichel, O. (1927), The Economic Function of Screen Memories. Collected Papers, I.
New York: Norton.
—— (1941), Problems of Psychoanalytic Technique. New York: The Psychoanalytic
Quarterly, Inc.
—— (1946), The Psychoanalytic Theory of Neurosis. New York: Norton.
Freud, A. (1936), The Ego and the Mechanisms of Defence. New York: International
Universities Press, 1946.
—— (1951), Observations on Child Development. This Annual, VIII.
Freud, S. (1887-1902), The Origins of Psychoanalysis. Letters to Wilhelm Fliess, Drafts
and Notes, ed. M. Bonaparte, A. Freud, E. Kris. New York: Basic Books, 1954.
—— (1899), Screen Memories. Collected Papers, V. London: Hogarth Press, 1950.
—— (1901), The Psychopathology of Everyday Life. New York: Macmillan, 1914.
—— (1905), Fragments of an Analysis of a Case of Hysteria. Standard Edition, VII.
London: Hogarth Press, 1953.
—— (1913), Fausse Reconaissance (Déjà Raconté) in Psycho-Analytic Treatment. Collected Papers, II. London: Hogarth Press, 1924.
—— (1914), Further Recommendations in the Technique of Psycho-Analysis. Recollection, Repetition and Working Through. Collected Papers, II. London: Hogarth
Press, 1924.
—— (1917), A General Introduction to Psychoanalysis. New York: Liveright, 1935.
—— (1918), From the History of an Infantile Neurosis. Standard Edition, XVII. London: Hogarth Press, 1955.
—— (1926), The Problem of Anxiety. New York: Norton, 1936.
—— (1937), Constructions in Analysis. Collected Papers, V. London: Hogarth Press,
1950.
—— (1938), An Outline of Psychoanalysis. New York: Norton, 1949.
Gero, G. (1951), The Concept of Defense. Psa. Quart., XX.
—— (1953), Defenses in Symptom Formation. J. Am. Psa. Assoc., I.

30 See Hartmann (1955), Kris (1955).

THE RECOVERY OF CHILDHOOD MEMORIES

—— and Rubinfine, D. L. (1955), On Obessive Thoughts. *J. Am. Psa. Assoc.*, III.

Glover, E. (1928), Psycho-Analytic Technique. In: *The Technique of Psycho-Analysis.* New York: International Universities Press, 1954.

—— (1929b), The Screen Function of Traumatic Memories. *Int. J. Psa.*, X.

—— (1940), An Investigation of the Technique of Psycho-Analysis. The Institute of Psycho-Analysis, London. Reprinted as: *The Technique of Psycho-Analysis.* New York: International Universities Press, 1954.

—— (1945), Examination of the Klein System of Child Psychology. *This Annual*, I.

Greenacre, P. (1949), A Contribution to the Study of the Screen Memories. *This Annual*, III/IV.

Hartmann, H. (1951), Technical Implications of Ego Psychology. *Psa. Quart.*, XX.

—— (1953), Contribution to the Metapsychology of Schizophrenia. *This Annual*, VIII.

—— (1955), Notes on the Theory of Sublimation. *This Annual*, X.

—— and Kris, E. (1945), The Genetic Approach in Psychoanalysis. *This Annual*, I.

Kaiser, H. (1934), Probleme der Technik. *Int. Ztschr. Psa.*, XX.

Kanzer, M. (1953), Past and Present in the Transference. *J. Psa. Assoc.*, I.

Katan, M. (1939), Der psychotherapeutische Wert der Konstruktionen in der Analyse. *Int. Ztschr. Psa. & Imago*, XXIV.

Kramer, P. (1955), On Discovering One's Identity: A Case Report. *This Annual*, X.

Kris, E. (1950a), Notes on the Development and on Some Current Problems of Psycho-analytic Child Psychology. *This Annual*, V.

—— (1950b), On Preconscious Mental Processes. *Psychoanalytic Explorations in Art.* New York: International Universities Press, 1952.

—— (1951a), Ego Psychology and Interpretation. *Psa. Quart.*, XX.

—— (1951b), Some Comments and Observations on Early Autoerotic Activities. *This Annual*, VI.

—— (1955), Neutralization and Sublimation: Observations in Young Children. *This Annual*, X.

—— (1956), The Personal Myth: A Problem in Psychoanalytic Technique. *J. Am. Psa. Assoc.*, in print.

Lamb, C. (1903), *Life, Lectures and Writings.* London: The Templeton Edition, III, pp. 39ff.

Lampl-de Groot, J. (1951), Re-evaluation of the Role of the Oedipus Complex. *Int. J. Psa.*, XXXIII.

Lewin, B. D. (1939), Some Observations on Knowledge, Belief and the Impulse to Know. *Int. J. Psa.*, XX.

—— (1950), *The Psychoanalysis of Elation.* New York: Norton.

Loewenstein, R. M. (1951), The Problem of Interpretation. *Psa. Quart.*, XX.

—— (1954), Some Remarks on Defences, Autonomous Ego and Psychoanalytic Technique. *Int. J. Psa.*, XXXV.

Mahler, M. S. and Elkisch, P. (1953), Some Observations on Disturbances of the Ego in a Case of Infantile Psychosis. *This Annual*, VIII.

Nunberg, H. (1931), The Synthetic Function of the Ego. In: *Practice and Theory of Psychoanalysis.* New York: International Universities Press, 1954.

—— (1932), *Principles of Psychoanalysis.* New York: International Universities Press, 1955.

—— (1947), Circumcision and the Problem of Bisexuality. *Int. J. Psa.*, XXVIII.

Rapaport, D., ed. (1951), *Organization and Pathology of Thought.* New York: Columbia University Press.

Reider, N. (1953), Reconstruction and Screen Function. *J. Am. Psa.*, I.

Riviere, J. (1952), General Introduction. In: *Developments in Psycho-Analysis*, ed. M. Klein, P. Heiman, S. Isaacs, J. Riviere. London: Hogarth Press.

Rosen, V. (1955), The Reconstruction of a Traumatic Childhood Event in a Case of Derealization. *J. Am. Psa. Assoc.*, III.

Sharpe, E. (1927), The Technique of Psychoanalysis—Seven Lectures. In: *Collected Papers on Psycho-Analysis*. London: Hogarth Press, 1950.
Siegman, A. (1955), The Psychological Economy of Déjà Raconté. *Psa. Quart.*, XXV.
Spitz, R. A. (1955), The Primal Cavity: A Contribution to the Genesis of Perception and Its Role in Psychoanalytic Theory. *This Annual*, X.
Waelder, R. (1951), The Structure of Paranoid Ideas. *Int. J. Psa.*, XXXII.
Zetzel, E. R. (1956), An Approach to the Relation between Concept and Content in Psychoanalytic Theory. *This Volume*, pp. 99-121.

RUDIMENTS OF THE EGO

SEYMOUR L. LUSTMAN, Ph.D., M.D.[1] (New Haven)

The most meaningful point of convergence of developmental research and psychoanalysis lies in ego psychology, more particularly in the development of the ego. While the most stimulating concepts of the earliest formative forces come from psychoanalysis, the nature of psychoanalysis as a research tool makes its use as an investigatory technique inappropriate to work with the neonate. In the presence of such stimulating concepts, the lack of verifiable data concerning the crucial early ego development has been deplored by many, and has turned sharp focus on the necessity for coordinated reconstructive and developmental research.

In his discussion of the import of psychoanalytic ego psychology, Kris (1950) points out that it "... re-emphasized the character of psychoanalysis as a psychology of adaptation, of learning, and clinical data have implemented these general assumptions as far as the child's earliest experiences are concerned." Actually, clinical data are most inadequate in terms of origins of ego function. Kris indicates this in noting the increasing research concern with the development of the ego, and the acceptance of the tendency to integrate observational data into the general flow of psychoanalytic thought. It thus appears that the earliest factors of ego development are beyond the powers of reconstructive psychoanalytic techniques, as they exist today.

Anna Freud (1954) has stated, "The rudiments of the ego, as they emerge gradually in the first half year of life, take their pattern from the environmental conditions which have left their imprint on the infant's mind by way of his early pleasure-pain experiences, the conditions themselves becoming internalized in the ego structure." Such a formulation is focused on a later stage of development, and begs the question of what precisely it is with which these environmental factors interact in the devel-

[1] Department of Psychiatry, Yale University School of Medicine.
The author would like to acknowledge his great indebtedness to Dr. Julius B. Richmond and to Dr. Earle L. Lipton.

opment of a rudimentary ego. In considering the "anlage" of a rudimentary ego, one is led to the study of the neonate, if not the fetus.

In the adult, as exemplified in studies of depersonalization such as described by Federn (1952), the bipartite structure of the ego seems most apparent. The primary functions seem to be perception in terms of body ego, and apperception in terms of mental ego. The proposition that the body ego precedes the mental ego in developmental sequence seems to be a clear-cut one, especially in terms of initial development. Indeed, in this regard, an extreme position is taken by Hoffer (1950) who speaks of a "mouth ego" in the development of the body ego. Although he stresses the importance of visual, auditory, and olfactory apparatuses to the seeming exclusion of tactile apparatuses, he makes the point that the structural entity ego, in infancy, has a definite physical, bodily connotation. This formulation again refers to the infant, and thus may have bypassed the precursors of the body ego which possibly are already apparent in the neonate.

Two concepts, as developed by Hartmann (1939), and Hartmann, Kris, and Loewenstein (1946), deal most directly with the earliest stages of ego development. Since the psychoanalytic definition of ego is in terms of functions, Hartmann emphasizes that in the earliest postnatal stage there is no ego. However, from his observation that in this stage, "it is difficult to disentangle the nuclei of functions that will later serve the ego from those that we shall attribute to the id," he arrives at a concept of the "undifferentiated stage." The second concept of a "sphere free from conflict" arises from the following observation: "Not every adaptation to the environment, not every learning and maturation process arises from conflict—I refer to the conflict-free development of perception."

There is, further, a recognition of inherent factors: ". . . the apparatuses serving perception, motility, . . . as well as those that account for the phenomena of memory, are partly inborn." Hartmann believes that although these functions come under the control of the ego, they also influence subsequent ego development. Actually, it is logical to think of these factors as exerting influence on original as well as on subsequent ego development. In a later paper, Hartmann (1950b) clarifies this further by stating, "Some aspects of early ego development appear in a different light if we familiarize ourselves with the thought that the ego may be more—and very likely is more—than a developmental by-product of the influence of reality on instinctual drives; that it has a partly independent origin—apart from those formative influences which, of course, no analyst would want to underestimate; and that we may speak of an autonomous factor in ego development in the same way as we consider the instinctual drives autonomous agents of development. Of course, this is not to say that the ego as a definite psychic system is inborn, it rather stresses the point that the development of this system is traceable not only to the impact of reality and of the instinctual drives, but also to a set of factors that cannot be identified with either one of them. . . . We come to see ego development as a result of three sets of factors: inherited ego characteristics (and their interaction), influences of the instinctual drives, and influences of outer reality." Thus, without minimizing formative forces, Hartmann calls attention to an autonomous factor in ego development which he relates in part to problems of maturation and growth, thus recognizing the physiological aspects of ego development.

To this point, it is pertinent to quote Rapaport (1951b), "Note the circularity; the ego is both born out of conflict and party to the conflict." In his explanation of this "seeming contradiction," he turns to the study of the infant, from which he concludes, "these apparatuses of perception, memory, and motility, are inborn and characteristic of the species and the biological individual, before they become expressive of conflict and experience. Memory, perception, and motility have already been existing and functioning before conflict ever occurred. Here, then, we see apparatuses which antedate conflict, and become the core of ego development." Speaking more specifically of perception, Rapaport (1951a) states, "Now psychoanalysis is beginning to take into consideration the fact that perception is built on constitutional endowments and is one of the pre-existing apparatuses which, once the ego and id have arisen from the undifferentiated phase, become ego apparatuses." He then formulates the following fruitful question, "does the individual's developing ego-structure, as it integrates the perception-apparatus, imprint its characteristics upon it?" To this we can add: do not the characteristics of the perception apparatus imprint themselves upon the developing ego? The question of individual differences in constitutional endowment has already been raised by Hartmann and Kris (1945), Rapaport, and others.

In following the sequence of these thoughts, one is led to inquire: what are the inborn, physiological precursors of id and ego, and how is subsequent ego development influenced? The importance—one could say, the vital nature of longitudinal developmental studies becomes apparent. One is directed to the neonate as a starting point only because the fetus is not as readily available for both observational and experimental study.

In an earlier study of autonomic function in the neonate (Richmond and Lustman, 1955), we had arrived at a concept of "inherent autonomic endowment" which we presented in terms of its implications to the development of psychosomatic disease. This concept was derived from clinical data, and the demonstration of statistically significant differences in autonomic reactivity already manifested by three-day-old neonates. Our study of changes in skin temperature and cardiac rate in response to a variety of stimuli, showed that the autonomic nervous system is already well differentiated by this time, and is neither characterized by a "physiological vagotonia," nor reactive in an all-or-none fashion. In terms of magnitude of change, the thirty-two neonates studied demonstrated individual differences falling into an approximately normal distribution curve, with clearly defined hyperreactors and hyporeactors.

While much of our special interest was directed to psychosomatic disease processes and manifestations, we are also concerned with the general effect of inherent autonomic endowment on personality development. We will try to show that inherent autonomic endowment, with its clearly demarcated individual differences, is one of the basic, inborn, autonomous precursors of ego function. We will attempt to formulate its possible role as one of the fundamental factors in the conflict-free sphere of ego development, and further its integration into the ego and its subsequent participation in and influence on later ego development through the effects of its involvement in conflict.

I might at the outset say something about sensation and perception. In contradiction to the opinion held by many, that sensation is the basis of perception, Schilder (1930) makes the assertion that it is incorrect to say that perceptions are built of sensations. For Schilder perception implies, "a) that which is perceived, b) my sensation, and c) my act of turning toward the world." Sensation is viewed as the subjective aspect of perceiving, and as such naturally has an impact on the meaning of what is perceived. For our purposes, we are willing to accept the formulation that sensation is the subjective aspect of perception, but with the emphasis that the nature of sensation will markedly influence perception, and that perception will in turn influence sensation. Such a reciprocal relationship is quite applicable to an already existing and functioning ego, but it is most difficult to apply to the neonate where such ego function does not yet exist. We must start here with what is possibly the most primitive kind of sensation since "that which is perceived" and "the act of turning toward the world" are quite likely beyond the capabilities of the neonate—or at least beyond our methodological techniques of study. Yet, as we shall show, there is a reaction to stimulation which indicates that sensations of some degree of differentiation exist. We think that such sensation precedes and molds the first rudimentary perceptions, but from that point on a kind of "feed-back" interaction may take place between perception and sensation.

We use autonomic reactivity as a measure of sensitivity not only in terms of possible afferent-efferent reflexes, but as evidence of already functioning higher corticoautonomic centers indicated by autonomic reaction to stimulation involving the other portions of the nervous system. This perhaps implies individual differences in central and peripheral nervous system organization and reaction. However, as it reacts, controlling the internal environment as it does, the autonomic nervous system can be thought of as participating in setting the bodily tone of sensation. In so influencing sensation, it influences perception. Indigenous to our concept of inherent autonomic endowment are the above-mentioned corticoautonomic relations.

We undertook, as part of a larger study, an evaluation of sensitivity of erogenous zones, using as our measure of such sensitivity the reaction of the autonomic nervous system. We elected to study the measured response to stimulation of the following zones: the lips, the skin (of the abdomen), the genitalia, and the anus. The neonates used in this work were between three and four days of age, and were randomly selected from the newborn nursery. A total of thirty-two full-term babies (sixteen males and sixten females) were used in the study proper, although many more were observed in the preliminary work. The experiment was conducted in a constant temperature and humidity chamber in which the temperature was maintained at 25° C. with a barometric pressure of 760 mm. Hg. All infants were nude for the duration of the experiment. The physiologic import of these conditions is discussed elsewhere (Richmond and Lustman, 1955).

For the purposes of this discussion, only the skin temperature responses of the four zones mentioned above will be considered. Skin temperature response was obtained by means of a copper vs. constantin thermocouple attached to the dorsum of the big toe of the right foot, and recorded continuously by means of a constant writing Brown electronic potentiometer. Prior to experimentation, the infant was permitted to adjust to the chamber temperature until the skin temperaure readings reached a constant level, which was considered the base line. The experiments were then performed, permitting a return of temperature to base line between each condition. Stimulation was for a one-minute period, and, due to the established lag in skin temperature response, the one-minute period immediately after stimulation was considered to be in response to stimulation.

Stimuli used were manual massage, and air stream, administered by the same person in the same sequence to all babies. We used air simply because at the time we wanted to work with a more readily controlled objective stimulus than massage. Obviously, massage by human hand is a more meaningful and realistic stimulus.

1. *The primacy of erogenous zones.* From the analysis of variance of the entire data, we can rank the above conditions with reference to the magnitude of the change produced:

FIGURE 1

	$\dfrac{(\Sigma d)^2}{n}$
1. Massage, lips	4.72
2. Air, genitalia	3.76
3. Air, lips	3.22
4. Air, anus	1.68
5. Massage, skin	1.53
6. Air, skin	1.44
7. Massage, genitalia	1.16
8. Massage, anus	.54

Before interpreting these findings, we must point out that we have serious doubts that the response to air stimulation of the genitalia would in general rank second, since the total of 3.76 was markedly influenced by the hyperresponse of one baby of 2.1° F. With this in mind, it seems quite clear that in the three-day-old neonate the lips represent the most sensitive erogenous zone. These data thus appear to be suggestive evidence for the psychoanalytic theory that in the neonate the oral area is the dominant erogenous zone. However, it must be emphasized that this is a relative, not an absolute, primacy. That is, oral sensitivity does not exclude sensitivity in other areas, but it is more intense.

2. *Individual differences.* The following graph (Fig. 2) represents the distribution of the infants studied with reference to the magnitude of change (as measured from prestimulatory baseline) in response to stimulation of the lips. From this, one can easily identify nonreactors and hyperreactors. We hesitate to use terms referring to divisions of the autonomic nervous system because of its complexity, and prefer to think in terms of hyperreactors.

For the purposes of this discussion we can select the one child who reacts with an increase in skin temperature of 1.4° F., the one child who reacts with a loss of 1.5° F., and one of the children who reacts with no change. This difference in reaction raises the question of neurological maturity. From our experience with other reflexes universally present in the adult, we know that some nonreactors are not necessarily phlegmatic, but too immature to respond. Not knowing what such experimentation would yield in the adult, we are really in no position to do more than consider this possibility. The only answer to this important question could come from a longitudinal study, and we deeply regret that circumstances turned this proposed longitudinal study into a cross-sectional one. But even if the varying rates and states of maturation are taken into consideration, it is significant that environmental factors, such as stimulation of the lips in feeding, the anus in toilet care, etc., interact with immature responses in some neonates.

FIGURE 2

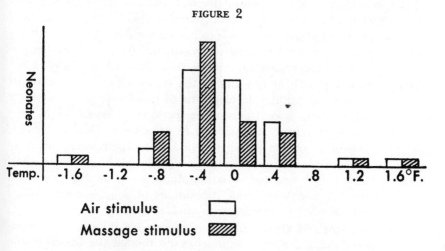

Air stimulus ▢
Massage stimulus ▨

To facilitate discussion, we shall for the moment oversimplify and arbitrarily assume an imaginary and impossible constancy of maternal care for these three neonates. It then becomes obvious that the experience of sucking must be a vastly different one for these three infants by virtue of their different sensitivity and response. These varying degrees of sensitivity and autonomic reactivity constitute the primitive sensation levels from which the subsequent perception of oral activity will develop. This is at first in terms of the autonomous factor in the conflict-free sphere of ego development (perception) proposed by Hartmann. In regard to the "undifferentiated stage" concept, one can again agree with Hartmann, since it is easily conceivable that sensitivity and autonomic reactivity participate in id impulses.

If we now carry the developmental process further to the conflict sphere, it is apparent that delay, deprivation, overindulgence, weaning will all be experienced somewhat differently by these three children. Thus the autonomous factor in the ego, if a persisting one, should have profound influence on subsequent pleasure-pain experiences, and hence on further ego development. It seems appropriate here to quote Hartmann once again; "Ego development, like libidinous development, is partly based on processes of maturation. And of the ego aspect too, some of us are agreed that we have to consider it as a partly primary, independent variable, not entirely traceable to the interaction of drives and environment."

So far we have considered only the different infants exposed to a hypothetically "constant mother." However, in reality the complexity of the individual mother's personality will add a vast number of variables. One aspect of this is suggested by Grinker (1953) who, in describing Mirsky's studies of pepsinogen levels in neonates, proposes the possibility that the hyperreactor is "destined to remain hungry and dependent on the mother whose integrative capacity becomes strained, resulting in her 'feeding back' rejection or hostility to the child. Thus a constitutional factor is responsible for the development of gastric symptoms of ulcer and for a dependent or oral demanding personality type." Thus, "the object which is perceived" may change in response to factors inherent in the endowment of the growing child. The repercussions of these tremendously complex responses and "feed-back" reactions which characterize the so-called symbiotic relationship between mother and child are apparent. When so considered, the number of possible permutations are astronomical—but in keeping with clinical data.

We can point out at this time that there were infants who hyperreacted in each of the zones stimulated, even though the lips were the most sensitive zone. The finding of such individuals is most interesting and adds perspective to the following statement of Hartmann, "Reaction formation, like orderliness or cleanliness, displacements, generalized attitudes, which we are accustomed to find correlated with the anal phase, may then appear before problems of anality have come to dominate the child's life." Thus, an infant who hyperreacts to anal stimulation may, though developing according to the phase concept, move more quickly in the area of anality—or, perhaps by virtue of greater sensitivity, provoke formative factors which produce reaction formations that appear to be "premature."

We might at this time mention some of our more subjective impressions which arose out of this study. In our experimental set up we had the opportunity to observe a fair number of babies while undergoing diaper change or cleansing of the perianal area. Again we were impressed that the reaction to this fundamental life experience for the child should be characterized by such wide individual differences. We are again tempted to predict that the anal hyperreactor might well be the one who will later develop those character traits related to anality. We do not in any sense mean to minimize formative forces, beyond saying that the soil is fertile for such developmental "arrests" or fixations. We think not only of the conflict-free ego sphere of perception of anal stimulation but also of soiling, training, and the effect of the mother's reaction to the child.

One other interesting observation, made in passing, is that while none of the neonates reacted to incidental noises such as talking or dropping equipment, etc., we were able to elicit reactions from some of the neonates by "gentle crooning." No attempt was made to study this.

In conclusion, we feel that this paper highlights the necessity for longitudinal studies of an experimental as well as an observational nature. We would like to emphasize that our discussion has been, in the absence of longitudinal data, a purely speculative attempt at integrating our cross-sectional findings into pertinent psychoanalytic concepts. We feel such speculation is warranted only if it is clearly recognized as such, and if its purpose is to stimulate further research. We conclude that inherent autonomic endowment (including corticoautonomic relations), demonstrable in the three-day-old neonate, is one of the factors making up the autonomous conflict-free sphere of ego development, and as such participates in and markedly influences subsequent ego development. We feel that our data give suggestive evidence for the phase concept by indicating that in the neonate the oral area is the primary erogenous zone, as analytic theory predicts. The finding of individual hyperreactors in other areas such as the anal zone adds perspective to reported clinical variations in phase sequence.

Inherent autonomic endowment is thought of as one of the nuclear apparatuses from which the primitive ego emerges, and upon which subsequent formative influences impinge, and with which they interact in the ultimate development of first body ego, and then mental ego. This is in keeping with Freud's (1937) postulated inborn, inherited ego factors; it seems to corroborate Hartmann's concepts of an "undifferentiated stage" and of a "conflict-free sphere of ego development"; and it seems to support the autonomy of the ego as formulated by Hartmann.

BIBLIOGRAPHY

Eissler, K. R. (1938), Zurgenaueren Kenntnis des Geschehens an der Mundzone Neuge-
    borener. Ztschr. Kinderpsychiat., V.
Federn, P. (1952), Ego Psychology and the Psychoses. New York: Basic Books.

Freud, A. (1954), Psychoanalysis and Education. *This Annual*, IX.
Freud, S. (1937), Analysis Terminable and Interminable. *Int. J. Psa.*, XVIII.
Grinker, R. R. (1953), *Psychosomatic Research*. New York: Norton.
Hartmann, H. (1939), Ich-Psychologie und Anpassungsproblem. *Int. Ztschr. Psa. & Imago*, XXIV. Translated in part in: *Organization and Pathology of Thought*, ed. D. Rapaport. New York: Columbia University Press, 1951.
—— (1950a), Psychoanalysis and Developmental Psychology. *This Annual*, V.
—— (1950b), Comments on the Psychoanalytic Theory of the Ego. *This Annual*, V.
—— and Kris, E. (1945), The Genetic Approach in Psychoanalysis. *This Annual*, I.
—— —— and Loewenstein, R. M. (1946), Comments on the Formation of Psychic Structure. *This Annual*, II.
Hoffer, W. (1950), Development of the Body Ego. *This Annual*, V.
Kris, E. (1950), Notes on the Development and on Some Current Problems of Psychoanalytic Child Psychology. *This Annual*, V.
Rapaport, D. (1951a), *Organization and Pathology of Thought*. New York: Columbia University Press.
—— (1951b), The Autonomy of the Ego. In: *Psychoanalytic Psychiatry and Psychology*, ed. R. P. Knight and C. R. Friedman. New York: International Universities Press, 1954.
Richmond, J. and Lustman, S. (1955), Autonomic Function in the Neonate: I. Implications for Psychosomatic Theory. *Psychosom. Med.*, XVII.
Schilder, P. (1930), Studies Concerning the Psychology and Symptomatology of General Paresis. In: *Organization and Pathology of Thought*, ed. D. Rapaport. New York: Columbia University Press, 1951.

AN APPROACH TO THE RELATION BETWEEN CONCEPT AND CONTENT IN PSYCHOANALYTIC THEORY

(with special reference to the work of Melanie Klein and her followers)

ELIZABETH R. ZETZEL, M.D. (Boston)

The relation between theory and practice is a central problem in the development of every branch of science. In the physical sciences, it is relatively easy to make a clear distinction between the objective data which lead to theoretical hypotheses and the objective experiments which confirm or validate theoretical hypotheses. With the growth and expanding applications of psychoanalytic thought not only to the problems of clinical psychiatry but to the related fields of anthropology, social relations and general psychology, there is inevitably increasing interest in similar methods of validation. In psychoanalysis, however, even more than in the other social sciences, both the lack of concrete objective data and the relative difficulty of repeating observational situations leads to special problems in respect to objective validation. In addition, however, to this problem which is well recognized in all social sciences, the development of psychoanalysis indicates certain inherent difficulties in making a clear distinction in our science not only between theory and practice, but also between theoretical hypotheses based on the interpretation of specific content, and theoretical hypotheses of a more general abstract nature concerning the structure and function of the mental apparatus itself. The development and validation of our science, in short, would appear to involve at least a threefold task; namely, first, the collection of clinical data; second, correlation and comparison of such clinical data leading to theories based on the content or meaning of such data; and third, general concepts of an abstract nature deduced on the basis of these formulations.

The development of psychoanalytic knowledge has from the outset been concerned with ever deeper and more penetrating investigation into the specific content of the unconscious mind, the nature of unconscious fantasies, the various mechanisms by means of which unconscious impulses are modified and controlled, the specific situations, both external and internal, which can be related to the development of the ego and the sense of reality. The correlation and comparison of the findings of different workers in respect to these problems has been a main preoccupation of psychoanalytic research. It would probably be correct to say that the general body of knowledge derived from these investigations into the content of the unconscious mind has in a number of respects reached a stage where certain formulations of a general nature have been embodied within our theoretical framework. The different stages of libidinal development, the specific content of oedipal fantasies, the essential nature of the definitive superego, for example, have been formulated in theoretical terms based on interpretation of content. In addition, however, to this type of theoretical formulation one must also consider another group of deductions which have been proposed as the basis for a framework of general theory. This aspect of theory is not concerned primarily with the specific content of the unconscious mind, but rather with abstract conceptual formulations which could account for the infinite complexities of other findings of a more specific meaningful nature.

The problem with which this paper is concerned, it will thus be seen, is related to general problems of validation concerned with the correlation of observed clinical facts with theoretical postulates. It is not, however, identical. In the first place, the question of objective validation is not under consideration. In the second place, this paper will attempt to concentrate mainly on the relation within the framework of theory itself between formulations concerned with interpretation of content and abstract deductions of a general nature. Certain generally accepted analytic hypotheses, mainly concerned with elucidation of content or meaning, form an integral part of psychoanalytic theory. Other basic premises, in contrast, refer to more general abstract concepts concerning, for example, the structure and function of the psychic apparatus, general instinct theory, and fundamental views regarding the nature of anxiety.

Freud's *Interpretation of Dreams* (1900) might be regarded as the model for the differentiation of these two aspects of psychoanalytic theory. The first six chapters of this book come mainly under the heading of content. The seventh chapter is mainly concerned with concept. It would be fair to say that in the earlier chapters, Freud is primarily concerned with a clinical approach to dream material; that from associations and the resistances thereto, he elucidates not only the latent meaning, or content, of the dream, but the various specific mechanisms by means of which the latent content is disguised and distorted in the manifest dream structure. He is able, by means of specific meaningful illustrations, to demonstrate the latent meaning of the dream and is also able to relate the dream work to both the nature and the content of the unconscious mind. In the seventh chapter, in contrast, he attempts to draw, from this essentially concrete material, general deductions as to the nature of the psychic apparatus which could account for his specific meaningful findings. Here, his approach is conceptual and abstract rather than meaningful in terms of the specific content of unconscious wishes or conflicts. In the earlier parts of the book, for example, he refers to the specific sexual nature of repressed material and is able to illustrate in a number of cases the underlying oedipal conflict. The final chapter of the book, on the other hand, is not concerned primarily with the meaning of the psychic or instinctual energy concerned, but formulates a conceptual approach to the psychic apparatus as a means of modifying and controlling instinctual energy, whatever its source.

These brief remarks indicate both the nature of contrast under consideration, and the difficulty in drawing hard and fast lines of demarcation. For example, from clinical observations of resistance and elucidation of its cause, Freud deduced the existence of the mechanism of repression. This was a theoretical concept with manifold implications familiar to all of us. At the same time, Freud also gave definite indications as to the nature of the repressed, at this time mainly limited to repressed sexual wishes at a genital level. The difference between content and concept may be clearly illustrated here. The concept of repression is a general concept which has altered very little in its fundamental meaning since Freud first defined it. This concept remains one of the basic concepts of psychoanalytic theory up to the present day. With regard to content we can also still agree as to Freud's correct elucidation of the importance of the oedipal conflict as an essential feature of the content of the repressed. Further work and deeper investigation has shown us that this early formulation, although correct, was by no means exhaustive so that we would now include in the repressed pregenital conflicts antedating the genital oedipal situation. This expansion of content, however, in no way affects the validity of the original concept and only indicates, here, the importance of distinguishing between these two approaches.

With regard to repression, therefore, alteration and expansion of our knowledge has not made necessary any radical alteration of basic concepts. On the one hand, increased knowledge of the content of the repressed does not invalidate the concept of repression; on the other hand, our expanded knowledge of the other mechanisms of defense, as Anna Freud (1936) has shown so clearly, although it has enriched, has not invalidated the concept of repression. In his earliest formulations, however, Freud made other tentative suggestions of a conceptual nature which have been vitally affected by later findings in respect to content. To give another example from Freud's own work: in his early formulations of instinct theory, he suggested a dichotomy between the sexual and the ego instincts. This dichotomy was originally based on the hypothesis that repression and the related defense mechanisms were set up by the ego or self-preservative instincts in opposition to dangers threatened by the sexual instincts. According to this formulation, mental conflict was ascribed to opposition between these two drives. Anxiety appeared as a result of the repression enforced by the ego instincts. Later, however, his investigation of the content of the fantasies and delusions of psychotic patients combined with a number of observations of the traumatic war neuroses indicated that the original dichotomy he had postulated between libido and the ego instincts could not account for the investment of the ego itself with libido, so clearly revealed in these and allied conditions. As a result of these observations, he recognized that it was necessary to alter his basic concepts as to the nature of the instincts. Further investigation as to the nature of anxiety, moreover, revealed the important function of anxiety as a cause of repression or motive for defense, which complicated his earlier concept of anxiety as the product of instinctual tension and frustration. The subsequent modification of his earlier conceptual framework, both with regard to the nature of the basic instincts and with regard to anxiety as a motive for defense, initiated the development of a structural approach with its manifold implications with regard to ego psychology.

It is clear, in following the development of Freud's theoretical work and correlating it with contemporary clinical findings of other pioneers in our field, that modifications of basic concepts have been, with one or two exceptions, closely related to the expansion of analytic knowledge regarding content. It was one of the special qualities of Freud's genius to combine in a unique manner intuitive understanding of the meaning of unconscious content with a capacity for conceptual deduction of a general abstract nature. He was able to recognize spontaneously the meaning of symbols, the manifold and startling manifestations of unconscious mental life and to interpret specific conflicts arising in the analytic situation. On the other hand, he never lost sight of the general, abstract or conceptual implications of his findings. It is desirable that every theoretical contribution to psychoanalytic thought should be oriented both to its implications with regard to content, and also to its conceptual significance. This type of correlation is, however, probably one of the most difficult tasks not only in psychoanalysis, but in psychological thought as a whole. As Brierley (1951) states in this connection, "There may be only one event, the psychological event, but there are very definitely two different methods of approaching it. As T. H. Pear (1948) says, 'Psychologists are often distinguished by the emphasis, theoretical and practical, which they place on one of two aims. The discovery of general laws of mind or the description or understanding of the unique and undivided personality.' The results of both approaches have to be correlated and can be used to correct each other. At the present stage of thinking development the distinction between them is readily lost and we should gain by choosing words which help to keep the difference clear."

The ability to maintain this distinction depends on a capacity to separate the concrete from the abstract which is extremely difficult in a science, the nature of which is essentially so subjective. Even Freud occasionally fell into the error of couching his theoretical propositions in too concrete terms. The first difficulty, therefore, in maintaining a clear distinction between concept and content can be attributed to the nature of the material with which we are dealing. As Hartmann, Kris, and Loewenstein (1946) have said, "Our reformulation shows that not the concepts which Freud introduces are anthropomorphic, but that the clinical facts he studied and described lead us to understand what part anthropomorphism plays in introspective thinking." In spite of this difficulty which is inherent in our material, it can probably be agreed that during the early stages of development of psychoanalytic knowledge and theory the practice and the science of psychoanalysis were inevitably so closely interwoven that almost without exception every new clinical discovery could be readily considered in terms of its theoretical implications. With the vast expansion of knowledge, clinical experience and literature, however, there has tended to be an increasing separation between those who are primarily interested in utilizing clinical material to enrich our understanding of the content of the unconscious, and those who are predominantly concerned with the clarification of psychoanalytic theory. Of recent years, there have been other analytic thinkers with at least Freud's capacity for abstract conceptual thinking, leading to valuable contributions, reformulating certain basic concepts, using the model set up by Freud (1900) in *The Interpretation of Dreams* and modifying it in the light of a more structural approach. Many of these papers have, however, been of an extremely abstract nature, leaving to the reader the burden of interpolating the significance of general hypotheses in terms of specific content. In spite of the very great value of such formulations couched in general abstract terms, there is, here, a potential danger that these formulations might be compatible with divergent interpretations of clinical material. This will be considered below in relation to Melanie Klein's work.

On the one hand then, there have been recent valuable contributions to our conceptual thinking which have been more or less divorced from specific content. On the other hand, there have been many gifted analysts with a deep understanding of the unconscious mental life of their patients, who have presented findings which to a greater or lesser extent have been correlated with the general body of psychoanalytic knowledge. In particular, there have been many valuable contributions proposing modifications and reformulations of our present views concerning the nature and meaning of conflict situations in the early months of life. Among these contributions, for example, one must include the work of Spitz (1946), Edith Jacobson (1946), Margaret Mahler (1952), Lewin (1950), Beata Rank, (1949), Phyllis Greenacre (1952) and Melanie Klein (1935, 1948). The formulations some of these writers have put forward are couched in general terms, but nevertheless should be regarded on the whole as interpretation of content rather than conceptual propositions. Edith Jacobson (1953), for example, in her important investigation of the metapsychology of depression and schizophrenia, has made suggestions regarding self-representation and object representation and the regressive reanimation of parental images in pathological situations. Greenacre (1952) has correlated her analytic reconstructions with certain objective observations and investigations of infantile behavior. She clearly indicates the possible pathological implications of excessive stimulation and severe frustration for future development of the ego and of the capacity to deal with anxiety. Spitz (1945, 1946) has made detailed observations of infants under institutional conditions and has drawn some general deductions as to the importance of the object relations in early infancy. Beata Rank (1949), from detailed analytic investigation of certain groups of abnormal children, has also drawn general deductions regarding the role of aggression and the fateful result of maternal deprivation. To discuss the conceptual implications of all of this valuable work would take us far afield. At this point the contributions of the most controversial of these writers, namely Melanie Klein, might be considered in order to indicate in some detail the relation of concept to content in her work and also to correlate in certain respects some of her views with recent reformulations of certain basic concepts. The aim here is not to give an exhaustive discussion of all of Melanie Klein's work which has been ably criticized by Waelder (1937), Edward Bibring (1947), Glover (1945), and Brierley (1951), but to select certain aspects particularly related to the topic under discussion.

In many ways, Melanie Klein's work is eminently suitable for this purpose. In the first place, many of the difficulties and problems raised by her theoretical formulations may be at least partially attributed to an inadequate distinction between observations enriching our knowledge of content and conceptual deductions as to the theoretical implications of these findings. Her work thus illustrates the vital importance of this differentiation in the development of psychoanalytic theory. In the second place, the overwhelming emphasis in Melanie Klein's work on unconscious fantasy as the mental expression of instinct; on concrete and specific fantasies as active from the dawn of life; on the ego as entirely derived from the id, mark an extreme contrast to the abstract conceptual approach exemplified by Hartmann (1950) and Rapaport (1951) who, following on the whole Freud's approach in the last chapter of *The Interpretation of Dreams* (1900), attempt to make general formulations relatively divorced from meaningful content. It should be possible, by discussing and comparing both the value and the possible disadvantages of these two extremes to indicate general problems which concern not only these specific contributors but also to illustrate the relationship here postulated between concept and content in the development of psycho-analytic theory.

From clinical observations derived from analyses of young children and later from analyses of borderline patients and psychotics, Melanie Klein (1932) became aware earlier than most analysts of the importance of aggression in early mental development. Moreover, from the same sources, she also recognized that depressive tendencies were far more important in the early stages of development than had previously been recognized. It would seem probable that the fact that Melanie Klein was a pupil of Abraham played some role in her search for and discovery of the importance of introjective mechanisms in these depressive aspects of early life. The close relationship between introjection and projection has long been recognized. In his discussion, moreover, of the metapsychology of psychotic depression, Abraham (1924) had clearly indicated the important role of objects introjected in an ambivalent or hostile manner in the genesis of depressive states. Melanie Klein (1932), applying these concepts to her analysis of young children, brought together her clinical observation of animistic fantasies both of a projective and introjective nature, and her increasing conviction as to the important role of aggression in the development of anxiety. She thus reached the conclusion that the infant's life is dominated by alternating processes of introjection and projection, caused by the infant's need to overcome anxiety with regard to his aggressive fantasies chiefly through the development of libido and its fusion with aggression. At the same time, however, this general proposition was amplified by increasing material regarding the specific nature of the fantasies by means of which these processes were expressed. She became increasingly convinced, from her clinical observations of young children, that there was strong evidence suggesting that these primitive fantasies contained elements of an oedipal conflict at a period far antedating the classical oedipal situation. This, she felt, suggested that the type of depression which she attributed to the early months of life could be compared in all essential respects with the structure of depression in the postoedipal period as described by Abraham (1924).

In other words, she did not feel that her findings necessitated any alteration of the analytic hypothesis that depression was related to a pathological relationship between superego and ego, even though the depression antedated the time usually ascribed to superego development. Pushing her investigations to an ever earlier period, she concluded that the depressive position of infancy represented a relatively advanced stage of development related to the acquisition of true or whole object relationship. Antedating this period, she suggested the infant's mental life was dominated by his anxiety with regard to his own aggressive impulses, proposing that his projection of these impulses onto the outside world could be described as essentially paranoid. During this early period, moreover, she postulated the existence of oedipal fantasies including genital impulses which she considered to be present from a very early period of life. Her assumption in this connection appeared to imply the existence of inborn, innate fantasies of an oedipal nature with some knowledge from the earliest days of life of the difference between the sexes, the relationship between the parents and the way in which babies are born.

To consider, briefly, in a preliminary fashion some of the controversial aspects of her point of view, without at present taking up in detail their full significance, her assumption that anxiety is ultimately attributable to the aggressive impulse is open to question on clinical grounds alone. Secondly, it is difficult to elucidate the evidence on which Melanie Klein (1932, 1948) bases her conviction that oedipal conflicts arise so early in life. As Marjorie Brierley (1951) has noted, "The ages given for the actual beginning of treatment (over two years of age in every case) appear to justify the views that the clinical evidence for Melanie Klein's reconstruction of the first year is mainly reference from the conditions observed at later ages . . . . and is the basis of numerous contentions that Melanie Klein reads back into early development conditions obtained only in later stages." The problem in this respect is a complex one. On the one hand, there is increasing evidence, as indicated for example by Greenacre's work (1952), as to the frequent occurrence of genital activity in the early months of life, particularly under conditions of overstimulation or frustration. That such activity should be related to the development of the oedipal conflict is undoubted. Most analysts, however, feel that such premature genital activity leads to distortion, both in the development of early object relationships and to pathological variations of the later true oedipal conflict. It is, in general, considered unlikely that oedipal fantasies of the type postulated by Melanie Klein are compatible with the general level of maturation at the period to which she ascribes them. The fantasies themselves, however, described by Melanie Klein (1932) have been confirmed by Edith Jacobson (1946), Beata Rank (1949), and others, but ascribed to regressive reanimation of earlier less specific fantasies rather than interpreted as evidence of the occurrence of such fantasies at the earlier period itself.

It may be helpful at this point to indicate the very real importance of certain of Melanie Klein's observations.

(1) Her recognition of the important role of aggression in early mental life has been confirmed by many other analytic observers.

(2) Her recognition of the importance of object relations, in particular, the early mother-child relationship with particular reference to the importance of this relationship in helping the child to master its aggressive anxieties and fantasies has also been widely confirmed by a number of child analysts.

(3) The relationship of difficulties in connection with the mother to early depressive tendencies has also been indicated by other workers. Here one might mention specifically the work of Spitz (1946) in New York and of Beata Rank (1949, 1950) and her co-workers in Boston.

(4) Melanie Klein's early recognition of the role of anxiety as a spur to development and of the part played by symbol formation in early play, in early fantasy and the development of sublimation is of the utmost importance.

From the point of view, therefore, of depth of clinical observations, there is no doubt that Melanie Klein has made very valuable contributions to our knowledge. It is noteworthy, however, that the contributions which appear to be most acceptable and which could be most easily integrated into the general conceptual framework of analytic theory come under the heading of content rather than concept. Through her recognition of the role of aggression and of introjective and projective mechanisms, Melanie Klein has enriched our knowledge of early fantasy life and has shown the derivation, from an early period of life, though possibly not as early as she suggests, of many of the animistic anxiety-provoking fantasies and delusions so familiar to us in the mental status of psychotic patients.

These remarks may now be amplified by more detailed consideration of the relation between Melanie Klein's (1948) views on aggression first to the recent papers of Hartmann, Kris, and Loewenstein (1949) and Anna Freud (1949), and second to Freud's theory of the death instinct (1920). It may thus be possible to illustrate the need to distinguish between propositions regarding content and fundamental conceptual orientation, and also to indicate the degree to which abstract formulations of fundamental concept may be compatible with essentially divergent interpretation of content. This point may first be illustrated by specific reference to the paper by Hartmann, Kris, and Loewenstein (1949) "Notes on the Theory of Aggression" and to show how closely the abstract concepts put forward in this paper may be correlated with many of Melanie Klein's propositions.

As already indicated, Melanie Klein, in her analyses of disturbed children and psychotics, became increasingly aware of the importance of aggressive fantasies and the profound anxieties to which they gave rise. She recognized how the conflict between love and hate and resultant difficulties in achieving a good object relationship played a crucial role in early development. These points have been discussed in an earlier paper (Zetzel, 1953). At this point, the questions previously discussed as to her timing of these conflicts will not be considered, nor at this point is detailed discussion as to whether the aggressive instincts are, in the first instance, directed toward the self or the outside world relevant to the point under discussion. In this connection, it is noted that Hartmann, Kris, and Loewenstein (1949) like Anna Freud (1949), in her recent paper on this subject, also avoid discussion of this aspect and consider the types of conflict aroused by aggression and the various means by which the aims of aggression are modified. Here, they suggest four main types of conflict.

(1) Aggression and libido may be involved in conflict when the cathexis of both drives is vested in the same object (instinctual conflict). (2) The reaction of the object to attempts at completion of aggressive acts may endanger the individual (conflict with reality). (3) This danger may be anticipated by the ego which is in part already identified with

the object, and the ego may be opposed to the completion of aggressive acts (structural conflict involving the ego). (4) The conflict may involve moral values (structural conflict involving the superego).

I should like to take up these general conceptual statements in relation to Melanie Klein's formulations.

(1) Hartmann, Kris, and Loewenstein (1949) referred to instinctual conflict when aggression and libido are directed toward the same object. They ascribe the relation of object development to fusion of aggression and libido and note the importance of libido development for the creation of good object relations. Melanie Klein makes many statements which are theoretically compatible with this formulation. Ignoring for the moment the degree to which she attributes early anxiety to the death instinct, she also notes the relation of ambivalence to instinctual conflict, and her concept of the depressive position and its mastery makes explicit reference to a development of libido, which in satisfactory development should lead to a creation of good object relations, threatened though they may be by the continued activity of aggression and its concomitant anxiety.

(2) Hartmann, Kris, and Loewenstein (1949) consider, under the heading conflict with reality, dangers which may arise as a result of aggressive acts, which precipitate retaliation on the part of the object. They do not clearly state how far this conflict with reality should be regarded as a real danger and how far the fears of retaliation may be limited to the realm of fantasy. They take into account, however, the possibility that the infant may respond to retaliatory or hostile impulses of which the object may be unconscious so that their work here may be correlated not only with the work of Melanie Klein, but with Beata Rank's proposals regarding the source of many early traumatic situations. While, therefore, Melanie Klein's greater preoccupation with the role of instinctual conflict and of internal objects colors her presentation of early anxiety situation in relation to their internal sources, there does not appear to be any serious conceptual conflict between her views and those of Hartmann, Kris, and Loewenstein. Both refer to the danger situation linked with fear of retaliation as a result of the expression of aggressive impulses; both also recognize that these fears may be colored by projective ,mechanisms. The distinction between the two points of view depends therefore not so much on differing concepts as to the mechanism by means of which conflict with reality is handled, but rather on different premises as to the role of external and internal reality in mental development, which I shall consider later.

(3) Hartmann, Kris, and Loewenstein (1949) discuss structural con-

flict involving the ego in a situation where the ego, because of its identification with the object, opposes the completion of aggressive acts. Here
too, we see a statement in terms of general concept which is compatible
with some of Melanie Klein's more specific formulations. There is general
agreement as to the vagueness of ego boundaries in the early months of
life. The close relationship between introjection and identification has
been stressed not only by Melanie Klein, but also by Hartmann, Kris,
and Loewenstein. It is clear, therefore, that the fear of destroying an
object with whom the ego is at least partially identified, comes very close
to Melanie Klein's (1935) conception of depressive anxiety where she
described so clearly the infant's anxiety lest his aggressive impulses should
result in the destruction of the good internal object. Identification with
this object is inevitably closely related to early ego development.

(4) Finally, Hartmann, Kris, and Loewenstein refer to structural conflict involving the superego. Here, the incompatibility between their
views and those of Melanie Klein does not concern the conceptual
description of conflict, but rather the nature and timing of early superego
development. Since this question was discussed in considerable detail in
an earlier paper (Zetzel, 1953), it will not be elaborated here. The main
point to be emphasized is the compatibility of the conceptual statement
with Melanie Klein's views with particular reference to the relationship
of a severe superego to the continued operation of aggressive fantasies
and impulses which have not been mastered.

Since these statements have been taken out of the context of the whole
paper, the correlation proposed here should not be taken too literally.
True correlation would depend not only on the possible vicissitudes of an
instinct, in this instance aggression, but also on other basic assumptions
regarding the nature and development of the individual as a whole.
Here, for example, there is a basic difference between the two points of
view with regard to the relative importance of internal and external
reality. For Melanie Klein, internal reality is primary and adaptation
to external reality dependent on mastery of the inner world. Hartmann,
Kris, and Loewenstein, on the other hand, have paid considerable attention to the autonomous development of reality adaptation and would
not agree that ego functions depend at every point on a specific mastery
of an internal conflict. Anna Freud's position in this respect would appear
to be intermediate. Melanie Klein pays minimal overt attention to the
role of maturation; in contrast, Hartmann, Kris, and Loewenstein are
very much concerned with this aspect of mental development. Nevertheless, and in spite of these important considerations, it seems that their
general formulations with regard to the aggressive instinct, like Anna

Freud's are not essentially incompatible with Melanie Klein's point of view.

When, however, an attempt is made to relate Melanie Klein's views with regard to aggression to the nature of the death instinct, more difficult conceptual problems emerge. Freud's (1920) conception of the death instinct, as is well known, was essentially a biological speculation which probably does not belong properly within the field of psychoanalytic theory. According to this view, the death instinct was closely related to the tendency of organic matter to return to an inorganic state of rest. The relation of this tendency to outwardly directed aggressive impulses and even to self-directed destructive impulses of an active nature is highly speculative and controversial. Anna Freud (1949), for example, although she refers to self-destructive behavior in certain pathological infantile conditions, is careful not to make basic theoretical assumptions on this basis. Hartmann, Kris, and Loewenstein take a similar position. Melanie Klein, however, had modified Freud's biological conception of the death instinct to put forward a concept of two basic instincts; namely, the libido and the death instinct, with the proposal that the death instinct must be considered as an active self-destructive tendency operative from the outset of life. On the basis of this assumption, Melanie Klein has also made the suggestion that anxiety derives from fear of the death instinct. She thus develops far-reaching conclusions both as to the nature of anxiety and as to the meaning or content of early mental conflict. Here, we must consider an interpretation of fundamental analytic concepts of quite a different order from the views already discussed with regard to the role of aggression. With regard to the latter, Melanie Klein is mainly concerned in expanding our knowledge of mental content to include deeper understanding of the role of aggression in early mental life. It is noteworthy, here, that many of her propositions regarding early mental conflict and the nature of ambivalence are fully compatible with the general concepts concerning the theory of aggression put forward by Hartmann, Kris, and Loewenstein (1949), and also by Anna Freud (1949). Where, however, she expands her own theoretical framework so as to explain her findings on the premise of an active death instinct, it is clear that her work is much more controversial. Here, she has left the field of content elaboration and entered the sphere of conceptual framework. While her elaboration of content, therefore, is not necessarily controversial, her conceptual approach must be regarded as open to question, since she puts forward as fundamental a conception of the death instinct which must be regarded as highly speculative and so far not easily acceptable within the general framework of psychoanalytic thought.

As indicated above, an essential feature of Melanie Klein's work is the emphasis which she places on internal as compared to external reality in the early phases of development. Her views on this question are closely bound up with her premises regarding the basic instincts. The overwhelming importance which she ascribes to inborn destructive impulses, which, in her opinion, constitute the existence of an internal threat from the outset of life combined with her assumption that the destructive impulses follow in their development the libidinal fixation to erotogenic zones, accounts for her preoccupation with the dangers of introjective processes during the early oral phase. This explains the emphasis placed by Melanie Klein and her followers (1952) on the relatively predominant importance of internal reality in early development and the related assumption that introjection and projection are the main, if not the only, mental mechanisms in the early months of life. As Hartmann, Kris, and Loewenstein (1949) suggest, however, our present state of knowledge does not allow us to accept the proposition that alternating processes of introjection and projection are the only possible explanation of early conflict, nor do they agree that the role of these processes can be solely ascribed to internal forces. Here, they raise the important and long-debated question as to the role of external reality and the degree to which aggressive responses can be attributed to frustration rather than to innate destructive tendencies. "Without discussing the problem whether or not instinctual drives tending toward destructive aims are part of the original equipment of man, one may be satisfied to assume that in the earliest phases of the infant's life any transition from indulgence to deprivation tends to elicit aggressive responses . . . . all human relations according to this suggestion may be permanently colored by the fact that the earliest love relations in the child's life were formed at the time when those whom the child loves are those to whom it owes both indulgence and deprivation" (1949). According to this view, in short, the relation of aggression to external frustration must be taken into account. From another point of view, Anna Freud (1949) approaches the same problem. It is her opinion that the existence of innate aggressive tendencies must be accepted. The mastery of these aggressive impulses depends in her view, as in Melanie Klein's, in spite of their somewhat different orientation in other respects, on the fusion of libido with aggression. Failure on the part of the external environment to provide adequate objects for libidinal gratification hampers this task and leads to the appearance of unneutralized aggressive tendencies.

Here, it will be clear, we are in an area where general conceptual thinking must still of necessity be somewhat speculative. The relative importance of object relations is still a matter of controversy. As already indicated, Melanie Klein puts major emphasis on internal factors; external factors are not, however, thereby relegated to a negligible role. Susan Isaacs (1952), for example, in her important paper "The Nature and Function of Fantasy," explicitly refers to the important role of external frustration as a stimulus for developments. She says, "Disappointment may be the first stimulus to adaptive acceptance of reality, but the postponement of satisfaction and the suspense involved in the complicated learning and thinking about external reality which the child accomplishes, can only be endured and sustained when it also satisfies instinctual urges represented in fantasy as well. Learning depends on interest and interest is derived from desire, curiosity and fear, especially desire and curiosity." This quotation indicates the difference in emphasis of the two approaches. Hartmann, Kris, and Loewenstein (1949) clearly indicate that frustration by a loved object is highly significant. Susan Isaacs, dealing with the same problem, stresses the significance of such disappointment in relation to already existing fantasy. In other words, there is an implicit difference between frustration as a source of conflict and frustration which will be interpreted in the light of inherent conflict and already existing unconscious fantasy. It is the relative importance placed on the latter which distinguishes Melanie Klein and her followers from more orthodox Freudian thought.

It is important to note the close relationship between Melanie Klein's views regarding introjection and projection, her assumptions regarding the nature of the death instinct, and her orientation toward the role of external reality. Since she specifically defines anxiety as a response to the death instinct, it is inevitable that internal danger situations should be regarded as of crucial significance. Since, in addition, she postulates introjection and projection as the main, if not the sole, defensive mechanisms operative in the early months of life, it is relatively easy to understand how far, in her opinion, reality experiences must be influenced by the infant's inner struggles. Moreover, the emphasis here given to a dangerous internal situation as operative from the outset of life explains the importance attached to the progressive internalization of better objects as a crucial feature of early development. Melanie Klein, in referring to internal objects, is concerned essentially with the content of inner fantasy regarding the nature of the inner world. The relationship of these fantasies to the actual environmental situation is implicit rather than explicit. In addition, the emphasis she places on an early differentiation between mechanisms of projection and introjection appears to imply some differentiation between external and internal from the outset of life. It is, therefore, difficult to correlate some of her views with basic Freudian concepts concerning the early development of the ego and sense of reality. Rapaport (1951), for example, has stressed the crucial importance of ego development implied in the achievement of a differ-entiation between external and internal reality. He regards the internali-zation of reality as one of the crucial characteristics of the function of the ego. Hartmann (1950) also refers to the necessity that the mental apparatus develops the capacity to recognize internal conflicts. Both of these writers, however, discuss this problem at an abstract level with little or no reference to the explicit fantasies characteristic of the early levels of mental development. The nature of mental conflict in the early months of life remains, of course, a crucial and controversial problem. On the one hand, Melanie Klein's emphasis on the internal situation, while at the same time implying sufficient differentiations between in-ternal and external to make a distinction between mechanisms of pro-jection and introjection, does not appear to pay sufficient attention to the role of external reality and the crucial step for ego development implied in the differentiation between external and internal reality. On the other hand, the abstract conceptual approach of Hartmann and Rapaport, while extremely helpful as a frame of reference, may not take into adequate account the possible role of early fantasy life in the devel-opment of the infant.

In this connection, it appears that theoretical premises concerning the nature and function of fantasy are of crucial importance. In particu-lar, we touch here on a basic problem as to the relation between reality thinking, autonomous functions of the ego, and their unconscious sources. Hartmann (1950), for example, although he indicates very clearly the way in which unconscious fantasy can interfere with secondary process thinking and the reality adaptation of the ego, nevertheless, places great importance on the concept of a conflict-free autonomous ego. It would appear implicit in his argument that conflict-free or autonomous ego functions are relatively, if not absolutely, independent of unconscious significance. Susan Isaacs (1952), on the other hand, states, "In our view reality thinking cannot operate without concurrent and supporting un-conscious fantasies. The fact that fantasy thinking and reality thinking have a distinct character when fully developed does not necessarily imply that reality operates quite independently of unconscious fantasy." This would imply that for Melanie Klein and her followers no mental activity, however functionally free, can be devoid of unconscious significance. Fantasy is, in Susan Isaacs' words (1952), "The mental expression of instinct"; fantasies therefore play a dominant role in mental life from the outset. According to this point of view, Hartmann's concept of neutralized instinctual energy would appear to be relatively unacceptable. The availability of this energy would appear to depend not primarily on neutralization but rather on the significance of the activity as a gratification of unconscious fantasy. Freedom of activity, in short, would depend on unconscious fantasies which endow the overt activity with unconscious value. It appears that on the other hand, Hartmann's emphasis is on neutralization as a means of liberating instinctual energy from its unconscious sources so that it becomes freely available for the ego.

Here, we appear to be concerned with a genuine difference of opinion as to basic concepts regarding the nature of the psychic apparatus. Although extremes of this difference are illustrated here in the contrast between Hartmann and Melanie Klein, the problem may well be of crucial importance for the development of psychoanalytic theory in general. Hartmann's concept, which is correlated with Freud's hints in "Analysis, Terminable and Interminable" (1950) as to the possibility of inborn ego attributes, stresses the relative unchangeability and autonomy of certain ego functions. Melanie Klein, in contrast, assumes that the unconscious significance of every mental activity may be ultimately traced to instinctual sources and related unconscious fantasies. It is obviously essential, if Melanie Klein's work is to be correlated within the main body of analytic theory, that she should indicate more clearly how and in what manner true reality testing and secondary process thinking can be understood in terms of her basic premises; how and in what manner inborn factors affect different phases of mental development; and how and in what manner maturation plays a role in different stages of development. On the other hand, it appears that valuable though Hartmann's conception of conflict-free autonomous ego functions may be from a conceptual and descriptive point of view, it is nevertheless desirable that these formulations be correlated more closely with detailed description as to the relationship between neutralization and specific fantasy and conflict. This correlation of concept and content is significant not only from a theoretical, but from a clinical point of view. The concept of autonomous ego functions relatively divorced from unconscious meaning and possibly arising from innate causes is likely to lead to relative skepticism as to the possibility of effecting major changes in character structure. Under certain circumstances this point of view could possibly encourage an attitude of pessimism and the acceptance of limited therapeutic goals. In contrast, the extreme emphasis placed by Melanie Klein and her followers on the instinctual basis or unconscious significance of all ego attributes with the related tendency to believe that most, if not all, of these attributes should respond to psychoanalysis may, under certain circumstances, encourage overoptimism and difficulty in accepting failure after many years of intensive treatment. Although, as already suggested, the implications of extreme attitudes in either direction are used for purposes of illustration, there are indications that differences in therapeutic approach based on the relative emphasis placed on inborn or autonomous ego features on the one hand, or on unresolved unconscious conflicts on the other, is a vital and open question in psychoanalysis today.

In connection with the subject of this paper, however, we are here concerned not only with the relation of concept to content, but with the influence of basic concepts on problems of clinical application and validation. It is, of course, inevitable that in the clinical practice of psychoanalysis, theoretical hypotheses influence clinical interpretation. It is, however, extremely important that as clear a distinction as possible should be made between interpretations based on understanding of the content of unconscious conflicts and interpretations based on conceptual hypotheses. Melanie Klein's work, for example, shows very clearly the degree to which conceptual hypotheses may influence interpretation of content. Susan Isaac's (1952) paper on fantasy illustrates this complicated interrelationship very clearly. In her opening more general remarks concerning the nature and function of fantasy, in her illustrations from the field of general psychology, and in her discussion of Freud's views, she makes contributions to our conceptual framework, which many analysts have found to be valid and significant. As soon, however, as she discusses content, her implicit acceptance of Melanie Klein's concept of the death instinct and her assumption of complex innate knowledge result in propositions regarding the specific content of very early fantasies which many psychoanalysts would find unacceptable.

In contrast, however, it has also been indicated that attempts to confine theoretical contributions to mainly abstract conceptual reformulations carry a risk, unless they are correlated with specific content of being compatible with divergent interpretations of clinical material. This has been illustrated by showing the compatibility of certain abstract formulations regarding the theory of aggression proposed by Hartmann, Kris, and Loewenstein (1949) with some of Melanie Klein's propositions.

Close study of the work of those analysts who have given us such valuable contributions toward the reformulation of basic analytic concepts indicates the advantage for such reformulation of considering the individual psychic apparatus in isolation. By this, it is not implied that the need for an object as a means of instinctual gratification is neglected, but that the Freudian concept of primary narcissism and autoerotism is retained as the model of psychic structure in the early days of life. The acceptance of this premise makes possible a consideration of mental development involving a very gradual growth of the ego, the sense of reality and true object relations. It also facilitates the reformulation of Freud's original views of the psychic apparatus as a means of modifying and controlling instinctual drives.

From many sources, however, we have increasing evidence as to the basic importance of very early object relations. The nature and significance of these early object relationships is still a matter of controversy. It is not impossible, however, that it may prove extremely difficult to conceptualize the meaning of early object relationships in terms of the concepts which form the basis of our present theoretical framework. A promising theoretical approach to this problem appears to be implicit in Lewin's (1950) recent work on dreams, in which he substitutes for regression to primary narcissism, regression to the most primitive object relationship. The implications of this attempt appear to be far-reaching. Unless some such theoretical hypothesis can be postulated, there is at least the possibility that just as Freud had to abandon his attempt to correlate his psychological findings with the findings of other disciplines, thus making his decisive step in setting up the concept of the mental apparatus, it may become necessary with our increased recognition of the importance of object relationships from the dawn of life to modify our conceptual framework to take fully into account the object needs of the human infant. Inevitably we will also be faced in this connection with an evaluation of the psychological significance of these early objective experiences with the possibility that Susan Isaac's approach to the nature and function of fantasy may prove to be of outstanding importance. It may, in short, be inadequate to retain a concept of primary narcissism and to include therein the lack of differentiation of infant and mother in the early days of life. Much as this might be desirable from the point of view of coherent theoretical formulation, it may indeed prove that psychoanalytic truth cannot be adequately expressed in abstract conceptual terms based on the individual psychic apparatus. Here, finally, we may be concerned with an insuperable limitation of the conceptual approach. This suggestion, however, may be premature at this point since, in the first place, we have by no means exhausted the possibilities of conceptual reformulation and, in the second place, the role of object relations in early infancy still remains open to debate.

An allied, but somewhat different, difficulty in the formulation of abstract concepts seems to concern the nature and function of the superego. Although there are many difficulties inherent in the conceptual reformulation of Freudian theory, using Freud's model of the mental apparatus as the basis for detailed consideration of ego structure, these difficulties do not appear to be inseparable, as David Rapaport's (1951) recent paper so clearly indicates. With regard to the superego, however, it seems that conceptual reformulation has, up to now, raised a number of difficulties. Some of these difficulties are intimately related to the present stage of theoretical knowledge. The attention paid by most analysts to superego structure and function in the early period of a struc- tural approach has, to a very considerable extent, now been overshadowed by the emphasis on the ego and its defenses. While the latter lends itself fairly readily to reformulation in abstract conceptual terms related to Freud's original conception of the mental apparatus, the superego is less easy to formulate in abstract conceptual terms. Glover (1947), refer- ring to the same problem, states "The superego concept is from first to last a clinical concept. It was founded on clinical analysis and retains throughout a clinical connotation. One must distinguish carefully be- tween descriptions of the superego and theories of its origin." This, too, is clearly indicated in the Hartmann, Kris, and Loewenstein (1946) paper on the "Formation of Psychic Structure." Although their formulation of the earlier period and of the development of ego functions remains fundamentally abstract and conceptual, their description of superego formation is formulated in terms of a specific meaningful situation, i.e., the oedipal conflict. Here, in short, it has not been possible clearly to separate concept from content up to the present time. A full discussion as to the reason or nature of this problem would involve detailed dis- cussion of controversial views regarding the origin of the superego, which would be outside the scope of this paper. The point is raised mainly to indicate the extreme difficulty of separating content from concept in rela- tion to certain aspects of analytic theory.

    While, therefore, there can be no doubt as to the extreme importance of as objective formulation as is possible of our fundamental concepts, I have tried to indicate some of the possible obstacles to achievement. The essentially concrete subjective nature of the material with which we are dealing leads to real difficulties in clear separation of theory from practice. This paper, however, is not primarily concerned with this basic problem. Our theory, according to this point of view, must be concerned not only with abstract formulations, but with interpretations of mean- ingful content, sufficiently general to be included under the heading of theory, rather than described as specific clinical observations. The analyst, for example, is definitely basing his deductions on a theoretical hypothesis of this nature when he interprets certain symbols, oedipal fantasies and well-accepted conflicts of the pregenital period. Both increased depth and wider applications of our knowledge lead to new findings with regard to content which, however valuable they may prove as a source of stimulation and the opening of new vistas into the unconscious mind, must be correlated with the general body of analytic knowledge. In addition, however, to this aspect of psychoanalytic theory, the search instigated by Freud (1900) in *The Interpretation of Dreams* for an abstract conceptual framework has been continued up to the present, as illustrated in this paper by reference to the recent work of Hartmann, Kris, Loewenstein, and Rapaport. It is essential for the progress of our knowledge, that, on the one hand, expansions of our theory mainly concerned with content should be correlated within this general conceptual framework. Equally important, however, is the need that abstract conceptual formulations should be related to interpretations of content. This need of mutual correlation is of importance not only in respect to our general body of theoretical knowledge, but also in respect to important clinical implications. The contributions of Melanie Klein, used as a basis for illustration in this paper, clearly show the disadvantage of inadequate distinction between content and concept. It is unfortunate that this confusion has inevitably led to relative neglect of many of her valuable contributions in the sphere of content.

As already suggested, this is a tentative and introductory paper in which an effort has been made to indicate certain patterns in the development of analytic theory. In addition to the task of clinical validation of analytic findings, it is essential that in our theoretical formulations we both distinguish between and correlate propositions mainly related to the content of the unconscious mind and propositions of an abstract conceptual nature regarding the nature and function of the mental apparatus. This thesis has been illustrated in the following ways. First, abstract formulations divorced from meaningful content may be compatible with divergent points of view, as illustrated in relation to the theory of aggression. Second, failure to make adequate distinction between concept and content may lead to semantic confusions, as illustrated in respect to certain aspects of Melanie Klein's work. It has also been suggested that possibly the abstract, objective, conceptual approach in a science based on essentially subjective, concrete data may have signifiant limitations. The development of psychoanalysis in its formative stages depended on the fusion in its founder of a capacity for both abstract and concrete investigation. It is essential for future development that this correlation should be maintained. It is necessary, in short, that we should distinguish clearly between that which is subjective and that which is objective, or in terms of the subject of this paper on the distinction between concept and content.

BIBLIOGRAPHY

Abraham, K. (1924), A Short Study of the Development of the Libido, Viewed in the Light of Mental Disorders. *Selected Papers on Psycho-Analysis.* London: Hogarth Press, 1927.

Bibring, E. (1947), The So-called English School of Psychoanalysis. *Psa. Quart.,* XVI.

Brierley, M. (1951), *Trends in Psycho-Analysis.* London: Hogarth Press.

Freud, A. (1936), *The Ego and the Mechanisms of Defense.* New York: International Universities Press, 1946.

—— (1949), Aggression in Relation to Emotional Development: Normal and Pathological. *This Annual,* III/IV.

Freud, S. (1900), *The Interpretation of Dreams.* London: Hogarth Press, 1953.

—— (1920), *Beyond the Pleasure Principle.* London: Hogarth Press, 1922.

—— (1937), Analysis Terminable and Interminable. *Collected Papers,* V. London: Hogarth Press, 1950.

Glover, E. (1945), Examination of the Klein System of Child Psychology. *This Annual,* I.

—— (1947), Basic Mental Concepts: Their Clinical and Theoretical Value. *Psa. Quart.,* XVI.

Greenacre, P. (1952), *Trauma, Growth and Personality.* New York: Norton.

—— ed. (1953), *Affective Disorders.* New York: International Universities Press.

Hartmann, H. (1950), Psychoanalysis and Developmental Psychology. *This Annual,* V.

—— (1952), The Mutual Influences in the Development of the Ego and Id. *This Annual,* VII.

—— and Kris, E. (1945), The Genetic Approach in Psychoanalysis. *This Annual,* I.

—— —— and Loewenstein, R. M. (1946), Comments on the Formation of Psychic Structure. *This Annual,* II.

—— —— —— (1949), Notes on the Theory of Aggression. *This Annual,* III/IV.

Isaacs, S. (1952), *Developments in Psycho-Analysis.* London: Hogarth Press.

Jacobson, E. (1946), The Effect of Disappointment on Ego and Superego Formation in Normal and Depressive Development. *Psa. Rev.,* XXXIII.

—— (1953), Contribution to the Metapsychology of Cyclothymic Depression. In: *Affective Disorders,* ed. P. Greenacre. New York: International Universities Press.

Klein, M. (1932), *The Psycho-Analysis of Children.* London: Hogarth Press.

—— (1935), Contribution to the Psycho-Genesis of the Manic-Depressive States. In: *Contributions to Psycho-Analysis, 1921-1945.* London: Hogarth Press, 1948.

—— (1952), *Developments in Psycho-Analysis.* London: Hogarth Press.

—— (1948), *Contributions to Psycho-Analysis, 1921-1945.* London: Hogarth Press.

Lewin, B. D. (1950), *The Psychoanalysis of Elation.* New York: Norton.

Loewenstein, R. M., ed. (1953), *Drives, Affects, Behavior.* New York: International Universities Press.

Mahler, M. S. (1952), On Child Psychosis and Schizophrenia: Autistic and Symbolic Infantile Psychoses. *This Annual,* VII.

Pear, T. H. (1948), Perspectives in Modern Psychology. *Brit. J. Psychol.,* XXXVIII.

Problems of Infantile Neurosis: A Discussion. *This Annual,* IX.

Rank, B. (1949), Aggression. *This Annual,* III/IV.

—— and MacNaughton, D. (1950), A Clinical Contribution to Early Ego Development. *This Annual,* V.

Rapaport, D. (1951a), The Conceptual Model of Psychoanalysis. In: *Psychoanalytic Psychiatry and Psychology*, ed. R. P. Knight and C. R. Friedman. New York: International Universities Press.
—— (1951b), The Autonomy of the Ego. In: *Psychoanalytic Psychiatry and Psychology*, ed. R. P. Knight and C. R. Friedman. New York: International Universities Press.
Spitz, R. A. (1945), Hospitalism. An Inquiry into the Genesis of Psychiatric Conditions in Early Childhood. *This Annual*, I.
—— (1946), Anaclitic Depression. *This Annual*, II.
—— (1951), The Psychogenic Diseases of Infancy: An Attempt at Their Etiologic Classification. *This Annual*, VI.
Waelder, R. (1937), The Problem of the Genesis of Psychical Conflict in Earliest Infancy. *Int. J. Psa.*, XVIII.
Zetzel, E. R. (1953), The Depressive Position. In: *Affective Disorders*, ed. P. Greenacre. New York: International Universities Press.

NORMAL AND PATHOLOGICAL DEVELOPMENT

UNUSUAL VARIATIONS IN DRIVE ENDOWMENT

AUGUSTA ALPERT, Ph.D., PETER B. NEUBAUER, M.D.,
ANNEMARIE P. WEIL, M.D. (New York)[1]

INTRODUCTION

Our work with young children has increasingly led us to a study of their endowment. We have become more and more impressed with the fact that children show manifestations of unusual drive equipment. This study is focused on the role of such unusual variations in the development of three children.

The cases selected show the following variations in drive endowment:

1. CARL —hyperlibidinal and hypoaggressive drive energies.
2. TONY —hyperaggressive and adequate libidinal drive energies.
3. SANDRA—hypolibidinal and hypoaggressive drive energies.

These are three separate studies, carried out by the three authors[2] and are presented as an initial report.

The clinical material led us to study drive endowment from the following viewpoints:

1. Quantity of drive energy;
2. Balance of drive energy;
3. Distribution of drive energy;
4. The study of drive endowment stimulated our investigation of its effect on ego development, as seen in the interaction with the environment.

In our concluding remarks, we shall indicate common principles.

1. A CASE OF ORAL FIXATION

Augusta Alpert, Ph.D.

Basis for Admission

Carl was brought by his parents to the Council Child Development Center at the age of two years and eleven months, because of persistent

[1] From the Child Development Center, New York.
[2] Many members of the Center's staff contributed to the material—too many to list their names. We wish to thank all for their part in this study.

thumb sucking, inability to be weaned from the bottle, feeding difficulties, some stuttering, aggression toward his younger sibling, then five months old, of which the first and last were most troublesome to the parents. Observation in the outpatient nursery group showed Carl to be a normally developed boy, sturdy in build and bland of face. He was clinging to the mother, passive, indecisive, for the most part keenly observant of surroundings, and at times withdrawn from it, but not sucking his thumb in this new situation.

History

Carl was the mother's second pregnancy, the first having terminated in stillbirth, due to delay in performing a Caesarian section. Carl was delivered by Caesarian section, at full term, condition normal, birth weight 6 pounds, 13 ounces, and was seen sucking his thumb "five minutes after birth," by his father. He was breast fed for three months, each feeding lasting 40 to 45 minutes, after which Carl would cry. Breast feeding was discontinued because the mother could not stand these prolonged nursings. He accepted the bottle well but was finicky about solids. He gained and throve until twenty months, when he developed a diarrhea, diagnosed as celiac, which lasted until thirty months. He was on the usual strict diet for five months, the acute phase, during which he "assumed responsibility for his diet," that is, he would reject proscribed foods. Weaning from the bottle started at sixteen months, but was given up when the "celiac" started. In fact, the number of bottles was increased, a characteristic restitution by the mother for all deprivations, frustrations and injuries. Thus, at twelve months, when Carl's thumb sucking had to be mechanically restrained because of a split lip from a fall, the mother offered more bottles; and again, when a sibling was born, Carl being then two and a half years old. At three Carl accepted milk from a cup for one week only and then demanded two bottles in a row, seemingly having already picked up mother's regressive cue! From then on, he became more dependent on his bottle than the sibling. Thumb sucking continued from birth, with peaks at the time of the "celiac" and the sibling's birth, and low points during summer vacations. In the nursery, it remained unchanged in intensity throughout his four years, with an increase just before his sixth birthday. It diminished somewhat, transitorily, with an increase in masturbation, noted in his fifth year. It acquired a more active concomitant of digging into his nose during the latter half of his fifth year. Perhaps it became more anal in character as a result of reactivating the anal phase in therapy.

Speech developed slowly, only a few words by one and a half and a few more by two, and remained indistinct. Mild stuttering developed at about three, when he tried to make sentences, and lasted for about three months.

He began to walk at seven months, fell and interrupted walking until nine months. He was always wiry and vigorous, so active since seven months that he "wore us out," according to the father. (This comment reflects parental intolerance, according to later findings.) By the time he entered nursery at three, his use of the body was considered less than age-adequate, moving the total body "like a two-year-old."

Sleep was good until eighteen months, but at this time he began to insist on being rocked, and once rocked himself vigorously until the crib "walked." This lasted until two years. Toilet training was undertaken at one, and by two Carl was dry and clean, day and night. "He trained himself" during "celiac"! As an infant of three months, Carl woke up dry after a night's sleep and the parents were worried enough to call the pediatrician, who reassured them that Carl was normal.

He always loved people, especially children, but was too devoted to the mother, and would not remain alone in his room, nor with his grandmother. He was inconsolable and refused to eat when his mother left for the hospital for the birth of his sibling, when he was two and a half.

Health, except for "celiac," was excellent.

The mother's memory for developmental history and early events was exceptionally poor, and she would turn to the father; but his was, if anything, worse.

Family

The *mother* was twenty-seven years old when Carl was born. She experienced anxiety during the pregnancy with Carl because of the previous stillbirth. She herself was a persistent thumbsucker as a child, and various restraints were used for many years, which she still holds against her parents. She was always a finicky eater. She had had globus hystericus twice: first at the age of twenty, probably at the beginning of sex relations, and again about the age of twenty-six. She may be described as an oral-castrative character, with strong penis envy and unresolved conflict between oral dependency and masculine phallic assertiveness. She is a good pianist, having studied with her father until eighteen, at which time she abruptly broke away. She worked as an interpreter before marriage.

The *father* was thirty-two years old when Carl was born. He, too, was a thumb sucker and had his bottle until the age of five. Both he and Carl are described as gulping their milk and letting it "run down" their throats. He is an orally dependent character, with passive, feminine identification, and suffers from ejaculatio praecox. The marriage has often been "rocky"; at present it is better. He works in his father's business.

Though the younger *sibling* is held up as the child who does not suck her thumb and who could be weaned easily (she was not breast fed, for fear it would make Carl jealous!), she is seen in the nursery behind a blanket strip, her "transitional object," sucking her tongue. During rest period, she makes strong sucking movements and sounds.

Effect of Hereditary and Environmental Determinants on Instinctual Development

Special scientific interest attaches to Carl's instinctual development, because heredity plays so clear a part in his oral fixation. Both parents show strong orally fixated characteristics, as do their parents. Thus, Carl can be said to come of "pure stock." The hereditary transmission of an easily and overly libidinized (sensitized) oral zone is assumed. The hereditary transmission of a relatively minus aggressive potential from the passive father to his son is not so clearly traceable; nevertheless, we assume it, not, of course, to the exclusion of environmental molding. The deviations of both drives will be traced genetically from phase to phase. Shifts in the distribution and balance of libido and aggression will be related to maturational and environmental determinants.

1. *Birth.* Taking Greenacre's "Biologic Economy of Birth" (1945) as the starting point, we consider the fact of Caesarian birth an important "environmental" molder of Carl's oral libido. Lacking as it is in the massage stimulus of natural birth, Carl's birth may have been prejudicial to motor discharge of tension and to have favored thumb sucking for this purpose, a pattern which was probably already established *in utero* (Mrs. S. Blanton, as quoted by Greenacre, 1945). It can be seen, therefore, as an instinctual response to shock (change) in favor of return to a previous condition of homeostatic equilibrium, that is, to the intrauterine state (Freud, 1920). Greenacre's speculation (1952) "that some libidinal phase, probably most frequently the oral, might be accentuated by being antici- pated in fetal life and a preliminary channelization for discharge estab- lished" has special cogency in Carl's case because of the strong oral heredi- tary endowment.

2. *Oral Phase.* The outstanding events are prolonged nursings, lack of interest in biting and solid foods, dietary deprivation, mother's oral fixation. The unusual duration of the nursings, 40 to 45 minutes, were obviously not accounted for by the infant's inability to suck, nor by the

insufficiency of milk. He sucked well and gained well. They seem to have been related to the mother's "reading" of the infant's sucking needs in identification with her own oral and manipulative needs. She enjoyed the breast feedings up to a point and terminated them in a state of mounting excitement and tension. The infant cried after nursing, which may have been his reaction to overgratification and stimulation, with sudden loss of the object. Though the mother's memory failed her on whether Carl sucked his thumb after nursing, it is hard to imagine that he did not replace the lost object in this way. This was both already a well-established response and also maturationally appropriate, since only a shadowy differentiation existed between self and object.

It is doubtful that the dearth of material on oral sadism is entirely explicable by parental amnesia. On biting, spitting, throwing of food, there is a blank. They remember only a lack of interest in solid and hard foods, until recently. Rather it seems to reflect the child's particular fusion of instincts on the oral level, in which the receptive libidinal component far outweighs the aggressive one. The ratio of aggression to libido is such as to yield pleasure in sucking, but less in biting, allowing, of course, for the aggressive component in sucking, in varying degrees.

That this constitutional preference was reinforced by parental handling was already seen in the increase in the number of bottles at every crisis. At twenty months, with the onset of "celiac," when Carl was beginning to give up bottles in favor of solids, the number of bottles were increased, thus artificially shifting the balance of oral drives in favor of the more passive component, at the same time exerting a backward pull on development, as described by Anna Freud (1954). The parents proudly stressed Carl's compliance during this period, his "voluntary" rejection of forbidden foods. Later, at the age of four, when the younger sibling was put on the same restrictions for the same reason, which his mother explained to Carl, he asked, "Was that when I was hungry and you didn't give me any breakfast?" At the time he made good the maternal deprivation by the substitution of thumb.

The parents' oral fixation, especially that of the mother, had a double fixating effect on Carl's orality. On the one hand, she was ashamed of his thumb sucking, as though it were her own, and equated it with masturbation. She would become very angry with the boy and banish him from her sight. On the other hand, she could not bear to stop him because of too strong an identification with an exaggeration of his frustration. The mother's ambivalent feelings increased the boy's fear of loss of love, and it also increased his oral intensity through identification with the mother's. The mother's strong aversion to male aggression carried an implicit sanction of her son's thumb sucking as the less threatening to her. Though I cannot at this time discuss in detail the dynamics of mother, father, and child around this fixation point, as other authors have done (Johnson, et al., 1953; Burlingham, et al., 1955), I stress here the *common* hereditary factor underlying the *common* fixation point.

3. *Anal Phase.* The outstanding event during this developmental phase was Carl's feat of "training himself" while suffering from diarrhea. This was all the more remarkable coming as it did when negativism and the sadistic drive component are normally at their height. His unusual readiness to give up his anal possessions was in part a reaction to fear of loss of love: his mother admitted that she would become very angry on the rare occasions of "accidents." To this day he gives away or "forgets" or discards possessions for which he had made a strong bid. A recent attempt at self-assertiveness with his mother ended with his remark, "All right, I give up," an anal expression of total renunciation (which roused mother's guilt). Currently, in the nursery he defies his teachers with "I won't give up," a response to educational and therapeutic support of assertiveness. It is interesting that he *holds on* only to objects he has made *himself*. It is questionable whether such compliance with mother's demands for cleanliness would have been possible without the constitutionally deficient aggressive drive already seen in the oral phase. To this, another constitutional factor, strong sphincteric control, is added. The strength of the urethral sphincter was referred to in his urinary *in*frequency from infancy; his persistent thumb sucking may have the additional determinant of a constitutionally strong oral sphincter. In a family where so much compliance and control are required, it is not surprising that aggression should be internalized, so early in the maturational sequence as to preclude neutralization, and emerge in psychosomatic symptoms, for both children (Hartmann, Kris, and Loewenstein 1949). In a sense, the liquification of the stool during "celiac," which thereby took on an early oral (and urethral) consistency, blurred the differentiation between oral and anal zones. The rapid passage of the stool without rectal friction, in which Carl was, so to speak, a passive participant, again shifted the instinctual balance from active to passive and in favor of oral retention, that is, thumb sucking.[3] As on the oral level, so on the anal, the sadistic component is not observable. Again we ascribe this primarily to the constitutional balance of libido and aggression, with parental influence and other specific events ("celiac") as secondary. The sudden loss of the anal object, feces, preceded as it was

[3] This line of thought was stimulated by a remark by Dr. Anita Bell Simmons.

by the imprint of sudden loss of the oral object, the breast, and the still earlier imprint of sudden loss of enfolding equilibrium through Caesarian birth, with probable separation from his thumb, built up a loss-of-object anxiety, to which Carl responded with an attempt at recovery of the object, through thumb sucking by now an overdetermined mode of anxiety relief.

4. *Phallic-Oedipal Phase.* This is an ongoing developmental stage at the time of writing and necessarily presents difficulties in abstraction. To understand the interplay of Carl's instinctual make-up with external events during this period, it is necessary to keep in mind certain facts about the parents. The father is a passive man with a symptom of ejaculatio praecox; the mother is an orally castrative woman; the parental roles are never clear-cut and often reversed; the sexual aspect of the marriage has been unsatisfactory until very recently when the father's symptom cleared up. Into this milieu and this developmental phase, Carl brought his overload of orally invested libido and underload of aggression.

The parents reported some infantile masturbation which stopped by two and a half, in response to a threat from grandfather, mother believes. But there were other *unspoken* threats. About this time, the mother would shower while Carl sat in the tub. She would encourage Carl's nude embraces, which both enjoyed. When this was interrupted by the mother, as she gained greater awareness in her therapy (when Carl was about three and a half), he continued sex play with older girls and with his younger sister. Once (?) he showed his erection to his mother, after such play with the sister. This premature sexual stimulation, chiefly by the mother, seems first to have mobilized enough instinctual energy, libido-aggression, for a more than phase-adequate response, but it must also have increased the threat of castration, probably more through recurrent exposure to the female genitals than from fear of the father (or grandfather), and must have again pulled him toward passivity. In any case, a cumulative susceptibilty for castration anxiety had already been laid down from birth on. About this time, Carl switched from the mother to the father and would get into bed with him at night. This was discouraged by the father through his therapy. The relationship with the father took on a "normal" look about Carl's fifth year: he was proudly exhibitionistic of his father's war medals and business; he enjoyed doing things and going places with him; he liked doing "hard things," which would at times interfere with realistic achievement. At times, anxiety would break through; that something catastrophic, which he had heard in the news, would happen to his father, and then he would anxiously telephone his mother. In his fantasy play with boys, such catastrophes or accidents would usually befall him, but in projective tests, the father figure would be killed by the little one. With his mother, he was overtly possessive, vis-à-vis his sister, afraid of her disapproval, compliant and submissive, as we have seen, but secretly angry and covetous. In projective tests the mother is seen as nourishing and punishing.

From four to five was Carl's most active period in the nursery, with a transitory decrease in thumb sucking and increase in manual masturbation, though both activities could go on simultaneously, as in fact most activities did. The typical pattern was a repeated alternation of doing something and thumb sucking, almost as though he had to recharge. From five and a half to six, Carl's activity range and duration began to decline, seemingly an inhibition of the aggressive drive, under the impact of castration anxiety. At home, he had given up the thumb sucking, at least in mother's presence, and at her insistence. When his best friend in the nursery (who had weaned himself from his thumb sucking about a year ago) told him it was time he gave up thumb sucking, Carl made a valiant effort, but his tension and restlessness increased to an unbearable degree, until thumb sucking was resumed. Toward this admired best friend, he was as submissive as to his mother, and as unable to express his resentment. It would seem that in the struggle of love, fear, and hate toward the loved and threatening object (fear of losing his friend's love was an ever-present realistic threat for Carl), his compromise was a passive surrender, probably accompanied by the fantasy of swallowing and being swallowed, expressed in the ensuing immobilization, except for thumb sucking.

Interaction of Drives and Ego Development

Thus far, the utilization of neutralized drive energy for ego functions has been referred to by implication only, and the direct emphasis placed on the quantity and balance of the drives. This has grown out of the focus set for this paper. But a brief review will now be made of those ego functions which clearly reflect deviant drive quantity, balance, and distribution.

Motility, by parental standards, was precocious. Already by seven months, he was so active, "'he wore us out." It is a fair guess that as Carl began to reach for things, to push, pull, throw, tear, he met with increasing disapproval, restraint, and confinement by the parents as a protection from being "'worn out." The parents reported that from eighteen months to two years, Carl demanded rocking at bedtime and was reported once to have rocked himself so hard, the crib "walked." We may assume that this was a reaction to too much restraint during the day, at a time when motility as an ego function is normally at its libidinal height (Mittelmann, 1953). It is interesting that even when ego and both drives converge in accordance with maturational expectations, the passive position is preferred (except for the one time he rocked himself). Though the environmental contribution is here more conspicuous than the constitutional one, there is no reason to regard it as basic. By the time he entered the nursery at three, Carl's motility was adequate in quantity, but not in quality; that is, in the differentiated, adaptive use of the body, it was rather like a two-year-old's. It was easier for him to become active through the stimulation of an active child. Even so, continuity and smoothness of motility was marred by the frequent interruption with thumb sucking. Recently, he interrupted a running game with his friends, with "I don't like to run too much. I get hot inside, don't you?" followed by thumb sucking. The fact that his motility did not suffer more is attributable to the nursery, where freedom and restraint are helpfully balanced.

Speech. Though no gross pathology is reflected in speech, such as there is, seems to be related to the central problem. The delayed and slowly developing speech is directly related to the established pattern of sucking movements of cheeks and lips, at the expense of explosive movements required for good speech. The result is slovenly enunciation, especially of labials. Transitory stuttering appeared just under three, which reflects a contamination by anal elements. Communication in the service of object relations was below par when he entered the nursery, still too much under the influence of infantile omnipotence and insufficient identification with his peers. This is no longer the case. But contact with the object is too often interrupted by thumb sucking and speech becomes unclear, especially as Carl is then partially turned away from the object as though in retreat. Communication breaks down noticeably when he cannot express his anger and resentment, but "accumulates it," as the teachers say, and sucks his thumb instead.

Defense Mechanisms. No ego function so sensitively reflects the balance between drives and ego as do defenses.[4] A strong fixation point, as in the case of Carl, is, of course, highly favorable to *regression* as a defense mechanism. There is, in fact, a to-and-fro movement of libido and aggression (the oral baby and the phallic boy) which has not grossly hindered the libidinal progression. This confirms Anna Freud's observations (1954). This fluidity is both an indication of his pathology and a

4 "Defense mechanisms are built on a two-fold basis: on the one hand, the ego, and on the other hand, the essential nature of the instinctual process" (A. Freud, 1936).

prognostic sign of health (A. Freud, 1945). *Reaction formation* against dirt was well established by the time Carl came to the nursery at three. This seemed to be another example of his too-ready compliance with parental requirements. But the *rigidity* of this defense was striking, especially since he seemed to have experienced no active anal pleasures during the anal phase (except in fantasy?). He would not play with dirt nor plastic materials. Rigid reaction formation, normally a brief maturational point in the anal phase between primary and substitute instinctual gratification, lasted well into the phallic phase in Carl's case, and would perhaps have continued to block the way to sublimation, if special educational and therapeutic efforts had not intervened. By providing an opportunity to relive the anal phase (especially in therapy) neutralization of libidinal and aggressive energies was facilitated. He now enjoys most plastic materials.

Discussion of Findings

I have described a child with the symptom of persistent thumb sucking from birth (or earlier) into the sixth year. This has been related to the hereditary strength of libidinal investment in the oral zone, and to the relative weakness of the aggressive drive, both interacting with environmental determinants. The insufficient admixture of the aggressive drive was especially evident at such maturational points where it normally predominates. For example, interest in biting and chewing did not come with the acquisition of teeth—not until much later. In the anal phase, there was no negativism, no demandingness, and no fight of any kind. There seems not to have been even any active phase-related pleasure. On the other hand, there was, as we have seen, mother's sexual stimulation outside Carl's developmental phase, which exerted a forward pull. For a time he made a more than adequate response. This was followed by a passive orientation toward the father, and a serious disturbance in the discharge of aggression in relation to the object.

In the sphere of the ego, no gross pathology was seen. Neither thinking, reasoning, reality testing, nor the synthetic function are impaired, according to observation and projective tests. Precisely speech, localized in the oral zone, is the ego function which has suffered most. But it is remarkable that an ego, which shows such ease of regression, should at the same time show so little impairment of its functions. It is as though the thumb sucking, present at birth, was an integral part of the "ego milieu," and, therefore, remained ego-syntonic, into the phallic-oedipal phase (A. Freud, 1954). The environment, mother and others, have increasingly interfered with this harmony between ego and instinct.

Focusing now on the economy and interrelationship of the two drives from birth, the following deductions are made:

1. The early availability of thumb sucking as a means of quieting tension also tended to delay externalization of aggressive energies.

2. Thumb sucking also served and still serves as a "neutralizer" of aggressive energies, which explains the relative absence of physical illness since the "celiac." (This corresponds to the findings of Levine and Bell [1950] that pacifiers reduce colic.)

3. The early and persistent thumb sucking was associated and equated with the introjected object (mother) and facilitated the internalization of environmental demands, especially those of the mother, which together with weak aggression accounts for the easy compliance. Later, as separation from the object progressed, fear of loss of love was added.

4. The entrenchment of such quantity of undifferentiated drive energy in the oral zone from birth also delayed adequate separation of the two drives, specifically in relation to the object. This presupposes delay in separation between self and object, especially in relation to the aggressive drive. When one would normally expect a child to discharge anger at the object, Carl switches to thumb sucking; that is, aggression is aim- and object-inhibited and is expressed by libidinal discharge on the self. (It is assumed that the thumb sucking includes an admixture of aggression, especially in view of the above statement regarding separation of drives.) It should be noted that this substitution of one drive for another is not in reaction to thwarting of drive discharge by an outsider, nor is it at the instigation of moral teaching (though the preference of the parents, as has been shown, is on the side of passivity), but comes from within. The thumb sucking here is also a defense against anger and reduces anger tension, as indicated by Hartmann, Kris, and Loewenstein (1949), and as seen in the case of Sandra.

5. We can speculate that the large quantity of unneutralized libido invested in thumb sucking reduced its availability for *better* ego functioning. Unneutralized aggression was seen in the early psychosomatic illness, now in the "pure" aggression, as expressed in fantasy, where there is no middle ground between "kill or be killed," and in the insufficient admixture of the aggressive component in all ego functions, as, in seeing an activity through, and in object relationship in the phallic phase.

These are different expressions of shifts in drive balance and distribution, overlapping and sequential, but not antagonistic or mutually exclusive.

Diagnostic Comment. Carl is a warm and likable child, but reminds one of a good dish with seasoning left out, to use an oral analogy. His oral fixation is now a symptom in a crystallizing intrapsychic conflict and is receiving therapeutic attention. He is of well above average intelligence, but concentration in a learning situation is poor, aggravated now that the conflict around thumb sucking is in the foreground.

2. A Case of Hypermotility

Peter B. Neubauer, M.D.

Basis for Admission

This family came to the Center to get help for their son, Tony, then almost three years of age. The parents were unable to cope with his disobedience, his temper tantrums, and his general hyperactivity. Their attempts to be permissive or to discipiline him had failed to evoke any improvement in Tony's manageability.

A few months after applying, this family was admitted to the Center, and Tony was enrolled in our nursery. Consequently, during the past three years, we have had an opportunity to study this child's development.

Family Background

Since we expect to trace Tony's development from infancy, it is important to understand the personality of his parents. We have, of course, more material than will be studied here. We have selected the data we think most significant for the topic under discussion.

Tony's parents are older than usual, above average intelligence, and from the lower middle class.

This is the *father's* second marriage. His history indicates that he keeps himself detached from close relationships, at least in his overt mode of behavior. This was as characteristic of his relationship to his mother and his first wife as it is in his present marriage.

This detachment covers a demand for dependency, which was disappointed early in his life. This disappointment created suspicion and hostility toward women. He makes strong conscious efforts to control his sexual and aggressive strivings. His defenses and conscious controls against these drives are not fully successful. His childhood history shows a repeated breaking down of these controls, in his participation in gang activities such as stealing, breaking of cars and windows, and early sexual promiscuity. Until recently, there have been episodes of gambling and extensive fantasies about keeping a mistress. Outwardly, he attempts to be calm, is critical of other people, condemning and admiring of their sexual activities. At times, his anger against this will break through, and he may punish his wife and child, with evidence of sadistic impulses, although this punishment is rationalized as necessary discipline.

At present, he tries to be calm, withdraws from social contact by reading books, and complains about his wife's inability to control the child. At times, these controls were not strong enough to avoid fantasy gratifications, and at other times they were strong enough to bring about episodes of depression.

The *mother's* behavior also indicates efforts at maintaining control. She is orderly and neat. In contradiction to the father, she uses activity as a source of pleasure. She appears to be a warm person, is obese, speaks freely, and gesticulates. She prizes action most highly.

She comes from a family in which sports were appreciated, and some members of the family excelled at some of them. These family members she admired and tried to compete with them. In speaking of her father, her pride in his "pep" is apparent. She imitated and competed with her older brother's athletic activities, worked very hard and successfully as a secretary, and kept this position until shortly before she gave birth to Tony.

That orderliness, which has compulsive coloring, and her need for activities and social contact are associated with a need for dependent relationships. She expects others to be warm and outgoing and to tell her what she should do. If they are not able to fulfill her needs, she overeats and is critical of them.

This similarity between herself and her husband does not lead to complementation, but exposes the insufficiency of each parent. Each looks to the other for qualities they are unable to provide. The mother cannot give her affection to a man who is quiet and detached. She looked for a man who was strong, which to her connotes being active and indulgent.

To these parents, and into this constellation, a *child* was born who showed characteristics from the first which could only accentuate some of the problems of both parents. Had he been just a warm child, ready to seek and to give affection, he might have stimulated different qualities. But, from birth, he appeared to be endowed with an exaggerated need for endless activity, based on a surplus drive energy. He carried into the family his problems of controls, exposing their own conflicts in this area.

We have a history of strong early intrauterine motility of this child. This was confirmed by nurses and doctors who predicted correctly that this would continue after birth, and that "he would become a future football player."

In spite of the mother's pleasure in having a boy, and a very active one, soon after his birth she became frightened of the child's hyperactivity and its accompanying requirement for continuous attention.

History of Motility

The history of Tony's maturational sequences manifests his precocious motility. During his second week of life, he tried to creep. He was able to sit at the age of five months, to stand at seven months. When he was able to walk, he could not tolerate restrictions. When he was one and a half years old, he broke the play pen. Speech development started very early.

We also get a story of his running away from his mother, but it would probably be more accurate to say that his urge for activity carried him away from his mother, instead of it being his intention to get away from her. Until the second year of life, he seems to have enjoyed escapades on the streets, visiting stores, and talking with strangers. The mother worried about this, because she feared he might get into troublesome situations. She herself did not feel that his running away was directed against her. He would hurt himself frequently, repeating activities which had proven to be outside his control.

At this stage of his development, there is no indication that fear was present, which could have exerted a controlling influence on his activities. Physical hurt through accident, and punishment by parents had no effect on his motor strivings. When frustrated, he would become destructive, break objects, tear clothes, attack his mother, or would have a temper tantrum with all its concomitants of aggressive discharge and loss of control. If by this period the ego had developed the capacity for reality testing, it was drowned by the overflow of drive discharge. The mother put a harness on him, and this was the manner in which he was brought to the Center.

It may be valuable to consider the following questions at this point:

1. It seems to be important to separate drive endowment from his maturation. It is interesting to speculate whether his surplus of aggressive energy has stimulated precocious maturational sequence, or whether this is due to an independent factor of endowment. In other children with hypermotility the sequence of their neuromuscular development may fall more within the normal range or perhaps be delayed.

2. To what degree does precocious development disturb the balance between the ego and drives? Or, more specifically, what kind of precocious maturation may assist the ego in controlling drive influences; what kind

may invite the drives to undermine the mediating functions of the ego? Has this early neuromuscular development facilitated drive expressions?

In order to gain further insight into these questions, we shall consider further Tony's drive endowment and maturation as well as his ego development. But, first, we shall summarize the libidinal phases of his development.

Libidinal Phases of Development

Oral Phase. This child showed early signs of, at least, adequate libidinal expression. When hungry, he would cry, suck adequately, and give expression to his oral pleasures. His crying imposed upon his mother the necessity for changing him from scheduled feeding to demand feeding, with increase in his formula. The fact that the mother could increase the formula without asking the pediatrician's permission is important to note. Unable to control her own food intake, she imposed her need on this child and could not tolerate it when, as she felt, he did not eat enough. She would then force-feed him. In spite of this, he seemed to enjoy his food. He accepted the bottle and solids without difficulty. Later he began to show certain disturbances around eating. He developed food fads and licked his lips. He did not eat at mealtimes. He expressed his opposition to the "when and what" of feeding, and not to "oral pleasure."

The mother would give him the bottle, not only when she thought he needed nourishment, but also to calm him when he was restless. When Tony watched television, which stimulated him into restlessness, she would push a bottle into his mouth to calm him. The mother tried to make him accept oral pleasures as a substitute for activity pleasures, but oral gratification could not stem the aggressive and libidinal overflow of energy through the channel of motility.

It appeared that eating could not make him restful. In the nursery, it was not possible for the teachers to keep him at the lunch table, although it was apparent that he was hungry. It was also impossible to calm him at the rest period. Nor was he sufficiently tired in the evening to fall asleep easily.

Signs of his orality continued into the anal and phallic phase. He continued to lick his lips when he was more than three and had food fads. He showed signs of oral dependency. His mother fed him and also had to dress him. He depended on others to help him in achievements. There are signs of disturbed object relationships.

In spite of his mother's inability to provide full satisfaction, he did not turn toward the self as his object for gratification. It may be that these children with hyperaggressive discharge are too outwardly directed to gain this advantage. This absence of oral-erotic activities, with the exception of one—licking of his lips—may be compared with Carl.

Anal Phase. Similar interplay between drives and object relationship was manifested in the anal phase. The mother made a feeble attempt at toilet training. When on the potty, he would either run away soon, or break it. She put him on the toilet seat before he was one year old. Later, she put him on a "toidy" chair, and he broke that, too. Still later, she gave up training him, and when he came to the nursery he still soiled himself and wet during the night.

Tony did not mind when he was soiled, and the mother kept a diaper on him until he was three, and let him stay in his soiled diapers. She is a very neat woman. She did this consciously, in order to teach him to be clean.

It may be because of the outward direction of his aggression that somatic illness did not occur. We have related this mode of energy distribution also to the absence of autoerotism. This is in contrast with the other children discussed. He showed a good deal of interest in smearing and spilling of water, and when he cleaned himself, he would use a good deal of soap. He used anal language freely. We have no evidence that this anal phase of development increased his hyperactivity.

It would be interesting to speculate about the reason for the absence of an increase in aggressive mobilization, during the anal phase of development, in a child with this endowment. It may be that only when the aggressive drive is partially internalized do we find, during this phase, an increased expression in motility (as in the case of Sandra).

There is another possibility. In addition to the spurt of action during this phase, associated with growth in neuromuscular development, a mother who had insisted on training might have increased negativism and thereby aggression. This mother has not been able to impose controls successfully on Tony. There was neither an increase in hyperactivity, nor a significant modification of it. We looked for signs of fusion of aggression with libidinal aims, but we found no convincing evidence of sadomasochism. It seems that he was not able to cathect sufficiently the object, nor secondarily, his own body. He behaved as if he were helpless. He had to be dressed and fed and did not wash himself without assistance. When he played, he needed the teacher to stand by to give him the tools he needed.

We find here a carry-over of the oral dependency. There were limited signs of reaction formation and no expressions of guilt connected with his inabilities and demands.

A significant change occurred after he attended our nursery school. He was then past three years of age, not toilet trained, and gave evidence of separation anxiety from the mother. We wonder now how much of his training difficulties were caused by his drive disturbance or by his mother's attitude. Similarly, we raise questions about the meaning of his separation anxiety.

1. Was this due to a precocious motility which led him away from maternal protection, before his ego was able to cope with a strange environment?

2. Was this separation anxiety a fear of loss of the mother with repressed aggression against her; that is, preneurotic in nature?

Our nursery provided the opportunity for more motility discharge in a protective environment. He could run and climb and be in motion as never before. The teachers aided him in his activities, in mastering his coordination in climbing and building, and did not restrict him. Furthermore, in this way they provided him with an opportunity for new and consistent object relationships. The separation anxiety disappeared after a few weeks, and he soon became toilet trained.

These reactions to his new environment enable us better to evaluate the contribution his mother has made to these disturbances. Still, the outstanding feature of his behavior was the endless need for activity, his still-limited ability for object relationships with teachers or other children, and his helplessness in taking care of himself. Oral and anal manifestations were carried into his fourth and fifth years.

Phallic Manifestations. We will consider the material to follow as early signs of phallic development. At four and five years of age, Tony had a heightened awareness of his age and size and the form of his relationship with boys and girls. There was genital masturbation during the last few years. While this, in itself, is not an expression of phallic manifestation, he had also taken girls into his play corner, built a house around them, and started sexual play with them. During this period, the teachers noted that his hyperactivity would become explosive in nature, would lead to a destructive, aggressive attack, and he would have a certain glazed look in his eyes, following the orgastic rhythm, according to Greenacre (1954).

He started to exhibit himself in the toilet. He was able to form a relationship with teachers and with other children. He was not only able to accept toilet training, but he was stimulated toward phallic strivings. It is true that most of the relationship focused around activities. His hide-and-seek play became more than a running away and being found, during this phase. It was an experiment in belonging and losing, but it seems also to have the quality of sexual seeking, of hiding and discovering, with its sexual secrets.

During this phase, we also see the emergence of certain fears. He would become cautious in climbing the jungle gym. He would not trust his body. Although in the first years of his life, fear of injury seemed to have no restraining effect on his activities, he would now become hesitant. He asked for help, which led him to a better object relationship. Fantasies, such as being Superman and flying through the air, or being a cowboy roaming through the Wild West, became interrupted by play which seemed to express the wish for limitations. He would build a house in which all windows and all doors would have to be carefully blocked. With these emerging anxieties and fears, there was the wish for limits, as concrete and specific as was his unbounded urge for freedom in activity previously.

While in the beginning of his school experience, he provoked the anger of other children by his disruptive acts, he became more and more accepted and sought after. He developed a dislike for "messy" material, such as clay, finger paints, and dough. He still had difficulty, however, in feeding himself and in resting. He became more mischievous than negative, more teasing than destructive. He became more exhibitionistic and, at the same time, more hesitant, when he made demands for help. We assume these to be expressions of phallic influences. We have seen that oral and anal problems were carried into the phallic phase. Conversely, phallic organization affected the previous phases correctively.

Aspects of Ego Development

Motility. We have discussed Tony's hyperactivity and his precocious neuromuscular maturation at length. We have seen this to be related to an overendowment of the aggressive drive. We have found that with his urge for activity, begun in his intrauterine life, he had no capacity for adequate control. His gross motor activities showed a lack of adequate coordination. He would fall repeatedly, injure himself, would not learn by experience. It is interesting to investigate here the mother's possible contribution to this development, as indicated by the Yale study on parental attitudes (Coleman, Kris, and Provence, 1953).

This was not a quiet introspective mother, who could not tolerate expression in activity. The area of conflict, therefore, between mother and son centered around different problems. In many ways this mother supported unconsciously the letting go and overindulgence. We find here therefore, overstimulation by the mother toward discharge, rather than frustration, which would have provoked aggression against her.

With the overflow of aggressive energy into motility, we find an inability to master control. This is not only true of his skeletal muscles, but this is found wherever aggressive strivings take part in the oral, anal, and phallic organizations. There, too, we find discharge problems with inadequate controls.

Until the phallic phase, object relationship suffered because Tony had little ability to tolerate frustration. To follow the point made by Hartmann, Kris, and Loewenstein (1949), "the ego could not use neutralized forms of aggression." There were certainly libidinal and aggressive aims satisfied in his motor discharge. In spite of his destructiveness, he did not find pleasure in inflicting pain. Fusion toward sadism as well as toward masochism is absent. He would hurt himself, but there were no signs that he enjoyed his pain.

This overflow of aggression into ego controls is also expressed in another important area of his development, namely, speech.

Speech. Again, he showed a similar pattern of development. He was an early speaker, has an excellent vocabulary, was very much stimulated by the mother, who sought premature companionship with her son. She spoke to him when he was a young infant, looking for "social" contact, which was denied her by her husband. Because of this, with his early speech development, he had speech problems. His speech was indistinct and slurred and improved at about the age of four. The control of his flow of speech came at a time when he was also able to control other functions of his body (drooling, toilet training, motor coordination).

Effect of Instinctual Balance on Ego Development

When we studied this child's hyperactivity, his object relationships and libidinal phase development, we had to go beyond the concepts of an inborn pattern of activity. This would have given too much consideration to ego functions and would not have answered the economic problem of distribution of energy.

We took into account the question of overstimulation by the mother, similar to Greenacre's (1952) outline about the libidinal drive.

Freud (1939) stated that "in a sequence of the relation which was already established between sensory perception and muscular action, the ego is in control of voluntary movement."

Tony has at least adequate sensory perception, and we have no indication of a faulty ego equipment. He has an excellent memory, was, therefore, aware of stimuli from without, and he could connect experiences. But he was, to follow Freud's (1939) outline of the principal characteristics of the ego, unable "by learning to bring about appropriate modification in the external world to his advantage through activity."

With his precocious maturation, his ego was certainly not sufficiently capable of controlling the surplus drive endowment. It was unable to postpone satisfactions. He had to satisfy the aggressive aim and jeopardize object relationships. The forming ego was largely unable to defend itself successfully against the flooding of the drive through the channel of motility.

The fact that the aggressive drive chooses motility predominantly as a form of discharge, instead of other avenues, does not exclude the assumption of surplus drive endowment. It does raise the question of the degree to which certain inborn aspects of the ego predispose the aggressive drive to choose this form of expression.

With the problem of the endowment in drives, we have to investigate the hereditary characteristics of the ego.

To follow Anna Freud's (1952) investigation into ego autonomy, we have little evidence of a defect in the ego apparatus, while we raise the question of predisposition in channeling of drive expression.

We have material which indicates overstimulation, in addition to failure, in normal drive development. Further, we assume the ego apparatus is not in control, due to a deviant drive quantity and distribution.

If we follow Tony's development into the phallic phase, we see that he chooses experiences connected with activities in order to gain increased object relationship. He follows the path of motor expression and makes this a part of the nature of his experiences. It appears that this could be considered as the secondary autonomy which Hartmann (1955) outlined.

Superego Development. Together with unusual drive endowment and interference in ego control, it is not surprising to find also disturbance in superego·development. The early years show Tony's lack of fears and lack of response with guilt toward his destructive behavior. The mother's indulgent attitude may certainly be one of the reasons for this.

In addition, it appears that the discharge in motility toward uncontrolled functions made his aggressive reactions less object-related. His destructive behavior was stimulated more frequently in connection with limitations on discharge and as a reaction to frustration, rather than in connection with the object. The wide discharge in action seems to have interfered with the cathexis of the object and its internalization.

We certainly find the fear of loss of the object, but not the loss of love. There was, therefore, less ability to internalize aggression, and with it, less development of guilt and superego. It needed castration anxiety to bring about the beginning of internalization. To express it more accurately, with the establishment of a more consistent object relationship which only came about in the phallic phase, castration anxiety was stimulated, and this, in turn, produced internalization of aggression.

Summary of Instinctual Development

We have selected a case history which we hoped would permit a study of unusual drive endowment.

Tony's history of unusual hyperactivity during intrauterine life, his continuous urge for motor discharge after birth, and his precocious neuromuscular maturation, offer evidence of factors of deviant endowment. This kind of data does not enable us to consider this problem as a reaction to environmental influences. If we had only studied the motility of this child, we might have arrived at a discussion of variations in activity pattern (Mittelmann, 1953). We found the overflow of drive energy, not only in the channel of neuromuscular activities, but closely tied to the erotogenic zones and their influence on libidinal phase development.

We have discussed these motility disturbances largely in connection with the aggressive drive, understanding that such activities also serve the libidinal aim.

Kris (1955) proposes that "maturational processes are more closely connected with noninstinctual energies and that the organization of action and problem solving is more dependent on the neutralization of instinctual energy."

We raise the question whether *precocious* motility may not impair the ego's ability to use neutralized drive energies; furthermore, whether a predisposition toward discharge in hyperactivity has not the characteristic of interfering with adequate object relationship and, therefore, ego development.

If we consider Hartmann's (1955) point that there are various degrees between instinctual and neutral energy available on which the ego has to draw, we may say from this history that the surplus discharge in motility seems to make neutralization particularly difficult, since it does not lend itself to modification through object relationship as much as do libidinal aims.

In order to understand the process of internalization, we have to differentiate between the object and the aim. While the aim of satisfying aggressive and libidinal demands was maintained in this child's activities, the object was more fleeting, and the aggressive intent was insufficiently object-directed. It spread to other parts of the environment with equal ease, and, therefore, the cathexis of the object and its internalization came about very slowly. Anxiety and guilt had to await this development.

Where we find flooding of motility with drive energies, we may find delayed superego development. The oral and anal phases seem not to have had sufficient effect on the ego modification of the drives, whereas the beginning phallic phase brought about the first marked modification. The question is whether we can generalize from this case.

We assumed where there is more externalization of aggressive than of instinctual strivings, there is less autoerotic and autoaggressive activity.

As to the prognostic outlook, Tony is now five and a half and has reached the phallic phase of development. There certainly will be delayed latency. To what degree will he continue to be hyperactive and later to act out? Will the oedipal phase bring about more anxiety and more inhibition of his drive? He uses actions as his important mode of expression and experience. Will there be a shift from the cathexis of function to the cathexis of objects?

3. A HYPOACTIVE CHILD

Annemarie P. Weil, M.D.

Sandra was referred by her previous nursery school to the Child Development Center when she was four years and seven months. A few months later, in the fall of 1955, the family was accepted into the Center and Sandra and her fourteen-month younger sister, Karen, entered our nursery school.

Outstanding in Sandra has been her lack of activeness, assertiveness and initiative, her physical slowness, as well as her lack of emotional responsiveness and her poor capacity to relate to people.

To us Sandra has been a marked example of the quiet, if not hypoactive, activity type, growing in an environment that made for its accentuation rather than "a development toward the median line" (Fries and Woolf, 1953; Wolf, 1953). The question arose whether in terms of drive endowment this means a deficient admixture of aggressive drive, possibly also a deficient endowment of libido, or whether it means not a quantitative but a qualitative peculiarity, i.e., unusual distribution. One can also question whether the apparent lag in ego development is the consequence of this drive endowment interacting with environmental forces, or whether an original constitutional weakness is at play.

Picture at Admission

Sandra is a nice-looking, blond, pigtailed girl, with unusually wide eyes. It needs to be said that there is a fascinating quality about her. Observed in the group, she stands out by her seeming detachment and her marked slowness. She seems to be much more an observer than a participant—an imitator rather than an initiator.

The referring nursery school described her as follows: "Sandra has been unable to make relationships, has not been able to join in group activities, and shows lack of initiative. Sandra will stand apart and watch; or she will bounce a ball for hours in a corner, her facial expression alternating between deadness ('a flatness which no other child in the group has'), and occasional interest. Outstanding from the beginning of her school career had been her lack of aggressiveness. She would never retaliate when hit, and she would submit if other children wanted her toy."

The parents reported that Sandra had shown slowness, unresponsiveness and lack of spontaneity practically from birth. At times they had even considered the possibility that she was retarded. Their description was: "Sandra does not move with the bounce and activity of other children. She can run, but she does not run fast. She does not laugh or smile, nor jostle and move around like the others. She does not play with the abandon and spontaneity other children have. She will build and call it a house, but then not continue any fantasy play with this house. In her talk, little is offered spontaneously; one has to feed her cues. She is 'shy, dependent, and an alien among children.'"

Areas of special concern to the parents were: demandingness toward her mother, with crying spells when frustrated; negativism; and enuresis. Enuresis had persisted with only short dry periods.

During the intake study Sandra, then four years and seven months, and her sister Karen, three years and four months, attended the outpatient nursery many times before Sandra was able to relinquish her mother and to mobilize herself. When Sandra finally let her mother go for an interview with the social worker, she became immobile again after a short while, to liven up only when her mother returned. With the gradual thawing out, there was some more and freer moving around, and at least passive participation in the group. Thus, she would sit at song time and answer a question, but not move as she was supposed to. She never initiated contact with other children and ignored their advances. Teachers and their suggestions were also often ignored. Sometimes Sandra would squirm so as not to be touched, but follow. (Striking was her behavior at one of the first snack times when she kept a piece of bread in her mouth way into the story time and just did not chew.)

Family Background

Sandra's father is a research scientist, devoted to his career rather than to remunerative advantages. He does not participate very actively in the upbringing, but applies his excellent capacity for observation also to his children. In his family background, the contrast between people who show overactiveness and others with underactiveness stands out and has left him with a tendency to discriminate between "thinkers" and "doers"; the former are represented, among others, by his father, the latter by his mother. His identification is clearly with the father.

Sandra's mother is an artistically gifted, intelligent person, who usually functions with superficial smoothness and gentleness. We have found her attitude characterized by anxiousness, hypersensitivity, at times overempathizing (equating her defeatist attitudes with Sandra's deficiencies), but also perplexity because of inability to understand Sandra's reactions. The middle child among brothers, the mother has not successfully achieved a feminine identification. She has a neurotic fear of failure and has given up a promising art career because of this fear. A tendency toward defeat has been most outstanding among a number of other neurotic symptoms. In the main, the marriage of Sandra's parents seems good. Both are moderately active, with a great tendency toward control of ambivalent striving. The climate at home is that of relative even-temperedness, thus neither arousing nor allowing much outward expression of aggression.

The mother's first pregnancy resulted in a premature mongoloid boy who died after two weeks while still in the hospital. Sandra had been very much wished for. The mother became pregnant again after six months, and there has reportedly been a positive feeling about Sandra's being a girl. The next two pregnancies were neither planned nor prevented. Karen was conceived when Sandra was five months old, and at the time of the referral the mother was pregnant again and in her fifth month. (The mother's seeming aceptance of the unplanned pregnancy with Karen, when Sandra was only five months old, may suggest that this pregnancy was unconsciously wanted to be more certain of having one normal child, since deviancy in Sandra was already evident in early months.)

Both parents had observed Sandra with anxiety from the beginning, and increasingly so when Sandra's initial reactions did not seem according to norm. We may assume that Sandra's immediately apparent specific make-up and this atmosphere of anxiety influenced each other in a circular way.

Early History

In the unfolding picture of Sandra's development the emphasis will be on the expression of drive energies, their interplay with ego development, and environmental factors—influencing drive expressions by way of the ego.

Birth to Six Months. Pregnancy with Sandra and delivery were uneventful. The mother had noticed, however, that the child was not very active *in utero*. Delivery was at term. Lack of activeness then was obvious from birth. Sandra did not signal hunger; her sucking was weak and she seemed to tire easily. She was nursed—and received a supplementary bottle—for three months, on demand. She never finished a bottle and never acted like a hungry baby. She seemed to be "too good a baby," except for certain hours when there was colic crying, which could be relieved by carrying. Colic continued until the third month, and then constipation set in.

Lethargic functioning continued also after the third month. She seemed content to just lie. The development of new motor patterns was slow. She was late in turning over. In spite of lack of spontaneous reactions, when given intense stimulation Sandra could react appropriately. Thus, she could smile at three months, point to her eyes, nose and mouth at six months (and, to look ahead a bit, could—although rarely—do "patty-cake" at nine months).[5]

Six to Twelve Months. The unusualness of Sandra's development now became even more conspicuous. She would not mouth, chew or handle things. She did not hold on to the bottle. She would not try to pull or tug at things in sight, and later would not reach for objects, although able to do so. She did not try to pull herself up (but at the end of the first year she could stand with support). If not stimulated, Sandra would just sit and look with big eyes. She did not laugh or smile spontaneously. However, her mother had found Sandra distinctly responsive and always very sensitive to her.

While there was lack of attempts at mastery of the outside world by means of skeletal musculature, vision started to assume unusual importance. This was *her* way of reaching out into the world, and associated

---

[5] These responses—as well as early talking and also her present functioning clinically and test-wise—prove that Sandra is definitely not a mentally retarded child. She now, without full cooperation, tests as of at least average intelligence—which, though adequate, is below family norm.

with this was perceptive discrimination. Not only did Sandra want the mother in sight and would whimper if mother disappeared for long, or appeared in a coat, but she did not allow anybody, even father or grand-mother, to do anything for her without whimpering. Speech development proceeded early and well. At nine months Sandra said "Mama." Thus, we find visual and vocal performance and contact prevailing over motor activity.

Toward the end of the first year, some kind of intense masturbation could be observed. Sandra would squirm in bed, perspire, and grunt. Masturbation by leg pressure has continued ever since. Around the age of one, Sandra's masturbation seemed to be the greatest expression of activeness encountered in her, albeit an activeness turned toward her own body rather than the outside world.

Discussion

Let us survey Sandra's development at one year of age, usually the highpoint of aggressive oral drives, of motor (hand and mouth) explora-tion of the world, and therewith of differentiation between self and non-self, of beginning individuation; and let us scrutinize the forces at work in Sandra's development.

Weak outward functioning of both drives from the beginning points toward an unusual *drive* endowment.

There is weakness of oral desires and activities.

There is weakness of motor activity. (We assume that visual and vocal performance needs less energy than that of the skeletal musculature.) Motor achievements come late and are slowly and infrequently per-formed. Pleasure in activity (*Funktionslust*)—a consequence of fusion of adequate amounts of both drives and cathexis of motor functioning—is conspicuously weak. This dearth of oral desires as well as of manipulatory reaching out, mainly a consequence of deficient drive endowment, may have been further fostered by environmental factors: the mother is a responsive rather than a stimulating person; and in her overconcern she may have reacted too quickly to weak signals. However, the picture San-dra presents goes far beyond the consequence of an anxious mother.

There is a weakness of emotional expressiveness, with only whimper-ing on the one hand and a slow smile on stimulation on the other.[6]

With so little evidence of the usual gradually increasing externaliza-

[6] Spitz (1953) described the instinctually better-endowed infant in the following words: "After about two months of life—we can begin to distinguish manifestations of pleasure from manifestations of unpleasure and frequently of rage. Phenomeno-logically we can speak of observable manifestations of the libidinal drive on the one hand and of the aggressive drive on the other."

tion of aggressive drive, providing strength to the expression of desires and activities, we may speculate whether the colic pains represent internalized aggression.[7] The subsequent long-lasting constipation may represent a continuation of this (it is, indeed, not of the conscious, anal, withholding type expressing externalized aggression), as well as being another indication of insufficient and insufficiently outward-directed drive energy.

As further evidence of deviant make-up, we find in Sandra an unusual phasic drive distribution. In contrast to minimal (for survival) expressions of orality, there is early and intense libidinization of the genital zone.[8] We can speculate whether the increasing, yet of necessity not always fulfilled, need for mother contributed to the intensity of masturbatory activity. Possibly the sensitive infant reacted to some slightly diminishing responsiveness of the pregnant mother at certain moments of increased tension with even less reaching out, putting what little active strivings there were into the service of autoerotic gratifications.

Ego Development. The weakness of Sandra's oral and muscular reaching out is—inadequately—compensated for by vision and perception (a heredoconstitutional anlage may play a role, since both parents are visually and perceptively gifted people). The lack of attempts at mastery—even with the prevalence of vision—have limited her familiarity with the outside world for a much longer time than usual to that part of it that consistently comes to her—the mother. Good discriminatory faculties (ego apparatus) and hypersensitiveness (to which I want to come back in my concluding remarks) of the dawning ego make for early—though limited—responses (smile; "Mama"), but also for early and intense eight-months anxiety. Parental anxieties may have made matters worse. Individuation, as a first step toward a future object relationship, seems to have started; but with anxiousness to the fore, and touching and grasping (now also in relation to mother) minimal, separateness could not be achieved. Eight-months anxiety continues in symbiotic needs. We see in Sandra increasing symbiotic dependence, on the basis of her specific drive endowment, some possibly innate ego weakness (hypersensitiveness), and in the setting of a mother's overresponsiveness, alternating with occasional withdrawal.

[7] Hartmann, Kris, and Loewenstein (1949) state: "Internalized aggression plays a relevant role in the etiology of illness."

[8] It is conceivable that masturbation started even earlier as a predetermined discharge channel (Greenacre, 1941) and that the motor components only became more evident at that time.

Fries and Woolf (1953) describe leg pressure in the startle response of a "quiet child," considering the possibility that by way of such self-stimulation future choice of areas of libidinization might be determined.

Development from One to Three and a Half Years

Environmentally important during this period is the birth of Karen, when Sandra was fourteen months old. With continuing overconcern for Sandra and minimal attention given to Karen, the latter developed fast into an active and easily relating toddler.

In Sandra, lack of reaching out to the nonmaternal environment and unusualness of drive expressions continued after one. Interest in locomotion and physical exploration lagged behind that in perception. Motility was slow, and motor achievements late. Sandra did not walk before seventeen months (mother's pregnancy may have contributed here). Sandra continued to be lazy to chew and did not eat meat until two. Speech development proceeded well, but its use was tardy and sparse. Passively giving in to environmental demands, Sandra took the cup easily after one and did not even request a bottle again when Karen was born. (However, she did request Karen's bottle once in her fifth year—a time of greater activeness—when told that a third child was coming.) Toilet training, like weaning, was achieved very easily, within days, at sixteen months, except for the remaining enuresis. Constipation had already yielded to cathartics since the child was one year old and stopped by the time training was achieved. Masturbation continued.

When mother gave birth to Karen, the situation was handled as well as possible. Yet it was too much for Sandra at that stage. While staying with her father and the maternal grandmother, who had come to the house two months previously, Sandra was passive and "extremely good." On mother's return, Sandra did not want to go to her, held on to her doll, cried and said: "Baby." She clung to her father and did not go near mother for the rest of the day. For the next two days she kept bursting into tears, but began to cling to her mother and practically rejected her father. Subsequently she did not allow him to fondle her or do anything for her, and continued to be very dependent on her mother. There was, however, no immediate reaction when she saw her mother handle the baby.

Weepy dependence on mother with passive compliance and anxious withdrawnness characterized Sandra's third year. She shied away from strange adults and children. Elaborate preparations had to be made whenever mother left; even so, there was a great deal of crying. After her third year, the situation gradually eased: she would stay with a neighbor if another child was present, and she again accepted her father.

Discussion

In Sandra this period is characterized by general anxiousness and by intense and persistent symbiotic needs.[9] Let us look at the factors contributing to this constellation.

Drives. Usually, during this period, libidinal strivings gradually shift to anal interest, and under the libidinal influence of the anal phase, expressions of the aggressive drive gain in quality and quantity. In Sandra, paralleling the weakness of the oral libido, direct expressions of anal striving have been practically absent (to this day she has never shown strong reactions for or against dirt, sand and messiness). Toilet training was easy; the constipation persisting throughout Sandra's first year, as discussed before, seems best understood as a psychosomatic disturbance due to the unusual distribution of aggressive drive energies. Indeed, its cessation as well as the eventual beginning of walking may be indicative of somewhat more outward-directed drive energy—though far from sufficient, as the whole behavior shows.

Weakness of aggressive drive admixture in Sandra's functioning parallels the weakness of libidinal expression: there is neither the increase of locomotion and mastery usually seen in the second year, nor the greater independence that follows in course in the third. The one exception to the weakness of expressions of the aggressive drive is the prevalence of a whiny, unhappy mood. We can speculate whether this represents— besides the consequences of sometimes unfulfilled symbiotic needs—an abundance of not externalized unneutralized aggression.

What is the interplay of this instinctual constellation with *ego development* and environmental factors? What is its relationship to anxiety? For reasons discussed, individuation was halted, and eight-months anxiety continued, with symbiotic tendencies. Naturally, anxiousness and with it symbiotic needs were bound to increase in Sandra, due to mother's pregnancy approaching term and the traumatic, practically preverbal separation it entailed. Symbiotic needs and their regressive increase after the separation were not transitory, as is usual. They were intense and long-lasting, again due to Sandra's specific drive constellation and concomitant poor resiliency of the ego. The parents' awareness of the trauma and increased concern, the mother's subsequent ready yielding, did not help matters.

We can speculate whether extreme compliance, as seen in Sandra at this age, represents another behavioral aspect of the instinctually weak,

[9] Although less sick, Sandra resembles the symbiotic children described by Mahler 1952).

not completely individuated child (preceding the stage of ego development in which compliance may be rooted in fear of losing love).

Beyond the role of Sandra's instinctual make-up in contributing to
symbiotic needs, the question arises whether her deviant drive endowment was not bound to increase anxiety for additional reasons. Normally,
the outside world is gradually established, cathected. The toddler's subsequent increasing active mastery of the world and practice of reality
testing diminish his fear of active approaches and happenings on the part
of this outside world. (This relates to the conquest of manipulation *and*
speed.) All of this is extremely laggard in Sandra: the outside world does
not exist beyond or without the mother, and there is neither activeness
nor speed. Another factor in the emotional mastery of environmental
occurrences is a child's capacity to actively play out whatever he has
passively experienced. Sandra did not avail herself of this mechanism
until very recently.

Development from Three and a Half to Five

This is the time of Sandra's first nursery school experience, and,
during her fifth year, of her mother's next pregnancy. Behaviorally, this
period is characterized by somewhat greater activeness, by gradually
decreasing anxiety, by cautious reaching out beyond the maternal environment, and even by some dawning negativeness. The following will
show this developmental spurt, but also how limited and unusual it is.

Social Development. Gradually, Sandra started to, at least, tolerate
strange adults or one child at a time without clinging to mother. She
would, however, remain unspontaneous and anxious. At three and a half,
with already some dawning improvement, Sandra started nursery school.
She allowed mother to leave her there after a few days—complying with
expectations. She would then stand watchfully—again with perception
in the fore—on the edge of the group, holding on to a toy animal or "just
to a piece of dough." It is interesting that clinging as such—rather than
a transitional object—substituted for the mother in this, until then, so
unmotoric child.

At the end of her first year at school, Sandra would at least sit with
the group, but would not speak or sing; and she would not even sit at
the table if there was a party and the general behavior was more active,
abandoned and noisy than usual. Whatever relationship she had been
able to make was to the teachers. She would sometimes cling to the
teacher in physical proximity, but never asked for help, and often withdrew if the teacher approached her. She sometimes talked to a teacher
over the telephone (rather freely) but then ignored her next day at

school. This lack of carry-over from one situation into another was evidenced at other times, too.

Karen entered the same school in Sandra's second year of attendance. Ignored as a baby by Sandra, she had grown into a lively, active playmate. Sandra had become quite dependent on Karen at home. There was a good deal of parallel play, and Sandra was most spontaneous and freest when with her. In school Sandra never asked to visit Karen who, on her part, visited Sandra. (However, Sandra once introduced herself to a worker: "My name is Sandra, I have a sister in the next room"—like a younger child, as if her identity needed Karen for its completion.) During her second year, Sandra, then four and a half, was able to make a fleeting relationship to one active little girl, Nora. When Nora was absent, Sandra would return to her solitary, watchful behavior. When she was present, Sandra would follow and imitate her.

In spite of apparently poor participation at school, Sandra's observation and retention seemed excellent. She would know the songs and stories and also occasionally report which child or teacher was absent. (Good observation was evidenced also in Sandra's occasional mimicry of adults she had met.)

More advanced achievements of motor development had been slow in coming and were usually slowly performed. On the playground Sandra had needed the incentive of an adult to start off on anything new, but then would learn quite well (sliding, bike riding). There was a certain pleasure evident now in stereotyped performances like bouncing a ball and swinging. As this period progressed there was somewhat freer play, and somewhat greater use of motility.

Expressions of negative feelings gradually became apparent. There were isolated instances of hitting back or asserting herself. In general, however, negative feelings were expressed in a much more passive way. The dependent, tearful demandingness for mother gradually took on a more provocative negativistic tinge. Yet, there was never an open refusal. Sandra expressed antagonism by ignoring mother's suggestions, by extreme dawdling over requested routines, or by not answering when spoken to—a passive resistance.

Anxious weepiness had given way to crying spells. "Frustration crying," as the parents called it, would follow a minor "No." Sometimes Sandra would, for instance, drop a spoon, scream, yet make no attempt to pick it up; or, again, she would cry when she could not do what she was otherwise able to do, instead of asking for help.

Masturbation reached its height when Sandra was about four years old. Sandra would press her legs and wiggle when lying across mother's lap or when playing with Karen in the room. She said to mother: "I do this in bed all the time." Sandra had never asked questions about sex, and mother had not volunteered. In her fifth year Sandra gave evidence of some sex interest. When bathed with Karen she once touched her genitals, saying: "You are just like me." After seeing a boy urinate, she attempted to sit astride the toilet seat and expressed the wish to urinate standing "like Daddy does." In contrast to this relative freedom is Sandra's not asking about mother's big belly, as Karen had done. When finally her mother told her about the new pregnancy, Sandra gave her a slight punch.

When Sandra was five, Mary, the second sister, was born. This time Sandra took the prepared separation from the mother well. It is interesting in the context of our scrutiny of instinctual expressions that at home Sandra has been observed playing with Mary in an aggressive way, pinching and pulling, and at the same time crossing her legs forcefully in a masturbatory manner.

Discussion

Sandra's behavior during this time is characterized by a slight increase in the outward expression of *drive* energies and by some decrease in anxiousness. Libidinal desires become stronger. There is a wish for the bottle, and we also learn about food preferences during this time. Masturbation increases, but as a continuation of the genital masturbation seen since infancy. Although now less exclusively self-related—lying across mother's lap—it shows the limitation of her relatedness, of her instinctual outward striving. The combination of autoerotic and alloaggressive activity—in her handling of Mary—looks like a transitory stage not usually seen. Without having lived out orality and anality, Sandra shows during this period some beginning phallic expressions, together with earlier, polymorphous perverse-like tendencies.

We can ponder whether the increase in drive expressions is due to an increase in libidinal strivings or to a greater admixture of aggressive drive energies making for more forcefulness of desires and interests.

Increased functioning and externalization of the aggressive drive can be seen in somewhat greater activeness, in greater demandingness and in Sandra's negative attitudes (giving to her behavior a belated tinge of anal characteristics).

Interaction of Instinctual Constellation with *Ego Development* and Environmental Factors. Contributing to the change in Sandra's behavior was a maturational spurt evidenced in greater outward expression of instinctual energies. This was bound to foster some further ego growth, the more so since environmental factors worked in the same direction. Nursery school experience gradually introduced more of the nonmaternal environment, enlarged the sphere of familiarity, lessening anxiety and fostering activeness (occurrences beyond the daily, known and predictable were still reacted to with anxiety and avoided). Object relation could now proceed from symbiotic clinging and passive compliance with the mother to somewhat greater independence. Remaining symbiotic tendencies were shifted to the sister and fleetingly to others. Karen, on her part, stimulated activeness and desires by way of imitation; while the year before—when actually generally more anxious—Sandra had been compliant, she could now insist on mother's staying in school. The birth of Mary acted similarly, stimulating regressive desires (for the bottle, which had not been expressed in their due time).

Progress, though, is still limited. Sandra's capacity for object relationship remains limited: in the relationship to the mother, we see symbiotic dependency decrease and a meekly sadistic demandingness and negativism increase. The father is still mainly accepted as a poor mother substitute; expressions of oedipal strivings are absent. Karen is needed for allaying anxiety, for borrowing identity and initiative (similar to the relationship of a younger child to an older sister).

Further Ego Functions. In line with this, we see Sandra still struggling with the reality principle and with omnipotence in her reactions to frustrations. With still deficient outward directedness, her reality testing is lagging behind. An interesting proof of this is Sandra's petting of dogs and screaming if they move. Of preferred defenses, avoidance is paramount in importance. Her motility often works in its service—not flight, but immobility. Introjection serves her limited feeling of identity and, as always, is put to use for learning.

Development from Five to Five and Nine Months

This period covers mainly Sandra's intake contact and her six months of attendance at the Center nursery school. There has been much improvement, with increased activeness, assertiveness and happier moods; yet there is still a great deal of pathological behavior, mainly seen in frequent slowness and lack of initiative. Sandra can assert herself for her turn or a wish, or defend herself with a "No, don't!" against teasing. There are expressions of real aggression, although rare and sometimes delayed. Thus, she may hit a child who had provoked her, but not until the next day. There are occasional spurts of quite abandoned and free behavior when she may climb up the jungle gym, show off and shout "Watch me!" There is better interchange with other children; Sandra can accept their advances and sometimes play more freely with them. There is also occasional playing out and pretending. Recently, she teasingly pretended to give the teacher an injection—an unprecedented event! In her occasional house play, identifications are not clear. She will put on a tie and man's hat as well as costume jewelry; she will want to be the father, but stay home and cook. In spite of a good deal of praise and encouragement, Sandra will give up whatever she may have quite successfully tried, like writing her name, when the more lively—and now also ambitious—Karen takes it up.

Conspicuous in Sandra's generally more active behavior is her negativism which is still marked. To any direct demand, Sandra may still react with an expressionless ignoring. That this causes no difficulties and that there has been so much improvement in spite of it can be related to the teachers' creating a very casual atmosphere for Sandra, in which suggestions are practically given sideways, passing on to the next child.

Discussion

The improvement has continued along the lines indicated before. We should like to add here some additional remarks on Sandra's *ego development*. In spite of some freer interaction, Sandra has not really been able to relate well to any child or teacher. There are beginning relations to other children, with imitation still prevailing over spontaneity. Communicativeness is unpredictable and scanty. Now, at almost six, Sandra's relation to her parents has still not reached even the oedipal level. Overt leanings toward the father are minimal, if not absent.

The struggle for sexual identification is still evidenced in Sandra's play as well as in the two now obvious neurotic symptoms—enuresis and avoidance of competition.

With somewhat freer motility, moments of a flaccid immobility stand out more clearly. Immobility and slowness sometimes serve Sandra's negativism; they still convey the "reluctance" to shift cathexis from one toy, activity, or situation to another. Possibly this "stickiness" of her cathexis is, or originally was, another expression of unusual endowment (since aggressive drive admixture makes for forcefulness *and* speed), taking on, with somewhat better ego development, the character of a defense. Immobility and slowness are still the most favored mechanisms to avoid anxiety. We will discuss the mechanism of inhibition later. Anxiety readiness still makes the group situation a threat. Sandra may become immobile even with a new outfit of her own, to which the other children might react in an unusual manner. However, at other times anxiety can now be handled with the help of newly gained activeness: in the morning Sandra may greet the teacher with a "Guess what?"

Diagnostic considerations are not in the scope of this paper, but the following may be said. In Sandra, deviational drive endowment caused, or is associated with, delayed ego development. The poverty of emotional response and modulation, lag in the development of object relationship and lack of communicativeness, as well as the general anxiety readiness—to mention only some criteria—put Sandra in the group of (schizoid) ego-disturbed or deviational children. The neurotic aspect of Sandra's personality points toward repetition of her mother's neurosis—struggle with the castration complex.

General Considerations

The unfolding clinical picture has shown marked deviancy throughout Sandra's life. We have tried to link these manifestations with unusual endowment of both drives.

There is no way of measuring quantities of drive energy. We are inclined to assume a certain innate weakness of both drives. Beyond this we see deviancy of distribution of drive energies. With regard to libidinal strivings, there was unusual phasic distribution. With regard to the aggressive drive, weakness of action and reaction revealed a minimum of outward-directed—fused with libido—expressions of the aggressive drive during Sandra's first four years. It seems that wherever we find expressions of aggressive drive admixture, of the different forms possible, the least active, the least aggressive, was chosen: visual and vocal performance rather than manipulation and locomotion; speech development preceded and was preferred to walking; Sandra's crying was weeping rather than rage; there was speech rather than action. (In song participation she said the words but did not move.) Even her negativism is one of "not doing" rather than of "doing what is prohibited." Conspicuous in the choice of the less aggressive modality was the scanty use of *the* organ of aggressive discharge, the skeletal musculature. Although still insufficient, we see spurts of greater externalization set in around four and with it Sandra's behavior has become freer.

Insufficient externalization of the aggressive drive is paralleled by manifestations of aggressive drive energies contained within. This is evidenced possibly in the early intestinal disturbances and in the prevalence of unhappy moods. Here also belongs the abundance of anxious tension (with hypersensitiveness and general anxiousness following in its path, as described by Greenacre, 1952). What is the connection of this tension, signifying preanxiety, with Sandra's drive equipment? Greenacre mentions Freud's concept of "dammed-up libido"[10] in relation to the frequency of erection in premature "preanxious" male infants. A case like Sandra's lends itself as well to considering the possibility of tension being due also to an abundance of unneutralized, unexternalized aggressive drive energies; the more so, since viewing Sandra's life, there seems to be a relation of reciprocity between inner tension and outward-directed functioning of the aggressive drive.[11] As a matter of fact, at all times we see this reciprocal relation of externalized drive energies and tension interact with ego development in a positive or negative circular way. There was minimal activeness with a great deal of tension and practically halted ego development between one and three years of age, increasing activeness, lessening tension, and gradual progress in ego development from three and a half on.

Several further questions arise. The relation of this specific drive endowment to ego development as evidenced in Sandra: With still adequate amounts of libido for cathexis of the first object (if one is present), but inadequate active mastery of the outside, as well as an abundance of tension (unneutralized, unexternalized drive energies) in the organism, ego development was bound to be disturbed. Early eight-months anxiety resonates with inner tension and increases instead of decreasing. The next step—recognizing that the rest of the world (beyond the mother) can be pleasure-bringing, too—cannot be made. The ego is flooded with anxiousness due to the circular interaction between symbiotic need and lack of activeness, until further developmental spurts make the circle turn in the other direction.

How do we understand the improvement? There may be maturational spurts of quantity. More conspicuous is the shift in the economy of the aggressive drive. There is increased externalization (fused with libido) making for greater forcefulness of drives and activity on the one hand, decrease of inward-contained drive energies on the other. The ego, freed from some tension, can then in turn more daringly explore the world, as well as allow more aggressive and negative expressions.

The relation of this drive endowment to inhibition: Sandra still appears like a greatly inhibited child. However, inhibition is a reaction of the ego to avoid anxiety.[12] Hence, it does not start at birth. We may however, speculate whether in children like Sandra the initially insuffi

10 Taking it from his writings before the introduction of the concept of the aggressive drive.

11 One may also speculate whether such early evident tension represents "not externalized" drive energies before "differentiation of drives out of the energy reservoir of the narcissistic stage set in" (Spitz, 1953).

12 Interestingly, Freud (1926) calls it an "impoverishment" of energies.

cient externalization of the aggressive drive finds its continuation in the later prevalent mechanism of inhibition.

The relation of greater amounts of not externalized aggression to fantasy: We cannot answer this yet for Sandra, but it is known that such children's fantasies often reveal a good deal of aggressive material.[13]

The causal relation between Sandra's unusual drive endowment and deviant ego development: Is the drive pathology paramount, and does it carry with it insufficient neutralization for the formation of a strong ego; or is there in Sandra's case also a constitutionally weak ego, one vulnerable to the tensions inherent in this instinctual make-up? We could then assume—what is most plausible—that a constitutionally deviant ego-id core continues after differentiation with pathology on both sides and with faulty interplay, as evidenced in Sandra.[14]

CONCLUSION

In our discussion of drive endowment, we used a three-way focus: quantity, balance, and distribution.

We have seen *quantitative* differences of innate drive energies as well as maturationally determined spurts.

The quantitative *balance* between initial libidinal and aggressive drive energies is another important variant in drive endowment.

Distribution relates to zonal-phasic[15] localization of drive expressions. (The factor of preliminary channelization is significant in Carl and Sandra; the factor of ego readiness and preference in Tony.) Distribution is also seen in degree of externalization. In our cases, we have seen a range from insufficient externalization (Sandra) to extreme externalization (Tony) from birth.

We have followed these variants in their bearing on the cathexis of the objective world as well as on *ego development*.

In Carl, localization of both drives in the oral zone from birth and insufficient externalization reduced the aggressive admixture in all ego functions and seriously limited aggressive discharge.

In Tony, a surplus of aggressive drive energies discharged in motility prevented sufficient focusing on the objective world.

In Sandra, deficient drive quantity, associated with insufficient exter-

13 Fries and Woolf (1953) confirm this. See also Dr. Alpert's Carl.

14 This would bear out recent—more biologically oriented—thinking about even sicker children, viewing their condition as a "basic disturbance of maturation on the embryological level of development" (Bender and Freedman, 1952).

15 We refer here to the libidinal erotogenic zones, as well as to discharge channels for aggressive drive energies.

nalization, seriously delayed cathexis of the objective world. It is interesting to note that in the deviant child we found the following constellation: deficiency of libidinal and aggressive energies, insufficient externalization, as well as a possible pathological ego core.

In addition to the relationship of these variants of drive endowment to ego development, we were interested as well in their interaction with maturational sequences and ego achievements. We discussed this in the individual papers and found significant constellations with regard to timing and quality of achievement.

In the development of our children, the resonance of similar drive endowment in both parents and child accentuated the imbalance discussed.

It is our assumption that initial variations in quantity, balance, and distribution of drives are found in greater or lesser degree in all children and have significant bearing on development—on the coloring of infantile neurosis, character disorder, as well as on deeper pathology.

BIBLIOGRAPHY

Bender, L. and Freedman, A. (1952), A Study of the First Three Years in the Maturation of Schizophrenic Children. *Quart. J. Child Behav.*, IV.
Burlingham, D., et al. (1955), Simultaneous Analysis of Mother and Child. *This Annual*, X.
Coleman, R. W.; Kris, E.; Provence, S. (1953), The Study of Variations of Early Parental Attitudes. *This Annual*, VIII.
Freud, A. (1936), *The Ego and the Mechanisms of Defense*. New York: International Universities Press, 1946.
—— (1945), Indications for Child Analysis. *This Annual*, I.
—— (1952), The Mutual Influences in the Development of Ego and Id. Introduction to the Discussion. *This Annual*, VII.
—— et al. (1954), Problems of Infantile Neurosis: A Discussion. *This Annual*, IX.
Freud, S. (1920), *Beyond the Pleasure Principle*. London: Hogarth Press, 1948.
—— (1926), *Inhibition, Symptom and Anxiety*. London: Hogarth Press, 1948.
—— (1939), *An Outline of Psychoanalysis*. New York: Norton, 1950.
Fries, M. and Woolf, P. J. (1953), Some Hypotheses on the Role of the Congenital Activity Type in Personality Development. *This Annual*, VIII.
Greenacre, P. (1945), Biologic Economy of Birth. *This Annual*, I.
—— (1941), The Predisposition to Anxiety. *Trauma, Growth and Personality*. New York: Norton, 1952.
—— (1952), Pregenital Patterning. *Int. J. Psa.*, XXXIII.
—— et al. (1954), Problems of Infantile Neurosis: A Discussion. New York: *This Annual*, IX.
Hartmann, H. (1955), Notes on the Theory of Sublimation. *This Annual*, X.
—— Kris, E.; and Loewenstein, R. M. (1946), Comments on the Formation of Psychic Structure. *This Annual*, II.
—— —— —— (1949), Notes on the Theory of Aggression. *This Annual*, III/IV.
Johnson, A., et al. (1953), Factors in the Etiology of Fixation and Symptom Choice. *Psa. Quart.*, XXII.

Kris, E. (1955), Neutralization and Sublimation: Observations on Young Children. *This Annual*, X.

Levine, M. I. and Bell, A. I. (1950), The Treatment of "Colic" in Infancy by Use of the Pacifier. *J. Pediat.*, XXXVII.

Mahler, M. S. (1952), On Child Psychosis and Schizophrenia: Autistic and Symbiotic Infantile Psychoses. *This Annual*, VII.

Mittelmann, B. (1955), Motor Patterns and Genital Behavior: Fetishism. *This Annual*, X.

Spitz, R. A. (1953), Aggression: Its Role in the Establishment of Object Relations. In: *Drives, Affects, Behavior*, ed. R. M. Loewenstein. New York: International Universities Press.

Wolf, K. (1953), Observation of Individual Tendencies in the First Year of Life. In: *Problems of Infancy and Childhood*. New York: Josiah Macy, Jr. Foundation.

EGO DEVIATION AND THE CONCEPT
OF SCHIZOPHRENIA

DAVID BERES, M.D. (New York)[1]

I. Introduction

The development of psychic functioning, the growth of the mind from its diffuse, unorganized state in infancy to its complex structure in adulthood, has always been a central interest of psychoanalytic research. From clinical experience and direct observation of children, psychoanalytic theory has postulated the differentiation, through maturation and development, of a complicated psychic structure, the parts of which are defined according to their functions and designated as id, ego, and superego. There is general agreement that into this developmental process many factors enter, internal and external, hereditary and environmental.

The interest in developmental problems is shared with other psychological disciplines and continues to take on increasing importance. In his introductory remarks at the Symposium on Genetic Psychology held at Clark University in 1950, Werner (1951) describes the difficulties that G. Stanley Hall encountered when he first introduced genetic concepts into child psychology. The role of psychoanalytic thought in this historical evolution is noted by H. H. Anderson and G. L. Anderson (1954) who say: "Freud not only introduced a new dynamic conceptual scheme of thinking about behavior and unconscious motivation but formulated the first systematic statement of personality viewed as a developmental sequence" (p. 1164).

The emphasis on problems of development has also brought into focus disturbances of development, which may take the form of arrested development, reversal of development or precocious development. Psychic phenomena, both in normal individuals and in psychopathological states, are subject to dynamic and genetic influences, with phases of progression and regression. This proposition has been discussed in great

[1] From the Pleasantville Cottage School of the Jewish Child Care Association, Pleasantville, New York.

detail in recent psychoanalytic literature, for example in a paper by Hartmann and Kris (1945). Measures of progression and regression may be applied to any of the structural components of the psyche—the id, ego or superego. In recent years psychoanalytic psychology has also directed its attention increasingly to sharper definition of the specific psychic functions which are subsumed under these three categories. This trend has been applied most energetically to the functions of the ego and the result has been an increasing clarification of the problems of ego psychology.[2]

The aim of this study is the application of recent theoretical advances in ego psychology to a specific clinical problem: the relation of disturbances of ego development to the concept of schizophrenia.

Direct observation of children in hospitals, nurseries, and in child-development projects has brought into purview a variety of clinical manifestations of arrested development and regressive phenomena. These cases have been described in numerous articles under different diagnostic categories, including: borderline cases, pseudo schizophrenia, ego deviation, atypical children, the autistic child, and childhood schizophrenia. This terminological profusion gives immediate evidence of the incomplete state of present knowledge in this area and activates the need to search for unifying factors.

Many questions arise. What, for instance, is the relation between specific external manifestations and underlying psychic functions of the id, ego and superego? And, further, should both processes, the developmental arrest and the regression, be called schizophrenia, or is there an advantage in distinguishing between them? There is also the question: what are the factors that determine arrest of development and regression, and what is their relation to normal development? The last question is beyond the scope of the present study, and it may be too much to hope that even the other questions can be answered at the present time with any degree of satisfaction, but the clinical importance of the problem warrants making the effort.

The evidence that I shall present consists of clinical examples illustrating various points. Case presentations cannot prove a thesis but they indicate the value of certain theoretical concepts in the understanding of clinical phenomena and they invite similar observations for further confirmation or denial of the value of these theoretical concepts.

2 See especially the paper by Hartmann (1950).

II. The Ego in Schizophrenia

In his earliest writings, Freud placed the ego in the center of the problem of psychosis. In 1894 he described the psychotic process as a flight of the ego from an unbearable idea. The role of defense mechanisms in psychosis was more sharply defined two years later when Freud (1896) described the use of projection in paranoia. In the Schreber case, Freud (1911a) approached the problem of psychosis from the libidinal energic view, the withdrawal of the libidinal cathexis from the object and the world in general. He says,"... in paranoia the liberated libido becomes fixed on to the ego, and is used for the aggrandizement of the ego. A return is thus made to the stage of narcissism (familiar to us in the development of the libido), in which a person's only sexual object is his own ego" (p. 459). But already at that time Freud recognized that libido vicissitudes alone are inadequate to explain the phenomena he was studying, and he adds: "We can no more dismiss the possibility that disturbances of the libido may react upon the egoistic cathexes than we can overlook the converse possibility—namely, that a secondary or induced disturbance of the libidinal processes may result from abnormal changes in the ego. Indeed, it is probable that processes of this kind constitute the distinctive characteristic of psychoses" (p. 461).

In recent years and with increasing abundance, the many studies on schizophrenia, especially those on childhood schizophrenia, have given evidence of the accuracy of Freud's early perception of the importance of ego development in the problem of the psychoses.

Glover (1949), in a discussion of the broader classification of psychoses, states that "sooner or later these groupings will be replaced by clinical divisions based on a developmental approach to mental function" (p. 203). He adds: "We must discover in each case the 'general fixation level' of the ego as well as of the infantile instincts . . . The final infantile level of ego development in the schizophrenic constitutes a base line, regression to which will, given an excess of excitation, disrupt the faculty of reality proving" (p. 221).

In 1937 Freud himself wrote, "Now every normal person is only approximately normal: his ego resembles that of the psychotic in one point or another, in a greater or lesser degree, and its distance from one end of the scale and proximity to the other may provisionally serve as a measure of what we have indefinitely spoken of as 'modification of the ego.' "

Most recently, Hartmann (1953), in his contributions to the metapsychology of schizophrenia, also has called attention to the value of consideration of developmental factors and ego psychology. He says:

> Historically we see in the analytic study of psychosis a mirroring of the trends of psychoanalytic psychology dominant at a given time. The next impulse might come from the advances in analytic child psychology, outstanding in the work of the last two decades. Actually, in saying this, I am not only speaking of the future; this trend has in part already been realized. For quite some time, the study of the regressive phenomena of psychosis has been utilized as one of the main avenues to our understanding of early childhood. While there is certainly no reason to assume that the promises of this approach are exhausted, we see today also a tendency in the opposite direction. What we owe to research in analytic child psychology—through retrospection or direct observation—is more fully utilized for a better understanding of psychosis and the disposition to psychosis. What has become known of the development of early object relationship, ego-id relationship, defenses, and reality testing, constitutes a vast reservoir of data which today we consider essential to any systematic approach also to psychosis.

At a round-table discussion of Childhood Schizophrenia (1953), the various discussants made repeated references to ego disturbances in their patients. A. M. Freedman described the observations at Bellevue Hospital under Lauretta Bender and defined childhood schizophrenia as a "dysmaturation, . . . a disorder of maturation within the embryological level of development in all the areas that are the basis or prerequisites of all future behavior in all fields, motor, adaptive, language and personal-social." In his short communication Dr. Freedman did not, however, relate his conclusions to the psychoanalytic concepts of ego functions, though some aspects of what he described would be so considered in psychoanalytic theory.[3] Similarly, Samuel Kaplan, reporting from the James Jackson Putnam Children's Center in Boston, spoke of "atypical development" as a diagnostic category defining these disturbed children. He also made the point that he prefers this term to either infantile autism or childhood schizophrenia because it "leaves open the question concerning the eventual outcome in these children." Margaret S. Mahler (1949, 1952), in her contributions to the subject, has emphasized the role of disturbance of ego functions and ego development. The publications of various authors differ regarding many points, such as the importance of organic or hereditary factors and the significance of mother-child

---

[3] For a more detailed presentation of the views of these authors, see Bender and Freedman (1952).

relationships, but all agree in the descriptive details of the behavior of these children and the importance of developmental disturbances. What is dealt with, under whatever terminology, is familiar to psychoanalysis in the context of ego psychology.

Thus, it is apparent that the "ego" has been involved in considerations of schizophrenia, both theoretical and clinical, for many years and increasingly so at the present time. What becomes essential, then, is a clear and precise definition of the meaning of "ego," specifically as it is used in psychoanalytic psychology.

III. THE EGO IN PSYCHOANALYTIC PSYCHOLOGY

The word "ego" has many meanings, in common usage, in psychological writings, and in psychoanalytic theory. It is important to establish this last meaning, which has become a tool to be applied to the elucidation of schizophrenia.

Allport (1943), writing as a psychologist in a psychological journal, commented that

> .... one of the oddest events in the history of modern psychology is the manner in which the ego (or self) became sidetracked and lost to view. . . . As if to compensate for the neglect of these interests within the field of psychology proper, psychoanalysis rose upon the horizon emitting a spectacular, if sporadic, light. Small wonder that the world at large turned to psychoanalysis for guidance in dynamic psychology. . . . Until psychoanalysis becomes finally fused into a broader and more adequate psychology, it may take pride in having preserved and advanced the study of certain functions of the self that positivistic psychology had consigned to oblivion. It may take credit too for preserving one term, more or less cognate with "self"* from the dark taboo of which I have spoken. "Ego" has featured prominently in psychoanalytic literature from its beginning.

The first point that demands clarification is the distinction between "ego" and "self." The words are not synonomous in psychoanalytic theory and much confusion in psychological writings has arisen from using them interchangeably. The "ego," as has already been noted, is defined by its *functions*. It is a substructure of the psychic apparatus which subserves certain specific functions. It is an arbitrary designation and, as future studies by both psychoanalysts and psychologists increase our knowledge of these functions, the definition of the ego will be altered correspondingly. The concept of the ego is a working concept and the danger of personifying it must be avoided. The "self" is a more inclusive term which is not specific to psychoanalytic terminology. The self may be defined in philosophical terms, in terms of any of various psychological disciplines, or in terms of psychoanalytic theory. In the latter instance, self has a broader implication, of which ego is a part, and one of the functions of the ego is in fact the awareness of the self. Psychoanalytic writings have contributed to such subjects as self-esteem, self-preservation, self-punishment, and other aspects of the self. These may include ego functions but may include other psychic functions as well. The subject of the self goes beyond the scope of this paper.[4]

The definition of the ego in terms of its functions is found in the early writings of Freud. In *The Ego and the Id* (1927, p. 15) he says:

> We have formulated the idea that in every individual there is a coherent organization of mental processes, which we call his *ego*. This ego includes consciousness and it controls the approaches to motility, i.e. to the discharge of excitations into the external world; it is this institution in the mind which regulates all its own constituent processes, and which goes to sleep at night, though even then it continues to exercise a censorship upon dreams.

Recent studies in ego psychology have added to this formulation the concept of independent energy cathexis of the ego. (See, for example, Kris, 1951.) Hartmann (1950), in a detailed analysis of ego psychology, has stated the problem precisely:

> "Ego" in analysis is not synonymous with "personality" or with individual; it does not coincide with the "subject" as opposed to the "object" of experience; and it is by no means only the "awareness" of the "feeling" of one's own self.... It is a substructure of personality and is defined by its functions.

The over-all function of the ego is to mediate between the instinctual drives and external reality, and this utilization of a mediating device is a specifically human attribute. In this sense the ego is unique to man and serves a group of functions which, in lower animals, are accomplished by the direct action of the "instincts." Freud (1939) speaks of the ego as "an intermediary between the id and the external world." Hartmann, Kris, and Loewenstein (1949) also point up the mediating function of the ego and indicate the importance of distinguishing between "instinctual drive" of man and "instinct" of animals. This distinction is relevant

[4] For a masterly discussion of this subject see Jacobson (1954a). For the point of view of a psychologist see Murphy (1947), who devotes six chapters to the self.

to the present discussion because the instinct of the animal is biologically adapted to respond directly to environmental stimuli, whereas the instinctual drive of man requires the intervention of the ego before it finds appropriate discharge.

Direct experimental confirmation of such concepts as those under consideration here is not easily available, and for that reason similar conclusions arrived at from totally different approaches have the confirmatory value of converging evidence, like sightings taken from different angles to determine a point in the heavens where direct measurements are not possible. So, for example Cassirer (1944), a philosopher, has concluded also, that in humans as distinct from animals there is a special psychic function that permits the delay of response to an impulse. He says:

> Yet in the human world we find a new characteristic which appears to be the distinctive mark of human life. The functional circle of man is not only quantitatively enlarged; it has also undergone a qualitative change. Man has, as it were, discovered a new method of adapting himself to his environment. Between the receptor system and the effector system, which are to be found in all animal species, we find in man a third link which we may describe as the *symbolic system*. This new acquisition transforms the whole of human life. As compared with the other animals man lives not merely in a broader reality; he lives, so to speak, in a new *dimension* of reality. There is an unmistakable difference between organic reactions and human responses. In the first case a direct and immediate answer is given to an outward stimulus; in the second case the answer is delayed. It is interrupted and retarded by a slow and complicated process of thought (p. 24).

The concept he expresses of a delayed response interrupted by a "slow and complicated process of thought" resembles the psychoanalytic concept of change from the primary to the secondary process with the binding of instinctual energy and delay of discharge.

There is then in man this unique structure, the ego, which in its full function allows for the expression of those qualities which distinguish the human from the animal and which, in their malfunction, give to his behavior and thought the characteristically human forms of mental illness. The significance of developmental disturbances of the functions of the ego and their influence on the psychopathology of childhood is our special interest here.

The functions which, taken together, comprise the ego are not evident in the newborn child. In his earlier writings on ego development, Freud

(1923) postulated the differentiation of the ego from the id, a process which results from the modifications in the id produced by external reality. In his later writings Freud (1937) indicated that the ego does not develop altogether by modification of the id through conflict with reality, but also that certain ego functions may have a biological basis inherent in the potential development of the individual. This concept was developed by Hartmann (1952), who postulated an early undifferentiated psychic state, a common matrix, out of which there later develop the differentiated structures of id, ego, and superego. According to this theory, the ego develops partly out of conflict between instinctual drives and reality demands, and partly out of autonomous, conflict-free growth. There is a combination of maturational and learning processes; inherent factors and environmental, cultural factors exert their specific influences in varying proportions on the growing psyche.

The development of the ego can be described only in terms of the development of its separate functions. The genetic approach assumes a progressive process of development and maturation in all areas of psychic functioning, as well as regressive manifestations, which may be normal or pathological. These processes will be illustrated below in the clinical examples.[5]

A complete listing of ego functions would be extremely difficult and perhaps not even feasible at this time. In the present state of our knowledge, any such list would have to be a tentative one. However, for the purpose of illustration of clinical data, the following ego functions will be discusssed in greater detail:

1. Relation to reality
2. Regulation and control of instinctual drives
3. Object relationships
4. Thought processes
5. Defense functions of the ego
6. Autonomous functions of the ego
7. Synthetic function of the ego

The interdependence and interrelationships of these functions will become apparent in the discussion that follows, as indeed will the fact that one cannot deal with any aspect of ego activity without involving the total personality.

[5] A number of authors have written excellent studies of the development of the ego and the reader may be referred to these. See, for example, Jacobson (1954a); various papers by Hartmann; and also Fenichel (1954, p. 468), for a summary of ego development.

IV. CLINICAL DATA

This study is based on observations of a large group of children in a placement agency. They were all in residence in a cottage school which is not a hospital, but which provides psychiatric facilities for the study and treatment of these children. The children were treated in analytically oriented psychotherapy. The children were placed in the cottage school for various reasons—death or illness of one or both parents; broken homes resulting from divorce, desertion or separation of parents; and, with increasing frequency, specific behavior or symptomatic disturbance in the child which required separation from the home. All of these children had to deal with the traumatic experience of separation and deprivation, some from earliest infancy, others more recently. To this were added other life experiences of varying degrees of traumatic significance, as the cases will show. All forms of psychopathology were noted in these children but the selection which follows is for the purpose of considering only one clinical problem, that of ego deviation. This is not a statistical study and the cases chosen are only a partial sampling of a much larger group showing various degrees of disturbed ego functioning.

The cases chosen have clinical manifestations in common which fall under the broad heading of ego deviation. Some of these children had been institutionalized previously at mental hospitals, some had been diagnosed as schizophrenic, and some had even received electric shock therapy before admission to the cottage school. The imperative need for this study was indicated, in fact, by the recurrent experience that many children were referred to the cottage school with the diagnosis of childhood schizophrenia on the basis of a single interview, a Rorschach test or even a period of hospital examination, where our own observations and the children's later development gave no evidence to substantiate the diagnosis. The application of recent advances in the knowledge of ego functions and their vicissitudes of development in the child seemed from the beginning to offer the most promising approach to the clarification of these differences.

In the child, growth is an active factor that must be considered in the evaluation of any manifestation of behavior or symptomatology. The ego of the child is, by the very nature of its biological state, an immature ego, and as such will introduce into the child's activities, both normal and pathological, evidences of this immaturity. Normal behavior may then carry the hallmark of what at a later age would be considered ego deviation, and psychopathology of every sort will carry a larger component of ego deviation than in an older child or adult. Anna Freud (1952), in a comparison of adult and infantile neuroses, emphasizes this. She points out:

> .... in the immature personality ... the ego does not stand firm under the pressure of instinctual regression, but regresses simultaneously. The gap between the two internal agencies is lessened in the event of such "total regression," i.e., the regressed ego becomes compliant toward the regressed id demands. This avoids the intensity of internal conflict for the child, but produces instead the multitude of abnormalities, hold-ups in development, infantilisms, failures in adaptation which we group together vaguely as "emotional disturbances of childhood development."

It is well known that some manifestations of childhood may closely resemble the behavior of psychotics, a point which Melanie Klein (1946) has developed in her concept of the universality of the psychotic position of the small child. She says: "In early infancy anxieties characteristic of psychosis arise which drive the ego to develop specific defense mechanisms. In this period the fixation points for all psychotic disorders are to be found." She makes it clear that she does not imply by this hypothesis that all infants are psychotic. Anna Freud (1936) also has described the bizarre behavior of adolescence which may closely resemble schizophrenia.

I hope to make it clear that this paper is not an essay on differential diagnosis. The cases which follow illustrate various disturbances of ego function. In each instance I shall try to point up the need to investigate the relation of the disturbance to the stage of development of instinctual drives and ego status of the child, the conflict situation, and the other aspects of the total personality. My purpose will be to recognize the dynamic interplay of forces in a still-developing organism. Questions of diagnosis will be secondary, though in some cases the profound pathology left little room for doubt. The terms "schizoid," "schizophrenia" or "psychosis" will be used descriptively according to the usage familiar to psychiatry and psychoanalysis, and I shall leave for another time the question of the definition of these terms.

The clinical considerations which follow can serve only to indicate the value of various theoretical concepts. Experimental validation of most of the concepts used in the study of human behavior is difficult to achieve, because the experimental method as it functions at present has not yet developed the tools to test these concepts, and not necessarily because

the concepts have no validity. In what is still the infancy of the science
of child development, a concept can, at best, be subjected only to the
test of clinical observation. If the concept is in accord with the observation, it deserves to retain its place. When new observations are made
which contradict the concept, a new concept will take its place.

1. *Relation to Reality*

According to Freud, the relation to the external world is "decisive
for the ego." The relation to reality includes several components—
adaptation to reality, testing of reality, and the sense of reality—all of
which form a central area of interest in the consideration of psychosis.
Adaptation to reality, which is most comprehensive, is the resultant of
many additional factors, including other ego functions, and will appear
in some form or other in all that follows in this paper. In this section
the emphasis will be on the functions of reality testing and the sense of
reality.

In 1894 Freud described flight into psychosis as a defense. He said,
"the ego has broken away from the unbearable idea; but the latter being
inseparably bound up with a part of reality, in so far as the ego achieves
this result it has also cut itself loose from reality, totally or in part."
Thirty years later Freud returned to this idea in his paper on "The Loss
of Reality in Neurosis and Psychosis" (1924a), in which he said, "A loss
of reality must be an inherent element in psychosis."

It is widely recognized that the sense of reality and the testing of
reality are complex processes which develop gradually in the child. This
has been described from different approaches, psychoanalytic and nonanalytic. In the "Stages in the Development of the Sense of Reality,"
published in 1913, Ferenczi dealt with this theme exhaustively and
elaborated on the transition from the pleasure principle to the reality
principle which Freud (1911b) described two years earlier. Werner (1948),
from his psychological studies, describes the gradual evolution of the
child's relation to reality from its early self-centered concrete physiog-
nomic attitude to the world to the later capacity to differentiate between
inner fantasy and objective reality. Piaget, especially in *The Child's
Conception of the World* (1929), illustrates this developmental process
with many examples of the productions of children observed at the J. J.
Rousseau Institute. When Bleuler (1912) introduced the term "autism"
he drew attention to a form of thinking "directed by strivings which
disregard logic and reality," and which is found in various forms in
both pathological and normal states, and especially in the mental activity

of children. Murphy (1947) summarizes experimental psychological data that give evidence of the "influence of need satisfaction on the movement of cognitive processes." Murphy supports the concept of the universality of autistic responses in thought and perception, in child and adult, which vary in degree according to individual differences determined by cultural, emotional and developmental factors.

The extremes of disturbances of reality function, such as hallucinatory activity or delusion formation, which are familiar clinical findings in adult schizophrenics, do not concern us here. Of more immediate significance is Freud's early observation (1911b) that every neurotic turns away from some fragment of reality. In a later paper (1924a) he said, "Neurosis does not deny the existence of reality, it merely tries to ignore it; psychosis denies it and tries to substitute something else for it." Freud returned to this problem repeatedly, and in a fragment published posthumously in 1938, he discussed the question of the splitting of the ego. In *An Outline of Psychoanalysis* Freud (1939) again described the concept of a *"split* in the mind [where] ... two mental attitudes have been formed instead of a single one—one, the normal one, which takes account of reality, and another which under the influence of the instincts detaches the ego from reality. The two exist alongside each other. The issue depends upon their relative strength. If the second is or becomes the stronger, the necessary condition for a psychosis is present" (p. 115). Freud described in detail the "split in the ego" which characterizes fetishism, but added that the fetishist "has never completely succeeded in detaching his ego from the reality of the external world." The fetishist has more accurately effected "a compromise formed with the aid of displacement." Freud expanded this concept to include the infantile ego which "often enough finds itself in the position of warding off some claim from the *external world* which it feels as painful, and . . . this is effected by *denying* the perceptions that bring to knowledge such a demand on the part of reality." He added that denials of this kind "turn out to be half measures, incomplete attempts at detachment from reality. The rejection is always supplemented by an acceptance; two contrary and independent attitudes always arise and this produces the fact of a split in the ego. The issue once more depends upon which of the two can command the greater intensity."

This phase of the development of the reality principle involves the distinction of inner reality and external reality. That it is a phase in a process that goes through different maturation stages has been recognized in nonanalytic writings as well as in psychoanalytic papers. Thus,

Koffka (1928) delineates the world of the child as one in which he goes from his inner world to the adult world of reality via a constant interplay of fantasy and reality. Piaget (1929) also gives numerous examples of this development and demonstrates its role in animism. A fundamental psychoanalytic contribution to the subject is to be found in Anna Freud's (1936) description of the child's use of denial in fantasy and in word and act, as early defenses.[6]

In an exquisitely detailed report based on careful observations by the mother of the child, Brenner (1951) describes a case of acute hallucinosis in a girl of three and a half years who was not psychotic. The development of the acute symptoms, in relation to the child's instinctual wishes and the anxieties produced by them, is presented by the author with convincing clarity. In this instance the child's ego, overwhelmed by wishes and fantasies relating to insemination, pregnancy and birth, and unable to mobilize more adequate defenses, resorted to a primitive regressive response including the loss of the ego's capacity to test reality and the substitution of hallucinations for external perceptions. In an older person such a clinical finding would suggest a psychosis. The age of the child and the relation of this isolated manifestation to her total personality made it clear that this was not a case of childhood psychosis.

In the children observed in our study there are numerous examples of similar distortions of the relation to reality which might be considered inappropriate for the age of the child but which, when evaluated in relation to the child's total responses, did not permit the diagnosis of a psychotic process.

The use of denial which characterizes the child facing an unpleasant aspect of reality is so familiar that it need not be illustrated here.[7]

[6] The interrelation of the ego function of relation to reality and other ego functions is here clearly evident. Defense functions of the ego and thought processes are especially important in this regard.

[7] More eloquent than any clinical example is William Wordsworth's poem, "We Are Seven." The poet describes his vain effort to convince an eight-year-old girl that she should not include a dead brother and sister among her numbered family. The last two stanzas follow:

> "How many are you then," said I,
> "If they two are in heaven?"
> Quick was the little Maid's reply,
> "O Master! we are seven."
>
> "But they are dead; those two are dead!
> Their spirits are in heaven!"
> 'Twas throwing words away; for still
> The little Maid would have her will,
> And said, "Nay, we are seven!"

Other manifestations of disturbed relation to reality in our cases included transient hallucinatory experiences, transient delusional states, progressive loss of contact with reality, and blurring of the distinction between fantasy and reality. Disturbed sense of reality was not easily demonstrated in these children. This may be due to the fact that such a reaction requires a degree of sophistication and language facility beyond the capacity of these children. Other observers working with children from a different background might have a different experience.

The following case is an example of transient hallucinatory experiences in a girl considerably older than the child described by Brenner.

Case A.[8] This twelve-and-a-half-year-old girl had been removed from her parental home by court order because of physical neglect when she was nine years old. Both parents were disturbed persons and the mother subjected the child to inconsistency in handling, ranging from actual neglect to overindulgence and an appersonified relationship, in which the child was treated as an extension of the mother by the latter.

From the beginning of her stay at the cottage school the child manifested evidences of severe disturbance of various ego functions. She had a fey-like quality, was usually withdrawn and isolated from the other children, but periodically broke out in aggressive actions, screaming and running around. Her school work was poor, and she tended to incoherence in her speech. She was subject to episodes of uncontrolled laughter and would say, "My heart is laughing." In striking contrast was a capacity for organized activity in certain areas, especially in drawing which was spontaneous, warmly colored, with rich content of persons, trees, houses, flowers, animals and other detail. She progressed slowly and in the later years functioned better in all areas, though still with evidence of great disturbance.

Her father had been ill for some years with a degenerative neurological disease. He had been abused by his wife, who, it was reported, used his crutches to beat him. The child had witnessed these altercations and was torn in her loyalties between her two parents. The father died in May, 1954. In July and August of that year the child had a number of experiences which she reported as visions of her father coming out of his grave and of seeing an angel wearing wings. The latter episode occurred during the day and the vision of the father

8 I wish to thank the members of the staff at Pleasantville Cottage School who helped me generously by supplying the data reported in the cases which follow. The psychiatrists who treated the children include: Drs. Jolan W. Blass, Alexander J. Friedman, Thomas Harper, Edith Jurka and Joseph Shectman. The co-operation of the casework staff and the cottage parents in supplying details of the living experiences of the children was of inestimable value. Special thanks are due to Mrs. Frances Dover of the casework staff for her help in culling over volumes of records. Mrs. Lila Oppenheimer, staff psychologist, made her protocols freely available to me, and she is now studying for future publication the data of the numerous psychological tests.

at night, but before she had gone to bed. She was convinced of the reality of the apparitions at the time of their occurrence, but by the next day admitted to their unreality and now, after some months, speaks of them as "dreams." Reality testing at all other times was intact.

The hallucinatory experiences that occurred in this girl were in relation to a specific stress, the death of her father. Their content suggests an effort to deny the reality of her loss, and at the same time contains elements which indicate a compromise formation, for example, the presence of angels which are associated with death and heaven. There is no doubt that some of the descriptive features of this case fit the rubric of schizophrenia, and the child has been so diagnosed by some psychiatrists who have seen her. This diagnosis deserves consideration if the intention is limited to designation of a descriptive nosological category. But it seems more rewarding to examine the hallucinatory experiences in this child in relation to her developmental status. It is then evident that the point of central interest is the persistent state of conflict in a still-growing child. Her earlier traumatic experiences had already resulted in marked deviations of ego functions in many areas. The added stress of her father's death tipped the scale in the direction of a psychosis, but the eventual outcome is not certain.

The second case, a girl of fourteen, illustrates another form of disturbed reality testing, namely, transient delusional states. As in the previous case, the central focus will be on the developmental details.

Case B. This girl was admitted to the cottage school at the age of ten. She has been there for four years. The parents are separated. The mother had been committed several times to a state hospital.

B. was subjected to a great deal of sexual stimulation, including primal scene experiences, dancing in excited fashion with mother and father, sleeping in the same bed with her father since the age of eight and most recently, direct sexual contact with the father, which apparently stopped short of intercourse.

B. was a nice-looking, moderately overweight girl who took average care of her clothing and grooming. With the onset of puberty she developed rapidly and took on an appearance that earned her the opprobrium of "sexy" from the other children.

The sexual experiences with her father were revealed by the girl, first to another girl, then to the cottage mother, and subsequently were discussed with the social worker and psychiatrist. The revelation was accompanied by a show of guilt, concern about "dirty thoughts" that filled her mind against her wishes, and the expression of a wish for an ideal life of great propriety and respectability.

Her relationships to other children were characterized by a tendency to form a clinging attachment to a "best friend" and this was also manifested in her transference behavior in her therapy, in which she developed a passionate "crush" on her female therapist, demanding long interviews and complaining of a lonely feeling. She baked a cake for her therapist and sent it to her with an impassioned love note.

With the revelation of her sexual experiences and the accompanying guilt feeling, the girl developed delusional thoughts that she was being watched by boys on the fire escape when she was in the shower or dressing. At the same time she expressed an aversion to traveling in trains or walking in the street because she felt that people were watching her. However, this aversion did not develop into an actual phobia.

The struggle in this girl between her sense of reality and the delusional thoughts could be observed in *statu nascendi*. Although she acknowledged the unreality of her thoughts, it was evident that she was not convinced. She said, "I know it isn't so, but I can't get rid of the feeling."

These manifestations disappeared gradually, but after an episode on a New Year's Eve almost a year later, when an uncle tried to kiss her, they returned in full force. On this occasion she refused the uncle's advances, but at the same time questioned the extent to which she had provoked the incident and sought reassurance that she had behaved correctly.

This girl gave a general impression of immaturity with a tendency to confusion and mood swings. She also was troubled by temptations to steal which she could not resist, despite a conscious struggle to stop her actions. The defective superego development in this girl will be discussed in the next section on control of instinctual drives. There has been progressive improvement toward increasing maturity in her general behavior, with, however, increasing evidence of neurotic conflict and rich fantasy activity.

The delusional states which involve the loss of the most primitive aspect of the function of reality testing, the capacity to distinguish perceptions from ideas,[9] are, if viewed in isolation and by definition, psychotic manifestations. But when they are considered as transient and recurrent phenomena related to specific stimuli, in this case sexual temptations which reactivated the memory of actual incestuous experiences, occurring in an individual with immature ego and superego development, the perspective goes beyond the issue of diagnosis. In this case, as in the preceding one, the conflict is still in a state of flux. At this point it is not possible with any certainty to foretell which form the predomi-

9 See Hartmann (1953).

nant defenses and other ego functions will take, and what will be the eventual clinical manifestations.

In other instances it was possible to follow the gradual deterioration of the relation to reality in a child to the point of overt psychosis. Cases of this kind are, of course, familiar to every psychiatrist and there is no need to describe one in detail. More important would be the documentation of long observation of children over many years as the struggle between progressive and regressive forces goes on, and the observer sees transitional and fluctuant states, with the disappearance and return of reality awareness. Although some of our children have been under the care of the agency since early infancy, early records do not supply the necessary documentation. This remains a problem for future study. Our direct observations, limited to seven years' duration or less, impressed us with the value of postponing a decision as to the ultimate outcome of the conflict until incontrovertible evidence for a diagnosis is available. The fact that in many cases our early concern was confirmed by the later development of an overt psychosis does not, in my opinion, detract from the validity of this point of view.

Case C. This brief description of a girl of thirteen and a half, whose mother was psychotic and whose father was dead, is an example of the deterioration of the relation to reality to the state of an overt psychosis. The child had been neglected since infancy but had developed a close attachment to the mother and fought against all efforts at separation. She presented severe aggressive behavior disorders at an early age. She was fearful, very withdrawn, and physically awkward and ungainly. She fought all routines, bit children who opposed her, and ate ravenously.

At the intake interview she was entirely relevant and coherent. Except for a marked tendency to deny her difficulties and to project onto others, she showed no loss of reality testing or of the sense of reality.

Immediately after placement, marked deterioration of reality functioning set in, and within six months a flagrant paranoid delusional state had developed which necessitated admission to a state hospital. Other ego functions showed a corresponding regression.

The reason for the rapid regression in this girl could not be determined, but two factors seem significant: the intolerable separation from the mother and the permissive atmosphere at the cottage school, which may have stimulated the irruption of instinctual drives that had been held in abeyance at home.

An important phase of a child's relation to reality is the role of fantasy. Fantasy in the life of a child has two important aspects: its role as a defensive operation and its role in the development and preparation for reality functioning. This subject is dealt with in detail by Anna Freud (1936) and Susan Isaacs (1948) from different theoretical approaches.

It is a common observation that the child may present a fantasy with such emphasis and conviction that the adult observer cannot determine easily whether the child distinguishes between the fantasy and actuality. The question resolves itself into the evaluation of the child's ability to test reality, his ability to recognize when he is in the realm of "make-believe," and when to accept the evidence of external facts. It is a well-known fact that this capacity is strongly influenced by the emotional significance of the content of the fantasy to the child. There are, of course, other factors—among them the level of education and other life experiences, which include exposure to the attitudes of the surrounding social milieu and the attitudes of the family. The latter factors may explain some of the divergences noted in studies by workers in different countries, e.g., Piaget in Switzerland, Werner in Germany, and Isaacs in England. In the adult, whether he be normal or pathological, there is a variable response to the impact of reality, and where unconscious factors are most prominent truth is most controverted, a fact which can be confirmed in everyday life as well as in the consulting room.

It is difficult to set exactly the age at which the child can definitely differentiate among fantasies, dreams and actual experiences. It may be questioned whether this is ever accomplished in an absolute sense even in the normal person. The borderline between real and unreal, between rational and irrational is not too sharply defined.[10]

Werner (1948), in a survey of 150 Hamburg children, reports that it is between the ages of six and eight years that "there arises a clear consciousness of the fictitious and the artificial, of a purely phantom reality." Isaacs (1930), on the other hand, believes that beyond the first three years the child rarely confuses thought and fantasy but, she adds in a footnote, "That is, of course, apart from neurosis, or from the temporary clouding of judgment under emotional stress."

But it is precisely the confusions which result from conflict and stress that impressed us in our study. Indeed, are they ever absent throughout life and do they not, in the child, even the normal one, assume especially great proportions? The following case illustrates this point.

Case D. This eight-year-old boy is the child of divorced parents. The mother was a harassed woman unable to cope with her many problems; the father was

10 For a detailed discussion of this problem see Hartmann (1947).

in prison for grand larcency and a half-brother was institutionalized for drug addiction. Another brother three years younger than D. lived with the mother. An attempt at foster home placement had failed and after a period of hospitalization the boy was admitted to the cottage school. He was described as overactive, aggressive and undisciplined in his behavior. His oral needs were so great that he is reported to have eaten out of garbage cans and drunk out of toilet bowls.

He was subject to vivid fantasy activity and gave the impression that he had difficulty recognizing his productions as unreal. For example, on one occasion, he appeared with a foreign stamp that a staff worker had given him, and with great excitement and serious mien imparted the information that the stamp was worth $1,800. He would sell it and with the money his mother would establish a new home. She would no longer have to work, and he would be able to return to her and they would live together as a family.

Within the limits that it is possible to be convinced in such a situation, the observer was convinced that to the child his fantasy was a realistic fact. Only slowly, under the pressure of discussion, did he relinquish his fantasy and accept the reality of his status in placement. His fantasy was not "make-believe" play: it was an earnest effort, though unconscious, to deny reality.

The mother never actually told the child that his father was in prison and wrote him letters explaining instead that he would be in a hospital "for a long, long time." The boy carried on this fiction although he knew the truth. Sometimes he discussed the problem of his father's imprisonment realistically with his caseworker or psychiatrist. At other times he reverted to the fantasy that his father was ill, and on one occasion even that his father was dead.

Over a period of more than a year the blurring of fantasy and actuality has gradually diminished and, although many pathological features remain, he seems capable of normal reality testing for his age.

The cases I have described in this section are not intended to exhaust the problem of the relation to reality, but only to illustrate some varieties of deviation of the function as they appear in the growing child where they may, by their extreme manifestations, raise the question of psychosis. The point of central interest is that in each instance a developing ego is caught in a violent psychic conflict, a fact that suggests the wisdom of a cautious approach to the question of ultimate outcome.

The function of relation to reality is closely tied up with disturbances of other ego functions, especially object relationships, the capacity to distinguish self and non-self, and the regulation of instinctual drives. It will be evident that a sharp distinction between the different ego functions cannot always be maintained.

2. Regulation and Control of Instinctual Drives

This is often described as the inhibitory apparatus serving postponement of discharge. It is manifested in the increasing capacity of the maturing ego to postpone gratification. It is part of the adaptation to reality and brings into play progression from the pleasure principle to the reality principle, and from the primary process to the secondary process. It must be distinguished from the delay of gratification that can be induced as a conditioned response in animals or infants, as, for example, in housebreaking a puppy or in premature toilet training of the infant.

The instinctual drives of the young child pass through a well-established developmental and maturational progression originally described by Freud and repeatedly confirmed by analytic and nonanalytic observers. These stages, known as the oral, anal, phallic, and genital, provide the basis of the behavioral and clinical manifestations of childhood. The development of the ego involves the interrelationship of these instinctual (id) drives, and their control by the ego. The maturing ego controls the discharge of these drives, both sexual and aggressive, according to the demands of reality. Hartmann (1953), particularly, has emphasized the importance of the process of neutralization, both desexualization and desaggressivization, of instinctual energy in the developmental process which leads to normal ego development and the control of instinctual drives. He says "the schizophrenic ego's capacity for neutralization is damaged" and "the lability of neutralization, or its impairment, is a fundamental character of the ego disorder in schizophrenia."[11]

Comparative psychologists have described in animals and in children the gradual development of discrete, specific differentiated and delayed responses out of a diffuse, unco-ordinated immediate response. Primitive activity is diffuse in its content, rigid in its application, and immediate in its discharge. Greenacre (1941) has described the diffuse response to stimuli in borderline cases, affording a clinical application of this principle.

Ego regression with access to id material and the irruption of id manifestations may occur within the limits of normal functioning in

[11] The recent papers by Hartmann and by Kris on ego psychology, including the concept of the neutralization of instinctual energy, have opened new vistas in child development studies and in clinical research. The role of neutralization in ego development, object relationships and sublimation assumes increasing importance as a working concept for the clarification of these complex phenomena. A related concept is that of the fusion of aggressive and erotic impulses in the course of development.

adults and even more strikingly in children. Kris (1952) has emphasized the role of ego regression in artistic creation where "the ego controls the primary process and puts it into its service" in contrast "with the opposite, the psychotic condition, in which the ego is overwhelmed by the primary process" (p. 60). In play, in wit, in the sexual orgasm, and in rage and temper outbursts the ego may temporarily surrender its control and permit the discharge of id energies. The determination of the point where such surrender of control and id irruption ceases to be normal and becomes pathological may be very difficult to determine, and especially so in the child whose ego has not yet established fully the function of control of instinctual drives.

Ekstein and Wallerstein (1954), in a study of borderline and psychotic children, discuss the "ego mechanism of control" and point up the significance of noting varying degrees of control in borderline patients and in overt schizophrenics. Geleerd (1947) also describes a group of children who displayed "a far lesser degree of control over their aggressive actions than do other children of the same age. Also, they show a lack of control over their anal and sexual impulses such as one would expect in a much younger child." These children also had disturbed object relationships and other manifestations of ego deviation from an early age. She suggests that these findings in young children may portend later schizophrenic outbreak, but she demonstrates the improvement in these children when given the opportunity to establish a completely dependent relationship to one adult.

Temper tantrums are a well-recognized externalization of uncontrolled aggressive impulses. Geleerd (1945) describes two varieties of temper tantrum—one, in children who have never developed past the stage of the early infant-mother tie or who have regressed, and who may show, along with the tantrums, breaks with reality, paranoid ideas and disturbed libidinal development; and, two, in children who, though also maladjusted, are able to respond to reality demands.

In a paper by the author (1952) on aggression it was concluded that outbursts of aggressive behavior may be expected as a regular concomitant of immature ego development and defective superego development. Several cases were described in which aggressive outbursts, temper tantrums and also attacks upon the self were considered as related to severe ego disturbance. Characteristic of these aggressive outbursts were: a lack of goal directedness, their diffuse nature, and a minimal relation to immediate frustrations. The ego deviation in these cases was related to severe disturbances of the mother-child relationship in early infancy.

It was found that the level of ego and superego functioning in each case was a direct determinant of the specific clinical forms of the child's aggressive behavior.

It is not only in aggressive manifestations that ego-deviant children evidence poor control of instinctual drives: a clinical manifestation also prominent in these children is the uncontrolled discharge of pregenital and genital sexual impulses such as bizarre eating habits, uncontrolled excretory function, and excessive masturbation. Such children function under the influence of the pleasure principle, and the disturbed behavior that results may suggest a lack of reality testing that descriptively permits the designation of psychosis. It is well recognized, however, that such behavior in children may not have the same serious significance that it would in an older child or adult, where uncontrolled outbursts of sexual or aggressive activity which disregard reality would be diagnosed as psychotic. The frequency of uncontrolled behavior in these children was remarkable and took many forms.

In presenting illustrative case material it is my purpose here, as in the previous section, to demonstrate the fluctuant nature of the child's behavior, indicative of a dynamic unsettled conflict situation. Irruption of libidinal and aggressive impulses may be followed by periods of controlled behavior; there are varying responses to the continued demands of reality, to the effect of new opportunities for identifications, and to new experiences. In any given instance it is not possible to be certain of either the immediate or eventual significance of a child's behavior, no matter how bizarre it may seem, until there is an opportunity to see the accumulated effects of all the factors enumerated and, in addition, to allow for an opportunity for further development and maturation—the factor of time.

Case C. is an example of a child whose inability to control her instinctual impulses progressed, along with other ego deviations, to the point of overt psychosis.

The following case also went on to overt psychosis but is presented to illustrate the intrapsychic conflict between instinctual impulses, ego defenses and superego demands that went on for years in a state of alternating dominance until eventually the ego surrendered and gave up its prerogatives and functions.

Case E. This boy was first seen when he was thirteen years old. The parents separated when he was four years old, immediately after a brother was born. The father was described as a rigid, punitive man who was alcoholic. He was a retired navy man. The mother, an intelligent person, was overwhelmed by her realistic problems and could not maintain a home.

E.'s early development was described as normal, with bowel training achieved at two and a half years but with persistence of enuresis. He was considered to be slow in learning but psychological tests later indicated normal intelligence. He was, however, considered to be a problem child from the end of infancy. This was evident mostly in his aggressive behavior, which took the form of assaulting other children, so that he could not be kept in school. In addition, he was disobedient, given to lying, to wandering away from home and to setting fires. He was hospitalized in several different mental hospitals from the age of six to eleven and different diagnoses were made in different places, from "primary behavior disorder" to "childhood schizophrenia." In one institution he received electric shock treatment.

After his discharge from the hospital when he was about eleven and a half, his father took him to live in another state, where the father maintained a home with another woman and her children. The boy was enrolled in a private school and made a fair adjustment for about two years. E. was returned suddenly to the mother when the father became ill and also because he had begun again to present difficulties. The mother immediately asked for placement, on the basis that she could not maintain a home for her children.

When he was seen at this agency the boy presented a pleasant, shy appearance. He was friendly in the interview and his productions were entirely relevant, but soon after his admission there was a marked isolation from the activities of the school and the other boys. The boy constantly read comics and sucked his thumb. His surface adjustment presented no overt problems except that he was unusually distrustful of both adults and children. Another bizarre manifestation was a tendency to wander off by himself into the woods, where once he built himself a hut in poison ivy and as a result suffered an acute generalized dermatitis. There were no difficulties with aggression at this time. Schizoid manifestations were clearly evident. Reality testing seemed intact at this time, although the boy had an active fantasy life.

Six months later a serious symptom became evident in the form of auditory hallucinations. He described these as "thoughts that talk." He said, "It is my conscience speaking to me from outside." The content of these hallucinations could not be determined. Control of instinctual drives seemed adequate. Despite the overt break with reality, the boy's behavior in general was not disturbing, and he was kept at the cottage school while plans for his future were considered. The hope was to avoid hospitalization.

This status continued for about a year, during which time the outstanding development was gradual loss of control of his aggressive drives. He was a huge boy, and, in behavior resembling that of Lennie in Steinbeck's *Of Mice and Men*, he became a threat to the other children. He was himself aware of the potential danger, tried to avoid hurting others, but invariably did so. On one occasion he killed a pigeon belonging to another boy, an action which filled him with remorse. He tried to please and was obviously distressed at the irruption of his aggressive drives. When he began a series of fire-settings it became necessary to send him to a mental hospital. From this hospital he was referred to another institution better equipped to deal with the dangers of his actions.

The striking feature in this boy over the years of observation was his effort to control his instinctual drives. From his early childhood these forces predominated. There was some cessation during latency, with recurrence in puberty.

The following case is one in which the outcome is still uncertain. The episodic outbursts of uncontrollable rage are the most striking of the clinical manifestations.

Case F. This is a thirteen-year-old boy, good-looking and of superior intelligence who has made a good surface adjustment at the cottage school, where he has been for more than two years. He was referred for psychiatric examination because of outbursts of rage which were associated with an acute sensitivity to what he construed to be criticism.

The boy's father died when he was eight years old. There was a history of profound overtly sexual involvement with his mother. This consisted of alternating episodes of seductive, affectionate, overdemonstrative behavior and violent quarrels and recriminations. The mother was under private psychiatric treatment and was described as having paranoid tendencies. Placement was indicated because of the realistic difficulties which the mother had to deal with to provide a home for the boy, but the deciding factor was the increasing conflict between mother and son, which was overtly sadomasochistic in character.

It was reported that the boy had on occasion dressed in his mother's underclothes. Other difficulties prior to admission included stealing, lying and unconcealed masturbation. In his behavior with other children he made great efforts to be involved in the typical activities of the other boys. He was considered to be a bright, resourceful boy who presented no particular problem at the institution.

In the psychiatric interview the boy at first presented a calm and reasonable front. He rationalized the need for placement, but when the discussion turned to his problems with his mother he began to cry. He refused to go further into the discussion insisting, "I can handle everything myself," and then veered off into an angry tirade against the cottage father. As he listed his complaints, his voice increased in volume to a scream, and he developed one of his typical rage reactions. His reaction was inappropriate and the tendency to projection was striking. In a subsequent interview the effort to direct the boy's attention to his conflict and his defenses of denial and projection resulted in an outburst of rage against the examiner.

There was evidence of profound conflict around bisexuality, masturbation, and oedipal problems as well as aggression. Some of his responses, when he was examined by the psychologist, were so unusual that a schizophrenic process was considered to be a strong possibility.

The questions opened up by this case go beyond the single issue of the ego function of control of instinctual impulses. The problems of choice of defenses and of object relationships particularly have important significance in the expression of libidinal and aggressive drives.

The slow increase of the ego's capacity to control instinctual drives is illustrated in the following case, in which there also was development of other ego functions. A point of particular interest is the marked libidinal conflict of this child, who never had a family of her own.[12]

Case G. At the present time this child is twelve years old. She was born out of wedlock to a psychotic mother who saw her only once a day for the first year during their stay in an institution, and rarely the following year. The father is unknown. The child was first placed in a foster home at fourteen months and in a series of foster homes after that, in none of which she succeeded in making a satisfactory adjustment. She was then referred for placement at the cottage school when she was eight years old.

She is a small, dark child, with an intensity and alertness that carry her into the midst of all activities around her. She has regular, delicate features and somewhat slanted eyes, which, with her impish manner, give her an unusual and attractive appearance. It was characteristic that in every foster home there was an initial period of acceptance of her which disappeared when her destructiveness, hyperactivity and impulsiveness took over the stage. She was demanding of attention, formed intense, clinging relationships, but quickly transferred her affectons to any new adult who became the center of her interest.

Reports show her early activities to have been characteristic of the institutionalized child. At about one year she was described as unresponsive and apathetic, with a strange limpness in her body tone noted by the nurses as a "lumpy feeling to her body." She sat up at nine months but subsequently lost this ability. At sixteen months she was considered to be a severely retarded child.

Feeding difficulties were an early manifestation in the foster home, with refusal of food and vomiting, but between the ages of two and four this disappeared and she became an active, talkative child. She was toilet-trained without difficulty. At this time her tendency to make friends with everyone was noted.

At about three and a half, overexcitability and destructiveness became apparent, with biting of children and adults and other aggressive attacks on children. Rocking was prominent. Enuresis and unconcealed masturbation appeared. These were met with severe restrictive measures by the foster mother. The child became extremely destructive, broke toys and other objects, cut up

12 This child was presented as Case VI in the author's paper on aggression (1952) to illustrate the interaction of aggressive and libidinal drives in the presence of ego deviation.

sheets and mattresses. At this time a preoccupation with keys and locks began, and has continued to engage her interest to the present time. It was reported that these disturbances appeared in relation to serious intrafamilial problems in the foster family which destroyed the warm atmosphere that had previously characterized the foster home.

In the next foster home where G. remained for two years till she was six and a half years old she was subjected to severe physical punishment and restraint, a fact that came out after she left the home. By this time new symptoms appeared, of a neurotic and phobic nature. She was in a panic at thoughts of injury or death, and became fearful of going into the street. She was wakeful at night and moaned in her sleep. She ate voraciously and her aggressive activities caused constant complaints at school. She would scream or laugh without provocation, roll in the mud and in other ways act unpredictably.

At the age of seven and a half, G. was sent to a hospital for study, where she remained for three months. Her case was diagnosed as a "conduct disturbance." She was then referred to the cottage school.

The outstanding characteristic of this child on admission was the wild quality of her uncontrolled behavior. All forms of instinctual drives were expressed: oral drives in biting and voracious eating; anal drives in soiling and defecating on the floor; phallic drives in exhibitionistic displays of her genitals and unconcealed masturbation. Her aggressive activities took manifold forms, as before her admission, and there were frequent violent temper tantrums. She was enuretic and urinated on the floor when she wished. Her hyperactivity took the form of wild running around in the classroom and inability to stay quietly in any one place—the dining room, the dormitory, the consultation room or the play room.

At one time, when she was about nine years old, there was a period of sexual activity with a group of slightly older boys, which involved actual intromission of the penis as well as mutual exhibitionistic play. On one occasion she tried to suck at her own breast, crying, "I want milk, I need milk, ooh good!" On another occasion she put a pencil in her rectum and said with glee, "Look at my tail, my tail, my tail." All of these activities were carried on quite openly so that the cottage parents became aware of them almost immediately.

She formed a very intense relationship with her therapist, a female psychiatrist, which remained constant throughout her varying responses in other areas. This attachment was strongly ambivalent and was punctuated by outbursts of rage, physical assault and, on one occasion, defecation on the floor. It was not possible to terminate an interview without a struggle.

Her fantasies revealed a preoccupation with the problem of the loss of the good mother, her replacement by a bad mother and the unremitting wish for the return of the good mother. There were also fantasies of the child who is beaten, which took the form of her demand to be spanked and her spanking games with dolls. In this play G. revealed her experiences in the foster home where she was beaten. She brought out oral and anal pregnancy fantasies and

the idea that the mother dies with the birth of the baby. She described fantasies
of playing with her father, swinging a doll over head and saying, "My father
used to do this to me." This may refer to experiences in the foster homes.

Although this child grew up without a family of her own and in a
series of interrupted foster home relationships, she shows the conflicts
of children with families, especially those of the preoedipal phases. To
these conflicts she brings an immature, inadequate ego, with the result
that the clinical manifestations are more in the nature of external behavioral disturbances than of intrapsychic conflict. Her inability to
postpone the discharge of her instinctual drives gives her psychopathology its most characteristic expression.

The poor ego development focused the therapeutic effort on the
need of satisfactory living experience and opportunities for identification with constant adult persons, rather than on direct interpretation.
Of special interest is the development that has taken place in her four
years at the cottage school. With the utmost caution, it may be stated
that considerable progress has been made by the child in all areas of
ego functioning. To what extent this is the result of maturation and
to what extent the result of experiences made available by the cottage
school environment and of direct therapy cannot be determined.

The ability to tolerate frustration and to postpone gratification has
increased, and the wild, uncontrolled behavior is no longer evident.
There are periodic outbursts of aggressive behavior but they relate more
to specific frustrations and are of lesser duration and lesser frequency.
Her involvement in premature sexual activity remains a prominent
danger. Though still not capable of a deep, sustained relationship, she
is less demanding of adult attention. Guilt reactions and early superego
formation become evident with questions about God, hell and sin in
association with incorporative fantasies. She speaks of sin as "a little
sickness which you can get all over your body"—and she points to the
left lower quadrant—"especially here." She shows fears of menstruation
which has not yet begun and she confuses it with anal functions. She
is obviously of normal intelligence, with an I.Q. of about 100, which
is considered minimal in view of her other difficulties. Her attitude to
the absent mother is now a more realistic acceptance of the incontrovertible facts.

In this child the uncontrolled behavior was perhaps more dramatic
than in most other cases, and her improvement points up the more
emphatically the importance of regarding this behavior not in isolation
but in relation to other ego functions and the changes effected by

continuing growth. The profound traumatic experiences which this child suffered have resulted in severe psychopathology. To what extent future maturation and development will compensate for this damage and whether this child will be able to cope with the conflicts of puberty, adolescence and adult life without regression to a psychotic state, cannot be answered at this time. I would suggest rather that in our present state of knowledge of growth processes in the human psyche these questions cannot be answered.

Superego functions are also impaired in the ego-deviant child, depending as they do for their development on the same factors that determine ego development, particularly identification. This subject requires more attention than can be given to it here, and the following comments are more in the nature of a digression than an exposition. Hartmann (1953) has described the superego defects in schizophrenia and has emphasized especially the low level of organization and integration, the lack of stability and consistency, and the archaization of predominant identifications. Róheim (1932, pp. 175 ff.) has described the severity with which the superego functions in primitive man, but only in those areas of behavior which are specifically significant to the group. There is a similarity in the disturbances of superego functions of the ego-deviant child, the schizophrenic and the primitive.

In Case E. above, the boy said clearly when his auditory hallucinations appeared, "It is my conscience speaking to me from outside." He could not cope with the conflict between his instinctual drives and his awareness of moral demands, and he regressed to the use of projection as a defense. In Case G. the instinctual drives slowly came under the control of the ego and, concomitantly, evidences of superego formation appeared with preoccupation with sin, God and death. In both cases what is relevant to the present discussion is the inconstant and disorganized superego functioning and the paralleling of disturbed ego and superego development.

In Case B. the role of the inadequate superego was especially clearly evidenced. This girl with strong drives to involve herself in sexual activities and to steal would try to talk herself into good behavior. She would say to herself, "I won't steal" or "You'll get caught." But then she could not control herself and actually carried out her actions in such a way as invariably to be caught. She has a powerful drive to confess and has become interested in religion. When planning a trip that might involve tempting situations, she would talk over every detail with some adult person, asking for advice, approval and support. The conflict

between instinctual drives and feelings of guilt was clear, with all the
forces in a fluctuant state and the outcome undecided, whether in the
direction of psychosis, neurotic acting out, psychoneurosis or normal
adaptation. In some children it was difficult to demonstrate evidence of
conflict, anxiety or guilt. These children with their incapacity to postpone gratification, their impulsivity, their antisocial behavior and their
narcissistic relationships manifested their ego deviations in an antisocial
character structure that foreshadowed the eventual development of the
clinical picture of the psychopath, as the term is commonly used.

3. Object Relationships

The development of object relationships out of the primary narcissism of the infant forms a long and still unfinished chapter in psychoanalytic research. The complex question of the separation of the self
from the non-self forms part of this chapter. Many factors enter into
these problems, including the neutralization of instinctual drives, the
vicissitudes of identification, the development of self-representation, the
concept of the body ego, bisexuality, and the development of the reality
principle.[13]

Anna Freud and Dorothy Burlingham, in their two books, *War and
Children* (1943) and *Infants Without Families* (1944), trace the child's
social development from early self-centeredness to the social relations of
the family and the group. They emphasize especially the significance of
a satisfactory relationship with a mother person during this period. The
theme has been amplified in numerous subsequent publications by Anna
Freud and others.

Hartmann (1953) describes two stages of object relationship: that of
the need-satisfying object, and that of the constant object. Object constancy begins to appear at about the sixth month of life, and from then
on goes through progressive development in the normal child. Disturbances of this developmental process may result either from retarded
development or from regression, from an inherent defect of the capacity
to develop object relations, or from a disturbed mother-child relationship. Piaget (1937), in his study of normal children, also describes the
gradual development of object constancy out of an early absence o
permanent objects.

Fenichel (1945, p. 415) has made regression from object relations to
narcissism a central manifestation of the schizophrenic process. Hart

---

[13] Jacobson (1954a) raises a number of penetrating questions regarding these
concepts, especially primary narcissism, self-representation and identification. It is no
necessary here to enter into these interesting theoretical considerations.

mann (1953) points out that ego disintegration is partly the result of object loss and deneutralization, while at the same time ego development determines the capacity for object relations and neutralization, thus indicating mutually interacting processes. In 1914, when he introduced the term narcissism into psychoanalysis, Freud described in detail the effects of withdrawal of cathexis from the object in various normal and pathological states, including schizophrenia. And in an earlier paper Freud (1911b) illustrated the transformation of the *pleasure ego* into a *reality ego* with the development from "auto-erotism through various intermediate phases to object-love."

In a thought-provoking study, Mahler (1952) describes what she considers to be two clinically and dynamically distinct groups of early child psychosis: one, the "autistic" psychotic child in whom "the mother, as representative of the outside world, never seems to have been perceived emotionally by the infant," and in whom "there are no signs of affective awareness of other human beings"; two, the "symbiotic" psychotic child in whom there is a persistence of the early mother-infant fusion without progression to the stage of object-libidinal cathexis of the mother. Mahler has particularly stressed the importance of constitutional intrinsic factors in the genesis of infantile psychosis, though she does not neglect environmental factors, particularly the mother-child relationship. In this and her other publications (1949), Mahler points up disturbances of reality testing, object relations and other ego functions in these children. Mahler's studies are an important contribution to clarification of the object relationships of the psychotic child, although the role of the etiologic factors in the different clinical types which she so definitively describes requires further confirmation. I cannot contribute further to this question of specific etiology because the children observed in this study were all subjected to such severe traumatic experiences, especially separation from the home, that it is impossible to separate hereditary and environmental factors.

The concept of the "autistic" child was introduced by Kanner in 1943 to describe a specific clinical entity in children which he defined in a later publication (1949) as "a profound withdrawal from contact with people, an obsessive desire for the preservation of sameness, a skillful and even affectionate relation to objects, the retention of an intelligent and pensive physiognomy, and either mutism or the kind of language which does not seem intended to serve the purpose of interpersonal communication." He considers this to be the earliest possible manifestation of childhood schizophrenia. Kanner's wide descriptive definition of the autistic child goes beyond the original use of the term, autism, by Bleuler (1912), who employed it primarily to designate a form of thinking. Careful reading of Bleuler's paper makes it clear that he was aware of the effects of this form of thinking, when it is preponderant, on other aspects of psychic functioning, including object relationships. He says: "One of the most important symptoms of schizophrenia is the preponderance of inner life with an active turning-away from the external world. The most severe cases withdraw completely and live in a dream world; the milder cases withdraw to a lesser degree. I call this symptom *autism*."

The concepts of autism and of the autistic child are thus seen to be very complex, including disturbed object relationships of a profound narcissistic nature, characteristic deviations of thought processes, and (in Kanner's definition) certain obsessive manifestations. It is important to keep clearly in mind in what sense the concept is used, whether to denote Kanner's clinical entity or whether to describe a less specific reaction of withdrawal which may result from various causes. In this paper the object relationships are considered in this section, the thought processes in the next section, and the obsessive features in still a later one.

The children in this study showed different varieties of disturbed object relationships, from the withdrawn, self-centered attitude of the narcissistic child to the undifferentiated, clinging adhesiveness to any available adult, also a narcissistic object relationship. These extremes sometimes occurred in the one child. There were also children who chose attachments to inanimate objects or to animals, or who remained in relation to a fantasied rather than a real object.

The following case illustrates the wide variation of object relationship in a child, though in all the overt manifestations the essential narcissistic orientation remained constant.

Case H. This is a twelve-year-old boy, the eldest of three children, whose father deserted the family when the boy was three years old. He was apparently a normal infant and the mother describes her early relationship with him as a warm and happy one. According to the mother, he was toilet-trained very early at three months. His development was reported to have been normal.

Difficulties appeared after the father left the home. The boy became aggressive, destructive and later a fire-setter. By the time he was at school he presented a severe behavior problem, especially because of his aggressiveness. There was a period of observation at a mental hospital before admission to the cottage school.

H. was placed at the age of eight. His behavior in the first few months after placement was marked by extreme withdrawal, crying by himself, apparent unawareness of surroundings, a game in which he played he was "dead," and trance-like state in which he would wander about the cottage at night. During this period he kept himself isolated from other children and adults, although he behaved appropriately in the various activities of the institution. In an early interview he revealed an interest in animals and elaborated a fantasy about some rabbits that he had caught in the woods and made into pets. There was disorientation regarding time and dates. He could not name the days of the week but, when told it was Wednesday, knew Tuesday comes before Wednesday and Monday before Tuesday. In this way he could finally list all the days.

In the course of his later development at the cottage school H. manifested a considerable change in his relationships. Toward adults, especially toward his therapist, he became a clinging demanding child with insatiable oral needs. He was eager for interviews and asked for more time. He achieved a relationship which was characterized by his narcissistic needs and by sadomasochistic fantasies. To his cottage parents he was responsive and attentive but distant. He was almost deferential in his attitude, with an opportunistic awareness of the proper action for the occasion. A landmark was the day that he voluntarily bought a gift for his mother out of his savings.

The early withdrawal from the other children was replaced by a complex and pathological relationship. He was frequently involved in fights, which he usually provoked. He also became a focus of perverse sexual activity among the children, acting as the aggressor in homosexual contacts and later making tentative moves toward heterosexuality. The manifestation of these object relationships was complicated by other ego deviations, such as the poor capacity to postpone gratification and the disturbance of thought processes. The latter included much magical thinking.

The case is presented here primarily to show the progression from extreme withdrawal to some degree of object relationship, though still narcissistic and pathological. Over the four years of observation the boy has improved in other areas also, including his ability to work at school and control his aggression. Bizarre fantasies are less evident.

Whatever form the disturbed object relationship might take in a child, it was in each instance a central question to determine whether there was retardation of development or regression from a more developed state. The characteristic progression of object relations in the child from narcissism provides a series of object relations which simulate the varieties of pathologic relationships noted in the adult schizophrenic patient, but in the former there is the added factor of an unsettled, growing psychic apparatus.

The separation of self from non-self is one of the first tasks that faces the newborn infant, and it is also one of the primary difficulties of the schizophrenic. Tausk (1919) was the first to speak of the "loss of ego boundaries" in schizophrenia, a concept that has been widely expanded by others (e.g., Federn, 1952). Winnicott (1953) describes the importance of the "first not-me possession" as a transitional object in the development of the reality sense in infants. This concept, in different terminological dress, is familiar also to the nonanalyst and has been described in detail by Werner (1948, p. 382), who illustrates the fusion of self and non-self in children and the syncretism of the personality of the primitive which also fuses self and non-self in daily activities and rituals (pp. 433 ff.).

The fundamental role of identification in ego development, especially the early identifications of the child with the mother, has been widely discussed. Freud (1921) describes identification "as the earliest expression of an emotional tie with another person" (p. 60), and in 1923 he speaks of "a direct and immediate identification [which] takes place earlier than any object-cathexis" (p. 39). This may be in part a basic human tendency toward unification with others, a phenomenon which at this time is not too clearly understood but is strongly suggested by the activity of a "primary identification."

The other factor which enters into the process of identification is the role of frustration and object loss. Fenichel (1926) especially emphasizes the second factor and explains even "primary identification" as a "reaction to the disappointing loss of the unity which embraced ego and external world."

Helene Deutsch (1942), in a classic paper, has demonstrated the clinical importance of pathological identificatory processes in schizophrenia and "schizoid" states. She describes a group of patients who form transient identifications with a passive suggestibility that makes them take on the characteristics of the immediate object of the moment. They go easily from one superficial object relationship to another, and the empty quality of their emotional life has led Deutsch to call these patients "as-if" personalities. Deutsch believes that "the schizophrenic process goes through an 'as-if' phase before it builds up the delusional form." Jacobson (1954b), in her study of psychotic identifications, defines "the essential differences between ego identifications and the early infantile identification mechanisms" and she shows how "in psychotic processes of regression, normal object relationships and identifications disintegrate and are replaced by ... preoedipal, magic identification mechanisms."

The cases already described under the other ego functions include many examples of disturbed object relationships and identifications. Either there was an inability to establish a sustained relationship or the relationship was transient and based on powerful preoedipal narcissistic needs, especially oral ones, similar to the descriptions of Deutsch and Jacobson. This was seen most clearly in Case G. and Case H. Case D. also presented a striking oral relationship to the persons in his environment. The clinging and demanding quality of the ego-deviant child has been described by many authors and, in our experience, it was prominent in the child's relationships in his daily living as well as in his relationship to the therapist. This was noted, for example, in the ease with which the children would accept the change from one cottage parent, social worker or even therapist to another, when this had to be done. It need hardly be said that every effort was made to keep the adult persons in the child's environment as constant as possible. However, it was not always easy to determine whether the narcissistic manifestations were aspects of retarded development or of regression. It was possible in some instances to observe the gradual development from self-centered, narcissistic and autoerotic attitudes to transient identifications and then to the establishment of more sustained relationships, with the suggestion of actual modification of the ego structure through these identifications. However, the readiness with which such changes broke down and regressed under stress or frustration was constantly noted, as for example, in Case G.

The fact that the children observed in this study share a specific background—they were all separated from their parents and therefore subjected in varying degrees to the trauma of maternal deprivation— undoubtedly makes certain aspects of their object relationships distinctive and perhaps different from what other observers have found in children from intact homes. In some of these children, where the history of maternal deprivation extends back for years or even to earliest infancy (e.g., Case G.), the object is apparently more important for the satisfaction of needs than as a constant recipient of cathexis, a quasi-experimental example of the two phases of object relations described by Hartmann.

Case I. An interesting demonstration of "the searching for the object" was the behavior of a nine-year-old boy with many manifestations of psychic immaturity. He came from a broken home where the parents were of different religions and he was the center of a fight for his custody which was marked by physical assaults by the father upon the mother and the boy. From an early age the boy presented evidence of disturbance in the form of severe temper tantrums. His aggression increased when he reached school age. Autoerotism included constant thumb sucking in addition to excessive masturbation. He slept in the same bed as his parents for years, in the intervals between their repeated separations. He was a regular witness to parental coitus. Bizarre actions were reported, such as pulling out his hair, urinating out of a window, inappropriate laughter and talking gibberish.

He had been sent to a hospital where a diagnosis of schizophrenia was made and he received twenty electric shock treatments. His admission to the cottage school followed the hospital experience.

At the time of placement he did not appear in any way disoriented, and his reality function seemed appropriate. His drive for close physical contact with his therapist (a woman) was marked by his hugging and kissing her in the manner of the deprived, clinging child. Most striking was a recurrent activity: with great intensity and absorption he would trace out the facial features of his therapist with his fingers. This boy, himself, sought out the kind of bodily contact described by Rank and Macnaughton (1950) as a therapeutic measure in the development of the ego in the "atypical children" reported from the James Jackson Putnam Children's Center. One might assume, however, that in this child the activity described was multiply determined. The preoedipal and oedipal fantasies produced by this boy in his therapy gave evidence that part of his behavior was related to the extreme sexual overstimulation of his early life and his disturbed relationship with his parents.

The basis for the definitive diagnosis of schizophrenia before admission to the cottage school was not made clear, nor was the rationale for the electric shock therapy. The clinging relationship to the therapist described above continued throughout his treatment but was considerably reduced as the treatment progressed.

The tendency to disturbed identifications was evident in cases in which the child took on the behavior of a psychotic parent, approaching the clinical picture of *folie à deux*. Such a case is the following:

Case J. This ten-year-old boy was the youngest in a family of four children. Both parents were diagnosed as schizophrenic, and the mother especially was notorious as a neighborhood character called "Gravel Gertie" and "the gypsy lady." The oldest sibling, a sister of twenty-seven, who rarely went out of the home, was probably also a psychotic.

The boy was fed from a bottle until he was seven years old. He came to the attention of the court through the school authorities because he came to school unkempt, with his clothing smelling of urine and feces. He soiled and wetted in school. He would sit in class without moving or talking, and refused to take part in any activity. The boy's mother frequently burst into the classroom with some unfinished family problem—the boy had left home without his underwear for example.

Before admission to the cottage school the diagnosis of schizophrenia was considered. He was sent to a hospital for observation, where note was made of his withdrawn and passive attitude. However, he did respond to attention and affection. He made no effort to protect himself against the other children when they attacked him or took his things. Separation from the home was recommended.

The striking passivity was immediately evident on J.'s admission to the cottage school. He made no move without permission. In response to questioning he seemed entirely relevant, and he also gave an impression of an underlying responsiveness.

Soon after admission remarkable changes took place in this boy and within six months he was far more alert and responsive, his face was more mobile and he smiled more quickly. His overconforming and passive behavior was still evident, although he began to voice some complaints about the institution. His wetting and soiling disappeared. He tended to deny difficulties at home. Despite the improvement, it was thought that there was profound psychopathology in the boy, and he was placed in psychotherapy. At this time he developed a great interest in gardening and he tended his garden with skill and care.

In his therapy he gradually established a friendly and warm relationship. It was apparent that he enjoyed being seen with his female therapist when she took him for a walk around the school grounds, especially when she was mistaken once by another child for his mother. His need for affection was dramatic. When his own parents, of whom he was ashamed, visited him, he would rarely bring them into the cottage but rather would take them off to some isolated spot. He also formed a warm relationship with his cottage mother, who became very attached to him.

J. became interested in drawing and on the occasion of a celebration drew an extraordinary greeting card "from the children" on a large piece of paper, depicting many gay children festooned with brightly colored flowers. The warmth and friendliness of this spontaneous action was in striking contrast to his initial isolation.

By the age of twelve it was possible to bring out in the boy expressions of concern about mental illness and his ambivalent feelings toward his family. He also brought to the surface his great sexual curiosity, especially about the hygienic activities of women, talk of which he had overheard in conversation of his sisters. At this time also his brother went into the army and the boy kept his picture in uniform on his dresser to show proudly to the other children.

These improved relationships were only partially sustained and now at the age of fifteen the boy is a thin, gaunt, shy adolescent. He is attending a public high school, just about holding his own. He has a place in the group but is usually quiet and passive. He is evasive and distrustful in his relation with his social worker. He is in conflict about his wish to return to his family and his awareness that this is not a feasible plan.

The complexities of object relationships and identifications make possible only this limited survey of the subject here. A few words may be added about the pathological development of the function of self-awareness and awareness of the body and its parts, the body image. This is influenced by disturbances of the early infantile identification mechanisms and may lead to distortions of self-representation in the sense that the term is used by Hartmann (1953) and Jacobson (1954a). Freud's well-known dictum (1923, p. 31) that "the ego is first and foremost a body-ego" assumes special significance when one views the distortions of body awareness in the child or in the psychotic. Scott (1948) has reviewed this subject, and Greenacre (1953) has pointed out the relation of early pregenital disturbances and "instability in the formation of the body image, with uncertainty as to outline, and fluctuations in the subjective sense of size." She refers to an increase of bisexuality and a corresponding split in the ego in these patients.

In the children observed in this study, disturbed body-image concepts were most easily demonstrated in their drawings. Children with sexual confusions gave free expression to fantasies of the phallic woman and other bisexual fantasies. What distinguished these productions from those more commonly noted in children was the minimal repression and distortion with which they were made manifest. An example is the nine-and-a-half-year-old boy, who will be described below as Case M., whose undisguised wish to be a girl was expressed in vivid fantasies. His concept of heaven was a place where boys became little girls. This boy's mother worked as a machine operator and was the dominant member of the family; the father was a quiet and passive person.

Problems relating to bisexuality have played an important role in discussions on adult schizophrenia since Freud's publication of the Schreber case (1911a). Indeed, Katan (1950) has made the conflict around bisexuality the central issue in schizophrenia. This conflict has been noted in some of our cases, but our observations do not confirm his sweeping conclusion that "schizophrenia is not preceded by an infantile psychotic state; that in this respect a psychosis differs radically from a neurosis, for which there is always an infantile basis." Katan questions whether the prepsychotic phenomena he describes in his cases have the same structure as the "infantile psychoses." According to Katan, in every case of schizophrenia the patient has a feminine attachment to the father figure in the prepsychotic phase. Katan's clinical reports only confirm the need to clarify the concept of schizophrenia so that his observations and those on younger children by other workers may be integrated. In our experience typical adolescent psychotic states have been preceded by ego-deviant manifestations in early childhood, and the two processes form a continuum in the life of the child.

Our experience confirms the conclusion of many observers—that the development from narcissism to true object relations, from inadequate self-awareness to self-identity, from transient identifications to the permanent identifications which lead to ego and superego formation, and from confusions of sexual identity to definitive sexual identity—that development in all these areas is in active dynamic flux in the child, subject to progression and regression according to various inner and outer forces.

4. *Thought Processes*

Disturbances of thought processes are emphasized in all studies of schizophrenia. Bleuler (1911), for example, states that "the disease is characterized by a specific type of alteration of thinking." The peculiarities of schizophrenic thought are to be found in the loss of its reasoning and logical character; schizophrenic thought becomes a device to serve magical control rather than communication.

Studies of the development of thought processes in the child indicate that there is a progression from early prelogical and irrational thought to the later reasoning and logical thought of the individual. In psychoanalytic writing this development has been described as the progression from primary process thought to secondary process thought. It may be noted that the progression from primary to secondary process, with its basic characteristic of the binding of energy, is found not only in thinking, but in other areas of psychic functioning also. The role of symbolism and the utilization of the primary process mechanisms of condensation and displacement characterize the thought processes of the child, the primitive and the schizophrenic. I do not assume an *identity* of the child, the primitive and the schizophrenic in their thought processes, and it would be a naive error to parallel them according to external manifestations; I do assume that a similar psychic process operates to a predominant extent in each of them—the primary process of psychoanalytic terminology, the syncretic phenomenon of psychological terminology.

The topographical aspect of the problem of thought processes lies in the question of accessibility of unconscious thought productions to consciousness. The passage of a psychic production from one state to another, from that of being unconscious to being preconscious and finally to becoming conscious is the result of alteration in cathexis of the fantasy, memory or idea, which in turn is related to the ego's capacity to utilize various defense mechanisms, especially repression. It is the aim of the psychoanalytic technique to facilitate this passage, but it occurs spontaneously and with various degrees of distortion in artistic creativity, wit, dreams and slips of the tongue. It also occurs characteristically in psychosis.

Freud, in *The Interpretation of Dreams* (1900), discusses psychosis from the topographical point of view. He describes the relaxation of censorship during sleep which permits unconscious impulses to express themselves by way of hallucinatory regression in the dream image, but with the safety factor that the motor apparatus is made unavailable in sleep. He continues:

The position is less harmless when what brings about the displacement of forces is not the nightly relaxation in the critical censorship's output of force, but a pathological reduction in that force or a pathological intensification of the unconscious excitations while the preconscious is still cathected and the gateway to the power of movement stands open. When this is so, the watchman is overpowered, the unconscious excitations overwhelm the *Pcs.*, and thence obtain control over our speech and actions; or they forcibly bring about hallucinatory regression and direct the course of the apparatus (which was not designed for their use) by virtue of the attraction exercised by perceptions on the distribution of our psychical energy. To this state of things we give the name of psychosis [p. 568].

In the child, also, an unconscious impulse, fantasy or thought is more easily accessible to consciousness than in the adult, a conclusion that can be confirmed in the undistorted dreams and fantasies of children, and in their productions at play and in drawings as well. In describing the process of communication between the systems Ucs and Pcs (or Cs), Freud (1915a) emphasizes the constant interchange which takes place through shifts in cathexis and indicates that "a sharp and final division between the content of the two systems, as a rule, takes place only at puberty."

The child, whose unconscious thought processes are so much more readily available to consciousness and with less evidence of anticathectic activity, will thus, more than the older person, possess primary process qualities. It follows that illogical, autistic, dereistic or irrational thought processes in a child need not necessarily imply a psychotic process. They may be evidence of a normal state of development in the child, with the normal manifestations of primary process which are characteristic of the child; they may be evidence of arrested development; they may be evidence of transient responses of a nonpsychotic child to conflict situations; or they may be evidence of a pathological state such as by definition is called schizophrenic. One might even question whether the designation of the "autistic child" as a subgroup of the schizophrenic child is not misleading, since autism in the child is normal, at first predominant, and only gradually gives way to nonautistic psychic activity. To determine in a specific instance whether the autism is pathological requires cautious consideration of the child's stage of development and of his total behavior in relation to surrounding persons and external reality. It is on this point that intensive work remains to be done in the correlation of psychological tests and clinical observations. An example of the complexities of the problem may be seen in Case D., whose wish-fulfilling fantasy of the valuable stamp must be evaluated in relation to the intense needs of the child and to his retarded ego development. Taken in isolation it appears as a psychotic thought.

Case K. Another example of autism in the sense of a distortion of cognition under the pressure of a wish is the long-continued, uncompromising demand of a fourteen-year-old boy that his social worker adopt him. He was a pleasant, friendly, co-operative boy of average intelligence, but the general impression he gave was one of marked immaturity.

He was an only child whose father was an invalid and had little contact with the boy. There was serious marital conflict ending in divorce when K. was about eleven years old. The boy was placed because the mother felt she could not take care of him. She visited him irregularly and when she felt upset would give up all responsibility for him.

K. fought vigorously against placement, but after it was effected he established a very close relationship with his female social worker. He asked for daily visits and he demanded that she adopt him and take him to live with her. He was fully aware of the realistic situation but reacted to all discussion as a rejection. He tried to get the other children to call him by the surname of his caseworker. He was jealous of other children on her case load.

K. was enuretic until the age of twelve. His mother subjected him to rapid alternation of overindulgence and physical punishment. His characteristic relationship to persons was a passive, demanding expectancy, mixed with widespread hostility and provocative argumentativeness. There was strong evidence of overt homosexual activity with younger boys. His school work was good.

There was a gradual disappearance of the unrealistic demand that the caseworker adopt him, and the boy eventually was placed in a foster home.

It must be remembered that in the adult also, primary process thought and autism are normal and play a role in artistic creation, fantasy, wit and play. The importance of primary process thought outside of deep regression was noted by Freud, and has been especially emphasized by Kris (1952) in his writings on the psychoanalysis of art. In fact, the inability to tolerate primary process activity may itself be a pathological manifestation.

The psychoanalytic concept of primary and secondary process is paralleled in the writings of comparative psychologists as has been indicated above. Werner (1948), for example, says:

In advanced forms of mental activity we observe thought processes which are quite detached from the concrete sensori-motor perceptual and affective sphere. In the primitive mentality, however, thought processes always appear as more or less perfectly fused with functions of a sensori-motor and affective type. It is this absence of a strict separation of thought proper from perception, emotion, and motor action which determines the significance of so-called concrete and affective thinking. Concrete and affective thinking are therefore characteristic examples of syncretic activity [p. 213].

Observations of children in psychoanalytic clinics and by psychologists have given abundant evidence of the special quality of thought processes in children. It is particularly noteworthy that the conclusions from different sources, both psychoanalytic and nonpsychoanalytic, correspond so closely. This strengthens the conviction of the validity of these conclusions, a validation that cannot easily be achieved in this area by direct experimental methods.

A difference in the thought process of the mature adult in contrast to the child or the schizophrenic patient is that the former is capable of abstract thinking but the latter can only cope with concrete content. Case D. again affords an illustration of primitive thought process in his approach to a concrete and an abstract problem. D. was very poor in arithmetic, especially in subtraction. He became confused in dealing with numbers and posed himself the problem of subtracting 9 from 3. He could not understand why this was different from subtracting 3 from 9. But when he was asked, "If you had 3 apples and I took away 9, how many would you have left?" he replied, "Are you crazy? You can't take away 9 apples from 3."

The accessibility of primary process thought to conscious awareness is illustrated in the following case, though the operation of defensive forces which result in displacement and distortion is also evident.

Case L. An eleven-year-old girl exhibited a profound fear of water. She would swim in the pool at the cottage school because "it is kept clean" but was in a state of panic when taken to a beach or to a picnic at a lake. She swam well and could dive. She stated, "There are spiders or things in the water. You can swallow those as you breathe swimming, and they go down your throat, and they grow in you and they can kill you—and they do. I heard of that. I was told so. I read about a boy in the newspaper, or somewhere. It happened to him and it killed him. I can see the spiders in the water because I swim with my eyes open." She related that these fears began after witnessing a TV show in which she saw "fish that eat up men—they just eat them up—there are many fish together and they eat up a person in no time."

This girl was born out of wedlock and abandoned by her mother immediately after birth. She was placed in foster homes but the father took her into his home after his marriage to another woman, when L. was about six and a half years old. She was referred for placement within a year because of conflict with the stepmother. She was an attractive child, with a charming manner which, however, quickly gave way to severe aggressive and destructive behavior. Stealing was another symptom. A central issue was her resentment, guilt and confusion about her rejection by her father. She did not learn that her step-mother was not her true mother until she was about eight years old.

She had a rich capacity for fantasy, would captivate strangers by her tales of being an abandoned orphan, and often received gifts from them. The fantasy of the spiders in the water suggests the child's unconscious preoccupation with oedipal conflicts which are colored by preoedipal and especially oral components. These conflicts remain unconscious, but her reactions go beyond what might otherwise be a neurotic fantasy. The child, in a way inappropriate to her age, insists that she sees the creatures she fears. The primary process, which operates in all fantasy production, has taken over here and she treats her fantasy as a reality. The function of relation to reality is here closely involved with the function of thinking.

Magical thought in the child is so familiar that it is hardly necessary to give an example. In 1914 Freud compared the mental life of primitive peoples and of children. He said:

In the former we find characteristics which, if they occurred singly, might be put down to megalomania: an overestimation of the power of wishes and mental processes, the 'omnipotence of thoughts'; a belief in the magical virtue of words, and a method of dealing with the outer world—the art of 'magic'— which appears to be a logical application of these grandiose premises. In the child of our own day, whose development is much more obscure to us, we expect a perfectly analogous attitude towards the external world.

The following short report will suffice to illustrate magical thought. This is the boy mentioned previously, whose wish to be a girl was expressed in vivid fantasies without distortion.

Case M. This nine-and-a-half-year-old boy, among other disturbances, had a preoccupation with telephones. He wrote enormous lists of telephone numbers, for example, of all personnel at the cottage school. He would seek every occasion to use a telephone and with a winning charm he was able to get the telephone operator to reverse charges when he wanted to call his family or even some stranger. In one instance an operator from the telephone company was fired from her job for doing this.

The boy continued his interviews with his therapist or social worker as though he were talking through a telephone. Whenever he did not like what was going on, he would announce, "You are disconnected." It was then of no avail to talk to him. He had magically broken the contact with the adult and until he was ready to resume the interview he only repeated, "I can't hear you. Sorry! You are disconnected. I can't hear you. Sorry."

M. was the only child of divorced parents. He was placed at the cottage school at the age of eight and a half, almost a year after the parents' divorce. Prior to the divorce he was closely attached to his mother, infantile in his ways, disruptive and aggressive. The divorce brought on a marked aggravation of his difficulties, especially an increase of aggressive behavior toward his mother and other children. This was related to sexual conflicts which manifested themselves in an unconcealed wish to be a girl. When he heard about the operation to change the sex of a male to a female, which was then being reported in the newspapers, he asked that this be done to him. At the same time he resented a play on his name used by the children who called him by a girl's name. It has already been noted that the mother was a machine operator, the father a quiet, passive man. On one occasion the boy inserted a crochet needle into the rectum of a younger male cousin, resulting in injury that required surgical treatment.

The magical use of the telephone game was presented here as an example of disturbed thought processes. It may also be considered as a defensive device in the boy's effort to deal with his aggressive and sexual drives, a phase of ego function which is dealt with in a later section. Other ego deviations in this boy included especially his narcissistic object relationships which took the form of a clinging, whining, demanding adhesiveness to adults.

Another common form of thought activity in children is that described by Piaget (1937) as "ego-centric"[14] thought. Here the child views the external world in terms of his own inner needs and drives. Self-centered thought is related to autistic thought and may be considered a variety of the latter. The following case illustrates briefly such a thought process in a child, with special emphasis on the relation to the specific conflict in the child.

Case N. This boy of twelve was extremely overindulged by his mother and manifested marked oral fixations. One visiting day he stood at the bottom of the hill waiting for his parents. He was found there shortly after lunch time whimpering. When told it was past lunch hour, he insisted that his parents had promised to come before noon and, since they had not yet arrived, it was not yet noon. The boy could not be convinced that he was wrong and only after his parents arrived a short time later did he come up the hill for his lunch. There were other severe deviations of ego function in this boy which can only

14 The term "self-centered" would here be more accurate. See above, on the distinction of ego and self.

be mentioned briefly here because the study of this child is still in its early phases.

Bizarre behavior prior to admission to the cottage school had led to a period of observation at a mental hospital where a diagnosis of childhood schizophrenia was made. The psychological examination at the hospital concluded that the boy was "schizophrenic, but not yet psychotic." The boy cut down his food intake after the other children began to call him a "fat, husky pig." He also refused to talk to anyone and said that if he spoke to his mother after she had eaten, her breath would go into his body and make him fat. He said that even if he only looked at an apple he would gain ten pounds. He could not swallow his saliva and would spit constantly, saying that he did not like the taste of his saliva. He was preoccupied with looking in the mirror and weighing himself. These manifestations were probably related to the boy's sexual confusions. The mother is the dominant member of the family, the father a nervous, irritable, quick-tempered but ineffectual man. There is an older sister of eighteen, who when the boy was less than a year old, accidentally scalded his penis and testicles.

The boy has since admission to the cottage school shown increasing progression in various aspects of ego functioning. The meaning of his bizarre thoughts, though clearly suggestive of feminine identifications and procreative fantasies, needs further study before their significance can be fully evaluated. His spitting activities persist but with less intensity, and he does not verbalize such fantasies as those which led to his hospitalization. At present N. shows increasing interest in participation with the group and acceptance by the other children. He works well at school and conforms with the routine of the institution. The place of the boy's peculiar thought processes, which according to the usual descriptive criteria would be called psychotic, remains to be determined in relation to his further development and to the other aspects of his personality.

A common experience is that of the child who becomes annoyed or irritated when the adult does not seem to understand him. He assumes magically that what is in his mind is known to the adult. This is noted also in children who are certain that adults can magically read their guilty thoughts and know of their wrongdoing.

Language, speech and the use of symbolism must be included in the consideration of thought processes, and in fact because of their relation to the capacity to conceptualize, are of unique importance in human thought.

Writing as a philosopher, Cassirer (1944) describes the progressive development of human thought when it is examined in historical perspective. He sees the concrete responses of primitive man to sensory stimuli as similar to those of animals, in contrast to man's later capacity to think in abstractions. It was not until the intellectual advances of

Babylonian and Greek thought that man was able to use abstractions such as those of time and space. Primitive man of today can lead a party down a tortuous stream through thick jungle without error, but he cannot understand a map. Cassirer has especially emphasized the importance of symbolism in human thought which he sees as the hallmark of the human mind. He says in a pithy sentence, "instead of defining man as an *animal rationale,* we should define him as an *animal symbolicum"* (p. 26). He indicates that in primitive thought there is a confusion between "the being and the meaning" of the symbol and adds, "But in the further progress of human culture the difference between things and symbols becomes clearly felt, which means that the distinction between actuality and possibility also becomes more and more pronounced" (p. ·57).

The most important instruments of symbolic activity are language and speech. The characteristic disturbance of language in schizophrenia is the loss of the capacity to differentiate the word as symbol from the word as thing. This was recognized by Freud (1915a) in his paper on "The Unconscious," in which he described how the *word* is subjected to the primary process with regression from its function as an abstraction to its use as a concrete thing. Cassirer's description of the confusion in primitive thought between the "being and the meaning" of the symbol, which was quoted above, is a corresponding concept.

Language, in its development serves different functions: expressive, magical and communicative, all of which may be observed progressively in children, and in various forms in schizophrenics. Hughlings Jackson, in his studies on speech affections from brain disease, published in 1874 and subsequent years, distinguished emotional from propositional speech, a distinction that has retained its validity through all the refinements of later studies (pp. 130 ff., 159 ff.). Jackson in these early writings described the loss of propositional speech in organic diseases of the brain with retention of emotional speech.

It is not possible in this paper to go further into the question of language and speech difficulties. Here again the reader may be referred to the detailed reports in the literature which give numerous examples pointing up the developmental aspects of the capacity to use language.[15] Clinical observations of adult borderline patients will often reveal peculiarities of language, even in well-educated persons. These include malapropisms, strange grammatical constructions and misuse of pronouns. In the children observed in this study similar observations were made,

15 See especially Piaget (1932).

but the two factors of incomplete development and disrupted school attendance added to the difficulty of evaluation.

It is most important to determine, from the clinical point of view, the variations in thought processes that may occur in a child and still permit later normal development. How far can a child deviate from a hypothetical norm and still be able to reverse the process and resume satisfactory growth? Many factors must be noted: for example, how long the deviations persist. In some children they appeared briefly, for a few moments as in a normal adult. But in some instances they persisted for long periods and were characteristic of the child's responses. Yet, after years, they gave way to more appropriate thought processes. However, it is not yet certain in any case how the child will react later in life.

This problem ideally requires extensive observations of children over long periods of time, under varying circumstances and with the opportunity for comparison of children from different cultural and social backgrounds. Careful studies such as those of Isaacs and Piaget bear witness to the complexity of the problem and indicate the need for further work to reconcile the apparent discrepancies in the conclusions of these authors.[16]

The present study is too limited to contribute to these basic questions. I have attempted only to demonstrate that where there is a freer interchange between the conscious and unconscious systems, primary process thought appears more readily and with different significance in the child than in the adult. Autism, magical thought, a tendency to thinking in concrete terms and language disturbances in childhood must be evaluated in relation to the developmental state of the child.

5. Defense Functions of the Ego

The ego, in its different phases of development, approaches the conflicts related to reality and to the instinctual drives with different defenses and different solutions, according to the specific phase. Thus, the defenses available to the immature ego are less stable and more primitive than those utilized later. In the course of development certain defense patterns establish themselves as characteristic of the individual and are called forth in various situations, even when not appropriate,

[16] Isaacs carried out her studies in a small school, the Malting House School in England, with children of very superior intelligence ("The mean mental ratio for the whole school was 131"); Piaget carried out his studies at the Institute J. J. Rousseau in Geneva and the children whom he observed were different from those reported by Isaacs in many respects, such as socioeconomic background, level of intelligence and family experiences.

to form the permanent character traits of the person. Hartmann (1952) notes that failure to achieve stable defenses is seen in various forms of child pathology and in schizophrenia. He postulates that this is to a large extent due to an impairment of the capacity to neutralize aggressive energy, so that neutralized energy is not available for use in counter-cathexis and in maintaining such stable defenses as repression.

The increased tendency to conflict in schizophrenia has been noted by Freud and others. Greenacre (1941), particularly in her paper on "The Predisposition to Anxiety," has emphasized the relation of anxiety to increased narcissism in severe neuroses and borderline states. The imma-ture or deviant ego is more vulnerable to anxiety and, *pari passu,* exces-sive early anxiety states lead to increase in narcissism, inadequate devel-opment of the sense of reality and other ego disturbances.

Jones (1929) described the fear of total extinction in cases of pro-gressive ego disintegration, a phenomenon that he called "aphanasis." Anxiety is an ego response to a danger situation, and, prior to the estab-lishment of the ego, one can only postulate a pre-anxiety state, a direct response to noxious stimuli similar to the responses of lower animals. Further, in its early stages, the immature ego reacts to a danger situation with a severe, immediate response, presumably because adequate defenses are not available and because the capacity to postpone discharge has not yet developed. This conclusion is in accord with that of Brenner (1953), who believes that anxiety is not present at birth or in early infancy, but that it appears as a reaction to danger as the ego takes over the functions of memory and sensory perception. Spitz (1950), on the basis of direct observations of infants, also postulates a pre-anxiety response to noxious stimuli in earliest infancy, especially separation from the mother.

Mahler (1952) has described the readiness of the young infant to be thrown into "affectomotor storm-rage reactions, which if not relieved by the mother's ministrations, may result in a state of organismic dis-tress," which she looks on as similar to the panic reactions of later life. Leitch and Escalona (1949) describe the variations in reaction to stress noted in different children. These studies support earlier observations by Fries, who classified infants according to the activity shown in response to certain stimuli, as "the congenital activity type."[17] The conclusions of Bergman and Escalona (1949) that unusual sensitivities in young children are related to later deviations in development (with four of five described cases later diagnosed as childhood psychoses) are of great importance and deserve extensive further study.

17 See her most recent publication with Woolf (1953) for a summary of these studies.

The sensitivity to stress and the lability of response of the young child is similar to that noted in the adult schizophrenic with a discharge pattern characterized by diffuseness, nonspecificity, and the utilization of organic channels, the psychosomatic response. This is related to the delayed progression from primary to secondary process, inadequate neutralization and binding of instinctual energy and impairment of the function of delayed response. Eissler (1953), in a detailed clinical study, describes the emotional responses of a schizophrenic patient who showed an incapacity to reduce emotions to signals, with a resulting intensity of emotionality. Glover (1949) also describes the incapacity of the immature ego to deal appropriately with stimuli and the resultant tendency to psychosomatic discharge. These psychoanalytic findings are in accord with the observations of psychologists who have described in the undeveloped organism the tendency to diffuseness of response. The progressive tendency from diffuse, global response to specific, individuated response is a basic biological principle that has been described in physiological and psychological studies of animals as well as humans.

As with other ego functions, the defensive function of the ego passes through progressive phases. The present state of psychoanalytic knowledge does not permit the setting up of a hierarchy of defense mechanisms, a problem posed by Anna Freud (1936) in *The Ego and the Mechanisms of Defense* (p. 54). But as early as 1915 Sigmund Freud (1915b) distinguished as more primitive the defenses of reversal into the opposite and turning round upon the subject, which precede the utilization of repression. In 1926 he stated more explicitly the relation of the differentiation of the components of the psychic structure—id, ego, and superego—to the development of specific defenses. He says, "It may well be that before its sharp cleavage into an ego and an id, and before the formation of a superego, the mental apparatus makes use of different methods of defense from those which it employs after it has attained these levels of organization" (p. 157). Most recently, Hoffer (1954) has discussed the problem of the developmental aspect of ego defenses and conceives of "the defensive processes and the defense mechanisms as being part of and as operating within a *defensive organization,* which is itself part of the total ego-organization, though not identical with it." Hartmann (1953) also points out that primitive defense mechanisms are more characteristic of schizophrenia. He includes among these denial, projection, turning against the self, reversal into the opposite and detachment of libido.

The ego establishes patterns of defense which may contribute to the formation either of character responses, or in other instances, of neurotic or psychotic symptomatology. Hartmann and others have brought out the importance of studying the precursors of defense in children as indications of potential dangers of neurosis and psychosis in later life. As already noted, Freud's earliest descriptions of the psychotic process were of its utilization by the ego as a defense against an unbearable reality. He has pointed out the characteristic use of denial and projection by the psychotic.

Anna Freud (1936), in *The Ego and the Mechanisms of Defense*, similarly describes the use of denial as a defense mechanism by the immature ego. She says, "The efforts of the infantile ego to avoid 'pain' by directly resisting external impressions belong to the sphere of normal psychology. Their consequences may be momentous for the formation of the ego and of character, but they are not pathogenic" (p. 75). The child's use of denial as a primitive defense has been discussed in the section on relation to reality. It is not necessary here to add further proof that children in their normal activities constantly use denial, projection and reaction formation as defenses. The question is rather when, in the course of development, do these defenses become pathological.

The defenses that characterize the more mature ego, particularly repression and isolation, are precisely the ones that are least evident in the schizophrenic and in the young child. The ability to accomplish repression and isolation develops only gradually in the child. These more mature defenses are more appropriate to the demands of reality; they are stable, and they permit more satisfactory expression of other ego functions. The loss of the defense of repression in schizophrenia is well recognized, and Eissler (1953) considers the inability to accomplish true repression in schizophrenia to be an ego defect. He has noted this also in delinquents.

The development of stable defenses is thus related to the development of other ego functions. The instability of defenses and the tendency to regression or change of defense is particularly evident in children. In the very earliest writings on schizophrenia, both Jung (1909) and Abraham (1908) pointed out that the essential conflicts in dementia praecox and hysteria are similar, the differences in the clinical picture in the two conditions stemming from the different ways in which the conflicts are dealt with, including, of course, different defenses. Freud reopened this question in 1926 when he outlined the different defense mechanisms that occur in different forms of psychoneurosis. Waelder (1951), in a recent paper, also underscores the central importance of choice of defense mechanism in different clinical conditions.

Freud has emphasized the role of defensive mechanisms in character development. In 1937 he wrote: "No individual makes use of all the possible mechanisms of defense: each person merely selects certain of them, but these become fixated in his ego, establishing themselves as regular modes of reaction for that particular character, which are repeated throughout life whenever a situation occurs similar to that which originally evoked them." He left open the question of what determines the choice of specific defense by an individual, whether constitutional factors, the nature of the trauma or the phase of development.

In young children where the characteristic defense patterns have not yet become set, where instability of defense and regression to more primitive defense mechanisms are expressions of normal development, responses to danger situations may vary widely from one time to the next, and result in dramatic differences in the manifest clinical picture. This normal variability is even more striking in the disturbed children whom we observed, where rapid shifts from "neurotic" to "psychotic" states and the reverse, descriptively considered, could be demonstrated repeatedly. Ekstein and Wallerstein (1954) have also noted dramatic changes in borderline and psychotic children which they similarly explain by assuming changes in defense patterns. They speak of "fluctuating ego states" which they relate to "different defense constellations."

These considerations are illustrated in the following case:

Case O. This is a boy who was twelve years old when he was admitted to the cottage school. He had already experienced two periods of hospitalization at mental institutions. His parents were divorced four years prior to his admission, after eight years of unremitting discord. The boy was the only child of this union.

O. was a bright, good-looking boy whose behavior most of the time was conforming and appropriate. He had a good sense of humor, was friendly in his relations with adult persons, but remained aloof from the other children. He could describe the conflict in his home and question why he had been placed, but could not express any hostility toward his parents. Reaction formations were evident in his overpoliteness and considerateness. He had a good relationship with his therapist but exercised a strong intellectual resistance throughout. He was always ready to discuss his problems but remained isolated from their emotional impact.

Periodically, according to the history, and twice while at the cottage school, O. developed a severe rage reaction. These followed minor frustrations and sometimes the precipitating cause could not be determined. On the two occasions when they occurred, these reactions were so violent that it was necessary to send him to a hospital on an emergency basis. He banged his head against the wall, frothed at the mouth, screamed uncontrollably and struck out at any object in his way, animate or inanimate. He had to be restrained to avoid injury to himself or anyone about.

By the next morning the boy was able to leave the hospital. He was again his usual quiet, conforming self. Although apparently out of contact with reality during his attack, the next morning he remembered what had occurred and expressed guilt and contrition. He stated that when he does not get what he wants he is overcome by a feeling of rage which he cannot control.

It was reported that O. had been hyperactive and aggressive since the age of three and a half. Temper tantrums were noted even before this, and it was their increasing severity which had necessitated hospitalization. The boy had been toilet-trained at nine months but had remained enuretic.

A more recent development was a preoccupation with guns which assumed the proportions of a compulsion. He collected all sorts of toy guns, talked about guns to anyone who would listen, and when asked to draw would cover sheets of paper with careful drawings of guns.

The interest in this case lies in the contrast between the clinical pictures at the time of the rage attacks and when he is well controlled, with special emphasis on the different defense mechanisms operating at these times. During his controlled periods reaction formation, isolation and repression were in evidence; during the rage reactions these were overcome by the aggressive drives. The defenses available when the more stable defenses disappeared, could not prevent the discharge of the instinctual drives, and an acute attack ensued that had all the quality of a catatonic excitement and was a psychotic episode in the descriptive sense of the term. In this phase of his behavior one might postulate the activity of primitive defenses especially regression, turning against the self and denial of reality. The regression involved a number of ego functions including object relationships, thought processes and control of instinctual drives.

The clinical experience described in Case O. is a familiar one which raises the question of the relation of the "neurotic" and the "psychotic" manifestations. Some authors speak of the "underlying psychosis" or of the "neurosis as a defense against the psychosis." For example, Freedman, in the round-table discussion on Childhood Schizophrenia (1953), says, "Clinical experience has shown that any severe psychoneurotic disorder in a child before puberty, obsessive-compulsive, hysterical, or severe anxiety state, is a reactive response to a deep threatening disorder, most often schizophrenia." Similarly, Pious (1950) speaks of the "masking of an underlying psychosis" by obsessive-compulsive symptoms.

An alternative approach would be from the direction of psychoanalytic characterology. This is based on the well-established observation, noted in the quotation above from Freud's "Analysis Terminable and Interminable" (1937), that for every individual there is established a characteristic pattern of response, including mechanisms of defense, which are brought forward in various situations throughout life.[18] It is possible by clinical examination and by psychological testing to recognize a patient's characteristic responses and defense mechanisms, and these may be the forewarning of a psychotic process. Such evidence of a potential psychotic reaction is, however, not the same as an "underlying psychosis." I believe the distinction to be more than a semantic one.

From this point of view one is dealing with a person who, under certain circumstances, utilizes defenses that result in a neurotic picture and under other circumstances utilizes defenses that result in a psychotic picture. Lewin (1954), in his discussion of the interrelationship of elation and depression, also supports the concept of different defenses being brought into play at different times. He indicates the confusion that results from the idea of "cover" of one clinical state by another. He prefers to view elation and depression as two different aspects of a conflict, each with its characteristic fantasies, defenses and symptomatic expressions. To speak of the neurosis as covering the psychosis, or the psychosis covering the neurosis, avoids the central question of an ego struggling to resolve a conflict among internal drives, in an ever-changing external world with mechanisms that themselves change as the person develops.

An important and familiar clinical observation is the close relationship between obsessive-compulsive manifestations and schizophrenia. Kanner (1949) includes in his definition of the autistic child an "obsessive desire for the preservation of sameness." The observations reported in this study confirm this finding in the striking prevalence of obsessive-compulsive manifestations in these ego-deviant children. The obsessive-compulsive phenomena were usually in the form of character disorders, less frequently as psychoneurotic manifestations. In each instance the clinical outcome is the resultant of a dynamic conflict and it is necessary to examine the relation of the underlying conflict, the defense mechanisms used by the ego and the adaptive value of the obsessive thought or compulsive act.

That obsessive-compulsive phenomena have a wider significance be-

[18] For a detailed discussion of psychoanalytic characterology, see Fenichel (1945, p. 463).

yond their role in psychopathology and that they appear in the ordinary
activities of human beings was recognized by Freud in 1907 in his study
of the resemblance of obsessive acts in neurotics and in religious practices.
The rigidity of primitive ritual has been illustrated by many writers and
in greatest detail by Frazer in *The Golden Bough*. Cassirer (1944) also
points up the universal need for conservativism, tradition and continuity
where the primitive mind must deal with problems beyond its understanding and actual control. What he says of the primitive mind may be
applied to the mind of the child and of the schizophrenic. The ego which
is faced with the threat of destruction seems under many different circumstances to seek safety by defenses that lead to obsessive-compulsive
acts, and the more so as other more appropriate defenses are unavailable
because of immaturity or regression. A clear distinction should be made
between the origin of the obsessive-compulsive manifestations and their
secondary utilization. The manifestations, under any circumstances, are
either character responses or symptoms resulting from conflict and defenses, more specifically from a conflict between instinctual impulses and
ego defenses; they may serve as secondary adaptive measures, accomplished, in part at least, by the synthetic function of the ego.

Case M., already described, is an example of obsessive-compulsive
features in an ego-deviant child which appear to be related to severe
conflicts around both aggressive and libidinal drives. The following case
illustrates a severe obsessive-compulsive picture in a boy, where the fluid
state of conflict and defense makes the outcome still undetermined.

Case P. This is a boy who was eight years old when he was placed at the
cottage school because his mother had to be admitted to a mental hospital.
The parents were divorced when P. was five years old. Prior to admission the
boy lived with the maternal grandparents in an atmosphere of extreme rigidity.
The grandfather, for instance, insisted that the child be in bed before his
return from work, though it might be as early as 5 o'clock in the afternoon.

It was revealed during the boy's therapy that the psychotic mother had always
been extremely seductive in her relationship with him, with close bodily contact, kissing, and sleeping with him. Exacerbation of symptoms could be related
to disturbing visits with the mother. The boy had been encouraged by his mother
and her parents to hate his father and, though he expressed overt hatred, it
became clear that this was a screen for a profound attachment, with memories
of early happy experiences.

The conflicts indicated in this familial background were underscored by
evidences of disturbances at all libidinal levels. P. ate voraciously, begging left-
overs from other children; he was orderly in his outer dress but filthy beneath;
he had a marked fear of bodily injury, especially to his eyes. Masturbation had

been an overt problem when he was at home. Until the parents' divorce he slept in their bedroom. He was a friendly but apprehensive child who impressed the observer by his awkward bodily movements. He avoided any show of aggression which, in an atmosphere where other children attacked one another and defended themselves freely, made him stand out startlingly. He even attempted to form a society to reward boys who settled their differences without fighting!

P.'s symptomatic manifestations were of two kinds, obsessive-compulsive behavior and schizoid reactions. P. first came under psychiatric observation at the age of six because of his restlessness at school and his compulsive mannerisms. On one occasion in a playroom he counted 197 blocks before he made any effort to play with them. He was also preoccupied with clocks and time. At the cottage school the preoccupation with numbers and time assumed increasing complexity as his mathematical abilities developed. In addition, he became adept at puzzles and checkers and became a collector of odd items, including bottle caps. A school assignment to list words containing a particular syllable brought on weeks of activity, resulting in lists that covered pages of carefully printed script.

P. developed an interest in the stars, with an ·extensive knowledge of astronomical detail, to which he added his own fantasies of travel in space.

Schizoid manifestations were noted in different areas of ego functioning. He kept himself isolated from other children, and a cottage mother described him thus: "He lives in the cottage, not with us." He had no significant relationships with any member of the staff, though he had an outward clinging manner. He clung physically to adult persons but at the same time seemed removed. Peculiarities of language were striking and included punning, nonsense jingles, neologisms and clang associations. He used language to achieve recognition by exhibitionistic clowning.

More striking were what appeared to be disturbed thought processes, which at times made his speech seem irrelevant and silly, with primary process qualities. But usually the connection of his productions could be established, and the irrelevancy was found to result from omission of the verbalization of a link in his thinking. There was a literalness in his play and use of language that suggested a confusion between the symbol and the thing. His intelligence was above average, but his scoring in subtests showed a wide range from 72 to 149.

Rationalizations were quickly brought into play and, along with the joking attitude, were used as defenses against the break with reality that his disturbed thought processes approached. The joking and clowning undoubtedly had other determinants as well.

The drawing that P. did was also significant. Drawing was a favorite activity and usually took the form of meticulously detailed plans of buildings or maps of streets, countries, and astronomical space. Human figures showed confusion of sexual differences, such as a woman with a mustache (which he rationalized by calling it a smudge of dirt), or a man drawn in Picasso-style with a full-front

body and profiled face so that the figure appeared finally with only one arm
showing.

The interplay of obsessive-compulsive and of schizoid manifestations
in this boy gave to his behavior and speech a peculiar, almost uncanny
quality. The pertinent question is whether the differences in the overt
manifestations can be explained by shifts in defense mechanisms. As in
Case N., here too one set of defenses gives way to another, though here
the different phases alternate more rapidly. In Case N., furthermore,
and not in this boy, there was the periodic explosive discharge of instinctual drives. Correspondingly, in Case N. the two forms of reaction
were easily distinguishable whereas in Case P. the rapid alternation,
almost simultaneity, of the different phases made the distinction more
difficult. In accordance with Freud's formulation (1924b), "Neurosis is
the result of a conflict between the ego and its id, whereas psychosis is
the analogous outcome of a similar disturbance in the relation between
the ego and its environment (outer world)," we may postulate that the
alternating phases and their defense constellations are related to different
structural conflicts: the one, intrapsychic, determining an obsessive-compulsive picture; the other between the ego and external forces resulting
in regression to narcissistic object relationships, to primary process
thought and to direct expression of instinctual drives—the schizoid
picture.

The outcome in this boy is not determined. He is still in the midst of
a profound oedipal and preoedipal conflict, and the opposing forces are
still jockeying for position. The prognosis is grave, especially in view of
the tendency to regression, but it is not determined. The case has been
presented to illustrate the uncertainty that attends the observation of
an active process in which so many fluctuating factors are operating.

6. *Autonomous Functions of the Ego*

In 1937 Freud, in his paper "Analysis Terminable and Interminable,"
postulated the existence of "primal, congenital ego-variations." Hartmann
(1950) has developed this concept in his writings on the autonomous
functions of the ego. These functions originate independently of conflict
(Hartmann's "conflict-free" sphere) but may secondarily become involved
in psychic conflict.

The functions which may be listed under this heading do not form
a fixed group in the present state of knowledge of ego psychology, and
future studies will surely bring many changes. Some of the ego functions
covered in previous sections of this paper may be listed as autonomous

ego functions, for example, reality testing and thought. Hartmann (1939) places in the conflict-free sphere of ego development the following: "perception, intention, object-comprehension, thinking, language, recall phenomena, and productivity, ..." also ".... the well-known phases of motor development, grasping, crawling, and walking..." and "... the maturation and learning processes implicit in all these and many others."

The autonomous ego functions provide a large part of the basis for ego interests and talents of the individual and thus become specially significant in consideration of problems of adaptation.

The autonomous functions may be brought into the area of conflict in the developing child. It must also be considered that along with other developmental arrests in the ego-deviant child these functions may also be retarded. Limitations of function may be found, but in some cases precocity or hyperdevelopment of specific functions appear in a child whose other functions are arrested. Hartmann (1953) points out that the ego apparatuses of memory and perception are usually intact in schizophrenia, an example of the preservation of some autonomous functions in the midst of regression of other ego functions.

Many examples of disturbance of autonomous ego functions may be found in the individual cases already presented. So, for instance, in Case P., mathematical aptitude was highly developed, whereas in most other cases reading disabilities and speech disturbances were common. School performance was in most instances retarded, though of course other factors contributed to this. It is very difficult to establish to what extent the disturbance of an autonomous ego function is the result of maturational arrest and to what extent of inhibition stemming out of an instinctual conflict. It is not surprising that sublimation is poorly achieved in most of these children where conflict is rampant and neutralization of instinctual drives is defective. Alpert (1949) describes a boy whose failures in sublimation ran a parallel course with the dynamics of his neurosis and reflected the major conflicts.

An important example of disturbance of an autonomous ego function is that of locomotion. Many examples of awkward gait, muscular incoordination and limpness of body posture, as well as hyperactivity of various forms, were noted. We could not find in any child the postural reflex responses described by Bender (1947), including the rotating and whirling phenomena reported in her cases. These phenomena require further study.

I avoid further discussion of the autonomous functions of the ego because it deserves more detailed consideration than I can give it. The corroborative efforts of psychologists are needed and, in fact, it is in this area that many activities of psychologists have been centered. My purpose in this paper is limited to drawing the attention of the clinical observer to the importance of evaluating the individual autonomous ego functions in their relation to the total functioning of the rest of the personality. As Hartmann (1939) has said: "The concrete study of many ego-disturbances in psychoses and of many psycho-physical interrelations must also take account of this conflict-free sphere. These problems cannot be completely resolved if only their drive and conflict aspects are considered."

It is the uneven progression and regression of individual functions that lie behind the impressive variations of the specific individual who may show startling aptitudes in one area with malfunction in others. An interesting illustration is the case of a mathematical genius described by Victor Rosen (1953).[19] This patient, along with precocious mathematical abilities, had a so-called "strephosymbolia" in reading and writing. Both the hyperfunction in one area and the malfunction in the other were related to underlying conflicts.

The interrelationship of primary and secondary ego autonomy is involved here but goes beyond the scope of this paper. (For a detailed theoretical study, see Hartmann, 1950.)

7. Synthetic Function of the Ego

The synthetic function of the ego has been studied intensively by Nunberg (1931), who describes "the ego's tendency to unite, to bind, and to create," which "goes hand in hand with the tendency to simplify and to generalize." It would seem that of all ego functions the synthetic function is most basic to sustaining the organism and to protecting it against dissolution. Even after a break with reality occurs, the synthetic function may remain, and may permit a degree of adaptation, though at a different level than before the psychotic break.

Nunberg has emphasized this point. He says, "It seems that in conditions such as that of schizophrenic disintegration, where Eros is most seriously menaced by the loss of object-libido, the ego makes the greatest efforts at synthesis." A striking example of this may be seen in the Schreber case, where the patient, with the most exquisite adherence to logic, developed a tightly knit pattern about his basic delusions. Nunberg (1920) describes a catatonic patient who early in his illness "was obviously still dominated by the general *need for causality*, common to all human beings."

19 See also Rosen (1955).

This function which tries to create order of some sort out of whatever material inner and outer perceptions supply, is also subject to development. Hartmann (1947) notes that the synthetic function of the ego is "not the most primitive regulating function we know from analytic experience; it develops only gradually parallel to the development of the ego." Hartmann suggests the use of the term "organizing function" as of wider significance, including elements of differentiation as well as integration.

The synthetic function cannot be examined in isolation. It always works with other functions, and evidence of its activity will be found in every action or thought of the person. Its tools, as well, are the other psychic functions, especially the thought processes. Binding of instinctual energy, progression from primary to secondary processes, the control of instinctual drives according to the demands of reality, the compromises of id and ego conflict that result in symptom formation—these and other aspects of ego activity exemplify the synthetic function. The justification of designating the synthetic function as a specific and separate one is in its operational value in describing certain clinical observations both in normal development and in psychopathology.

In the productions of children, in dreams, and in the confabulations of organic brain disease, there is always evident an effort to bring together the thought or image within some recognizable organization. This is familiar to the analyst in the secondary elaboration[20] to which the dream is subjected. The child's need to explain what is happening to him or to explain the phenomena about him are met in accordance with the limitations of his experience, knowledge and the maturational state of his instinctual drives and ego functions.

Kestenberg (1954), in a detailed study of an "autistic" child, describes defects in the synthetic function of the ego, as well as other ego deviations. She suggests the theory that the primary disturbance is an interruption of action and perception in their natural course from tension to discharge.

Piaget, in *The Child's Conception of Physical Causality* (1930, p. 258), traces the evolution of the idea of causality, through many steps, from the child's tendency to take his psychological motive as the true cause of everything to the reasonable explanation by logical deduction. In *The Origins of Intelligence in Children* Piaget (1936) speaks of the function of organization, which he considers a biological function, as

---

[20] "Secondary revision," in the recent new translation of Freud's *Interpretation of Dreams.*

well as of a regulating function of the intellect. These concepts approximate the concept of the synthetic function of the ego in psychoanalytic theory. Piaget (1936) concludes that "intelligence constitutes an organizing activity whose functioning extends that of the biological organization" (p. 407), the latter being present in animals other than man. The specific differences between the synthetic function in man and the biological organizing function in animals pose a challenging problem for future study.

To illustrate the role of the synthetic function as a uniting force in the children we have studied would require not only a recapitulation of all the clinical reports already included in this paper but adding to them. In Case A. it is evident in the child's attempt to reconcile her hallucinatory experience with the attitudes of the persons about her, by her reluctant admission that she dreamed the vision. In Case B. it is to be seen in the effort to reconcile the strong sexual impulse with the prohibitions imposed by the social mores with which she is familiar, a conflict unreconciled intrapsychically, in part because the components of her psychic structure are still in process of development.

A point of some interest is the retention of a surprising capacity to create in drawing or sculpture a production which seemed integrated and well organized in certain children where ego deviation seemed severe in terms of object relations, reality function, thought processes or other functions. The prognostic value of this finding remains to be determined. Child A., already described, is a case in point.

The importance of the synthetic function is more dramatically evident when it breaks down. So, for instance, in Case C. and Case E., progressive deterioration of other ego functions appeared along with loss of the synthetic function. In these two cases and in other children, a frequent finding was an increasing sense of confusion, which could be related to disturbance of the synthetic function.

Winnicott (1945) postulates a "primary unintegration" which may reappear in regressive states. In his opinion this and other primitive psychological tendencies exist which are normal in early infancy, and which reappear regressively in the psychoses. Such an "unintegration" corresponds to the loss of synthetic function and would subjectively appear as confusion.

The following case is that of a child in whom a progressive deterioration of ego function was accompanied by an increasing sense of confusion.

Case Q. This girl was admitted to the cottage school at the age of nine and a half. She was originally placed at the age of nineteen months because of the mother's inability to take care of her children, the result of her own mental illness and the father's desertion of the family. Before she came to the cottage school, Q. had eleven different placements, including foster homes, institutions and shelters.

Her overt difficulties consisted of aggressive and negativistic behavior, inability to get on with other children and adults, and frightening dreams. In addition, she appeared unusually confused. She had difficulty in pronouncing words and sometimes could not make herself clear in speaking. She would say, "I got that wrong," or "It is not coming out right." Drawings were confused and disorganized. The confusion was especially evident in psychological tests. For example, in the assembly test, she left the trunk of the man upside down, attaching the head to the trunk where the legs should be. The assembly of an automobile was done quickly and without error. There was also a marked confusion in the use of pronouns. She was of average intelligence.

These difficulties persisted as the child continued in placement. A surprising finding when she was twelve was that according to psychological test results, she was able to size up situations in a logical way and her judgment in handling everyday problems was superior. This was in sharp contrast to her overt social difficulties and her confusion in day-by-day situations. She did her daily chores poorly. She overlooked the obvious, seemed to work without a plan, and used her hands in a poorly co-ordinated way. Her thinking also seemed confused, though reality testing was intact.

At about the age of twelve there was a sudden change, with symptoms suggesting an acute psychotic episode. For a few days she behaved as though in a fugue state. She expressed homicidal impulses and her fear of these. She could not remember the street on which her family lived. She made several attempts to run away at night and described hallucinatory experiences of seeing members of her family in front of her. She said, "It is just that you don't believe me, but I tell you it was so real, I did not know what to do—I dashed down the fire escape, out of my room, into the fresh air."

Her struggle to maintain the integrity of her personality was dramatic in its intensity. She asked for help and appeared at the therapist's or the social worker's office several times a day.

There has since followed a state of fluctuant behavior which is still unresolved. Predominant is a sense of confusion, verbalized as such. The therapist has an impression that there are elements of depersonalization which the child cannot express, perhaps because of her lack of language facility. In these periods her speech becomes confused; she becomes amnestic about details, sometimes claiming she cannot remember her name. She becomes aggressive and assaultive, agitated and depressed, and she expresses delusional ideas such as the existence of a "spy system" at the cottage school. In addition she disregards all rules of the institution and makes crude sexual overtures to boys.

These serious states alternate with periods when she is quiet, amenable, and friendly. But the confusion remains, at this time with an Ophelia quality of bewilderment and helplessness. In this phase she approaches different adult persons about her in her inarticulate search for reintegration.

The emphasis in this case has been on the failure of the synthetic function to effect a reconciliation of the conflicting forces, and its manifestation as confusion. What the eventual outcome will be, in terms of the potential development of a full-blown psychosis and the form it will take, remains to be seen.

The final case which I shall present allows the demonstration of a deficiency of the synthetic function and, at the same time, a survey of the other ego functions and their deviation.

Case R. This twelve-year-old boy was admitted to the cottage school at the age of nine after a stay at a mental hospital for a period of observation. He was an only child. The father was away in the army during his infancy and returned to the home when the boy was just less than three years old. Within two weeks the father developed an acute psychotic state and was sent to a hospital where he has remained until the present time. He has been diagnosed as a paranoid schizophrenic. The child remained with the mother after this. She also manifested depressive reactions and when R. was eight years old, she attempted suicide by slashing her wrists and jumping out of a window. This took place in the presence of the boy, and he tried to prevent his mother's actions but failed. She has subsequently been hospitalized at a state hospital where she is still a patient.

The boy was always a feeding problem but other details of his early development are not available.

After the mother's suicide attempt R. was taken into the home of the mother's brother and his wife, a very young couple. The wife was in the middle of her first pregnancy. They wanted to help the boy but could not cope with his difficulties. He was aggressive and on several occasions he kicked his aunt, actions that later assumed greater proportions when the pregnancy miscarried. R. also exposed himself to other children in the neighborhood, and he demanded to be allowed to fondle his aunt's breasts. This brought to light the fact, confirmed by the mother, that she had engaged in play with R., fondling his penis, cuddling with him and allowing him to suck and fondle her breasts. This play continued until the separation when R. was eight years old. About a month after his relatives took him into their home he threatened to commit suicide. He was found in the bathroom with a razor, saying he would cut himself as his mother had done. It was at this time that he was sent to a hospital for observation and subsequently to the cottage school. He is now a totally abandoned child.

He went to see his mother once and his father was brought to the cottage school to see him. These visits were very disturbing and he does not want to visit either one again. He receives an occasional letter from one or the other. His other relatives have stopped writing to him and he has had no visitor in two years.

When R. first came to the cottage school he was nine years old. He was small for his age, disheveled and unkempt. He was so attached to his caseworker from the hospital that it was necessary for the latter to accompany him to the cottage school and stay with him part of the day. He seemed fearful, wept uncontrollably, and gave an impression of "falling apart." When his hospital caseworker left he cried again for a few minutes, then clung to his new social worker. He was oriented in relation to the reality aspects of the situation.

Throughout his placement this boy has shown no gross disturbance of his *relation to reality*. His *capacity to test reality* was repeatedly demonstrated. On one occasion he received a letter from his father expressing the pious wish that they should all be reunited during the approaching Passover holiday. The boy took this to mean that he would return to his parents and his home, and when his misinterpretation was explained to him, he appeared crushed but accepted the realistic situation. He denied his disappointment which was, however, obvious in his contorted features. He explained his mistake by saying that the children who read his letter for him (he is a nonreader) had misread it. The *sense of reality* also seemed intact. During a psychological test when he was producing rather bizarre fantasies he showed some concern when he saw the psychologist writing. He tried to reassure her, "I'm just dreaming. Read it to me. It was funny. I was dreaming." He showed a strong tendency to denial and projection in dealing with the difficulties of his everyday life. He was very hostile to a teacher who, he said, reminded him of a neighbor whom he considered responsible for his mother's illness. Similarly he blamed his difficulties on his cottage mates or cottage parents.

In his early months at the cottage school episodes occurred in which he would roll on the floor, make unintelligible sounds and act as though in a trance. Such episodes have not been noted for several years.

The *regulation and control of instinctual drives* posed a constant problem. When he first came to the cottage school his aggressive and libidinal drives sought immediate gratification as manifested in his seductive behavior with his aunt, his aggressive attacks upon her and upon children, and his insatiable demands on the adults about him. In the course of the years the disturbance in this area has lessened and there is increasing capacity to control his drives with more acceptable behavior as well as evidence of the development of compulsive patterns of response. The early impulsivity has progressively decreased and episodes of disturbed behavior are uncommon. There was one experience of fire-setting about a year ago.

There have consistently been deviations in his *object relationships*. His extreme clinging and rapidly shifting relations to adult persons have been described. His identification with the psychotic mother appeared in his suicidal gesture. In his early relationship at the cottage school he was withdrawn and cautious, but he made steady progress in involving himself in group activities. His relationships with adult persons remain on the level of seeking for satisfaction of his narcissistic needs, demands for money and objects such as stamp books, a bicycle or a watch. There is a profound wish to return to his parents, but an acceptance of the futility of the wish. There is still no indication of a true object relationship.

His figure drawings give further evidence of his distorted sense of self-representation and object representation. The drawings are characteristically primitive, distorted and without detail or form. His figure of a man is a small, mousy creature with big ears (like his). His figure of a woman turned into a "vampire" with unformed appendages for legs, huge teeth, and blood dripping from her mouth. He drew a dead man nearby whose flesh the vampire-woman eats. It was in creating this fantasy that the boy expressed the reassuring thought that it was only a dream. His figure drawings showed no improvement over the years.

Thought processes presented many deviations. His intelligence was definitely superior though his test responses varied. He had difficulties with the naming of common objects and in his earlier period at the cottage school could not name the days of the week. The four seasons of the year he named as "Spring, Summer, April and May." His difficulty with abstraction and conceptualization appeared in his speech disturbance and also in such an incident as when undergoing a psychological test, he had to touch his hair before he could draw the hair on a figure.

The *defenses* which the ego mobilized to deal with his drives and conflicts showed wide variation. Denial and projection as characteristic defenses have already been mentioned, the latter manifesting itself in a persecutory attitude of schizoid quality. A peculiar response in this boy when his defenses appeared to fail him was an abandoned outburst of crying which was so intense and pitiable that it aroused in observers the impulse to pick him up and rock him in their arms. This could be brought on by a specific frustration or after a prolonged situation of tension such as an impending visit from his father. Even more striking was the suddenness with which these outbursts disappeared, and the boy in a few minutes would resume his previous activities. There seemed in this to be operative the sudden reappearance of defenses, however primitive these were. The outbursts have become less frequent.

Recently the appearance of compulsive patterns of behavior such as preoccupation with time have given evidence of the increasing use of the defense of isolation. Rorschach studies also have shown the "isolation of his aggressive and sexual impulses so that he has little contact with his own feelings." His compulsiveness also appears in his drawings which contain many small repetitive figures. In his behavior and actions toward other persons, reaction formation is seen with ever stronger distinctiveness.

Autonomous functions were disturbed, probably because of disturbed development as well as because of their involvement in the child's conflicts. The boy had a marked speech difficulty and often used his body with gesture or movement to express himself, and he is described as having a dance-like quality in his movements in his efforts to communicate with others. His reading disability was so severe that he was almost a nonreader. At the same time he showed a striking aptitude in arithmetic and quickly reached a level of performance normal for his age. This, it is to be noted, took place along with a striking difficulty in dealing with abstract concepts. There was a poverty of verbal capacity below the level of his intelligence. Motor co-ordination was poor. There were no disturbances of memory or perception.

The *synthetic function* has shown over the years a progressive development but even after three years there is still a marked disorganization in his general behavior and speech. His sentences are left incompleted, with dangling phrases and misplaced parts of speech. His productions sometimes seem incoherent and he jumps from one subject to another, failing to follow through on any line of thought. At the same time there is increasing control and organization in his general behavior and his play activities. He is usually not hyperactive. He can, with encouragement, work steadily and persistently at a task.

The most striking characteristic of this boy when he was first admitted to the cottage school was his state of disorganization. This was so marked that the other children, many of whom were themselves severely ego-deviant, would help him in many little ways to carry him through the demands of his daily living. One worker said of him that he seemed unable to stand by himself, that he had to lean against a wall to support himself, or he would fall to the ground. Winnicott's "primary unintegration" was a most fitting designation for this boy. The severe deprivation of his early infancy, the inconsistent relationship to a psychotic mother, and the absence of contact with his father are undoubtedly significant factors in the etiology of this deficiency of the synthetic function of the ego as well as the other ego deviations that have been described.

After three years at the cottage school there has been demonstrable growth in the synthetic function though it is still markedly disturbed. Other ego functions have shown progressions and regressions. The main effort has been to provide the boy with stable living conditions, consistent adult figures for identification, educational opportunities including remedial teaching and direct psychotherapy. Grave pathology persists and the outcome is still undecided.

V. Discussion

In this paper I have attempted to demonstrate by clinical examples the central role of the ego in the problem of schizophrenia, continuing in this a line of thought that has remained unbroken from the earliest psychoanalytic writings on the subject. Recent studies in ego psychology have with increasing sharpness delineated the specific ego functions which comprise the ego, but in clinical articles dealing with schizophrenia most

authors have continued to discuss ego dysfunction as a general phenomenon. There do appear in these articles references to one or more specific
ego functions, usually object relationships, relation to reality, and thought
processes, but not as the central point at issue. I have made the specific
ego functions, their development in children, the resultant ego deviations,
and the relation to the concept of schizophrenia the focus of consideration.

In 1951 Hendrick described psychosis as "primarily the result of defect
of functions usually considered components of the ego." He deals primarily with the details of early identifications. Maenchen (1953) sees the
core of psychosis or psychosis-like illness in children to be the arrest of
ego development. Weil (1953a, 1953b) also stresses disturbances in ego
development in these cases, with special emphasis on so-called constitutional factors. Stern (1945) and Bychowski (1947) discuss ego disturbance
in a general sense in adult borderline cases, the former speaking of the
"warped ego," and the latter emphasizing splitting of the ego and disturbance of the synthetic function.

Considerations of ego strength and ego weakness play a prominent
role in many studies. But in each instance the author is forced eventually
to express himself in terms of some specific functions of the ego and to
leave the global approach to ego strength vague and unanswered. Nunberg (1942), in his paper on this subject, shows how tentative our knowledge is and that one can only describe the *"relative* weakness of the ego
in definite situations." He also states, "It seems that the *arrest of development* of the ego is the most important factor in predisposing it to weakness." Which is the best measure of ego strength remains at this point an
open question, though some fruitful suggestions have been offered. Hartmann (1952) considers the resistivity of ego functions against regression as
the best measure of ego strength, a concept that seems very useful. Glover
(1943) suggests that "harmonious adaptation to the total (ego-syntonic)
requirements of instinct depends to a very large extent on the mechanism
of displacement" and he sees a "capacity for harmonious adaptation
through displacement" as a sign of ego strength. Bellak (1955) recognizes
that ego strength is a global concept and that "any attempt to test ego
strength would actually have to consist of many subtests."

It is obvious that a more precise instrument than the general concept
of ego strength is needed in the study of ego deviation and schizophrenia.
Such an instrument is the detailed analysis of the separate ego functions,
and I have in this paper tried to demonstrate its usefulness. The seven
headings I have used are to be considered a working list only, and future
studies will surely bring many changes.

Recent studies by Beck and his associates (1953, 1954) consider the problem of loss of ego functions in schizophrenia, but the approach is quite different from mine, especially in the definition of specific ego functions which I emphasize. The authors list 120 behavior items classified according to "defenses, ego functions lost, primitive functions revived, emotional forces and restitutional forces." On the basis of a "trait universe" they define six forms of schizophrenia, using both clinical observation and Rorschach diagnoses. Two of the types are impermanent ones, seen only in children and on Rorschach tests, which later develop into one of the other forms.

In discussing the value of studying individual ego functions, however they may be defined, it is not my intention to urge a return to a variation of factor analysis. On the contrary, I would emphasize the ultimate goal of an approach which treats the human psyche as a unit reflecting in any given manifestation the resultant of many forces, genetic and dynamic, hereditary and environmental, inner and outer, conscious and unconscious.

Every child is exposed to the forces of growth, conflict and stress, and phases of progression and regression are inevitable. No absolute norms are available, and it becomes a matter of clinical judgment when a specific aspect of behavior is defined as ego deviation. It may be questioned whether any child, as he passes through the successive phases of instinctual drives, with their successive danger situations in relation to the demands of reality, can avoid some transient expression of ego deviation.

In the children who made up this study there were unusual stresses. They were all subjected to separation from their parents and in each instance there was a serious disturbance of the mother-child relationship, of varying intensity, duration and quality. It is not feasible to go further into a discussion of the etiological factors behind ego deviation, nor is this necessary for the purpose of this paper. This question requires considerable further analysis before definitive answers are available. Starr (1954) has examined this question with special emphasis on the "symbiotic union of mother and infant" as the nucleus of psychosis.

Concerning every child presented in this paper, at some point the question of a diagnosis of schizophrenia has been raised, either in our own thoughts or prior to his admission to the cottage school. But in this paper I have made the ego deviation the issue of primary interest, with the concomitant emphasis on growth processes. I have tried to avoid the question of diagnosis. What comes out of this study, I suggest, is the value of applying to the child's clinical manifestations the measures of ego development and other aspects of dynamic psychopathology. It has not been my intention to minimize the gravity of the psychopathology encountered in these children, and the prognosis in many instances is very serious; my attitude is an expectant one, not necessarily an optimistic one. I have used freely the various diagnostic terms in common usage, though I believe it may be said that there is an increasing trend away from sharp distinctions of nosological nomenclature to the more precise definition of the vicissitudes of ego functions, ego defenses and ego development in each case.[21]

Schizophrenia is useful as a term to describe a characteristic response to stress. It is, in fact, a process, and has been so described by many writers. This is, of course, not a new idea, and may be found in the early writings of Adolph Meyer, for example in a lecture he delivered at Clark University in 1909, at the same celebration of the Twentieth Anniversary of the University to which Freud was invited. It has been suggested that when this form of response, this process, is established in an individual, he can never change. This opinion is held by many, for example, Beck (1954), who says: "The conclusion: schizophrenia is a permanent character structure. Once schizophrenic, always schizophrenic" (p. 143). To this statement I respond with two questions: Is it not perhaps too early, in the present state of knowledge of ego development and ego pathology, to draw so definitive a conclusion? And, most emphatically, in cases of children, where the factor of growth introduces an immensurable variable, does not scientific caution suggest the wisdom of a more expectant attitude?

Extreme cases in adults may warrant such positiveness but our interest is rather in the case which is not extreme, the borderline case, the individual who oscillates between psychotic and nonpsychotic states—and the child in whom deviations of ego function are so common and often so marked. It is in this area that the problems of ego deviation and schizophrenia share the to-be-explored potentials of ego psychology.

The child in his development only gradually assumes those qualities which in time give him the unique status of a human being. The capacity to form concepts; the use of language, symbols and tools; the capacity to form identifications; the distinctive thought processes, both primary and secondary process; the postponement of gratification; the organizing or synthetic function—these and other human functions develop in the child and are part of his ego. In the course of this development, whether

21 For a different approach which sets out detailed criteria for the exact diagnosis of childhood schizophrenia, see Bender and Helme (1953).

normal or pathological, there will be manifestations of immature functioning which will be similar to the disturbances seen in schizophrenia. In fact, if one accepts the concept that schizophrenia is primarily the result of ego regression, then it may be said that it is the breakdown of these unique human qualities that comprise the schizophrenic process.

Comparative psychologists have made it abundantly clear that, despite certain superficial similarities in the psychic activity of humans and animals, the basic differences are of fundamental character. The physiological and biochemical substrata, the primal sensory and motor-effective organs may be very similar, but in certain areas man remains unique. These areas are precisely the ones that have been defined as ego functions. The question of the uniqueness of man has engaged the interest of the biologist (Huxley, 1948), the comparative psychologist (Katz, 1953; Köhler, 1927), the philosopher (Cassirer, 1944), the anthropologist (Muensterberger, 1955), and the psychoanalyst (Kubie, 1953). Freud (1915a) touches on this problem when he questions the existence of consciousness in animals. The concept of primary identification (Freud, 1923, p. 39) also suggests a unique human capacity. Cassirer (1944, p. 94) describes this tendency in a broader context. He speaks of a rudimentary belief of mankind found in all peoples, a "sympathy of the Whole." It is a tendency to a pervasive unity found in the "mana of the Polynesians, the Iroquois orenda, the Sioux wakan, the Algonquin manitu." It is close to the Eros of Freud and suggests a fundamental human quality that enters into the vicissitudes of identification.

These considerations are all related to the problems of ego deviation and schizophrenia. They extend these problems into areas beyond the scope of a psychoanalytic inquiry, but they emphasize all the more the tentative state of our present knowledge.

It is clear by this time that the reader who has been expecting a solution to the problem of schizophrenia will have been disappointed. I can only take refuge in the dictum that there is value in asking of questions as well as in answering them. Certainly, more questions have been raised than answered in this study. But this is in the nature of the problem, and I conclude with even more questions. Ego deviation in the child is related to disturbance of the growth process. What then are the means that may bring on re-emergence of growth potential? What, in therapy, education, living experience and maturation, will keep open the door to further growth? How long are new identifications still possible after the child has been deprived of the usual identifications of early infancy? How long before the pathological process becomes irreversible?

In the answers to these questions will lie the therapeutic hope in working with the ego-deviant child, regardless of whether or not one calls him schizophrenic. There is definite value in an attitude of expectancy where ·certainty is not available, as long as one reaches out in a direction where certainty may be found.

BIBLIOGRAPHY

Abraham, K. (1908), The Psycho-Sexual Differences between Hysteria and Dementia Praecox. *Selected Papers on Psycho-Analysis*. London: Hogarth Press, 1927.
Allport, G. W. (1943), The Ego in Contemporary Psychology. *Psychol. Rev.*, L.
Alpert, A. (1949), Sublimation and Sexualization. A Case Report. *This Annual*, III/IV.
Anderson, H. H. and Anderson, G. L. (1954), Social Development. In: *Manual of Child Psychology*, ed. L. Carmichael. New York: John Wiley.
Beck, S. J. (1954), *The Six Schizophrenias*. American Orthopsychiatric Association, Research Monograph, VI.
—— and Nunnally, J. C. (1953), Two Researches in Schizophrenia. *Am. J. Orthopsychiat.*, XXIII.
Bellak, L. (1955), Toward a Unified Concept of Schizophrenia. *J. Nerv. & Ment. Dis.*, CXXI.
Bender, L. (1947), Childhood Schizophrenia. *Am. J. Orthopsychiat.*, XVII.
—— and Freedman, A. M. (1952), A Study of the First Three Years in the Maturation of Schizophrenic Children. *Quart. J. Child Behav.*, IV.
—— and Helme, W. H. (1953), A Quantitative Test of Theory and Diagnostic Indicators of Childhood Schizophrenia. *A.M.A. Arch. Neurol. & Psychiat.*, LXX.
Beres, D. (1952), Clinical Notes on Aggression in Children. *This Annual*, VII.
Bergman, P. and Escalona, S. K. (1949), Unusual Sensitivities in Very Young Children. *This Annual*, III/IV.
Bleuler, E. (1911), *Dementia Praecox or the Group of Schizophrenias*. New York: International Universities Press, 1950.
—— (1912), Autistic Thinking. In: *Organization and Pathology of Thought*, ed. D. Rapaport. New York: Columbia University Press, 1951.
Brenner, C. (1951), A Case of Childhood Hallucinosis. *This Annual*, VI.
—— (1953), An Addendum to Freud's Theory of Anxiety. *Int. J. Psa.*, XXXIV.
Bychowski, G. (1947), The Preschizophrenic Ego. *Psa. Quart.*, XVI.
Cassirer, E. (1944), An Essay on Man. New Haven: Yale University Press.
Childhood Schizophrenia. Round Table (1953). *Am. J. Orthopsychiat.*, XXIV, 1954.
Deutsch, H. (1942), Some Forms of Emotional Disturbance and Their Relationship to Schizophrenia. *Psa. Quart.*, XI.
Eissler, K. (1953), Notes Upon the Emotionality of a Schizophrenic Patient and Its Relation to Problems of Technique. *This Annual*, VIII.
Ekstein, R. and Wallerstein, J. (1954), Observations on the Psychology of Borderline and Psychotic Children. *This Annual*, IX.
Federn, P. (1952), *Ego Psychology and the Psychoses*. New York: Basic Books.
Fenichel, O. (1926), Identification. In: *Collected Papers*, I. New York: Norton, 1953.
—— (1945), *The Psychoanalytic Theory of Neurosis*. New York: Norton.
Ferenczi, S. (1913), Stages in the Development of the Sense of Reality. In: *Sex in Psychoanalysis*. Boston: Richard G. Badger, 1916.
Freud, A. (1936), *The Ego and the Mechanisms of Defense*. New York: International Universities Press, 1946.

—— (1952), The Mutual Influences in the Development of Ego and Id: Introduction to the Discussion. *This Annual*, VII.
—— and Burlingham, D. T. (1943), *War and Children*. New York: International Universities Press.
—— —— (1944), *Infants Without Families*. New York: International Universities Press.
Freud, S. (1894), The Defense Neuro-Psychoses. *Collected Papers*, I. London: Hogarth Press, 1924.
—— (1896), Further Remarks on the Defense Neuro-Psychoses. *Ibid.*, I.
—— (1900), The Interpretation of Dreams. *Standard Edition*, IV, V. London: Hogarth Press, 1953.
—— (1907), Obsessive Acts and Religious Practices. *Collected Papers*, II.
—— (1911a), Psycho-Analytic Notes Upon an Autobiographical Account of a Case of Paranoia (Dementia Paranoides). *Ibid.*, III.
—— (1911b), Formulations Regarding the Two Principles in Mental Functioning. *Ibid.*, IV.
—— (1914), On Narcissism: An Introduction. *Ibid.*, IV.
—— (1915a), The Unconscious. *Ibid.*, IV.
—— (1915b), Repression. *Ibid.*, IV.
—— (1921), *Group Psychology and the Analysis of the Ego*. London: Hogarth Press, 1940.
—— (1923), *The Ego and the Id*. London: Hogarth Press, 1927.
—— (1924a), The Loss of Reality in Neurosis and Psychosis. *Collected Papers*, II.
—— (1924b), Neurosis and Psychosis. *Ibid.*, II.
—— (1926), *Inhibitions, Symptoms and Anxiety*. London: Hogarth Press, 1936.
—— (1937), Analysis Terminable and Interminable. *Collected Papers*, V.
—— (1938), Splitting of the Ego in the Defensive Process. *Ibid.*, V.
—— (1939), *An Outline of Psychoanalysis*. New York: Norton, 1950.
Fries, M. E. and Woolf, P. J. (1953), Some Hypotheses on the Role of the Congenital Activity Type in Personality Development. *This Annual*, VIII.
Geleerd, E. R. (1945), Observations on Temper Tantrums in Children. *Am. J. Orthopsychiat.*, XV.
—— (1947), A Contribution to the Problem of Psychoses in Children. *This Annual*, II.
Glover, E. (1943), The Concept of Dissociation. *Int. J. Psa.*, XXIV.
—— (1949), *Psycho-Analysis*. London: Staples Press.
Greenacre, P. (1941), The Predisposition to Anxiety. *Psa. Quart.*, X.
—— (1953), Certain Relationships Between Fetishism and the Faulty Development of the Body Image. *This Annual*, VIII.
Hartmann, H. (1939), Ego Psychology and the Problems of Adaptation. In: *Organization and Pathology of Thought*, ed. D. Rapaport. New York: Columbia University Press, 1951.
—— (1947), On Rational and Irrational Action. *Psychoanalysis and the Social Sciences*, I. New York: International Universities Press.
—— (1950), Comments on the Psychoanalytic Theory of the Ego. *This Annual*, V.
—— (1952), The Mutual Influences in the Development of Ego and Id. *This Annual*, VII.
—— (1953), Contribution to the Metapsychology of Schizophrenia. *This Annual*, VIII.
—— and Kris, E. (1945), The Genetic Approach in Psychoanalysis. *This Annual*, I.
—— —— and Loewenstein, R. M. (1949), Notes on the Theory of Aggression. *This Annual*, III/IV.
Hendrick, I. (1951), Early Development of the Ego: Identification in Infancy. *Psa. Quart.*, XX.
Hoffer, W. (1954), Defensive Process and Defensive Organization: Their Place in Psychoanalytic Technique. *Int. J. Psa.*, XXXV.

Huxley, J. (1948), The Uniqueness of Man. In: *Man in the Modern World*. New York: Mentor Books.
Isaacs, S. (1930), Intellectual Growth in Young Children. London: Routledge.
—— (1948), The Nature and Function of Phantasy. *Int. J. Psa.*, XXIX.
Jackson, J. H. (1874), *Selected Writings*. London: Hodder & Stoughton, 1932.
Jacobson, E. (1954a), The Self and the Object World: Vicissitudes of Their Infantile Cathexes and Their Influence on Ideational and Affective Development. *This Annual*, IX.
—— (1954b), Contribution to the Metapsychology of Psychotic Identifications. *J. Am. Psa. Assoc.*, II.
Jones, E. (1929), The Psychopathology of Anxiety. *Brit. J. Med. Psychol.*, IX.
Jung, C. (1909), *The Psychology of Dementia Praecox*. New York: Nervous and Mental Disease Monographs, No. 3.
Kanner, L. (1943), Autistic Disturbances of Affective Content. *Nerv. Child*, II.
—— (1949), Problems of Nosology and Psychodynamics of Early Infantile Autism. *Am. J. Orthopsychiat.*, XIX.
Katan, M. (1950), Structural Aspects of a Case of Schizophrenia. *This Annual*, V.
Katz, D. (1953), *Animals and Men*. London: Penguin Books.
Kestenberg, J. S. (1954), The History of an "Autistic" Child. *J. Child Psychiat.*, II.
Klein, M. (1946), Notes on Some Schizoid Mechanisms. *Int. J. Psa.*, XXVII.
Koffka, K. (1928), *The Growth of the Mind*. London: Routledge and Kegan Paul.
Köhler, W. (1927), *The Mentality of Apes*. New York: Humanities Press, 1951.
Kris, E. (1951), The Development of Ego Psychology. *Samiksa*, V.
—— (1952), *Psychoanalytic Explorations in Art*. New York: International Universities Press.
Kubie, L. S. (1953), The Distortion of the Symbolic Process in Neurosis and Psychosis. *J. Am. Psa. Assoc.*, I.
Leitch, M. and Escalona, S. K. (1949), The Reaction of Infants to Stress. A Report on Clinical Findings. *This Annual*, III/IV.
Lewin, B. D. (1954), Sleep, Narcissistic Neurosis, and the Analytic Situation. *Psa. Quart.*, XXIII.
Maenchen, A. (1953), Notes on Early Ego Disturbances. *This Annual*, VIII.
Mahler, M. S. (1952), On Child Psychosis and Schizophrenia: Autistic and Symbiotic Infantile Psychoses. *This Annual*, VII.
—— Ross, J. R., Jr.; and De Fries, Z. (1949), Clinical Studies in Benign and Malignant Cases of Childhood Psychosis (Schizophrenia-Like). *Am. J. Orthopsychiat.*, XIX.
Meyer, A. (1909), The Dynamic Interpretation of Dementia Praecox. In: *The Collected Papers of Adolph Meyer*, II. Baltimore: Johns Hopkins Press.
Muensterberger, W. (1955), On the Biopsychological Determinants of Social Life. *Psychoanalysis and the Social Sciences*, IV. New York: International Universities Press.
Murphy, G. (1947), *Personality*. New York: Harper.
Nunberg, H. (1920), On the Catatonic Attack. In: *Practice and Theory of Psychoanalysis*. New York: International Universities Press, 1955.
—— (1931), The Synthetic Function of the Ego. *Ibid.*
—— (1942), Ego Strength and Ego Weakness. *Ibid.*
Piaget, J. (1929), *The Child's Conception of the World*. New York: Humanities Press, 1951.
—— (1930), *The Child's Conception of Physical Causality*. New York: Harcourt, Brace & Co.
—— (1932), *The Language and Thought of the Child*. New York: Humanities Press, 1952.
—— (1936), *The Origins of Intelligence in Children*. New York: International Universities Press, 1952.

—— (1937), Principal Factors Determining Intellectual Evolution from Childhood to Adult Life. In: *Organization and Pathology of Thought*, ed. D. Rapaport. New York: Columbia University Press, 1951.

Pious, W. (1950), Obsessive-Compulsive Symptoms in an Incipient Schizophrenic. *Psa. Quart.*, XIX.

Rank, B. and Macnaughton, D. (1950), A Clinical Contribution to Early Ego Development. *This Annual*, V.

Róheim, G. (1932), Psychoanalysis of Primitive Cultural Types. *Int. J. Psa.*, XIII.

Rosen, V. H. (1953), On Mathematical "Illumination" and the Mathematical Thought Process: A Contribution to the Genetic Development and Metapsychology of Abstract Thinking. *This Annual*, VIII.

—— (1955), Strephosymbolia: An Intrasystemic Disturbance of the Synthetic Function of the Ego. *This Annual*, X.

Scott, W. C. M. (1948), Some Embryological, Neurological, Psychiatric and Psychoanalytical Implications of the Body Scheme. *Int. J. Psa.*, XXIX.

Spitz, R. A. (1950), Anxiety in Infancy: A Study of Its Manifestations in the First Year of Life. *Int. J. Psa.*, XXXI.

Starr, P. H. (1954), Psychoses in Children: Their Origin and Structure. *Psa. Quart.*, XXIII.

Stern, A. (1945), Psychoanalytic Therapy in the Borderline Neuroses. *Psa. Quart.*, XIV.

Tausk, V. (1919), On the Origin of the "Influencing Machine" in Schizophrenia. *Psa. Quart.*, II, 1933.

Waelder, R. (1951), The Structure of Paranoid Ideas. A Critical Survey of Various Theories. *Int. J. Psa.*, XXXII.

Weil, A. P. (1953a), Clinical Data and Dynamic Considerations in Certain Cases of Childhood Schizophrenia. *Am. J. Orthopsychiat.*, XXIII.

—— (1953b), Certain Severe Disturbances of Ego Development in Childhood. *This Annual*, VIII.

Werner, H. (1948), *Comparative Psychology of Mental Development*. Chicago: Follett.

—— (1951), The Conception of Genetic Psychology. *Am. J. Orthopsychiat.*, XXI.

Winnicott, D. W. (1945), Primitive Emotional Development. *Int. J. Psa.*, XXVI.

—— (1953), Transitional Objects and Transitional Phenomena. *Int. J. Psa.*, XXXIV.

ON MATERNAL OVERSTIMULATON AND EGO DEFECTS[1]

L. BRYCE BOYER, M.D. (Berkeley, Calif.)

The infant is born with a physical and physiological status which makes the perception of stimuli less efficient than subsequent growth will potentiate. In *Beyond the Pleasure Principle,* Freud (1920) chose to call the high perceptive threshold of organisms a stimulus barrier. He stated ". . . the mass of excitations coming up against it (the *Reizschutz*) will take effect only on a reduced scale; towards what is within, no protection against stimuli is possible." Concerning inner excitations, he continued, "There will be a tendency to treat them as though they were acting not from within but from without, in order for it to be possible to apply against them the defensive measures of the barrier against stimuli." He defined trauma as "such external excitations as are strong enough to break through the barrier against stimuli" and further stated that "an external trauma will undoubtedly provoke a very extensive disturbance in the working of the energy of the new organism." The implication that internal stimuli which accumulate will likewise cause trauma in the same sense seems strongly indicated. To quote further, "The flooding of the psychic apparatus with large masses of stimuli can no longer be prevented: on the contrary, another task presents itself—to bring the stimulus under control, to bind in the psyche the stimulus mass that has broken its way in, so as to bring about a discharge of it."

It is outside the scope of this presentation to outline possible steps in and requirements of the process of the neutralization or binding of libidinal and aggressive drives. Their essential features, so far as our current stage of knowledge is concerned, are covered by the series of theoretical articles written by Hartmann, Kris, and Loewenstein (Hartmann, 1939, 1950, 1952; Hartmann et al., 1945, 1946, 1949; Kris, 1950, 1954; Loewenstein, 1950).

Freud (1924) stated that neurosis is the result of a conflict between

[1] Presented in modified forms, under the title "On the Stimulus Barrier and Schizophrenia," before the East Bay Psychiatric Association, November, 1955, and the Midwinter Meeting of the American Psychoanalytic Association, December, 1955.

ego and id and that, analogously, psychosis is the result of a disturbance between the ego and its environment. He thought that the conflict with reality and the subsequent break with reality could be traced either to the features of reality itself or to increased pressure of the instinctual drives, and that an ego which reacted in such a manner to the rivalizing demands of id and reality on the ego must have already been disturbed (Freud, 1939). Hartmann (1953) added a third possibility, suggesting that for some reason the ego's role as a mediator between the drives is impaired: "either the defensive countercathexis of the ego, or those ego functions that maintain the contact with reality, may be incompletely developed or weakened. Thus, while a break with reality could ensue in all these situations, 'conflict with reality' can, as to its causative impact, only be evaluated in relating outer frustration not only to the instinctual, but also to the ego aspects of the situation." Thus, there is an increasing tendency to conflict and the ego is incapable of dealing with it by the usual methods. The reader is referred to Rapaport's recent paper, "The Conceptual Model of Psychoanalysis" (1951b), for further clarification of this point.

Bergman and Escalona (1949) described five children who were markedly hypersensitive to external stimuli. Four of the five revealed congenital physical abnormalities. Quantitative and qualitative hypersensitivities to stimuli in the visual, auditive, gustatory, equilibritory and temperature spheres were demonstrated. The mothers of these children strove to protect them from outer excitations and to relieve their inner tensions. The maternal roles were in the form of what could be termed a supplementary barrier against stimuli. Nevertheless, the children described became psychotic. Bergman and Escalona suggested a hypothesis to be investigated, stating "that the infant who is not protected sufficiently from stimuli either because of a 'thin protective barrier' [Reizschutz], or because of the failure of maternal protection, may have to resort for such protection to premature formation of an ego. When this premature ego breaks down, possibly as a consequence of trauma, the psychotic manifestations are thought to set in." The implication was clear that ego defects would result also if the maternal protective barrier were too "thin"; this could be the result of "maternal deprivation" which might lead to an increase of tension through not removing excessive external stimuli or not satisfying drives; or, on the contrary, the mother, through her handling of the infant, may herself add excessive stimuli to the precarious balance.

Spitz's (1946, 1949, 1950, 1954, 1955b) observations of infants developing anxiety at about eight months of age apparently indicate that "At this stage at which the Ego is still nonexistent, its defense functions are partly replaced by an exceedingly high perceptive threshold which acts as a biological stimulus barrier . . . this stimulus barrier will serve later as a model for certain Ego functions in the nature of defense, more specifically those on the lines of repression. But before that can come to pass the threshold must be progressively reduced and finally disappear, to be replaced by Ego functions" (Spitz, 1950). His now famous illustrations of hospitalism (1945, 1947) can be justifiably interpreted to mean not only that the stimulus barrier begins to recede in its effectiveness during the third month of life but that inadequate protection from traumatic stimuli through the administration of care and handling by mothers during the crucial period when the biological protection recedes, results in a lack of psychical and physical maturation and development. Some analysts, as Melitta Sperling (1955), believe that psychosis is largely the result of outright maternal rejection. She sees this phenomenon as the fundamental difference in the mother-child relationship between the psychosomatic pattern and some psychotic patterns of response. The literature is replete with references to deleterious effects on children of maternal neglect and rejection (Aubry, 1955; Gelinier-Ortigues and Aubry, 1955; Klimpfinger, 1950a, 1950b; Langford, 1955; Mohr et al., 1955; Morrow and Loomis, 1955).

In the schizophrenic the ego's role as mediator between id and reality is impaired. The defensive countercathexes or those ego functions that maintain contact with reality are incompletely developed or weakened. What is most obviously lacking is the organized, ego-integrated stability of the defenses, compared to what is found in normals and neurotics. Primitive defensive mechanisms are more characteristic, such as turning against the self, reversal into the opposite and the detachment of libido. Such defenses are those which do not utilize large quantities of neutralized aggression in countercathexis (Hartmann, 1953). Unneutralized or deneutralized aggression is absorbed by the superego and turned toward the individual or may be directed externally (Nunberg, 1920, 1932; Pious, 1949).

Defenses against the without as well as the within develop in close interconnection with object relations (Arlow, 1952; A. Freud, 1949; Hartmann, 1953; Kris, 1950).[2] Trouble in the development of object relations

[2] The importance in all living systems of four points more or less directly indicated in this brief review pertaining to one facet of the development of an infant in his environment can be found in the illuminating paper of Beach (1954). The four are: the interaction between the organism and the environment, the sequence of development, the importance of time phases, and the ways in which development can be held back or made to increase, depending upon the environmental influences.

may interfere with growth of stable defenses which may again stultify development of object relations. Distorted object relations predispose to schizophrenia. One decisive factor on the side of the ego is the level of neutralization. In dedifferentiation of the ego, more differentiated forms of object relations can no longer be maintained. Self-object and ego-id relations run parallel. Withdrawal of object cathexis may well lead to loosening of ties with reality. The dedifferentiation of reality testing may be related to deneutralization; inner reality as well as outer reality become distorted.

The communication between mother and infant during the early period of babyhood is a subject pregnant with difficulties. In the book by Ruesch and Bateson (1951) no chapter is devoted to relationships between mothers and infants; their index contains neither the word mother nor the word infant. However, one facet of the hypothesis of this study involves an assumption that a mother can communicate demands to a nursling.

We know that in this earliest relationship cooperative actions are required on the parts of mother and baby for such a basic phenomenon as survival. Escalona (1953) cites the case of a mother whose eager baby was simultaneously unable to suck. Therefore she cupped the infant's face in her hand, adapted herself to his breathing and took over the job of moving his jaws. It was six weeks before this "division of labor" could be abandoned. Escalona suggested the possibility that "the importance which breast feeding can have in the developing mother-child relationship is anchored in the fact that breast feeding required mutual interaction of a delicate kind, mediated by bodily processes in both mother and child." The ability of the child's regulatory mechanisms to handle the problem of belching, his sensitiveness to stimuli awake and asleep, his levels of innate activity: all these and numerous other phenomena bespeak the great variability of the individual child. They limit the kinds of behavior which can be used in his care. Then there are the mothers. Some for various reasons reduce physical contacts with their children to a minimum. Others cannot leave their babies alone. The reasons for both types of maternal behavior and the varying intergradations are legion in the psychic structures of the mothers. If we recall the innumerable degrees of skin sensitivity, to mention only one facet, with which babies are born, the potential problems of interactions and adjustment unfold before our eyes. The mother has the upper hand in determining the kinds of behavior on the part of the infant she will accept and encourage. Likewise, through varying degrees of handling of the infant in all spheres, she will communicate through her muscular tension, her noises and expressions, her approbation or disapproval of the child's actions. Among his first memory traces will be the communicated attitudes of the mother. Spitz (1946) has indicated that most probably muscular tensions and the degree of smoothness of motion employed will be more significant during the phase when the ego has not yet developed to the stage of the smiling response. The personal demands of the mother can be made known to the nursling through all her means of care for him. This we know from clinical observation. The precise mechanisms involved still remain mysterious.

Obviously, internal levels of stimuli and thresholds of perceptive sensibility will interact in diverse ways with excitations from the environment. A child with a low threshold to perception who has an average inborn level of impulses (Fries, 1944) will more easily perceive tension or sharpness in the mother through his tactile, auditory, visual, proprioceptive and perhaps gustatory receptors. Her permission of ingress of light and colors will affect his psychological state. Her neglect to relieve his tensions through the means at her command will result in higher states of frustration. The child with a higher stimulus barrier and average impulse tensions will be less perceptive to both inner and outer excitations. He will be able better to tolerate relative neglect and handling which is not gentle or is chronically increased because of maternal factors. There is no need to enumerate the possibilities which offer themselves. Even this rough description of means through which mothers can communicate their demands to the tiniest infants suffices to remind us what will be necessary for the child to develop the basic sense of trust to which Erikson (1950) refers and upon which so much depends for the development of object relations and ego growth.

A striking example of what may be relatively permanent effects of early childhood perceptions is to be found in the case reported by Seitz (1950). A girl of two and a half years was seen because she pulled hair from her head and held it near her lips while she was nursing from a bottle and held in her mother's arms.[3] Such behavior had begun during rather strict toilet training at the age of eighteen months. She had been weaned before she was three weeks old. Seitz suspected that her mother's aureolae were hirsute. Such was true. A nipple was constructed with human hairs projecting from around its base. When the child was given

[3] Hallopeau (1889) coined the term "trichomania" or "trichotillomania" for compulsive hair pulling.

the bottle and the hairs were brushed against her mouth, she stopped plucking her hair.[4]

Eventually, no doubt, observational studies will be employed which can convincingly test the hypothesis of Escalona and Bergman. Recent studies of family interaction have revealed that the parents' unconscious desires exert extreme influences upon children (Jackson, 1954; Johnson, 1953; Szurek, 1955). However, just how to go about testing their hypothesis presents difficulties. It is risky, at best, to attempt to extrapolate backwards into infancy data received from adult patients. Neverthless, this is what will be attempted in the material to follow.

To recapitulate, the infant is born with a physical status which makes the perception of stimuli much less efficient than later growth will make possible. A baby possessing such a relative inability to perceive excitations can be thought of as having an inborn stimulus barrier. During the period in which the *Reizschutz'* efficiency diminishes, object relations develop. The primary development of such object relations is with the mother or her surrogate. Before the nursling can adequately perceive and both defend itself against and utilize stimuli to its advantage, the ideal mother serves as a supplementary stimulus barrier. Infants whose mothers supply deficient protection during this period develop ego weaknesses and inadequate differentiation of ego and id. If we consider an equation similar to mathematics, the situation would be: stimulus barrier plus maternal protective barrier plus growing psyche yield normal ego development. On the other hand, ego development would be disturbed if the stimulus barrier or the maternal protective barrier be deficient—and all possible gradations of both phenomena may exist in individual situations—or if the strength of the child's drives be unusually increased—that such varying intensities of drives exist seems to be demonstrated by the observations of Fries (1944) and Wolf (1953).[5] It follows that if the infant has or has not a "normal" stimulus barrier and drive potential and the mother adds traumatic stimuli to those to which the baby is optimally subjected, the net result might be similar.

It is the hypothesis of this study that a mother who adds to ordinary stimuli during this early period of ego development contributes to inadequate ego growth. A fragment of the case history of a woman suffering an acute catatonic state will be employed. From it, I hope to demonstrate

---

[4] Studies of psychophysiological responses to the environment have been conducted by a number of investigators. Although the references given here are to studies which included some children of slightly older ages, they seem applicable (Mangham and Tjossem, 1955; Ripley, et al., 1955; Tjossem, et al., 1955).

[5] See also *this Volume*, pp. 125-163.

that this mother added problems of her own to the child, was overrigorous in communicating her demands to the baby, thus adding stimuli for which the child was not ready, and that the mother's shrill, constant nagging resulted in a specific sphere of overstimulation. The effect on this child, as I interpret the situation, was a flooding of the immature psyche with stimuli both from the child's frustrated desires and from the side of harmful external stimulation. This particular mother provided over-gratification in the feeding sphere. The combination of these phenomena resulted in growing dependency upon the mother and confusion of iden-tities, that is, inadequate development of ego boundaries. Later separa-tion threats resulted in this woman's unconsciously perceiving the love object who might be lost to be her mother, and his or her parts, mother's parts. Such traumata contributed to the development of her psychosis.

CASE PRESENTATION[6]

Mrs. Maria P. was the twenty-six-year old daughter and only child of immigrant, uneducated Italians. Her mother was a garrulous, shrill, con-trolling, nagging, opinionated woman who seldom stopped talking.[7] No arguments could sway her. She spent her life interfering with others' affairs; directing her husband and daughter. She was nosy and gossipy. A hypochondriac, much concerned with her own bowels, she had odd, fixed ideas about food and health-giving mechanisms. Her conscious goals in life were headed by the acquisition of money. As a child, she experi-enced a hard life and felt deprived in many ways. She had had little food and no opportunity to rest in the daytime. Maria's father was a lazy, taciturn janitor who, despite loud, cursing protestations, submitted to his wife's intense domineering. His mother had been similar to his wife. Maria's mother had married him because she had not been asked by anyone with more money. She had held him in conscious contempt. Dur-ing the years before Maria's birth, mother worked and accumulated money.

Maria was unwanted except as a device. Her mother had feared she

6 Although the information regarding the parents and the girl's life history in-cluded in this presentation were obtained initially from the anamnesis offered by the patient, no data are included which have not been confirmed by a reliable informant, a sister of the mother, and, in large part, by the mother herself.

7 Galvin (1955) has presented evidence that the mother of a schizophrenic does not enjoy being a woman and wants continuing control of her child. The control typically has a secret quality. The mother of Mrs. P. was such a woman, with a slight modifica-tion. Her control of Maria was obvious to outsiders and to herself, but the control urges were quite successfully rationalized. That is, her daughter was incapable of some decisions, therefore it was necessary for mother to make all her decisions.

would lose her husband, so became pregnant to keep him. Just before the child's birth, the mother ceased her work as seamstress and saleslady, to devote her life to her daughter's care. Until Maria was somewhere between three and six months of age, she was breast fed whenever she whimpered and often when she did not. Weaning was the result of loss of milk, according to the mother. Maria's version was different. She had heard a family story stating that one time her mother had nursed her on church steps. Someone had looked "strangely" at the scene. Thus mother stopped nursing her daughter because of fear of the evil eye. Even after the weaning, Maria was never allowed to get hungry. Though she was constantly handled, the baby was never sung to. Her father was considered too clumsy to care for her. During infancy and early childhood, she was force-fed and became quite fat. She was completely toilet trained for soiling and wetting somewhere between twelve and eighteen months. As soon as Maria was old enough to be fully awake part of the time, mother set her sleeping patterns. Even though the baby was not sleepy, mother lay and held her as mother slept. In later preschool childhood, this pattern annoyed Maria, but she had no choice. She judged the sleeping to have been done when mother wanted to nap. All the girl's activities were prescribed. Her likes and dislikes were ignored. Maria's clothes were laid out for her every morning until she graduated from high school. During her preschool years, mother took her to the toilet, pulled down her panties, frequently actually fed her, dressed her, bathed her and so forth. Maria's chief memories of her childhood before she went to school were concerned with her mother's insistent, nagging instructions and her own frustration because she was not allowed to do things herself, such as housecleaning, cooking and sewing.

When Maria started school, mother abruptly returned to work. Her parents left before she awoke. A neighbor woman came in, dressed her, fed her and sent her to school. She went to the neighbor's for lunch and was fed whatever mother had dictated. As soon as school was over, she ran to the neighbor's and sat there until her parents returned from work. She had withdrawn into friendless loneliness. During the week she was dressed unbecomingly. She was supposed to have been fat and was fat. On week ends, she was lavishly clad and exhibited to mother's relatives.

After high school graduation, she became a clerk-typist. She continued to live at home. Now mother's attitude changed precipitously. Maria was to be gaudily dressed, wear makeup and flirt with men, to seduce them to the altar. She was instructed to marry a monied Italian Catholic. According to Maria's understanding, this meant that he was to have been a philanderer, brutal sexually, require her to be just a housewife, and insist on her having many children. Through her lifetime, she had heard nighttime noises and fights and had decided men were bestial. She had listened to mother's complaints of lack of sexual gratification and father's similar protestations. She decided that to keep a spouse, one must be sexual. But she considered her father to have been her mother's asexual son. She attempted to comply with mother's demands to find the right man, but failed. She met a soldier who was neither Catholic, Italian nor rich. They kept company for two years. He made no overt sexual advance and had no interest in marrying her. He just came around. He criticized nothing she did or wore. When she was with him, she was pleased at the absence of nagging criticisms and directions. His voice made her feel "full." She built up romantic fantasies. When he left without bidding her farewell, she frantically sought to find him. She began to imagine sexual experiences; went uninvited to her boss's apartment to start an affair. She thought the man's landlady was cold and suspicious, however, and fled. She was soon a sleepless, immobile hulk.

She was hospitalized for three months and given electroconvulsive and insulin coma therapies. Following her release, her mother's efforts to dispose of Maria through marriage redoubled. Mother now more than ever had the helpless child she herself had wanted to be, but the disadvantages apparently outweighed the pleasures derived. Maria met and married a man like her father, a Catholic Italian, lazy and taciturn. He was the antithesis of the prescribed partner. In her fear she would lose him, she became pregnant with the thought he could not then leave her. With a baby inside her she felt more whole than before. With her son's birth, however, she felt empty and unreal. Three months later, at New Year's Eve, a woman enthusiastically kissed Mr. P. Maria became intensely anxious, demanded frequent sexual relations and rapidly regressed into another catatonic state which was similarly treated. During the next year she was more markedly dependent upon her mother. Simultaneously, mother was more dependent on her. At times, Maria's solicitude for her son was strong; at times absent. The boy was never restricted by anyone. No toilet training was undertaken, nor has it been at the time of this writing although he is over two years old.

Fourteen months after her second acute psychotic episode, her husband injured his back. Her fantasies that he might die resulted in terror and marked preoccupation with having intercourse. Unable to use his penis successfully as the substitute for the breast which would dissolve the feared separation, she very rapidly reverted to catatonia.

She was hospitalized under my care. She was found to be mute and motionless. She obeyed commands but displayed no initiative. When food was brought near her mouth, her gesture inquired whether she should open her mouth. She let the food lie in her mouth until she was told to chew and swallow it. Her behavior was that of a small child who has been taught she must have permission and orders to act. She had to be told to take down her panties to urinate, to relieve herself into the toilet, and so on. Against my wishes but for reasons that need not be discussed here, electroshock therapy was begun. It had no discernible effect during the two weeks of its administration. For the first week of her hospitalization, she refused to acknowledge my presence. One day after I suggested that she was angry with me because she felt I had betrayed her, a dramatic episode transpired. I sat by her bed for thirty minutes. No word was spoken. She looked constantly and inquiringly at my face. After twenty-five minutes, her eyes rolled from side to side, with her gaze focused on my eyes, nose and forehead. I had the strong impression that she was imitating a nursling. The next day she voluntarily left her bed when I entered the room. She said she had heard a man's voice during the night, saying "Baa, baa, baa." The sound reminded her of a cow. She began to point to various objects and name them. Her speech was monosyllabic and her tone was inquiring and approval-seeking. The naming behavior continued for two weeks. Her need to be instructed regarding actions did not change.

Two days after her last (ninth) electroshock treatment, which had no observable effect, she began to speak short sentences. She revealed falsification of identity with other women in her three-bed ward. Her speech showed sexual curiosity and confusion and a desire to be handled like an infant, all expressed in symbols. The next day she had again withdrawn into silence. I said she had left me in anticipation that I would leave her after she had revealed sexual curiosity. In the following interview she became talkative once more. Intermixed with the naming, pointing behavior, she spoke with such words and innuendoes that I understood the presence of a desire to feel my body and know whether I had sexual reactions similar to her own.

Until this time her hostility had been handled by utter passivity which forced others to do things for her and seemed to ridicule her mother, in effect saying, "See what a bad mother you are, you've taught me nothing." There were also the withdrawal maneuvers. However, she now mentioned some realistically annoying actions of nurses and other staff members. I answered by stating that the nurses and doctors were responsible to me, that she did have to obey them but did not have to like the compliance. With this assertion of my power, willingness to accept responsibilty, setting of limitations and permission for her to be angry, she smiled and called me by name for the first time.

Because Maria still refused to eat unassisted and because she requested insulin therapy, subcoma doses were given. For three subsequent interviews, she continued to talk of confusion about identity and obligations. She began to test whether she could wheedle and cajole for unreasonable promises. When I was quietly firm, she laughed. Then she reproached me for not seeing her more often. She said her husband had promised her candy, but she thought he would not bring it. Understanding this to be a request for a gift of candy from me, I ordered a pound box of chocolates to be given in my absence. She ate all the candy within an hour. From that moment her behavior altered startlingly. Now she ate enthusiastically and socialized with the other patients. She was active and pleasant. She greeted me by name. No further hallucinations were admitted. She felt refreshed after sound sleep. The change in her actions was truly noteworthy.

Ten days before a planned absence, I informed her I would be gone for about a week. Her immediate response was withdrawal. As soon as I told her where I would be and gave her permission to call, contact was reestablished. The next time I saw her, she complained she had always been constipated. She did not want laxatives. She requested a lettuce salad. I inquired whether she wanted a lettuce salad from her husband. Her firm reply was, in that case, she'd take pills. Then she made an open, but apparently offhanded, request that I bring her a miniature doll from my trip. Instead of agreeing to give her the baby so directly, I told her I would order lettuce for her. With a happy smile, she promptly fell asleep. After a few minutes, she awoke and told me her baby slept at 6:30, 10:30 and 2:30. She soon amended her statement, averring he had done so before her second hospitalization.

Before I left, she asked permission to have sexual relations with her husband; then denied she wanted them. Previously, as will be recalled, when she said she wanted candy, she first stated she wanted it from her husband and then denied the wish. On the day of my departure, she pleaded with me to return safely because she felt she would regress into psychosis and be immured forever, should I not.

A brief evaluation of the preceding vignettes seems indicated. The oral gratification of the candy insured her of my good will. I did not fear her introjection of a part of me. She could then take into herself her concept of me and behave both as she thought I did and wanted her to. With my threatened withdrawal, the introject was ejected and psychosis supervened. However, told that although I would be absent physically, she could make a part object of my voice, the good object was reintrojected. The subsequent material could be interpreted to mean she perceived all gratifications to be the same. Conversely, any refusal was felt to be the original trauma, epitomized by the withdrawn breast. The gratification of her request for the lettuce meant she was permitted to eat things of mine, perhaps parts of me, that she could safely express aggression, namely the feces, that I accepted her since I did not reject her wish to give me feces, and that I gave her permission to have sexual experiences, that is, produce a baby. The baby was in the first instance my gift to her, but her falling asleep upon the granting of her wish meant that in return for my giving her the lettuce-baby,[8] she was giving me a baby, herself. Her messages before my departure confirmed her wish to have sexual experiences, really again with the aim of taking my penis-breast-milk into her and preventing or removing the separation.

To continue the story: Upon my return she had no use for me. When I suggested she was angry with me for having gone, she laughed, sighed with relief and requested permission to come to the office after she left the hospital.

Mrs. P. summarized, I think, material which supports the thesis of this study. Following her hospitalization, she commuted to my office alone from another city and was seen twice weekly, vis-à-vis. Three months after office visits were begun, she reported spontaneously in one interview: "My husband is trying to make me ill, now. He's told me he wants a divorce. He tries to provoke me with his voice and his words." I asked why she obeyed his commands. "That voice scarces me. It leaves me completely alone. It's the same as when Tom (her soldier who left) disappeared. Maybe I'll get sick. It takes him out of me in every way possible. I put him completely into my mind when we married. I felt blank and lost after Tom left. With him I had grasped something human. I feel emptied out with that voice. So I mind him. But then he does it other ways. He gets my opinions and then ridicules me. He dances close to other women. When he did that that New Year's Eve, it emptied me out. Then we had relations and his body was next to mine and he was inside me with his body but that didn't make me feel full even though my body felt full. I got that full feeling from Tom's voice. Like in the hospital. My husband said I said the candy made me well. It was your voice. Even when you said the wrong things. Your sweet, purring voice, like a cat. It babies me in my mind. It says, 'You're a nice girl. You've got a nice figure.' You like me and that makes me feel well. You just

---

[8] See Sechehaye (1951) for a discussion of the role of "symbolic gratification" in the treatment of a schizophrenic girl.

want to help me for myself. You don't try to make me do things for you."
She went on: "I'd rather live with my husband, even like he is, than to
return and live with my parents. That's horrible. Inside of me I couldn't
get away from them. Now I don't let my mother's voice go inside of me.
It's not my husband made me sick. It was my parents' voices. I want to
be empty of them. They didn't give me a full feeling after Tom left.
Instead it was a dominating feeling. I had to do what's best for them and
not for me. I was supposed to solve her problems. Marry the kind of man
she wanted to marry. She didn't want to do housework or cook or sew,
so she wouldn't let me learn. She had no interest in *me*. I could have
stood on my own two feet if she had taught me to do things for *me*."

DISCUSSION

The anamnestic material from Maria, her mother and the aunt, reveal
that mother was hostile to this girl and minimized Maria's needs. The
girl's wants were ignored and mother's were heeded. Mother could not
let the child be separate and bound her through feeding experiences
(among others). The type of feeding experience, while gratifying in one
way, should be considered as overgratifying, that is, frustrating. The girl
was not permitted to learn to be hungry. Foods shoved into the mouth
in the absence of hunger adds unnecessary stimuli, perhaps similar quali-
tatively to an enema administered in the absence of an urge to defecate.
Such an interaction between mother and child could result in the young-
ster's defensive development of an ego-alien identification. To return,
mother kept Maria helpless. The disregard of the child's own wants
resulted in unceasing inner tensions which she learned to attempt to
handle according to mother's formula, through the mouth or other
orifices which could be equated with the mouth, the anus via enemas, the
vagina via intercourse, and the eyes and ears. There are hints that her
skin itself was utilized as a similar orifice. Although there were denial
actions, she seemed also to remove separations by skin contacts. The
historical material obtained from the girl's memories and other stories
obtained reveal a clear utilization of the daughter by the mother to solve
the problems of the latter, at least during and subsequent to childhood.
Confusion as to identity ensued. Not only did she and mother constitute
a symbiotic psychological syncytium, but in this woman persisted a fusion
of roles of men and women as well as of mothers and children, even after
her overtly psychotic episode was no longer present.

In the hospital she acted like a hyperobedient little girl whose apparent willingness to comply disguises ruling through helplessness. After

I interpreted her anger at me, she convincingly imitated a nursling. She hallucinated my presence, acting in accord with the primary model of thinking mentioned by Rapaport (1951a). She transiently regressed to a preverbal state. Then came a prolonged reliving of the period of babyhood in which the infant learns to talk. Her behavior at that time revealed a clear object confusion and a simultaneous listening for verbal clues. She expected to be told everything she was to do or think. Subsequently appeared confusion about bodily functions and differences. When I called her attention to reality, that I was her doctor and unafraid to accept my own identity and responsibility, she was relieved and understood I would not add my problems to hers. When I gave her the candy as well, without telling her I had sacrificed myself and she should feel guilty, as was mother's wont, she introjected a new figure to mime on the one hand, and behaved as she thought I wanted her to, on the other. The lettuce-doll episode was a dramatic illustration of the thesis that, for an orally fixated patient, every frustration and every gratification are perceived as oral experiences.

Granted that no certain evidence is present to indicate that the mother superposed her wants upon the infant Maria, there are indirectly derived data, obtained through repetition of her infancy, if my conviction be accurate, during her hospitalization. I am indebted to a suggestion of Bertram D. Lewin, with which I agree, that the fact of my conviction that this is a reliving phenomenon, although subjectively received, should nevertheless be considered as additional confirmatory evidence.

The interview which was reported in detail, plus the fact that each time I saw her after she left the hospital she referred to mother's voice and its frightening aspects, combine to suggest a specific means through which this particular mother added traumatic external stimuli to the baby: that of the voice, its quality and amplitude.

That she grew up with ego defects is clear. Among them was inadequate development of ego boundaries. To retain identity at all, she had to feel she had someone or a part of someone inside her. With each threatened separation, she both returned to mother in actuality and/or sought reunion through a man's penis as a source of milk. It is less obvious to me whether she developed premature ego segments, as hypothesized by Bergman and Escalona (1949).

If this material is considered from the standpoint of the stimulus barrier, the hypothesis tested appears to have been confirmed. It may be that a specific manner in which the infant's stimulus barrier was broken was through the agency of the mother's voice.

In his thoughtful discussion of this study at the Midwinter Meeting

of 1955, Martin Wangh has called attention to a publication of Spitz
(1955a) which appeared after the present study was written. I shall quote
from Dr. Wangh's discussion notes, but shall not attempt to answer the
important theoretical question raised, since I do not feel qualified. Instead I refer my readers to the article of Spitz mentioned above and to
Hartmann's "Contribution to the Metapsychology of Schizophrenia"
(1953). Dr. Wangh states:

> Dr. Spitz, in his recent paper, "The Primal Cavity," has thrown
> new light on his concept of the stimulus barrier. His view seems to
> me to raise the question as to whether this concept is at all necessary
> when we are trying to formulate intrapsychic hypotheses. Perhaps we
> may well consider it to be supplanted by that of countercathexis. Dr.
> Spitz writes, "The newborn is incapable of perceiving the outer world
> . . . the sensorium is not yet functioning, in terms of the dynamic
> viewpoint, the newborn has not yet cathected it . . . the stimulus
> barrier is not to be understood as an obstacle in the path of the
> reception of stimulation originating in the environment. It is to be
> understood as consisting in the uncathected condition of the sen-
> sorium." I ask then: can we not assume that parallel with the gradual
> cathexis of the infant's sensorium, countercathexis too develops in
> the same way under normal circumstances. Possibly the latter with a
> temporal lag to the former. This would mean that we could think of
> a gradual transition from the uncathected to the cathected and then
> to the countercathected state of the sensorium. Cathexis and counter-
> cathexis would be necessary for optimal function in the same manner
> that agonists and protagonists in the muscular system make for
> orderly functioning. Following this line of thought we would then
> have to say that the mother of Dr. Boyer's patient interfered with the
> establishment of countercathexis in the course of the infant's devel-
> opment. I would recall to you Dr. Hartmann's (1953) views on the
> defective countercathexis in schizophrenia. He states: "These counter-
> cathectic energy distributions are essential, for instance, for the
> acceptance of outer reality. Without them, not even the separation
> of inner and outer world can come about." I would add here, not that
> of self from nonself.
> [Dr. Wangh made other comments which seem to demand further
> information and perhaps speculation from the present author. He
> went on:] The mother in Dr. Boyer's case treated her child as a part
> of her own body, her own self. And so it is most interesting to find the
> patient felt herself to be such a part, needing completion. This com-
> pletion she achieved only when her boy friend or his penis was in
> turn available as a part object. She also felt completed when she was
> pregnant. Then she was "full." Her identity was established. That the
> feeling of fullness was acquired through the combined oral and audi-
> tory route is most intriguing. The voice becomes an introject. Dr.
> Spitz traced the common pathway of orality and the visual sensorium.

Here, we may have a common path of orality and the auditory sensation. Optic overstimulation we can avoid by some physical mechanisms: we can close our eyes or avert our gaze aside from reinforcement of countercathexis. Is it not possible that in the case of auditory overstimulation we need an extraordinary amount of countercathectic energy in order to avoid traumatization? The infant cannot plug its ears. Hence the great vulnerability of this perceptive route and therefore the frequent finding of auditory hypersensitivity of schizophrenics?

Maria had, so far as I know, no visual hallucinations. She reported only two hallucinatory experiences during the time I saw her, although she said she had heard indistinguishable noises and words when previously hospitalized. Following an interview in which she revealed through symbolic language a desire to feel my body to determine whether I had sexual reactions similar to her own, she reported she had spent the night with her (nonexistent) brother. Their bodies had been near each other all night. No sexual relations occurred. The identity of the man in bed with her was overdetermined. At one time she said it was her son. None of her relatives, to my knowledge, had blue eyes. I do have. The man who lay with her and whose body filled her through tactile contact, she thought, even though she denied having seen him at all, had blue eyes. This hallucination, so far as reported, involved tactile and proprioceptive spheres. I assume that enteroceptive sensations were likewise involved. In the hallucination which succeeded the episode of imitating a nursling, the total related content was that she heard a man's voice saying "Baa, baa, baa." Although this hallucination appeared to fit the primary model of thinking delineated by Rapaport (1951a), it is possible that more was involved. It may be that her confusion of names contributed to her using the sound of a sheep to represent the sound of a cow. Nevertheless, one might speculate whether her sheeplike behavior and her attempts to make sheep of her mother surrogates through her helplessness contributed to her word confusion. It would appear that this particular sort of behavior on her part involved both primary and secondary autonomous agencies, similar to those utilized for explanation by Brenman (1952) in her discussion of the psychodynamics of the teasee and emphasized by Hartmann (1953) and Rapaport (1951b). Be that as it may, in this case we have what appears to be primarily an auditory hallucination.

In Spitz's article (1955a) referred to by Wangh, we find:

Lewin (1946, 1948, 1950, 1953a, 1953b) . . . deduces logically that if a regression occurs from the visual imagery level at which the dream functions, then there should be memory traces older than these pictures. Thus, as I do, he sees these memory traces "more like pure emotion," made up of deeper tactile, thermal and dimly protopathic qualities which are in their way "memory traces" of early dim consciousness of the breast or of the half-sleep state. And, if I read him correctly, he believes it is to this level of integration that the subject regresses in the so-called blank dream. It follows that the level of regression involved in the Isakower (1938, 1954) phenomenon harks back to an earlier period, that which precedes the reliable laying down of visual mnemic traces or at least to a period at which a significant number of visual mnemic traces has not yet been accumulated. I would be inclined to say that while the regression of the dream screen goes to the level of the mnemic traces laid down somewhere between the ages toward the end of the first half year and reaching to the end of the first year, in the Isakower phenomenon the regression reaches to the traces of experiences preceding this period. Obviously these age ranges represent extremely wide approximation.

In the case reported by Seitz (1950), tactile memory traces appeared to play a role in the little girl's action of putting hairs around her mouth while nursing, despite her having been weaned at two or three weeks. This case is so startling when we consider the diffusion of sensations experimentally observed—or, stated differently, the relative absence of sensorium cathexis during such early stages of life—that we must wonder whether indeed all the necessary information is available to us for making a clear statement regarding the meaning of Seitz's findings. All the same, the case is temptingly suggestive. If it occurred in the manner there described and there are no further important data which should be employed in its interpretation, the significance is that at least some infants do indeed develop strong memory traces of sensory perceptions and integrate them with phenomenological Gestalten at very early ages, although we are generally inclined to agree with Spitz (1955a): "The sensations of the three organs of perception—hand, labyrinth, and skin cover— combine and unite with the intraoral sensations to a unified situational experience in which no part is distinguishable from another. This perceptive experience is inseparable from that of the need gratification occurring simultaneously and leading through extensive tension reduction from a state of excitement with the quality of unpleasure to quiescence without unpleasure. *We do not postulate any memory traces, be they even unconscious, of this situational percept of the newborn.*" (My italics.)

But to return more directly to the issue at hand: in the hallucination in which Maria slept with a man, one of the men in the condensed figure was her therapist, at that time her clearest mother surrogate. She was then deeply regressed. The perceptions involved in the hallucination appeared to be primarily tactile, proprioceptive and, perhaps, enteroceptive. We know that in the case of Maria and her mother, much bodily contact was employed during her infancy. It may very well be that the level of her regression is indicated by the fact that previsual elements were at least predominantly employed. It could be that even in later periods of her infancy, such sensorial phenomena were of more importance than visual. In the case of the "baa, baa, baa" hallucination, we have no direct evidence to enable us to conclude that more than auditory perceptions and their projection contributed to her model of primary thinking, as there illustrated. We would assume that, if it was an episode of primary ideation, the absent mother surrogate was the object of an aim, namely an aim to be held and nursed. Thus, indirectly, we could guess that proprioceptive, tactile and enteroceptive perceptions were involved.

Spitz (1955a) has already called attention to the importance of the labyrinth in the nursing situation. To quote him further: "When we lift the newborn from his cot and place him in the nursing position, we set in motion in the labyrinth a neurophysiological process of a very special nature. This process is a gravity-induced shift of the endolymph within the labyrinth, resulting in two sensory stimulations of a completely different nature. . . . The pressure of the endolymph on the lining of the semicircular canals results in changes of the equilibrium sensation; the same pressure will simultaneously provoke auditory sensations in the organ of Corti in the cochlea. . . . The sensations connected with the stimulation of the semicircular canals will be dizziness and vertigo, those connected with the stimulations of the Corti organs will be auditory, probably vague rushing, murmuring, roaring noises which may be similar to the sensation described by Isakower and Lewin."

It would appear that the case of Maria might give us information to substantiate a hypothesis that under special situations of infancy, in which certain auditory stimuli are repetitively associated with the experience of being mothered, they may become more clearly and persistent accentuated facets of the oral sensorium. It might, as Wangh suggests, give us some clues as to why in schizophrenics it is not unusual to find great vulnerabilty in the auditory sphere.

Summary

According to one formulation, the physical status of the newborn makes the perception of stimuli less efficient than later growth potentiates. Freud formulated the concept of the stimulus barrier. As the *Reizschutz'* efficiency diminishes, object relations develop; the primary figure of importance in the development of object relations is the mother or her surrogate. Before the nursling can adequately perceive stimuli, the ideal mother serves as a supplementary barrier against traumatic external and internal excitations. Infants whose maternal protective barriers are deficient develop ego weaknesses and inadequate differentiation of ego and id. If the stimulus barrier or the maternal protective barrier is deficient, or if the drive strength of the child is unusually increased, ego development may be disturbed. It follows that if the infant has or has not a "normal" stimulus barrier and drive potentials and the mother *adds* traumatic stimuli, ego development might be abnormal.

A fragment of the case history of a catatonic woman provides information which can be interpreted to mean that her stimulus barrier was broken by the mother's adding external stimulations and failing to relieve inner tensions by adding her problems to the child's and using the baby to solve her own problems, and specifically through continual auditory excitation.

Certain speculations are made which lead to a tentative conclusion that under certain conditions of mother-child relationship in infancy, the accentuation of auditory stimuli cause an unusually strong bond between the Gestalt of being mothered and the auditory sensorium, that is, the development of a strong link between oral and auditory sensorial spheres.

BIBLIOGRAPHY

Arlow, J. A. (1952), Discussion of Dr. Fromm-Reichmann's Paper. In: *Psychotherapy with Schizophrenics*, ed. E. B. Brody and F. C. Redlich. New York: International Universities Press.

Aubry, J. (1955), The Effects of Lack of Maternal Care: Methods of Studying Children Aged One to Three Years, Placed in Institutions. In: *Emotional Problems of Early Childhood*, ed. G. Caplan. New York: Basic Books.

Beach, F. A. (1954), Ontogeny and Living Systems. In: *Group Processes*, ed. B. Schaffner. New York: Josiah Macy, Jr., Foundation.

Bergman, P. and Escalona, S. K. (1949), Unusual Sensitivities in Very Young Children. *This Annual*, III/IV.

Brenman, M. (1952), On Teasing and Being Teased. *This Annual*, VII.

Erikson, E. H. (1950), *Childhood and Society*. New York: Norton.

Escalona, S. K. (1953), Emotional Development in the First Year of Life. In: *Problems of Infancy and Childhood*, ed. M. J. E. Senn. New York: Josiah Macy, Jr., Foundation.

Freud, A. (1949), Aggression in Relation to Emotional Development. *This Annual*, III/IV.

Freud, S. (1920), *Beyond the Pleasure Principle*. London: Hogarth Press, 1948, pp. 33-34

—— (1924), Neurosis and Psychosis. *Collected Papers*, II. London: Hogarth Press, 1948

—— (1939), *An Outline of Psychoanalysis*. New York: Norton, 1949, pp. 62-63.

Fries, M. E. (1944), Some Basic Differences in Newborn Infants During the Lying-in Period. Teaching Film with Guide. New York University Film Library.

Galvin, J. A. V. (1955), Mothers of Schizophrenics. Read at the First Western Divisional Meeting of the American Psychiatric Association, a Joint Meeting with the West Coast Psychoanalytic Societies, San Francisco, October 28.

Gelinier-Ortigues, M.-C. and Aubry, J. (1955), Maternal Deprivation, Psychogenic Deafness and Pseudo-Retardation. In: *Emotional Problems of Early Childhood*, ed. G. Caplan. New York: Basic Books.

Hallopeau (1889), Alopecia par grattage (trichomania ou trichotillomania). *Annales de dermatologie et syphilologie*, X.

Hartmann, H. (1939), Ich-Psychologie und Anpassungsproblem. *Int. Ztschr. Psa. & Imago*, XXIV; translated in part in: *Organization and Pathology of Thought*, ed. D. Rapaport. New York: Columbia University Press, 1951.

—— (1950), Psychoanalysis and Developmental Psychology. *This Annual*, V.

—— (1952), The Mutual Influences in the Development of Ego and Id. *This Annual*, VII.

—— (1953), Contribution to the Metapsychology of Schizophrenia. *This Annual*, VIII.

—— and Kris, E. (1945), The Genetic Approach in Psychoanalysis. *This Annual*, I.

—— —— and Loewenstein, R. M. (1946), Comments on the Formation of Psychic Structure. *This Annual*, II.

—— —— —— (1949), Notes on the Theory of Aggression. *This Annual*, III/IV.

Isakower, O. (1938), A Contribution to the Psychopathology of Phenomena Associated with Falling Asleep. *Int. J. Psa.*, XIX.

—— (1954), Spoken Words in Dreams. *Psa. Quart.*, XXIII.

Jackson, D. D. (1954), Some Factors Influencing the Oedipus Complex. *Psa. Quart.*, XXIII.

Johnson, A. M. (1953), Factors in the Etiology of Fixations and Symptom Choice. *Psa. Quart.*, XXII.

Klimpfinger, S. (1950a), *Der Kindergarten als familiensoziologisches Problem*. Wien: Bundesverlag.

—— (1950b), *Zur Psychologie des Kleinkindalters*. Wien: Bundesverlag.

Kris, E. (1950), Notes on the Development and on Some Current Problems of Psychoanalytic Child Psychology. *This Annual*, V.

—— (1954), Chairman, Problems of Infantile Neurosis, a Discussion. *This Annual*, IX.

Langford, W. S. (1955), Disturbance in Mother-Infant Relationship Leading to Apathy, Extranutritional Sucking and Hair Ball. In: *Emotional Problems of Early Childhood*, ed. G. Caplan. New York: Basic Books.

Lewin, B. D. (1946), Sleep, the Mouth and the Dream Screen. *Psa. Quart.*, XV.

—— (1948), Inferences from the Dream Screen. *Int. J. Psa.*, XXIX.

—— (1950), *The Psychoanalysis of Elation*. New York: Norton.

—— (1953a), The Forgetting of Dreams. In: *Drives, Affects, Behavior*, ed. R. M. Loewenstein. New York: International Universities Press.

—— (1953b), Reconsideration of the Dream Screen. *Psa. Quart.*, XXII.

Loewenstein, R. M. (1950), Conflict and Autonomous Ego Development During the Phallic Phase. *This Annual*, V.

Mangham, C. A. and Tjossem, T. D. (1955), Locomotor Behavior in Young Children, Relationship to Mother and Child Interaction. Read at the First Western Divisional Meeting of the American Psychiatric Association, a Joint Meeting with the West Coast Psychoanalytic Societies, San Francisco, October 28.

Mohr, G. J.; Richmond, J. B.; Garner, A. M.; Eddy, E. J. (1955), A Program for the Care of Children with Psychosomatic Disorders. In: *Emotional Problems of Early Childhood*, ed. G. Caplan. New York: Basic Books.

Morrow, T., Jr. and Loomis, E. A. (1955), Symbiotic Aspects of a Seven-Year-Old. *Emotional Problems of Early Childhood*, ed. G. Caplan. New York: Basic Books.

Nunberg, H. (1920), On the Catatonic Attack. In: *Practice and Theory of Psychoanalysis*. New York: International Universities Press, 1955.

—— (1932), *Principles of Psychoanalysis*. New York: International Universities Press, 1955.

Pious, W. L. (1949), The Pathogenic Process in Schizophrenia. *Bull. Menninger Clin.*, XIII.

Rapaport, D. (1951a), *Organization and Pathology of Thought*. New York: Columbia University Press, p. 690.

—— (1951b), The Conceptual Model of Psychoanalysis. In: *Psychoanalytic Psychiatry and Psychology*, ed. R. P. Knight and C. R. Friedman. New York: International Universities Press, 1954.

Ripley, H. S.; Ax, A. F.; Dorpat, T. L.; Strand, G. T., Jr.; Kogan, W. S.; Quinn, R. D. (1955); Multiple Psychophysiological Responses in Psychiatric Patients and in Control Subjects. Read at the First Western Divisional Meeting of the American Psychiatric Association, a Joint Meeting with the West Coast Psychoanalytic Societies, San Francisco, October 28.

Ruesch, J. and Bateson, G. (1951), *Communication: the Social Matrix of Psychiatry*. New York: Norton.

Sechehaye, M. A. (1951), *Symbolic Realization*. New York: International Universities Press.

Seitz, P. F. D. (1950), Psychocutaneous Conditioning During the First Two Weeks of Life. *Psychosom. Med.*, XII.

Sperling, M. (1955), Psychosis and Psychosomatic Illness. *Int. J. Psa.*, XXXVI.

Spitz, R. A. (1945), Hospitalism, *This Annual*, I.

—— (1946), The Smiling Response: A Contribution to the Ontogenesis of Social Relations. *Gen. Psychol. Mon.*, XXXIV.

—— (1947), Hospitalism: A Follow-up Report. *This Annual*, II.

—— (1949), The Role of Ecological Factors in Emotional Development in Infancy. *Child Development*, XX.

—— (1950), Anxiety in Infancy: A Study of Its Manifestations in the First Year of Life. *Int. J. Psa.*, XXXI.

—— (1954), Genèse des premieres relations objectales. *Rev. Franç. Psychanal.*, XVIII.

—— (1955a), The Primal Cavity: A Contribution to the Genesis of Perception and Its Role for Psychoanalytic Theory. *This Annual*, X.

—— (1955b), A Note on the Extrapolation of Ethological Findings. *Int. J. Psa.*, XXXVI.

Szurek, S. (1954), Concerning the Sexual Disorders of Parents and Their Children. *J. Nerv. & Ment. Dis.*, CXX.

—— (1955), Childhood Schizophrenia, Psychotic Episodes and Psychotic Maldevelopment. Read at the Meeting of the San Francisco Psychoanalytic Society, May 16.

Tjossem, T. D.; Leider, A. R.; Deisher, R. W.; Holmes, T. H.; Ripley, H. S. (1955) Psychophysiological Studies of Skin Temperatures in Young Children. Read at the First Western Divisional Meeting of the American Psychiatric Association, a Joint Meeting with the West Coast Psychoanalytic Societies, October 28.

Wolf, F. M. (1953), Observations of Individual Tendencies in the First Year of Life In: *Problems of Infancy and Childhood*, ed. M. J. E. Senn. New York: Josiah Macy, Jr., Foundation.

ON THE DEVELOPMENT OF MATERNAL FEELINGS IN EARLY CHILDHOOD

Observations and Reflections

JUDITH S. KESTENBERG, M.D. (New York)

Introduction

Although Freud wrote several papers on the development of female sexuality, his references to maternal needs are few and far between. When they do occur, they disclose a concept of motherhood which is consistent with his interpretation of female development. Freud could readily accept new contributions of female analysts to this subject. He considered the female psyche quite enigmatic, possibly more accessible to understanding by women than by men. But he could never agree with theories of the universality of early vaginal sensations. In one case he did find a possible evidence of such an occurrence (Freud, 1925), but as a rule he thought that memories of early vaginal sensations were displacements from other libidinous zones. To Freud, the little girl was essentially masculine up to the time she turned to her father because of her disappointment in her mother, who had failed to give her a penis. The girl's early preoccupation with dolls was explained in terms of the young child's need to reverse the mother-child relationship. Freud consistently called activity masculine and passivity feminine, but conceded that the activity involved in the little girl's maternal play was "the activity of femininity" (1931).

While the relationship between maternal activity and femininity remained somewhat obscure, two sources of a baby image emerged clearly throughout Freud's writings: the "anal-baby" associated with the passive feminine attitude, and the penis-baby equation derived from the active masculinity of the phallic phase. In discussing the fantasy "A Child Is Being Beaten," Freud (1919) made a fleeting reference to the girl's identification of her clitoris with a child. The vagina, emerging late in female development, was considered a successor to the rectum or its subtenant. Its symbolic representation was that of a receptacle for the penis. Inasmuch as the wish for the child is eventually replaced by the wish for the penis, the vaginal cavity became also a host of the child.

Various authors[1] enlarged, modified or contradicted some of Freud's views. Two schools of thought emerged, one most consistently represented by Horney and the Kleinian school; the other, expounded by such adherents of Freud as Deutsch, Mack Brunswick and Bonaparte. The former believed in the existence of early vaginal sensations which were repressed in time, thus assuming an early femininity; the latter followed Freud in his concept of the girl's initial masculinity. Klein drew attention to the child's concept of babies residing in the maternal abdomen, and consistently maintained that children had an unconscious, inherited "knowledge" of the vagina as an organ. Brierley and Payne, especially emphasized the equation of the vagina with the mouth, pointing out that vaginal contractions were sometimes associated with suckling Deutsch described passive feminine masochism preceding the appearance of the vagina as an organ, while Payne spoke of receptivity rather than passivity, and of a capacity to tolerate and adapt to periodical variation rather than of masochism. It was Brierley who suggested that feminine normality depended on a particular kind of coordination between the clitoric and the vaginal functions, getting away from the idea that one supplanted the other.

One gets the impression that the proponents of early masculinity in women followed Freud's concept of maternal activity, while those who assumed early vaginal participation in female development were more inclined to see the mother's role as oscillating between activity and passivity, according to the changing needs of the child. It was Freud himself who drew our attention to the fundamental change of maternal attitude which occurs when the small infant grows up to be a child. In his paper on Leonardo da Vinci (1910) he says: "The love of the mother for the suckling whom she nourishes and cares for is something far deeper reaching than her later affection for the growing child. It is of the nature of a fully gratified love affair, which fulfills not only all the psychic wishes but also all physical needs, and when it represents one of the forms of happiness attainable by man it is due, in no little measure to the possibility of gratifying without reproach also wish feelings which were long repressed and designated as perverse" (pp. 92-93). The reference to all bodily needs may be taken as a hint that pregenital and genital desires find fulfillment in the care of the infant. In this reflectio

1 See particularly Bonaparte (1935, 1953), Brierley (1932, 1936), Deutsch (1933, 19- 1945), Fenichel (1934), Ferenczi (1919), Hitschmann-Bergler (1936), Horney (1926, 19: 1933), Jacobson (1936, 1937), Jones (1927, 1933, 1935), Klein (1932), Lampl-de Gro (1928, 1933), Lorand (1939), Mack Brunswick (1940), Müller (1932), Payne (193 Riviere (1934).

Freud does not speak of any difference in the handling of male and female infants. Later he describes the mother's need to realize her frustrated wishes for a penis in the achievements of her son (1932). Inasmuch as the male child substitutes for a penis, we have to expect that the mother's attitude toward her son will not change fundamentally when he grows up. She still will take narcissistic pride in his adult achievements. The maternal bliss in caring for her infant, regardless of sex, seems dependent on the child's smallness and helplessness. Freud's remarks can be developed further to mean that mothers enjoy the care of their infants in substitution of their early repressed wishes to handle their own genitals. I suggested a similar interpretation of a mother's need for a small child, in the hypothesis that early undischarged vaginal excitations were the basic source of the girl's need for a child (1956).

The localization of the vagina, its inaccessibility and the diffuseness of its excitations make it impossible for the child to explore it fully. The infant can be handled and fondled while the early vaginal tensions are usually not discharged on the organ itself. The young girl has to find substitute channels for discharge. Even in the rare cases where children do experience an orgastic vaginal discharge, it does not seem likely that the anxieties connected with the excitement can be fully mastered. Other libidinous zones are accessible to continuous experimentation and can become incorporated in the body scheme; their excitations cease to be sources of anxiety when their boundaries and functions have been sufficiently explored. The vaginal tensions can find a certain modicum of discharge by displacements to other parts of the body. This neither constitutes full discharge nor does it allow for the creation of an organ concept. In her search for an explorable object, the little girl identifies herself with her mother and chooses a baby as a suitable substitute. The wish for a child can thus be traced from a biological need. This need is, in turn, influenced by psychologically determined attitudes, such as the identification with one's mother and the wish for a penis. With such speculations[2] we come closer to the subject of maternal "instinct."

MATERNAL "INSTINCT"

The question of instinct has been a long-standing bone of contention in the development of psychoanalytic theory. Hartmann, Kris, and Loewenstein (1946) clarified this issue by pointing out that instinct, as evident

[2] In consideration of the scantiness of the clinical material, available to me, and a recognition of a certain amount of bias in favor of one's own interpretation, it is important to stress the speculative aspect of the concept, developed here.

in animals, is largely lacking in the human species. Erikson (1950) stated: "Man's 'inborn instincts' are drive fragments to be assembled, given meaning, and organized during a prolonged childhood by methods of child training and schooling which vary from culture to culture and are determined by tradition." Helene Deutsch (1945), evaluating the maternal instinct in the human female, finds it difficult to decide "to what extent the complex emotional attribute that we call 'motherliness' expresses a biologic condition." In adult women, Benedek (1952) was able to find an experimentally established correlate between maternal qualities and hormone fluctuations. Deutsch (1945) is inclined to stress the psychological meaning of motherhood in the present society. Still she says: "Possibly part of the deeply feminine quality of intuition is a remnant of that strong instinct, to which we are told woman once owed her dominant position in primitive society."

It is undoubtedly true that today's woman does not approach childbirth and infant care as if she were guided by a maternal instinct. She has no inner wisdom which would prompt her to find a nesting place, to bite off the cord, and to suckle the infant as long and as often as he needs it. She uses substitute equipment in the care of the child's excrements. She seems singularly unprepared for these maternal functions and often afraid to exercise them. Nevertheless, our ideal picture of a truly maternal woman is one of an omnipotent, all-knowing mother who knows what to do with her infant by sheer intuition. Our present culture has contributed a great deal to the estrangement of the woman from her biological functions. While I may return to the question of cultural influences later, I want to mention in passing that both vaginal sensibility and motherly behavior have suffered from the increasing masculinization of women, largely due to environmental changes.[3] Despite their flight from feminity, women cannot escape womanhood when, with the onset of puberty, they become subject to regular hormonal fluctuations. We have learned from psychoanalysis and from research on maturation that adult functions are foreshadowed in early development. We wonder, then, how the adult woman, whose psychological attitude undoubtedly depends on her specifically female hormonal cycle, has been prepared for the cyclic nature of her femininity as well as for the events of pregnancy and infant nursing, which periodically interrupt her cycles. We postulate a preparation, and doubt that such a preparation has only psychological determinants. We expect to find a biological substrate to maternal behavior which operates since early childhood. Whatever such

[3] This factor in itself contributes largely to the obscurity which envelops our understanding of feminine development.

a biological factor may be, we are inclined to think of it as a substitute for the animal instinct, and we expect to find a correlation between the biological factor and the specifically maternal intuition of women. Let us turn to observations of children to gather traces of later motherliness.

VAGINAL STIMULATIONS IN THE ORAL PHASE OF DEVELOPMENT

Early in his writings Freud (1905, 1906) drew our attention to the role of the mother as seductress of the infant who, ministering to his bodily needs, awakens such sexual urges as are attached to the erogenous zones of the infant's body. While there is a succession of dominant needs during infantile development, the infant's mother not only satisfies the phase-specific needs but also acts as premature stimulant of zones which are destined to become erogenous at a later time. Greenacre (1952) pointed to a possibility that genital discharge may occur prematurely when, under deprivation, the infant responds with an unspecific totality of discharge through all channels. More frequent is the situation in which a mother cleanses the anal and the urethrogenital zones after a child has been fed, i.e., under conditions of oral satisfaction. Brierley and Payne thought in terms of spontaneous overflow of excitation from the oral to the vaginal zone. This is quite feasible in view of the fact that in the first few weeks the whole female genital is frequently enlarged and swollen, so that a local response of vaginal "sucking" may develop in association with oral sucking. The ministrations of the mother, such as bathing, oiling and diapering, may have a further stimulating effect not only upon the external but also on the internal genital of the girl. Soapy bathing water can flow into the vagina, wiping of the introitus mucosa can have an indirect effect on the vaginal mucosa which it adjoins. There are other sources of excitations in the vagina early in life. The pressures exerted on the adjoining vaginal walls by a full rectum or bladder are probably only fleeting, because in the average infant a discharge follows the fullness almost immediately. Such stimulations become more important with the establishment of sphincter controls. The pressing of the infant's abdomen, widely practiced calisthenics and the playful tossing up and down also contribute to vaginal excitations. Some girls recapture during analysis the memory of inner genital excitement produced by jumping up and down in early childhood. The attachment to transitional objects in boys seems to have a connection with early genital sensations (Wulff, 1946; Greenacre, 1953, 1955). Such a connection is not all too clear in girls.

TRANSITIONAL OBJECTS

Toward the end of the oral phase and sometimes earlier, children often get addicted to articles which they need to touch or rub while going to sleep (Wulff, 1946; Winnicott, 1953; Stevenson, 1954). Some of these objects are quite inappropriately called "baby," as they rarely resemble babies. Winnicott rightly pointed out that these possessions, to which the child clings at moments of separation, represent both the absent mother and the child itself. One can easily recognize from the demeanor of the infants that they are repeating the nursing situation: they suck with one hand and clutch an article with the other. The fingers substitute for the breast or bottle, while the touching of the cherished item revives the sensation of handling the mother's clothes or breast. Yet, one must not forget that the most frequent appearance of transitional objects coincides with the time when the child has already been able to reach his genitals. Not only has he already the awareness of the lower part of his body, but he is also beginning to recognize dimly the connection between abdominal sensations and elimination, a problem which has held his attention rather early in life. I am inclined to believe that the transitional object serves a multitude of needs. It represents an ideal solution for the infant who cannot cope with so many tensions stemming from the outside as well as the inside of his body, tensions which overcome him with greater force when the waking activity ceases and the immobility and aloneness of the sleep separation brings about a unique intimacy with his own body. Oral, anal as well as genital needs seem to be met in holding on to articles of special texture which feel like mother's breast, like the tissue cleansing the anal and genital regions, all areas where the "me" and the "not me" meet. At that stage inner sensations are most probably still fused with, and projected to the outside, so that they too can be mastered by the method of delineation of boundaries between oneself and others. Some children indicate that a special softness of the texture is important, as if they wanted to reproduce the feel of mucous membranes, which are the mediators between outside and inside. The connection with anality is indicated by a special smell important in some cases. A clear substitution of anal manipulation by rubbing of a silk fringe (changed later to silk pants) was observed in P. Her first action on lying down was putting her fingers into her mouth and scratching her anal region with her other hand. Only after her mother removed the child's hand from this place twice, did the child turn to handling the silk piece as a substitute.

The primary transitional objects lay the foundation for secondary preferred toys, many of whom represent anal babies. In this phase of transitional phenomena there is no evidence of vaginal excitations. The child is entering an abdominal stage in which most probably all inner sensations are fused and predominantly projected upon the anal orifice.

The Anal-Baby Phase

The little girl develops sphincter control earlier than the boy. This is generally assigned to the girl's greater dependence on her mother, her more obedient and passive attitude. It is quite possible that the girl is more dependent on outside help because she has an additional inner tension which adds to the child's difficulties in coping with bodily stimulations. Also, the girl finds additional pleasures in the exercise of sphincter control which the boy does not have. There is a general tendency to contract vaginal muscles alongside with the contraction of sphincters. Contraction of laminal muscles, which we find so rigidly established in cases of vaginism, seems to be the girl's pastime of the anal phase, of which no conscious representation is possible because of the simultaneous contractions of sphincters and laminal muscles. Holding back of feces and urine for a good long time is a play preferred by girls. The resulting fullness of bladder and rectum may be kept up until abdominal pain develops. The feeling of fullness, which the child experiences, seems to foreshadow the pleasure of a full vagina which she cannot experience until much later. The period of holding back is often interpreted as production time. What is discharged after the withholding is considered "made" (formed) by the child, while immediate release is experienced as surrender to both bodily demands and mother's commands, in contrast to active voluntary "work." Feces are particularly suitable for the development of this concept, as the child apprehends that holding back will result in solid, formed bowel movements, while feces discharged in great urgency tend to be fluid or "torn" ("in pieces"). This work principle seems to be intimately connected with the "anal baby" concept. Knowing clearly where the feces come from, and the experience of making them, is a practical creative situation which follows the illusory creativeness of the transitory phenomena. The transitional object seems to lay a foundation for the baby concept in the sense of "something of me and something of mother." The anal baby is not only possession but also a product from which the child parts with sorrow before he is able to give it away to his mother as a present.

Nelly, a two-and-a-half-year-old girl, came to analysis because she was not able to solve her oral and anal problems and was already overburdened with genital excitations. During her treatment, her mother was advised to allow the child to hold back her excrements as long as she wished. Immediately after the mother stopped reminding Nelly to go to the bathroom, the child held back her urine and feces for a long time. During this withholding period she "worked" ironing and washing. In the middle of this work she developed abdominal cramps whereupon her mother told her that going to the bathroom would relieve the pain. Nelly seated herself on the toilet in such a way that she could observe how her feces left her anus. When a tiny piece of b.m. adhered to her skin, she anxiously asked her mother why this piece kept dancing on her and would not go into the toilet. The slight incident apparently detracted from the feeling of control over her products the child was about to acquire. She quietened down when her mother wiped the disobedient piece away. Two days later she became quite excited in what seemed a generalized genital excitation. At night she made several attempts to seduce her mother and asked her what it means to "eat me up." The following morning she was curious why her mother's "wee-wee" was brown, and was told that what she saw was hair, which she too would get when she grew up. Nelly replied that she was a big girl and wanted hair right away. The same day she showed her mother her b.m. and pointed to the big pieces, calling them "mommy ballies." The small pieces she named "brother ballies" (her brother then was a small baby). The following day Nelly jumped on her mother's bed and in her excitement urinated on it. This loss of urinary control distressed her greatly. In her analysis, Nelly had been discussing eating of feces as well as her fear to displease her mother if she soiled herself. The withholding of urine and feces followed such a session. In the next hour Nelly indicated a preocupation with an earlier sexually tinged episode, the nature of which she would either not disclose or not remember. The sexual excitement, the questioning of her mother and the "ballie" episode occurred after this hour. In the next session Nelly returned to what seemed to be a confession of seeing adult sex relations of some kind, but again could not tell what had happened. She made it quite clear, however, that she had reacted with a lot of bowel movement to the traumatic scenes she must have witnessed. After leaving her session Nelly vomited her meal, a symptom she had suffered from before the onset of her analysis.

Because of the overlapping of oral, anal and genital problems, Nelly originated several theories of sex relationships and childbirth, in quick succession. The clearest theory of all was the anal-baby idea which developed after she linked up "the triad" of withholding, work, and control over the abdominal content. She produced two kinds of babies, just like her mother. The baby making was intimately connected with her sexual feelings toward her mother. In identification with her mother, and with a simultaneous reversal of roles, she gave birth to her mother-baby Also in identification with her mother she delivered a fecal penis-boy We can guess that Nelly was also busy with a cannibalistic sex, birth o impregnation theory. In addition, her genital excitement directed toward her mother expressed itself in jumping associated with urethral discharge. Whether the last activity was also connected with babies remains an open question. The nature of her generalized excitement revealed a genital component, but we have no evidence of vaginal participation in the oral, anal and urethral discharges which overlapped with the child's need to create a baby. The vagina was silent and the anal dominance overshadowed all other recessive zones. The anal baby emerged as a product which the child wanted to control by herself. Possibly because of a recognition of her helplessness, she turned to her mother, inviting her to participate in her baby production. She seemed to present to her mother the shaped ballies (and her vomit) soon after she had recognized her need of mother's help, and immediately after she was confronted with her mother's anatomic superiority. At an earlier time, Nelly has shown an interesting transition from the fear of losing her feces to an attitude of generosity, in which she wanted to give them to another child whom she liked. In this fantasy she identified herself with her own bowel movement, as she was also afraid to be flushed down the toilet as a whole. An attempt was made to explain the sewer system to her in order to allay her fears. She listened carefully, and at the end of the explanation cheerfully exclaimed that the pipes land in the house of her favored girl friend, whom she had never visited. Thus, her philosophy seems to emerge as sharing what she cannot produce by herself, and giving what she does not want to lose. Her sharing and giving are attached to persons she is fond of.

In summary, we may conclude, that the anal baby is a mixture of possession, creativity, sharing and generosity. It is intimately connected with withholding, abdominal sensations and ejection of the abdominal content. There is no direct evidence that vaginal excitations contribute to the prevailing abdominal pressures. From analyses of older girls, it seems likely that the abdominal fullness creates vaginal tensions which cannot be discharged adequately through the available anal and urethral channels. The overwhelming anal preoccupation of the anal stage may, however, absorb a good deal of vaginal tensions. In the postanal, prephallic phase of development, maternal activities show a trace of the earlier anal-baby concept. We may wonder about the nature of the organic tension which supplies the fuel for the ardent maternal urges of the toilet-trained clean girl. Or to paraphrase it colloquially: now that the baby is born, why does the little mother still need it so much?

THE BABY OF THE EARLY MATERNAL STAGE

I have the impression that with the passing of the anal phase, vaginal excitations become an important, at times discernible source of tension.

This could not be deduced from direct observation of young children, but seems a possible turn in development from the retrospective analysis of young girls and women. In immediate observation it becomes evident that the girl's maternal interest in that stage is much more pronounced than that of the boy.

A.[4] who distinguished himself early by his unusual independence and persistence in his own ways, initiated his self-feeding by first feeding his mother and then eating from his mother's plate rather than his own. Prior to this, he had gone through a difficult feeding period which seemed to end with complete recovery. He responded to weaning from the bottle by a spurt of independent behavior in keeping with his early intolerance of passivity. When A. became proficient in walking, he became increasingly interested in his brother's and sister's toys. He loved to wheel his sister's doll carriage. On seeing his sister's doll he would kiss it and go off to other interesting play. To my knowledge, his mother never discouraged doll play. His siblings' refusal to give up their toys to A. for a prolonged period would only increase his interest in them. Yet, A. did not develop more than a fleeting interest in dolls. Before he reached his second year he became inseparable from a cap which he wore all day and hung on the bedpost at night. When he was about two he was given a rag doll of his own which he kept in his bed alongside with an array of other toys such as guns, but which he did not carry around with him.

A. was probably aware of sex differences by that time as he could observe his mother and sister freely and for a time slept in one bed with the sister. Shortly before he was two and a half he told his mother repeatedly that a dog had bitten his "boy" (the brother's word for the penis). This he would do when she touched his penis while washing him. At that time A. was completely toilet trained. He used the big toilet, holding on to the sink for support. Being too small to reach the bowl in standing, his mother would hold his penis while he urinated, thus helping him to direct the urine into the toilet. A few days before he was two and a half he refused the mother's help stubbornly but began to ask her again to assist him after several experiences with spilling of urine on the bathroom floor. Shortly after that he was observed at a time when his two siblings and his father were away from home. Soon after his sister left, A. took her doll and brought her into the living room. He had begun to be interested in this doll and at the same time lost interest in his rag doll, when the sister used a bottle to feed her. When the bottle was lost his interest in the doll had waned. Today, even though he had taken the doll out of the sister's bed, he was busy with some "repair" activities when I arrived for my period of observation. He greeted me with a large screw driver in his hand, which he held very expertly. He was given a set of

4 A summary of A.'s behavior up to the age of eight months was presented, in cooperation with J. Friend, in a short communication "Preliminary Report on Three Infants" in the Arden House Conference, 1954.

tiny baby dolls in bunk beds, a set of hollow cubes and a doll bottle. He
became very interested in nursing the two little dolls, but concentrated
more on his sister's doll. He alternated between feeding her with the
bottle and with a hollow cube, which he probably used for a cup. He
asked me to help him with such things, as putting the nipple on the
bottle and other menial tasks he could not accomplish. But his whole
demeanor to his mother showed that he shared the doll with her. He
would get up and hand her the doll for feeding. He tried to sit next to
her and alternate with her in the nursing process. As she encouraged him
to sit next to me, he would comply, but with each feeding spurt he would
gesture and talk to his mother, showing her what he did with the doll.
Conspicuously he corrected his mother each time she referred to the doll
in feminine terms such as "she" or "her." He would turn to her intently
and would say "boy" in a tone of firmness and finality. It must be noted
that the doll was unmistakably dressed like a little girl and had braids
to boot. Nevertheless, when I asked him to show me the "boy" of the
doll, he uncertainly pointed to the navel and around the abdominal
area. When asked where the "wee-wee" came out, he was quite sure in
pointing between the legs of the doll. He did not correct me and showed
a hesitation as to the doll's sex when confronted by my question. He was
reluctant to interrupt his play when his mother called him into the
kitchen for his own meal. Nevertheless he put the doll away and began
to stuff the doll bottle into one of his pockets and two little cubes into
the other. This accomplished, he went into the kitchen where he refused
to sit down until his mother suggested that the doll would eat with him.
The doll was placed on the table in front of him. He refused to eat his
soup and fed it to the doll instead, until his mother made some eggs for
him, which he ate himself with great gusto. At times he fed the doll and
at others he asked his mother to do so.

During the earlier bottle feeding he once handed the bottle to me,
giving the impression that he thought the bottle was empty. To show
him that there was still some water in it, I spilled some water on my
hand. He proceeded to spill water out of the bottle on the doll's hands,
wiping them carefully afterwards. In an almost imperceptible transition,
he turned to sprinkling the water on the rug, making wider and more
vigorous movements and getting away from doll play. He held the doll
closely only when he bottle fed her, and the only expression of affection
for the doll was a gentle patting of the doll's shoulder which he did between feeding her the soup in the kitchen. This gesture suggested an
imitation of burping the baby.

Quite different was the behavior of P.,[5] a little girl of two and a half.
She has had already a vast experience of playing with a number of dolls.
To her, the affectionate hugging of the doll was the most important part
of the play. She would be busy with the doll's clothing, bathe it, put it
on the pottie, and lay it down to sleep, making sure that her "baby" had
silk pants in bed with her, in imitation of P.'s own transitional object.
When she was given a new big boy doll on her second birthday, she

5 Also presented in the Arden House Conference.

carried it around with her incessantly, this being the highlight of the birthday party. All these were serious activities in which she would use the mother or me to help her, where her motor skill lagged behind her maternal ambitions. When embracing her doll, however, she would look blissfully happy, press it affectionately to her "bosom" and would repeat with great conviction "my baby." When she needed a helper in the doll care, she insisted that things be done exactly to her specification. Whenever I came to visit for the observational period, she looked for a baby doll in my bag, and was keenly disappointed and almost unbelieving when I gave her another present. On testing, she excelled early in all items in which a doll was used, losing interest quickly when the doll was removed. During the second year of her life, every doll was called "baby" but this did not seem meaningful at first, as her mother introduced the dolls by that name. However, there was no mistaking of the doll's sex, a factor which was not encouraged by the mother. Every doll was clearly referred to as girl. The boy doll too was treated as a girl. About a month or two after her second birthday I had occasion to ask her about this boy doll's sex. Her reply was "girl." Some weeks later she was already aware of the fact that this doll was considered male by the environment. When asked about any doll's sex she would answer "baby." When the question was repeated she would say "baby doll" (a term she had reluctantly adopted recently, after having heard repeatedly that the object she played with was a doll. In the tone of her voice she revealed that she was making a concession to the demands of the adults).

When further pressed to specify the doll's sex, she would either ignore the matter or would repeat the last word of the question in an automatic obedience. Some months later she devised a new answer in an effort to settle the problem for good. Her reply would be "girl boy." Confronted with a real baby before she reached two, she would treat this baby very much the way she treated her dolls, stroking and hugging it, but also pinching and poking her finger in the baby's eye. When the baby would cry as a result of these doings, P. watched the child's face with the curiosity of a scientific observer. However, this real, crying baby was clearly not her own. When her doll was presented to her in the small child's presence, she smiled with exalted happiness, pressed the doll, hugging it with great affection and saying "my baby."

P., like A., was well acquainted with sex differences. Some time during her second year she had begun to pull her older brother's penis when she followed him into the bathroom. This seemed to be integrated into a phase in which she was very greedy, and in her mother's words "everything was hers." Similarly it was difficult for P. to give things away, while she wanted to grab all of her brother's toys. Yet, even in this phase, P., given a definite choice between a gun and a doll, was primarily eager to keep the doll although she wanted the gun too. By the time she was two and a half P.'s interest in her brother's toys seemed to diminish, while her play with dolls not only persisted but also became more meaningful.

When P. was a little over one year old she seemed quite worried about the face of a colored doll. Much later she was reminded of feces on seeing a colored boy, and also indicated to her mother that she did not want her to take a colored baby home. At the time of my first observation it impressed me that P. was concerned with the blackness of the doll's face because she felt that there was something wrong with her. It is very likely that anal components played a role in P.'s distress. Yet, she was able to overcome her worries about this doll toward the end of her second year, at a time when her toilet training was far from being accomplished, and way before she was able to express her equation of the dark face with feces. She was shown that the dark face can be whitened with a white crayon and she immediately proceeded in this task, switching rather quickly to smudging her white doll's feet with a pencil. From that time on, P. no longer minded the dark doll, though she was still in the middle of her anal conflicts. At two and a half she was preoccupied to some extent with cracks and "boo-boos" of different dolls. She treated such injuries with bandages and did not show undue concern over them. She wanted her mother to fix (glue together) broken things and also small items which she detached from dolls. She would, for instance, remove a bow from the head of a little doll, would demand that this be repaired, but would tear it off again as soon as the repair was done. Throughout such play she would remain placid. On seeing a paper doll which was headless and legless, P. was not alarmed. When asked where the missing parts were, she pointed happily to the empty space where they should have been. In manipulating the head, which could be put in the empty space, she pulled it and almost tore it, on finding it in an upside-down position. The "injury" which she inflicted herself frightened her. The combination of the "upside-down head" and the twisted neck was too much for her. Again, it seemed that distortions of the body image (earlier through color difference, which the child could not correct until she was taught how to do it, now through reversal of accustomed configurations) were much more disquieting to P. than injuries such as cracks or losses of limbs. Anal preoccupations as well as fears of injury played a role in P.'s experimentation with dolls. Her main interest, however, centered on efforts to preserve the baby image of her dolls. Cracks and limbs could be filled in fantasy, but distortions were too difficult to overcome, and therefore frightening.

Clearly, both children took on their mother's roles in their doll play. Both identified the dolls with themselves. Both were in a stage where turning from passivity to activity was of paramount importance. A., however, acted out a special traumatic area of feeding, while P. was universally maternal. Furthermore, to A., the bottle and the feeding cube were the significant objects in the process. The identification of the bottle with the urinating penis broke through during the nursing game. A. wanted to be in control of the mother's feeding activity, the feeding tools being of special oro-phallic significance to him. P. wanted to possess a baby as her very own. A. shared the doll feeding with the mother. He acted as if it was important to him that the child was his and his mother's, with the distributions of roles clearly indicating that A. was the director, corrector and dictator of the whole affair. He was already more of a tender father than a mother. P. wanted her dolls at all cost and would renounce masculine toys for them. She yearned to be given more and more babies, over which she wanted full control. Sharing was acceptable if necessary, and even that was tolerated for a short time only. Alongside with her possessive pride, P. used dolls a great deal to solve her own body problems. She was not a child who frightened easily, yet she would get quite upset if something in a doll's countenance would detract from her baby qualities. When she was able to control the color of the doll's skin, which worried her at first, she proceeded to equalize her babies, making one doll whiter and some other dolls darker. Loss of control over her "baby's" bodies filled her with fear. Injuries, which did not distort the baby image of the doll, she could fix with ease. Neither was she compulsive about small matters like a doll's bow. She even enjoyed such little deprivations that she herself could inflict upon the doll. Important was that the "babies" were hers and that they were girl dolls, shaped like she was herself, treated the way she wanted to be treated. They were part of her.

Castration fear and penis envy played a tangential role in doll games of both children. To A., it was important to have a boy with his mother, although he knew that the doll was supposed to be a girl. To P., it was equally important that the doll was a girl like herself, compromising under pressure for a bisexual child, but certainly not for a boy. Nelly, who has abandoned a transitional object in favor of a doll only after the birth of her brother, also insisted that her doll must be a girl. She would play with boy dolls only for very short periods, and would cling tenaciously to her girl doll. Only after she has been assured that in contrast to boys and men she had a "bottom" like mommy and all other women, did she permit her girl doll to play the role of a boy, for brief periods, in which she imitated her mother's behavior toward her brother. Before this, she would act out, on the distinctly female doll, her mother's activities on herself as well as those on her brother. She too, like P., had her doll very much on her mind. She would interrupt her play with other toys and would ask in a tone of anxious concern: "Where is Hedy?" She too made it quite clear that this baby was hers and nobody else's. She too, despite her penis envy, insisted that the doll was shaped in her image. Only when she knew that she had some kind of an organ, specifically feminine, could she unqualifiedly allow her girl doll to assume the role of a male, but only for a short time. The girl doll seemed to represent both the child herself as well as that part of her which she intuitively perceived as an organ important for her feminine identity.[6]

We recognize in the two-year-old girl's attachment to the doll not only the continuation of earlier oral and anal possessiveness, but also elements familiar to us from the behavior with transitional objects. Winnicott (1953) says that the transitional objects and phenomena belong to the

---

[6] The toy industry, which is usually quite sensitive to both permanent and transitory childhood needs, teaches us that boy dolls are items of small demand.

realm of illusion, an illusion that what the infant creates really exists. He says further: "This intermediate area of experience, unchallenged in respect of its belonging to inner or external (shared) reality, constitutes the greater part of the infant's experience and throughout life is retained in the intense experiencing that belongs to the arts and to religion and to imaginative living, and to creative scientific work." While both sexes live for some time in this world of illusion where reality and imagination flow into each other freely, the little girl singles out the illusion of motherhood as her most cherished creative experience. What Winnicott describes seems to be identical with the intuitive quality inherent in creativeness. The peculiar transition from reality to irreality in the games of the two-year-old "mother" is an all-pervasive phenomenon of her acting out of the maternal role. It is not even quite correct to call her activity a play or game. It seems more like a creation of a dramatic role, in which reality and imagination merge.

Two-year-old P., surrounded by her dolls when I arrive for my periodic visits, is very happy to let me undress and dress her dolls. She understands a role game and participates in calling different dolls by such names as are familiar to her as titles of different members of her family. She also readily consents to my pretending that some of P.'s dolls are mine. Both P. and I are sitting on the floor, each hugging a doll and saying to the respective "babies" with great affection "My baby." For a few minutes P. is enjoying herself, then she gets up, runs to her mother, vocalizing plaintively, and pointing to me with an accusing finger. She condenses her complaint in a sentence that sounds like "Lady, my baby." Suddenly she has become afraid that the play is real, and that the lady is taking one of her babies away from her.

Nelly who frequently treats her analyst like a baby demands that the analyst cry for various childish reasons. She puts the analyst to sleep, covers her, gives her candy or withholds it. But foremost she insists that the analyst should cry because some object is "not for you." In one such crying episode the analyst unwittingly begins to smile. Nelly runs to her mother and joyfully exclaims: "Dr. K. is only kidding." She does so despite my repeated statements that I was merely playing. When presented with small pipe-cleaner dolls, Nelly insists that the analyst should put pants and shoes on them. One such doll has shoes painted on her feet. Nelly demands that the analyst take them off. When I explain to her that these are toys with which we can play make-believe games, but we cannot really do them, she consents with an air of an indulgent adult, who caters to the whims of a child. At another time she puts a big doll to sleep in another room. Upon her return to the analyst she insists that she hears Daisy's crying and it does not disturb her in the least that nobody can really hear a sound. She acts the role of an intuitive mother with an extrasensory perception. When she creates the crying, it exists. When the analyst wants her to imagine shoes on the dolls, she becomes a representative of reality and doubts the existence of something she cannot see. She does not take seriously the adult's assurances that the doll is only a toy. In patting a big doll, Nelly discovers a "crying whistle" in the doll's body. She repeatedly asks what this is and gets the same answer to the effect that the man who made the doll put a whistle in, to imitate a real child's crying. Nelly listens to the explanation each time. Then she gives up asking and runs behind me, hugging me and asking me to cry (this time for no apparent reason). She presses me in the region corresponding to the same place on the doll in which she discovered the whistle. Obviously Nelly does not believe the story about the toy manufacturer. She wants to find my whistle to prove her belief in the doll's identity with a living being. Only her own imaginative creativeness becomes reality, she neither accepts the adult's make-believe nor the adult's reality when they interfere with her own magic world of pseudo reality. For her, the doll is not a toy with a whistle, but just as alive as the analyst and built the same way.

Whence does the inanimate doll get the quality of aliveness, which permeates the "play" of the two-year-old girl? The answer sometimes comes from the analyses of older girls and women.

A young woman in analysis had great difficulties in understanding female anatomy. She had been fully enlightened as a child. She has read relevant books on the subject, both in her childhood and recently. Yet she could not grasp the shape and location of the vagina, uterus and tubes. She thought of the vagina as a line rather than an organ. Throughout her associations there were sporadic references to dolls from her childhood. A vague fantasy or screen memory of her mother throwing the head of a doll out of the window and into the garden, where the patient played, appeared as the first doll reference, and was repressed during the analysis. The doll theme vanished for a long time. The completely frigid patient was busy with castration fears, dreaded injuries of her inner genital, penis envy, and with fears of her mother and her sisters. Memories of exploration of the labia had occurred much earlier. Now, however, clitoric sensations became apparent to her, though not clearly remembered from childhood. A vague awareness of deeper genital sensations followed in time. She was uncertain whether she really felt anything inside, and was most uncertain about the localization of the sensations. Experimentation with retention of feces and urine seemed to be the main source of vaginal excitation. When she began to worry that she might get a baby, the doll theme reappeared. Under some pressure she was able to recollect a great many of her childhood dolls, but she could not think of any doll she may have had at about one or two years of age. She used the recollection of one doll who had a very wide skirt for speculations about mechanisms of childbirth and pregnancy. She could not understand how a baby could come out in one piece, and was afraid that her baby would be cut up during delivery.

One of her persistent complaints in connection with dolls was a still intensely felt frustration because her mother would not let her have a doll which looked like a real baby. I had the distinct impression that she repressed the memory of an early doll which might have represented a real baby to her. Such a recollection did not appear and I abandoned my initial impression, assigning it to the realm of the "analyst's wishful thinking." After some weeks, a lucky set of circumstances uncovered a definite evidence of a "baby doll" which the patient had possessed at the age of about two. She reacted to this discovery with amazement, but could not yet remember this particular doll. But the associations which came up now were clearly connected with the phase of the patient's development in which she played with the forgotten doll. Her feelings of inadequacy in caring for a baby became adamant, and she came close to a state of panic when thinking of a possible pregnancy. At the same time her confusion about her vagina returned. She bought a children's book about female anatomy, studying the diagrams carefully. She had been irrationally preoccupied for some time with short-sleeved blouses, and it occurred to her now that the diagram of the vagina looked like a blouse, the fornix indicating the sleeves, the rest of the organ representing the main body of the blouse. The image was strikingly similar to shapes associated with the "wide skirt doll." While working out the blouse-vagina equation, the patient measured in fantasy different-size breasts. She understood then why she had been preoccupied with blouses for such a long time. She associated motherliness with large breasts and was jealous of her motherly sisters and still doubted her ability to produce an uninjured, live baby. The anticipation of caring for an infant filled her with intense anxiety. She stressed particularly that she did not want to raise a boy at this time. Her confusion about vaginal sensations and the shape and localization of the vagina reigned supreme. Oral, anal and phallic representations distorted and confused her intellectual knowledge of anatomy as well as her memory of recent experiences in which the vagina played a role. Defensively she retreated to her past "feelings" that her inside was empty, her vagina virtually nonexistent, merely a line or at best two-dimensional. The defensiveness as well as the rapid stream of confused and contradictory representations of her genital ceased when she realized that she had accumulated several images of her vagina, which, superimposed over each other, created a chameleon-like object, and forever changing and impossible to fathom.[7] She would see in the diagram of the vagina a headless and legless baby. (Compare P.'s lack of concern when she saw the headless and legless paper doll picture.) She could also see the uterus as a head of a baby or as a headless and legless child, the tubes representing the arms.[8] Superimposed images of her mother's body as well as those of her own body were related to her blouse-vagina concept. She mistook the contours of the vagina diagram as well as those of the uterus for the outside of the female body. Con-

[7] Greenacre (1948) described identical body image confusions in discussing the influence of anatomical structures upon the development of the superego.

[8] The equation of womb and baby in the unconscious has been pointed out by Jacobson (1950).

flicting with all these representations, there loomed the shape of the
penis, giving content to the empty space created by the female outside.
When she thought of the outer lines of the diagram as outlines of the
female body, it seemed that the vagina and uterus were empty shells.
When she thought of the vagina as a penis container the feeling of
emptiness left. The "inner penis" fantasy has been worked out a long
time ago, so that she did not linger on it too much now. Also, earlier
ideas of a connection between mouth and a vagina-rectum (cloaca) did
not add too much to the confusion at this time. But her dread of the
"mutilated baby" image could be linked up now with oral and anal
aggressions. The "inner penis" fantasy elicited a fear that the baby would
not have enough space for the development of its whole body. Many
of the conflicting ideas were supported by various vague vaginal sensations, which fused with anal, clitoric and urethral sensations, and therefore could not be localized. The appearance of vaginal sensations would
give her a feeling of having something inside. Disappearance of these
sensations confirmed the ideas of having nothing inside. She seemed to
feel that sensations could only come from a solid, moving, if not visible
part of the body. It took her some time to realize that the walls of the
vagina consisted of living tissue, capable of excitation. She linked up such
inner sensations, as came from the vagina, with ideas of a solid baby or a
solid penis inside, or else projected them outside when she shaped the
baby after the outer contours of the mother. Sensations associated with
"water waves" could be traced back to excitations of the anterior wall of
the vagina. When she finally understood that there was a solid interior
wall of the vagina adjoining the bladder, she still kept calling it bladder.
Fears that she would defecate during intercourse led to the realization
that the posterior wall of the vagina were separate from the rectum. She
worried how the penis could reach the fornix where she seemed to feel
a tension, expressed as a need for the penis to get in deeper. She thought
of the fornix as a bilateral excrescence, identified with the tubes and the
arms of the baby. The usual fears that the vagina was too small for the
baby was easily worked out, as she herself experienced the vaginal wall as
flexible ("can be pushed out"). Clitoric sensations seemed an easy challenge, as compared with vaginal excitations, which were scattered all
over, unclear and unlocalizable. She never was quite sure where they
were. In an effort to decide whether they were inside or outside, she
would touch her clitoris. She deduced from lack of excitement in the
clitoris, as determined by touch, that the sensations must be elsewhere.
She was keenly dissatisfied with direct explorations of the vagina, as she
could not find solid unshiftable boundaries, and could not get the image
of the vagina as a whole organ, being unable to encompass the whole
structure at once. Active experimentation would follow the passive perception of sensations, coming from different parts of the vagina as well
as from the clitoris. She was less frightened by and surer of her vaginal
contractions, which she could produce at will. Wonderment about the
motility of the vagina was worked out in connection with mechanics of
intercourse. These she associated with a contraption easily recognizable

as a spinning top, a toy from her childhood. She speculated helplessly, asking like a very small child whether the whole body of the top moved or merely the outside, with the axle remaining stationary. She worried about not being able to spin the top if it fell sideways, an idea linked up with earlier lateral shifts of the vagina image. It was conspicuous that the patient's thinking showed unmistakable characteristics of a two-year-old child's reasoning. In one session she kept using the words "vagina" and "baby" interchangeably, so that I could not understand what she was saying. When I asked her what she meant, she glossed over the confusing aspect of this condensation in the same way a two-year-old ignores the gaps betwen reality and fantasy. When she finally got to understand that there was meaning to her using these terms as if she was speaking of one and the same object, her ego functions lifted to the level of an adult, but she could no longer remember what she had said.

Only after the vaginal confusion was thus worked through, did the patient express fantasies associated with the positive and negative oedipus complex, as they related to her wish for a child. She also returned then to a preoccupation with the mechanics of defecation, dwelling for some time on the withholding-work-production factor in anal birth, which she developed along lines identical with Nelly's ideas. Withholding was linked with vaginal excitations. Much earlier she was able to recover the memory of fused clitoric-vaginal sensations which occurred during the excited jumping in her childhood. Needless to say that castration wishes and fears as well as penis envy entered into the fantasies connected with the positive and negative oedipus wishes.

A girl in prepuberty, displayed conspicuous symptoms of penis envy in her analysis. She seemed forever arrested in the negative oedipal phase, woven through with anal sadistic and genital masochistic wishes. She too showed a confusion between a vagina and a baby, in her own drawings of the inside and in her understanding of diagrams. An extremely articulate child, she called her vaginal feelings "yearnings" in contradistinction to clitoric sensations which were associated with masochistic fantasies of being raped, enslaved herself, and enslaving others. In trying to explore her vagina through the small opening the hymen allowed, she fantasied that a child is coming out, and was keenly disappointed because she could not get very far with her finger, and could not touch anything tangible inside. The unfulfilled yearning and the disappointment after the fruitless exploration would enhance her penis envy as well as her resentment of her mother, who neither satisfied the yearnings nor gave her a penis. When she reached puberty, she was able to stop clitoric masturbation, but her sadomasochistic genital fantasies were either acted out or filled her thinking to a point where effective functioning became impossible. When she understood that the new fantasies were replicas of her earlier "slave and torture" ideas, she found herself incapable of imagining them any longer. Instead painful vaginal sensations appeared for the first time. I reminded her how she used to interrupt her earlier clitoris masturbation each time when she felt that she had hurt herself. The physical part of her masturbation ran parallel to her stopping of masochistic fantasies, before the actual rape occurred. Other pain factors, which she had overcome in analysis, were connected with rashes she used to develop when she would try to stop masturbation. She scratched until her skin bled painfully, knowing that she enjoyed it. As a child, she had a habit of wetting her pants and holding her feces until she developed severe abdominal cramps. These cramps were continued into the phase of menstrual cramps. In the anal withholding as well as in the clitoris handling, excitement, pain, anxiety and relief were typical sequences which could not be adequately explained until the contribution of vaginal excitations to these processes became apparent. She had associated feces with inner little people, her slaves, and this had led to links with anal birth and anal penis ideas. Only when she found that she could not continue her sadomasochistic daydreams any longer no matter how hard she tried, she found that instead of these fantasies there appeared unpleasant burning sensations in her vagina. She had no control over their coming and going, but the sequence of excitement, pain, fear and temporary relief remained. She was glad to cooperate to the utmost hoping to get rid of the uncontrollable feelings. She associated the burning with the pain of delivery. She wanted to stop the sensation before an injury would occur, while at the same time she could not wait to get the baby, she needed it so badly. Delivery would stop unbearable inner sensations, yet feelings of loss, injury (her vagina falling to pieces) and let down were associated with continuing the sensation to the peak of delivery (equation of genital discharge with child delivery). A similar set of fantasies interfered with the older patient's ability for orgastic discharge. To her, excitement was life; the end of excitement was death. Projection of the life-giving vaginal sensations to the outside, to an already delivered baby, circumvented the feeling of vaginal loss and injury. That kind of solution was only temporarily successful in the life of the younger patient, when she had revived doll play shortly before the onset of her menstruation. She gave the new doll complete bodily care and fantasied that her boy friend was the doll's father. Only when playing with dolls became unacceptable as too unreal, was she able to express the connection between vaginal sensations and her need for a baby. After the baby-doll experience, turning to penis envy and urgent but passive wishes toward her father could be seen. They were followed by a relapse to phallic, sadomasochistic wishes toward her mother, the analysis of which revealed the underlying unbearable tensions, which she wanted to eject into the form of a baby.

Helene Deutsch (1945) recognized the importance of organ lack in the development of the girl. Both observation and analyses seem to indicate that the girl's first substitute, created to compensate for the organ lack, is a baby. Vaginal tensions appear to urge the girl on in her need for an organ of discharge. The difficulty in localization as well as the enigmatic quality and multilocality of fleeting vaginal sensations create a confusion in the young girl, which she tries to solve in two ways. In one type of solution she fuses vaginal tensions with others coming from the inside of her body and projects their common bulk to orifices with which she has become familiar, such as mouth, anus and the urethral orifice, neighboring the clitoris.[9] Fusion is facilitated by the simultaneous occurrence of various sensations. The second solution appears to be a projection to solid outer objects, at first to a child (via the anal-genital baby route), and then to a penis. The latter projection, normally regresses to the earlier child wish via the substitution of the penis by a child. Fusions and projections do not give permanent relief and are therefore abandoned over and over again, throughout the girl's development, thus creating a psychological readiness for the adult cycles in maturity.

Externalization of inner sensations is reiterated in the cathecting of bodily orifices, in the attachment to transitional objects, and in the girl's creation of her very own "fetish," her doll baby. The image of that baby is molded after the child's own body as well as after that of the mother. The vagueness of early vaginal sensations and the lack of differentiation of vaginal and sphincter contractions create a fertile atmosphere for the development of intuition, rather than knowledge, about the existence of a female inner organ.[10] This intuitive quality is projected, alongside with the vague tensions, onto the relationship of the little girl with her baby doll. In a period in which turning of passivity into activity predominates, the little girl has a strong need for mastery which she can achieve in relation to her doll, while discharge on and mastery of the inner genital is not feasible.[11] Where the environment does not furnish a doll, siblings and the mother herself are used for the same purpose as the doll. Fantasies about making the mother small like a baby belong to this period (Deutsch, 1933; A. Freud, 1949). Children, who do play with dolls, alternately use people and dolls for the achievement of mastery. The intuitive quality of the early doll play is reinforced by the girl's identification with her own intuitive mother.

Where clearly localized vaginal sensations, introduction of foreign bodies into the vagina, and even orgastic masturbation in the vagina,

[9] Another projective connection is that to the nose, a connection referred to by Freud in his early writings.

[10] Greenacre (1948) described an intuitive knowledge of the vagina. In what measure the phylogenetically determined "unconscious knowledge" (Klein) or rather, readiness for knowledge, contributes to intuition is difficult to say on the basis of clinical observation. The universality of such symbols as jewel boxes makes us inclined to believe that there is a readiness in the depth of the unconscious to accept the hollow quality of the female genital.

[11] Exceptions reported in literature will be discussed later.

have been reported as experiences of childhood, the published clinical
material (Müller, 1932; Hann-Kende, 1933; Eissler, 1939; Kramer, 1954)
does not lend itself to an evaluation of motherliness in such deviant
development.[12] A reverse relationship between vaginal sensitivity and
maternal needs in adult women has been clearly elucidated by Helene
Deutsch. Adult vaginal satisfaction in coitus and masturbation brings
relief of sexual tension, but does not allow for active mastery of the
organ.[13] The girl has to yield the exploring, fear-conquering activity on
her vagina to the man. This she normally does in her role as the receptive, passive partner in intercourse, as well as in her role as a dependent
of her husband. The active manipulation and mastery of her infant substitute for her inability to develop a clear image of her inner genital.
Following Freud's concept of motherhood as an active occupation, Wittels (1933) suggested that motherhood was in part a sublimation of
masculinity. Undoubtedly the wish for masculinity is operative in the
desire to have a child.[14] Underlying the wish for masculinity is the more
fundamental urge to respond with active motor discharge to sensory
stimuli. In the ego, this biological urge is represented in the wish to
experiment actively with organ boundaries and organ qualities, crowned
by the achievement of a secure body image. In terms of object relationship, the same sphere of interest is expressed in the small child's eagerness to show his discoveries to his mother, and to exhibit proudly not
only what he or she had, but also what he has achieved.[15]

The Passing of the Early Maternal Stage

Just as the real mother has to accept the giving up of her infant
because he grows into a child, and countless times before had to renounce
a hoped-for pregnancy with each return of menstruation, the illusory
little mother goes through similar experiences. Various episodes in which
the unreality of the doll baby becomes apparent contribute to the girl's

[12] In Kramer's cases (1954) there is some indication that neurosis broke out in
connection with childbearing.

[13] For the most lucid discussion of the masculinity-activity versus femininity-
passivity see Nunberg (1949). For a consideration of organ activity see also Kestenberg
(1956).

[14] Bonaparte (1935) thought that the apparatus of maternity exercises an inhibiting
influence upon the virility of the female organism. She considered female genital
pleasures to be virile and stressed the feminine-masochistic aspects of pregnancy and
delivery. Still she kept in mind the activity involved in baby care.

[15] Ferenczi (1919) illustrated this theme beautifully in his description of Cornelia,
mother of the Gracchi, who felt the need to exhibit her children, saying: "These are
my treasures, there are my jewels."

growing understanding that she is merely playing with a doll and has no baby. Sometime during the third year, traumatic incidences of doll mutilations are linked with ideas of the baby's death. In a way, with the "death of the doll,"[16] the world of unreality and magic creativity seems to die too. The girl may now pass through a phase of dull obedience and lack of productivity. Depressions varying from brief let-downs to prolonged periods of depressive inhibition occur now.[17] With the devaluation of the doll, the little girl's inside becomes devaluated too. She withdraws from the doll as well as from her mother, who neither gave her genital satisfaction nor a substitute for it, a real child. The "major withdrawal and shift of cathexis from the object to the self-representations" (Jacobson, 1954) leads her to transitory "inactivity or general inhibition of the ego activity." After the recovery from this depressive phase, in which the loss of the baby was equated with the loss of the mother, the little girl returns to her mother as a love object in the new phase of phallic orientation.

It is important to consider the role of aggressive impulses and actions in the behavior of the "little mother," because they have a decisive influence upon the form and length of her prephallic depressions. Needless to say, that unresolved oral and anal sadistic problems enhance a more regressive form of depression. In her maternal behavior, the little girl acts out on the doll her aggressions against the mother, as well as the hostility which her mother inflicts upon herself. Parallel to these phenomena which belong to the realm of object relationships, there goes on in the girl a latent battle between herself and those parts of her body which disturb her equilibrium through increase of tensions. Deep-seated autotomic impulses to destroy the sources of unbearable itching, swell-

[16] Compare Stevenson's warm account (1954) of the death and funeral of Goggles, seven-year-old Janet's shapeless wooden doll. In my experience, such an incident during the latency period usually functions as a screen for much earlier doll events which occurred during a less realistic phase of development.

[17] The depression ending the early maternal stage requires further exploration. The greater proneness to depression in women, as compared with men, has been noted long ago (see Lewin [1950] and the literature cited in his book). The precipitating factors of such depressions are frequently severe labors or deliveries, but, paradoxically, easy deliveries as well. It may not be necessary to evoke the thesis of increased feminine orality (Gerö, 1939) in all such cases. Depression, connected with childbearing and related functions may turn out to have a history of a traumatic ending of the early maternal stage of development. The resulting early depression may have been very severe in such cases, not necessarily because of an orally determined predisposition, but also because of the individual circumstances operating in this phase, which could have enhanced an oral regression. A loss of the baby would be anticipated in such cases, and the trauma of the early maternal stage repeated, regardless of the reality of a good delivery of a healthy baby.

ing, yearning, are associated with fears of bodily harm, which the small child gleefully projects upon the mother and her doll.

Nelly, whose bodily excitations made it difficult for her to fall asleep and once asleep to maintain sleep, accused her mother of waking her when she got out of bed or screamed for someone to come to her at night. She scolded her doll severely for screaming, and threatened to take her to the analyst if her bad behavior would not stop. Other children, who are freer in expressing their aggression and who show more intense oral and anal sadism, sometimes attack a doll with a fury very similar to the rage expressed by a depressive adult patient who fantasied pulling out her excited vagina and losing it in the bloody menstrual discharge. She hoped that such a loss by self-inflicted injury (which she also dreaded) would rid her of undischargeable sexual tensions forever. She acted out this fantasy by repeatedly losing her pocketbook. While in other phases of her analysis she wanted to be a boy who could get rid of sexual tensions on his penis, in the moments of greatest excitement and rage she wished for aphanisis (Jones, 1927) rather than for a penis. The young woman, described earlier, remembered biting one of her early dolls. In her fears of delivery, the image of mutilation of the baby in the birth process was linked to memories of injuries inflicted by herself upon various dolls and to fantasies of her mother who threw the doll's head out of the window "and would take away her baby" once it were safely delivered.

Spitz (1949) described a typical group of depressed mothers whose children developed coprophilic tendencies. They presented a picture of the self-sacrificing, self-debasing mother who envelops her child with love. Their worries about their infants expressed themselves in anxious questioning whether the baby was blind or deaf. The incidence of injury of the children at the hands of their mothers was great. Such a maternal behavior is identical with the play behavior of the "little mother who loves her doll to death" and examines it anxiously, worrying about any little defect.

Nelly, for instance, playing with tiny dolls, asked the analyst compulsively what the side seam on the doll was. She was sure it was an injury. On seeing a microscopic protuberance on the doll's foot, she asked anxiously who pulled it out. She refused to let anyone play with one of the little dolls who had a small hole in the foot. She ruminated about the question who had broken the doll and how it was done. She wondered whether she might have crashed it with her foot, as she remembered stepping carelessly over a number of small toys lying on the floor and breaking some in the process. P. dropped her dolls suddenly, and used to stick her finger in the doll's eye, although she had a faint awareness that such an act hurts people and can lead to a disfigurement of some dolls. One must not forget, in this context that not every care-less action of the "little mother" is due to an aggressive impulse. Much of it is a result of the two-year-old girl's lack of skill, her poor sense of reality and her sudden shifting of cathexis with which she reacts to new pleasurable stimuli. A feeling of being a little child, incapable of handling a real baby, might have contributed to a repetition of early lack of skill, in the behavior of Spitz's depressive mothers. Such a self-evaluation is typical of infantile mothers, who have to be helped in every step of child care. A transitory feeling of her own lack of qualification for infant care, confronts every new mother who grows up in our culture.

FURTHER DEVELOPMENTS OF THE WISH FOR THE BABY

Except in cases of very early intense penis envy, the girl in the phallic phase not only explores her outer genital but also masturbates. She continues her interest in her genital, which had started sometimes during the first year when she discovered it manually. Now she frequently succeeds in getting a visual experience by bending down and looking between her legs. In the course of her handling of her genital, she experiments not only with the shape and consistency of all parts but also tries out different movements which in turn produce different sensations. Just as the boy is worried about a possible self-injury, she too at that time develops castration fears in connection with present and past scratches and hurts. In her first genital strivings she had passive aims[18] and often expressed the wish to be handled by her mother in her genital region.

Soon the clitoris is singled out as a more sensitive and distinct organ which conveys the qualities of aliveness she had lost earlier in the discovery of the inanimateness of the doll. Frequent complaints about the flabby consistency and the undefined borders of the rest of the genital highlight the clitoris as a very special organ, which the girl hopes to enlarge by various manipulations. Fantasies about growing a penis (illusory penis [Rado, 1933]) seem to alternate with hopes to grow a baby externally. At the height of the phallic phase the girl cathects the clitoris in the sense of an active masculine organ. She develops a sense of organ belonging. Because this organ gives her a great deal of satisfaction she feels that it might satisfy her mother too. Both the baby and the penis which she wants to develop there are meant to be presented to her mother now. But the baby idea is mostly condensed with the penis representation, as the penis itself is valued as a baby-making organ. A frequent speculation of this time concerns impregnation with a penis which,

---

[18] Compare here the early passive strivings of the boy (Loewenstein, 1935).

deposited in a mother, transforms into a baby. This in turn leads to ideas of multiple penises, as many as necessary to produce a lot of babies. Such thoughts are also used for consolation about the smallness of the clitoris, which "was big once and will grow back to make another baby." The girl eventually gives up her mother attachment and this libidinous zone because of her disappointment in the zone itself and in the mother who failed to give her an organ more suitable for satisfaction and baby making. Many a time the clitoris is only given up as an organ of satisfaction for the mother and remains active in connection with fantasies directed toward the father.

During the play with the outer genital, the child is able to discharge a great many vaginal tensions, as the clitoris seems to draw from all genital zones. On the other hand, the handling of the clitoris, labia and the introitus region stimulates the vagina much more than the earlier pregenital activities. Both the discovery of the introitus and the increase of vaginal stimulation connected with its explorations contribute to the now ensuing denial of the introitus and vagina. The girl, who had become bolder and had come closer to the vagina in her explorations, now withdraws and goes further and further away from it. She will either retreat swiftly to the clitoris or else remain only active on the periphery of the labia and the skin around the genital. Her castration fears are denied along with the denial of the hole she has discovered on the genital. In her play with dolls, she may now act out her fears of injury. Pregenital fantasies contribute to her playing that the doll is being wet, soiled, stamped and torn. In this play, the doll represents the girl herself as well as her mother and father, but also her own genital. The preoccupation with castration fears occupies the child so much that the baby wish, latent in the early phallic phase, recedes more and more.

The long identification with the father prepares a fertile ground for the development of a positive relationship to him. When the girl hopes for genital gratification by the father, her castration fears transform into castration wishes. The desire for the child is revived, as it substitutes for the missing penis and is considered a gift indicating the father's love for the girl. The fantasy of an incorporated penis[19] has succeeded the idea that a penis will grow on the outside. This thought of vaginal ingestion of the penis, and the masochistic desire to be injured and penetrated, lead to a recathexis of the inside of the body. If the girl has stopped masturbation she has no discharge channels for external and internal

19 Edith Jacobson (1937) recognized this fantasy as favorable for the development of femininity, as she found that it paved the way for the acceptance of an inner genital organ.

excitations. She may revive the early doll play with added features, which indicate that the baby of this period is identified with a penis. Toward the end of the oedipal phase and carried through into latency, the games with dolls are used to express oedipal wishes. Princess dolls are in vogue now. The girls play out fairy stories of princesses who, first persecuted by a mother figure, eventually marry the king, get children and live happily ever after.

In this last phase the girl may come closest to an awareness of vaginal sensations. When resolution of oedipal wishes prompts the girl to postpone her hope for marriage and children, she can express her wish for a baby with greater ease than her wish for sexual gratification. The baby image, and with it the doll play, has become desexualized. Preoccupation with dolls' clothes substitutes for the earlier baby care games. Costume dolls, sewing of doll's dresses come into the foreground. As the girl grew, her child-doll has grown with her. Revivals of earlier forms of play occur both in latency and prepuberty, even in adolescence.[20] The form the play takes in each individual instance reveals the phase that is being relived. Age-adequate modifications as acting out with puppets, marionettes, and costume dolls, contribute to such extensions of doll play. In each successive phase the girl acts on her doll what she wishes would happen to her. But she identifies herself with a mother of a growing child too. The doll is still used to express and act out genital wishes which the girl herself is unable to admit and experience. The projection of genital tensions and genital wish fulfillment upon the doll continue. We can see here the similarity to the mother of a growing girl, who eventually has to give up her youthful sexual aspirations and tends to relive sexual gratification by identification with her daughter (Freud, 1913). She not only shares the daughter's gratifications, but also projects upon the girl her own forbidden or repressed sexual wishes. Where parents expect their children to fulfill their thwarted ambitions, the behavior of the father can be identical with that of the mother. But the boy neither experiences as intense a yearning for a child as the girl does, nor does the father involve himself with his children to the extent a mother does.

[20] I was once able to witness group doll play in a residential school. Children in latency, prepuberty and puberty participated. Each child maneuvered a doll, spoke for her and dressed her according to her own taste. In an atmosphere of giggling initiated by the somewhat embarrassed older girls, they all enacted dressing for a ball and dancing there. The end of the game was crowned by a ceremony in which the king chose the fairest for his bride. Other dolls ended up with sweethearts of lesser rank, one (interpreted by the youngest child) married a cowboy.

The Boy's Wish for a Baby

In the transitional object, common to both sexes, we have seen the early model for a child.[21] In the anal phase, the boy also tends to identify his feces with a child. At the end of the anal phase passive and active phallic strivings conflict with each other (Loewenstein, 1935). The boy wishes to have a baby with his mother in identification with her, and he varies his fantasies from wanting to get a baby from the mother, sharing one with her and finally giving her one. He identifies the child with a penis. He hopes to take his father's place, he wishes to have a larger penis than he has now, and also would like to give his mother bigger and better children. A small baby does not become too meaningful to him, neither does the female child. The wish to keep the child to himself has its roots in anal retention, but it occurs in the phallic period also when the child-penis is hoped to become the extension of the boy's own genital. These ideas are side issues of the phallic development and gain importance only in pathological cases. Yet, they contribute in a great measure to a father's feeling that his son is an extension of himself.

In the passive oedipal phase, the identification with the mother as well as wishes to be penetrated by the father contribute to the renewal of the wish for a child (Freud, 1923). Anal birth and oral impregnation theories are regressively revived at that time. From analyses of men who suffer from a strong identification with their mothers, we can learn about two distinct types of wishes for a baby in a feminine way. (1) The man who identifies himself with the phallic mother repeats the mother-child relationship when he chooses a person to represent himself while he takes on the role of a mother. He rarely wants a child as a result of this union, since the relationship in itself is satisfactory enough as long as it lasts. But he will choose people who can stand for a boy child for his love objects. (2) Later identification with the mother which occurs during the negative oedipal phase is, to my knowledge, always preceded by a turbulent anal phase. The psychological content is expressed by passive desires toward the father and uterus envy of the mother. The physical

21 It is interesting to note that in the boy a continuation of transitory phenomena into adulthood leads to fetishism (Wulff, 1946; Greenacre, 1953, 1955). In the girl, such a continuation sometimes develops into a tendency to use her child like a fetish. Some such women need the presence of the child for sexual stimulation, although they are rarely conscious of the connection. They use various rationalizations to have the child sleep in one bed with the parents and, also by other means, continuously involve it in their sex relations. A mild variation of this fetishistic attitude is displayed by "saintly" women who consider intercourse, removed from the anticipation of a child, a sin.

sensations which underlie the fantasy stem from abdominal tensions and anal sensations. Confusion and helplessness analogous to that of women confronted with vaginal sensations is related here to abdominal pain and distension, cramps, burps and countless other unfathomed sensations. There is a difficulty in turning from passivity to activity. (Activity in normal development produces a shift of cathexis from abdominal and anal zones to the penis.) Instead of displacement onto the genitals, we see in such cases primitive fusions of genital and anal sensations. Erections are tied up with sphincter contractions, and anal sensations become one with those of the penis.

In the case of a patient of this type, periodic acting out of delivery during analytic sessions brought about extreme passivity, relaxation to the point of sleep and incoherent talk. During these episodes the penis was erected. Only bits of the incoherent, later repressed associations would betray abdominal sensations, wishes to be penetrated, and disguised hopes to deliver a baby safely. On one hand, the erection of the penis served as a signal that all this was only a game; on the other hand, the penis represented the child who came out uninjured and in one piece. At the end of the delivery game, the patient would jump up, practically sit up on the couch and would suddenly be able to act his usual masculine self. The erection would go down as soon as the sleepy period would end. The penis was used here as an accumulator, condensor and reactor for abdominal and anal sensations; it also represented a child. Early in the analysis before the development of these sleep attacks, this patient brought his analyst a toy figure which was given to him by his mother. The statue was a symbolic representation of a little boy and was called by a nickname which was also used for the patient, hence an object equivalent to a doll.

The development of the wish for a baby in boys is similar to that of girls, inasmuch as in boys there also occur identification with the mother, reversal of roles, the wish to get a baby from the mother and, later from the father, and the wish to give a baby to the mother. It seems also that abdominal sensations, when unbearable, call for externalization and may be projected onto a doll or doll-like object in boys too. The dominance of the phallus, which is apparent already in infancy, influences the viccissitudes of the anal phase, so that toward the end of this period phallic needs predominate over any tendencies to have a child. (A.'s play behavior with dolls seems to be typical of that stage.) Successful shifts of undischarged abdominal tensions bring about a parallel shift from the anal to the penis baby. Experimentations with the enlargement of the penis, erections and relaxations of this organ, are used for the mastery of genital as well as of abdominal-anal excitement. Disappointments in the size and performance of the penis bring about a defusion of genital and anal components with a tendency to revive the wish for a baby. The active phallic boy scorns doll play, but he accepts children again in his role as a father who gives presents to his wife. A boy-child fills earlier needs for the extension of the penis, for a reserve penis and for the revival of the father. The girl-child seems more of a successor to the anal baby and a reincarnation of the mother. In normal development, the predominance of phallic interests combines with cultural influences to create an estrangement of the growing boy from babies and dolls.

The Influence of Tradition and Culture on the Choice of Baby Substitutes in Children's Play

In discussing the concept of doll-child = vagina in early childhood, Benedek (1952) emphasized the girl's identification with her pregnant mother and questioned the emphasis on dolls, as developed in my previous paper on female sexuality. Why children chose particular toys such as dolls to act out their libidinous problems, seemed to me a question well worth an investigation.

I am indebted to my husband for the suggestion that dolls of today may be descendants of idols, the formidable inanimate representations of parental figures. Many data from the spheres of language development, anthropology and fairy tales, tend to confirm this idea. For example, the word "doll," according to one theory of language development, is derived from the word "idol" (Daiken, 1953). The symbol of a child is traced from the symbol of a parent. In traditions and superstitions of many people, the female child appears to be a reincarnation of the grandmother, while the male child is taken for a reincarnation of the father. We are reminded here of unconscious fantasies which play a role in the early development of the wish for a baby in both sexes. ("When I grow big and you grow small.") In one primitive society, after a festival in which gods have been celebrated, the children are given the divine images to play with.[22] In this aftermath of a ceremonial, we possibly encounter a condensed repetition of prehistory. Parents, through tradition and language, encourage the small child's belief that the doll is a baby. Thus, in the doll custom of today we may find the condensation of old theories of reincarnation of ancestors through the equations ancestor = child, ancestor = stone, child = doll. The mother, who calls her little girl's doll a baby, is not the deceiver; the child believes her to be when she begins to appreciate the inanimate quality of the doll. In the lan-

---

[22] Communication by Dr. Margaret Mead.

guage of the primary process, in the unconscious, the doll apparently is a child. How ingrained the doll-baby equation used to be in our language can be shown from the following examples taken from Daiken's book *Children's Toys Throughout the Ages* (1953). Until 1850 the word "dollhouse" was not used in England. The then existing term was "baby-house." The dictionaries of that time defined a doll as a "child's baby," although some began to be more realistic and called the doll a "girl's toy baby." (Compare P.'s transition from calling her doll a "baby" to "baby doll.")

An alternate theory about the derivation of the word "doll" connects the doll with femininity. It has been thought that "doll" was derived from the name "Dolly." The doll as symbol of femininity also appears in the Japanese doll festival. The girls' festival is celebrated by a display of dolls, the boys' festival is distinguished by waving phallic symbols in the form of kites depicting fishes. Thus the boy's sex is defined by the phallus, while the girl's sex is defined by a doll. The size of the kite flown during the boy's festival is directed by the size of the child to be celebrated in the household. The fish kite seems to stand for the whole male child as well as for the phallus. By analogy, the doll probably represents the female child as well as the female genital.[23]

The theme of inanimateness of the stone image, as contrasted with the alive qualities of real babies, is preserved in such fairy tales as the one about the wolf who stole and ate the babies of the goat. The mother rescued her live children by cutting the wolf's belly open, and replaced the babies with stones.[24] An identical theme appears in the custom of primitive shaman, who in imitation of delivery, retire into the woods where they are supposed to deliver stones (Mead, 1949). The absence of the inner genital in the male shaman prevents the delivery of live babies. Similarly, the inner genital of the little girl, which is not ready to deliver a live baby, psychologically appears inanimate, empty, dead, stonelike. In folklore, an intercourse in which the woman is frigid, is said to be incompatible with conception. The presumably lifeless, stone

[23] Freud (1917) was of the opinion that a "child" (*Kleines* = "little one") symbolically represents the genital, male or female. He also pointed out that raw material, such as wood, is a symbol of femininity, and objects made out of raw material, such as a wooden table, are also feminine. Primitive images are made of stone or wood. Thus, the inanimate wooden doll symbolically may stand for a child, for the genital and for femininity.

[24] Klein believes that in the pebble play of toddlers, the little stones represent babies (personal communication). "Jacks" which are used in a typical girl's game of skill (Kestenberg, 1956) are successors of Jack-stones. Primitive jacks were small stones, the modern jack is made out of metal.

cold vagina of a child, when externalized, can be only transformed into an inanimate baby, not a live one.

The masculinization of the inner genital, which develops in the late phallic stage, gives the little girl new hope for a real, live, now male baby. In Bali, where the phallus is overcathected, little girls carry cucumbers in the same position their mothers carry the babies.[25] In a society like the Sioux (described by Erikson, 1950) where the relationship of a mother to her infant takes preference over her relation to her husband and great value is placed upon the preservation of the hymen (the guardian of the vagina) before marriage, little girls are given dolls to play with. Thus, the baby substitutes may differ from culture to culture. The environment may encourage the prolongation of one developmental phase and diminish the impact of another. Accordingly, the baby substitutes with which the children play will differ.

Conclusions

The question of vaginal sensations in early childhood is still controversial. The average little girl seems to fuse her vaginal excitations with sensations stemming from other zones.[26] In addition, she projects vaginal tensions to the outside of her body. Unable to experience a direct vaginal discharge and unable to master vaginal excitations by active exploration, she tends to externalize her wish for mastery. In the baby-doll she finds a suitable substitute for the lack of an organ of discharge. Where the aforementioned mechanisms break down, denial sets in. Where vaginal sensations threaten to invade consciousness, repressive forces may be set in operation, which can be lifted during analyses. At the end of phallic development during which the baby-wish has become attached to the penis-wish, the inside of the female child is recathected, as the girl wishes to be penetrated and hopes to receive a baby.

These vaginal desires undergo further repression at the time the girl abandons her oedipal wishes and enters the latency period. This seems to be the average development, while cases in which vaginal sensations became fully conscious in childhood appear to be few and exceptional. Various fusions, projections and externalizations of early vaginal

25 Personal communication by Dr. Margaret Mead.

26 Simultaneous excitations can extinguish one another depending on the dominance of the stimulated zone (Linn, 1955). Since the vagina hardly ever is cathected as an organ or libidinous zone before the experience of intercourse, it cannot function as a dominant zone of the body scheme earlier than that. It is not surprising that reports of vaginal sensations in childhood are rare. The absence of sensations, however, does not disprove the existence of excitations.

excitations seem to contribute to the changing image of the girl's inside, which is later used for the development of the image of the vagina as an organ. Successive oral, anal, baby and phallic representations eventually merge with the final, more realistic image of the vagina. Each of these developmentally fixed representations can contribute its useful share to the various functions of the adult woman in her role as a mother. The oral representation, modeled after the primal cavity (Spitz, 1955), can foster the vaginal incorporation wish, so necessary for the initiation of pregnancy. The anal image can contribute to the retentive aspects of pregnancy. Both the anal and urethral images may serve as a model for the expelling in delivery. The baby image seems to enhance the mother's need to take care of her infant. The early female-baby concept coupled with the later penis-baby image make it possible for a mother to accept female and male children. Clitoric representations and fantasies may underlie the maternal concern with the steady growth of her small child. The many times in which the girl gives up her hope for a baby during her early development may well prepare her not only for the cycles of her adulthood, but also for the time when she eventually has to give up her children, so that they may form intimate relationships with others.

The more the wish for the baby is based on the underlying desire to master the genital as an organ, the more desexualized are the maternal functions. If there is a predominance of a need for discharge of vaginal tensions over the wish for mastery, the child is primarily used for discharge purposes and treated like a sex object. If it is true that the unfulfilled need to discharge and master early vaginal tensions creates the typically feminine wish for a child, the hymen, specific only to the human species, may prove to be the necessary prerequisite for the acceptance of children and thus a safeguard for the preservation of the race. Possibly with the development of the anterior extremities into prehensile organs, the vagina became more accessible to exploration so that a new protective device was needed to prevent premature sexual involvement. Undischarged vaginal tensions may serve as the biological vector of motherhood, substituting for the animal instinct. The intuitive "knowledge" of the vagina, derived from the unclear, shifting, projected vaginal tensions, may be the source of the mysterious maternal quality called intuition. The yearning of women for children of both sexes as the ultimate fulfillment seems to be due to a long preparation for that kind of satisfaction. Children gratify the mother's desire for a reunion with her parents, and for the perpetuation of the parent-child relationship. A child also represents an ideal solution for the problems arising from the inaccessibility and enigmatic quality of the inner genital.

290 JUDITH S. KESTENBERG

BIBLIOGRAPHY

Benedek, T. (1952), *Psychosexual Functions in Women*. New York: Ronald Press.
Bonaparte, M. (1935), Passivity, Masochism and Frigidity. *Int. J. Psa.*, XVI.
—— (1953), *Female Sexuality*. New York: International Universities Press.
*Brierley, M. (1932), Some Problems of Integration in Women. *Int. J. Psa.*, XIII.
—— (1936), Specific Determinants in Feminine Development. *Int. J. Psa.*, XVII.
Daiken, L. (1953), *Children's Toys Throughout the Ages*, New York: F. A. Praeger.
Deutsch, H. (1933), Homosexuality in Women. *Int. J. Psa.*, XIV.
—— (1944-1945), *The Psychology of Women*, 2 Vols. New York: Grune & Stratton.
Eissler, K. R. (1939), On Certain Problems of Female Sexual Development. *Psa. Quart.*, VIII.
Erikson, E. H. (1950), *Childhood and Society*. New York: Norton.
Fenichel, O. (1934), Further Light upon the Pre-Oedipal Phase in Girls. *Collected Papers*, I. New York: Norton, 1953.
Ferenczi, S. (1919), Cornelia, the Mother of the Gracchi. *Further Contributions to the Theory and Technique of Psycho-Analysis*. London: Hogarth Press, 1950.
Freud, A. (1949), Über bestimmte Schwierigkeiten zwischen Eltern und Kindern in der Vorpubertät. In: *Die Psychohygiene*, ed. M. Amande-Pfister. Bern: Hans Huber.
Freud, S. (1905), Three Essays on the Theory of Sexuality. *Standard Edition*, VII. London: Hogarth Press, 1953.
—— (1910), *Leonardo da Vinci: A Psychosexual Study of Infantile Reminiscence*. New York: Moffart Yard, 1916.
—— (1913), The Horror of Incest. *Totem and Taboo*. New York: Norton, 1952.
—— (1917), *A General Introduction to Psychoanalysis*. New York: Liveright, 1935.
—— (1919), "A Child Is Being Beaten." *Collected Papers*, II. London: Hogarth Press, 1924.
—— (1923), A Neurosis of Demoniacal Possession in the Seventeenth Century. *Collected Papers*, IV. London: Hogarth Press, 1925.
—— (1925), Some Psychological Consequences of the Anatomical Distinction between the Sexes. *Collected Papers*, V. London: Hogarth Press, 1950.
—— (1931), Female Sexuality. *Collected Papers*, V. London: Hogarth Press, 1950.
—— (1932), *New Introductory Lectures on Psychoanalysis*. New York: Norton, 1933.
Gero, G. (1939), Zum Problem der oralen Fixierung. *Int. Ztschr. Psa. & Imago*, XXIV.
Grenacre, P. (1948), Anatomical Structure and Superego Development. *Am. J. Orthopsychiat.*, XIII.
—— (1950), Special Problems of Female Sexual Development. *This Annual*, V.
—— (1952), Pregenital Patterning. *Int. J. Psa.*, XXXIII.
—— (1953), Certain Relationships between Fetishism and the Faulty Development of the Body Image. *This Annual*, VIII.
—— (1955), Further Considerations regarding Fetishism. *This Annual*, X.
Hann-Kende, F. (1933), Über Klitorisonanie und Penisneid. *Int. Ztschr. Psa.*, XIX.
Hartmann, H.; Kris, E.; Loewenstein, R. M. (1946), Comments on the Formation of Psychic Structure. *This Annual*, II.
Hitschmann, E. and Bergler, E. (1936), *Frigidity in Women*. New York: Nervous and Mental Disease Publ. Co.
Horney, K. (1926), The Flight from Womanhood. *Int. J. Psa.*, VII.
—— (1932), The Dread of Woman. *Int. J. Psa.*, XIII.
—— (1933), The Denial of the Vagina. *Int. J. Psa.*, XIV.
Jacobson, E. (1936), Die Entwicklung des weiblichen Kindeswunsches. *Int. Ztschr. Psa.*, XXI.

* I am also indebted to Dr. Brierley for her personal communications.

——— (1937), Wege der weiblichen Überichbildung. *Int. Ztschr. Psa.*, XXII.
——— (1950), Development of the Wish for a Child in Boys. *This Annual*, V.
——— (1954), The Self and the Object World. *This Annual*, IX.
Jones, E. (1927), The Early Development of Female Sexuality. *Int. J. Psa.*, VIII.
——— (1933), The Phallic Phase. *Int. J. Psa.*, XIV.
——— (1935), Über die Frühstadien der weiblichen Sexualentwicklung. *Int. Ztschr. Psa.*, XXI.
Kestenberg, J. S. (1956), Vicissitudes of Female Sexuality. *J. Am. Psa. Assoc.*, IV.
Klein, M. (1932), *The Psycho-Analysis of Children.* London: Hogarth Press.
Kramer, P. (1954), Early Capacity for Orgastic Discharge and Character Formation. *This Annual*, IX.
Lampl-de Groot, J. (1928), The Evolution of the Oedipus Complex in Women. *Int. J. Psa.*, IX.
——— (1933), Problems of Femininity. *Psa. Quart.*, II.
Lewin, B. D. (1950), *The Psychoanalysis of Elation.* New York: Norton.
Linn, L. (1955), Some Developmental Aspects of the Body Image. *Int. J. Psa.*, XXXVI.
Lorand, S. (1939), Contribution to the Problem of Vaginal Orgasm. *Clinical Studies in Psychoanalysis.* New York: International Universities Press, 1950.
Loewenstein, R. M. (1935), Phallic Passivity in Men. *Int. J. Psa.*, XVI.
Mack Brunswick, R. (1940), The Preoedipal Phase of Libido Development. *Psa. Quart.*, IX.
Mead, M. (1949), *Male and Female.* New York: William Morrow.
Müller, J. (1932), A Contribution to the Problem of Libidinal Development of the Genital Phase in Girls. *Int. J. Psa.*, XIII.
Nunberg, H. (1949), *Problems of Bisexuality as Reflected in Circumcision.* London: Imago Publishing Co.
Payne, S. (1935), A Conception of Femininity. *Brit. J. Med. Psychol.*, XV.
Rado, S. (1933), Fear of Castration in Women. *Psa. Quart.*, II.
Riviere, J. (1934), Review of *New Introductory Lectures on Psychoanalysis. Int. J. Psa.*, XV.
Spitz, R. A. (1949), Autoerotism. *This Annual*, III/IV.
——— (1955), The Primal Cavity. *This Annual*, X.
Stevenson, O. (1954), The First Treasured Possession. *This Annual*, IX.
Winnicott, D. W. (1953), Transitional Objects and Transitional Phenomena. *Int. J. Psa.*, XXXIV.
Wittels, F. (1934), Mutterschaft und Bisexualität. *Int. Ztschr. Psa.*, XX.
Wulff, M. (1946), Fetishism and Object Choice in Early Childhood. *Psa. Quart.*, XV.

SOME EVIDENCES OF DEVIATIONAL DEVELOP-
MENT IN INFANCY AND EARLY CHILDHOOD

ANNEMARIE P. WEIL, M.D. (New York)[1]

This paper deals with certain early phenomena encountered in infants and prelatency children who—according to the severity of their disturbance—are later called deviational, ego-disturbed, atypical, or even childhood schizophrenias (Putnam, 1948; Rank, 1949; Weil, 1953; Mahler, 1940, 1952; Bender, 1947). Many of us have come to recognize that this group covers a rather wide range of disturbances of varying degrees of severity, with the near-psychotic cases at one end, and much milder and much less conspicuous disorders at the other.

Severely pathological development, usually evident earlier, as well as less severe disturbances with clearly pathological behavior only in latency have been described before. We shall present here mainly some of the finer signs of such disorders in infancy and early childhood. Such manifestations, although different because of the age, then indicate the same basic pathology: it seems that the development in such children lacks integration at all times. They show peculiarities and unevenness of their general maturational patterning, of their physiological functioning, and of their psychological apparatus. They show delay in ego development[2] and, frequently, deviations in the expression of libidinal and aggressive drives. This is often associated with an overload of tension evident from an early age, and with various manifestations of anxiousness.

Distortion of ego development at the various age levels (from the beginning to age six) becomes evident if one scrutinizes the different facets of the growing ego. The gradual development of object relationship is one such facet, one which is most dependent on drive endowment. Adequate endowment of libidinal and aggressive drives *and* their fusion[3]

[1] From the Child Development Center, New York.

[2] "Ego functioning" or "ego development"—in what follows—does not refer to the initially nonconflictuous sphere, the apparatus (which sometimes shows outstandingly high or outstandingly low equipment), but refers to the conflictuous portion of the ego.

[3] According to Hartmann, Kris, and Loewenstein (1946), also neutralization of residual drive energies is needed.

are needed if what is usually gradually achieved by latency is to be achieved (A. Freud, 1949). We scrutinize the stages of an unfolding object relationship leading to complete individuation—giving up of the autistic as well as the symbiotic position—with the resulting feeling of self-identity and the capacity for identification with others (to which I want to come back later). We observe the attitudes which gradually evolve with a maturing capacity for object relationship in such a young child: giving up of omnipotence, of magical thinking, and acceptance of the reality principle. Other behavior phenomena to be observed include the child's developing reality testing and his use of defenses as related to his age. Disturbances in these spheres are less conspicuous in a young child, yet recognizable if compared to age-adequate functioning and its usual variations. With such knowledge, we can detect lags in the very dawn of ego development, starting in infancy, and continuing throughout. We then also recognize that in such children—whether less or more ego-disturbed —there will appear only the usual phenomena of childhood, though at an inappropriate time and thus in a distorted constellation, and often with a deviational intensity. In many of these children, *the ego continues to grow,* although at a slowed rate and hence with a great deal of distorting effect on the personality. Only some—the near-psychotic and psychotic cases—show standstill or even permanent regression. However, in those children that do progress, as well as in those that do not, we often find reduced resiliency: overfacile transitory regressions as a reaction to minor frustrations;[4] or somewhat more substantial and longer lasting regressions —in ego achievements and/or in libidinal level—as a reaction to the usual inadvertent events in a child's life (such as birth of a sibling, illness or death of grandparents, etc.).

As these children grow up, their deviational make-up and development does not exclude neurotic symptom formation. Rather it seems that there is a relation of reciprocity. The milder the basic personality distortion, the more distinct will the neurotic symptomatology be. With some ego and superego development, the possibility is given of unconscious conflicts and neurotic elaboration of conflicts. Therapeutic planning for a given child will need consideration of both: the deviational development and the neurotic symptoms shown.

In surveying the evidences of such disturbances in infancy and pre-latency, well-known phenomena will be only briefly mentioned.

Deviant physiology and erratic patterning often seem to make for a bad start in life for such infants. To name only some manifestations: hypertonic states, excessive crying in spite of yielding care; persistently

4 Cf. Kris (1951) on "regression rate" and "constancy of behavior."

erratic patterns of eating and sleeping; constant regurgitation and vomiting, or diarrhea without detectable cause; or, e.g., voracious intake without adequate weight gain, etc.

Deviant drive endowment of many such children—another expression of their deviational psychobiological anlage—makes for conspicuous disturbances in the sphere of impulses, evident from the very beginning and remaining throughout. We find apathetic infants who do not cry, do not signal their needs, take hours to drink the bottle, tend to sleep too much;[5] babies who are found where and as they were put down, who are lazy to grasp, and who do not mind being kept in bed or playpen for longer periods and until later ages than usual. Other children are sleepless, restless—possibly hypertonic—and later show extremes of hyperactiveness and aggressiveness, especially obvious and disturbing after walking. Growing physical potentialities make such children increasingly difficult as they grow up.

Maturational sequences are often unusual: children who do not stand but walk right away, or who are mute until four, then talk perfectly well. We also encounter sequences of gain-loss-gain, talk-muteness-talk, instead of the usual fairly steadily rising curve of achievements. In some, deviational maturation is evidenced predominantly in the sphere of neuromuscular development, with prolonged athetosis, thrashing movements, convulsion-like phenomena, etc. Such children look like primarily organic, sometimes even like defective organic, children for a long time, until their further development clearly disproves this assumption, with organic signs waning and the ego distortion coming distinctly to the fore.

The overload of tension may often be evidenced from earliest infancy. Hypertonicity has already been mentioned. Some such infants show extremes of autoerotic or autoaggressive habits (sucking, rolling, rubbing, head banging, etc.). A deviant anlage of hypersensitivity to sound, light, even touch sensations, often adds to the state of tension, and makes for early fright reactions. (These start earlier, are much more extreme and more persistent than those sometimes transitorily seen in toddlerhood.)

Forerunners of fears are found in early dislike of any change. With such babies, routines have to be handled always on the same spot and in the same way. It is in line with this that many such children, though neuromuscularly capable, falter at a developmental step—such as swallowing solids, holding a toy, or walking—for a long time.

Sometimes the overload of anxiety is channelized into the still too undifferentiated relation to the mother and a symbiotic attachment i

---

[5] These may be Fries's (1944, 1953) hypoactive children. Sandra, in "Unusua Variations in Drive Endowment," is also a case in point (see *this Volume*, pp. 146-161.)

maintained for years (Mahler, 1952). Or various more concrete fears may color the second year, and find verbal expression in the years to come. Sometimes they are relieved by or alternate with compulsive mechanisms (light on, out . . . door open, closed . . .) much more extreme and persistent than such passing fancies of that age.

Most important as finer evidences of such disorders are the disturbances in the dawn of ego development. Among the criteria are manifestations (or, rather, lack of manifestations) that indicate difficulties, delays, relating to the first beginnings, pre-stages in the development of object relationship. Thus we see infants who—in their maintained autistic tendencies—do not smile back in response to mother's face for months or years (Spitz, 1946); who do not show the anticipatory gesture when about to be picked up (Kanner, 1943) and do not hold on when carried; infants who do not respond to cuddling, or do not themselves start to touch and experiment with mother's body, especially her face, and thus miss this important early experience of learning separateness; or they may, somewhat later, show incapacity for imitation—primary identification—which is such an important step in the beginning of object relationship, and which, beyond furthering separateness, may serve as a bridge for the toddler's attempts (e.g., through imitation of facial expressions and gestures) to "feel with" the other, to grasp the other's feeling. No wonder that among our cases are also the toddlers who often cannot engage in any back-and-forth or give-and-take play until a much later age than the average child with better drive and ego endowment.

Another important indication of the child's developing capacity to relate, can be observed in his communicativeness—first gestural and then verbal. The capacity for gestural communication alone can already be revealing. Some of our toddlers do not even gesture their needs: they scream without pointing or signaling of any sort, and the mother has to guess what action or object will appease his wish. How much more capacity to relate and identify is shown by an otherwise equally developed toddler who will direct his mother with grunting and gestures alone to perform complicated tasks for him, or who will start to gesticulate even in situations that do not serve his immediate need fulfillment.

Still more obvious does this relatedness become in the verbal stage. All toddlers will use language first for the expression of needs and wishes, as for food, or for the opening of the door or to learn the name of a new object.[6] However, with growing individuation and object

[6] K. Buehler's (1924) three phases in the functional development of language (indication, release, and representation) can be understood in terms of growing object relatedness.

relationship, the wish to share an experience develops, and—if it has not been experienced together—it has to be verbalized. This is when true communication sets in. In my opinion, it is a big day in the emotional development of a child when he, as a toddler, returns from the park and tells the parent who had stayed home: "Lady fed pigeons," or "Soldiers marched"—nothing in the line of a wish, only an expression of the dawning need truly to intercommunicate. Here again, the considerable difference of reactions is not dependent on verbal capacity or intelligence, but solely on the capacity and need to relate. The deviational toddlers often show considerable lag in this sphere (since some of them do not even verbalize or signal requests).

The indicators just mentioned—no smile, no imitations, as well as such lack of communicativeness—are not always found in deviant children; since object relationship is only one facet of ego functioning. The significance of the presence or absence of these early emotional reactions, for the child's further development arises from the fact that these very reactions can, by their seductive winsomeness, make for good emotional interplay between mother and child.

In the light of what has been said, we do consider certain transitory difficulties in infancy and early childhood as positive factors with regard to early ego development. Thus the so-called "stranger-anxiety" ("eight-months anxiety") occurring somewhere between the seventh and twelfth months is a sign of individuation and differentiation (Spitz, 1946, 1950). The "stranger-anxiety" implies that the mother's face is not only pleasurefully recognized as that of a separate individual who brings fulfillment of needs and gratifications, but that it is differentiated from strange faces, which then seem to be less promising, even startling. Similarly with a passing sleep disturbance within the second year. At this period—normally—a fair degree of individuation has occurred at the cost of narcissistic libido. An increase of this object cathexis, probably associated with a greater awareness of the dependence, makes the child experience sleep, especially falling asleep, as an unpleasurable separation, and resist it. It seems as if many stages in the development of object relationship are associated with such passing experiences of unpleasure. However, usually the next step of development brings relief; the infant learns that the mother will be there as well, behind the stranger; and that the stranger may be pleasure-bringing too; and the toddler learns that the separation at night is followed by a reunion in the morning. Again, it is only those deviational children with the overload of innate tension, who do not find the next step, and persist in a continuous anxious response to the not-maternal environment with a symbiotic clinging to the mother, or who persist in a severe and lasting sleep disturbance. (Poor handling of such a symptom as a sleep difficulty, which usually passes, can make for a neurotic fixation of the disturbance in any child. However, we then find this symptom in a different constellation of previous development and symptomatology.)

The more marked deficiencies in emotional development that become conspicuous in late toddlerhood hardly need to be discussed. In some of them the autistic position still remains in the fore, with unreachability and unresponsiveness, usually without much evidence of fear; in others, a little further developed, the symbiotic clinging to the mother remains in the fore, with anxious shutting out of anybody else. Refusal to develop self-help may be a manifestation of such symbiotic attachment; we encounter children who, throughout prelatency, do not eat unless fed by their mothers—so much in contrast to the average child's "do it myself, myself," apparent after two.

Sometimes we find the opposite, namely, precocious and extreme independence, as a marked and outstanding symptom. Instead of the normal transitory negativism, in such children antagonism and unpredictability set in too early, are too extreme, and do not wane. This may contribute to another frequent problem of such toddlers: difficulty in training. No wonder, since in this early learning experience the interplay between mother and child—beginning object cathexis, as well as delay of gratification for the sake of the mother—is of greatest importance (Hartmann, Kris, and Loewenstein, 1946).

As such children go through prelatency, we can frequently observe other facets of disturbed ego development. We sometimes find that omnipotent demands have a far greater impact and persist longer than is usual: temper tantrums on the slightest frustration, insatiable demandingness and impatience, typical in the inability to delay and in the slow adjustment toward the reality principle. Violent upsets then persist as a reaction to any unexpected happening. Again, this type of response to a "disturbed anticipation" (Ch. Buehler, 1943) is a well-known transitory phenomenon of the two- to three-year-olds, usually waning as omnipotence decreases and better acquaintance with reality and potential happenings in the outside world grows. Or sometimes, unfocused expression of aggression and destructiveness continue, as would befit only the beginnings of toddlerhood. We assume that in such children delayed ego control is associated with lack of fusion of the—sometimes overly strong aggressive—drives. Others are involved in fantasies and fantasy play too intense, too lost, withdrawn from their real environment (and continue in this way over too many years), and their reality testing conspicuously

lags behind. As a child approaches latency, another indication of this
can be found in the extent to which his thinking and talking reveal a
prevalence of secondary processes: how much and how long do primary
processes remain in the fore, especially outside of play, silliness or emotionally charged situations?

Two more phenomena that give us finer gauges of ego development in
the preschool years are the role of imitation and the dawning development of discrimination and tact. We have mentioned the setting in of
imitation of a gestural—primary identification—type, so important
around the end of the first year. Only with the growing ego's deeper
capacity for object relationship, and furthered by the renunciation of the
oedipal phase, does secondary identification set in, and with it imitation
on a higher, also more conscious, level. While some of these children
show no capacity for imitation at all, as said before, others, although
already beyond this stage, show extremes of imitativeness of the primary-
identification type and continue to do so. They imitate others, instead of
making friends with them; they play not *with* but *after* some other child.
Besides relating in this primitive fashion, it seems as though some of these
children—with delay in the consolidation of ego boundaries and weakness
of outward-directed drive impulses—need to borrow identity and initiative in this way.

In line with the prelatency child's increasing capacity to relate and
gradually also to empathize with other persons, there are usually recognizable signs of growing tact and discrimination, of a feeling that we
approach different people in different ways. (In some cultures this is
nicely laid out for the child of beginning school age by the introduction
of "you" instead of the indiscriminate "thou" to everybody—the acceptance of which will depend on environmental pressure as well as also on
the individual child's feeling and need for such discrimination.) Such
growing capacity for discrimination is often conspicuously lacking in
these cases. Even though these children may be highly intelligent, and
approaching latency, they do not start to whisper in talking about others,
especially about the defects of others; they continue to say everything to
everybody at any time out loud (or, the opposite, nothing ever); and,
typical also, many of these children develop no variation or modulation
whatever in their tone of voice.

As said in the beginning, the described phenomena are all typical
for some period of a child's life. However, in these deviational children
they appear at an inappropriate time, hence in a distorted constellation.

If one has become aware of the described facets of behavior indicating the rate at which the ego develops, one is bound to detect in

deviational children delays beyond the range of usual variations in many spheres, and often in spite of environmental support toward ego growth. No doubt lack of such support may make for delays too; however, it seems that these children need even more and steadier support than is supplied by an average environment—one not guided by awareness and understanding of the specific pathology.

BIBLIOGRAPHY

Bender, L. (1947), Childhood Schizophrenia. *Am. J. Orthopsychiat.*, XVII.

Buehler, C. (1943), *From Birth to Maturity*. London: Kegan, Trench, Trubner.

Buehler, K. (1924), *Die geistige Entwicklung des Kindes*. Jena: Gustav Fischer.

Freud, A. (1948), Aggression in Relation to Emotional Development, Normal and Pathological. International Congress on Mental Health, London 1948. Vol. II. *Proceedings of the International Conference on Child Psychiatry*. New York: Columbia University Press.

—— (1949), Aggression in Relation to Emotional Development: Normal and Pathological. *This Annual*, III/IV.

Fries, M. E. (1944), Psychosomatic Relationships between Mother and Infant. *Psychosom. Med.*, VI.

—— and Woolf, P. J. (1953), Some Hypotheses on the Role of the Congenital Activity Type in Personality Development. *This Annual*, VIII.

Hartmann, H.; Kris, E.; Loewenstein, R. M. (1946), Comments on the Formation of Psychic Structure. *This Annual*, II.

Kanner, L. (1943), Autistic Disturbances of Affective Contact. *Nerv. Child*, II.

Kris, E. (1951), Opening Remarks on Psychoanalytic Child Psychology. *This Annual*, VI.

Mahler, M. S. (1952) On Child Psychosis and Schizophrenia: Autistic and Symbiotic Infantile Psychoses. *This Annual*, VII.

—— and Ross, R., Jr.; De Fries, Z. (1940), Clinical Studies in Benign and Malignant Cases of Childhood Psychosis (Schizophrenia-like). *Am. J. Orthopsychiat.*, XIX.

Putnam, M. C.; Rank, B.; Pavenstedt, E.; Andersen, I. N.; Rawson, I. (1948), Case Study of an Atypical Two-and-a-half-year-old. Round Table. *Am. J. Orthopsychiat.*, XVIII.

Rank, B. (1949), Adaptation of the Psychoanalytic Technique for the Treatment of Young Children with Atypical Development. *Am. J. Orthopsychiat.*, XIX.

Spitz, R. A. (1946), The Smiling Response. *Gen. Psychol. Mon.*, XXXIV.

—— (1946), Anaclitic Depression. *This Annual*, II.

—— (1950), Anxiety in Infancy. *Int. J. Psa.*, XXXI.

Weil, A. P. (1953a)), Certain Severe Disturbances of Ego Development in Childhood. *This Annual*, VIII.

—— (1953b) Clinical Data and Dynamic Considerations in Certain Cases of Childhood Schizophrenia. *Am. J. Orthopsychiat.*, XXIII.

CLINICAL CONTRIBUTIONS

OBSERVATIONS ON THE PSYCHOTHERAPY OF BORDERLINE AND PSYCHOTIC CHILDREN[1]

RUDOLF EKSTEIN, Ph.D and JUDITH WALLERSTEIN, M.S.W.
(Topeka)

In a previous paper (1954) we reported several observations regarding the ego psychology of borderline and psychotic children. We described the fluctuating availability of different ego organizations in these children, ranging from psychotic manifestations to advanced achievement appropriate to chronological age. These observations have various implications for psychotherapy. In this paper we shall attempt to examine some of the technical problems of interpretation which arise in the treatment of these children. Furthermore, since our primary goal is the enrichment of clinical skill, we shall describe some technical modifications which gradually took shape in accommodating to the particular ego attributes of these clinical groups.

We may take the well-known story of Hansel and Gretel as our common point of departure. For the psychoanalyst and the small child, the fairy tale of Hansel and Gretel is a story of conflict which gathers dramatic strength as it moves regressively from one level of ego organization to another. The mother image in the fairy tale appears in at least two successive guises: first, as a stepmother plotting to banish the children and separate them from their loving father, and later as a witch inside a candy house who means to devour them. Thus, the story follows a regressive pathway in developing the theme of the rejecting and vengeful mother figure, and the children's attempt to master this threat. For it retreats from secondary-process thinking, moving from the suspiciousness of the children at the outset to the paranoid projection of the devouring witch. In libidinal terms, the dominant oedipal and phallic elements in the stepmother figure give way increasingly to primitive,

[1] Report from a Current Psychotherapy Research Project at Southard School. This report is based on the work of a research seminar conducted by Dr. Rudolf Ekstein for the professional staff of Southard School. In addition to the authors of this report, Seymour W. Friedman, M.D., Mrs. Dorothy Wright, M.A., and Helen Sargent, Ph.D. have provided special time for this project. We are indebted to Mrs. Dorothy Wright for permission to utilize her case material.

oral, cannibalistic fantasies. (We say increasingly, since the witch certainly has attributes associated with stages more advanced than the oral stage, as do regressions in our patients as well.) On an ego level, action begins with an attempt to outsmart the parents and eventuates regressively in destruction by incorporation, accompanied also by trickery.

The divergence between the children's relationship to the stepmother and to the witch additionally points to the changing dominance of different ego organizations. The hostility to the stepmother is within the confines of an established object relationship, and the solution proposed, namely separation, reflects a neurotic ego with a consolidated core of identity and beginning capacity for independent activity. The relationship with the witch, by contrast, falls within primitive "either/or" bounds suggesting a predominantly hostile symbiosis, and the major solution offered is the incorporation of the bad object.

It is important to bear in mind that the Hansel and Gretel story expresses the repetitive statement of conflict at different levels of ego achievement which can be distinguished primarily in terms of the degree of dominance of one ego organization over others. Clearly, ego organizations are numerous and overlapping. Their complex hierarchical structure and functional interrelationships range along a continuum which does not permit absolute distinctions.

We may now transpose the fairy tale to the clinic and assume it to be an original fantasy of little Gretel in therapy. If we assume Gretel to be suffering with a neurotic illness, the therapist has a variety of interpretive choices which are well known in child analysis. He may, for instance, link the content of the stories of both stepmother and the witch directly to conflict with the mother. He may alternately stress defense against conflict by calling attention to the significant resemblances between the two story parts and noting the regressive transition from stepmother to witch. Or he may employ what we shall call "metaphoric interpretation" and fashion his remarks around the witch and the frightened children in order temporarily to help maintain a distance of the fantasy from the conscious awareness of the child. He can, in effect, move with relative freedom in appropriately making use of the range of interpretive possibilities. For he can rely upon his patient's achievement of a neurotic level of ego functioning, upon the relative stability of the child's ego state, and upon the relative strength of neurotic defenses. To return to our example, he can depend upon the immediacy of Gretel's conflict with the mother which has its roots in early fixations expressed in the fantasy of the witch, and can gradually bring this conflict into the realm of full recognition.

If we assume little Gretel to be a borderline or psychotic child, however, several inferences can be drawn regarding her ego organization which operate to constrict the therapist's freedom of interpretive choice. For such a child, the "neurotic"[2] relationship with the stepmother represents, in Knight's metaphor (1953), only an outpost of advanced ego achievement whose connection with earlier and more primitive ego achievements is tenuous and intermittent. Accordingly, for a borderline or psychotic Gretel, the image of the witch draws the main cathexis and the associated fantasies of cannibalistic fusion are experienced as fearsome reality. Moreover, the fragility of the neurotic defenses exposes the child to the imminent threat of psychotic upheaval.

In the therapy of neurotic children, interpretations are addressed primarily to the more mature ego achievements. In the treatment of borderline and psychotic children, however, such interpretations often result in panic and the precipitous disruption of contact. Or they may succeed in superimposing a pseudo-secondary process upon a shaky foundation, as a concession to an outer demand for social adjustment and conformity.

We have had many opportunities in residential treatment to observe the extensive use which borderline and psychotic children make of imitation and cue-taking. These imitative mechanisms are of considerable help to these children as they try to find their way through the intricacies of social intercourse and daily routine. But the very success of these mechanisms should not obscure the dangers of perpetuating and strengthening their use in psychotherapy.

Clinical material from the second year of treatment of an eleven-year-old schizophrenic child, whose impulses and fantasies are closely akin to our psychotic fairy-tale Gretel, may serve to illustrate the consequences of interpretive techniques addressed to different levels of ego organization. In this first excerpt the therapist offers an interpretation which would be appropriate in the treatment of a neurotic patient. This interpretation, focusing on a transference displacement which the child had employed for several weeks, triggers a psychotic regression.

Ann found a piece of paper in the playroom where one of the other children had printed, "Jimmy will be upset and he will act it." Ann asked, "Dorothy, did you write this?" I asked if she thought I would write something like that. Ann replied that she did not think so because I would use script if I had written it. I asked if that was the only way

2 Our use of term "neurotic" refers to the neurotic manifestations of the ego which may be present in different kinds of personality organizations, including psychotic personalities.

she was sure that I hadn't. Ann disregarded my comment and went on to try to figure out which one of the children had written the note. She assured me Jimmy was doing better. "Sometimes," she said, "Jimmy is very aggressive, but that is good for him because he needs to get it out of his system." She then said Mary was at it again. Mary had told Ann that all the kids did not like her and that was not true, was it? I thought that Ann would be the one to know if it were true. Ann said she was trying to figure out these old problems. Wasn't she stronger than her problems? I thought perhaps she was. But, she continued, she was still so afraid of Mary, and what was she going to do about that? I told Ann I thought the feeling she had toward me and the feeling she had toward Mary were both expressions of the feeling she had toward her mother. At the present time Mary stands for the bad mother whom Ann fears, and I at the present time am the good mother whom Ann tries to please and who doesn't hurt her. Ann said, "Oh, dear, Dorothy, this mother problem is a big one." I thought so too. Ann continued that this mother problem was about the biggest she had now. Would her mother understand if she had to act silly? I thought so, although it was hard for mother always to be understanding. Ann was sitting in the chair beside me and said, "Oh, Dorothy, here it comes. I feel like being silly. What will I do? What will I do?" She began rolling around in the chair, smelling her hands and squirming. She exclaimed: "Dorothy, what are you going to do?" I said I would like to try to help her understand these feelings. Ann got up and said she needed to tell me about a number that had to do with the numbers in the 20s. She used to have several numbers that bothered her, 9, 12, and 15. But these don't bother her any more. This last number is the only one left now, but it is the biggest one of all. She began rolling around, saying, "Oh, how often does this have to come up? Oh, Dorothy, what will I do?"

It is likely that the therapist was misled at the beginning of the hour by what seemed to be the child's relatively "neurotic" functioning, and accordingly interpreted the displacement to Mary, much as one would with a neurotic child. Ann's response demonstrates the tenuousness of her adjustment: it could not be sufficiently maintained to permit either the integration of the interpretation or its rejection by neurotic means. For as the displacement was interpreted, transference feelings and impulses previously bound by this mechanism could be warded off only by regression. In effect, the therapist's interpretation was directed at secondary-process thinking and was understood, but without consolidated secondary-process mediation and without capacity to synthesize or defend against the implications of this interpretation on a neurotic level. Consequently it triggered a collapse of ego boundaries and the ensuing invasion of the ego by primary-process material—an action accompanied by acute suffering.

Ann's use of displacement is relevant to the problem of interpretive choice. In general, the mechanism of displacement represents a relatively advanced achievement in the hierarchy of defenses. For it is associated with the differentiation of self from the outer world, and its efficacy as a defensive maneuver can be said in large part to be predicated upon the stable cathexis of ego and object boundaries. In the neurotic patient, displacement is a mechanism available prior to therapy which becomes manifest within the context of the transference neurosis. For the psychotic child, however, the ability to use displacement as a defense frequently signals a significant progress because it is associated with a growing capacity to maintain object cathexis.

The interview cited occurred at a time in treatment when the transference was in the process of becoming consolidated on a neurotic level, but when psychotic transference manifestations were still very much in evidence. Consequently, the interpretation was premature in its failure to appreciate the fragility of the newly acquired ego functions and to recognize their close interdependence with the cathexis of the therapist. Ann's capacity to displace certain hostile and sexual impulses was of central importance in safeguarding the relationship with the therapist. And, as the displacement yielded, associated functions of ego-boundary maintenance and object cathexis became strained to the breaking point.

To return briefly to Hansel and Gretel, our selection of this story was based in part on the ending of the fairy tale. When the children came home, they were surprised to learn that the stepmother somehow had died in their absence. The fairy tale thus conceals the connection between their murder of the witch and the nondisplaced death wish toward the stepmother from the conscious awareness of the children, and thereby makes it possible for them to return safely home. In keeping with the views offered here, the fairy tale maintains the psychological distance between witch and mother and refrains from adding to the already overburdened children a direct recognition which they could not bear.

The following interview excerpt which is drawn from approximately the same general period of treatment is offered to illustrate a successful attempt to employ interpretation within the mode of thought and level of ego functioning as manifested in the child's communication. For the understanding of this material it should be known that Ann's father had been mentally ill and committed suicide while undergoing therapy.

Ann came in with a big package wrapped up in foil paper and told me she had brought me a present. There was a piece of cake for herself and for me. I exclaimed how wonderful it was that we could have a party. Ann barely touched her cake and wandered aimlessly about the room and finally stopped and stared for a long time at a smear of ink on

the far wall. She turned to me and said, "Dorothy, see the sign of death."
I repeated, "Yes, Ann, the sign of death." She stared at it and then put
her arm out straight and started walking toward it, slowly saying in a
frightened voice, "How close am I to it, Dorothy? How many inches?"
I gauged the inches and when she got real close she drew back. Then she
silently went toward it again and as she drew close to it, she asked me
how close she was. Then she touched it and in a wild panic turned and
ran back toward me, holding out the finger which had touched the sign
of death, saying, "Oh, Dorothy, do something." I took hold of her hand
and kissed her finger at the end. She said, "Oh, Dorothy, you saved me."
I said, "Yes, I would never let the sign of death hurt you, Ann." She
quickly left me and went over to the mirror and started sucking with her
lips pressed hard against the glass. Then she came back to the table and
took a small piece of clay which she placed just barely below the sign of
death and told me that the clay was on her side and it was safer. I said I
was on her side too, and did we also need the clay? Ann affirmed that the
clay was safer. I asked if it would save her better than I could. Ann said
no, that the clay and I would both save her. I suggested maybe that was
a good idea because the clay wouldn't frighten her as much as I did.
Ann made no reply but again went through the approach to the sign of
death, but only touched the clay. Then she took a pencil and approached
the wall, telling me it took 15 seconds for the sign of death to run
through the pencil and into her arm and for me to keep track by the
clock and tell her when 10 seconds were up. I warned her at 10 seconds
and she threw the pencil into the sand pile, asking anxiously what would
happen if she had held it the full 15 seconds. I told her I would not have
let her hold it that long. I was here to keep her from getting hurt and I
wasn't going to let anything happen to her. Although she felt very close
to the sign of death at times, I would never stop looking after her and
we would never leave her alone, as they had left her father. Ann said,
"Johnny is a poor little kid. He doesn't have a mother and I don't have
a father." I repeated, "Yes, poor little kids." Ann said, "Dorothy, I wish
you would have Johnny in therapy because he needs a therapist. And I
think you're the best therapist in the School." I replied that that pleased
me because maybe she thought she was getting help from me too. Ann
said she knew she was better, but after all they had thought her father
was better too. I asked: "Yes, and you wondered whether we might be
mistaken too about your being better?" Ann said, "Sometimes my father
scared me."

The child employs the magic thought and gesture of the primary
process as her only available way of expressing suicidal impulses. She
requests and receives help from the therapist in terms of the primary
process. As the interview proceeds, her anxiety noticeably lessens and she
is finally able to discuss, in secondary-process language, her relationship
with her father. We note, therefore, a shift from psychotic to neurotic
ego state which, we suggest, resulted primarily from the therapist's under-

standing of the most central aspect of the child's communication, and the therapist's ability to interpret effectively within the context of the regression.

In the first part of this hour Ann recaptures a magical mode of thought deriving from a developmental stage when reality and fantasy are blended and when the secondary process has not yet become sufficiently established to separate thought from action. Magical thinking is commonly synonymous with omnipotent thought. Yet, from the vantage point of maturity, thinking which is inseparable from action fails to achieve the primary purpose of all thought which is trial action. Therefore, magical thought from the perspective of the mature ego is ineffectual thought; its use bespeaks the weakness of the ego.

Ann's regression and mounting panic culminating in her cry of "do something" arise from an immobilizing dilemma. Her urgent need to confess her suicidal preoccupations is opposed by her terror that in so doing she will be compelled to act them out. In acceding to the child's frantic request by means of a magical protective gesture, the therapist deliberately employs the primary-process language of the child's communication. In this way the therapist expresses understanding not only of the affective content of the communication but of the ego weakness to which the child confesses and of the psychotic ego state itself. Furthermore, the assurance of protection combined with full acceptance of the child's terrifying fantasy is designed to help drive a wedge between thought and action. Ann responds by regaining sufficient psychological equilibrium to express the same content in a more mature, more reality-anchored way. Thus, by taking hold of the therapist's hand and symbolically, in primary-process language, of her strength as well, the child has for the moment achieved the capacity to separate thought from action and is enabled thereby to proceed.

This kind of interpretive response which we have variously called "interpretation within the regression" or "interpretation within the metaphor" involves, to paraphrase Coleridge, "A willing suspension of disbelief in unreality for the moment." Such interpretation rests upon the temporary willingness to assume that the patient's grossly distorted perceptions reflect outer reality, because they accurately reflect his inner psychological reality and the state of his ego which has temporarily lost the capacity to differentiate inner and outer reality. At the same time, the interpretive response remains firmly anchored in the secondary-process world. For it is predicated upon the therapist's conscious metaphoric use of the patient's regressed language in order to convey understanding of his inner world and feelings in the only way immediately available to the patient, namely, the language of regression. Accordingly, in the material cited, the therapist accepted the projection of omnipotence and acted in a manner entirely consonant with the child's magical expectations. In this way, she employed the primary process of the child's communication as a metaphor designed to convey her assurance of continuing love and protection in direct response to the child's expressed fears of being deserted and left to commit suicide.

It may be helpful to distinguish briefly between interpretation within the regression and the kind of metaphoric interpretation which can be used with any neurotic patient, depending upon the personal style of the analyst. In metaphoric interpretation, in which the therapist's immediate response uses the metaphor of the patient's communication, there follows rapidly an explication which elaborates meaning and intent in mature secondary-process language. Interpretation within the regression, however, is predicated on the assumption that the patient's ego state directly reflects the extent of his ability to come to terms with the conflict. Therefore, communication remains within the confines of the patient's expression until some future time in the treatment when the patient himself indicates his capacity for fuller understanding.

Interpretation within the regression, furthermore, is often a direct result of the therapist's primary aim which is to maintain the relationship and prevent the disruption of contact. Borderline and psychotic children readily regress to a prior stage of development in which human contact was tenuous. Consequently, such regressions threaten rupture of all object relationships, including the relationship with the therapist. We recall that in the last interview cited, Ann screamed for help almost as if the therapist were not present. By attempting to follow the child into this state of attenuated human contact, the therapist tries to uphold the object ties on whatever level possible. For by returning with the child to ego stages where contact is almost disrupted and by reliving early experiences, primitive transferences are evoked or maintained which can serve as the foundation for new and more mature identifications. This maintenance of the therapeutic relationship, often made possible by interpreting within the regression, thus lays the foundation for the new development of identificatory processes rather than the superimposition of an imitative façade. And it is by the continual repetition of such experiences that the secondary process can emerge and extend its dominance.

As in any other therapy with children, interpretive work with the borderline and psychotic child proceeds gradually to more mature levels. Clearly, every psychotherapy seeks not only to comprehend the child's world but must ultimately help the child to understand the world of reality. As regressive trends lessen and as the neurotic aspects of the child's ego become stabilized, interpretations aim at giving insight and thus eventually approximate those used with the neurotic child.

Sometimes these changes will appear very slowly over a long period of time. Sometimes the child will mark the turning point dramatically by describing a previously highly cathected fantasy as science fiction, by projecting responsibility for its emergence upon the therapist, by stating, as did one nine-year-old to his therapist after months of painstaking work, "Space patrol? Really this is 1953, not 2053. *You* must have been dreaming." These are among the clinical signs which indicate that the child's ego has achieved sufficient strength for the therapist to relinquish the special interpretive measures which had been previously required.

From its beginning, analytic work with children has been based upon departures from the basic model of classical analytic technique as originally worked out for adult patients. These changes were necessitated by the special psychological attributes of childhood, namely, by the immaturity of the child's ego and consequent inability to maintain a relatively intact level of ego functioning and by the resulting dependency. In their impact upon the basic treatment model, the special ego attributes of borderline and psychotic children can be viewed as extensions of psychological attributes common to all children in comparison to adults. The interpretive techniques here elaborated also represent not innovations so much as further adaptations of methods which have already been constructed for the therapy of the neurotic child.

The chief technical difficulty in the psychotherapy of borderline and psychotic children is how to respond to the rapidly changing need systems and modes of expression of these children in order ultimately to develop secondary-process potentialities to their fullest. The approach described essentially aims at working with that part of the ego that is intact, at whatever developmental level that may be, in this way enabling the ego ultimately to achieve a higher level of functioning. Communication remains within primary-process fantasy and modes of expression *until the patient has acquired on each such occasion the strength to move to a more mature position.* Interpretation within the regression, in the sense here defined, is an effective tool for the accomplishment of the therapeutic task.

BIBLIOGRAPHY

Ekstein, R. and Wallerstein, J. (1954), Observations of the Psychology of Borderline and Psychotic Children. *This Annual*, IX.
Knight, R. P. (1953), Borderline States. *Bull. Menninger Clin.*, XVII.

AN EGO DISTURBANCE IN A YOUNG CHILD[1]

ERNA FURMAN (Cleveland)[2]

CLINICAL PICTURE

Carol was referred to University Hospitals Nursery School by the local child guidance center at her parents' request.

Carol was three years, four months old, rather small and thin for her age, but well built and physically healthy. She looked very dainty with her dark hair, big brown eyes, and delicate complexion. Quite often, however, her features and her whole body became rigid, tense, and distorted, and she would stare in an intense, blank fashion which seemed to repel, rather than absorb, whatever she saw. Even in her more relaxed moments she could not smile or laugh. In observing Carol, it became evident that she was not able to relate to adults or children and that she could not comprehend the meaning of everyday events around her. She would sometimes stand apart with a withdrawn expression, or she would for longer periods monotonously pour water from one can into another, or shovel sand in the play yard; but she seemed to pay little attention to what she was doing, apparently absorbed in thought. Then her placid attitude would suddenly change: her body stiffened, her hands and arms began to wave excitedly, and she would rather rigidly dance around on her tiptoes, showing tremendous over-all excitement. At such times she talked excitedly to herself or to others, but one could not understand her in spite of her clear articulation. Here is an example of her speech recorded at that time:

Carol picks up two wooden blocks and hands them to the teacher. She talks in a loud voice, accompanied by much dancing and waving of hands. "You hold this, that, eat it—perfume. Feels good, it's an airplane.

[1] Presented at the June 1955 meeting of the Philadelphia Association for Psychoanalysis.

[2] From the Department of Psychiatry, University Hospitals, Western Reserve University School of Medicine.

I am most grateful to Dr. Anny Katan, head of the child psychiatric services of University Hospitals, and to Dr. M. Katan, for their continued interest in this case, and especially for their valuable suggestions and comments during discussions of this case at staff conferences.

Things buy cans, 50 cans, a Monday can, a Peter can." The teacher asks her what a Peter can is. Carol responds with even more excited waving and tiptoeing and says, "One beer candle, candle out, smell it, sure enough two bottles. Feels acri, a madri, put it like this. Bottles acation, three, five bottles. A chey. R T B is E T R S 9 8 2. Uncle bitch poo for bottles. We bought a truck tractor. S B 8 she, in the morning talk about the letters. What's the number of the fox?" Carol is now at a pitch of excitement, dancing, waving, and shouting, "Take all this cabbage bottles. Take the chey." The teacher asks, "Why do you feel so excited?" And Carol shouts at her, "Cuz S T R T 9. What's your name? Want E T overs and B 2 R."

It was impossible to interrupt Carol or to calm her down by diversion. She never responded to being talked to. Her speech appeared to be a discharge of excitement rather than a means of communication. Sometimes Carol approached an adult and asked in a high-pitched tone of voice, "What's your name, what's your name?" She did not listen to a reply, did not remember what she was told, nor did it stop her excited, repetitive questioning. Her motor control was very poor. She handled materials requiring small-muscle coordination like a much younger child and could not climb, swing, or jump. She did not appear to remember anything, not even recent events. Thus her ego activities were greatly impaired in every sphere: lack of reality testing, no relationships with people, poor motor control, meaningless speech, no apparent memory. She cooperated very poorly in an intelligence test and achieved an I.Q. of 68. Carol had a number of other difficulties: she was ridden with innumerable fears to such an extent that shortly before her admission to the nursery her mother had had to allow her to stay in bed for several days because Carol was so afraid of stepping out, as well as afraid of every object, person, and activity. Carol would make sudden aggressive attacks on other children, biting and scratching them or holding them in an iron grip. At the same time she showed tremendous fear of her victims and was quite confused as to whether she had hurt them or they had hurt her; in her panic she often felt more injured than the attacked child. These attacks were very different from the screaming fits with which Carol tended to react to frustrations by an adult. Carol hardly ate at all, and it was difficult to suggest foods to her or to feed her because she became so excited and tense. During a meal at the nursery she sometimes started with diffuse hand waving and nonsense talk, would then suddenly throw off all her clothes and roll on the floor, kicking her legs. Occasionally Carol masturbated and tried to insert objects in the genital area; this seemed to be part of her over-all abreaction of excitement.

FAMILY BACKGROUND

Carol came from a lower middle-class family. She and her young parents used to live in an apartment but moved to the second floor of a duplex when Carol was three years old. The father served in the Army and then became a truck driver for a bakery. At the time of Carol's referral he was still in psychiatric treatment for an anxiety neurosis which had started acutely when Carol was only a few weeks old. He had held Carol in his arms, suddenly felt terrified that he would die, and dashed out for help. His main conflict was related to a revival of his experiences around a younger sister's birth. His early relationship to Carol was therefore very tense and inconsistent. At times he could not tolerate her childish behavior and turned away from her or spanked her in sudden outbursts; at other times he overstimulated her by playing exciting games, kissing and hugging her. He felt very guilty about Carol's difficulties, and the child in turn was terrified of him, although she provoked him to exciting interplays.

Carol's mother was an outgoing woman with a hysterical character make-up. She sometimes lost her temper with Carol, but was generally warm and understanding and maintained a basically good relationship with the child. Her feelings about Carol were much less complicated than the father's. She genuinely loved Carol and tried to be patient and reassuring with her. For a long time the mother was the only person who could handle Carol and whom Carol trusted, but at the time of referral even she could no longer understand Carol's nonsense talk and was at a complete loss as to how to approach Carol. In meeting the mother, it was very striking how much and how compulsively she talked, and it became apparent later that she used her speech both aggressively and as a means of discharge when she felt anxious. Both parents showed considerable preoccupation with oral matters: eating, talking, biting. Both of them were also impulsive and sensually very demonstrative. This was further exaggerated in their home life by the father's constant need for loving reassurance from his wife. In spite of occasional loud arguments, the parents seemed very fond of each other.

Several members of the father's and mother's families were emotionally so disturbed as to require psychiatric help. Since the families were rather close-knit, Carol came into regular contact with them. One aunt, who had had a postpartum depression and who later suffered from severe outbursts of aggression, actually shared the duplex house with Carol's family.

Carol had only one sibling, a sister who was born when Carol was three and a half years old, shortly after she entered the nursery school.

Personal History

Carol's history showed a number of features which could make for developmental difficulties, but none of the events seemed incisive enough to account for the very poor functioning of her ego or her diffuse, great excitement.

Carol had a difficult feeding period. It was hard to find the right formula for her; she was always a poor eater and did not take to mixed foods. During her second year Carol did not feed herself, refused to eat, and the mother spoon-fed her with very little success. At the time of referral Carol ate hardly at all. She was weaned from her last bottle at the age of two years. She never had any oral autoerotic habits, but did a good deal of rocking and head banging during the first fourteen months.

Her physical development was normal. She was somewhat fearful of walking, but then suddenly learned to run at thirteen months. She spoke her first words at one year of age and acquired a good vocabulary during her second year. She could then make herself understood very well until her disconnected nonsense talk began in her third year. The toilet training was uneventful. Her mother began to put her on the pot at about one year; Carol cooperated well and was clean at about two years. Carol was never ill or separated from her mother. She is said to have been a rather timid but normal toddler and had no disturbances aside from her eating disturbance. She never suffered from a sleep disturbance or separation anxiety.

Although Carol had always occupied her own room, she shared the parental bedroom during a week's vacation when about thirteen months old. At home the parents would dress, bathe, and use the toilet in front of Carol, and she occasionally came into their bed in the morning. In addition, Carol observed much sensual behavior between the parents, which the father demanded as reassurance against his anxieties.

Carol's first fear was supposed to have centered around a Johnny cardboard figure, a cigarette advertisement in her grandparents' store. When Carol was about two years old, this figure fell on her and completely terrified her. Her other fears and difficulties started at about that time and were intensified during the following months when her mother was often bedridden during a difficult pregnancy.

First Phase of Treatment

Carol was observed for one month, attending sessions five times weekly. During this period she formed a relationship with the therapist, recognized her, and expressed both positive and negative feelings about coming to her. She also soon showed understanding of the treatment in that she told her teachers she was coming to therapy because she was afraid and because she had hurt Leslie, a little girl whom she had repeatedly attacked in the nursery. Occasionally her responses to interpretations were normal; in fact, they were the first understandable, coherent sentences she spoke. For example, when told in connection with her play that some little girls like to hit people, Carol quickly replied, "I am not such a little girl, not me."

In view of these hopeful diagnostic signs, treatment proper began when Carol was three years, eight months old and has continued for almost three years. Carol always attended five times weekly except for the usual vacations. Throughout this period the therapist also had weekly interviews with the mother in order to gain detailed information about Carol's daily life, to advise the mother on educational measures, and to help her adjust her handling so as best to support the analysis in its various phases. The father was seen only occasionally.

The first task was to help Carol to improve her testing of reality by analyzing some of her main defenses.

Carol used internal and external denial extensively. She would not see or hear. She would repeatedly ask, "Who is it? What's his name?" but did not comprehend the replies. For about four months after the beginning of therapy she did not even acknowledge the existence of her baby sister, so that she did not have to show any signs of feeling about her. It was pointed out to Carol that she did not perceive things around her because they made her angry and scared. As she began to express herself verbally, she summed up her defense once, when she saw a block building, by saying, "Sometimes I am angry with the building, and then it's not a building." Similarly her nonsense talk served the purpose of denying any unpleasant feelings within herself; as she later put it, "If nobody knows what I am saying, then nobody knows that I'm angry."

Another of her most crippling defense mechanisms was the severe restriction of her ego activities: Carol could not dress herself, she could not handle play material, she could not even open a door or lift up a small chair. She only started to use her energy a little when she could say, "I can't do it because I'm angry."

Turning passive into active was also very pronounced and persisted for a long time. Carol had to be active in all play, especially in situations relating to eating. For months she would play at pretend-feeding by aggressively stuffing the therapist's mouth, but was quite unable to change roles. Similarly she could not passively take in with her eyes but could only attack with them. She would pick up toys and hold them close to her face, staring at them, yet could not comprehend what she saw. An eye examination proved that she had no organic visual handicap. Interpretations of her compulsive need to be active led eventually to a fuller understanding of the many traumatic situations which she had endured passively, and threw much light on the conflicts behind Carol's eating and learning disturbances. It was striking that in a repeat intelligence test, after one year of treatment, she scored an I.Q. of 76 in a test requiring passive cooperation, but in a test which allowed for active expression without many verbal instructions she achieved an I.Q. of 93. Her most bizarre defense mechanism was her confusion of attacker and victim, which at the time seemed to be the result of primitive introjection and projection. The full meaning of this defense was not understood until a number of years later. In her everyday life it could be observed in her confusion during attacks on other children. In the sessions she acted this out with toys; e.g., she once picked up the scissors, then retreated with them to the other end of the room, crying in terror, "You are going to hurt me!" Another time she grabbed a toy man aggressively and screamed out, "The man is going to break me all up!"

Lastly, Carol used displacement so persistently and to such an extent that she invested all reality with the fears and impulses which she had experienced in specific situations.

While interpreting Carol's defense mechanisms, it was also necessary to help her cope with her inner tensions by other means. It seemed that a great part of her ego was instinctualized and she did not have at her disposal the usual means of mastery, namely, verbalization of feelings and neutralization of instinctual energy. Carol's uncontrolled bodily expressions were linked with her feelings of anger and excitement. She gradually learned to use words for their verbal expressions and began to direct her movements more specifically; e.g., her excited waving of arms turned into hitting her thighs, then into tentatively hitting the therapist, and finally into verbal aggression. This ranged from a timid "It's hard to like you always" to eventual forceful threats: "I want to break you all up and throw you in boiling water!" Carol in this way learned to channelize her feelings, but her threshold of self-control was low. Therefore her libidinal expressions had to be limited, and in many instances discussion of exciting material had to be postponed; e.g., talking about sex differences would lead to her dancing around tensely, undressing, and masturbating. She had to be told, "We cannot talk about pipis and show them. That makes you too excited." (Pipi was her term for genitals.) At home, educational changes had to take place along similar lines, and Carol herself learned to dose her excitement; e.g., she would say to her father, "Daddy, don't kiss me goodnight. You make me too excited."

As Carol's defenses lessened, it was possible to observe the functioning of her ego. She seemed to have reached the level of a two-year-old: her conceptions were animistic, and the reality which she now absorbed and described was completely swamped with aggressive and libidinal meanings. Carol could not cut out paper because she feared it would hurt her in revenge; when she finally mastered the skill, she still did not dare to cut off a piece, saying, "I mustn't cut all of it." She needed repeated reassurances that it was quite safe to push buttons or handles because it did not hurt them. She could not eat food because she equated it with eating people. She treated toys and make-believe as live reality and therefore was practically unable to play; e.g., she wished very badly for a doll's house in the therapy room, but when it finally arrived she became so jealous of the doll's having a house to itself that she only wanted to snatch the house away from the doll and destroy it, since she could not live in it herself. As some of these meanings were clarified for Carol and she learned to distinguish people and things from herself, she cautiously started to discover the world around her. Many sessions were spent in reassuring, supporting, and teaching Carol as she found out about trees, blossoms, snow, rain, sun and shadows. She was delighted with her new knowledge, yet for a long time continued to approach facts and concepts with mistrust. After initial questions about a well, for example, she inquired anxiously, "Does it hurt? Does it make a noise?" All her early ego activities were acquired in the treatment and to a large extent depended on it. Even after two years she tended to produce much better work in the sessions than at home or at the nursery. Only in the last year of treatment, after the analysis of her learning disturbance, could she effectively learn from the teacher or her mother and proudly exhibit her skills to the therapist.

Throughout the first twenty months of treatment, Carol's conflicts centered around phallic and oral material. Her penis envy and fears about the loss of her penis were clearly manifested in her behavior. She lived in constant fear of bodily injury. She could not perform the simplest task, such as reaching up for a toy, lest she fall down and hurt herself. She was terrified of doctors and of men in general. She viewed injections as sadistic attacks, and later on repeatedly equated gunshots with shots of medicine. Carol would deny that boys had a penis or that she was a girl. She was compelled to show off bodily and was very conscious of pretty clothes. Sometimes she would say, "You know, I have a big pipi inside and it's—it's yellow." Her confusion about colors could later be linked with her denial of having observed the colors of real genitals. Carol expressed her wish for a penis by being demanding and possessive to an incredible degree, mainly toward her mother and the therapist; e.g., she was unable to settle down to drawing a picture because, in getting a sheet of paper, she became so preoccupied with wanting all the paper that the originally planned activity deteriorated into snatching paper and hoarding it, which finally led to an outburst of anger. She was of course quite unable to share, which, in addition to other difficulties, prevented her from even attempting to participate in group activities or play with other children. Her main fantasy was that she had lost her penis by having it bitten off by a man. It was possible to show her that she had projected her own oral aggressive wishes, and this was brought out more clearly in her eating disturbance. Only subsequent material showed that Carol's fantasy was strongly reinforced by actual sexual experiences and observations.

When Carol began to play with dolls and puppets, she would become extremely excited and would make them kiss and hug each other, push into and bite each other. At times she accompanied her play by speaking in an assumed, excited voice, "Honey, I'm going to tear off your clothes and eat your pipi. I'm going to bite it, honey. I'm going to put it in." Carol would attempt to act this out with the therapist, and when stopped and asked who said such things, she would quickly cover up with nonsense talk. Later she was able to relate her observations of fellatio and other sexual activities verbally, and her parents confirmed her material. Carol's emerging intercourse fantasies were mainly oral; e.g., "They eat their pipis and then throw them into the garbage can." "Mummy bites off Daddy's pipi." "Daddy bites off Mummy's pipi." She regarded eating together as a sexual activity, which accounted for her tremendous excitement during mealtimes. Carol's occasional anal and urethral intercourse fantasies were not difficult to correct, but her oral ones persisted for a very long time. Her observations of parental activities evoked so much fear, excitement, and anger in her that she had to deny them or pretend, through nonsense talk, that they had not been real happenings. She displaced all her feelings onto daily routines, filled them with great libidinal excitement, and would not hear therapeutic attempts relating the feared observations to her own sexual wishes. At that time Carol's general fears became more specific: she was terrified of anything that made a noise and would react to it by covering up her eyes and refusing to look at the source of the noise. Gradually Carol began to protest openly against noises, dared to find out about them, and accepted interpretations on the displacement from the parental bedroom.

After several months of treatment, Carol showed considerable improvement in all areas of ego functioning, her excitement subsided, and she could relate to people. Suddenly all her original symptoms of diffuse excitement returned and her reality testing deteriorated. She was again extremely fearful and demanded a good deal of physical closeness with the therapist. She staged a number of games of "going to the basement": she would lie down with her legs apart, waving her arms excitedly. Soon she accompanied these games by whispering to herself, "He touches my pipi. You must not tell your mummy. Mummy won't like it. She'll be angry. He is going to hurt my pipi. They are angry. You are going to bite off my pipi. They will be home." Another time she would add, "He kissed my pipi and bit it, and I bit his pipi. Don't tell Mummy. You mustn't tell Mummy." During these excited monologues Carol would mention the name of her father as well as the names of other men, especially her Uncle Jay. Carol had to be reassured that nothing was going to happen to her again, that she could tell the therapist and need not tell her mother. Her words and actions made it clear that she had undergone fellatio and possibly other sexual experiences with a man. The parents could give no information; to their knowledge, Carol had never been with anyone except members of the family. The father was a suspect for some time, since it was known that he had had a compulsive need for sexual reassurance at the height of his anxiety neurosis, but his attitude toward this material and his cooperation with Carol's treatment made it seem unlikely that he was personally involved. Several months later, however, Carol's Uncle Jay became very anxious and sought psychiatric help at the clinic of University Hospitals. According to his psychiatrist's confidential information, this uncle's chief complaint was his compulsive thoughts about performing perverse oral sexual acts with little girls. It was also known that this uncle often indulged in stimulating games with Carol when the family visited the grandparents, with whom he lived. The parents had to stop him repeatedly and protect Carol, who was afraid of him. In the analysis, Carol's material was interpreted from the point of view of her fears and was linked with her fantasies about the loss of her penis. Later Carol wanted the therapist to go to the basement to re-enact the scene with her. She also actively used toy animals and toy men to repeat in games the sexual activities that she had talked about. At that time she needed to be very active in every situation and could not endure passivity: she would stuff people with food and was very bossy. Her wish to master the experience actively was interpreted and later linked with her eating disturbance and her own sexual wishes. Every new exposure to seeing somebody naked or to witnessing a fight reactivated this type of material and was marked by a temporary return of the old symptoms. It seemed that Carol had never repressed the original incident but could relate it in an understandable manner only after her ego was capable of some verbal means of expression and she had enough confidence in the therapist to tell her what she had been forbidden to tell her mother.

Throughout the first two years of Carol's treatment, the analytic work centered largely around her severe eating disturbance. This symptom served to express a series of main and subsidiary conflicts. Sometimes it was used as a defense against fears on a phallic level, but mainly it seemed to be linked to fixated oral experiences and to attitudes in her home environment. At first Carol's greatest conflict was whether one eats what one likes or what one does not like. This confusion was partly the outcome of her experience of fellatio and of her own oral-sadistic fantasies and animistic conceptions; partly it had been encouraged by the mother, who frantically tried to persuade Carol that she "liked" certain foods in order to make Carol eat something. Grandmother added to this confusion by hugging Carol affectionately and saying, "I love you so much I could eat you all up." Carol's wish to eat up objects and people was so strong that she had to inhibit all her aggressiveness and thus could not eat. She would hold objects close to her eyes, staring at them aggressively. This subsided when she was shown that she even used her eyes to incorporate objects, which in turn often prevented her from looking at them with comprehension. Her oral aggression was particularly aimed at phallic objects. At one time Carol could eat only phallic-looking foods, like carrot sticks and wieners. She wished to bite off a penis and in this way acquire one for herself, as she thought her mother obtained a penis by biting off father's genitals. At times Carol was so envious of other people's food that she could not eat because she was too preoccupied with taking, or wishing to take, food away from others. To Carol, eating represented a sexual activity. She endowed it with her exciting observations and sexual fantasies, reacted to it with tremendous excitement, and, while unable to eat herself, interfered with everyone else's meals. In this way she acted out her wish to stop her parents' sexual activities and made up for the passive role of witness which she had had to take. One of Carol's main difficulties in eating was her inability to be the passive recipient of food. In her play she was always the active server of meals: she pretend-spoon-fed the dolls and the therapist, urged them to try to eat various items, and never allowed expressions of dislike. Although her mother had long since allowed Carol to select items she liked from the family menu and to help herself, Carol persisted in her aggressive feeding games. They were her active reaction to the passively endured oral experiences. They were linked to her helpless position during her seduction and later led to the uncovering of the anal component of her eating disturbance.

Anal material was largely absent during the first one and a half years of treatment. It seemed that the activities originating from sublimations of the anal drives were much more at Carol's disposal than energy from any other level. When Carol entered the normal positive oedipal phase, she expressed her aggression against her mother in the form of teasing her by not eating. At the same time she began to smell foods and her hands; foods which looked messy were repulsive to her, and she refused to touch anything dirty. When her underlying wish was interpreted to her, Carol went through a period of messing with and spilling food, eating with her fingers, and talking constantly during mealtimes in an attempt to "mess up" the meal for the others. She became very provocative and even soiled and wet on several occasions.

In the sessions she re-created the early feeding situation by acting like a baby who had to be fed by the therapist; instead of eating, however she would turn away her head and demand foods which the therapist had not listed in the pretend menu. It became evident that Carol had wanted to eat dirty substances as well as her own bodily products and, if not allowed to do so, had refused to eat altogether as a form of aggression against the mother's toilet-training demands. After this conflict was worked through, Carol's eating difficulty subsided. She enjoyed eating and gained over ten pounds within four months, which brought her up to the average weight for her age and height. Although the anal material was a strong component of Carol's eating symptom, it seems that otherwise her personality had dealt with the anal conflicts relatively normally, and they do not seem to have contributed to the overwhelming of her ego as was the case with her sexual experiences.

Because of Carol's disturbance, her positive oedipal phase was delayed. After about ten months of treatment, at the age of four and a half, she showed slight signs of wanting to be with her daddy and of becoming more angry with her mother, but she always quickly withdrew with fearful "I don't want him to do anything to me."

For a long time Carol persisted in the negative oedipal phase because her wish to get a penis from her mother contained all her early aggression against the mother. Until then she had been unable to show any hostility toward the mother directly, perhaps because the mother was the only safe person in her surroundings.

A few weeks after Carol's fifth birthday, her mother had to be hospitalized for a short period. Carol was prepared for this separation. Upon the mother's return, Carol developed her first neurotic symptom: she refused to open doors. In this way she demonstrated her wish that her mother would not return home so that she could continue her pleasant time alone with her father. This marked the onset of her positive oedipal phase and was accompanied by a great attempt to master her instinctual excitement at all levels. During the sessions she reprimanded the therapist, "Pull your dress down! It's not very ladylike." Upon being reminded of her earlier hostility toward her baby sister, she said, "Oh, yes, I used to scratch Lillie a long time ago, when I was very little. But now I watch her for Mummy." She was also very critical of other children's behavior and work output, while she herself tried hard to conform. For a long time Carol displaced her jealousy of her mother onto secondary attributes, such as the mother's belongings, and she resisted interpretations relating her feelings to the parental relationship. One day she said sadly, "You know, I can really have a lipstick and real perfume, but can I really have a husband to sleep with and two babies?" Carol's death wishes were so strong that she developed a transitory fear of death and a slight separation fear. It was much easier for her to express her hostility and jealousy in the transference. She was furious with the therapist for being married, and would say, "You can't have a husband. You can't even cook and you don't even have a room to sleep in with him." Her poor tolerance of frustration made her oedipal wishes into essential demands. When I expressed sympathy and told her that it was certainly very hard to wait until she would become a big lady and could have a husband to herself, Carol replied, "But I need a real husband very badly, right now." In relation to her father and to other men, Carol's behavior varied. At times she was overaffectionate and excitable; at other times she defended herself against her feelings by pretending not to like men. Increasingly she learned to have a good time with her father without becoming overwhelmed.

Carol's relations with other children lagged far behind her ability to be friendly with adults. For a long time she showed no interest in children, except for occasional hostile outbursts. Later she was greatly handicapped in her interaction with other children by being unable to share. Although Carol's rivalry with her baby sister contributed to this, she mainly related her behavior to her feelings about her mother: "My mummy is selfish. She won't let me have anything that belongs to big ladies, so I'll be selfish at the nursery." After one year she brought up the concept of friendship for the first time in response to a disliked interpretation by saying, "If you talk about such things, I won't be your friend any more." From then on she at least was able to tolerate her fellows, and by the time she left the nursery she was relatively capable of getting along with other children; occasionally she even enjoyed playing with them.

At the age of five and a half, Carol was ready to enter the kindergarten class of a public school. By this time she could test reality well. Her excited hand movements, tiptoeing, and nonsense talk were no longer in evidence; her pathological fears had subsided, except for a fear of dogs; she commanded a large vocabulary and could handle her aggression verbally; she also showed initial signs of identification with her mother. Her weakest points were her variable work output, her difficulty in following directions, and her relationships with other children.

Second Phase of Treatment

During the summer vacation Carol had a very good time and changed a great deal physically, giving the appearance of a much bigger, stronger girl.

A week before returning to treatment and entering kindergarten, Carol witnessed an automobile accident. She was riding with her aunt and her grandmother in her aunt's car when the car knocked down a woman carrying her little girl. The child fell to the pavement, was severely injured by the car, and later died in the hospital. An immediate scene ensued between the aunt, who was panic-stricken, and the child's mother, who loudly blamed the aunt for having killed her child. It was some time before Carol's mother was called to take Carol home. Although Carol's parents tried to discuss the incident with her, Carol at first denied how much she had seen, talked about it fairly calmly, and seemed to isolate the event. In the sessions she soon tried to master the experience by experimenting with hurting herself and asking, "Did it hurt more than that?" As her ego began to absorb the shock, she developed a number of fears of cars and of traffic in general. In addition, some of her nonsense talk and inability to see and to hear returned. It was pointed out to her that in this way she wished to pretend to herself that she had not seen or heard anything when witnessing the accident. Then Carol's underlying feelings emerged: she was mainly concerned with the idea of whose fault it had been. She projected her own hostile wishes against her mother onto the little girl, imagining that being dropped by the mother and being injured was the deserved punishment. Carol's reaction was determined by her acute oedipal complex and by the fact that, several months earlier, she had met a little girl whose mother had died in an automobile accident. Carol had very much envied that little girl for being able to have her father all to herself and had often wished that her own mother would disappear in a similar way. Although her conflict was worked through within a relatively short time, it caused her to inhibit her hostility toward women for a time and complicated her adjustment at school.

During her first few weeks in kindergarten Carol refused to participate in any activities, acted stupid, and did not respond at all to the teacher's gentle approach or her saying, "You can join us when you are ready." In the sessions Carol misused the teacher's kind words by postponing all discussion of the material and saying provocatively, "I'll tell you when I'm ready." Later she would play school but always had to take the active part of being the teacher. She tried to teach the therapist many activities on which she had blocked at school. Interpretations of her active defense, as well as of her negativism at school, brought out Carol's difficulties more clearly. She was extremely critical of herself and frustrated at not being able to do things perfectly; she could not bear her inferior role in relation to the teacher and was unable to comply with requests or to follow instructions. In so far as she wanted to learn at all, she showed interest only in inappropriate subjects, unsuited to her age and ability; e.g., reading, writing, and embroidery. Dynamically, this seemed to be due to a number of factors: her poor ability to tolerate frustration; the intensity and acuteness of her oedipal wish to be the mother, which she still hoped would be fulfilled magically and suddenly upon entering school; her compelling mechanism of taking the active role, which prevented her from tolerating the passive position of pupil; and, finally, her real inability to take in, which persisted in the area of learning although it had subsided with regard to eating. In the sessions, she mainly displayed various forms of "passive into active": she would feed the therapist with talks she thought the therapist liked, often adding, "Want to talk about it a little more?" much as one would feed a child with suggestions of different foods; she would also very aggressively feed the therapist with repetitive phrases, becoming more and more insistent when the therapist did not respond, yet when the therapist did respond, Carol did not take in what was said; in her fantasy play she would become the aggressive, punitive mother or the sadistic doctor or dentist, while the therapist had to be the patient or the child who had instruments, pills, and food stuffed into her mouth; her need to be active went so far that during the story time at school she could not listen but had to disrupt the period by telling her own stories to the other children. Another defense was to assume a different identity: she would act and talk like the mother, the teacher, her younger sister, or just like another child. Very often, of course, Carol would pretend to talk about her problems and to remember incidents that had really happened to her. Finally she reverted to her old defense of nonsense talk, primarily to saying that all the things she had previously told in the analysis were nonsense, that they had not been real, that she had just made them up.

Her behavior was accompanied by extreme guilt and the need to pro-voke punishment; e.g., she would be most apologetic in response to a defense interpretation, would say she knew she was really terribly bad to do what she had done, would promise never to do it again—and could one possibly love such a bad girl? In short, she was crushed. She also became very concerned as to where her mother was during our sessions. Could her mother hear her? What would her mother think if she heard that she, Carol, was so resistant? Yet at the end of most sessions she had to confess to her mother how very bad she had been. Although Carol was very resistant and often threatened to leave the room, she demanded much physical closeness and was often so upset that she had to sit on the therapist's lap, repeating how much she had missed her. This last be-havior pattern recurred every time the seduction material came to the surface, and it was later possible to point out to Carol that it reflected her great wish that her mother had been with her and protected her at the time of the original incident.

Carol's behavior and defenses were interpreted to her, and she was asked repeatedly why it was so bad to be herself. What had she done or seen that made her wish it had been unreal? This finally brought much new material about Carol's experience of seduction, as well as about her observations of parental intercourse, and led to a better understanding of her inability to take in visually or to take in according to verbal in-structions. It also cast some light on the nature of Carol's penis envy.

Although seduction and intercourse material were closely interwoven they are presented separately for purposes of clarity. In contrast to Carol's previous recollections of this material, her ego now seemed to participate much more actively; i.e., the material was not just brought in the form of overheard words and actions, which she reproduced almost unaltered while in a state of over-all tremendous excitement. The ma-terial now came mainly in the form of repetitive nightmares and trans-tory symptoms, accompanied by a great deal of real affect; in particular there was no hand waving or rolling on the floor, although she did become rather tense, had to go to the bathroom quite often, and reverted to being unable to see or hear so that interpretations could not reach her at times.

When it was pointed out to Carol that she wanted to learn only things which she was not supposed to learn, she began to mouth inedible objects such as toys, pencils, and tassels of Venetian blinds. Sometimes she would actually bite them so that they cracked. This would make her feel extremely guilty: she would worry about whether the objects could be fixed, and yet at the same time she aggressively wanted to keep the broken toys: "I didn't really break it. I did break it, but I didn't mean to. Can it be fixed? I broke your toy and I am going to take it home with me and keep it all the time. I am not even going to bring it back." She once brought a red balloon, which she managed to blow up in such a way that it entered her mouth fairly big, but the moment she tried to enlarge it, it wrinkled up and she feared she had spoiled it. She defied all attempts to refer her back to previous material about the seduction; she seemed to have repressed it completely. At times she wanted to be told about it as if it had been the therapist's.experience and to her was just nonsensical news. Then, following a visit to her grandparents and her Uncle Jay, she had a nightmare from which she woke up vomiting. She was quite shaken by this and had to stay home from school because she felt so upset and ill. In the dream a big dog had sat on top of her and poked holes into her all over with his big fingers and with his knife; he started poking her in the legs and belly, in her genitals, and finally in her eyes. At this point she felt like throwing up, and did. It was pointed out to her that it was strange she felt like vomiting when actually nothing had happened to her mouth in the dream. She then related another dream of the same night in which several dogs were in cages "so that they could not bite me." Carol's further association led to playing dentist: she wanted to stuff instruments from the doctor's kit into the therapist's mouth, became very tense, aggressive, and upset, and suddenly stopped, saying, "We mustn't play this. It makes you too excited." The nightmare could be worked on further only when it repeated itself following another visit to the uncle later that week. This time Carol woke up with the feeling that she was going to vomit, but did not actually do so. While talking about the dog's poking, Carol began to play with a large lipstick, which she wanted to stuff into the therapist's mouth, saying at a pitch of excitement, "You just open your mouth nicely, Honey. You'll be okay." Upon interpretation of her active defense, Carol pushed the lipstick into her own mouth, gagged, and in panic gurgled, "I can't talk, can't talk!" Carol was reassured that now she could take it out and could talk because nobody was really doing this to her. Carol shouted out,

"He put it in, and I bit it, and then it was gone, and he got so mad at me!
And I mustn't tell, I mustn't tell!" She was able to identify her Uncle Jay
and described having lain down with her legs apart while he touched and
tickled her and inserted his penis into her mouth. After she had recovered
a bit, she said, "Now I can tell it myself, and you can just listen." Following this material, Carol became overtly angry when asked to take in, in
contrast to her previous passive pretense of not understanding or of not
being able to learn. She began to follow instructions for work at school
and received a number of stars for her efforts. This made her simply
furious in the sessions afterwards: she was angry because she had really
done what the teacher had told her to. She became quite angry with her
Uncle Jay, and on one occasion when he was playing an exciting game
with her sister, Carol shouted at him, "You stop it, you stop it! You
mustn't do that to her!" Around that time Carol received her Christmas
and birthday presents, which were a great disappointment. Nothing short
of a penis or a husband could please her. As Carol put it, "Little girls can
do nothing about it. They have nothing, and everything can happen to
them." Carol had a fantasy of wanting to be given a big man who could
not move at all; only his penis could move; she would make it move and
would put it into her special hole. Carol's experience had accentuated her
developmental wish for a penis rather than a wish for more passive
feminine enjoyment. Interpretations are only partially effective in helping to overcome the past reality. Undoubtedly the repeated observations
of the primal scene and of parental fellatio have contributed to this all
the more, as there too she was the passive witness. When Carol's seduction material was discussed with her mother with a view to limiting
visits to the uncle and never leaving Carol alone with him, the mother
told me that she had always suspected this uncle because of his need to
excite, pat, and touch little girls, and his complete denial that this might
have any effect upon them. She also spontaneously contributed her idea
that Carol's original sudden fear of the Johnny cardboard figure must
have been related to an overwhelming experience in that house, especially since Carol had never wanted to visit there on Sundays, i.e., the only
day when the uncle was at home.

Carol had great difficulty in looking. She would watch television
intently staring at it, yet she could not take in the contents of the show.
In discussing this, Carol brought much material pointing to the idea of
how naughty it was to watch and to know what was going on. At first she
displaced, e.g., how naughty it was to want to look at the tooth fairy who
brought her money at night (she knew, of course, that the parents were
the fairy). She enacted short television shows which she would pretend to

watch very guiltily. With the help of defense interpretations, she later staged exciting interplays between puppets who were hugging, kissing, tearing off each other's clothes, poking into each other. Then she would suddenly ask, "Was I very bad to watch?" At this time Carol's looking inhibition became particularly pronounced: she actually could not see objects in the room, not even the therapist, nor could she hear her. Carol finally staged an intercourse scene herself: she lay on the floor with her legs apart, moving rhythmically while she tried to push big objects into her belly and between her legs. While doing so, she repeated phrases of endearment, orders about what to do next, and noises which she had obviously overheard. This was the first time that Carol had enacted such a scene by being the passive and the active partner at the same time, unable to distinguish the two or at times distinguishing them only in so far as she spoke the part of the active partner and acted the part of the passive one. This mechanism was discussed with her, and her observations were again explained. Retrospectively, this helped me to understand the nature of her early attacks on other children, her reactions to other scenes of violence, and her bizarre behavior with the toys at the beginning of treatment, e.g., her terror that the scissors in her own hand would attack her. Following this hour, she brought verbal accounts of observed fellatio and intercourse which she had viewed as a sadistic-libidinal attack, and she also had a number of dreams about it. Because this material was much less frightening than the seduction material, she would distinguish her dreams about it by qualifying the dog in these dreams as "the nice dog and not so big as the one that poked me in the eye." As Carol worked through this material, she became more active. She would now stage intercourse scenes between the puppets and suddenly shout at them in anger, "You stop it!" At the same time she could master her own excitement much better and could verbalize her libidinal wishes. Confronted with this material, Carol's mother admitted for the first time that although Carol had never been in their bedroom when they were having relations, she had ample opportunity to watch the parents because they used to have relations in the living room right outside Carol's bedroom door.

Although temporarily relieved, Carol soon became very concerned about being curious with her eyes. She would not tell me anything, accusing me of being "just a nosey so-and-so" and saying, "You don't really want to help me. You just want to know about everything." What was wrong with being nosey? Why should not she or I know anything we wanted to know? Who had told her off? I pointed out to Carol how very closely she was observing me, how greatly concerned she was about a little scratch I had, and in particular how increasingly anxious she was about her own little injuries, especially when they were bleeding. This finally led to Carol's observations of menstruation. She had seen blood-soiled pants in the hamper, was certain that her mother lost her penis this way, and she related it to herself, i.e., she believed she must have lost her penis by pulling it so that it bled and came off. Again Carol defended herself by repeatedly assuming another identity. This time she did so in order to avoid her own guilt. As she put it, "I shall be some other girl. I shall be Marilyn or Susie, and then I won't be the bad Carol." It was not so terrible to be a girl. The worst was to be a bad girl.

The interpretative work during this period was concentrated mainly on clarifying Carol's ideas about her observations of intercourse, fellatio, and menstruation and showing her that she had extended fear, anger, guilt, and excitement to quite harmless areas of looking, which consequently made it impossible for her to learn by taking in with her eyes. Also, her persistent dog phobia subsided as she began to understand that her dreams about frightening and exciting dogs really related to her feelings about her father.

Although Carol had been able to relate her traumatic experiences in so much detail and in a much more active way, and although it had been possible to show her that her fellatio experience and observations had been not only very frightening but also very exciting, that she had wished to participate in the parental activities and had wished to bite off and swallow Uncle Jay's penis, Carol continued to have the greatest difficulty in taking in verbal instructions and in learning through verbal explanations. She would listen to the words and then repeat them exactly in the manner and tone of voice in which she had heard them, but was quite unable to act accordingly. For example, she would ask me how to make a certain letter because she wanted to learn to write her name; as soon as I wrote out the letter and told her how it was done, she would pretend to try to copy it, pretend to try to please me, yet she would persistently start the letter in the wrong way and would end up with a scribble, while repeating my instructions or corrections. The persistent stupidity of her attempts and the monotonous repetitiveness of her imitation of me had such an aggressive affect that it belied her apparent wish to please and to learn. Around this period she again reverted to stuffing me with food in play, and in anger she began to spit. It was possible to show her that she was really spitting back all that she had been told, much as she used to spit back food that her mother would feed her. The mother confirmed that during Carol's second year, and later, Carol would constantly spit back what had been spoon-fed to her; she never digested anything to throw it up later, nor did she actually refuse to take food into her mouth. Carol's past hostile reaction to the mother's feeding was linked with her present hostile spitting back of words. It was pointed out to Carol that she equated food with words, that she resented her mother's compulsive, forceful talking just as she had resented her earlier feedings, and that she had extended this reaction to all verbal instructions. Carol re-enacted her early feeding difficulty in the sessions: for a while she had to spit so compulsively that she would spread out a sheet of paper in the closest and spit and spit. Her hostility in spitting back was discussed with her at length and also linked to her fellatio experience when she wanted to spit back the penis but could not.

Gradually Carol's actual and verbal spitting back subsided, yet she still could not take in at all. Sometimes as she listened to me, I would notice sudden chewing movements and finally realized that she was indistinctly repeating my lip movements; she would chew, then swallow, and looked quite blank by the time I had finished talking. Carol became extremely guilty when this was pointed out to her. She became verbally very aggressive and threatened, "I'll chew you up to bits, and you'll be inside me and gone!" It became clear that Carol's spitting back had been a defense against her aggressive wish to devour and to destroy by incorporating. It was also evident that she treated any part of a person, even that person's spoken words, as if they were the whole person. She could now begin to understand why it had been much safer to spit back her mother's food, for otherwise she would have eaten up all of her mother, and why she had reacted with such guilt to her Uncle Jay's anger, namely, she had not only gagged and therefore bitten his penis but had actually wanted to devour and destroy the penis inside her. With the help of this new insight into the nature of Carol's different oral mechanisms, I could now review the manner in which Carol had related her seduction and intercourse observations when she came for treatment. The first time, she recalled the traumatic incidents in the form of "spitting back" what she did not like; the second time, she brought out how she had reacted by wanting to incorporate or devour the object of her aggressive and libidinal wishes. It thus showed her not only as an overwhelmed, passive participant but also as an active participant, although mainly only in thoughts and wishes. The earlier spitting back of unabsorbed material therefore appears partly as a defense against the very active oral-sadistic and libidinal impulses which had been evoked.

In her daily life Carol tried to defend herself against these impulses which she experienced in every learning situation. She would be unable to learn on the spot according to instructions, but would produce what she had learned in a different setting; e.g., what her teacher had taught her she could show in the sessions, and vice versa, or she would learn something at once but would insist that she had taught herself or had done it right just by accident. Her tremendous wish to incorporate was discussed with her, as well as the fact that she had to take in so aggressively that it became impossible for her to store the acquired information inside herself and to remember it. Anything that she took in had to be destroyed, the partial object standing for the whole object. In fact, Carol could learn from and identify herself with adults only in areas where she could learn by visual means, i.e., by imitation and observation. For example, she understood and was interested in movies and plays, magazine and picture stories, and she could also learn a number of household chores. Yet the moment that verbal directions were issued, she had to incorporate them destructively and could hardly profit from them. Not only was this linked to her past oral experiences but proved to be greatly influenced by her still acute penis envy and oedipal aggression. She badly wanted for herself all knowledge that she did not have; since she equated everything she did not have with a penis, learning immediately brought up her oral-sadistic fantasy of acquiring a penis. Similarly, she very much wanted to take her mother's place in relation to her father and also in order to avoid being a helpless little girl, yet the wish was so strongly reinforced by the earlier feeding situation that she could become the mother only by taking her in orally and thus destroying her. As we worked on this material, Carol's learning improved considerably but showed a strange peculiarity: she could now learn very well as long as the teacher did not insist that she do so, and she also profited most from interpretations that were not directed specifically toward herself. She showed the same tendency more clearly one Sunday when she could not eat a meal she usually liked because her Uncle Jay was present and she imagined he had urged her to eat. On the other hand, Carol would often readily take in words directed to her provided she liked their content, and she would insist upon being told things she liked to hear, e.g., praise for her work. It was pointed out to her how confused she still was as to whether she should take in what she liked or what she disliked, what was urged on her or what was not urged on her, whether it would make people more angry if she did or did not take in. Apparently Carol's aggression was still so great that she often refused to take in, in order to preserve the object.

Although this material requires much further working through, Carol has improved greatly during recent months. She has been able to keep up with her class in learning. More recently she has managed to follow verbal directions and has shown interest in and remembers stories, games, and other activities taught in kindergarten. She enjoys school and is eager to compete. Her teacher feels that Carol learns best when she is not personally urged to do something but when it is left up to her to do as well as the other children. She will start the first grade in autumn. Her social relationships are quite good. She plays well with girls but tends to become overexcited with boys, whom she provokes by her very coyness. This difficulty is at present being worked on in the analysis. At home Carol is no problem except for her cheeky talking back in response to requests. She is quite independent in dressing, washing, and looking after herself. She loves working around the house, is a good cleaner, dishwasher, and table setter, and regularly takes care of some chores for which she receives weekly pocket money. Although Carol has become more reserved and more aware of social habits, she tends to speak her mind very freely and impulsively, as younger children do. She has an excellent sense of humor and is an astute observer. Her teacher believes her to be of superior intelligence, but it is doubtful whether she can yet cooperate satisfactorily in a testing situation.

It is evident from the course of the treatment that Carol's relationship with the therapist is a very close, basically positive one. She still needs the therapist as a reassuring, supporting person. On occasion, especially at the beginning of the analysis and sometimes in connection with the material, Carol has regarded the therapist as the feared father or uncle, and she has also equated the therapy room with the scene and objects of her traumatic experiences. She would become anxious, would leave the room, or would spend much of the time hiding in the closet. For many months the therapist was the only person to whom Carol dared to voice her hostility, and for an even longer period later she treated the therapist as the envied mother. However, she was also always able to express her positive feelings, the therapist being the first one with whom Carol could share and to whom she brought spontaneous gifts. She has nearly always been eager to come and is fully aware of the help she receives. One day her mother's car broke down on the way to the session. It had to be towed in, and the mother prepared Carol for not seeing the therapist that day. Carol became quite upset and started to cry loudly, "But whom shall I tell my worries to?" until a customer at the garage overheard Carol and offered to drive her and her mother to my office. In spite of her dependence, Carol never regressed during long vacations or temporary interruptions for which she had not been prepared. On her return she never had difficulty in verbalizing her sadness and anger over the separation. Carol has an excellent understanding of the treatment task. For example, during a Friday session Carol was resistant and wanted to leave earlier; when this was pointed out to her, she said, "Yes, I don't like it. But I guess I better get down to it, because tomorrow is Saturday and you won't be able to help me, and then I'll go yak-a-ti-yak all week end." Provocative talking was one of her most conspicuous symptoms at the time.

The analysis presented a number of technical difficulties. Particularly in the initial phases it was very hard to work with Carol, since she could not express herself in play because of her animistic concepts, nor could she verbalize; even later talking about instinctual material would lead to her being overwhelmed with excitement. Another difficulty has been to keep Carol's ego development and the analytic material in step. Much time had to be spent in helping her to find out about reality, in learning, and in education in general. In addition, Carol needed a good deal of physical comfort to be able to tell about her frightening sexual experiences. However, the therapist refrained from bodily handling as much as possible and never introduced the eating of real foods. An attempt was also made throughout to adopt an attitude different from that of Carol's parents by being very passive— at times even walking around in the treatment room would frighten Carol; by talking little and by insisting on a direct approach to reality—the parents are excessive talkers and neglect actual experience to help Carol clarify simple concepts.

Carol's relationship with the therapist is a reflection of her basically good relationship with her mother. Both parents have been most cooperative throughout Carol's analysis. The mother in particular has shown good insight and has been able to profit a great deal from her interviews with the therapist. She has handled Carol well and has been helpful in encouraging Carol to refer her problems to the treatment sessions, yet allowing her to express at home the appropriate feelings. The mother tries to control her own weaknesses to a certain extent in relation to Carol, yet she remains an aggressive talker and prefers to argue about matters rather than to insist on firm, quiet discipline. It has been interesting to observe that the mother has the same disciplinary difficulty with her younger child, although Carol's sister has developed fairly normally and has no eating or learning problems. Carol's father is still preoccupied with his own difficulties; therefore the main burden of education falls upon the mother. It is extremely hard for the father to handle the children firmly because he himself is so often irritable and fears they may reject him.

During the last six months, Carol's analysis has dealt mainly with two aspects, namely, her relationship with boys, and her adjustment to a new teacher and to more formal learning in the first grade.

Carol's earlier coy provocativeness with boys subsided as she gained further understanding of her oral-aggressive wishes toward them. Her attitude was patterned after her reaction to her traumatic experience with her uncle and was reinforced by her still acute penis envy. At present she prefers girls as friends, but she also makes normal contacts with boys and enjoys playing with them.

In the first grade the new teacher found Carol very cooperative, socially accepted, and eager to do good work. There are, however, some traces of her previous difficulties: she is sometimes slower than her classmates in completing her assigned tasks, and at first she asked the teacher for repeated individual instructions. The analysis so far has shown that Carol's slowness in comprehending and working occurs in situations which arouse her anger toward the teacher, and she tends to cope with this by restricting or slowing up her ego activities. The cause of Carol's hostility appears to lie in her envy of the adult woman whose greater knowledge makes Carol feel very inferior. Carol's aggression is becoming embodied in her superego so that she herself is the sternest critic of her work. In spite of these difficulties, she is able to keep up with the teaching program.

BIBLIOGRAPHY

Freud, A. (1936), *The Ego and the Mechanisms of Defence*. New York: International Universities Press, 1946.
—— (1946), The Psychoanalytic Study of Infantile Feeding Disturbances. *This Annual*, II.
—— (1949), Aggression in Relation to Emotional Development: Normal and Pathological. *This Annual*, III/IV.
—— (1952), The Mutual Influences in the Development of Ego and Id: Introduction to the Discussion. *This Annual*, VII.
Fraiberg, S. (1952), A Critical Neurosis in a Two-and-a-Half-Year-Old Girl. *This Annual*, VII.
Greenacre, P. (1950), Special Problems of Early Female Sexual Development. *This Annual*, V.
—— (1952), *Trauma, Growth and Personality*. New York: Norton.
—— (1954), Problems of Infantile Neurosis: A Discussion. *This Annual*, IX.
Hartmann, H. (1952), The Mutual Influences in the Development of Ego and Id. *This Annual*, VII.
—— and Kris, E.; Loewenstein, R. M. (1949), Notes on the Theory of Aggression. *This Annual*, III/IV.
Lehman, E. (1949), Feeding Problems of Psychogenic Origin. A Survey of the Literature. *This Annual*, III/IV.
Maenchen, A. (1953), Notes on Early Ego Disturbances. *This Annual*, VIII.
Mahler, M. S. (1952), On Child Psychosis and Schizophrenia: Autistic and Symbiotic Infantile Psychoses. *This Annual*, VII.

CLINICAL CONTRIBUTION TO THE PROBLEM OF THE EARLY MOTHER-CHILD RELATIONSHIP

Some Discussion of Its Influence on Self-destructive Tendencies and Fugue States[1]

ELISABETH R. GELEERD, M.D. (New York)

In the last few years a great deal of work is being done in order to shed some light on the earliest mental processes. The Symposia published 1950 and 1952 in *This Annual* reflect the approach and the points of view of the various authors.

Anna Freud (1953), in her paper "Some Remarks on Infant Observation," elaborates on Freud's concept of the pleasure ego. She vividly describes how the young infant does not differentiate between himself and the outside world. Under the influence of the pleasure principle, the infant builds a "pleasure ego": what is pleasant is considered to be himself, what is painful is considered to be outside himself. While on the mother's lap, he does not know where he himself ends and the environment begins. Even in the second year, children may still occasionally behave with their mothers as if their two bodies were one. A child who likes to suck his thumb will suddenly take the mother's thumb instead of his own; or, while feeding, will put the spoon into his mother's mouth.

One may surmise that what goes on on the mental side of the newborn are the contrasting feelings of pleasure and pain. It is on the strength of these sensations and of their contrasting nature that the infant organizes what he will later feel to be his self. Only through the painful experience of losing his mother periodically does the child learn, very gradually in the course of the first year, that the big pleasure self he believes to be his own is not all his own. Parts of it walk away from him and become environment, while others remain with him for ever.

Hoffer (1950), in "Development of the Body Ego," points out, as a

1 Presented at a meeting held in connection with the Freud Centenary at the Hampstead Child-Therapy Clinic in London, May 3, 1956.

decisive factor in the delineation between the self body and outer world, the unique experience of the infant touching itself. He then states: "the self emerges as a function of interaction between inner drive and apparatus (bodily organs like the mouth) through which the drive acts."

In his paper on "The Mutual Influences in the Development of Ego and Id," Hoffer (1952) characterizes the sleep of the infant as the essence of primary narcissism, a state where there is complete lack of all qualities discriminating between self and not self. Referring to the view expressed by Brierley (1951) that it is a state of feeling awareness which cannot be devoid of sensory impressions, he reformulates this to mean that a fusion of sensory and affect awareness takes place.

Edith Jacobson (1954), in her paper "The Self and the Object World," writes that there is a continuous, silent discharge toward the inside in the sleeping infant. This is the earliest form of discharge on the self.

From the academic psychological point of view, Piaget (1950) states that the psychic activity of the infant begins with the attempts at mastery of the environment. Simple perceptions become meaningful very early; e.g., the sight of the mother or the breast means that food is coming. With maturation, actions become purposeful; thus the infant moves its hands to grasp an object. The sensations of effort and achievement as well as those of impatience, waiting, satisfaction, etc., are the first emotional experiences of the self.

Heinz Hartmann (1950) and Ernst Kris (1950) again call attention to the fact that the understanding of the development of the ego will have to come from a collaboration between direct observation and reconstruction from clinical work.

It is the purpose of this paper to present fragments of the analyses of three adult patients where the analysis of the early relationship to the mother played a decisive role.[2] This relationship might be described as one in which the patients to some extent experienced themselves as being one with the mother and re-experienced this in the transference with the analyst.

Two of the patients could be diagnosed as character disorders; the third presented a more disturbed picture due to alcoholism. All three led active, full lives and, though hampered by their many neurotic difficulties, were able to function.

[2] Manifestations of disturbances of early mother-child relationship, resembling those here to be described, may be found in the cases of fetishism reported by Bak (1953) and Greenacre (1955). Their patients, due to early traumata, had failed to achieve a complete differentiation from the mother. This resulted in intense separation anxiety and clinging reaction as well as in increased primary identification and impairment of the sense of identity accompanying fetishism.

Case 1

A male patient in his thirties at a certain stage of his analysis became aware of a sudden upsurge of obsessive thoughts with anal content about his analyst. The childhood memories centered around his mother's uninhibited behavior in the bathroom and led to the discussion of his masochistic fear of the woman whom he always was driven to pursue. This partially explained why he had to put her on a pedestal, adore her, recite poetry about her, looking upon her as an untouchable queen; but the moment a girl showed willingness for a relationship, his interest in her diminished considerably.

Early in his analysis, the patient had related a dream in which he went in a rocket to the moon. There he found huge, pear-shaped objects of which he wanted to get more than his share—or he would be left out. However, he only managed to get two; some other people got less. These pear-shaped objects were bottles containing a most precious liquid. They looked "shitty" on the outside. About their shape he said: "Well, maybe it looked like a penis, maybe it looked like a breast"; but this seemed an intellectualization. He extensively described the power of the rocket, the agility of the machine and its speed.

In the period which followed, the patient became aware of increased sexual excitement. Simultaneously there was in his behavior something best described as hyperactivity, while at the same time he complained about stomach aches. In the transference as well as in memories his sibling rivalry came to the fore. There was a growing awareness of the patient's intense feelings of need for the analyst. He could only describe it as something engulfing him, something in which he lost all his feelings of self. It reminded him of the times in childhood when he was delirious with fever and felt he was becoming part of his pillow. At the same time he mentioned how important it was to him to feel powerful; he wished he had a profession enabling him to decide over life and death. Apparently his need to feel powerful was directly connected with his feelings of being completely dissolved in his relationship to the analyst.

In fact, he suffered from intense feelings of inefficiency; he wished closeness with the analyst in order to become powerful, he felt depressed because he could not obtain her; but then suddenly something came over him which he could only describe as a hypomanic feeling, like "to hell with her, let's get drunk, let's find another girl."

It is generally assumed that feelings of omnipotence have their origin in early infancy when the cry of the baby makes the mother appear and bring satisfaction of bodily needs. In this case the fantasies of power became conscious in the analysis simultaneously with the emergence of feelings of intense longing for the mother.

Gradually there emerged dreams and fantasies of an oral nature. The patient had more need for taking a cocktail, here or there, and drinking wine. At this point he reported an inability to read and would become very sleepy whenever he was reading. He also would fall asleep in concerts, which annoyed and shamed him no end, since he was a great music lover. There seemed to be a generally increased need for sleep. The patient had always appeared highly active in his life and work, keeping very busy, going to many places, filling up his time to the utmost, with a strong feeling that no time should ever be wasted. He now recalled a period of his life when he had been really overactive. He had been most busy, felt he could think much faster and more clearly than ever before, and this was when he had been asked to be a witness in a lawsuit. One of his friends was in serious trouble, and the patient could save this friend by giving testimony in his behalf. In his feeling, this came close to being involved in decisions over life and death.

He now brought to attention the dream he had related earlier, about going in a rocket to the moon. He elaborated on it, mentioning that in adolescence he had been most interested in science fiction and had actually had fantasies of going out into space and becoming a great astronomer and physicist in these pursuits. He suddenly recognized that the pear-shaped objects reminded him, in their shape, of baby bottles with nipples which he remembered seeing around the house when his siblings were small. He recalled one story he had read that always stood out in his mind. This was a tale about an inventor who went out into space with his rocket. But since our universe is expanding, he expanded with it, becoming bigger and bigger, and finally became so strong that he got out of our universe into a new universe. There he discovered that our own universe actually was but an atom in a gigantically sized superuniverse, of which he (the hero of the story and the patient through identification with the hero) then became a part.

Now the dream became understandable. "The moon," said the patient spontaneously, "that is the breast," and the fantasy of going out into space to retrieve the bottles with the precious liquid was an expression of an early union with the mother.

After this session the patient felt depressed. He took a long walk near the river and, although he never had been suicidal, he now longed to jump into the river and just drown. The reason for the depression was that after the session it had dawned on him so clearly that he would never be able to possess the analyst. Thus, the fantasy of going into space meant not only reunion with the mother but also a sense of isolation from her, a going away from everybody; to have no attachment, to be all alone and to die. "The suicidal fantasy," he said, "is like the space fantasy. My wish to possess you is based on dreams; it's completely air, gas, like a planet. Even if you were free, I could never have you. I have this hunger for you, and it is all a dream. It is like a hungry man getting into a desert; but he realizes that the whole world is a desert, it's all inside himself. Those fantasies I have about you, to chew you and to eat you, they are a terrific feeling; they are a compulsion. I have got to have you, and there should be no danger of losing you. If I could only be inside of you, or eat you up. I could travel to the end of the universe to do this; I'll build my own rocket ship, but once I'm out in the universe I must forever starve because there is no one and I will be all alone." In the midst of the drowning fantasy he had had a feeling as if he were an infant and someone strong and maternal and prohibitive like the analyst were holding him up. They were together in the water; it was like playing as well as holding him up. Then there came a desperate feeling: "You cannot let me go. Drowning is terrible, because it means separation. It is this terrible fear of death that I have." He started worrying that I would think he was so impossible and had such terrible symptoms and did not get any better, so that I would be fed up with him and kick him out. "But," he said, "I won't go, I'll cling, I'll stay forever." Here the patient remembered with affect the situations in childhood when his mother had cruelly punished him by putting him on top of a shelf above the cellar steps, in the dark. He realized that those repeated episodes of standing immobile on the shelf in the pitch-dark must be related to his space fantasies, because on the shelf he had felt suspended in space and absolutely deserted.

All these fantasies seemed to prove Lewin's contention (1950) that suicidal fantasies and sleeping are closely linked to the early infantile fantasies of falling asleep at the breast, reflecting the whole complexity of the mixture of union with the mother and separation from her in those very early, undifferentiated object relationships. It is noteworthy that this patient's increased need of sleep also confirms Lewin's contention of the oral triad.

At the same time when the patient was talking about feelings of deep longing for the analyst, as expressed by the obsessions about eating and chewing her, there were also obsessions to hurt her. The ideas would stick in his mind and plague him, and they would give him no peace until he had been able to think the worst; namely, that her son would die. First of all, it would render me helpless and I would need him.

(Needless to add that the dead son was the patient himself as well as a displacement from his younger brother.) Then the horrible self-reproaches would start: what a terrible monster he was, and how the analyst would certainly not want to deal with him any more—on and on, in a circle, because then the next thought would be: "I will cling to her," etc.

Freud wrote that obsessive-compulsive phenomena stem from fixations to the anal-sadistic stage of libidinal development. He also stressed that obsessive phenomena might be due to a precocious ego development. The oral regression of the patient simultaneously with the obsessions raises the question whether the latter do not, in this case, stem mainly from oral fixation. Possibly we are dealing here with one of the instances noted by Hartmann (1950), when he suggests that the formation of obsessional phenomena may be tied up with the development of ego phenomena which need not necessarily be linked to certain stages of the libido.

CASE 2

The next patient to be described is a young, unmarried woman who came to analysis because of alcoholism. She was an intelligent business woman who periodically had to get drunk. She would drink until she had "knocked out her faculty of restraint," as she put it, and then would go out and get herself into all kinds of dangerous and compromising situations. She would pick up strange men, indulge in various perverse activities with them, and generally wake up with great memory defects or complete amnesia as to what had really happened.

When she started her analysis she decided that she would stop drinking. She wanted to obtain a prohibition from me about it and was resentful that none was given. When she herself stopped the drinking, she became a compulsive eater. This disturbed her intensely, since she was an attractive girl whose appearance was important to her. As a matter of fact, also her mother had always been proud of the patient's good looks. She was well aware that she made herself look ugly this way and also that it made her look much more like her mother who, ever since the patient knew her, had been an obese woman.

For a long time her attachment to the man, her father, and her rivalry for him with mother and sisters had been discussed in the analysis. Then followed a period in which the analyst and the mother became the center of the analysis. Intense rivalry for the mother had existed not only with her older sister but, much more so, with her brother who was two and a half years younger. At this point her overeating and drinking suddenly made themselves felt with the utmost intensity and became uncontrollable. To mention a dream from this period: There is a lot of candy wrapped in paper; the patient eats much more than her share, and should stop but cannot. This dream was elicited when I had announced an interruption of the analysis for a period of three weeks. In her associations to the dream she made a slip: "You are leaving me for three months," and then, with a start: "my mother nursed all her children only for three months."

With the increasing awareness of her need for her mother, the sexual nature of the relationship could also be analyzed. A dream confirming this material was as follows: someone, a man or a woman, was performing cunnilingus on the patient; it was like a calf drinking from a cow, without the cow paying any attention to what the calf is doing. The patient felt that she was the calf as well as the cow. This dream seemed to open a direct way to an understanding of the patient's need to drink. She then could elaborate on many of the perverse oral activities which had taken place when she was drunk. On one occasion there had been a homosexual episode. It became clear that the men, who previously had been understood as father figures, represented much more strongly the mother.

For the first two years of her analysis she hardly ever took a drink, even socially; but gradually the drinking increased. She tried not to drink, but compulsively had to. The way she described it was that at night when she came home from work, she just could not stand her apartment. She felt restless; she felt as if she were "a disembodied body in search of a body; everything seems to be in a fluid, and I am part of it"; and she had to drink in order to stop this agony. She felt that with her drinking she could "get herself into oblivion until nothing exists and nothing is anything," and although some awareness continued, the drinking somehow stopped the mental agony. It seemed self-evident that to reach a state of oblivion must have been one of the reasons for the serious drinking that had occurred before the analysis.

The patient's anxiety in her home, with the feeling that she could not stand it, seemed like a form of claustrophobia. She would walk from room to room, but no room gave her peace. There was a strong urge to go out, but going out would have meant the repetition of her past behavior: going to a bar, getting drunk, etc. She then would take a drink and, in spite of the alcohol, when she finally went to bed could not fall asleep. Then she would start to take sleeping tablets, all of which only made her more awake.

Lewin (1952) discusses in detail how in claustrophobia many elements of the oral triad are present. He approaches the problem through symbolic interpretation. The analysis of the patient's feelings about her house, her mother and herself showed definitely that the claustrophobia was rooted in the early mother-child relationship. Many of her symptoms confirmed Lewin's thesis.

A few dreams of the patient from this period of her analysis are reported here. For instance: "There were two women, a mother and a little girl; they have a hole in the chest, and they are actresses; they are wearing pale pink drawers; but instead of their legs, their arms are through these; one of the women had a hoarse voice, she was the tougher of the two." *Euridice* was the first association to this dream—thus the search for a loved one who has disappeared. The patient also believed that she had a hoarse voice from drinking too much the night before. The dream also seemed to indicate that the breasts now were the object of sexual interest. The subsequent night she dreamed that an awful woman was clawing her with her nails and biting her, and she tried to escape. She then woke up, and in the state between dreaming and waking she felt there was someone on top of her, a figure hard to describe: big and fat like a sack of meal, or like a fish without a head or a tail, or a mother rolling over on a baby; "the body is undifferentiated, fat like my mother."

She recalled the hypnagogic phenomenon of seeing a lot of cooked oatmeal, which repeatedly had disturbed her while in college. "This must be my mother's breast," she suddenly remarked; "it is mottled, like skin must look when you see it from close by."

Another dream was: She was in analysis; both analyst and analysand were sitting in rocking chairs, across from each other; and she made it clear in relating the dream that there was some doubt, in the dream, as to who was analyzing whom.

In another dream again there are loads of mashed potatoes, a barrelful of them; she has a feeling that she should eat them because they are available, not because she really wants to. She has the identical feeling when she goes on her compulsive eating and drinking binges.

The patient in her childhood had lived near a convent. She now brought into focus the fact that since the age of two and a half, which was the date when her brother was born, she had spent most of her daytime life there. Some people actually had thought she belonged to the convent. She had spent most of her time in the kitchen where the nun who cooked was a fat woman with heavy breasts. The nuns always had stood in her life for what is beautiful and good. As she defined it, they stood for "ascetics and aesthetics." It also is interesting to note here that the nun is a good prototype of the vague, nondescript, early oral libidinal object; her face is almost entirely hidden by a coif, her figure completely wrapped in her garments; she is as nondefined as the "bag-of-meal" figure in the dream. The patient recalled that in the afternoon all the nuns used to take a rest upstairs and no uninitiated persons were allowed inside the convent. But generally the patient was hidden by a lay worker in the kitchen (interestingly enough, in the larder). But one afternoon, she related, while the nuns had their—and here the patient made a slip and said—"Fiesta—oh no, siesta," one nun apparently had taken her upstairs. Here the memory was very vague, but something had happened. The nun had started to take the patient's clothes off; she has a feeling, also her panties; but then they were disturbed by someone. The patient felt most guilty and unsure of herself when telling this, but still said that definitely something like that had taken place.

In this period of the analysis the homosexual aspect of the relationship stood in the center of interest. But then another element came more and more into focus; namely, the feeling of being part of the mother, as if the patient and her mother or analyst were one unit.

During this time I had to keep the patient waiting a few minutes for her appointment, and when the patient came into the office she was in a rage. She had first wondered whether she came at the wrong time or whether I had not heard her ring the bell, then thought she had been forgotten, and to vent her rage she could only think she would like to jump through the window. "I know I was mad at you, but it didn't make any difference if *I* jumped through the window or made *you* jump." And she added: " a real temper tantrum."

The patient lately had mentioned that she was not able to stand herself. She looked fat, her clothes did not fit, she felt sloppy, her complexion was sallow from drinking and lack of sleep, and she used the same terminology about her apartment: "The place is sloppy, in disorder, things are all over the place." Moreover, when discussing her mother she would again use the same words: how fat the mother was, how careless of her looks; how the home had always been a most hospitable place for friends, with lots of food, but never neat and never attractive.

It was interpreted to the patient in this connection that her eating and drinking were not only the expression of a need to be united with her mother, but also a punishment for the mother. The mother had always shown off the patient and all her accomplishments; thus, to be unsuccessful and ugly is not merely a self-destructive act. At the present stage of the analysis it was not clear whom the patient was hurting: her mother, herself or the analyst.

In the next session, the patient said that while going home she had found herself in the strangest state: "It all sounds wacky and crazy, but

I can only describe it in this way: after I left, I had the feeling as if between you and me there was a pure love, something spiritual, something like the holy communion. I have read about the 'return to the womb'; but this was not a return to the womb, because we can only return to the womb if there is an 'I,' as a person, who can go in there; but it was much vaguer than that. You and I were like one." After she came home, there was an intense conflict about whether she would be able to do some intellectual work and read. Instead, she was again compelled to take a drink, to cook herself some food and then, while she had another drink, to call up a maternal friend. But all this time, while drinking, she was trying to resist the effect of it. One of the reasons for not wanting to go into her state of oblivion was that she was afraid of it; it seemed like a dissolution. To fall asleep had the identical meaning.

The patient was a person who easily made friends, who superficially had an easy way of talking and making contact with people. With superiors she was either overapologetic and self-depreciative, or had a manner of "hail fellow well met." Her free and easy manner, at times almost hypomanic, was an expression of "the unity between mother and child." There is no difference between us, we are equals, we are the same, we belong together. It also meant: "You are as low, bad and dirty as I am," as well as a complete denial of her own feelings of unworthiness.

Thus, as the patient unraveled it in her analysis, feelings of being part of the mother coexisted with sexual fantasies about the mother. Clinically and dynamically one might say that the patient identified herself with her mother. It is important to see that genetically this particular identification was the result of a regression to that period of early infancy where, to use Anna Freud's example, the patient when sitting on her mother's lap was one with the mother, but also considered herself as being the same person as her mother. Chronologically the analysis of the sibling rivalry preceded that of the homosexual aspect of the relationship to her mother. Then followed a period in which the fantasies of being a unit with the mother were the main topic. It may well be that the history of the relationship with the mother was rolled back in reverse in the analysis.

CASE 3

Another young woman, who had come to analysis because of a character disturbance and had revealed a number of masochistic traits, gradually became more and more aware of her dependency upon the analyst as a mother figure. Simultaneously she discovered that, although being sweet, pliable, and submissive in her overt behavior, she had a great need to control and to be "bossy," as she put it. A few nights following this insight, the patient dreamed that she wanted her way in a certain situation and, because people would not let her have it, committed suicide. She then continued dreaming that she was drowning in a bathtub but really out of anger. She woke up with anxiety because she thought she might bite into a penis. There were no further comments to the dream; she felt there was nothing to explain, the dream had said it all. She could only repeat: "I was so angry in the dream, and that's why I committed suicide; I was so angry at everybody."

The patient at this period of the analysis found herself fighting a battle not to yawn whenever she was reading to her children, until it dawned on her that her mother had used to read bedtime stories to her. She became aware of various parapraxes. She had always had certain fastidious habits as to the use of towels in the bathroom, but now repeatedly caught herself taking her children's wash cloths or towels. Several times she wanted to hand her toothbrush to her youngest child. The children had their own silverware, but now she repeatedly made mistakes when serving them and especially used theirs for herself. These actions revealed the wish that there were no real difference between mother and child, that they were interchangeable or part of each other.

The patient had been a profuse daydreamer in childhood and adolescence. As an adult she often appeared absent-minded, seeming not to be "quite there." At this period of the analysis she realized that it meant a reunion with her own mother. Her mother was always distracted; the patient often had to shout or pull at her to get her attention. In childhood the daydream had been a common meeting place for mother and child. Absent-mindedness and being lost in daydreams thus could be understood as a temporary, partial regression to the early phase of mother-child relationship.

This patient had an intense awareness of the moods of the people around her, which made her into a perceptive person but led to gross overreactions. It gave her a feeling, as she complained, of having "no personality," since she would react with an identical mood. This also could be understood as the reaction to her moody and depressed mother and meant not only to be like the mother, but to be one with the mother.

The patient now recalled having heard her family mention that in her early childhood she had had great difficulty in learning to walk freely. Long after she could walk, she had to hold on to her mother or to some furniture. It is possible that this was already an indication that the patient had difficulty separating from her mother. One might wonder how far this also was a reaction to the mother's depression.

The Problem of Self-Destructive Acts

The anger at the world, which in the dream of the third patient ended in suicide, seems similar to the wish to jump through the window out of anger at the analyst in the case of the second patient. It is generally assumed in psychoanalytic practice that self-destructive acts are aggressions toward an object, which subsequently have been turned against the self out of guilt feeling. As Freud (1915) says in "Instincts and Their Vicissitudes," the object has been turned into the subject; or, as he describes it in "Mourning and Melancholia" (1917), the love object has been incorporated in the ego, and the superego now punishes the ego as if it were the object.

It seems that in the two cases presented, something more primitive takes place. There is no difference between ego and love object, since we deal here with a partial regression of certain ego functions to the state where differentiation between the two has not yet taken place, where they are still one unit. Therefore it does not seem to matter toward which of the two the punishment is directed. This regression occurs under the impact of strong emotions, such as intense longing for the mother figure and the disappointment when she did not come, in the case of the second patient. In the third patient it was the rage about not being all-powerful which brought about the partial regression.[3] The fantasy of being all-powerful belongs to the period before differentiation between ego and outside world has taken place. The child's realization that neither the mother nor he himself are all-powerful is one of the painful experiences referred to by Anna Freud. Experiences of this kind lead to the transformation of the "pleasure ego" into the "reality ego."

A dream of the third patient, while working through this problem, clearly showed the ambivalence which takes its origin from this close tie to the mother. She dreamed about Spain and Portugal. Geographically they are one unit, the Iberian Peninsula; their division is completely artificial. But the people of either country hate the other because they cannot stand to be so close.

One might consider the possibility that some remnants of the early mother-child relationship persist in the adult personality in the relation between ego and ego ideal. The ego ideal is the carry-over of the image of the mother' who in early childhood appears to be all-powerful while the child is completely dependent on her. This situation also is repeated

---

[3] Loewenstein (1955), in his paper on masochism, also mentions masochistic reactions in which the aggression is bent inward without intervention of guilt feeling.

in reality situations, such as hypnosis, infatuation and the relationship of the individual to a leader, as Freud pointed out (1921).

RELATIONSHIP TO FUGUE STATES

In "Contribution to the Study of Amnesia and Allied Conditions," published in 1945 in co-authorship with Frederick J. Hacker and David Rapaport, we made certain postulates which might now be viewed with a slightly different slant and somewhat elaborated upon in considering the relation to the early, undifferentiated mother-child relationship.

Fugues and allied states all are characterized by an altered state of consciousness. There is amnesia for all essential facts of the previous life experience and, on awakening, for the content of the episode itself, although the extent of the amnesia may vary from one case to the next. Not all fugue states are similar. Some are short in duration, others last years; sometimes a new name is assumed, even a completely new personality may develop. Some patients act in a strange way, so that they are detected immediately; others may live socially acceptable lives under a new name in a new environment. In all fugue states the sense of personal identity, of the person's "self" or "me"-ness, has been lost.

In our paper we compared these states with dreams and sleepwalking. Their main difference from the dream state is that the ego still maintains full cathexis of motility, perception and many other integrative functions of waking-state living. But there is no doubt that in both dream and fugue unconscious wishes have an opportunity for expression, albeit in disguised form, to a far greater degree than in the waking state.

Since sleep is one of Lewin's "oral triad" phenomena, the fugue—an altered state of sleep—may well be closely related to the oral phase.

Although in classical psychiatric nomenclature fugues are labeled hysteric, we were able to show that they may appear in the most varied clinical conditions and character structures, as a symptom at the onset of a schizophrenia as well as in compulsion neurosis, depressions and hypomanic states. As a matter of fact, two of the cases we studied were hyperactive in their fugue states; these were the ones that were detected immediately. One of them, a few years prior to his amnestic disturbance, had had an episode of strange behavior after suffering a leg fracture. At that time the patient had become fearful lest he lose his mind, was "through with life" and wanted to leave home. A few years later, apparently under too much pressure of work, he began to act strangely, as if he were an automaton. This became progressively worse and ended in a hypomanic state with confusion in which the patient lost his sense of place and time. There was complete amnesia for this episode.

Karl A. Menninger (1919) described a case of a man who for years lived away from home under a new name and could not remember his previous existence. When he "woke up" he returned home, picked up his former life and was completely amnestic for the fugue state. Later on he developed a hypomanic state for which he was hospitalized. During this state the amnesia for his fugue was lifted; but on recovery from the hypomanic episode, repression for it set in anew. The close connection between the fugue and the earliest phase of the libido is shown especially clearly by this case, since in hypomania a regression to the oral phase of libidinal development takes place.

The first patient described in this paper, whose space fantasies could be analyzed as a return to unity with his mother, also seems to prove this contention. Although he did not actually go into fugue states, he described phenomena which could be understood as last-ditch struggles to prevent a fugue. He suffered from two different kinds of depressions. When he could cry during the depression, there were no feelings of estrangement. He remembered having cried in childhood, in the hope that his mother would see the tears and accept him again. His mother's habitual threat was to send him away if he did not do well in school or was bad. But on those occasions when he could not cry, he started to feel strange, out of contact, depersonalized. "I fear to lose my ties, because then I lose my identity." In this context he reported a dream in which an adolescent boy announced that he was going off and would walk and walk until he would dissolve into nothing. In the dream the patient begged the boy's father not to let him go. The boy had done something to a girl, made her pregnant or so, was his explanation. The associations led again to the hallucinations, in childhood, of becoming one with the pillow. The patient, full of affect, remarked: "The boy is going to vanish, he is going to lose his identity." It reminded him of a story he had read, about a man who ceased to exist because the girl with whom he had had an affair was not known at her address and her name was not even in the phone book; then a friend of his vanished, and another was unknown; and the story ends with, first, the man sitting dazed in an empty luncheonette, and then even he has vanished and all that is left is an empty chair in front of a half-finished sandwich. The patient also brought in the space dream, and his next associations opened up the whole problem of his guilt about masturbation.

He remembered a period of great shame in his life, where he thought to have degraded himself, and at that point a feeling of being lost had set in. He had wandered aimlessly through the city. But then he began actively and compulsively to seek all sorts of contacts with acquaintances and former schoolmates. This seemed to be a clinging to reality.

At this point in the analysis the patient complained about a lifeless feeling in his penis, and the idea came to cut it off. He also had suicidal fantasies again, realizing that he wanted to cut himself off entirely. He believed that if he killed himself the analyst would not reject him, since by his suicide he would have shown that he realized his unworthiness. Thus, suicide was the price he was willing to pay in order not to lose his analyst or mother. Losing her, he said, was equal to losing his identity.

The second patient described her states of amnesia as similar to nightmares. She would wake up thinking that she had had a bad dream and preferred not to remember it. But it would plague her, and certain elements gave her the conviction that it must have had some reality. Sometimes there were circumstances proving to her that it could not have been a dream, but the quality of the experience was as if it had been one. It was most difficult in analysis to bring back to memory and to reconstruct the complete chain of events of the episode.

The third patient had a dream in which the analyst and her husband were sitting at a table in a self-service restaurant. The patient tried to find food for herself and wandered aimlessly around searching for a tray, for food. Although it stood there, served on a large table, she could not get to it and could not find a place to sit. The dream obviously refers to a primal scene and to the patient's feeling of being left out. Since this dream occurred during the reliving of her early mother relationship in the transference, the primal scene was the situation of most intensely felt desertion. Interestingly enough, as an association the patient brought the novel *The Spear in the Sand,* by Raoul Faure. This is a story of a man shipwrecked on a deserted island. The book describes wih great lucidity his gradual disintegration because there is no contact with anybody or anything; he finally wanders into the sea. Thus it seems that the loss of an important object may lead to disturbances of ego functions, which can be viewed as a partial regression taking place to the earliest mother-child phase.

In the paper which I mentioned before, we stated that in the fugue state the pleasure ego of early development is recathected under pressure of specific traumatic circumstances or when particular fantasies are being reactivated. The satisfaction of unconscious repressed fantasies in the fugue state was likewise established there. The fugue seemed a compromise between living and dying; it is a partial suicide. The patient with the space fantasies described in this paper clearly shows how closely the fugues and suicidal fantasies were connected.

Although the third patient in the waking state had no symptoms of a fugue-like nature except the repeated periods of nonattentiveness, her dream indicated that in fantasy it existed. This patient also revealed that in rage she had suicidal fantasies. She considered both choices: suicide or the fugue, which one may conceive to be a suicide equivalent.

All three patients were analyzing their early mother-child relationship when they brought into the analysis ideas and fantasies centering around self-destructive tendencies as well as material related to fugue states. The material as presented by these patients gives evidence that fugues and allied states and, in some instances, self-destructive tendencies as well, are partial regressions to the undifferentiated phase of the early mother-child relationship.

BIBLIOGRAPHY

Bak, R. C. (1953), Fetishism. *J. Am. Psa. Assoc.*, I.

Brierley, M. (1951), *Trends in Psycho-Analysis*. London: Hogarth Press.

Freud, A. (1953), Some Remarks on Infant Observation. *This Annual*, VIII.

Freud, S. (1915), Instincts and Their Vicissitudes. *Collected Papers*, IV. London: Hogarth Press, 1925.

—— (1917) Mourning and Melancholia. *Collected Papers*, IV. London: Hogarth Press, 1925.

—— (1921) Group Psychology and the Analysis of the Ego. *Standard Edition*, XVIII. London: Hogarth Press, 1955.

Geleerd, E. R.; Hacker, F. J.; Rapaport, D. (1945), Contribution to the Study of Amnesia and Allied States. *Psa. Quart.*, XIV.

Greenacre, P. (1955), Further Considerations regarding Fetishism. *This Annual*, X.

Hartmann, H. (1950), Psychoanalysis and Developmental Psychology. *This Annual*, V.

—— and Kris, E., Loewenstein, R. M. (1946), Comments on the Formation of Psychic Structure. *This Annual*, II.

Hoffer, W. (1950), Development of the Body Ego. *This Annual*, V.

—— (1952), The Mutual Influence in the Development of Ego and Id: Earliest Stages. *This Annual*, VII.

Jacobson, E. (1954), The Self and the Object World: Vicissitudes of Their Infantile Cathexes and Their Influences on Ideational and Affective Development. *This Annual*, IX.

Kris, E. (1950), Notes on the Development and on Some Current Problems of Psychoanalytic Child Psychology. *This Annual*, V.

Lewin, B. D. (1950), *The Psychoanalysis of Elation*. New York: Norton.

—— (1952), Phobic Symptoms and Dream Interpretation. *Psa. Quart.*, XXI.

Loewenstein, R. M. (1955), A Contribution to the Psychoanalytic Theory of Masochism. Paper read at the Midwinter Meeting of the American Psychoanalytic Association, New York, Dec. 3.

Menninger, K. A. (1919), Cyclothymic Fugues Associated with Manic-Depressive Psychosis: A Case Report. *J. Abn. Psychol.*, XIV.

Piaget, J. (1950), *La construction du réel chez l'enfant*. Neuchâtel: Delachaux et Niestlé.

Symposium on Psychoanalysis and Developmental Psychology (1950). *This Annual*, V.

Symposium on the Mutual Influences in the Development of Ego and Id (1952). *This Annual*, VII.

THE RELATIONSHIP OF PSYCHOLOGIC STATE AND EPILEPTIC ACTIVITY

Psychoanalytic Observations on an Epileptic Child[1]

LOUIS A. GOTTSCHALK, M.D. (Cincinnati)

In the investigation of epileptic phenomena, there are few detailed clinical reports available that describe the epileptic activity and the sequence of interpersonal and intrapersonal events during which the seizures take place. In certain types of paroxysmal activity, variously called "psychic equivalent seizures," "affective epilepsy" (Wilson, 1940), and so forth, it may become impossible to differentiate between epileptic experiences (and behavior) and nonepileptic experiences (and behavior). This is especially likely to be so when the presumed seizure activity involves complicated and highly integrated patterns of behavior and psychologic processes. On the other hand, just as the clinical phenomenon of the "Jacksonian march" gives a rough representation of neural structure and function, so the detailed description of more complex types of epileptic sequences may reveal relationships of brain structure and function to psychopathologic processes or relationship of psychologic stresses to brain function. Previous reports (Gottschalk, 1953, 1955) have provided evidence that psychologic factors, as well as other factors, can contribute to the form and frequency of seizures and associated clinical manifestations.

The present paper is about a ten-year-old boy, Ned, who was observed in psychoanalytic psychotherapy for a period of twenty-eight months and who was followed by correspondence and occasional interviews for another period of five years. This boy frequently had one of his three types of seizures during the therapeutic sessions in the playroom; and the type

---

1 From the Department of Psychiatry, University of Cincinnati, College of Medicine. Part of this study was done while the author was a Research Associate at the Institute for Psychosomatic and Psychiatric Research and Training, Michael Reese Hospital, Chicago, Illinois.
Presented in condensed form at the Chicago Psychoanalytic Society, March, 1956.

of seizure repeatedly observed during psychoanalytic sessions can most accurately be labeled as an "atypical or psychic equivalent" seizure. The observations made with this patient illustrate not only the therapeutic value of psychoanalytic psychotherapy in the management of certain types of epileptic individuals, but also demonstrate the value of psychoanalytic study of epilepsy as an important avenue of furthering our understanding of the neural basis of emotional disorder.

A brief summary of the kinds of seizures Ned developed in the chronological order of the appearance of the manifestation follows:

1. His atypical seizures were precipitated usually by looking through an ordinary window screen or occasionally by looking at checkered or striped patterns on clothes, tablecloths or drapery. (These seizures will henceforth be designated as "screen spells.") These episodes had had their onset when he was five years of age, soon after the father had to leave home to enter active duty in the army. The fits consisted of spells of staring through a window screen and were accompanied by unco-ordinated, generally symmetrical stereotyped shaking of the upper extremities. According to the parents, the arm movements, with accompanying head and neck motions, suggested to the parents protective or warding-off actions against some threat to the child's head and neck. These seizures lasted from one to forty-five minutes. Ned would generally remain standing, would only rarely fall or bite his tongue, could not be communicated with during the spell, and could not recall what he had been doing during the spell. Neurologists, pediatricians, psychiatrists, and electroencephalographers who studied the boy between the ages of five and ten concurred in the opinion that these episodes were of an epileptic nature.

2. His grand mal seizures were rare. The first one had occurred at the age of nine years, and one such seizure had occurred each year thereafter, accompanied by tonic and clonic phases and biting of the tongue on two occasions. The grand mal seizures all evolved during "screen spells."

3. The psychomotor seizures appeared at the age of ten years. Typical in their pattern, lasting from fifteen to thirty minutes, these were paroxysmal episodes of complicated and rather highly organized motor activity, with a prominent destructive component, e.g., tearing clothes to shreds or breaking furniture. The boy had no notion what led to these seizures and could not be communicated with during them. After the seizures he could not recall what he had done during them. It was these seizures that motivated the parents to bring him for psychiatric evaluation and treatment.

Possible Pathogenic Factors in the Epileptic Syndrome

There was no familial history of epilepsy or migraine and no relevant history of trauma or infection. The patient's birth and development during infancy were free from any known symptomatic disorder. All neurological examinations revealed a normal state except for bilateral construction of the peripheral visual fields ("tubular vision"), first appearing at the age of ten years four months and lasting two months. Thorough neurologic and ophthalmologic studies revealed that a disturbance of the form fields and not of the color fields was involved in this visual symptom, but there was no detectable structural or anatomical basis for it. The visual field defect cleared up soon after the advent of psychotherapy and did not recur.

The first electroencephalographic recording, done when he was six years old, showed 3 c.p.s. spike and wave discharges, a little more pronounced from the right hemisphere.

Electroencephalograms done at the ages of seven, ten, and eleven were generally similar to the first electroencephalogram but showed a progressive trend to irregular slow wave activity (3-4 c.p.s.) without regular spiking. An electroencephalogram at thirteen, taken shortly after the termination of psychoanalytic treatment, gave evidence of focal slow activity in the right parietotemporal region.

Ned was described by his parents as a boy who, except for his seizures, was customarily conforming to their standards, though clinging and demanding of indulgence. He was adjudged by psychiatrists who had seen him previously on consultation as "very immature and rather effeminate" and as "a boy with whom it was difficult to establish close rapport." He was an only child.

Psychiatric and social casework studies of the mother revealed that she was a compulsive, perfectionistic person, whose relationships with others were characterized by very little investment on her part. She was mainly interested in people in order to get support and approval from them. She was inclined to be overindulgent and unduly intimate in Ned's rearing. She kept in constant attendance during his baths and frequently undressed in front of him or slept with him up to the time he began psychologic treatment. On the other hand, she showed poor tolerance to the least signs of independence and hostility he manifested toward her. She encouraged him to learn to cook and do housework. She had a tendency to tell him in what respects she considered the father inadequate.

The father was a passive, self-depreciative person who had difficulties in dealing with men in competitive situations or adequately asserting himself when someone's demands were actually excessive, e.g., an employer's. As the oldest son in the family, the father had had to take over the financial support of his own siblings at the age of fifteen because of the economic failures of the paternal grandfather, a temperamental chronic alcoholic. The father worried that the patient wanted to replace him, just as the father had replaced the paternal grandfather. The father dealt with his rivalry with his son by reaction formation, by constantly giving him gifts, exposing him—when not pushing him—to the mother's confusing intimacy, aloofness, and compulsive demands for cleanliness and orderliness. Though the father wanted to do so, he had difficulty in experiencing a warm interest in and real companionship with his son.

Events Occuring at the Onset of Patient's Seizures

The onset of Ned's first seizures ("screen spells") occurred at the age of five years, in 1943, shortly after the father departed for active duty in the army. Interviews with the mother revealed that at this time she turned to the patient for security and that she also directed some of her anger, aroused by her husband's leaving, at the patient. Her inconsistent seductiveness and compulsive restraint were most pronounced toward him at this time.

No life situations of significance are known to have occurred during the time of onset of Ned's grand mal seizures, at the age of nine years, and his psychomotor seizures, at the age of ten years.

Effect of Anticonvulsant Medication on Clinical Manifestations Before the Start of Psychoanalytic Psychotherapy

From the time of onset of his first seizures, the "screen spells," many of the standard anticonvulsant regimens, including use of a ketogenic diet and administration of bromides, phenobarbital, diphenylhydantoin, and trimethadione (tridione), or combinations of these, had been tried. Such medication had effected no essential change in the frequency or form of his seizures. At the time psychotherapy was started, however, the patient had not taken any medication regularly for about one year, being given only a capsule of phenobarbital (30 mg.), usually after a fit.

Because of the distressing effect on his parents of the destructive aspects of his psychomotor seizures at the time psychotherapy was started, another trial of diphenylhydantoin medication was made—diphenylhydantoin, in a dose of 0.09 gm. twice a day. With the disappearance of the psychomotor spells after the first six months of psychologic treatment, the administration of diphenylhydantoin was discontinued. No anticonvulsant drug of any sort was administered during the remainder of the course of psychotherapy.

Psychoanalytic Observations

At the initial interview, Ned was observed to be a large boy for his age, plump, pink-skinned, with regular facial features. He wore glasses. Throughout this session he kept a knitted cap on his head. He was restless and moved about the playroom continually, sometimes apparently for purposes of exploration and orientation, but oftener without discernible reason. He glanced out of the playroom window through the window screen furtively, without any immediate or noticeable reaction. He then began playing actively with a dart gun and holster, while explaining he had seen several doctors previously at the clinic. It seemed, he explained, that he had "hypnotic powers," could hypnotize himself by looking through a screen, "a habit, very silly." He went on to say that he wanted to get rid of the habit because Dr. H., his pediatrician, told his mother he should. As soon as any questions were asked, he regularly responded with the remark, "I don't know," but often would later elaborate spontaneously with a more detailed and pertinent answer. He volunteered tensely that he liked to come and see doctors, psychiatrists, because he liked "to be amused." When his next responses were awaited without his implicit plea to be entertained being satisfied, he remarked petulantly, "I love to play and amuse myself." He did so for a while with different play materials. Returning to the gun and holster and strapping it onto himself, he tried pulling out the gun rapidly and pulling the trigger, observing that he had to practice because he "might be slow on the draw, the gun could get caught in the holster . . . happens sometimes to cowboys." At the close of the session he said he had to shoot the dart gun four or five more times. He did so and then observed, in a tone of threatening reminder, "I like to be amused so much; do I have to go?"

During the next several treatment periods Ned revealed that he thought his psychomotor spells were like uncontrollable attacks of rage. He indicated these seizures were precipitated by seemingly trivial frustrating incidents, such as the interruption of a radio program he was listening to with an advertisement by the program's sponsor. His demands for dependent gratification (to be amused) increased in the playroom setting and when frustrated in these demands he appeared to express his reaction in his play: for example, he would build high towers of blocks and then invariably knock them over and remark that tall towers always topple over easily. He then began to confide, anxiously, his fear of hurting someone in a display of aggression, citing instances at the age of five and later when he threw snowballs or rocks at passing autos, once broke a window, and feared he injured someone. The following hour he announced he had had a psychomotor spell after his pediatrician had put him on a diet because of being overweight. Then he related how he had once had a fight with a boy who made a slanderous remark about his parents. He said, with flashing anger, that he could kill somebody who said anything against his parents; he could even kill a "grownup" like me if I said any such thing.

He now attempted to express and to check his rage and to communicate the reason for it. These activities became the central issue of treatment. In games, such as checkers, he attempted to control my moves by sounds and gestures, drumming on the table, muttering, whistling. When reality testing exposed the lack of magical effect of these procedures, he became provocatively hostile, shooting at me with a dart gun. At the same time, he sought control of and protection from his destructive fantasies and impulses and I informed him I would check him if he could not do so himself. A rigid self-control over affective displays began to show itself.

During the first three months of treatment the "screen spells," which had occurred one to several times a day, became decreasingly frequent and disappeared for about six months. In the meantime the psychomotor seizures became more frequent, the number ranging from two to eight a month. No grand mal seizures occurred during this period. Then, as the patient began to be able to communicate the various components of his psychomotor seizures, i.e., the thing he was doing and what feeling he had about it at the moment just preceding his psychomotor spell, and what he did, thought, and felt during and after the seizure, his psychomotor seizures disappeared fairly rapidly. No further frank psychomotor episodes occurred after the sixth month of psychotherapy. In view of this, the diphenylhydantoin sodium, which had been administered with the beginning of psychotherapy was then discontinued. In these circumstances, no recurrence of the psychomotor fits was noted. Situations which previously had been followed by psychomotor spells were then followed by typical temper tantrums, which the patient could describe and discuss fully. He could also give a more detailed report of his emotional reactions during the temper tantrums. The incidence of these temper tantrums gradually decreased during therapy and became progressively milder and briefer. During the last eighteen months of treatment they occurred only rarely.

On the other hand, as psychomotor seizures waned and disappeared, the "screen spells," which had practically stopped at home, began to recur first at home and, by about the fifth to the sixth month of treatment, they began to occur during the therapeutic sessions in the playroom.

About this time, he asked several times whether I had been in the army, and told me that his father had. He scrutinized my face carefully and observed that I looked as if I had been in the army, meanwhile pounding a ball of clay with his fist, rolling it into long thin cylinders and naming his creation "snakes that could bite." He made a pouch-like receptacle of the clay and then suddenly smashed it flat as a pancake and made a hole in the middle of it. Then he rolled another thin cylinder of clay, wound it into a flat spiral with a knob protruding from the center, and cut the knob with scissors and then with serious preoccupation, without any show of feeling except slight tension and a startled reaction after completion, he unraveled the thin cylinder of clay and cut it into even one inch sections. On my asking, "Are you frightened?" he retorted, irritably and seemingly obtusely, "I'm not angry!"

Now he became resistant to coming to the sessions, covered his head with his jacket in the waiting room, imputed magical powers to me, and expressed suspicions I would tell people his secrets. I informed him I knew he was anxious about his secrets, I did not know why, and I would not know any of his secrets as long as he did not want to tell me about them. Then he had his first screen spell during a treatment session. It lasted four or five minutes. He stood before a screen, tended to look upwards, made masturbatory movements on a pencil he held in his hands, while he rubbed his genital region against the wall and made jerky ducking movements with his head as if suffering or dodging some dangerous object. During the spell he dropped the pencil out of his hand, bent over to pick it up, and resumed his jerking. The seizure lasted until I told him the session was over and then without a pause he turned away from the window and screen and walked out of the room. The resistance to coming to the treatment sessions continued. He explained, "I don't like coming because I have secrets I don't want to give up." I reiterated that I would never know any of his secrets as long as he did not want to tell them. And I added that the only thing I knew about him was that he was a very angry boy. He seemed somewhat relieved, remarked that he knew he had a bad temper and that was why he was afraid to argue with anybody. Outwardly he became more friendly to the idea of therapy, several times put his arm up across my shoulder as we walked to the playroom, asked for rules of various games, asked for help to solve jig-saw puzzles. Now screen spells occurred in the playroom clearly whenever some dependent demand was frustrated in the transference. He would get up and walk to the screen and soon start shaking. During one of these episodes, while carrying on a conversation with me, he simultaneously reported he was having "a dream." In this waking or hypnagogic "dream," he said he was with many little people, all very much smaller than he; suddenly in the "dream" he wanted to return home with his parents, he did so and felt better.

Though no associations to the dream were provided, I privately speculated that the "dream" represented the ambivalent attitudes he had about his treatment—a wish to be in the clinic where other children ("many little people") were, and to get help for his problems and also a contrary wish to escape from the possible exposure, in the treatment, of his overwhelming hostile emotions and conflicts. I also considered the possibility that the "dream" represented a wish to be the center of attention and care rather than to tolerate the frustrations of sharing affection with rivals.

Subsequent sessions tended to confirm these speculations. Ned made further abortive efforts to effect control of me by magical wishes and gestures in competitive games; and when these did not suffice, he openly asserted his rivalry with me with the addition of some element of compromise, e.g., he said that though I could defeat him in most games of pick-up-sticks, he was better than I in picking up difficult sticks.

Furthermore, he now began to request, then demand, to be taught how to hypnotize, and to be hypnotized. If I hypnotized him, he said, then I could get secrets out of him. I told him if he wanted to talk about his secrets he had my permission to do so. Hypnosis was not necessary, I said. Persistently and in a whining manner, he elaborated that it was very important for him to learn how to hypnotize. Then he could hypnotize others, his friends, particularly his mother. He could make his mother do things for him, wait on him. He could control her. (With an air of finality I declined, saying that hypnosis was not so powerful as he thought.) With this, in crescendo order, he worked himself up from desultory and increased motor activities to a full-blown temper tantrum, threatening to throw playroom objects at me. When I indicated no alarm at this display and casually but firmly told him he was not to throw things at me, he appeared relieved. Still somewhat restless and excited, he became confidential and teasing; he kept looking out of the window without having a spell and repeatedly invited me to look and peek out of the window with him at events going on outside, mentioning that there were some pretty nurses he could see. I told him to enjoy himself, but at the moment I did not care to look out the window.

Now a period ensued of open cooperation in the treatment. He showed growing interest in the precipitating factors for and the frequency of his various kinds of paroxysmal motor excitement. The nature and function of the "screen spells" continued to remain unknown for a time. But it became clear that what once had all the clinical earmarks of true psychomotor seizures, the spells that had developed relatively recently in his life, became, during the process of treatment, an explosive affective and motor discharge, about which he could report the precipitating situation, the overwhelming impulses he experienced, and the fear, shame or guilt he felt about putting these impulses into action. The realization that it was possible to describe to someone else (in verbal terms) his subjective experiences was associated with a dramatic decrease in the frequency and a change in the quality of the psychomotor seizure. Concomitant with his increasing ability to master the mode of expression of his chaotic affects, the psychomotor type of fit was successively replaced by an exacerbation of the "screen spells" and finally by temper tantrums of shorter and shorter duration.

His parents began to regard Ned as a much more reasonable, understandable boy, who asserted himself angrily when blocked from doing what he wanted to. He was gradually able to win some independent privileges, by his self-assertions. He got a job as a delivery boy. He started coming to the clinic without the company and protection of his mother. But his increased openness and frankness confronted his parents with new problems difficult to cope with. For example, in the presence of his parents, he would caricature them, putting on either his father's or mother's hat, demanding in appropriate intonations that his father, and likewise his mother, do that or this—a kind of play acting in the role of the aggressor that the parents found amusing at times, more understandable certainly than fits of anger. But his role playing became distressing to both of his parents, more so to the mother, when his play became vituperative and caustic, as it frequently did.

Fortunately, the transformation of his "psychomotor seizures" to attenuated temper outbursts and his improved social and school adjustments led his parents to enthusiastic and staunch cooperation with the psychotherapeutic program. Their cooperation in encouraging Ned to continue his psychologic treatment was important at this time, for Ned's screen spells—which had temporarily abated in the beginning of treatment—now recurred as frequently as ever and became a focal point of the therapeutic interviews. It seemed that one means of discharge of instinctual tensions, derivatives, and defenses against these drives had been abandoned for another channel of discharge, older in the patient's life history and more complex.

His investigatory interests in the playroom and his transference reactions began to change and became more specific. He stated: "Not long ago I wanted to be a doctor. You know, now I don't want to be a doctor any more? Not a regular doctor anyway. I'd rather be the kind of doctor they have in a crime laboratory. That would be more exciting! I visited an FBI crime lab. with my father not long ago."

He evidenced increasing interest in and use of certain playroom materials about which he had previously showed only brief curiosity— a magnifying glass and kaleidoscope. During one session while playing with the kaleidoscope, he suddenly became tense, put it down, and asked me whether I would play checkers with him. When I declined, he returned to the kaleidoscope, became aimlessly restless and went up to the window screen in the room, looked through it for a while, without developing a spell. (I observed casually to him that I noticed he did not have one of his usual spells when looking through the screen in the room.) Very seriously he explained that the playroom screen faced the wrong direction—it should face south. Also, he added, he had to look upwards for a while to have a spell. At this point, he did so without having a spell and then explained that yesterday he had been looking through the kitchen screen door, was shaking, and had scraped and hurt his nose against the screen.

At the next session he at first reported that he had got tense and angry when an uncle had clipped a bit of his hair to get gum out of it. On talking more about this experience he indicated that he expected that his uncle was going to cut his scalp or clip his ear, and he was prepared to defend himself aggressively against this fantasied attack. He was relieved to experience no injury.

With anxieties about the matter temporarily allayed, he apparently felt reassured enough to proceed spontaneously with the recital of some "new discoveries" about himself. He recognized, he related, that when he stood at a screen and had a screen spell, he "shook all over like a hula dancer." He continued, "I try not to do it but I can't help it. The screen ought to be on a certain side of the room for me to have a spell." Later, on questioning him about spatial relationships, he drew diagrams of room arrangements of the homes in which he lived from age three to five and from five to the age of ten. In both plans it was obvious that he could see directly into his parents' bedroom from his bedroom. In the apartment where the patient had lived from the age of six to the age of

ten, the doorway to his parents' bedroom was noted to be on the same
side of the room he indicated a screen should be to produce a screen
spell on looking through it. It developed that there was actually no
door—but only an open doorway—between his room and his parents'
and by lying on his bed he could see his parents' bed. He could not remember that there were any curtains or checkered screens present between his room and that of his parents during the last five years, but there
had been checkered bedspreads and tablecloths in the household. He
appeared astounded after drawing the diagrams of the living arrangements that the sensation that he must look to the left and upwards
through a screen to have a spell was coincidental with the direction he
would have to look when lying or sitting on his bed to see through the
doorway into his parents' bedroom. He anxiously denied ever seeing any
sexual activities going on between his parents—though he did not deny
looking. He suddenly disgressed, however, and burst forth with associations about his own sexual activities and conflicts. He denied any masturbatory activities: "I never did anything of that sort—well hardly ever.
It can lead to a rupture. I only touch it when I wash or urinate or when
it itches. The fellows in the neighborhood talk dirty about sex. I think
some of them are going to drive themselves insane." With this beginning,
he began to elaborate on his sexual activities, fantasies, and play with
other children. Although he could not be explicit why he felt so, his
attitude about his own sexual interests and play were that they were
dangerous, forbidding, and could only eventuate in his own or someone
else's destruction and that it was equally dangerous and forbidding to put
any of his erotic thoughts and wishes into words. It is interesting to note
that at this time all screen spells stopped for a period of a month. He
timidly acknowledged masturbatory activities and sexual interests in girls
but did not feel inclined to elaborate on these topics. On the one hand,
he stated he knew all about sex and how babies were made because his
mother told him. (It turned out later, he was quite confused about these
matters.) On the other hand, he displayed an ambivalent urgency to know
more. He put two airplanes in front of the playroom window screen and
shot at them with a dart gun, while talking about his parents' not understanding the needs of a young boy. He reported dreaming of a dead uncle
who looked at him from a coffin with his eyes closed; he worried that his
uncle's spirit might throw a curse on him. He said he was having trouble
going to sleep at night, suffering headaches "behind my eyes," first behind one eye and then the other eye. At this time he broke his glasses
and though he got a new pair, he generally refrained from wearing them.
He reported that he looked out of the window only in the daytime when

he could see. At night he had tried looking but could not see because of the darkness; so he did not look then.

His anxiety mounted and he volunteered he felt uneasy when he came to see me, he did not know why, but felt scared; but also he felt he needed my help. He briefly again begged to be hypnotized, and he asked, "Why does a hypnotist look in a person's eyes?" Then, still discussing the matter, he volunteered, "I hypnotize myself at the screen, you know? I get in complete control of myself, like in a trance or having a dream." Then he expressed some preferential interest in the women's role. He complained that his father had to go to work and he had to go to school in the morning, while his mother stayed home, and all she had to do was a little housework. He himself liked to cook and clean he said. He would rather be like mother and stay home and rest and loaf.

He related that he was having distressing dreams but could not tell me about them—they were "too personal." Finally, asking for a pencil and paper and saying, "This is safer," he wrote: "I was pretending I was fucking a girl in my dreams." And, "Somehow I like to see girls tortured, I don't know why." Elaborating on these written statements, he confessed he had had sexual dreams nightly since the age of five. And at the age of eight he had tried performing sexual relations with a girl per rectum, had been caught by his mother and father, was scolded and threatened but not whipped. He had fantasies of raping a girl in an alley and having people watching him from their kitchen window; they would call the police and get him jailed. He said that he used to sleep in bed with his mother when his father was away on a trip, as late as one year ago, and he would start jerking and shaking, kicking at his mother, and he would pull the covers away from her. "I got an urge to look up a girl's dress or see through their dress." This burst of confessional material was accompanied by vasomotor reactions, tension, and finally mild crying as he left saying, "I needed to get this load off my mind."

A long period of confessions and relatively free reporting of fantasies, affects, and conflicts followed. Oral incorporative preoccupations were prominent. He said he had the idea that something bad, something alien, was inside of him. With a tone of revulsion in his voice, he reported that he liked to eat phlegm from his throat and "buggers" from his nose. When he was "a very little boy" he urinated in a cup and drank it. And now he loved to eat raw meat, raw hamburger and garlic. He wondered whether these habits had something to do with his trouble, whether there were some impurities in these things. An aunt had told him it was bad to eat raw meat because he might get a tapeworm. His trouble was that he

364 LOUIS A. GOTTSCHALK

ate too much. His mother and pediatrician had said he was overweight. (He weighed 125 lbs. and was now eleven years old.)

The following hour he talked about how much fun it would be to break all the windows in the apartments on Lake Shore Drive. This reminded him of the time he threw a rock at a passing car and broke a window; it was dangerous and someone might have been killed, he reflected. At this moment, he walked to the playroom window and looked out through the screen and his arms and legs jerked briefly. He stepped away from the screen and reported that he jerked because he thought he might get hurt if he hurt someone. He channelized these conflictual fantasies into hyperactive shooting with the dart gun for a few minutes and then expressed a more elaborate fantasy. He wondered, he said, when a gangster shot a girl why the gangster did not have sexual relations with the dead woman; he would think of doing it. Continuing, he reported that he played with two boy friends at this sort of game. One played the part of the gangster; another, the part of the girl: "He is a good actor." He himself took the part of a detective, most of the time. And they played at having sexual intercourse in various ways. Near the end of this session, he touched on a matter that, presumably, was a stimulus for some of his hostile fantasies. He mentioned that he loved movies. "One movie actress, Oh, boy! her legs when she dances, how sexy she is!" This reminded him that he had often seen his mother with her corset or girdle on (glancing through the window). He could see the door of his parents' room from his bed. He ventured that he would like to see his parents have intercourse; he never had, but he usually imagined they were having intercourse when he looked at the door. He remembered feeling left out, hurt, and angry when his parents went to their bedroom and made him stay alone in his own bedroom.

The next session he reported having had a nightmare. In the dream he was sleeping and someone came in and removed his covers. He awakened, felt anxious, went to his parents' room, and complained to his mother that someone removed his blankets. He did not speak to his father. His mother told him to return to bed. Associative material, verbal and nonverbal, revealed his rage at the parents' interest in one another exclusive of him, and secondarily his rage that his father interfered with his dependent and erotic interests in his mother. A diffuse pervasive fear of retaliation for his destructive rage was present. The jealous rage and fear of retaliation was interpreted.

He accepted the interpretation with a conditional "maybe," looked out of the window through the kaleidoscope, briefly jerked his arms and legs defensively—like a prolonged generalized startle reaction—and said:

"I jerk like I'm afraid of something." Then he reiterated in more detail: "I'd like to see my parents screwing. I've always wondered what they do at night. I was always curious about what went on in their bedroom and wanted to be in there with them too."

There followed several hours during which he elaborated on his erotic fantasies and indicated further information about the function of the screen and his "screen spells" as a substitute means of discharging inhibited conflictual tensions. The recurring conscious conflictual theme presented at this time was a wish to rape a girl, blocked by the fear of incarceration or injury by the police. He revealed some common childhood misconceptions about the processes of procreation, parturition, and childbirth. Sexual intercourse, he figured, occurred via anal copulation. The baby developed in the stomach and was given birth via a process of defecation. The fetus' umbilical cord was attached to the mother's navel from the inside. And a woman with an injured breast could not, he felt, conceive another baby; one of his mother's breasts was injured when he was a baby and she was going to have an operation on it soon. She could not have any more babies. (A breast operation on his mother was actually impending.)

He wondered whether he was nearsighted and had to wear glasses because he had hurt his eyes by looking through screen, especially because he kept trying to look through the tiny holes in the screen. He related that when he went to the screen he would first start looking downwards through the small holes and then his eyes seemed pulled upwards, into the sky area, and to the left. Something attracted him toward the left and upwards. At this point he demonstrated exactly what happened to him at the screen and developed one of his characteristic spells of jerking and shaking his arms and shoulders. But at my encouragement he continued talking, telling of a series of three visual hallucinatory experiences he was having, in the following order:

(1) "I see a farm woman, wheeling a wheelbarrow toward me from my left. A package is in the wheelbarrow. Wrapped. A toy for me. It might be a red light, a railroad crossing bar, a caboose. The woman with the wheelbarrow is sexy. I'd like to f— her" (giggling and jerking).

(2) "A ray of light, powerful, is coming from the upper left, down across the blue sky."

(3) "Two' sailors are sitting in a boat, stripped to the waist, one behind the other, talking. The boat is next to a dock."

While he was still standing facing the window screen, I asked him for his associations to certain items in the waking dreams. He responded as follows: "I get that idea about the woman whenever I think of anything bad. I jerk as if something stops me from thinking or doing anything more. A caboose is the rear end of a train. The ray of light is like part of God, letting me know he knows everything and to beware. I don't know what else to say about the two sailors, except that one was behind the other."

I told him I realized he was in a hurry to copy a grown-up man and have sex relations, but he was terribly afraid someone would get hurt and he was trying to figure out what to do about this problem. He responded to this interpretation with the equivocal statement that he liked to cook, stay home, be like his mother, but he would rather be like his father.

For a period of many sessions thereafter he frequently went to the screen and had spells, the form of the seizure and the content of the verbal productions undergoing remarkable transitions:

(1) (#48). He looked through the window screen for a while and reported that he saw a man pulling on a rope. At first he seemed to be pulling it downwards from the roof of a house. Later, the man seemed to be pulling it out of the ground. The patient had occasional jerking and shaking movements of his arms while looking through the screen. He rubbed his eyes after reporting what he saw and sat down and complained that looking strained his eyes. He said he thought a lot about seeing naked women, and that he had a feeling of pleasure going to the screen and looking through it. The rest of the session he indulged in compulsive play by himself with the pick-up-sticks, not asking for my participation.

(2) (#49). He was generally uncommunicative and sulky. At the screen, he put his hands in and out of his front and back pockets, sometimes grabbing through his pockets at his genitals or buttocks. Between these movements he made other motions that looked like he was hitting himself or defending himself. I commented he looked like he was having a fight. He immediately walked away from the screen and asked whether he could go to the toilet and have a bowel movement. Upon returning, he volunteered that his parents tried to stop him from looking through the screens at home and he resented their interference. I reminded him I had not been stopping him.

(3) (#50). At the screen he revealed offensive and defensive, well-coordinated movements with his arms and hands. He touched and grabbed briefly at his buttocks; then jerking his hands away, he grabbed briefly at his genitals—going rapidly from one to the other for about ten minutes. I said I wondered why he never finished doing what he wanted with his hands. He said nothing, but the jerking, defensive and offensive movements with his hands stopped and he began to masturbate genitally

with some coital movements. When told at the end of the session that it was time to leave, he reported he did not recall what happened while he was at the screen. I told him what had occurred and he appeared surprised.

(4) (#51-53). Screen spells continued occurring in the playroom. During one of the spells he remembered that, though there was no door, there was a checker-painted screen between his room and his parents' when he was between the ages of three and five.

Masturbatory activity during the spells was accompanied by visual imagery of having sexual relations with a girl and hurting her. At the screen he acted out terror, guilt and self-punishment at his own erotic and hostile impulses. After I described his screen spells to him, he remarked that he did not ordinarily express his feelings well and that he had a difficult time communicating what he wanted except in his spells. He now related that he masturbated regularly in his bed or on the screen porch. He reported feelings of depersonalization and dissociation when he masturbated; for example, he said, "I'm a brave, dirty guy, I'm somebody else when I masturbate." And then he claimed that he clearly remembered biting his mother's breast when he was a baby, and it was because of his biting that his mother had to have a breast operation not long ago. Also, he said his mother told him he used to bite her breast and she had said it was his fault she had to have an operation. (The mother denied ever having said such to the patient, but she probably said something like this which the patient unconsciously distorted.)

(5) (#54-58). The screen spells began to occur with decreasing frequency in the playroom. Instead, he spent the time in activities of open rivalry and aggression in games, play, and talk with me.

He confessed that he went to the screen when something happened that made him angry. The anger was aroused by the frustration of dependent wishes and the frustration of erotic wishes, especially by his mother (but also, by other adults, including me, as was repeatedly observed in the playroom sessions). When he was so angered, he became afraid he would "go crazy," would kill someone, felt anxious and guilty and punished himself (actually hit himself, as was seen during the therapeutic sessions).

(6) (#90). The destructive, magical potentialities of looking were the prominent theme of this session. After having a screen spell he reported he had the impression that while he was pushing and leaning against the wall, looking out the window, the wall seemed to move out, as if he had pushed it out with his knees. He reported that it was terrifying for him

to imagine he had such powerful thoughts, looks, or movements, and it was reassuring to learn he did not have them.

(7) (#92). When he first came into the playroom, he reported becoming periodically enraged at his "boy friend," E., for looking or staring at him. For doing so, the patient had wrestled with E., had become so infuriated at him, he had nearly strangled E. Ned's mother warned him not to become so violent in his wrestling with E. because "it might be fatal."

The immediate question that occurred to me was: what provoked the patient's fury in this situation? Some answer was given by the patient himself during this session as he stood at the screen and reported a vivid visual fantasy, accompanied by appropriate motor accompaniments. He saw E. coming at him with a long pole with a big ball at the end; the ball was burning. Ned was terrorized because he had the idea E. was going to ram this pole up his rear end. So, it appeared that Ned's anger was a fear-inspired warding off of a fantasied brutal anal attack by his "boy friend" and the idea of E.'s attacking was a projection of his own sadistic concept of the masculine role.

Because the patient always turned his back to me when he looked out of the playroom window screen, I ventured to ask him whether he had the idea he had to get hurt physically if he depended on me too much. He started to say something, blocked, left my side and went to the screen, had a brief episode of his old stereotyped screen spell, came back and sat down near me, went back to the screen, returned to his chair, all the while speechless. I stopped his returning to the screen after he made several such trips back and forth and asked him what was the matter. Rather tangentially he first told me that he lost contact with me when he went to the screen and he was not sure whether or not he wanted to do so. Then he said he had thought sometimes maybe it would "be nicer" being a woman in sex relations. Then, apparently digressing, he said he had learned to get along well with all his teachers at school; he was using "psychology," which on further explanation by him turned out to be a kind of extremely unctuous courteousness. Now he complained of having had pains recently in his penis, recalled that E. carried a knife and had once accidently stuck him in the belly with it when the blade was closed. He made no connection between these associations, but he became immediately more relaxed and comfortable.[2]

2 Such a sequence of clinical observations might be interpreted in a number of ways. I saw the chain of Ned's reactions and associations as a transference expression of his rebellion against his passive, masochistic concept of the dependent, submissive role, and this type of adaptation was temporarily brought to the fore in connection with conflicts about oedipal wishes. No interpretation was made at this time.

In subsequent sessions, his masochistic concept of the submission or feminine role and his sadistic concept of the dominating or masculine role were acted out less in his play with contemporaries and in his screen spells. Instead he put his ideas and concepts more and more into words and on such occasions he experienced "scared feelings" that were clearly anxiety attacks.

When he became openly competitive with his peers, his father or me, he was less inclined to overshoot the mark and worry that he was supposed to destroy ruthlessly his rivals. When he became openly dependent and submissive, he became less fearful of losing his individuality or being damaged. But a restless attitude of wanting to be done with boyhood and a premature desire to assume the sexual prerogatives of manhood and fatherhood persisted. This attitude seemed almost indelibly implanted in his mind by the experience of having been designated by his mother as the "man of the house" during the period his father was away in the military service for three years starting when Ned was five years old.

Unfortunately, the regular psychotherapeutic work with Ned had to be discontinued at this time before it could be completed, for I was obliged to move to another city for military service. But by correspondence with Ned and his parents and through occasional interviews, a five-year follow-up of Ned's condition was made possible.

At the time when his treatment was interrupted, his "screen spells" occurred rarely in the playroom and infrequently at home. No psychomotor seizures had recurred for two years and none were manifested for a five-year period following termination of his treatment. Two grand mal seizures occurred during the twenty-eight-month period he was being observed intensively. They appeared at a time when he was making efforts toward breaking away from parental supervision. The first grand mal spell happened after eighteen months of observation when he prepared to come, on his own insistence, to the therapeutic sessions without the company of either of his parents. The second one occurred the day after termination of his treatment, although he was superficially gleeful about the ending of treatment because he wanted to regard the termination as a sign he had matured and developed to the point where he could be the master of his own strong chaotic impulses, he was still fearful what he might do without the limit-setting of a good parental figure.

One year after the termination of treatment, at the age of thirteen years and ten months, with his parents' permission, he went away from home to a summer resort to work as a bus boy and waiter. His parents allowed this because he had been free of all seizures during this time and because he had grown rapidly in the ensuing year and was now almost as tall as his father. They reasoned, incorrectly, that he was as mature in his psychologic integration as he looked physically. Within a week after arrival at the summer resort, there was a recurrence of his grand mal seizures, each one occurring during the course of a "screen spell." The compulsion to stare through window screens had recurred soon after his arrival at the place where he was to work for the summer months. The boy's father wrote me on July 24, 1952:

> On the 28th of June, Ned went to a camp in the north woods to work as a waiter and bus boy. We did not tell the owners of the camp about Ned's ills. Ned did not want us to do so. He said he would not go to the screens and therefore would not have any seizures. On July 11th, Ned had a seizure early in the morning while in bed, looking out of the screen. His roommate told us that he did foam at the mouth. After that he went back to work, but did not feel well, complained of pains in his stomach.
>
> On July 19th my wife and I went out to visit Ned. We saw him and he did not feel well and wanted to go home. On July 21st Ned had another seizure the same way. We can now put his seizures as definitely coming on from the screens.
>
> I asked Ned why he didn't stay away from the screens. He said that it feels good while he stares through them and he wants more and more.
>
> Now that they have returned what do you suggest we do? . . .

From our previous work together and additional information Ned was able to tell me later about his experiences that summer of 1952, it was possible to piece together the psychodynamic mechanism leading to the seizures.

The temptation to act out his aggressive sexual fantasies and the fear of retaliation or loss of parental care should he gratify these impulses became overwhelming in the setting of the summer resort.

The outcome of these inner conflicts was a pleasurable compulsion to go to a window screen and look through it. Thereupon, as our previous studies revealed, he re-experienced and acted out on himself in an abortive way, his forbidden impulses and the punishments for them.

After further correspondence with Ned and his parents, Ned was advised to resume taking anticonvulsant medication, namely, sodium diphenylhydantoin .09 gm. twice a day. Though his "screen spells" had never been blocked by this medication, there was sufficient reason to expect that the final consequence of some of these "psychic seizures," the grand mal seizures, could be blocked by dilantin. Furthermore, Ned was now aware of the sources of his anxiety about his dependent and sexual urges and was not so desperately self-critical and punitive about the sexual and hostile reactions he had to seductive or controlling women, such as his mother. Therefore, it was believed he might find a better way to handle the tensions generated by these conflicts than by compulsively acting them out while looking through a window screen. His parents never did understand the full details of his emotional problems and I did not pass along to them the "secrets" that Ned had entrusted to me in strict confidence. He told them himself, however, much more about his inner experiences and conflicts than he realized he could, and he found them, as might be expected, quite understanding and accepting of him in comparison to his threatening fantasies of parents or other authority figures.

After the brief episodic recurrence of the screen spells and grand mal seizures in 1952, there was no recurrence of any seizures throughout the next three years. From the viewpoint of his parents, Ned matured well without any notable signs of emotional instability. Quotations from a chatty letter about Ned from his mother illustrate his clinical course, from one point of view.

Dec. 12, 1954

. . . We have lots of good news to report. So here we go.

Ned was very good all summer. He did not stand at the screens, and he would say to me that the screens do not bother him any more. He feels that he has the screen spells licked.

Ned has been taking the sodium dilantin twice a day, and he has not had a grand mal seizure since starting this medicine (in 1952).

He is feeling less nervous than he was, accepts things in a different light, gets along better at school (with a G average). He has a tough time though on his tests. Can it be that he gets too nervous and can't think? Algebra is his tough subject. He was warned against taking it by his advisor in school, but Ned wanted to take it so that he can go to college. However, he is getting some outside help and seems to be catching on.

He was 16 years old Sept. 26th, has learned to drive the car, has not applied for his driver's license as yet. He is sort of afraid on account of the passage in this booklet which I am enclosing. [The booklet cited State regulations disallowing the awarding of a driver's license to an epileptic person, except with a physician's statement that the seizures were well controlled.]

Dr. Gottschalk, I want you to know that Ned has been doing everything a boy his age should do. He plays a fair game of golf and his social life has been good.

Ned has had a part-time job after school but he quit because he found it too much for him. He had to travel quite a distance.

Ned is a fine boy, and we are proud of him, the way he has accepted his sickness and hasn't been ashamed of it.

We are very thankful to you for the help you have given us, for alone we would have been lost. We are always thinking about you and will never forget you. So the best again to you and yours.

A follow-up interview with Ned when he was seventeen showed that he was still seizure-free. He was dating girls and was comfortable in his relationships with them. Compulsively looking through window screens no longer attracted him. He was advised to continue taking sodium dilantin medication, .09 gm., twice a day, because it was felt that this medication, though it had not been found previously to stop his screen spells, did block the grand mal component of his epilepsy.

Whether the emotional trigger mechanism for his seizures is less likely to operate as he continues to mature and find more adequate ways of managing his psychologic conflicts will have to be determined in the future.

Discussion

A resumé of the psychological factors activating Ned's seizures is helpful as a point of departure for discussing the theoretical implications of the empirical observations made during this boy's psychologic treatment.

Screen Spells. A characteristic chain of events was observed to culminate in screen spell in the playroom. (1) Ned would be either engaging the therapist in some play or talking with the therapist. In this interaction, an incident would occur which Ned would presumably experience as a frustration, the frustrating agent being either someone that Ned was telling the therapist about or the therapist himself, e.g., the therapist or someone else did not fulfill some explicit or implicit demand of Ned's. (2) The pattern of Ned's immediate activities would abruptly change, whatever he was doing or saying. He would turn and walk toward the window, on reaching it would glance slightly upward through the screen, and would often reiterate that at times he was unaccountably and irresistably drawn to the screen. (3) Generally, staring less than half a minute through the screen did not lead to a typical screen spell. During this half minute, verbal interchange with Ned was open. When questioned, he never saw any relation between his compelling feeling to go to the screen and the context of the immediately preceding interactions with the therapist. He never volunteered that he experienced any feeling of anger, fear or frustration. In fact, he usually denied any such feeling when he was asked. But an accurate and acceptable interpretation of the preceding situation and Ned's presumably covert aims and feelings could at this point prevent the development of a screen spell. (4) If Ned looked through the screen for longer than about half a minute, a screen spell of varying duration invariably occurred during the first year of psychotherapy. Thereafter, modified screen spells, during which he was communicating his subjective experiences, lasted as long as five to ten minutes and could be terminated voluntarily by himself or on request.

Grand Mal Seizures. Grand mal seizures were never observed in the playroom. In all instances in which they occurred, however, it was observed by his parents, or other observers, that grand mal fits developed some time during prolonged screen spells. Psychiatric investigation added the information that the infrequent grand mal seizures tended to occur during a period when he had been making efforts, often premature, toward independence from parental control and support.

Psychomotor Seizures. No psychomotor seizures were observed during sessions in the playroom. Retrospective verbal comments by Ned about the situations and his personal feelings and aims just preceding the onset of such seizures gave evidence that a sequence of events obtained somewhat similar to those with the screen spells. That is, Ned experienced some feeling of deprivation which was shortly followed by a psychomotor seizure. The deprivation, as reported by Ned, was typically of a trivial variety. For example, on one occasion he reported that he had been listening to a cowboy radio thriller and the program was interrupted by the announcer making a commercial; Ned felt furious, briefly, at the interruption, and a psychomotor seizure occurred. Ned could not report what he did during the seizure. Only his parents could give a description of the behavioral details. Nor could Ned recall any of his thoughts or feelings during the seizure episode. On another occasion, he reported he had been bouncing a tennis ball against a backboard. He missed several shots, felt furious, and started to break his tennis racket. A psychomotor seizure, with the usual wantonly destructive components, followed.

A perhaps essential differentiating characteristic of the intervening variables in the psychologic precursors associated with the psychomotor seizure as distinguished from the screen spell was the fact that Ned could report feeling angry (out of proportion, of course, to the situation) just before the onset of the psychomotor spell; whereas, he was aware of no emotion or frustration just before the onset of a screen spell—only a compulsion to go to and look out of a window screen.

Psychologic State and Epileptiform Activity

An unusual feature of this boy's behavior was the phenomenon of the so-called "screen spells."

From the psychoanalytic point of view, these episodes would, at first sight, appear to be a kind of hysterical conversion phenomenon. Various aspects of the seizure manifestation lend themselves well to the inference that a forbidden impulse and the punishment for it is being expressed. Also, condensed and symbolized in these spells appear the scoptophilic activities of the little boy trying to discover what his parents are doing in their bedroom, the jealous rage concerning the father's prerogatives with the mother, the guilty fear of his sexual impulses to the mother and aggressive impulses to the father, the attempted solution to these forbidden impulses by displacing the one impulse to the other parent or to the self, and by the converting of the elements of the psychologic conflict into somatic manifestations. Finally, there is the regressing to earlier psychophysiologic levels of integration and the forgetting (or lack of awareness) of the psychologic experience and motor behavior while at the screen. Supporting evidence that Ned was capable of dealing with emotional stress through conversion mechanisms was the episode he had of "tubular vision" for which no structural basis could be demonstrated and which cleared up soon after psychotherapy started.

Further evidence of the importance of the role of psychologic conflict in not only the content but also the pathogenesis of the screen spells was the fact that the frequency and form of the usually stereotyped screen spells could be modified by psychotherapy. During psychotherapy these spells were modified to the point where the boy was able to report, just before or during a spell, thoughts and feelings that were highly unacceptable to himself, and concomitant with these communications to the therapist, his motor behavior during the seizures changed and typified the elements of the psychologic reactions he was in the process of putting into words. The boy revealed a terrible fear of punishment and abandonment for his forbidden impulses and primitive tensions. As he learned, from experience with me in the treatment situation, that his aggressive fantasies and fears of retaliation were not appropriate to current realities, he found more effective ways of integrating and discriminating between his perceptions of his past experiences and his expectations accompanying his preparations for action in his current adjustment problems. With these dynamic changes in his personality, a pronounced decrease in the frequency of his seizures occurred.

But the presence of these emotional conflicts and psychologic mechanisms, and the repeated observations that their stirring up could precipitate the screen spells, do not completely explain the mechanism of this epileptiform activity. Other boys have similar conflicts and psychologic mechanisms without having any seizures at all. And there are other features of the patient's clinical manifestations not accounted for very well by a primarily psychological theory. When these spells began, at the age of five, an electroencephalogram revealed 3 c.p.s. spike-wave rhythms that, in terms of our present-day knowledge, are thought to signify the presence of a neurochemical disturbance (secondary to many different possible factors) involving thalamocortical function (Williams, 1953). The screen spells were quite stereotyped for years, which is customary with an epileptogenic seizure; in fact, they did not vary in form until the boy was in psychoanalytic therapy. Though they were not blocked by anticonvulsant medication he had received (diphenylhydantoin, mesantoin, tridione, phenobarbital), the occasional frank grand mal seizures developed only during screen spells. These aspects of the screen spells cannot be accounted for by psychoanalytic theory alone, although the idea of a neurochemical factor in the pathogenesis of personality disorder is not inconsistent with psychoanalytic theory.

In this case, then, both psychologic factors and a focal disturbance in cerebral functioning are necessary to account for the pathologic clinical manifestations. Without either factor, the presenting clinical epileptic syndrome would not have occurred. As a means to test this statement it is obviously not possible experimentally to cancel out one factor to observe the effects of the other factor alone. The supporting evidence for this hypothesis comes from certain relevant clinical observations. The psychomotor seizures stopped after the first six months of psychotherapy and did not recur, although diphenylhydantoin was also discontinued after these six months. A discontinuation of grand mal seizures was associated with the administration of diphenylhydantoin, but screen spells were not blocked by this anticonvulsant. Psychologic factors triggered screen spells and screen spells triggered grand mal seizures. Reducing the effect of psychologic factors through psychotherapy was associated with the absence of all seizures for more than a year after the discontinuation of the psychotherapy during which the patient received no anticonvulsant medication. New external stresses were associated with the recurrence of screen and grand mal seizures during the follow-up period. The patient has now been seizure-free for four years on small doses of diphenylhydantoin. This boy's emotional conflicts have not been canceled out by psychotherapy, but the effectiveness of the emotional factors in stimulating seizures has been reduced. The effect of the cerebral functional disorder which has been shown to be associated with a lowered seizure threshold (Liberson, 1955) presumably persists (as adjudged from a recent electroencephalogram), but its potency has been reduced too, by the diphenylhydantoin (and possibly by the psychotherapy). These points plus the detailed observations of the relationship between the patient's psychologic state and his ictal activity, recounted in the above description of the therapeutic process, attest to the necessity of both psychologic factors and the presence of a paroxysmal cerebral functional disorder (involving corticothalamic and associated pathways) to produce his clinical syndrome.

A search in the medical literature for reports of epileptic reactions associated with looking reveals some highly relevant observations. Bickford et al. (1953) studied the convulsive effects of light stimulation in children. They found twenty-seven children who had convulsive reactions of varying degrees to stimulation by light. Most of the children had convulsive reactions, substantiated by electroencephalograms, to intermittent light. Some had epileptic reactions to steady, nonflickering light. One case, a six-year-old boy, is reported who developed petit mal seizures, accompanied by typical spike-waves in the electroencephalograph, when staring at a window screen, window curtain, finely woven cloth or his father's corduroy jacket! Robertson (1954) has recently reported seven cases of "photogenic epilepsy" in which epileptic attacks were self-precipitated in the patients by movement of the fingers or hand in front of the eyes or by blinking while looking at the sun or strong light. In the case of Ned, his convulsive episodes—"screen spells"—developed when perceiving continuous illumination and there was no rapid interruption of the light by his fingers, hands or eyelids. The similarity of Ned's case to the six-year-old boy reported by Bickford et al. (1953) is striking. The psychoanalytic study of Ned's case provides evidence that psychologic conflicts about looking may be one of the determinants in epileptic susceptibility to visual stimulation. Also, the fact that self-precipitation of such seizures has been commonly observable elsewhere makes more understandable Ned's remarks that he could "hypnotize" himself, for this was the way he saw his role in initiating the seizure state.

Problems for Further Psychophysiologic Research

No extant hypothesis explains satisfactorily the triggering of paroxysmal neural activity and an altered state of consciousness by a self-induced or externally stimulated psychologic conflict or state. In a recent study (Gottschalk, 1955) where paroxysmal slow electroencephalographic activity was correlated with an epileptic subject's tape-recorded verbal associations, it was found that the arousal of separation anxiety facilitated epileptic discharges in this patient's electroencephalogram. Such observations, however, only illustrate that the phenomenon can occur, but they do not explain the mechanism.

A resumé of the observed relationship between Ned's psychologic state, his psychic seizures, and finally his grand mal seizures will be sketched out to indicate some of the gaps in our understanding of this sequence of events. Either a meaningful external situation or a self-initiated series of thoughts aroused in the patient memories of recent and past experiences having to do with dependent, sexual, and aggressive interchanges between key people of the past and recent present. These old perceptions were associated with various feelings—pleasure, displeasure, fear or anxiety (of punishment, of ridicule, of loss of parental support), frustration, and anger. The psychologic compromise between these conflicts was experienced as a compulsion to go to a window screen and look through it. If looking through the screen was not interrupted for 30 seconds, a screen spell invariably started which could, after Ned had been in psychotherapy a while, be modified by maintaining verbal communication with the patient. Presumably, memories and thoughts (cortical activity) and the emotional components (subcortical activity) of these ideas modulated 3 c.p.s. spike and wave activity that in itself was not sufficient to cause a seizure. Under some unknown set of circumstances a psychic seizure, with highly integrated motor activity, could ensue. This seizure was associated with an altered state of consciousness from which the subject could sometimes be aroused. Sometimes—it is not clear how or why—the relatively localized epileptic cerebral discharges (involving predominantly one frontotemporal cortex, the diencephalon, the reticular substance) could spread further and become a diffuse epileptic discharge manifested as a grand mal seizure. As previously indicated, a necessary condition for this sequence of events was a specific anatomical structure and neurochemical basis, without which the behavior associated with the psychologic state would probably have been otherwise.

Some Recent Research, Contributions from Physiologists and Neurologists

There is information which has accumulated elsewhere that fills in some of the gaps of our understanding of the mechanism by which emotions may be associated with epileptic phenomena. Liberson (1955) has recently indicated that emotional stimuli may induce a convulsion through (1) either the creation of a "general excitatory state" with an excessive formation of either acetyl choline (see also Forster, 1945) or insulin, or (2) a preliminary conditioning of certain stimuli which set up epileptogenic states in those areas of the brain which participate in the control and release of emotional processes, such as the rhinencephalon, diencephalon, and mesencephalon. He has collected evidence which shows that rhinencephalic structures, which appear to be involved in the integration of emotional reactions and visceral activity (see also Mac-Lean, 1949, 1952; Papez, 1937; and Yakovlev, 1948), have the lowest threshold to epileptic discharges and that these discharges can be induced by visual and auditory stimuli. Epileptic discharges can be induced experimentally similarly in diencephalic and mesencephalic structures. It is additional data of this sort which is required to account for the general and specific mechanisms of the association of psychologic conflict and epileptic states.

The Epileptic Seizure as a Symbolic Expression of Emotional Conflict

Other authors have seen epileptic seizures as symbolic expressions of repressed desires that are unconscious. The seizure, particularly grand mal seizure, has been described variously as an expression of inhibited rage (Freud, 1928; Bartemeier, 1932), inhibited sexual desire (Greenson, 1944), and frustrated dependency (Heilbrunn, 1950).

The present study found no evidence to support any of these views in so far as the grand mal seizure is concerned. Though Ned's grand mal seizures were observed to occur when he was making premature attempts to establish independence from parental figures, this does not tell us that his grand mal seizures symbolize his conflicts with authority figures or with dependency problems. It simply tells us that such a situation has a temporal relationship, and possibly a causal relationship, with a final event. The testing of any hypothesis one might have about the symbolic function of the experience for the person having the grand mal seizure is virtually precluded by the impossibility of verbal communication with a person having such a seizure. The present study, however, does reveal that condensation and symbolization are demonstrably important processes in certain types of minor epileptic spells where higher levels of cerebral integration are maintained and during which some verbal communication may take place, such as during the patient's "screen spells."

In my opinion, the grand mal seizure probably has no symbolic significance, though it may be precipitated by various kinds of emotional conflicts. My impression is that no symbolic activity is possible at the psychologic level without effective cerebral cortical functioning or, from the psychologic frame of reference, without the intactness of cognitive processes. In grand mal convulsions, integrated functioning of the cerebral cortex does not occur. When cortical functioning is not completely impaired—as in certain types of focal epileptic reactions—symbolic activity may be possible. A grand mal seizure is a kind of mass reflex which is the end product of a potential series of noxious stresses (trauma, electric shock, drugs, metabolic disturbances, emotional problems) to the organism, but it is not specific to any one kind of stress. And the grand mal seizure does not signify the nature of the stress precipitating it. It has no more symbolic function than the circulatory dysfunction of ulcerative colitis or essential hypertension. In less generalized forms of epileptic discharge, however, such as in psychomotor epilepsy and related automatisms or in certain manifestations of petit mal epilepsy and especially in "psychic equivalent seizures," it is likely that epileptic manifestation may symbolize in microcosmic forms some aspects of the subject's old and recent emotional conflicts.

Summary and Conclusions

The psychoanalytic study and treatment of a ten-year-old epileptic boy are reviewed. Particular emphasis is laid on the sequence of psychologic conflicts and states associated with one type of seizure that was repeatedly observed in the playroom sessions with him. This type of seizure was an atypical, so-called "psychic equivalent" seizure, with motor components. Interseizure electroencephalograms showed a 3 c.p.s. spike-wave pattern. Also, the psychic equivalent seizures were the prodromal manifestation of infrequent but clear-cut grand mal seizures.

The features and psychologic conflicts of a hysterical character, although manifested both during seizure and interseizure periods, were not found sufficient in themselves to account for the epileptiform manifestations of this patient. The presence of a type of paroxysmal cerebral functional disorder, which has elsewhere been found to be associated with decreased seizure threshold, could not alone account for the epileptic behavior, particularly that manifested during the psychic equivalent seizures. Both complex factors (the hysterical character disorder and the paroxysmal cerebral functional disorder) were considered necessary to produce the clinical syndrome.

The therapeutic problems encountered in this patient illustrate the therapeutic value of psychoanalytic psychotherapy in the management of certain types of epileptic individuals.

The case study is also considered to illustrate the value of psychoanalytic study of epilepsy as an important avenue of furthering our understanding of the interplay of the neural and experiential bases of emotional disorder.

BIBLIOGRAPHY

Bartemeier, L. H. (1932), Some Observations on Convulsive Disorders in Children. *Am. J. Orthopsychiat.*, II.
Bickford, R. G.; Daly, D.; Keith, H. M. (1953), Convulsive Effects of Light Stimulation in Children. *Am. J. Dis. Child.*, LXXXVI.
Forster, F. M. (1945), Action of Acetylcholine on Motor Cortex. *Arch. Neurol. & Psychiat.*, LIV.
Freud, S. (1928), Dostoevski and Parricide. *Collected Papers,* V. London: Hogarth Press, 1950.
Gottschalk, L. A. (1953), Effects of Intensive Psychotherapy on Epileptic Children. Report on Three Children with Idiopathic Epilepsy. *Arch. Neurol. & Psychiat.*, LXX.
—— (1955), Psychologic Conflict and Paroxysmal EEG Patterns. *Arch. Neurol. & Psychiat.*, LXXIII.
Greenson, R. R. (1944), On Genuine Epilepsy. *Psa. Quart.*, XIII.
Heilbrunn, G. (1950), Psychodynamic Aspects of Epilepsy. *Psa. Quart.*, XIX.
Liberson, W. T. (1955), Emotional and Psychological Factors in Epilepsy: Physiological Background. *Am. J. Psychiat.*, CXII.
MacLean, P. D. (1949), Psychosomatic Disease and the Visceral Brain. *Psychosom. Med.*, XI.
—— (1952), Some Psychiatric Implications of Physiological Studies on Frontotemporal Portion of Limbic System (Visceral Brain). *EEG Clin. Neurophysiol.*, IV.
Papez, J. W. (1937), A Proposed Mechanism of Emotion. *Arch. Neurol. & Psychiat.*, XXXVIII.
Robertson, E. G. (1954), Photogenic Epilepsy: Self-Precipitated Attacks. *Brain,* LXXVII.
Williams, D. (1953), A study of Thalamic and Cortical Rhythms in Petit Mal. *Brain,* LXXVI.
—— and Parsons-Smith, G. (1949), The Spontaneous Electrical Activity of the Human Thalamus. *Brain,* LXXII.
—— —— (1951), Thalamic Activity in Stupor. *Brain,* LXXIV.
Wilson, S. H. K. (1940), *Neurology,* Vol. II. Baltimore: William Wood.
Yakovlev, R. K. (1948), Motility, Behavior, and the Brain. *J. Nerv. & Ment. Dis.*, CVII.

CLINICAL OBSERVATIONS ON THE "LITTLE MAN" PHENOMENON

WILLIAM G. NIEDERLAND, M.D. (New York)

Recently Paul Kramer (1955) has focused attention on a developmental phase of which comparatively little seems to be known. K. R. Eissler (1950), in an earlier study, had already spoken of a stage in the child's development "which can be called the discovery of the ego" and had stated: "Comparable to the phase in which the child discovers that there is an outer world and familiarizes himself with it, there must be a developmental phase in which the child discovers that 'he' is 'he' which means that there is not only an outer world but also an ego as a distinct entity."

Johnny, a little boy of two years and ten months, who was watching his one-year-old brother Charlie crawling on the floor, succinctly expressed it this way: "Charlie is a Charlie, daddy is a daddy, mummy is a mummy, grandma is a grandma, Johnny is a Johnny." It was not coincidental, perhaps, that the child, while slowly enumerating and emphatically identifying the population of his immediate environment, mentioned his own name last, thus possibly indicating that the discovery of himself as a separate entity was preceded by that of the significant persons around him.

More specifically, Kramer's interesting case report deals with the emergence, in analysis, of an isolated, separate ego segment, termed by his patient the "little man," which had persisted throughout his life. The analytic penetration of the patient's earliest memories and fantasies enabled Kramer to demonstrate in some detail how this part of the ego came into being, under the influence of certain traumatic events in childhood, and how it continued to lead "a sort of autonomous existence," unchanged and unmodified, as an ego part separated from the rest of the personality. Because of the scarcity of such observations in the literature, it may be of interest to present a comparable case. Though some features of the case to be described appear rather similar to those observed by Kramer, a number of differences in the psychopathology will be easily noted. My data stem—like Kramer's—from a middle-aged male patient.

The following presentation will focus chiefly on the material pertaining to the study of the "little man" phenomenon as a pathological ego formation; other factors of the case history will be omitted or greatly condensed. Preliminary observations on a possible variant or precursor of the phenomenon, gained from the still incomplete analysis of another patient, will also be presented.

Of European extraction and single, patient A had successively been a businessman, hotel manager, manufacturer, free-lance writer, newspaper reporter, and professional man of various kinds. He came for treatment in his thirties with few initial complaints, vaguely speaking about "a certain restlessness" which would at times assail him and impel him to change his job, domicile, and occupation. Though fairly successful in his variegated activities, he felt increasingly dissatisfied. He also mentioned unsatisfactory relations with women whom he would befriend rather easily and quickly, but after a brief and often hectic relationship discard in short order. Sexually he was aggressive and potent. He gave the outward impression of an easygoing, optimistic, bright individual whose genial and debonair behavior seemed designed to charm and please; but there was an almost palpable note of bravado, if not outright insolence in his demeanor, which can perhaps best be described by the word *brash*.

It soon became apparent, during the course of treatment, that the patient's object relations were of an extremely tenuous nature. In fact, they were little more than narcissistic pseudo-object relations. Emotional ties of others to him were ruthlessly exploited and were maintained chiefly in the service of narcissistic gratification. If they failed to provide such gratification, they were promptly abandoned. He manipulated and exploited people as well as situations in the typically cold-blooded, callous, and often cruel manner of the psychopath, cleverly maneuvering under the cloak of respectability and using considerable "predatory skill" (Devereux, 1953) in his exploits. No sooner had he gained the trust of some unsuspecting man or woman than he began to exploit them. He borrowed money which he did not return, or interested them in business operations in which he did not believe but from which he expected some advantage for himself. He was extremely stingy and would keep substantial amounts of cash on his person, usually in the back-pocket of his trousers, "to be ready for any eventuality."

The patient's utter callousness, lack of emotional depth, and flourishing megalomanic ideas—during the war he likened himself to Roosevelt, Churchill, Mussolini, etc.—were at times reminiscent of a latent psychotic process. There were also considerable distrust and suspiciousness accompanied by paranoid ideas, especially about money and banks which, he feared, would take his money away from him. With all his fantasies of uniqueness and personal grandeur, however, he was sociable, active, even animated by and well oriented toward reality which to him—like to Helene Deutsch's (1955) impostor—was but a stage on which he felt destined to play a great and leading role "with the rest of humanity as admiring audience." He was rebellious against all authority, belittling and devaluing it constantly. In brief, the patient presented the picture of a severe character disorder with all the typical earmarks of a psychopath.

The "little man" phenomenon first emerged in a dream. One day, after the patient's attention had been focused on his stinginess, questionable business deals, lying, and fraudulent behavior on various occasions, he reported that he had dreamed about *a little man who looked like an ugly, deformed dwarf and who in a dirty, cellar-like basement was turning somersaults among garbage cans, discarded vegetables, and other litter. The dwarf was jumping around in the cellar, hiding behind the garbage, and generally behaving in a sort of provocative as well as merry-making manner.* In his associations the patient spoke first of the dwarf Alberich presiding over the hoard of gold in the Nibelungen saga, of other dwarfs in mythology and literature, such as Rumpelstilzkin in Grimm's fairy tales, the hunchback of Notre Dame in the story by Victor Hugo, and finally of himself. He felt that the little man in the dream was he. Following this he began to speak more and more of himself as "the dwarf" whenever he mentioned some shady business deal he had engaged in, some act of provocation or aggression he had committed, his dishonest behavior with people, predatory exploits, fraudulent practices, and the like. He would report, for instance, "the dwarf was loose yesterday" or "the little man is active again," in describing antisocial impulses or activities which he experienced as coming from that inner agency named the "dwarf," occasionally also using the terms the "sneak" or the "dirty pig." As a rule, the patient was fully aware that he used these expressions to designate a part of his own personality—"the dirty and sneaky part of myself," he said. Occasionally, however, when he went on describing the "dwarf's" aggressive or fraudulent behavior in boastful detail, it proved helpful to point out to the patient that the sneaky, aggressive "dwarf" was himself. As in Kramer's case, the patient thus learned to distinguish between the "dwarf" segment of his ego and the ego proper, a distinction which initiated a very slow therapeutic process and contributed a great deal to the ultimately favorable outcome of the treatment.

The patient depicted the "dwarf" as a little man, less than a foot tall, ugly, deformed, and hunchbacked, with a big square head resting on a tiny, almost boneless and muscleless body. The large head was completely out of proportion to the rest of the body. The dwarf's face was angry and mischievous looking. The whole creature was forever bent on committing misdeeds, attacking and ridiculing others, being insolent and cruel, lying, deceiving, provoking, rebelling, bullying, boasting, sneering, hiding, enjoying other people's trouble, and having lots of fun in general. The "dwarf" felt superior to everyone and everything, and was sure that nothing bad could happen to him. In his omnipotence he resembled Eissler's (1950) patient who had lived with a syphilitic girl for many months and remained absolutely convinced that he could not become infected. The "dwarf" also felt immune to any disease.

The anal-sadistic components contributing to the "dwarf's" libido reservoir, character, and conduct were perhaps even stronger than in Kramer's patient, as evidenced by his cruel, aggressive behavior, secretiveness, stinginess, and chosen domicile. The patient expressed it this way: "As Alberich of the Nibelungen lives in a cave filled with gold and treasures, the dwarf resides in my rectum from which he can emerge at will and to which he returns at will after having done his dirty work— and nobody knows about him but me." He repeatedly returned to this theme of utter secrecy and the "dwarf's" safe abode in the rectal hideout, often quoting Rumpelstilzkin's triumphant lines:

> "Ach wie gut dass niemand weiss,
> Dass ich Rumpelstilzchen heiss!"

As was said above, the "dwarf" considered himself immune against disease. At one point during the treatment a short intercurrent infection necessitated the patient's hospitalization. When this happened, and the infantile omnipotence was temporarily shattered by the physician who ordered hospitalization, the patient meekly accepted the doctor's advice; but he took all the cash money he owned in a big wallet with him to the hospital. There he kept it next to himself, hidden in his clothing, through the days of his stay in the hospital. He said later that he could not have stayed in the hospital for a single day without the money next to him. He would have been in the most terrible panic without it. We shall presently see that this behavior toward illness still had further implications for the patient. As soon as the acute danger for the "little man's" existence subsided, the reverse process occurred. The illusion of omnipotence promptly re-established itself and the patient felt that the "little man" knew everything, accomplished everything, and could overcome every obstacle in his path. On such occasions he would compare himself to the frog in the ancient fable that blew itself up to the size of the elephant and more. The patient stated that the "dwarf," in his moments of triumph, did precisely that. It became clear that in these triumphant reactions the "dwarf" segment of the ego became the dominant element in the ego organization which was thus put in the service of its infantile grandiosity. It was under such circumstances that the patient felt that he possessed the statesmanship of Roosevelt, the courage of Churchill, the genius of Napoleon, the determination of Bismarck, and the scholarship of Kant, all wrapped in one and located, as it were, in the big square head of the "dwarf."

As the treatment progressed, it became apparent that the agency named the "dwarf" was instituted in the ego as a massive narcissistic defense against overwhelming castration anxiety and represented a kind of internalized fetish, serving—to use Freud's (1927) original formulation on fetishism—as "the token triumph over the threat of castration and a safeguard against it." That the castration fear assumed the severe and disruptive quality observed in this case had its roots in the patient's developmental history, especially during the first two or three years of life. Greenacre (1953) speaks of "primitive disintegrative anxiety" in serious disturbances of the early body image. From the multitude of data I shall select such material as is relevant here.

There had been gross nutritional disturbances from the very beginning of infancy. The mother was hospitalized for several months following the patient's birth, and he was bottle fed by a succession of apparently indifferent maids, for some time also by the mother's unmarried sister and the usually very busy father. There was evidence that the patient experienced near-starvation during infancy.

The nutritional disturbances as well as the patient's bizarre behavior to physical illness became clearer when he began to speak about certain body-destruction fantasies like dismemberment, mutilation by bone breaking and bone crushing, cutting and chopping up, cannibalistic devouring, tearing and hacking to pieces, etc. In early childhood, the patient had suffered from severe rickets which continued at least through the first two or three years of life and left permanent bodily changes on his chest and, to a lesser degree, on his head. The thoracic deformity moderately affected the arcus costalis. The cranium had some minor, groove-like deformities near the parietotemporal sutures which were partly hidden beneath the hair. It is worth noting, in this connection, that the patient's physical appearance as an adult did not reveal any of these abnormalities, not outwardly at least. He was well above average height, normally built, broadshouldered, and physically healthy in fact as well as appearance. Perhaps the only external circumstance reminiscent of early rickets was his relatively large head which seemed like a faint reminder of the *caput quadratum* the patient attributed in his fantasy to the "dwarf." There were, however, indications that some of the skeletal sequelae of the rachitic illness had been much more pronounced through the years of latency and early puberty. In grammar school he was among the smallest of his classmates who would call him "shortie" or "big head," occasionally also "little monster." His brother, several years his senior, would call him hunchback, or threaten that he would become one. The patient withdrew from all bodily competition with the athletically active brother. Physical activities, especially in the form of sport, gymnastics, and competitive games, were severely inhibited. Characteristically, in most intellectual subjects he succeeded in reaching the head of the class.

Due to the advances in nutrition and vitamin therapy rickets has ceased to be a major pediatric problem today, at least in this country. It is well to bear in mind, however, that active rickets is essentially a debilitating disease of the first two years of childhood, that it usually starts at the age of three months or shortly thereafter, and in severe cases may well continue into the third or fourth year of life. When the illness persists beyond the first year, thoracic changes as well as marked cranial deformity are frequently found, the head being enlarged out of proportion to the rest of the body. The English word "rickety," which originally meant affected with rickets, clearly denotes the state of severe musculoskeletal weakness and general helplessness produced by the disease. There can be little doubt that at the time the child learned to stand or walk—though nothing definite about this period became known during the treatment—the interference with both the development and function of normal skeletal and muscular activities must have been considerable. It seriously disturbed the integration and development of the body ego. Abundant material indicated that the aggression normally discharged through the motor system not only became heightened in form of murderous, sadistic fantasies, but also focused on and was partly discharged by the anal-secretory functions, with particular emphasis on the sadistic components of these pregenital processes. Retaliative castration anxiety with increased tendency toward feminine identification and general passivity was intense. The patient blamed the mother for his rachitic deformities and hated her consciously for her supposed negligence.

This was further reinforced by the arrival of a sister during the patient's second year of life, presumably at the height of his rachitic illness. Whereas the patient had been separated from the mother, due to her hospitalization, and bottle fed, the sister was breast fed by the mother at home and given special care because of a pulmonary infection. (These data were later corroborated by the surviving parent.) The patient dated his lifelong resentment toward his mother from these two events, the birth of the sister and the rachitic disease which he attributed to his mother's neglect of him.

It will be recalled that the patient depicted the "dwarf" as an angry creature almost without bones or muscles. Shorn of his infantile omnipotence and other concomitant features, the "dwarf" thus could be recognized as what he must have been originally modeled on: the body image of a rachitic infant desperately struggling against multiple dangers which threatened his body integrity through the rachitic process, his security through separation from the mother during her prolonged hospitalization and later the birth of the sibling, and his survival through severe nutritional disturbances to the point of near-starvation. This series of traumatic events during the first two years of life was soon augmented by certain occurrences in the phallic phase. The at least partial blocking of the skeletomuscular system of discharge at a period when such avenues for discharge were most urgently needed, had far-reaching effects. The child entered the phallic phase with a few minor bodily defects, but with a severely disturbed body image.

The beginning of the phallic phase was ushered in by some type of allergic reactions or attacks, the exact nature of which has never been fully established. It may have been an angioneurotic edema, a kind of giant urticaria, or some other allergic syndrome. The patient called it "an idiosyncrasy to red foods such as red beets or strawberries." It lasted through the years of latency and puberty, and disappeared in midadolescence. He described it as an acute swelling and reddish discoloration of the skin areas around the forehead, cheeks, nose, chin, and neck, which came regularly after eating red beets or strawberries, sometimes also spontaneously. These attacks occurred without pain, apparently also without major discomfort otherwise, and lasted for several hours. They were mainly characterized by the marked swelling and reddening of the facial tissues. The patient stated that at the height of an attack he had the feeling that his head doubled in size and dimensions. Though this appears exaggerated, it is certain that at the age of four or five his father, worried about the boy's "big head" during such an attack, took him that same day to the University Clinic of the capital city some hundred miles away. When they arrived there, after a long railroad journey, the symptoms had subsided and the medical examination was negative. The question as to the nature and type of the attacks remains undecided. It can be said, however, that these periodic spells of cranial tumescence and detumescence further contributed to the patient's unstable, distorted, and fluctuating body image. The narcissistic fantasies about the "dwarf's" head and his extraordinary capacity of rapidly increasing his size now become more fully understandable. The phallic significance of this intermittent cranial tumescence-detumescence process is, of course, obvious.

At this point some remarks about the patient's parents are indicated. He described his father as a powerfully built, robust man, colorful and fear-inspiring; the mother as a completely passive, unassuming, and inept woman who was mainly concerned with the father's welfare and terrified by the latter's whims and angry outbursts. The father, in his youth, had allegedly been an actor or musician of some sort, later a traveling salesman, a wine merchant, and a manufacturer of leather goods who had gone into bankruptcy leaving many unpaid debts. About the time the patient was born he was an overseer at the municipal abattoir and had also started a part-time business of his own. This business, which had apparently become quite active by the time the patient was three years of age, consisted of buying and slaughtering chickens, ducks, geese, turkeys, etc., and selling the killed animals to the local butcher stores and grocers. The slaughter of the animals was done by the father in a backroom of the apartment, occasionally also in the kitchen, with the patient as an eager bystander. At times the young boy was also taken to the abattoir where he not only witnessed the slaughter of cattle but also the flaying and cutting up of the carcasses. "The most impressive sight was the blood," he related, "as it came streaming out of the animals' throats cut wide open by the butcher's knife." A question, unanswered, poses itself immediately: Was there any connection between these bloody scenes observed by the child and the allergic reactions to red foodstuffs which developed about that time?

Greenacre (1953, 1955) has in some detail discussed the particularly traumatic effects of witnessing mutilating events in early childhood. Besides the extremely intense castration anxiety engendered by such experiences, there was in this case still another aspect to the frequent bleeding, cutting, killing, dismembering, knife wielding, chopping up and flaying observed by the patient. The little boy soon noticed that the animals, especially the bigger ones like cows and pigs, did not always die instantly. There was for several minutes a final life-death struggle with violent bleeding, convulsive movements, and muscular vibration in the slaughtered animal. The termination of this struggle, i.e., the arrival of death, was sometimes indicated by the emergence of fecal matter from the animals' anus. It became the boy's habit, whenever he visited the slaughterhouse, to look eagerly for this sign of death which he saw in the last and final defecation of the animal. As long as ther remained some feces left inside, he thought, however little and insignificant, there was life and not everything was lost. When the last bit of fecal matter left the body, then life left the body, too, and could never be regained . . . never. The question of "feces in the rectum" thus became almost literally a matter of life and death. It will be remembered that the "dwarf" not only resided in the rectum, but could also make his emergence from it as well as his return to it at will—a striking example of the "dwarf's" protective, lifesaving capacity for automatic reversal of these bloody, mutilating, and terrifying experiences. The "dwarf" was always full of life, immune to injury and disease, and practically invulnerable.

Coming back to the patient's hospital visit at the age of four or so, he vividly recalled that he and his father had to wait a long time in some anteroom or hallway of the clinic until they were admitted to the consultation room. While waiting, the child caught sight of a number of patients lying on stretchers, and when he noticed that some of these patients were carried or wheeled by the nursing personnel to another room in the rear of the building, he was sure that they were taken to a backroom in order to be slaughtered there. He became panicky, started crying and screaming wildly, imagining that he would be the next to be put on a stretcher and taken to the slaughter room. He did not stop crying until his father handed him his money bag with all the money in it as a token promise that nothing was going to happen to him. With father's purse in his possession, he calmed down and stayed in the clinic until the medical examination was over. When he had to go to a hospital for the second time in his life, as described earlier, he took his wallet with all his money to the hospital room as a safeguard against imminent castration.

It is noteworthy that some of the traumatic events in the early development here described were paralleled in the childhood history of Kramer's patient. The latter also experienced a severe organic illness during his first year of life; when he was twenty months old, a sibling was born whose arrival resulted in "constant rage against the mother and newborn child." In both patients a marked mother-child disequilibrium was predominant from early infancy. In both cases, to borrow from Kramer's description, "a succession of narcissistic injuries on every level of early development resulted in the loss of the feeling of infantile omnipotence . . . compensatorily, a separate structure in the ego was erected, and this proved of fateful significance." In both patients these separate ego elements named by the patients the "little man" drew to themselves substantial amounts of libidinal energies from all phases of libidinal development, a fact that led to a tremendously heightened secondary narcissism, possibly superimposed on pre-existing primary narcissism, thus devitalizing as well as impoverishing the ego proper. The "little men" formed no true object relations, both being extremely hostile to objects. Under certain conditions, the "little men" took over important aspects of ego functioning and seriously interfered with the respective patients' activities. They both represented isolated ego elements which had remained fixated on narcissistic pregenital levels and did not participate in the further development of the ego to higher levels. Inasmuch as these segments remained essential, albeit crippled parts of the ego organization, they also remained ego-syntonic, of course, and it was impossible for the patients to distinguish between the pathological ego formations called the "dwarf" or "little man" and the nondeformed part of the ego. Only after these ego segments emerged into consciousness and the patients acquired the capacity to make a definite distinction between the two agencies in question, did therapeutic efforts become effective.

This last point seems to me of considerable clinical significance. I am at present analyzing a very ill patient B, a college student in his early twenties, who through most of his life has been confused about his sexual identity. His aim in life was not to exert himself and to be taken care of. Though being a physically healthy six-footer and walking erect, he spoke of himself as an invalid and said that he was "a cripple on crutches" who was bent in the middle, leaning forward on the crutches and was "all out of shape or joint." For a long time this ominous description of his own body image remained strange and incomprehensible until certain fantasies emerged which centered around his congenital funnel chest. He perceived this thoracic deformity as "a hole in the center of my body . . . it is such a bad deformity," he said, "because it is a hole. It does not let me feel like a man." Later on, talking about his passivity, this extremely slow-moving, slow-acting, slow-speaking patient compared himself to an amoeba and stated: "I really like to cuddle up and do nothing, think nothing, say nothing. Being active and doing things is like stretching out pseudopods, and that is terribly dangerous. A pseudopod can be chopped off . . ." Against his intense castration anxiety he defended himself with the help of the amoeba fantasy which allowed him not only to withdraw his pseudopods at will, later re-creating as many pseudopods as he wished, but also to encapsulate himself like an amoeba and practically to disappear. The process of partial encapsulation was acted out by him in early puberty when he built for himself, in his room, forts and strongholds out of blocks and placed himself in the middle of the fortress. The confusion about his sexual identity is also part of the amoeba fantasy: while the pseudopods represent typical tumescence-detumescence organs like the penis, the indented space between the pseudopods and the vacuole of the amoeba are the female genitals and, as the patient himself says, "my hole in the chest." It is interesting that the Rorschach protocol on this patient discusses him as "a helpless, crawling creature begging for sustenance." It is further remarkable that this undoubtedly very sick man is an excellent student, married, sexually potent, and has successfully worked on several jobs, though his passivity is apt to cause occasional difficulties in his work. I am inclined to see in the amoeba fantasy a variant of the "little man" phenomenon, that is, to regard the amoeba as an isolated, separate ego segment, though ontogenetically and structurally considerably less differentiated than the "little man" and, in a sense, perhaps its forerunner.

Certain developmental data seem to support this view. From the history I can here give only two sets of data. From the end of the first year or the beginning of the second year of life well into the third year the patient suffered from frequent and severe diarrheas which were diagnosed as mucous colitis. In a number of analytic sessions he vividly described these diarrheas, speaking of his "loose bowels flowing out like water from a faucet . . . everything rushing out of me, blood, and phlegm, and water pouring out through my rear end . . . everything about me feeling phlegm-like and fluid, my body feeling fluidy, soft, jelly-like, and everything flowing out of me . . . like, yes, *like an amoeba,* soft, melting and pouring away . . ." Here is the early body image (or, should I rather say, *body feel?*) which centers around a physical sensation of watery dissolution through the anus—a bodily feeling which was relived in analysis with great intensity. The other facts I wish to mention briefly are that until his eighth or ninth year the mother would wheel the patient in a carriage, spoon feed him, and in all ways treat him like a helpless infant. Up to the age of seven he would sleep in the parental bedroom. Primal scene experiences which also played a great role in patient A, were dramatically described by him on numerous occasions. B was an only child until the age of ten when a brother was born. During the mother's pregnancy and for some years following the brother's birth he played the "encapsulation game" mentioned above.[1] He often felt "boiling mad inside," and at school began studying the natural history of protozoa,

---

[1] The "encapsulation game" probably is overdetermined. It is an attempt to cope with the dreaded sensation of body dissolution. At the same time, it also represents the patient's wish to be the protected foetus in utero as well as his identification with the pregnant mother.

particularly amoeba. He later wrote several scholarly essays on the subject. The aggression in this patient—much of it nonneutralized aggression, in Hartmann's sense—was enormous and mostly expressed on the amoeba level, so to speak: breast, penis, semen and other body elements were engulfed and incorporated in typically amoeba-like fashion.

When some of this material was worked through in analysis and the patient's attention was drawn to the "amoeba segment" of his ego, its development, vicissitudes, clinical manifestations, and anal connotations, a striking symptomatic act occurred in the transference which the patient interpreted himself. He always used to hand me his monthly check folded in the middle. For the first time in almost three years of treatment he then handed me the check unfolded and commented: "I never could give you a check unless it was folded in half. Today, for the first time, I did not fold it. Folding it in half was like two parts of me not being together, separated, or being bent in the center . . . like me bent with my caved-in chest in the middle, like being broken in half . . ." It is, of course, too early to add more to these preliminary observations. All that can be said at the present time is that with the growing distinction between the "amoeba segment" of the ego and the ego proper further developments may be expected.

It may be noted, furthermore, that in the three examples here discussed, Kramer's case as well as the two patients observed by me, a number of ego functions derived from "two psychic localities within the ego," as it were. This had far-reaching consequences. The ego behaved in this respect like an army whose operations are directed from two headquarters simultaneously, one of which functions in accordance with the realistic exigencies of the situation, while the other one operates in a completely different manner, basing its decisions not on sound strategic principles valid today but on tactical moves and impulsive responses which were established at a time when the original setup was organized and which have remained essentially unmodified since then. This could be observed both in the "dwarf" and the "amoeba" patient. The patients' ego organizations were operating in a Janus-like fashion, that is, two-faced, with the "dwarf" or "amoeba" segments of their respective ego agencies turned to the past and their intact ego parts turned to the present. Since the reality testing of the latter was preserved, the individuals functioned on the whole in a nonpsychotic way. It was only when the "dwarf" or "amoeba" elements took over and subjugated the rest of their respective ego organizations that the reality testing became precarious and at times quite poor.

As to the two kinds of anxiety found by Kramer in his patient, they could also be observed fully in the "dwarf" case and could be understood in accordance with the psychic locality in the ego where the anxiety originated. As a rule, little conscious anxiety was felt by the patient, and if so, it was of a vague, pale, rather shadowy quality. In situations, however, in which the "dwarf" felt directly threatened and his secret existence exposed, for instance, when he was caught red-handed in an act of fraud, the anxiety became acute. It grew to panicky proportions each time the "dwarf's" infantile omnipotence was shattered by a more "powerful" event, such as physical illness, loss of home, destitution, and immobilization in a hospital. Then the "little man" felt really little, helpless, forlorn, and the anxiety flowing over to the rest of the ego became an annihilating, all-pervading experience of utter despair and distress. Similar reactions could be seen in the "amoeba" patient; with the analysis still in progress, their clinical evaluation will have to be postponed until a later date.

Returning to the comparison between Kramer's patient and the "dwarf" man, the presence of sharp differences must also be noted. While both appeared to be isolated, infantile segments of their respective ego organizations, the "dwarf" appeared closely related to, if not identical with, the pleasure ego. The patient came to understand this himself. He stated: "The dwarf is interested in pleasure only, in having fun and power. He does not let me be a decent person." In Kramer's case, there was stern opposition to enjoyment of pleasure and the patient complained to the analyst that "the little man won't let me live," because he sharply opposed pleasure and freedom.

K. R. Eissler, in the aforementioned paper (1950), makes some comments on the ego pathology of delinquents which seem to me important enough to the understanding of this type of patient to be included here:

> In the type of delinquency discussed . . . one encounters a noteworthy pathology of the feeling of omnipotence . . . These patients must sometimes have had a disastrous experience in a situation in which they expected protection, help, or love from the persons whom they endowed with omnipotent powers. *This trauma must have kept the child fixated to the phase of omnipotence* . . . The quick succession of feeling immune to any attack followed by the feeling of complete helplessness, reflects the early traumatic situation when the child tried to counteract the inroad of the omnipotent forces by using his own omnipotence against the supposed adversary—only to fail. The predominantly hostile coloring which the environment takes on for them makes *these patients quite frequently appear paranoid,* but their history and their clinical symptomatology make it possible *to differentiate them from their schizophrenic counterparts* [italics mine].

It seems to me that the trauma or series of traumata postulated by Eissler (1950) as an essential factor in delinquent patients with "the psychopathology centering around the maintenance of a feeling of omnipotence" has been amply demonstrated in the "dwarf" patient here presented. The sequence, severity, and phase specificity of the traumatic events reported, especially those of a bloody, mutilating quality, and thus directly challenging the infantile omnipotence, were apparently absent in Kramer's case. Equally absent in the latter—or at least unrecorded in his report—was the role of the aggressive, fear-inspiring father who, while blatantly acting out himself, apparently achieved vicarious gratification by unconsciously or consciously goading the child into acting out, too. This is perhaps the way in which, according to the studies of Johnson and Szurek (1952) on the genesis of antisocial acting out, the father's taking the three- or four-year-old boy to the public abattoir can be understood. The fateful interaction between significant parent and child, to which these authors point, led the "dwarf" patient to massive acting out, in contrast to Kramer's patient who—with essentially the same omnipotence disturbance—became a greatly inhibited, masochistically oriented individual.

At any rate, the necessity to differentiate these nonpsychotic patients from "their schizophrenic counterparts," as Eissler has it, is of great practical significance. With their severe psychopathology, persistent ego split, infantile megalomania, emotional callousness, and sometimes bizarre behavior, such patients lend themselves to be classified as psychotics or psychotic-like individuals. The "little man" phenomenon in particular, so conspicuously reminiscent of Schreber's symptomatology,[2] is apt to arouse ominous doubts in the observer's mind about the patient's clinical condition. Closer study, however, reveals the essentially traumatic origin of many of the more puzzling features in a clinical picture which, I think, is basically a severe character disorder, in which the "little man" phenomenon can be viewed as an attempt at perpetuation of the infantile omnipotence and as a special, albeit pathological, solution of the castration threat.

2 The anal-sadistic connotations of Schreber's "little men" were shown by me in a previous paper (1951). The anal meaning can also be found in a case report by Bychowski (1950) who described the bathroom fantasy of a young girl during the act of defecation; while sitting on the toilet and pressing with her foot on the floor, she imagined that a dwarf-like, cruel Chinaman would either be kept inside or come out of her, dependent on her will. Johnny, the three-year-old boy mentioned earlier, pointed proudly at a copious piece of feces just produced by him and exclaimed: "Look, *a carrot man!*"

BIBLIOGRAPHY

Bychowski, G. (1950), On Neurotic Obesity. *Psa. Rev.*, XXXVII.

Deutsch, H. (1955), The Impostor. *Psa. Quart.*, XXIV.

Devereux, G. (1953), Cultural Factors in Psychoanalytic Therapy. *J. Am. Psa. Assoc.*, I.

Eissler, K. R. (1950), Ego-Psychological Implications of Delinquents. *This Annual*, V.

Freud, S. (1927), Fetishism. *Collected Papers*, V. London: Hogarth Press, 1950.

Greenacre, P. (1953), Certain Relationships between Fetishism and the Faulty Development of the Body Image. *This Annual*, VIII.

—— (1955), Further Considerations regarding Fetishism. *This Annual*, X.

Johnson, A. M. and Szurek, S. A. (1952), The Genesis of Antisocial Acting Out in Children and Adults. *Psa. Quart.*, XXI.

Kramer, P. (1955), On Discovering One's Identity: A Case Report. *This Annual*, X.

Niederland, W. G. (1951), Three Notes on the Schreber Case. *Psa. Quart.*, XX.

THE EFFECT OF EXTREME PASSIVITY IMPOSED ON A BOY IN EARLY CHILDHOOD

ELEANOR PAVENSTEDT, M.D. (Boston)

Many years ago, while working with adult schizophrenics, I was struck by the frequency with which I found that they had undergone a personality change at the time of a serious, often very painful illness in childhood. The illness itself was many times a long one and its effects had prevented the child from returning to his normal active life for many months. Theraupeutic procedures during the illness had often forced the child into a particularly passive masochistic attitude. Sometimes special rehabilitative measures were instituted during convalescence, and derivatives from these were always prominent in the later pathology of the patient.[1] In one case the father, in another an important father substitute, had charge of the case. In retracing the very early history of these patients, there always seemed to be indications of stress prior to the illness but not to the extent of creating obvious personality disturbances.

In the past eight years I have had under observation a boy, Brad,[2] now twelve years old, concerning whom I was able to obtain a very detailed history[3] by cross-checking the information from his father, his maternal grandmother, and his pediatrician (who knew him from birth), with repeated accounts from his mother in the course of three years of intensive casework.[4]

The reconstruction of his history appears to throw considerable light on the factors which were operative in preventing an adequate and orderly modification of his primitive drives; and in interfering with his

---

[1] One case, a boy of six, was treated by his father for pleurisy with drainage and frequent lavage of the pleural cavity. He was later given jars with colored liquids and instructed to blow bubbles into them to expand his lungs. His paranoid delusions at twenty-five centered around his breathing.

[2] First seen at the James Jackson Putnam Children's Center.

[3] For a more detailed history, see Pavenstedt (1955).

[4] Undertaken by Irene Andersen, M.S.

establishing an identity, particularly a sexual identity for himself. His drive to mastery and his active assimilation of reality were thus drastically curtailed.

PRESENTING PICTURE

Brad, when I saw him at four, was a very attractive little boy, well proportioned and holding himself erect. He was tastefully dressed in colors that suited his reddish hair, his blue eyes and fair complexion. Had he not been in constant motion or deeply absorbed by his preoccupations with little awareness of people around him, one would have looked upon him as a particularly handsome sturdy child.

Much of the time he moved in little volleys on his toes. He shook one hand or both, twirling them in rotary motion at shoulder height. At times his head was thrust forward and often his jaw moved up and down. When he spoke it was mostly too indistinct to be understood; the sentences were apt to be unfinished and trailed off into space. The mother could interpret much of his talk which was usually related to stories that had been read to him. She made the impression of someone who handled him with dexterity and kindliness, but as though a part of herself were detached from the situation.

He became absorbed in the piano, for fully fifteen minutes striking the keys and watching the hammers move. He moved the piano away from the wall to see what was behind it and said, "You push it and movement comes out." Anyone watching him would have been impressed with how much this piano was a part of himself. From there he turned to the one-way screen, pointed to it and said: "Is that a radio? Is it playing? Play the radio"; and a moment later: "Brad's a radio," which mother corrected. Although he spoke of not wanting to lie down, he sometimes lay flat on a table for a second, only to spring up again.

Later in the yard he was more withdrawn, walking around in circles, shaking his hands while talking loudly to himself. He was keenly aware of noises. Once when a plane passed overhead, he ran and twirled more excitedly than ever. While talking about a bicycle he said, "I live the bicycle"; he then ran straight ahead, twirling his right hand as if it were a motor or a wheel.

Usually, he was unaware of the other children, but at times a screaming child would catch his rapt attention. Occasionally he stood, a fascinated bystander, and the presence of other children then would seem to excite him a great deal.

He often seemed to want to join in activities on the swings, etc., but then froze—the more his mother urged him, the more he resisted.

In the therapy room feminine activity predominated. He gave baby care to a doll that he handled quite carelessly, and dusted the walls. His mother reported that he had been asking for hair ribbons.

When we said good-by to him, he became distressed: "You don't want me to go." A few minutes later he was engrossed in something else.

FAMILY HISTORY

Brad had grown up in rather exclusive contact with his father, mother and maternal grandmother. I shall describe them briefly so as to make the story of his development more vivid and understandable.

The mother whose adjustment was basically very frail, was experienced by the members of her family as overpowering. The only way the maternal grandmother and the father knew of staving off her furious outbursts was to be completely submissive and placating. The mother herself reported, and the grandmother confirmed, that as a child she had manipulated her parents and asserted herself by fainting and going into "hysterical spells." She said grandmother had always been too patient; she had felt in comparison hateful, mean, nasty, too bad to live with her family, a villain who was going to do something terrible to someone. She wondered why her mother had allowed her to get away with it and determined to raise Brad differently and not to spoil him. Even as a child she had clearly demonstrated her division of herself into the good and bad part by splitting off the good part onto a girl doll which was for seven years her constant companion and was given the presents that she could not accept directly. Her jealousy of her older sister had continued in an extremely hostile relationship. She had succeeded in covering up her intense jealousy toward her younger brother, even to herself, by making him dependent, showering him with gifts, dressing him up like a doll, and seducing him to admire her. In her dramatic accounts of tragedies with which she had come in contact in her youth, Brad's mother betrayed her primitive feelings as well as a distinct paranoid trend. One such was the story of her father's sudden death at night in her arms. Shortly thereafter she had provoked the man she had loved to break off their engagement. She attempted to expiate her guilt feelings over her strong attachment to her father by at times giving Brad over to her mother, who had lost everything at the time of her father's untimely death when Brad's mother was nineteen; this alternated with her need to possess Brad completely, by pushing the grandmother out of the picture.

The father was the studious type whom mother married because he accepted her completely. She described him as plodding and slow, need-

ing to be pushed in order to accomplish odd jobs around the house. The
mother showed the social worker sores in her palms, where she dug in her
finger nails in her impatience with him. The loss of his mother at four,
absence of intimacy with his father and harsh treatment at the hands of
his stepmother appear to have contributed to his passivity. At fourteen
he ran away, assisted by his older brother, and thereafter lived with his
paternal grandparents. He was always retiring, never allowing himself
to be drawn into arguments or fights, turning all his energy to his intellectual pursuits, in which he succeeded in making a moderate career for
himself. He allowed his wife to take over the management of their son,
as she had made him feel so inadequate in "getting anything out of
Brad." When Brad returned for treatment at the age of nine, the father,
during a brief period of therapy,[5] expressed fear of being attacked by
the patient and a feeling of frustration because Brad made it impossible
for him to be the good protective person (seemingly maternal) that he
would have wanted to be.

The third member of the household, the maternal grandmother, who
made her home with Brad's parents but was away for months at a time
when her other two children needed her, was a gentle and timid old
lady, concerned for Brad and for her daughter, grateful toward the latter
for giving her a home, yet well aware of her dominating ways and of her
harsh treatment of the patient. She herself had given Brad tender care,
rocking him and cuddling him, feeding him and reading to him for
hours. Her many absences, however, and her fear of arousing her
daughter's anger often kept her away from him, thus making her an inconsistent and untrustworthy provider. At times she interceded for him,
warning the mother that she would regret her severity, which only redoubled the mother's determination to deal with him as she saw fit.

THE PATIENT'S HISTORY

Everyone agreed that the mother—and the father too—had wanted a
girl, and that she tried from the time of Brad's birth to conceive again
to satisfy this longing. She had miscarried her first fetus and throughout
her pregnancy with Brad had been obsessed by the fear of losing this
baby too and had vomited the entire time. Delivery, although by breech
presentation, was uneventful and the baby was fine. Nursing was re-
pugnant to her and he did very well on bottle feedings in his crib, was a
healthy, happy and responsive baby of whom the mother was proud.[6]

[5] Carried out by Louis Sander, M.D.
[6] Many historical details were confirmed by perusal of the patient's Baby Book
kept up at the time by his mother.

She seldom picked him up for fear of spoiling him, and the grandmother was away from his second to his fifth month. The mother told of feeling disgusted at "the looks of the penis," particularly when she had to pull back the foreskin to keep it clean. She apparently did this vigorously because it once became so enflamed and swollen that it required medical treatment. The mother began in his fourth month to hold Brad's head and force pablum down his throat in the amount she felt he needed, whereupon he began vomiting. Thumb sucking, which started at six months and increased when he was easily weaned from the bottle at eight months, was actively interfered with by strapping his hands at eleven months and putting him into metal cuffs at thirteen months. At eighteen months, when the mother had put bitter fluids on his hands and slapped him hard, he finally abandoned it. The mother is almost certain that his hand waving, which was still present at age ten, had begun then. When toilet training was instituted at six or eight months, he was such a docile baby that the mother bragged about him to her friends. The grandmother remembered his kicking a cradle gym hours on end, sometimes laughing hysterically, watching it spin. As far as we know, he was allowed to abandon himself to this activity at will. When Brad sat at eleven months but would not stand, the mother took hold of him and shook him and stood him up, and from that time on he stood. By fourteen months she spanked him hard every time he wet. He responded by giving up wetting in the daytime. When he began running he had to be tied so that the mother could keep track of him. He would often run from one shade-pull to the next, keeping them spinning. He had a few well-enunciated words at fifteen months; however, he would not feed himself, continued to vomit, and screamed with rage at the sight of a stranger. Eight years later when her little girl—then a baby—bit her, the mother realized that Brad had never even attempted to bite her. She could not leave him alone; he had to do just what she wished; she couldn't help it, she said then. She guessed she just couldn't stand him because he was a boy. We can see that Brad rebelled against the treatment he received, but his rebellion broke through often belatedly and in a very distorted way, thereby remaining ineffectual.

Although his pediatrician recognized behavior problems, he declared his general mental and physical condition to be normal at eighteen months.

There followed at twenty-one months a three-day diarrhea with temperature around 103 degrees and a rectal prolapse, during which the mother was terrified of losing him. His pediatrician noted it without alarm; there was no specific organism isolated. The mother says they were told to have him have his bowel movements lying flat on his back for six months thereafter. There is no mention of this in the pediatrician's report.[7] Brad was put through a ritual every evening before supper: the father at first held him down with his legs up over his head while mother gave him enemas or suppositories, but after a few weeks his bowel movements came naturally. His grandmother was amazed at and concerned over his complete absence of resistance. According to all reports, speech dropped out completely at this time and his extreme fear of shampoos and baths began. It was followed closely by his fear of lying down in general; he refused to lie on his back even in bed until four when this subsided during treatment. His grandmother spontaneously dated the end of his normal development to this time. There was nevertheless in the midst of this period a push of activity: when his mother on his second birthday abruptly refused to continue spoon feeding him, he ceased vomiting, gradually began (with grandmother's help whenever the mother was out) to feed himself and recommenced speaking. However, his words were at first much less distinct than they had been. His with-holding of feces for three to four days at a time, which has persisted till now, began when he was allowed to resume having his bowel movements on the toilet.

At two years and five months when the pediatrician saw him again, he noted that his physical condition seemed normal but that "his behavior was at a standstill." Brad was referred for consultation four months later with the diagnosis of arrested development from some unknown cause with the statement that he had not had any severe enough illness to suggest encephalitis.

The mother tried to comply with the advice given her at this time not to put pressure on Brad or spank him and to give him plenty of love. "He went to pieces," was very demanding, screaming and overactive, and began sucking and chewing anything he could lay his hands on. There was, however, a great spurt in his speech development: within a week he learned to say sentences.

At three and a half we have a report from the pediatrician that he was crying hard at night and hardly sleeping. His nightmares began about this time. The mother attributed these to a change in his routine as she had been putting him to bed earlier. He had started stuttering and the mother had thought that he needed more rest. She never connected it with her second miscarriage, which took place just about this time. She told about that in another interview. This fetus was six months along

---

[7] Many pediatricians since have told us that such preventive measures are not customary.

and when she lost it the mother became extremely depressed and is sure that she completely neglected Brad. Shortly before she came to us, she had gone back to the spankings, trying to control him within certain limits, and found that they were just about back where they were before they went for the consultation, in that he was good on the whole but still extremely queer.

She said she just hated to hit Brad but couldn't help it because he annoyed her so. It hurt her deeply to know that he was afraid of her. How afraid he was she confided only five years later when she said she shook and shook him sometimes till she actually got frightened that she would murder him. His reaction to her anger was to become pale, frightened and limp. She would be overwhelmed then with remorse and would try to make up for it by showering him with affection and gifts.

During the summer vacation when he was four, there were two significant events. Once while paddling in the ocean he fell flat on his face and apparently made no effort to pick himself up. The mother tells the story in her usual dramatic way: she tore down to pick him up; he was breathless, choking and terrified. Rescue fantasies remained prominent and were often played out later. When the family visited Niagara Falls, he was beside himself with fear. On his return home he evinced great fright of the noise of water in the pipes in his bedroom and screamed at night that it was coming down on him.

OBSERVATIONS DURING TREATMENT

Our observations in the course of treatment illustrate the alternation of extremes of this child's passivity and aggression and the mechanisms he used in his attempt to deal with these extremes. Brad reacted to my (and gradually also his mother's) decreased coercion with overactivity, self-assertion, some destructiveness, increased waving and particularly again with mouthing—his cuffs, his collar, his shoulder straps, wash cloths, rags, etc.—sucking, biting and ripping. He had already bitten his teddy bear so frequently in the genital region that the mother had made him a large leather patch there.

As it became possible for the social worker to convey to Brad's mother that punitive control did not have to yield to complete laissez faire and as he began to relate to the therapist, he started to communicate and to show interest in things outside his fantasy world; his anticipation anxiety decreased and his hand waving became less frantic. Gradually his preoccupation with housework waned and he began to roughhouse with his father, often biting him. After a while the excitement subsided and he became what his father called companionable. He grew increasingly aware of people, wanted to touch them on the street car, responded for the first time to the neighbors' greetings. The fight for control between him and his mother seemed to be subsiding. Brad pushed his teddy ahead of him now as he began to explore and to master courage. He began to lie down on his back, once even when his mother was in the room with him, and proudly demonstrated it in bed to his father. His mother was able to tolerate our permissive handling of Brad during this time by developing a kind of hypomanic acceptance of our "magic cure" and acted this out by grossly exaggerated permissiveness toward him at home.

This encouraging period of growth and expansion was disturbed by his mother's fourth pregnancy which, coming only a year after her second miscarriage, must have had many painful associations for Brad. For the first time the mother continued to feel fine and declared it a miracle. Brad reacted by regressing and with self-destructive impulses. He wanted to be carried, to throw his legs away; he tried to pull off his ear and the doll's hand and became absorbed in what went down the toilet; he began performing a touching ritual of his body parts. The mother's abortion, which she openly blamed on Brad because she had fallen and bruised herself when he inundated the kitchen floor, led to a renewed outburst of resentment at the Center. She expressed fear of insanity for both herself and Brad. The spell of our treatment was broken and the mother was never really won back—she remained thoroughly ambivalent thereafter.

Brad became intensely disturbed and anxious, and attempted repeatedly to do himself damage. He asked his grandmother one day whether she had a penis and whether she wanted one. When her answer to both these questions was "no" he said "mine will drop off." He told his parents that night he was afraid of the water in the walls but loved it. He demanded long pants to hide his legs and talked of boys going down the sewer. While playing with a baby doll (about a month after the mother's abortion), he became suddenly frightened: "It's real, tear off its arms and legs" and again "Is she real? Pull her lip off. Am I a nice boy?" His behavior at the Center was extremely disorganized. He withdrew from the therapist, had a "crush" for a time on the Nursery School teacher and then turned against her. Treatment thereafter accomplished little. After recovering from the effect of the mother's abortion, Brad attempted to grow up by making a kind of token identification with an older boy in the neighborhood. He was calmer for a time and the mother was quite encouraged. Once when he was shaking less, his mother told him she would play him a certain record provided he not shake while it played: he managed to control himself but with rising tension and finally caught hold of his penis and shook that. The mother was horrified and decided she would make no more such attempts.

His passive compliance at childrens' parties and in Sunday School gave his mother sufficient assurance to take planning for Brad's future out of our hands. She entered him in a small kindergarten the following year. In spite of his failure there, she insisted on his going on to public school for three years where he learned nothing. They complained that he was too good. When the teacher stood beside him, initiating his activity, he would work. As soon as she left his side, he just sat looking out the window. His mother forced him to learn some things at home; she said she always had to start him off on any activity.

At nine when the mother at last had her little girl, therapy was resumed; much more verbal now, Brad made many things very clear. For the first seven weeks he was seen in the playroom. He began immediately to focus his talk on "my brother Tarboy" who, at once the aggressor and the object of aggression, seemed to represent (1) his little sister, in relation to the aggressive feelings he wanted to take out on her; (2) his mother, scolding, spanking and berating him; and (3) the therapist against whom he expressed hostility, particularly when it came to a struggle of allegiance between her and his mother. He acted all this out very forcefully with a large rag doll.

At times when Tarboy represented the asocial side of himself, he insisted that the only way to treat him was to beat him up, put him in jail, electrocute him, murder him, and spoke of his intense hatred of him. He had said of Tarboy: "I can't stand him, he's a dope, he won't even defend himself," which his mother had said of him many times. Through him Brad expressed various hypochondriacal fantasies such as having all his blood removed because it was bad, and of dying. I introduced some solicitous care by nursing a sick doll: Tarboy and Brad approved of it one moment, only to say "he must die" the next.

Soon a new theme emerged—of being eaten by lions and monsters. At the end of an hour he suddenly darted behind me and grabbed a large mouthful of the clothes on my back, in his teeth. When I turned to say I couldn't let him do that he ran to the door with a shriek, grabbed his jacket and left. There was considerable magic play too, turning the therapist into an animal, a devil, a prisoner, etc.

As he began again to have some confidence in the therapist, he administered a shampoo and a bath quite realistically talking to me soothingly and speaking of caring for me as he no doubt had been seeing his mother care for his little sister. He played dentist and barber with me too, taking pains to contain his aggression. He expressed great hostility toward his mother, saying Tarboy had killed her.

At home his rebellion and hostility were just pouring out, and his mother, responding in kind, often spoke of feeling like choking and killing him. The only peaceful and friendly times they had together were on their drives to and from the clinic.

Gradually his need to be hurt, punished, beaten for his desire to hurt were expressed directly, without projection onto Tarboy. We had long, quite thoughtful conversations about the violent feelings in everyone which had to be controlled as we grew up and that parents punished children in order to help them with this. He spoke of the Tarboy in himself as though that made things hopeless, and then one day he said: "The trouble is: my mother has some Tarboy in her too." I attempted to convey to him that this was a general phenomenon, not something so bad as to warrant severe punishment. One day when I said that all children wanted to learn to be good because they wanted to be loved, he leaned over quickly on his way out and gave me a moist peck on the cheek.

These conversations began when we moved from the playroom to my office. Here his extreme restlessness and at times violent destructiveness diminished. The attacks on the therapist's hair and back, however, recurred intermittently.

In connection with entering the cub scouts, Brad talked about the many things Tarboy had to learn. I introduced the idea of the satisfaction and pleasure one could get from learning. He played around with it a bit, often sarcastically, and it seemed clear that he had never experienced it. Later, in his few attempts at games with me, I saw that he could not allow himself to try. In a competitive game, he said he was not supposed to be glad when the opponent lost. Reassured, he became scathingly critical of me, but his expressions of pride in his own success sounded hollow.

Later a new theme was his fear of a "bent light," at night on his ceiling. He identified it for his mother as a certain light at home which she said came out of the wall above the bathinette where he had had his movements lying down.

His tendency to project and displace was very clear when he talked at length about the therapist's having to be locked up in a small, smelly jail; the next time he remonstrated loudly about having to stay in the office, using exactly the same words to describe it. He attacked me several times during that interview, but could be warded off easily. I pointed out that he could open the window and that I was not even holding him. In a totally different voice he then began complaining of his mother's hard treatment, of her criticism of his school work, of her making his father punish him when he wasn't at all bad. He continued: "You're just the opposite and it makes things hard for me." I accepted his dilemma and henceforth kept giving this as my reason whenever I restricted him. Sometimes he desisted, sometimes not.

He wanted to know for what kind of crimes a judge could send one to jail; would he if a boy didn't go to school? When he mentioned in the course of this conversation that his father and mother wouldn't let him go to school, I laughed, whereupon he pounced on me, almost tearing my clothes off and said he couldn't stand being laughed at. He had the same kind of fury when he dropped something.

In the fourth month of this period of treatment he began to be openly erotic. Once in the course of dramatizing a nightmare, he exposed himself. Later he said people paid him for it but denied this when closely questioned. He told a long story about a boy at camp who had put his penis out the window and had been sent to the infirmary for punishment. Actually Brad had spent two weeks there the previous summer and felt his parents were abandoning him when they left him there after a visit. Once when he had taken a hunk of hair from the back of my head into his teeth, he said, with rising excitement, "I want to love you up." When he was warded off, he responded with genuine feeling: "You make me angry." I felt that a kind of sing-song toying with sounds "a-wee-tee-tee-ai" in a high falsetto voice, which he had combined often with silly giggling, probably was intended seductively.

Gradually his extreme sensitivity about being different, stupid, a dunce, a dope, became the central theme. This was followed by ideas of grandeur; for instance that he knew everything, that he was a mind reader,—that these ideas were very powerful and could murder people; he would leave each interview declaiming loudly, "Brad Grimes wins again!"

Once he astounded me by this bit of insight; I suggested that we learn subtraction together and surprise his mother with his new knowledge. "I know better than that," he said seriously and positively. "You mean she wouldn't like it that someone else had taught you things?" I asked. "Yes, that's just it. She would rather teach me than do anything else in the world—she'd rather teach me than take care of us and feed us. We have long conversations about numbers." I asked: "What's wrong with that?" He replied: "It's all wrong. She thinks I was born careless." When I defended him, he went on with: "I have a bad mind—just bad, that's all." Did he mean it had bad thoughts? "It doesn't think bad things all the time—just sometimes. When you get that worried feeling —you know." He then went off into his falsetto sounds and interpolated: "Sometimes I go off the beam." He complained about his inability to learn to ever make anything of himself. He expected to be a criminal, to land in jail or the electric chair, to lead a "bent life." He complained at length about his mother's discipline, threatened to run away and accused me of doing nothing for him because I left him with his mean parents.

Gradually he began to be provocatively erotic at home. As the mother became frightened by his demands to remove father from the house, by his pushing against her, and finally by exposing himself to her, she revealed how very seductive she had been with him over the years.

The following dramatization of a "nightmare" clarifies the importance of father's passivity for Brad in his oedipal conflict. Brad decided to play father and told the therapist to be his little boy—no his little girl. He turned out the light and said she was in a spooky room. He screamed loudly as an intruder, at first frightening only the little girl. "Father" overheard the girl crying, told mother she must be dreaming again of that frightening man, went to her to reassure her. Gradually the spook became more and more threatening to father who admitted he shared his little girl's fears. Thereafter the play consisted of dramatic fights between a weak frightened father and "the man." As father continued to talk sotto voce to mother, the therapist asked why the man only wanted to get father and the girl, and did nothing to mother? "He's in love with mother" was the unhesitating reply. Thereafter father was actually killed, then dying. Brad said, father didn't know where he was— he was going up into the air, nowhere, then drowning; he said what was the use of going on living, he was just a rag, to be thrown out.

Brad had often spoken of his fear of drifting off into the sky or the ocean. He associated fear, badness and lonely feelings, and was afraid of falling asleep at night because he was lonely. He repeatedly said that if he drifted off, his father and mother would not care, they didn't love him.

SUMMARY

Brad was described as a healthy, happy and responsive baby. It is my impression that for his mother, he represented a number of things: a guilt-laden oedipal child, her own brother of whom she had been so fiercely jealous, and that part of her body that she so resented not having, that one didn't touch, completely controlled and that had to be perfect.

For all these reasons she consciously rejected a boy child. She failed to respect his spontaneous developmental patterns, interfered with his sources of gratification, denied him free motor activity through which he could have discharged some of his tension, and forced him to submit to her will. We have seen that his father was too passive to provide him with either protection or an upstanding manly example. The grandmother by her inconsistency increased his ambivalence.

He became caught in a pattern of reaction that began in the oral phase. Whereas he finally yielded with passive surrender to his mother's disciplinary measures toward his thumb sucking, he had a delayed reaction: his hand waving was a displaced and distorted gratification.

He yielded with a similar pattern to the assault of being made to have his bowel movements lying down; he later refused to lie on his back and withheld his movements.

It was this event which continued for six months, around the age of two, that became the culmination of his masochistic experiences. He became fixated at this period in the struggle between aggression and passivity, for which his earlier development had laid the foundations. This episode was particularly overwhelming for the following reasons: (1) because of the *timing* just under two when instincts are particularly stormy and as yet poorly controlled; when the child feels threatened by his discovery that he can assert himself but cannot control himself; before speech is established which strengthens the security the child derives from his relationships; and when body integrity and body image are so vulnerable; (2) because the *part of the body* invaded was at this age especially anxiety provoking; (3) because the *individuals* engaged in the assault were the powerful figures of his environment. He was so overwhelmed that inhibitions and regression followed. Furthermore, our material confirms the fact that passive subjugation to having his bowels emptied was accompanied by sexual stimulation and experienced as masochistic pleasure; his conflict now became essentially a sadomasochistic one. His anxiety over a "bent light" and his attacks from the back on the therapist's hair exemplify the two opposing trends springing directly from this experience. The trauma was immeasurably intensified because of the disturbed development that had preceded it.

In the genital sphere I suspect that Brad's mother neglected to confide to us that her punitive treatment of his hands was aimed at keeping Brad from playing with his penis, as well as from sucking his thumb. We observed that he never touched it subsequently, even when urinating. He was willing at times to relinquish his penis and later developed touching rituals.

He became so frightened of his environment that he was never able to master his fears. When his mother was twice induced to remove her controls, all his inhibited primitive aggression emerged. The mother's miscarriages and subsequent rejection of Brad each time forced him into an even stronger ambivalent attachment to his mother. His fear of drifting off into limitless space was the expression of his slender object relationships, so threatened by primitive sadomasochistic fantasies; his fear of isolation drove him back into his erotized subjugation to his mother.

Finally the nightmare dramatization portrays his bisexual struggle— he sees himself as the helpless little girl whose fears are shared by her weak father; he enacts both the weak father and the murderous mother-loving intruder, whom the timid father cannot combat.

Brad's rebellion was totally ineffective. However, when mother and father were helped to endure it and to deal with it realistically, and when he was encouraged to accept his aggression as a necessary part of himself, he became gradually a little less frightened. In an excellent remedial school for over two years now, he has begun at last to learn and has given up his waving. Some part of his aggression at least seems to have been transformed into energy available for work.

However, he remains a psychotic child. Bender (1947) believes that some children with deep anxiety due to disturbances in interpersonal relationships may react with profound biological disturbances and regressive behavior akin to the schizophrenic child. Mahler (1954) would presumably class him with "the induced or *folie-à-deux* type of infantile psychosis"—a subtype of symbiotic psychosis.

It is not my purpose here to make a differential diagnosis. I wished simply to report a case in which a specifically traumatic event—specific in early childhood for the various reasons I have outlined, and particularly traumatic because of what had preceded it—seems to have contributed so clearly to a conflict which could be dealt with only by psychotic mechanisms.

BIBLIOGRAPHY

Bender, L. (1947), Childhood Schizophrenia. *Am. J. Orthopsychiat.*, XVII.
Burlingham, D. (1953), Notes on Problems of Motor Restraint During Illness. In: *Drives, Affects, Behavior*, ed. R. M. Loewenstein. New York: International Universities Press.
Freud, A. (1951), Observations on Child Development. *This Annual*, VI.
Mahler, M. S. (1954), Round Table on Childhood Schizophrenia. *Am. J. Orthopsychiat.*, XX.
Pavenstedt, E. (1955), History of a Child with an Atypical Development, and Some Vicissitudes of His Treatment. In: *Emotional Problems of Early Childhood*, ed. G. Caplan. New York: Basic Books.

A MOTHER'S OBSERVATIONS ON THE TONSILLECTOMY OF HER FOUR-YEAR-OLD DAUGHTER

JOYCE ROBERTSON (London)

With Comments by

ANNA FREUD, LL.D. (London)

At four years and three months, Jean was in hospital for three days, accompanied by her mother, for the removal of tonsils and adenoids. This was a well-managed hospitalization and the outcome was good, but it is clear from the record that the experience was fraught with anxiety for the child.

A PLANNED HOSPITALIZATION

My husband and I believed that hospitalization for tonsillectomy could be traumatic to a child of this age, but that if the mother were present to play a supportive role throughout, the risk of aftereffects could be greatly reduced. The children's physician and the ward sister (charge nurse) were specially sympathetic to our views and interested in the possibilities of nursing by the mother. We discussed the practical implications of my wish to be present during all of Jean's conscious experience.

It was eventually agreed that I should be with her until she became unconscious, and again immediately after the operation. There was initially some reluctance to allow me to be present during the early stages of returning consciousness. They then believed that she would have no awareness in that phase, and that I should therefore be spared the anxiety of witnessing an unfamiliar scene of blood and apparent distress.

Jean and I would share a cubicle in the children's ward. She would be allocated to one nurse in accordance with the practice of this ward, but in fact I would do everything for her except the technical nursing.[1]

1 We wish to thank the staff of the children's ward at Guy's Hospital, London, and in particular Dr. Ronald MacKeith, Children's Physician, and Miss J. Tanner, Ward Sister, for their cooperation in this experiment.

Previous History

From birth Jean suffered from eczema and food allergy, which created problems in feeding and management. The eczema was managed with a minimum of restraint. There was inevitably some frustration and interference during the first two years of her life, but there were no disturbing investigations or treatments and no hospitalization. The eczema then cleared, except for mild spring outbreaks, but left a tendency for common colds to develop into bronchial asthma.

Her social development was slightly retarded by the difficulties of the first two years, but by the age of four this had been largely made up. She had friendly relationships with the children of the neighborhood, and with adults whom she knew well, but was noticeably slow to accept the advances of strange adults. In illness she tended to be more negative and withdrawn than most children.

During the winter preceding her admission to hospital, she had several attacks of otitis media and tonsillitis, and during treatment was found to be allergic to the antibiotics. Since the attacks were becoming more serious and could not be satisfactorily dealt with medically, it was reluctantly accepted that her tonsils and adenoids should be removed.

I intended to say nothing about this to Jean until about a week before the operation, which was arranged for six weeks ahead. But as will be seen from the Diary, I was compelled to begin telling her almost immediately.

Preparation for the Operation

I decided to make no reference to the possibility that she might be subjected to enemas, injections, blood tests, urine tests. I judged that such procedures were best explained immediately before they happened, and that earlier explanation might arouse unnecessary anxiety. I covered procedures in general by saying that in hospital we did not always like what the doctors and nurses did, but that they were always trying to make us better.

When I first told her of the operation I gave no details other than that it was her tonsils which kept making her throat and ears sore, and that in hospital the doctor would make her go to sleep and take them out. I told her she would be three days in hospital, and that I would be with her all the time.

During the next five weeks I gradually expanded this first statement, following the lead given by her questions and behavior. This is the essence of the picture I built up for her:

There would be doctors and nurses looking after her and the other children. On the first day the doctor would look in her throat and ears, and listen to her chest. Next day at breakfast time she would be given a pill. Later she would smell the "funny smell" and would go to sleep for just a little while—it would be a special "tonsils sleep" and not ordinary sleep. She would go on the trolley to have the doctor take out her tonsils, and then he would carry her straight back to her cot in our little room. When she awoke her throat would be very sore, just like a really bad cold. It would be because her tonsils were out. Tonsils were like the loose skin which sometimes hangs painfully around a fingernail—it is sore after it is cut off, but next day it is better. When her tonsils were first out she would not feel well, but I would sit by her cot and read the stories she liked best. Although her throat would be sore, it would be getting better all the time. Her throat would bleed, just like her knee when she fell on it. Some of the blood might go down into her tummy, and then she would spit it up. She would feel better when she had spat it out. We would both want to go home to Daddy and Katherine (her sister), but would have to stop until the doctor told us her throat was better.

Since long before it was known that Jean would go to hospital, there had been in our home two pamphlets showing picture sequences of children in hospital (Robertson, 1953a; Connell, 1953). She became suddenly interested in these and, as will be seen in the Diary, she repeatedly asked to have them explained to her—which I did, in a way I thought applicable to her situation. The first of these Jean refers to as "Laura," and she selected for special attention four pictures showing— Laura sitting in a hospital cot hugging her favorite toys and looking rather sad, being visited by her mother, putting on her shoes to go home, and finally walking out of the hospital gates with her mother. The second pamphlet she calls "Tonsil Boy." This shows a boy going to hospital to have his tonsils out, being undressed, looking at books with his mother and a nurse, being examined by a doctor, smelling the anesthetic, sleeping in a cot with his mother by his side, sitting up to have a meal after the operation, and finally home again.

The Diary

I decided to keep a diary of events in the hope of recording a follow-through account of the reactions of a young child to tonsillectomy that would add to understanding of how a child might best be helped to cope with such an experience. In this I shared the interest of my husband who has published on the problem, notably his film "A Two-Year-Old Goes To Hospital."[2]

DIARY[3]

BEFORE ADMISSION TO HOSPITAL

March 1st. Jean was seen by the surgeon today, and he recommended removal of her tonsils and adenoids. This was said in her presence, but as she has been rather deaf because of the ear infection (otitis) she seemed not to have heard. The operation was arranged for six weeks ahead, and I have decided not to say anything to Jean about it until about a week before she goes to hospital.

March 2nd to 5th. During these few days Jean became increasingly difficult about her food. She ate little and appeared angry or unhappy at mealtimes. This puzzled me until I overheard her say to herself, "Don't eat it. Better not eat it or you'll go to sleep." So, although I had planned to give her only about a week to adjust to the idea of an operation and a stay in hospital, I decided to begin telling her at the first opportunity lest her eating disturbance was in fact connected with fantasies about anesthetics.

March 6th. Today I told Jean that she would go to hospital one day to have her tonsils taken out. I chose a moment when she was complaining about having to stay in the house because of a sore throat and cold. Together we looked out of the window and named the children who had been ill and were now well again. I pointed out two children who had had their tonsils out, and Jean added two more names to the list.

She said, "I wouldn't like to go to hospital without you. I would want you all the time. I wouldn't stay there." I told her that I would stay with her in the hospital. She said, "All the mummies don't stay with their children all the time in hospital. Why don't they? Susan's mummy didn't stay with her." I reminded her that Susan's mummy had visited her every day instead: "Susan is a bigger girl than you are. She goes to school and is used to being away from her mummy." Jean said, "Susan didn't like it when she didn't see her mummy in the night, did she?" I agreed that Susan had been a bit unhappy, but because she was seven she could wait until the morning for her mummy; and told her I knew that girls of four wanted their mummies to stay with them, but added that when she was bigger she wouldn't mind sometimes being without her mummy.

I told her very briefly what would happen in hospital—that she would go to sleep, her tonsils would be taken out, and that we would stay in hospital for three days. She did not ask for more information.

[2] Robertson, J., "A Two-Year-Old Goes to Hospital." (Film, 16mm., black and white, sound, 45 min.) London: Tavistock Clinic, 1953. Robertson, J., "A Two-Year-Old Goes to Hospital; An Illustrated Guide to the Film." London: Tavistock Publications, 1953.

[3] Events were usually recorded immediately after their occurrence, and never later than the evening of the same day.

March 7th. Jean began eating again almost normally. She searched among her Daddy's papers for the pictures she called "Tonsil Boy" and "Laura." She brought them to me and asked to be told the "hospital story." She searched anxiously for a picture she remembered, showing child and mother going home, and when she failed to find it she appealed to me.

March 8th. At breakfast she examined her fork, and said, "This fork would dig right into my throat, and it would hurt. I've got a big hole in my throat, haven't I?" Later she asked for the stories of Laura and Tonsil Boy. "Why do the doctors wear that thing on their faces? Why must they not cough germs at the ill children? Can I cough at you?"

March 9th. Jean saw me open a tin with a tin opener as she had often done before. She handled the tin opener for a few minutes, and then asked: "What's this for? What do you do with it?" Twice during the day she asked to be told the story of Laura and Tonsil Boy.

When an ambulance stopped outside our flats she said, "Look! The ambulance has stopped because someone is ill." And later, "It's all right, it has gone now." (There is an ambulance station in our road, and she sees many ambulances every day.) Later when she saw an ambulance driver walk by she remarked, "It's all right now. He is going home to tea round the corner."

March 10th. Jean stopped in the middle of her lunch, lay back and sucked her thumb. I asked if she was tired. She sat up and said, "A little girl has died. Michael said she didn't die, but she has." I asked, "Why did she die?" and Jean answered, "Because it was time for her to die." I told her that little girls did not die when they had their tonsils out. She asked, "Why don't they? They might if the Doctor couldn't get their tonsils out properly."

I again explained the hospital procedure, and Jean ran to get the Laura and Tonsil Boy pictures. As I went through them with her, she added some remembered explanations. She counted each picture as a day. For the rest of the day she was active and cheerful, but she slept badly.

March 11th. At breakfast Jean made a fuss about the salt cellar. She refused to let anyone else have use of it, because she wanted to have one of her very own. "Can I buy one for myself on Saturday with my own pocket money?"

March 12th. At teatime she cut her poached egg very carefully, saying, "I want it [the yolk] to run out." She watched her Daddy having tea half an hour later, and said, "Look, when Daddy cuts his egg it all runs out." (A week before this record started Jean had said, "When all the blood runs out of cut and hurt people they die.") She put her thumb and first finger in her mouth and pinched the back of her tongue, remarking "It hurts when I do it."

March 14th. Jean saw a picture of a man, a prisoner being led between two policemen; and for the next twenty minutes she questioned me persistently about "naughty men." "Do children go away when they are very naughty? Were you naughty, Mummy? Did you go away when you were little?" I spoke of the coming hospitalization, and we talked about the reasons for it.

March 15th. At lunch she talked again of knives and forks being sharp. "They could poke our throats," she said, then ate her lunch mostly with her fingers. She pretended to cut my hand and arm with a knife. She asked to be shown the sharp end, then pushed it into her mouth very slowly and carefully until it appeared to touch the back of her throat. She then withdrew it. She said nothing.

March 16th. After breakfast Jean had a temper tantrum and aggressively banged a drum until the top caved in. In the afternoon, while listening to a radio program playing records for children in hospital, she sat handling a little fruit knife. For a quarter of an hour as she listened she made cutting movements on the chair arm, the table, the cushions, my arm, hand and face. When the program had finished, she asked, "Why are those children in hospital? When will they go home again? Read me Tonsil Boy and Laura."

March 17th. Several times today I saw Jean standing quietly putting her thumb and first finger far into her mouth with a pinching movement.

March 19th. Jean bought a gun with her pocket money, and played shooting for the rest of the day. Later she wanted explosive caps to make bigger bangs.

March 20th. She had no interest in games other than shooting—the bigger the bang the more she liked it.

March 21st. This was the first fine day of spring, and our family went strolling in the park. Jean drew attention to herself by shooting everyone she met. When her explosive caps were finished, she wanted to go immediately to buy more and was furious when told it was Sunday and the shops were closed. She could find no pleasure in the park, and asked to be taken home.

March 22nd. There has been no mention of hospital for several days, but Jean has become very aggressive toward me and has scratched and bitten her sister with very little provocation.

March 23rd. Her very aggressive behavior continues.

March 24th. Today Jean overheard an adult talk about a child who had been killed on the road. I spoke with her later about it, but she would not admit that a child could be killed on the road in this way.

March 25th. Her aggressive behavior continues. Temper tantrums in which she throws herself on the floor at the slightest upset have become rather frequent. As she had not mentioned the coming operation for a week, I decided to reintroduce the topic.

After a tantrum I linked her behavior to the operation, and she talked willingly about it. "They will hurt me. Very ill people go to hospital, and they have to go in an ambulance. I don't want to go." At bedtime she said, "Wash my hands when I'm in bed. I'll shut my eyes tightly, then I won't know that you are doing it."

March 26th. Jean awoke in the night screaming. She complained tearfully, "It hurts, it hurts!" and pointed into her mouth as if at an aching tooth. After an aspirin and half an hour in my bed she returned to her own room and slept. This morning I took her to the dentist, but he could find nothing to cause toothache.

This morning Jean did not notice when I undid her nightdress because we were talking. With delight and surprise she explained this to me. "It was just like my tonsils, I did not feel you do it."

March 27th, 28th, and 29th. Many aggressive outbursts.

March 30th. When asked not to scratch her sister, she said, "Well, we didn't talk about the hospital yesterday. That's why!" She found Laura and Tonsil Boy and asked to be told and retold their stories. She dug her fingers into her mouth, and asked, "Which bits of skin will the doctor take away?"

March 31st. At bedtime Jean asked with a whisper for both hospital stories. A few minutes before she had been examining her navel, asking what it was and how it came.

April 1st. We bought some puzzles and other oddments to occupy her while in hospital, and Jean put them in a case under her bed. This evening she took longer than usual to settle down. When I gave her her usual dose of Anthisan (the drug used to control her allergy) she told me to put the bottle into the case with her hospital things. When I said the Anthisan should not go into the case, because it was not yet her turn to go to hospital, her restlessness subsided and she slept.

April 2nd. Today has brought many minor accidents—for instance she caught her thumb in her tricycle and later caught her foot in a chair. Her skin is more sensitive than of late, her eyes and chin become inflamed very easily, and her tummy and thighs show signs of having been scratched a lot.

April 4th. Several of the children were playing hospital in the garden, and Jean was the patient.

April 5th. She talked of other children known to her who had been to hospital. Some time after she had been settled for the night, she called out, "I want to play with the hospital puzzle."

April 6th. Jean had a very active and happy day. When I discussed with her sister the arrangements for her care while Jean and I were away, Jean asked "Why?" as if the whole idea were new to her, and added, "But I don't want to go to hospital."

At teatime Katherine complained of stomach-ache. Jean asked, "Has Katherine got a pain like Susan? Will she have to go to hospital?" Later she asked me to list those of her friends who had been to hospital. She agreed to some names, but denied others. She asked to have a bandage over her eyes.

April 8th. When I told Jean that this was the day for us to go to hospital, she flushed and said, "I don't want to go to hospital—not today. Let's go tomorrow." Half an hour later she said, "Can I take my party dress? Can I take three dresses, and three cardigans? I'll play outside for a few days (!) first." And later still she said, "I might not want to come home again. I might want to stay there."

Saying that she might want them, she asked to take two dollies, dolly blankets, a windmill, and many other toys. To her sister she said, "Mummy will be with *me* and you won't see her."

She played in the garden with her friends for the next hour, dancing and skipping about and behaving as if she were going to a party. She boasted of where she was going. Now and again she came in to me with an anxious face. "I don't want to go to the hospital today," and almost in the same breath, "When is Daddy coming to take us to the hospital? —Daddy must come and bring stamps to me every day.—When my tonsils are out I won't keep getting ill.—When I come home my tonsils will be all gone.—I won't know when the doctor takes out my tonsils."

IN HOSPITAL

On the way to hospital in her Daddy's car she sat quietly, remarking on things seen from the window. She held my hand tightly and seemed apprehensive as we walked into the office to register, and as we went into the ward. She said several times, "I don't want to have my tonsils out. I don't want to stay in this hospital."

When the doctor and the ward sister (charge nurse) spoke to us she kept very close to me and said nothing. At lunch she ate little, saying it was not the same as we had at home. And again and again she said, "I want to go home. I don't want to have my tonsils out." She showed no interest in the other children. She was cross with me when I picked up a toy for a crying child.

For an hour I sat in our cubicle while Jean went to and from the balcony, reporting back to me every few minutes as one child after another was examined by a doctor in the open ward. She stood watching a toddler who cried loudly when his ears were examined. Her report was: "The doctor tickled him, but he didn't laugh."

We were invited to join some of the "up" children at play on the hospital lawns. Jean soon joined in the games, and all her anxiety seemed forgotten. Her good spirits remained during tea which we had together in the cubicle. After tea she ran on to the balcony and peeped through the window into the ward. When she saw the children were being prepared for the night, she too wanted to have her nightie on; but she agreed that as it was only 4:45 it was too early for her. Instead, she played in her cot and pulled a hospital screen around to make a little house.

At 5 o'clock she was invited into the ward to see television, but unluckily the anesthetist came just then to examine her. She cried when I brought her back to the cubicle, and made examination almost impossible by her struggling and screaming. She took no notice of the friendly advances of the anesthetist.

After the anesthetist had gone I explained the nature of the examinations to Jean, and when the houseman came half an hour later to examine ears, nose, and throat she seemed rather less difficult. But shortly afterwards when she was required to sit on a very small chamberpot to provide a urine specimen she was greatly offended by its size and only used it after much persuasion.

At 6 o'clock she undressed herself and climbed into her cot. She slept immediately. During the night she scratched restlessly in her sleep for two hours, in a way reminiscent of her eczema days two years before.

April 9th. Jean awoke at 6:30 A.M. and wanted to get dressed, saying, "I don't want to have my tonsils out, I want to go home." She played with toys in her bed for a short time, but without interest or concentration.

At 9 A.M. the ward sister came on duty and told Jean she could get up and walk around in slippers and dressing gown. Jean commented, "I like that Big Nurse. She is kind, because she lets me get out of bed." For the next hour she walked about aimlessly, saying again and again, "I want to go home.—I don't like doctors and nurses.—I don't want my tonsils out."

At 10 A.M. she took her premedication (two pills) from me with great difficulty. She could not swallow them, and vomited one. Then she had another in jam. She was very upset by this episode, and I found myself trembling at the knees. She sat quietly on my knee for half an hour, and then had an injection (Atropine) which made her cry bitterly.

She was by now very sleepy and asked to lie in her cot. When I suggested that she should go to sleep on the trolley which was already in the cubicle, she said, "That's only for very ill people, because it has a red blanket." She roused when I carried her to the trolley at 11 A.M., but when I spoke to her she relaxed and slept. In the induction room she roused again at the first whiff of the anesthetic, but seemed to go under quickly. She was wheeled into the operating theater, and my husband and I had an uneasy walk round the hospital block. Twenty minutes later she was brought back to her cot, the operation over.

As she returned to consciousness she became very restless. She kept trying to sit up, with eyes closed; but her movements were so uncontrolled that she had to be protected from hurting herself against the sides of the cot. I talked to her, saying several times, "Lie down, Jean. Put your head on the pillow and I'll tell you a story." But she did not respond, and the ward sister intervened to give a morphia injection which quietened her. It was then mid-day.

She roused every ten minutes and cried a little, but slept again when she heard my voice. At 12:40 she asked for her special "Noddy" story (the story I had promised during the preparation for hospital). At 1:30 she opened her eyes for the first time and looked around the room. She asked quietly, "Are my tonsils out? I didn't feel them come out."

She slept again but awoke every fifteen minutes or so complaining of pain. She calmed down again each time when I spoke or read to her. At 4 P.M. she asked for a drink, took one sip and cried with pain. She continued to awake every fifteen minutes and to say a few words and complain of pain until about 6 P.M.

At 6 P.M. she asked for the potty, but insisted "Not in my bed—on the floor." This was allowed. As she sat she said in a bright voice, and as if both surprised and impressed, "You were quite right, Mummy. My throat *does* hurt a lot—but I didn't feel them come out." She drank a little and cried again. From 6 till 7 she dozed restlessly, whimpering and coughing at intervals.

At 7 p.m. she vomited a fair amount of blood. She had been told that this might happen, and though made miserable she showed no fright. She said, "I dribbled out all the blood, didn't I?" She drank a little water and dozed restlessly again.

Her restless doze continued until 3 a.m. when she became fully awake and apparently properly oriented to her surroundings for the first time since the operation. She asked to use the potty on the floor again. She drank with less discomfort, "I like this drink." She talked a lot: "My tonsils are out now.—I won't keep getting ill.—I didn't feel my tonsils coming out.—When did the doctor take my tonsils out?—Were you there?—My throat does hurt me now.—You said it would hurt.—Can I get dressed when it is morning?—I didn't smell the funny smell to make me go to sleep.—I didn't like the pills, or the prick in my leg.—I didn't feel my tonsils come out; that's funny, I thought I was in my cot all the time.—Can I go home the very next day now that my tonsils are out?—Where is Daddy? Will he come every day to bring me stamps? Why can't Daddy and Katherine stay here too?"

After this barrage of question and comment, which lasted for half an hour, she sang a nursery rhyme, then slept peacefully for two hours. (And so did I.)

April 10th. At 6 a.m. she surprised herself by eating some breakfast. From 7 till 9 she stood in her cot, talking and jumping about and very impatient to get dressed and on to the floor. She said, "My throat doesn't hurt a bit." I was sure it did hurt and told her so. I told her again that her throat would be sore but would get a little better each day. A minute or so later she cried and said, "Yes, it really does hurt."

At 9 a.m. the ward sister came on duty and brought in the mail. She promised that at 10 o'clock Jean could dress and sit on the balcony. Jean was a little shy at first, and would not accept her letter; then with a laugh she snatched it from the sister's pocket. When sister asked, "Do you know where you are going tomorrow?" Jean brightly replied, "Yes—home!" When the sister left Jean said, "That Big Nurse is nice. She gave me postcards. She lets me get up and go home."

A little later she said, "I might want to stay here all the time, and not go home. I might like it here so much I'll just stay."

When I had to leave the cubicle for twenty minutes I gave her pencils and paper to play with. She seemed not to mind my going, but said, "Put up both sides of my cot, and lock them. Then no one can hurt me when you are gone."

She would not let any nurse take her temperature; and each time I acted in their stead she resisted, saying, "I'm not ill. I haven't got a temperature." (Her pulse was always taken when she slept.)

Many times during the day she asked me to tell her how she got her tonsils out. Each time I reminded her of what she already knew: "You had pills and a prick in your leg, and you sat on my knee going to sleep. I was going to put you on to the trolley with the red blanket, but you didn't want that so I put you into your cot. When the doctor was ready to take out your tonsils I carried you to the trolley and I took you to the special room. I was with you when you smelled the funny smell, then you slept the special tonsils sleep. The doctor took out your tonsils and carried you back to your cot. Then I sat next to you and read you a story."

After each telling she was ready with questions: "Where is that doctor now? Where does he live? Will he come again? Where is the special room? My nose hurts. Were my tonsils in my nose too?"

At 10 A.M. we sat on the balcony and played with cards. Although she had been jumping around in her cot, now that she was up she was limp and listless. She objected to my showing interest in another child.

At lunch she tried several times to swallow some semolina, but turned away in pain. I left her alone in the cubicle while I went to the kitchen to find jelly. When I returned five minutes later she was near to tears. Her tumbler of aspirin drink lay broken on the floor. She said, "I couldn't help it. I did drink some of it. I didn't cut myself." She had picked up the pieces of glass and placed them on the side of the sink. When I reassured her that no one would be cross about it, she said, "The nurses are nice. They don't mind."

She went gladly to her cot and slept for three and a half hours. After tea she played on the balcony, then walked with me on the lawns. She was bright and cheerful, saying repeatedly, "I didn't feel my tonsils come out. I didn't know, did I? Which room did I go into to have my tonsils out?" Again I told her how it had happened—the pills, the trolley, the anesthetic, the operation, and return to her cot.

At 6:30 P.M., the time when parents could visit their children in the open ward, we sat and played with a child who had no visitor; and stayed for ward prayers. Ward sister arranged that the hymn should be one known to Jean, and this pleased her very much: "My Big Nurse knows that hymn too."

When she got to bed she seemed very wide awake, and was unwilling to be left alone in the cubicle. She asked me to read a story, then another and another, as if to keep me with her; and she said often, "I want to go home now." She knew that next day she would go home.

April 11th. From 5 A.M. she was impatient to get dressed. She whimpered if my movements in the cubicle took me near the door; she complained that her throat hurt, resisted having her temperature taken, and refused breakfast. I moved her from her cot into my bed, gave her some toys and she cheered up a little. After a while she worried again to get dressed, with such insistence that I dressed her but put her back into her cot. This satisfied her for a while, but soon she became fretful again.

At 9 A.M. the ward sister came on duty and allowed Jean to walk about. She played happily in the open ward, talking to the children there and looking for her favorite hospital toys. She spoke in a friendly way to her Big Nurse, but then shot a flying toy which hit the Big Nurse's leg.

She was glad to see her Daddy when he arrived about 10 A.M. to take us home, but was a little reserved toward him. When the houseman wanted to take a final look at her throat she clenched her teeth and then cried.

AFTER DISCHARGE FROM HOSPITAL

She dozed in the car on the way home, obviously tired, but when we reached home she strongly resisted being put to rest. She silently watched her playmates for a while from the window, then slept for two hours. She awoke in good spirits, and played actively and happily all afternoon.

That evening she would not be left alone in her bedroom. She asked for several readings of Tonsil Boy. I sat on her bed until she was asleep. At 9 P.M. she awoke coughing and crying, "My throat hurts. But I'm crying because I'm by myself." I was unable to settle her, so took her into bed beside me and there she slept restlessly throughout the night.

April 12th. Second Day Home. There were several aggressive outbursts today. Immediately after a drink which hurt her throat, she slapped me hard, saying, "I don't like you, because you took me to the hospital." She saw an ambulance from the window: "There is an ambulance; perhaps someone is in it."

On leaving hospital yesterday we had unexpectedly been presented with Jean's tonsils and adenoids in a small glass jar. This morning Jean held the jar for a long time, peering intently at the contents and tilting them this way and that. I asked her what should be done with them. With great tenderness she said, "I'll keep them. I'll put them on the shelf in my room." I queried this: "Do you *really* want to keep them?" She replied emphatically: "Yes, I do!" She disappeared into her room with the jar in her hand, then returned ten minutes later with a flushed face: "No, Mummy. Let's throw them away."

She herself threw them into the dustbin.

April 13th. Third Day Home. I told Jean that we had been invited back to the hospital to have tea with the Big Nurse. She replied, "Yes. But just to see her, not to stay there." She added, "Why did you take me to that hospital? I wanted to come home the very first minute I was there." She recalled with a laugh how her flying toy had hit the Big Nurse. "I shall get my gun and shoot you all away."

She sat bending her hand to and fro, and pointing to the creases on her wrist, "Look at my hand. There are the lines where it could break off."

She saw three off-duty nurses in the street. She looked casually at them and said, "Yes, they do wear dresses like that." And as we passed the local hospital she remarked, "That's another hospital—not mine."

April 14th. Fourth Day Home. This was a good day. Jean seems to have found her place in the group again. She ate a little at each meal with enjoyment, and asked for her after-meal toffee.

This evening she was asleep by 6 P.M., but awoke at 8 with a heavy nosebleed. She was very uncooperative, would not have a compress applied to her nose nor would she suck ice. This inevitably caused some tension between us, because I knew we might have to return to hospital to have the bleeding checked. But by 10:30 P.M., however, the nosebleeding had subsided and she was asleep in my bed. We both spent a restless night.

Because of the bleeding the hospital doctor ordered 48 hours bed rest.

April 15th. Fifth Day Home. Jean was cheerful and looked well. She wanted to get up, so I let her get dressed and she spent the day on a settee in the living room.

She played a game of not being able to see or hear. She dug a finger into each ear, shut her eyes, then asked me to speak to her, saying, "I can't hear you now, and can't see you."

During the day she displayed and examined her genitals, laughing and looking at me to bring her behavior to my notice.

At bedtime she talked for a long while about her hospital experiences: "When I had my tonsils out I didn't feel it. I didn't hear and I didn't see. Why didn't I? It was funny. First of all I was ordinary asleep, then I smelled the funny smell, but I didn't know because I was asleep. Then I had the tonsils sleep. I would know if I was ordinary asleep."

She was rather lively, and kept bouncing her head on and off the pillow. This seemed to bring a hazy recollection. She said, "Was it yesterday you kept telling me to lay my head on the pillow? I didn't want to— I wanted to sit up." (Her recollection was in fact from the half hour immediately after the operation six days previously, when she had been extremely restless and apparently disoriented and I had tried to get her to keep her head on the pillow. It had been thought unlikely that she would have memory of that phase of recovery.)

She asked again for many bedtime stories, and clung to my hand when I eventually tried to leave the room. She made no complaint when I left the room, however, and was probably helped by the fact that her sister had just come to bed in the same room. She called out several times, but not with anxiety. She fell asleep with a penicillin tablet in her mouth. I opened her mouth to remove it, and was surprised that instead of resisting she seemed to open her mouth still wider and did not wake.

April 16th. Sixth Day Home. When she awoke she sang a song about "wobbly" (her own name for penis). She wanted very much to be active, but had to continue resting on the settee. I said she could get up when her tonsils were better, and she corrected me, "I haven't got tonsils, only a throat. The dustman has taken my tonsils away. I wonder where he puts all the rubbish?" She exhibited her genitals several times during the day.

In the afternoon I allowed her up to play quietly at a table. She resented the restriction on her movements, and was aggressive until the further concession was made that she could walk about. Later she was aggressive again when, after eating a nutcake, her throat pained her.

Looking out of the window at a strange family passing in the street, she said, "That girl was in hospital with me." She went to her room, dressed in her nurse's uniform, and played with her dollies and pram.

At bedtime she insisted on "five" stories. She was quiet for a few minutes after I left her, then cried out for "just one more story." She was obviously tired, held her cuddly, put her thumb to her lips but not into her mouth—she just stopped short of her usual relaxed sleeping position. She asked me to sit on her bed and to sing songs. While I did so she wriggled about, still resisting sleep. She slept well.

April 17th. Seventh Day Home. A good day with only two negative patches. When put to bed she asked for "two stories," then cried when I proposed to leave the room, saying "I don't want to be all alone. Did the hospital doctor talk to you on the telephone today?" I sat on the bed and she fell asleep within a few minutes. She did not suck her thumb. Once during the night she cried in her sleep.

April 18th. Eighth Day Home. Quite a good day, with only occasional aggressive and negative patches. For the first time since the day before the operation she asked to have long plaits in her hair.

At bedtime she refused to be washed or get undressed, and screamed when I insisted. She asked for "four bedtime stories." First of all I retold her own hospital story, and during the telling she made such remarks as, "Yes, I am cross with you for taking me to hospital. I didn't want to go. There was a little child there without his Mummy. I am sure he wanted his Mummy. The big boy won't be cross with his Mummy because he is big. He knows that sometimes children just have to go to hospital.— Yesterday you asked me to shut the door, but I wouldn't. I pretended that I couldn't. I opened it wide and put a chair there, and then I fell down."

Five minutes later while I was reading her stories she sat up, held my hand to her face, and cuddled round my neck: "I *do* like you Mummy. I *do* like you. I liked the Big Nurse—she brought letters to me. I didn't answer when she first asked me, and she walked away—then afterwards I took the letters from her pocket and she didn't know who had taken them." I said, "Shall we go to see the Big Nurse one day?" and she answered, "Yes, just to see her, just to have tea with her."

April 19th. Ninth Day Home. Rather more aggressive and temperamental behavior than during the past few days. She showed more anger against her Daddy. "We could have put a bed in our hospital room for Daddy."

April 20th. Tenth Day Home. A day somewhat like yesterday, with some aggressive and a few tyrannical outbursts. There were many "Why" questions.

She saw a large building which had two open swing doors. A baby lay in a pram outside. She looked intently, and after we had passed she kept looking back. Then she said, "Why is that baby going in there?" I told her that the building was a library. She said, "It looks like a hospital, but it isn't." In the evening she was loudly good-spirited and more affectionate to her Daddy.

April 21st. Eleventh Day Home. A good day. I was out for the whole of the afternoon, and Jean stayed happily with her Daddy. She showed him much affection.

She did not want to be left alone at bedtime. I read many stories, and then sat on her bed until she slept.

April 22nd. Twelfth Day Home. For most of the day she was active and in good spirits, sometimes with a slightly manic tinge. When crossed, however, she immediately threw temper tantrums. She behaves like the so-called "spoiled" child. The "Why" questions today were more specifically about marriage and conception.

April 24th. Fourteenth Day Home. The "Why" questions continued throughout yesterday and today. At bedtime she asked, "Who takes people to prison?" I assured her that children did not go to prison. She said, "When children are naughty, their Mummy and Daddy make them good again, don't they?" I suggested that children were sometimes naughty because they were worried and unhappy about something they could not understand. She said "Yes," thoughtfully, and twenty minutes later went on: "I don't know what makes me unhappy. Perhaps I won't be naughty tomorrow, and won't hit you." She slept easily.

April 25th. Fifteenth Day Home. At breakfast Jean lay back, quietly licking a grape. With a puzzled frown she said, "It was my Big Nurse who pricked my leg. I didn't like it. Why did she?" (This apparently referred to the injection given before the operation by the ward sister—Jean's "Big Nurse." Until today Jean had insisted that the prick had been given by a student nurse with whom she had no relationship.)

April 26th. Sixteenth Day Home. She told her sister Katherine with impish laughter of the time when her flying toy hit the Big Nurse's leg. She is very keen to have fairness. "She hit me, so I hit her. She hurt me, so I hurt her" is a recurrent theme. She watched two playmates fighting: "It's all right, Tommy. You can hit Betty because she hit you. Go on, Tommy, it's all right."

Later she said, "Hazel nearly died today—she was so sick. She did, she nearly died. I was sick with all the blood" (recalling her own postoperative blood vomit).

April 27th. Seventeenth Day Home. During last night she had a nightmare, with "doggies" in her bed. At breakfast she grumbled about not being given a tomato with her bacon; and when given a tomato she complained that it was too firm. She said often, "I don't like you."

She asked to have her toast cut into little pieces, and then divided them according to size into "mummies, daddies, and children." "I'll eat the children first. What was the name of the little baby who cried in hospital? Was it a boy or a girl?—Its Mummy wasn't there and it cried." I reminded her that the Mummy had in fact visited the child each day. She said, "But perhaps the baby wouldn't know which was his very own Mummy. Perhaps they would all wear the very same coats." I asked: "Do you think perhaps the Mummy wouldn't know it was her very own baby?" She nodded.

A letter came from the Big Nurse and I read it to her. She took possession of the letter and said she would like to go for tea with the Big Nurse. She went to her doll's pram and said, "I want a coat for my dolly. I can't find it, I'll put on her nightie instead. Doesn't she look sweet in her nightie?"

A few minutes later I heard her singing in her room. "And then her tonsils popped out, and if I do she'll be sure to die." (In this she was parodying the end of the nursery rhyme "Little Boy Blue": "Will you wake him? No not I, For if I do he'll be sure to cry.")

Shortly afterwards she came to me and said, "I won't ever have to go to hospital again, will I? I don't want to." When I reminded her that mummies go, for instance to have babies, she said, "When I'm a mummy I won't mind, because then I'll be big."

A little later she came in from the garden to ask: "What is a stomach? Peter [a playmate who had recently had his tonsils and adenoids removed] had something in his nose." I explained about adenoids, and linked it with her nosebleed after the operation. She stood quietly pinching her tongue with finger and thumb, as she had done often before the operation.

Later she was playing doctors with a little boy with dolly for patient. She said, "We must have a doctor, and you be the doctor. You must hurt her leg and then you must make her quite better."

April 28th. Eighteenth Day Home. "I didn't like the Big Nurse pricking my leg. Which leg did she prick? Did she make a hole?" She fell over many times during the afternoon, and each time she came to show me the cuts and bruises on her legs.

April 29th. Nineteenth Day Home. At breakfast she recalled: "When I cut my finger the blood came out. I licked it and the blood went down into my tummy. It doesn't matter, does it? Blood can go down?"

Ten minutes later she called me to the lavatory and said very brightly, "Mummy, I feel sick." I did not take her seriously, and she said again: "I do feel sick—something might dribble out—I did dribble out all the blood, lots of it. Why did I? Why do tonsils make blood in my tummy? I want to go to see the Big Nurse today."

April 30th. Twentieth Day Home (Day of Return Visit to Hospital). She seemed happy to be going to visit the Big Nurse. As we approached the hospital a mother and two children were ahead of us. One of the children carried a case. Jean made a quick inference: "That little girl is going to stay in the hospital. I'm not, am I?"

She showed no anxiety as we went into the hospital. When we reached the ward she skipped ahead of us, almost dancing, and went straight to her former cubicle. She showed it to Katherine, and then took her on a tour of the ward and showed her things with a proprietorial air. She pointed to where the ward sister's hat and cloak hung: "That's my Big Nurse's." She did not talk to the nurses, but smiled and nodded in answer to the ward sister.

Her ball ran into the induction room, and she was hesitant to go after it until encouraged by the ward sister. She tiptoed in, and in picking up her ball she peeped quickly into the operating theater which lay beyond, then hurried out with a flushed face. (She knew the purpose of these two rooms.)

She saw a little girl walk about the ward asking and looking for her mummy. Later she asked: "Where was that little girl's mummy?"

On the way home she said, "I want to visit the Big Nurse again."

At this point it seemed that Jean had worked through her hospital experience. She looked well, ate and slept normally, spoke little of hospital, and showed no special anxieties. She had started nursery school for the first time, and settled quickly and happily. After a few days she insisted that I should not accompany her to school, and went cheerfully with a neighbor and her children. Her increased confidence and independence of me was commented on by our neighbors. Her extreme fear of dogs had almost disappeared, as she herself remarked, "That dog looked at me, and I wasn't even afraid."

For these reasons the Diary was discontinued at this point, three weeks after the operation. But the following narrative, which begins eleven weeks after the operation, shows how external events reactivated her anxieties.

June 23rd to August 28th. Eleventh to Twentieth Week Home. During the first week of this period Jean's behavior suddenly deteriorated. She cried easily, grumbled at everything, threw temper tantrums, refused to go to the lavatory alone "because it comes too quickly," and in general acted much as she had done immediately before going to hospital.

After a few days during which we could not account for the change, we realized that three external events had reactivated her anxieties. These were:

a. one of her playmates went to hospital to have her tonsils out;
b. the mother of a neighboring family went away from home for two weeks and left two young children in the care of their father;
c. the anticipation of our annual seaside holiday.

The Playmate's Tonsillectomy. On June 23rd a five-year-old girl living in the block made it known that she would soon go to hospital, by herself, to have her tonsils out. The other children in the group appeared to take no special notice, but Jean and Hazel became inseparable. Although hitherto they had been only casual playmates, they now held hands, walked about with arms around each other, and whispered together.

A week later, Jean saw Hazel go off by car to hospital; and during the day she spoke of it many times. For the next two days she wore her nurse's uniform most of the time, and came in from play often to ask: "Is Hazel in hospital now? Are her tonsils out? Will her mummy go to see her?"

Hazel in fact suffered a setback. On the second day she had a hemorrhage and a policeman came to tell the mother to go to the hospital. This was known to all the children and there was much talk and reminiscence about blood and operations. Hazel's return was delayed, and Jean became increasingly anxious because Hazel did not come home on the expected day. She asked many times for her, and was irritable, fretful, and easily provoked into tantrums.

Hazel came home after a week, and had to stay in bed for three days. Each morning Jean called up at her window, and became very excited when Hazel appeared and waved down to her. Four days after Hazel had resumed play in the garden, Jean again called up to her window. Hazel was slow to appear and Jean greeted her with, "Hello, Hazel. I thought you were dead. You didn't come when I called you."

Children Left by Their Mother. On July 8th, the day after Hazel's return from hospital, the mother of another family had to leave home for two weeks to care for a sick relative—leaving two children to be looked after by their father. A week later, in response to a remark of mine about mothers looking after children, Jean exploded with: "They don't always. Mary's mummy has gone away for lots of days and left her alone."

Anticipation of the Holiday. From the beginning of July there was much talking over of arrangements for the family holiday which was to begin on August 1st. Toward the end of the month I realized that this was adding to Jean's anxieties, because there were similarities between this waiting period and that which had preceded her going to hospital. I was using similar phrases to deal with her impatience for the holiday as had been used to prepare her for hospital: "Soon we will be going. We will put these things ready in the case. We will have to wait a few more days, because it isn't our turn yet." I talked with her about this similarity, and during the whole of the next day there were no temper tantrums.

Her behavior gradually improved, and by the fourth day of the holiday she seemed to be over this period of difficulty and anxiety. This good state continued when these notes were written up which is three months after our holiday and eight months after the tonsillectomy.

ANNA FREUD, LL.D.

In a recent paper on "The Role of Bodily Illness in the Mental Development of Children" (1952), I stated with regret that professional workers have little opportunity to follow without interruption what happens in a child's mind during the complete course of an illness. I attributed this to our present conditions in child care when doctors and nurses lose touch with their patients when they recover, while teachers, child-therapists or analysts do not meet their charges when they are ill. There remain only the mothers who see their children in both health and illness and in the transitional states between them. But mothers, as I said then, are bad observers at such times, preoccupied as they are with their own anxieties and with the task of nursing.

It is this latter statement which I want to withdraw after reading Joyce Robertson's account of her four-year-old daughter's tonsillectomy. This mother's outlook on her daughter's inner experience remained objective during all the intricacies of the child's disturbed, occasionally negative, at all times highly exacting behavior. She never lost touch with the underlying trend of affect by which the child's reactions were determined and to which her own responses were directed. In following her account we are presented therefore not only with an interesting description of a small girl's behavior under the stresses of operation and hospitalization but also with a convincing and consistent report on the inner struggle between the anxieties which were aroused by the experience and the infantile ego's attempt at dealing with them.

From the first part of the diary which covers the preparatory period we learn that Jean confirmed almost all our theoretical expectations of what operation and hospitalization may mean to children of her age. There was, in the first instance, the threat of the anesthetic, conceived by the child as an oral attack against which she defended herself by a refusal of oral intake. Only the quick understanding and interpretation from the mother's side interfered with more permanent displacement of this phobic attitude onto food, prevented symptom formation and rendered the child amenable to a rational discussion of the danger situation. Separation anxiety arose next with which the mother could deal by reassurance since she had permission to accompany the child to hospital. Next came castration fears, centered around the frightening image of a body hole. Again, Jean had recourse to a phobic defense which made her reject temporarily the use of knife and fork and eat with her hands, an attitude which changed almost immediately to the active use of knives. Jean placed herself in the role of surgeon and operated tentatively on herself. Alternating with this identification with the aggressor, she turned aggression outwards, against members of the family, furniture, etc. Death fears and the fantasy of being robbed of body content (blood) were mobilized next on the id side. To these the superego added an equally frightening moral version of the impending dangers in which the hospital took on the aspect of a prison, the surgeon that of a policeman, and the operation was turned into a major punishment. The anxieties from these sources which flooded the child's mind produced in manifest behavior an increased demandingness, irritability, uncooperativeness and indiscriminate aggressions toward the environment (cutting and shooting). Conversely there appeared also a certain measure of accident proneness and self-injury, the defenses regressing increasingly toward primitive types (psychosomatic symptoms, temper tantrums) as the date of the operation drew near. In the last days of waiting, denials of external reality and internal feelings were most prominent: children are *not* killed, they have *not* gone to hospital, hospitals are nice places where children wear their party dresses, where they want to stay for ever. Jean's final protest against going to hospital may be regarded as belonging to the same defense, i.e., less as a refusal to cooperate than as a vehement denial of her sense of helplessness and impotence to do so.

With the operation accomplished the diary presents a very different picture of Jean's state of mind. We find the diffuse anticipatory anxieties swept away and the child more concerned with the reality aspects of the situation. Even the actual sight of her own blood did not revive her former fantastic anxieties and left her unafraid. What disturbed her most at this time was the interruption in conscious experience caused by the anesthetic. Apparently this connected with some unconscious fantasy of passive surrender to attack. She reacted with a "barrage of questions," i.e., an insatiable demand for reassuring details which might serve to fill the gap. One can well imagine another child answering to the same experience with a phobic attitude toward sleep as the state of unawareness in which "anything might happen." Further, there were the indications of a proprietory and positive attitude toward the hospital and staff which so many children manifest after medical or surgical interventions; in Jean's case this well-known passive-masochistic trend was tempered by an aggressive retaliating wish (hurting the nurse who had hurt her). A heightened impatient irritability on the morning before leaving hospital may well have been due to the child's disbelief in the promise of release.

In the three weeks after their return home, the diary shows how mother and child dealt with the emotional aftermath of the operation. Unlike children who have been to hospital on their own, Jean showed no excessive clinging to the mother. An exception to this was bedtime when —contrary to former habits—she refused to be left alone. We may ascribe this difficulty to the prolonged fear of the passive experience of anesthesia which leaves her suspicious of sleep and increases—at this time only—her infantile dependence on the mother's presence.

There is, further, the interesting incident when Jean decided to discard her cut-out tonsils. Here, the reader is reminded of similar infantile behavior during toilet training when children find it easier to be active themselves in throwing out their own highly cathected body products than to be deprived of them passively. One concludes that Jean's mother had used the device in earlier years of allowing the child to empty her own pot.

Another interesting characteristic of the postoperative period was the marked increase in Jean's ambivalence toward her mother which reminds us of an infant's primitive distinction between the "good" and the "bad" mother.[4] At this time Jean saw her mother actually in a double role, as her protector against danger as well as the person responsible for delivering her to danger. Accordingly, gratitude and anger, love and hate, appeared in quick succession in her conscious feelings, causing difficult and unpredictable behavior. This regression in the relationship to the mother also reawakened the primitive anxieties and, with them, some of the defensive behavior of the preparatory period.

On the other hand, with the operation safely behind her, Jean showed herself less overwhelmed by her anxieties than she had been before and better able to cope reasonably with some of the undigested memories of her hospital experience. She returned gradually to more cooperative and independent attitudes with the need for constant reassurance markedly diminished. The emotional relapse after an interval of two months, although bearing witness to her prolonged vulnerability, also provided an added opportunity for working over and assimilating the experience.

While following the sequence of happenings in Jeans's mind, we cannot help speculating how she would have dealt with the events if— as happens to most children—she had been less well understood, or

4 See Melanie Klein.

among strangers, and deprived of help and support at the critical time. As it was, her battle between id anxieties and ego defenses was played out against the background of her mother's reassuring presence. There was in the child a constant urge to distort and magnify external danger situations and use them as representations of internal threats. This was met by the mother's equally constant, tolerant and understanding behavior which served to undo the distortions, to separate fantasy from reality and, thereby, to reduce the quality and quantity of anxiety to levels with which the child could deal. That she accomplished this without falsifying the unpleasurable aspects of reality is greatly to the mother's credit.

Mrs. Robertson's account of Jean's tonsillectomy seems to me an instructive contribution to our psychoanalytic studies of small children, not diminished in value by the fact that her observations were carried out in the original setting of the child's life and relationships instead of in the analytic setting as we construct it artificially to provoke the repetition of internal events before the analyst's eyes and in the transference relationship.

In her role as mother, Mrs. Robertson kept her account strictly within the limits of her own child's experience and refrained from generalizations. As analytic readers, we may permit ourselves to go a step further and extract from her study some points of general validity. There are, in my opinion, two main respects in which the foregoing description confirms and illustrates our knowledge of the working of a child's mind.

First is the fact that a young child's emotional balance is shown here to be no more than a matter of quantities, i.e., a function of the relation of strength between the id and ego forces. Anxieties are mastered by the ego while they remain below a specific threshold. They become pathogenic, creating neurotic symptoms or behavior problems when they rise above that level, that is, when the defenses are overtaxed or overthrown. If the ego is successful in its mastery of anxiety, the child feels encouraged and relieved. Progress within the province of the ego has been achieved and a potentially traumatic event has been transformed into beneficial and constructive experience, as it has happened in Jean's case.

Second, there is ample confirmation in Mrs. Robertson's account that it is not the external danger, real and serious as it may be, which accounts for the traumatic value of an experience. Injections, loss of blood, surgical interventions, etc., are shown to remain manageable events unless they touch on and merge with id material which transforms them into experiences of being assaulted, emptied out, castrated or condemned.

When looking at the two aspects of Jean's fears, one is tempted to reopen an old theoretical controversy which has been neglected by analysts in recent years; I mean the question whether the phenomenon of "real" anxiety exists at all. Most analytic authors insist that, by the working of our mind, external danger is inevitably and automatically transformed into internal threats, i.e., that all fear is in the last resort anxiety with regard to id events. Personally, I find it difficult to subscribe to this sweeping statement. I believe in a sliding scale between external and internal threats and fears. What we call "courage" in ordinary language is, I believe, no more than the individual's ability to deal with external threats on their own ground and prevent the bulk of them from joining forces with the manifold dangers lurking in the id.

It is this last consideration which may help us also to assess the nature of the mother's achievement in Jean's case. Mrs. Robertson helped her child precisely in this way: to meet the operation on the level of reality, to keep the external danger in consciousness to be dealt with by the reasonable ego instead of allowing it to slip to those depths in which the rational powers of the ego become ineffective and primitive methods of defense are brought into action.

Child analysts and therapists may wonder where, with a mother of such rare insight, her province ends and theirs begins. I suggest the following answer. Mothers—unless specially instructed and guided to do otherwise—should, as Mrs. Robertson has done, limit themselves to assisting the child's ego in its task of mastery, lend it their strength and help to guard it against irruptions from the id. Analysts work in the opposite direction. Under carefully controlled conditions, they induce the child to lower his defenses and to accept the id derivatives in consciousness. The contact with the id impulses which is obtained thereby is used then to effect a gradual transformation of these strivings to which all neurotic anxieties and symptoms owe their origin.

BIBLIOGRAPHY

Coleman, H. (1942), The Psychologic Implications of Tonsillectomy. *N. Y. State J. Med.*, L.

Connell, L. F. (1953), Tonsils: In or Out? *Parents' Magazine*, Oct. 13.

Deutsch, H. (1942), Some Psychoanalytic Observations in Surgery. *Psychosom. Med.*, IV.

Faust, O. A. et al. (1952), *Reducing Emotional Trauma in Hospitalized Children: A Study in Psychosomatic Pediatrics.* A Report by Departments of Pediatrics and Anesthesiology. Albany, N. Y.: Albany Medical College.

Freud, A. (1952), The Role of Bodily Illness in the Mental Life of Children. *This Annual*, VII.

Jackson, K. (1951), Psychologic Preparation as Method of Reducing Emotional Trauma of Anesthesia in Children. *Anesthesia,* XII. Also in Faust et al. (1952).

—— (1953), Behavior Changes Indicating Emotional Trauma in Tonsillectomized Children. *Pediatrics,* XII. Also in Faust et al. (1952).

—— et al. (1952), Problem of Emotional Trauma in the Hospital Treatment of Children. *J. Am. Med. Assoc.,* CXLIX. Also in Faust et al. (1952).

Jessner, L.; Blom, G.; Waldfogel, S. (1952), Emotional Implications of Tonsillectomy and Adenoidectomy on Children. *This Annual,* VII.

—— and Kaplan, S. (1949), Reactions of Children to Tonsillectomy and Adenoidectomy: A Preliminary Report, with Discussion. In: *Problems of Infancy and Childhood,* ed. M. J. E. Senn. New York: Josiah Macy, Jr. Foundation.

Levy, D. M. (1945), Psychic Trauma of Operations in Children. *Am. J. Dis. Child.,* LXIX.

MacKeith, R. (1953), Children in Hospital: Preparation for Operation. *Lancet,* II.

Miller, M. L. (1951), The Traumatic Effect of Surgical Operations in Childhood on the Integration of the Ego. *Psa. Quart.,* XX.

Pearson, G. H. J. (1941), Effect of Operative Procedures on the Emotional Life of the Child. *Am. J. Dis. Child.,* LXII.

Pickerill, C. M. and Pickerill, H. P. (1954), Elimination of Hospital Cross-Infection in Children: Nursing by the Mother. *Lancet,* I.

Pillsbury, R. M. (1951), Children Can Be Helped to Face Surgery. *The Child,* XVI.

Prugh, D. G. et al. (1953), Study of Emotional Reactions of Children and Families to Hospitalization and Illness. *Am. J. Orthopsychiat.,* XXIII.

Robertson, J. (1953a), A Two-Year-Old Goes to Hospital. *Nursing Times,* XLIX.

—— (1953b), Some Responses of Young Children to Loss of Maternal Care. *Nursing Times,* XLIX.

Spence, J. L. (1947), Care of Children in Hospital. *Brit. Med. J.,* I.

Winkley, R. (1952), Caseworker's Participation in Preparation for Tonsillectomy in Children. In Faust et al. (1952).

APPLIED PSYCHOANALYSIS

THE SCHOOL'S ROLE IN PROMOTING SUBLIMATION

LILI E. PELLER (New York)

Over the years a number of studies have re-examined the concept of sublimation. These, and particularly the panel discussion (1955), have greatly clarified the theoretical aspects of sublimation. My own interest is far more limited and I shall confine myself to some practical implications of our knowledge of sublimation for education.

With the term sublimation Freud originally referred to the process by which the primary aims of instinctual drives are given up for certain cultural or otherwise highly valued achievements. Repeatedly he points to the gratification, the discharge of tension which sublimation provides. Today, we would add that in sublimation primary and secondary processes interact, with secondary processes prevailing. Activities based on sublimations are, at least to a large extent, communicable, not idiomatic, not part of a person's private world. They may yield pleasure of high intensity as well as lasting contentment.

Bernfeld (1922) at one point suggested to redefine the concept of sublimation in such a way as to eliminate the implied value judgments and to speak of ego-syntonic aims instead. However, there is behavior which has ego-syntonic aims, yet offers no gratification. If we accept Bernfeld's suggestion, then all behavior which comes under the reality principle might be based on sublimation. In my opinion, the term sublimation should be restricted to processes leading to ego-syntonic actions which retain a libidinal investment and have a discharge value. In this study our attention will be focused on those ego interests and attitudes which are highly invested.

Sublimation may serve defense, but is hardly a "mechanism" in the usual sense. Pleasure is yielded also by other defense reactions but is seldom of comparable intensity, or not so securely anchored in reality. In sublimation the pleasure is inherent in the process itself, not only in the attainment of the goal. Already en route to it, tension may be discharged and gratification may be harvested.

Not all processes of sublimation have an adaptive function. They occur also when our essential needs are not covered. Even in a situation of marginal existence (see, e.g., recent reports from detention camps) a prisoner may trade badly needed food or other essentials for paper scraps and a pencil, or for chess figures. In this connection, Hartmann's (1948) statement that the id of human beings is further removed from reality than the instincts of animals is relevant and could be expanded to include these aspects. From the point of view of self-preservation or survival the substituting of chess play for essential food is not adaptive.

A child may take his play—which is his main avenue toward sublimation—seriously, an adult may invest a stupendous amount of libido in his work. "Every playing child behaves like a poet, creating his own world. . . . It would be wrong to assume that he does not take this world seriously. To the contrary, he takes his play very seriously." Freud's phrasing (1908) indicates that he is disputing a generally accepted view— namely that "taking something seriously" and "playing" are mutually exclusive or at least represent contrasts. Everyday psychology considers play the opposite of serious pursuits. Procuring (directly or indirectly) life's necessities is considered "serious," while activities not connected with useful goals, as play or leisure-time activities, are rated "not serious."

No doubt, play has a quality of levity, of lightheartedness (I almost said of playfulness) and yet children and adults as well may take their respective play activities very seriously. How can we solve this apparent contradiction? Could we define what is implied by "taking something seriously"? Before attempting this, Freud's comments concerning a completely different field, namely *rational thought*, might be helpful. He considers thinking essentially a trial action with small quantities of energy.

In rational thinking there is less expenditure of physical effort than in action—this is obvious. Moreover, a trial action has no immediate consequences in the world of reality, hence there will be less anxiety than in action (or more correctly: no anxiety). To these signal features of rational thought I may add that the ideas involved in thinking are invested with neutralized energy. (The pleasure inherent in intellectual work, in functioning per se is a different matter.) Rational thought is thus characterized by the absence, or near-absence, of physical *effort,* of *anxiety* and by the cathexis of ideas and images with *neutralized energy.*

We may now examine whether this little excursion can solve the apparent contrast between the levity of play and the fact that it may be often taken seriously. Applying to it the same three criteria we find: great physical and/or mental *effort* can be called forth in play and its *libidinal cathexis* may be high, but only mild degrees of *anxiety* are compatible with play. Mounting anxiety (arising in play) will disrupt it. However, anxiety which is of low intensity, i.e., which is experienced as a challenge and not as a threat to ego organization, adds spice to play.

The absence of anxiety characterizes rational thought. With other aim-inhibited activities, anxiety is compatible as long as the ego is not threatened to be flooded by it. (According to Hartmann [1955], the threat of anxiety eruption characterizes sexualization but is absent in sublimation.)

Sublimation is a kind of hybrid concept in so far as its definition includes both psychological and social elements. Behavior which at one time is socially acceptable in one society may not be so in another. Something similar may be said about activities based on reaction formations.

We have indicated the importance of sublimations for our libidinal balance, because activities so derived bind psychic energy while retaining a high libidinal investment. Another economic aspect concerns *fatigue*. Obviously action demands expenditure of energy and is in the long run tiring. But there is no straight positive correlation between investment of effort and feeling tired, neither for the adult, nor for the child. Expending energy in disliked or indifferent work may lead to exhaustion. Yet the same amount of energy will be spent with little or no fatigue in an activity based on true sublimation. This may be an extension of the truism that sublimations always bring pleasure. In true sublimations great expenditure of effort will result in very little fatigue. The pleasure gain seems to counteract it. Descriptively this is correct, but we would like to put this in psychoanalytic terms.

In sublimation ego, id and superego are on excellent terms. Their actions are synergic, not antagonistic (Hartmann, 1955). When a distasteful task is replaced by well-liked work, the change from fatigue to a surplus of vigor may be dramatic. Here an earlier simile of Freud may help our understanding. He compares ego and id to a rider and a horse. When a rider has difficulties in making his recalcitrant horse trot on the path he has chosen—a short distance will wear out his strength. But if the horse comes along willingly, a long stretch can be covered with but minor exertion.

We return to an already mentioned characteristic of sublimation: the discharge of tension and the gratification attached to the process. In other reality-syntonic activities we try to reach the goal on the shortest route and with the smallest expenditure of energy. In sublimations the pleasure hinges not only on the goal—the acting, the doing, the functioning as such is gratifying and hence the joyful, often lavish expenditure of energy and effort.

We may speak of *functional pleasure* if we keep in mind that this describes the phenomenon without explaining it. In academic psychology, the term has been introduced to obviate the search for other causes, to account for behavior. Waelder (1932) has pointed to its limitations, yet in recent years it has shown up quite often in psychoanalytic literature.

Academic psychology needs the term because it makes the implicit basic assumption that our everyday behavior is rational and instigated by goals. When a person stirs without a strict goal, the needed explanation is found by assuming that the doing, the functioning per se yields pleasure.[1]

In psychoanalysis we see that the pleasure in functioning is related to specific symbols and fantasies, to specific zonal tensions, to the desire for mastery. Not only the choice of an aim-inhibited activity, but also the intensity of the pleasure derived from it, is highly variable. What seems a trifling outer or inner change, may completely destroy the gratification value of an activity.

In sublimation, there is the process and there is a goal. The latter may be a tangible product or it may be a skill, an ability. According to Kris (1952), every sublimation solves a conflict. Kris probably has creative activities in mind; however, his statement is valid for all sublimated activities in the sense that lessening of tension also is a kind of conflict solution.

It is about time to point out which pursuits we consider to be based on sublimation: creative achievements in the arts, in science, philosophy and religion come to our mind first and this large group is mentioned in psychoanalytic literature most often. Well-liked work, even quite humble work, represents another group.[2] Many hobbies, leisure-time pursuits and

---

[1] Academic psychology provides us with a number of concepts which are descriptively excellent, e.g., "habit" or "drive to imitate" or, of more recent vintage, "emotional insecurity." They fit so well phenomena we all know and thus seem to explain them. Actually they explain too much. Thus they blur the issue and, far from uncovering the motives, interfere with even a clear statement of the problem. Because these omnibus terms explain too much, they cannot be used to predict when a phenomenon will not occur.

Functional pleasure is a striking phenomenon and easy enough to observe. So is the urge to imitate. But these "concepts" fail to tell us why, in certain situations, the desire to imitate will not show up, no pleasure in functioning will be observable, or why a well-established habit pattern will be broken.

[2] See Freud's footnote in *Civilization and Its Discontents* (1930) about tending a garden.

play activities can be similarly regarded. In characterizing the aforementioned groups of sublimations, we may say: in a creative act the path to the goal seems to lead through territory where nobody set foot before—hence the proverbial toil and pain, the steep joy and anguish of the artist. The person whose sublimations lie in the realm of well-liked work moves on a well-traveled path. And what happens in the area of hobbies and avocations? There is neither a hazardous lonely trail nor a smooth public thoroughfare. The amateur moves through a park-like area, whether he strolls this way or that is of little consequence. Needless to say that these are prototypes. In life situations mixtures of these types will be encountered just as we will meet mixtures of behavior based on sublimations and other processes.

In a highly industrialized society there are fewer jobs entailing hard labor and back-breaking toil, but there are also more and more routine jobs which do not invite libidinal investment. There is in our society a great flowering of all kinds of hobbies, sports and spectator activities which are sometimes seen as related to the longer leisure hours that a growing segment of the population enjoys. I think avocations and leisure-time skills become a necessity when bread-earning activities do not yield libidinal gratifications. The less personal fulfillment or challenge there is in a person's daily work, the greater the need for hobbies and amusement. The unexpected does not happen in life, so one turns spectator and identifies oneself with the person in the arena, on the screen, the stage or inside the book covers. Hence, the ever-growing variety of colorful hobbies and sports offered in our society. Whether the mental stability of a society is furthered more by work which carries libidinal investment or by routine jobs combined with a wide range of hobbies is a question which may be raised, but will be hard to answer.

Another aspect may be relevant in the context of the present paper: What becomes of children growing up in such a society? It has been emphasized that in our days children see less of the work of their parents and can understand but little of what goes on in their professional lives. Now we add: What happens to children when the work of their elders is predominantly void of libidinal investment, when it has hardly any sublimative aspects?

THE SCHOOL'S CONTRIBUTIONS

It is the function of the school to supplement the child's life experiences. Under certain cultural conditions the school's task is very simple: mainly to teach the three "R's." Everything else the child is supposed to acquire outside the school, without formal teaching. As society becomes more complex, as there are more and more compartments in the adult's life in which the child cannot take part, the program of the school grows and grows. And because the adult's work is so often unrelated to his interests and preferences, it becomes especially important that the school provide the child with work which fosters true sublimation.

Every educational system has a central concept to which it adheres. The old-fashioned school stresses discipline, obedience, while some modern schools make the avoidance of frustrations their main concern. Neither type of school emphasized work which is well liked, irrespective of whether or not it requires effort and self-denial. Such work facilitates sublimation and a variety of factors may further or interfere with its development. We will point to a few only.

Which factors determine that a particular activity or interest is chosen as the main goal of drives, thus permitting their sublimation? One among them is certainly natural endowment. Frequently the assumption is made that talent will manifest itself if only the child is well cared for, receives love and intellectual stimulation. Yet psychoanalytic experience indicates that a child may possess many more abilities than actually come to fruition. A chance success, e.g., an unexpected narcissistic gratification may result in the development of a talent. This is obvious, but the opposite experience, i.e., a narcissistic injury may also open the door. Anna Freud (1936) cites the case of a boy who after a frightening dream gave up his beloved football playing and started writing good stories and poetry. Here an ego restriction opened the path to a sublimation.

THE TEACHER

An object libidinal core is seldom or never missing in sublimation. The child's desire to please a teacher or to identify with him may lead to a genuine interest which will outlast the personal tie which started it. New interests are acquired through identification with an ego ideal. And the child entering school is usually eager to identify himself with his teacher. Let us repeat briefly what preceded this development. The infant identifies himself with the *function* of a needed or loved person before he identifies himself with the person. As Ruth Mack Brunswick (1940) put it: "The child attempts to repeat actively every detail of physical care which it has experienced passively. . . . Each bit of activity is based to some extent on an identification with the active mother." Thus the development of identifications parallels the development of object relations: a true object relationship is preceded by the relationship with a need-gratifying object. Earliest attachments as well as early identifications relate to need-gratifying functions or body parts, not to persons.[3]

In the oedipal phase he forms ties of love and of identifications with his parents. While these early intrafamily identifications by far over-shadow all later ones, they also pave the way for new ones. Thus, the six-year-old entering school is ready to identify himself with his teacher.

What is the specific feature of a good teacher-child relationship? The child forms a strong attachment to a person who does not share the intimacies of his home but remains at a certain distance. The fact that there are other children competing with him to be noticed by the teacher arouses his jealousy, but it also intensifies the child's admiration for her and it confirms the existing distance. As long as no one receives too much, the child can accept the limited share given to him. Consciously each one in class would ardently like to have a greater part of the teacher's personal attention—and yet in the latency years when the child strives to escape from oedipal entanglements it may relieve him to know that the distance to the admired object is not likely to shrink much.

In progressive schools a teacher sometimes tries to eliminate this distance and to become entirely the child's buddy. In nursery school she may sit on the floor while telling a story, although this is uncomfortable for her, makes her squirm, and makes it harder to hold the attention of her listeners. By eliminating the traditional aura surrounding the function of the teacher, by dispelling the awe and the projections of the young school child, it was hoped to eliminate anxiety and to solicit the child's fuller participation in the school program and a more relaxed use of his abilities. This expectation failed.

The teacher who puts herself on the child's level all the time, who encourages indulgence, who shows lavish admiration for any scribble—this teacher fails to inspire the child's wish to identify himself with her. Much as she tries to captivate the children's interest, she fails to get it. This does not imply that the so-called old-fashioned school has the most effective ways to promote learning and growth; it only indicates that conditions are more complicated than we thought. Basically a school program must be geared to children's abilities and interests. But the latency child also expects the teacher to make demands and is disap-

---

[3] This is also true of my observations of early play. The very young child who "mothers" a doll or another child does not dress up for his play. His interest is riveted on feeding, caressing, or punishing the doll, on mothering it, not on playing the mother's role, and he plunges into it without wasting time on preliminaries. This changes with the onset of oedipal play. Now the child dresses up, hunts for scenery and props for his play, he imitates the mother, not only her actions. The character of his play changes, although the content—mothering—may remain the same.

pointed when he receives no assistance from her in dealing with his instinctual pressures.

It seems that identification depends on an optimal blend of gratification and deprivation and that either extreme disfavors them. The identifications which are most relevant in school may follow the lines indicated by Waelder (1939) in his examination of group processes. He speaks of the type of identification that "contributes to the establishment of an agency which stands back from the ego and watches it critically. What happens in this type of identification is not that the child feels that he is like his father, or that he does really become more like him, but rather that he criticizes and punishes himself just as he was formerly criticized and punished by the father."

If the child's teachers change every year or even every term, or if on the higher school levels a teacher has a "student load" of over one hundred, then the teacher-student relationship is reduced to a mechanical level. The recent development of teaching several hundred students simultaneously through a closed T.V. circuit carries the deficiency, the lack in personal relationship even farther. The detriments to the student are not nearly as drastic as they are to an infant whose mother figure has changed several times. Yet without the mutuality of a personal relationship a teacher can pass on information, but he cannot inspire and thus the development of identifications will be impeded. Indeed, the outstanding book has a better chance to stir the reader than the gesticulating screen teacher.

THE GROUP

Once we realize the importance of identifications as *catalysts* of development, not only stable identifications, but also a wider choice of them become imperative. This leads to a consideration of the group in which the child finds himself in school.

A child entering school must be ready for a group of age-mates. Without this readiness for a wider circle of friends he will receive custodial care only—even in the best school, i.e., a school offering excellent opportunities for identifications and sublimation. A child needs others who are about his age, but the strict segregation according to age levels which most schools practice today limits his friendships and deprives him.

If a class consists of children of the same age, then ties of affection and admiration toward an older child or a paternal protective attitude toward a younger friend cannot develop. A narrow age range increases competition and comparisons between the members of the group, making the child more conscious of his limitations. It increases the pressures inside the group, and it does so even in a school which has a highly permissive attitude. Ironically some of the most advanced and progressive schools take at present pride in the fact that the age range in their classes has been reduced from twelve to six months! Fortunately a few schools are experimenting with arrangements making the mixing of age groups possible. The advantage of mixed ages are so obvious—especially in these days when families are small and most teachers are women, thus reducing the boys' chances for identifications—one wonders that this problem has received so scant attention. There are several reasons for this. The mutual educational influence of children of different ages is hard to assess. There may be an old puritan view that innocent young children learn "bad things" from older children. Moreover, there are the very real dangers of abuse. Indeed, autobiographical and fictional stories of British public schools can be amply quoted for instances of institutionalized or personal abuse and exploitation of younger boys by older ones.

Among another group of educators we may find the belief that a friendship with a younger child increases the attraction of childish behavior and thus detracts from the child's eagerness to go ahead—in other words, association with a younger child may encourage childish behavior labeled as regressive in the older child. Many modern teachers have learned about the norms for each age level before they ever enter a classroom. These teachers may have a static conception of those norms and be unaware that everyday life normally encompasses considerable fluctuations back and forth. A play interest which, according to the book, is below the child's age is easily seen as indicative of pathology. The close association and even interdependence of growth and regression are overlooked.

Observations by Fraiberg (1952) may be relevant in this context. A child treated by her also attended nursery school and the teacher reported an interesting pattern of growth: "Before Sally took each major step forward in the acquisition of new skills or new relationships, she would regress for a while to thumbsucking and withdrawal or to infantile behavior and speech." It was also typical for Sally that after achieving one level of performance or acquiring certain elementary skills she seemed for some time to have little desire for mastery and moving on to new levels.

With the spread of psychological knowledge the tendency to "observe" a child and to evaluate all his doings has also entered the home, so that now parents get alarmed when their child seems to be intrigued by play material designed primarily for a younger child. Manufacturers cater to this by printing age levels on equipment and toys. Thus, the range of "approved" activities which give pleasure and provide avenues for the discharge of tension becomes narrower.

There are several trends in today's education likely to interfere with the goal set forth in this paper. Modern education wants to integrate the child into the community and exercises gentle or not too gentle pressure on doing things *together*. Teachers with a certain amount of psychoanalytic training are aware that the lonely child is at times queer and that the distance between queerness and schizophrenic trends may be short—hence they reason that solitary play will in turn favor schizophrenic trends. In their thinking cause and effect are reversed. I have seen teachers in progressive schools go to all lengths to prevent a child from playing or working alone—even for a short time. They seem obsessed with the fear that the lonely child may indulge in daydreaming or in fantasies along the lines of primary process thinking. Of course he may, but he may also be absorbed in highly constructive work or thought.

Here I would like to return to the initial proposition of this paper. It is the libidinal charge of an activity which really counts. The child who shares a collective activity with lukewarm interest profits less than the child deriving a deep gratification from a solitary pursuit.

ANTICIPATION

The dimension of time does not seem to exist for the deepest strata of the id. The meaning of a deprivation remains the same, whether occurring now or later. But for the ego's capacity to deal with it, it makes a great difference whether something occurs suddenly, as a kind of surprise attack, or whether there is the possibility to anticipate it. According to Hartmann (1952), anticipation is one of the most important achievements of early ego development; it is also a prerequisite for the development of action and participates in every action to some degree. The school's setting can give wide scope to this ego development, or it can nip it.

A sudden change or deprivation may harm a child, yet the identical deprivation introduced in a way allowing anticipation, will lead to adjustment. Anna Freud and Dorothy Burlingham (1943) give an example which many of us can duplicate from our everyday experience.

Hetty and Christine were of comparable age and background and both their mothers expected another baby. Both children were placed in a residential nursery. In Hetty's case this was done with foresight and intelligent planning from the mother's side. She entered the nursery as a day child, her mother helped her through a period of adaptation. Christine, on the other hand, was brought in and left at once, though she had never before left her mother's side. In the completely strange surroundings she reacted in a most bewildered way. She did not respond but stood around quietly or crying and would only say at intervals: "Mum Mum." She fell ill a few days after her arrival.

Both children suffered the same deprivation yet Hetty adjusted while Christine developed neurotic symptoms. Hetty had been able to anticipate the changes ahead of her. On her visits to the nursery she had experiences which later were "copied" by reality ("I will eat here, sleep here, like these children do"). Through this preliminary inner rehearsal she had a grip on the situation *before* it occurred (anticipate = *antecapere*).

Here anticipation was used to prevent pathology. But anticipation has a less dramatic, though not less important, function in a child's everyday life. A good deal of a child's play helps him in looking ahead. Many features of a good nursery school come under the heading of making anticipation possible. If dangers are excluded and if—indoors or outdoors—spatial boundaries are well defined, then many choices can be left up to the child, even a very young child. The limits actually increase his freedom by reducing the need for close surveillance.

The young child lives in a world where he is taken by surprise many times a day. To compensate for this a school for young children should provide a place where they can do things for themselves—as has been rightfully stressed for many years—but it also should permit a maximum of anticipation. A stable order and a simple intelligible organization will assist him in looking ahead. Each thing, each tool he uses has its definite place. If he knows where to look for it, he is never quite separated from it; he can command its presence. The area where an inner planning precedes reality action widens.

The young child's ability to *select* is limited, even under very favorable conditions. His schoolroom needs to be uncluttered, simple, serene. Recently Alpert and Krown (1953) suggested that not all drawings of a child should be displayed on the walls of the nursery in order "to avoid reinforcement of the distorted image . . ." Walls covered with the large sheets of children's drawings may add confusion and disorganization to the room. Yet this kind of conspicuous display which makes children the prisoners of their own imperfections is today an accepted practice in many schools. Let us remember, however, that similar attempts have been made earlier; e.g., in the 1920's the very progressive Berthold Otto school

in Berlin taught reading by the use of books written by other children
of the same age. The readers were printed, with great care to preserve
the age-specific punctuation and sentence structure of the child authors.
Such an attempt seems rather ridiculous today. Here a school went out
of its way in order to prevent the child's exposure to correct grammar
and syntax. Yet other practices of isolating children in an artificial child-
centered world still occur today.

CONCLUSION

Freud (1909) postulated as the task of education "to enable the individual to take part in culture and to achieve this with the smallest loss
of original energy" ("*das Individuum kulturfähig machen mit der klein-
sten Einbusse an Aktivität.*" The meaning of the German word *Aktivität*
is, in my opinion, not adequately rendered by "activity.") This statement takes the multiple function of education into consideration. Education aims at enabling the child, on the ego level, to participate in
cultural pursuits, and on the drive level, to preserve the original energy.

Education fails when too much of the original strength of the instinctual drives becomes invested in rigid reaction formations, repressions, or neurotic symptoms. This energy is then not available for other
ego purposes which may be less rigid and more adaptive. But education
also fails when the child does not become ready for cultural interests,
when he receives too little guidance—in short, when he is neglected.
Neglect may be unintentional, for instance, when it is due to poverty,
or intentional as in a certain brand of progressive education or in mis-
understood psychoanalytic education.

Good education is not characterized by its degree of permissiveness or
strictness. A school with inadequate teachers or with a poor program
cannot be improved by loosening (or tightening) the reins. There are a
few indications that the dominant educational climate may change radically. The pendulum may swing all the way back from overindulgence
to strict discipline and still miss the essential. A school may be very
permissive, take a very lenient attitude toward some of the child's instinctual needs and consider academic work a necessary evil, something
that children naturally dislike. In consequence it will postpone academic
learning, reduce the study load, and for the irreducible rest impose passive acceptance upon the child. This is exactly what some schools do
today.

In terms of Freud's postulate for education such a school is not successful. The child's cultural activities are fed by a trickle of his energy—they are not effectively connected with the deeper wells of his being.

Activities and interests which are highly cathected and stable may be a better indication of what has been done to enrich the child's life, and to promote his capacity to sublimate. The process of sublimation follows certain laws which are by no means new in psychoanalytic thinking, but have been pronounced with greater emphasis and clarity in recent studies of ego development.

BIBLIOGRAPHY

Alpert, A. and Krown, S. (1953), Treatment of a Child with Severe Ego Restriction in a Therapeutic Nursery. *This Annual*, VIII.
Bernfeld, S. (1922), Bemerkungen über Sublimierung. *Imago*, VIII.
Brunswick, R. M. (1940), The Preoedipal Phase of the Libido Development. *Psa. Quart.*, IX.
Freud, A. (1936), *The Ego and the Mechanisms of Defence*. New York: International Universities Press, 1946.
—— and Burlingham, D. (1943), *War and Children*. New York: International Universities Press.
Freud, S. (1908), The Relation of the Poet to Day-Dreaming. *Collected Papers*, IV. London: Hogarth Press, 1925.
—— (1909), Analysis of a Phobia in a Five-Year-Old Boy. *Collected Papers*, III. London: Hogarth Press, 1925
—— (1930), *Civilization and Its Discontents*. London: Hogarth Press.
Fraiberg, S. (1952), A Critical Neurosis in a Two-and-a-Half-Year-Old Girl. *This Annual*, VII.
Glover, E. (1931), Sublimation, Substitution and Social Anxiety. In: *On the Early Development of Mind*. New York: International Universities Press, 1956.
Harries, M. (1952), Sublimation in a Group of Four-Year-Old Boys. *This Annual*, VII.
Hartmann, H. (1948), Comments on the Psychoanalytic Theory of Instinctual Drives. *Psa. Quart.*, XVII.
—— (1952), The Mutual Influences in the Development of Ego and Id. *This Annual*, VII.
—— (1955), Notes on the Theory of Sublimation. *This Annual*, X.
Kestenberg, J. S. (1953), Notes on Ego Development. *Int. J. Psa.*, XXXIV.
Kris, E. (1952), *Psychoanalytic Explorations in Art*. New York: International Universities Press.
—— (1955), Neutralization and Sublimation. *This Annual*, X.
Lantos, B. (1955), On the Motivation of Human Relationships. *Int. J. Psa.*, XXXVI.
Panel on Sublimation (1955), reported by J. A. Arlow. *J. Am. Psa. Assoc.*, III.
Peller, L. E. (1954), Libidinal Phases, Ego Development, and Play. *This Annual*, IX.
Sterba, R. (1930), Zur Problematik der Sublimierungslehre. *Int. Ztschr. Psa.*, XVI.
Waelder, R. (1932), The Psychoanalytic Theory of Play. *Psa. Quart.*, II.
—— (1939), Psychological Aspects of War and Peace. *Geneva Studies*, X.

ANALYSIS OF A JUVENILE POEM[1]

MARTHA WOLFENSTEIN, Ph.D. (New York)

I wish to analyze here a poem written by an adolescent. The poem is one by A. E. Housman, which he wrote in his fifteenth year. He produced it for a play on which he and his younger brothers and sisters were collaborating: The Tragedy of Lady Jane Grey. It was a song to be sung by Lady Jane in prison while she awaited execution.[2] I shall try to show how many major fantasies of Housman's were involved in this poem, what their sources were in his life, and to what extent they anticipate A Shropshire Lad, as well as other later poems. Let me, however, first briefly indicate the main formative events of Housman's early years.

I

Alfred Housman (born March 26, 1859) was the eldest of seven children.[3] Four of his younger brothers and sisters were born before he had reached the age of five. He claimed that he could remember the baptism of his brother Robert when he was two, and that this had revived in him the memory of his own baptism. During the ceremony the thought had struck him: "But this is something I've seen before; only then they were doing it to me" (L. Housman, 1938, p. 20). This, which we may take as a screen memory, probably has condensed in it a great many early experiences, where the eldest child, so quickly superseded, had to watch his mother doing things for the younger ones which had briefly been his prerogatives. He must have felt great resentment toward his mother and strong aggressive feelings toward the little brothers and sisters, but there

[1] This paper is part of a study now in preparation on the life and work of A. E. Housman.

[2] See L. Housman (1938, pp. 37-38; 1937, pp. 100-101) and Symons (1937, p. 20).

[3] Biographical data are drawn from the sources already cited, and Mrs. E. W. Symons' (Kathrine E. Symons) introduction to Grant Richards' Housman: 1897-1936 (1942). The latter volume also contains a family chart drawn up by Housman. The younger Housman children, with their birth dates, are: Robert (August 30, 1860), Clemence (November 23, 1861), Katharine (December 10, 1862), Basil (January 16, 1864), Laurence (July 18, 1865), Herbert (July 19, 1868).

is evidence (some of which I shall bring out presently) that these hostile impulses were strenuously fought down.

Housman's mother died on his twelfth birthday. It seems likely that he mistook her last illness for another pregnancy. In his later poetry, death is recurrently associated with birth, sex, and love. While these are common associations, they probably gained uncommon intensity in one who had not only seen his mother undergo the pains of birth so many times (as was customary in Victorian households, the children were born at home), but whose fate it was to have his mother die on his birthday.

The depressive tendencies, derived from Housman's early disappointments, which I shall not elaborate further here, were confirmed by his mother's death: he seems to have mourned her all his life. His father was of quite a different disposition. Not inclined to be long cast down, he married again a little over two years later. His second wife, Lucy Housman, was a first cousin.

Not long after his mother's death, Alfred instituted the custom of collaborating on literary productions with his brothers and sisters. These younger children seem to have been greatly under the sway of their admired and rather imperious older brother. The various games, literary or otherwise, in which he was the leader held much fascination for them. The series of communal literary activities began with his ordering them to produce a poem, with a stanza by each, on Death. The contribution of Laurence, the second youngest, has been recorded: "Death is a dreadful thought,/ And every person ought/ To think of it with reverence/ Before they go forever hence" (Symons, 1937, pp. 17-18). Alfred and the grownups had a good laugh over it. Thus the older boy found an escape from his solitary brooding in making the younger children occupy themselves with the same themes, as a literary exercise, and discovered a way of turning grief into laughter by displacing emphasis from the subject to the unintentionally comic qualities of the children's style. There were also other occasions when the poems undertaken were meant to be comic.

Alfred frequently contributed to these joint literary productions (though he had not participated in producing the poem on Death), and entered poems of his own in the family competitions for which he would set the subjects (the younger children sometimes suspecting that he had prepared his own poem in advance) (ibid., p. 18). Here he was apparently seeking to establish that community of daydreams which reduces guilt (Sachs, 1942). Not only did Alfred mingle his own productions with those of his brothers and sisters, he also sometimes foisted his work on them. According to Laurence's reconstruction of a childhood incident which he did not quite understand at the time, Alfred, who had written a sonnet which he did not think good enough for him but did not want to suppress entirely, got together with Laurence and told him that he (Laurence) was to write a sonnet. Alfred then proceeded to extract from his brother by questions and suggestions the text which he had already formulated (asking him, for instance, for the name of a waterfowl, rejecting "duck" and "goose," and giving his approval when Laurence finally came up with "swan") so that the younger boy thought the poem was his own. As Laurence puts it in retrospect: "He had a tough task, stuffing it down my throat and getting it out again" (L. Housman, 1937, p. 20). Here, besides sharing responsibility, Alfred was acting out certain fantasies: one of poetic inspiration as a penetration of the throat, another of delegating to a brother the execution of important wishes. I shall go into both these fantasies more later on.

Shortly following their father's remarriage the Housman children, as always under the direction of Alfred, put on a parody of *Hamlet* with Alfred in the title role. It is not hard to see the association between their own family history and that of the play: "The funeral baked meats did coldly furnish forth the marriage tables." And the marriage of first cousins might well be considered incestuous. The comic treatment, of course, helped to ward off and to master the painful feelings connected with these themes. In one of the lines recorded by Laurence, Alfred in killing Polonius cried: "A rat, a rat, my kingdom for a rat!" (L. Housman, 1938, p. 37).

About the same time, Laurence began composing a play in verse about the death of Lady Jane Grey. When Alfred discovered this, he immediately took it over, decreeing that each of the children should write a scene, and announcing that he would take the role of Bloody Mary (L. Housman, 1937, pp. 100-101; 1938, pp. 37-38). While this play was never completed, it was in preparation for it that Alfred composed the poem which I shall analyze here, the only part of the play which seems to have been preserved. His sister Clemence was working on the scene of Lady Jane in prison on the eve of her execution. She had the thought that it would be fitting to have her heroine sing a song during this scene, and she asked Alfred to write it for her. Thus in the accustomed context of shared responsibility for literary productions, Alfred was able to write in the character of a young queen about to die, and to express what I would take to be some of his central adolescent fantasies.

Before coming to the poem itself, let me remark on the appeal of this episode in English history for the Housman children. In the background of the story is Henry VIII, who married so often, and killed so many of his wives. In the foreground is Bloody Mary, who succeeded Lady Jane as queen, and whose possession of the throne was made secure by Lady Jane's death. These events correspond to what must have been two of the main fantasies of the Housman children about their mother's death: either father (the king who married so often) killed her, or the stepmother (the new queen) disposed of her predecessor. That Housman's mother's name had been Sarah Jane no doubt contributed to the selection of Lady Jane to represent her.

II

Here is the song of Lady Jane Grey in prison, which the adolescent Alfred Housman composed (L. Housman, 1938, p. 38):

> Breathe, my lute, beneath my fingers
>   One regretful breath,
> One lament for life that lingers
>   Round the doors of death.
> For the frost has killed the rose,
> And our summer dies in snows,
>   And our morning once for all
>   Gathers to the evenfall.
>
> Hush, my lute, return to sleeping,
>   Sing no songs again.
> For the reaper stays his reaping
>   On the darkened plain;
> And the day has drained its cup,
> And the twilight cometh up;
>   Song and sorrow all that are
>   Slumber at the even-star.

It is, I think, a rather lovely poem. The already accomplished craftsmanship of the young poet has achieved a gently sad, melodious effect. The words, however, which go with this pleasing sound speak not only of regret and sorrow but of death and killing. Beneath the graceful façade of the lady singing to the accompaniment of her lute there is the foreboding of imminent fatality.

Anticipation of death was to be a major preoccupation of Housman's later poetry. More than half the poems of A Shropshire Lad contain this theme. If we consider the setting of the drama for which this early poem was intended, the situation is a special instance of anticipation of death, that of one awaiting execution. This theme also reappears in Housman's later work: he imagines himself watching through the night while a friend in jail awaits execution the next morning (ASL IX). In "The

Carpenter's Son" he makes Jesus, about to be executed, speak ironically, warning others against coming to such a bad end (*ASL* XLVII). In "The Culprit" a man about to be hanged blames his father and his mother for his fate (*Last Poems* XIV). "Eight O'Clock" deals with the sounding of the hour when a hanging is to take place (*LP* XV).

In the Tragedy of Lady Jane Grey it is a woman who is about to submit to the executioner. This subjection of a woman to a man's violence recalls another, common theme of childhood fantasy, and one which again occupied Housman in his later poems: that of the sexual act between the parents as a sadistic attack of the father. This is expressed most forcefully in a poem called "The Welsh Marches" where, by putting the union of his parents in the historical setting of the Saxon invasion, he associates it with violent death and rape.

> Ages since the vanquished bled
> Round my mother's marriage bed
> .　　　.　　　.　　　.
> Couched upon her brother's grave
> The Saxon got me on the slave.
> (*ASL* XXVIII)

Housman's poetry abounds in images of the primal scene, though often more disguised than this one, evoking "Horror and scorn and hate and fear and indignation—" (*ASL* XLVIII) as well as feelings of painful helplessness at not being able to interrupt it (one of the determinants of his recurrent theme of the futility of trying to save).

It seems likely that Lady Jane about to face the brutal headsman signified in Alfred's imagination his mother about to submit to his father's attack. Perhaps Lady Jane's executioner was condensed in fantasy with the background figure of Henry VIII, the king who killed his wives. Such images of the sadistic primal scene are of course very common. They perhaps gained, as I have suggested, more than usual hold on the imagination of Housman because of his mother's early death which followed on what seemed to be an incessant series of pregnancies.

If we supply the latent meaning of a sexual consummation to the encounter of Lady Jane with her executioner, we find a parallel to another later poem, "The True Lover" (*ASL* LIII), in which a young man cuts his own throat before going to join his beloved: his first amorous embrace will be his last, and the fulfillment of his love will coincide with his death. Here we have the substitution of a man for a woman as the one who dies (as also in the later poems about execution). Although the True Lover has a partner, a cruel woman whom he reproaches for having precipitated his death, in effect he enacts himself both roles in the sadistic primal scene: he is the one who wields the lethal instrument and the one who is penetrated by it.

In "The Welsh Marches," which I have already quoted, Housman expresses the sense of being both the brutal conqueror, the father, and his victim, the mother:

> None will part us, none undo,
> The knot that makes one flesh of two,
>
> . . . .
>
> When shall I be dead and rid
> Of the wrong my father did?
> How long, how long, till spade and hearse
> Put to sleep my mother's curse?
>
> (*ASL* XXVIII)

Thus he is haunted by the sadistic primal scene, identified with both participants, at the same time that he finds both positions unbearable.

There is another, related theme in Housman's poetry in which love and death are associated with more manifestly positive feelings. This is the theme of dying for a beloved person. To take one of numerous expressions of this (from the posthumously published *Additional Poems*):

> I shall not die for you
> Another fellow may;
>
> . . . .
>
> For I was luckless aye
> And shall not die for you.
>
> (*AP* XX)

This wish to die for the one he loves (frequently combined as here with the regretful acknowledgment that he cannot do so) would seem to express in part the wish to die trying to save mother from father. Partly it may express inverted oedipal strivings: to die as he imagined mother did for father's sexual pleasure. A variant of mother's dying for father is exemplified in the lines from Euripides' *Alcestis* exalting the queen who died to save her lord, one of the few passages of Greek poetry which Housman chose to translate. (A further motive behind the fantasy of dying for another would be that of saving the other person from his own destructive impulses by turning them back against himself.)

III

In writing the song of Lady Jane Grey, the young Housman was, I think, putting himself in the place of his mother about to go to her love-death with his father. The importance of this fantasy for him is attested by his life history, both earlier and later, as well as by his poetry. However, it does not preclude his having imagined himself in other roles in the drama. He had originally intended to take the part of Bloody Mary. This role no doubt had multiple appeals. In other joint literary productions he had written the part of the murderer of the character portrayed by a brother. Thus in a collaborative novel, for which Laurence had provided a curate with a beautiful long beard, Alfred improvised the character of the villain who would strangle the curate by winding that beard around his neck (L. Housman, 1937, p. 100). Bloody Mary's situation in life had certain resemblances to Housman's own. She was the eldest child of a father who put her mother aside in favor of another wife; and she was herself superseded by younger rivals. But I would suppose that on a less conscious level Bloody Mary was again the mother attacked, made bloody, destroyed by the father. This presumption that the roles of Lady Jane and Bloody Mary coincide seems borne out by a piece of humorous verse which Housman wrote years later, in which a woman who is cut to pieces has the name of Mary Jane. This was intended as a parody on the Salvation Army:[4]

> 'Hallelujah!' was the only observation
> That escaped Lieutenant-Colonel Mary Jane,
> As she tumbled off the platform in the station,
> And was cut in little pieces by the train . . .

Lieutenant-Colonel Mary Jane differs from Lady Jane mainly in her absurdly euphoric feelings about being cut up; though the manifestly inappropriate affect, which produces a comic impression, may correspond to a real, but deeply unconscious emotion. In this case, it would be the expectation of overwhelming pleasure in the sadistic attack of the father.

Attempting to reconstruct the development which led the adolescent Housman to imagine himself in his mother's place, let us look back to the initial oedipal period in his life. I would suppose that when he entered it his aggressive impulses were already excessively interfered with. He had had much occasion for rage against the mother who had given birth to so many more babies in such quick succession, and at these

[4] L. Housman (1938, pp. 59, 133). These verses were enclosed in a letter to Housman's stepmother around 1897. Housman from boyhood on produced humorous verse for family consumption.

younger children who supplanted him. But he had also felt that this anger was extremely dangerous, as wounding to his mother and as threatening to alienate her from him. Laurence Housman, in his autobiography (1937, p. 36), recalls his mother's particularly impressive way of arousing guilt for unkindness to a brother. The recently published fragments from Housman's notebooks contain a piece which bears on the same point:[5]

> If you'll be good to one another,
>   That's the coin would pay me best;
> But if man still must hate his brother,
>   Hate away, lads, I will rest.

I think we may hear in this an echo of the mother's reproaches for the fights and quarrels between the brothers, and the overt or covert threat that she would just as soon be dead if they could only be so hateful to each other.

The aggressive impulses of the oedipal phase probably evoked exceptional distress and alarm in Alfred because of the great conflicts about such motives in the preceding years.[6] In consequence the impulse to contend with the father and the aspiration to take his place could not develop fully. I believe that a major oedipal fantasy of his was one in which he delegated the killing of the father to a younger brother—an Ivan-Smerdyakov fantasy (as elaborated in *The Brothers Karamazov*). This is expressed in a complicated poem (which I shall not otherwise analyze here), "Hell Gate" (*LP* XXXI), in which a comrade with whom the speaker of the poem communicates only by looks is emboldened to kill the "father" and lord of the underworld. Underlying the song of Lady Jane Grey there were varied and conflicting feelings of the young Housman toward his father. That this fantasy of renouncing the role of oedipal hero to a brother was one of them is suggested by distinctive analogous phrases in the song of Lady Jane and "Hell Gate": "doors of death" and "gate of hell." (In an early draft of the latter poem there was also the phrase "doorway of the lost" [Haber, 1955, p. 116].) These related phrases are practically unique to these two poems.[7]

---

[5] See Haber (1955, p. 67). The fragments in this volume, such as the one quoted, were not considered as having sufficient literary merit for publication either by Housman himself or by his brother Laurence as his literary executor.

[6] Cf. Phyllis Greenacre's remarks (1955, p. 217) about similar difficulties in the emotional development of Lewis Carroll.

[7] The only other occurrence of a like phrase is the ironical use of "at death's door" in speaking of the condition of the lover brought low by pangs of love: "If at death's own door he lies,/Maiden you can heal his ail." (*ASL* VI). *A Concordance to the Poems of A. E. Housman,* compiled and edited by Clyde Kenneth Hyder (1940), lists the lines in which each word used by Housman occurs in his poems.

We have seen that the father of the fantasied sadistic primal scene aroused feelings of horror and indignation in Housman, combined with a sense of incapacity to interfere. In the complex of his positive and negative oedipal feelings there was also some contempt and mockery of the father. In a school prize poem on Sir Walter Raleigh (L. Housman, 1938, p. 30), which he wrote at about the same time as the song of Lady Jane Grey, he inveighed against James I as:

> A King who sought the land to bind
> Down to the meanness of his mind,
> A man to coming times exempt
> From every feeling but contempt.

It seems likely that the adolescent Housman, with a dawning awareness of his own superior intellectual powers (he was by then carrying off most of the prizes at school), had some sense of surpassing his father. That the father had nothing like the gifts of his eldest son is implied in the succinct remark of Housman's sister about him: "Mentally, his great abilities were probably derived from his mother" (Symons, 1937, p. 9). The little that is said about their father by Housman's sister and brother in their various memoirs suggests a good-natured, absent-minded, optimistic, and garrulous man, who was unsuccessful in his profession of country solicitor. He is described by the sister as "a man of many hobbies —too many," ranging from horticulture to fireworks; and she adds that all the children except Alfred participated in these varied activities with him (Symons, 1937, p. 12). Alfred Housman's character developed to be strikingly opposite to his father's.[8] That this rather scatter-brained and undistinguished father offered numerous points for criticism and mockery to his exceptionally gifted eldest son did not, however, weaken the earlier image of the violently overpowering father, nor did it reduce the son's attachment to the father seen as a diminished and rather silly figure. There is not space here to document these points fully.[9] However, let me

---

[8] To cite only one instance of this extreme contrast, while the father scattered his energies among his numerous hobbies, the son was later to impose on himself the strictest concentration. Thus he gave up his work in Greek scholarship to devote himself exclusively to Latin. "He was once asked why, when his early work had been so impartially distributed between the two languages, he had ceased to write about Greek; his reply was 'I found that I could not attain to excellence in both'" (Gow, 1936, p. 15).

[9] It was Housman's inability to take his father's place when he was later called upon to do so that precipitated the major tragedy of his life. At the time when he was about to take his final examinations at Oxford, he heard that his father was very ill and not expected to live. The family looked to him, the eldest son, who had shown so much promise, to pursue as quickly as possible a prosperous career; and, the family fortunes

recall the line from his parody of Hamlet in which Alfred, stabbing Polonius, cried: "A rat, a rat, my kingdom for a rat!" There in the guise of a joke (in which the contemptible rat is condensed with the more noble animal invoked by the dying Richard III), the young Housman expressed his longing for his father, however devalued.

I would suppose that following his mother's death, Alfred turned with intense feeling toward his father, with the unconscious wish to take his mother's place. This reaction was prepared for in part by the weakened form of his original positive oedipus strivings which I have indicated, partly by tendencies already present and now strengthened to identify with his mother. It would seem that in his early efforts to master his hostility toward his younger brothers, Alfred assumed something of his mother's attitude toward them. This is reflected in the recurrent expressions of good-will, understanding and compassion for younger "lads" in his later poems. The tendency to identify with his mother gained in strength after her death. The common mechanism of internalizing a lost love object was reinforced by feelings of guilt toward her and the judgment that he deserved to undergo a fate like hers. The mother's death must have roused self-reproaches for early hostility toward her and particularly the idea that unkindness to his brothers could lead to the loss of the mother. Further he may have believed that his own birth had damaged her irreparably. He must have heard it told that his birth had been a particularly difficult one (L. Housman, 1938, p. 19). That his mother died on his birthday may well have seemed a confirmation of this connection. The fantasy that he must die in turn in giving birth is expressed in "The Immortal Part" (ASL XLIII):

> 'Tis that every mother's son
> Travails with a skeleton.
>
> Lie down in the bed of dust;
> Bear the fruit that bear you must.

---

being at low ebb, to provide for the schooling of his younger brothers (Symons, Introduction to Richards' Housman, p. xiv). Housman's biographers have been understandably puzzled as to why this brilliant student, who was later to become one of the foremost classical scholars of his time, failed his final examinations at Oxford. I believe that it was because of his inability to accept the role of head of the family which was about to be thrust upon him. Ironically, his father did not die at that time. Housman paid a crushing price for his examination failure. Excluded from an academic career, he was forced to take a job as a clerk in H.M. Patent Office, where he remained for ten years. By producing classical studies at the same time, he managed to establish himself sufficiently to gain an appointment as professor at University College, London. But it was almost twenty years more before he attained a position appropriate to his gifts and accomplishments, as professor of Latin in Trinity College, Cambridge.

The skeleton may be taken to be the internalized mother; by a reversal he must bring her to birth and in so doing die.

We may suppose that Alfred also felt impelled for a number of reasons to turn toward his father for love. His early disappointments with his mother, who was so soon nursing another baby, may well have impelled him to seek gratification instead from his father who, according to Laurence's recollection (1938, p. 22), had as a distinctive trait the generous giving of sweets to the children. In addition to the weakening of aggressive positive oedipal strivings, which I have already suggested, another factor would seem to have weighted the balance toward an inverted oedipus. A sister had been born when Alfred was two and a half, and another a year later. They seem to have inspired him with a horror and disgust which was to be transformed in later years into a mocking contempt for their sex.[10]

The tendencies to identify with his mother and to turn to his father for love were, as we have seen, given increased impetus by his mother's death. His emerging adolescent sexual impulses were the more strongly invested with sadomasochistic imagery through his mother's death coming at just this time. His sense of grief and loss, his longing for love, his identification with his dead mother, his fantasies of retribution and death, of the love act as one in which the father had destroyed the mother, his love for his father all combined in the fantasy of himself as a young queen about to go to her execution. The decapitation may be taken as standing for castration, the price that must be paid for becoming the object of the father's love.

IV

The intensity of Alfred's regret that he could not take his mother's place with his widowed father, and that his father took a second wife instead, is reflected in a poem of later years, "Epithalamium." This was written on an occasion which repeated the ordeal of having to resign his claims to a beloved man in favor of a woman. The one great friend of

---

10 Housman's sister Katharine remarks with evident feeling on his readiness to "belittle the opposite sex because he felt himself superior—very often quite untruly" (Symons, Introduction to Richards' *Housman*, p. xiv). Richards, Housman's devoted publisher, demurs at a statement that Housman hated women, but acknowledges that one might say "he had a real contempt for the sex" (1942, p. 309).

The phrases "doors of death" and "gate of hell" (in the song of Lady Jane Grey and "Hell Gate") may be taken as signifying, among other things, the female genitals. This horror of the female was, however, largely transmuted into mockery. The words "sister" and "daughter" appear only in Housman's humorous verse, in contrast to "brother" and "son" which, with one exception, occur only in his serious verse (Hyder, 1940).

Housman's life, and apparently the one person outside his family whom he ever greatly loved, was Moses Jackson, whom he met as a student at Oxford (L. Housman, 1938, pp. 43, 56; Richards, 1942, pp. 306-307). Housman's "Epithalamium" (*LP* XXIV) commemorates the marriage of this friend:

> Friend and comrade yield you o'er
> To her who hardly loves you more.

This poem is linked to the song of Lady Jane Grey, written so shortly after the father's remarriage, by similar passages about the evening star. The word "even-star" occurs only in the song of Lady Jane Grey, its counterpart "Hesper" only in "Epithalamium" of all of Housman's poems (Hyder, 1940). In the song of Lady Jane:

> Song and sorrow all that are
> Slumber at the even-star.

In "Epithalamium":

> All whom morning sends to roam,
> Hesper loves to lead them home.
> Home return who him behold,
> Child to mother, sheep to fold,
> Bird to nest from wandering wide:

This latter passage is modeled on a parallel one of Sappho's.[11] When at fourteen Housman wrote the lines about the even-star, he had probably not read Sappho, but the emotional connotations were similar. Perhaps in the later poem Sappho as a participant in responsibility for the feelings expressed replaced his sister Clemence who was his partner in originating the earlier poem. There was equally a male partner in both cases, his brother Laurence in the first, and Catullus in the second, one of whose Epithalamia,[12] written on the marriage of a close friend, provided the model for the opening of Housman's.

I should like to add a further point about the impact of his father's second marriage on Housman's development. The father, as I have mentioned, took as his second wife a first cousin whose family name was also Housman. The young Housman must have felt, I think, that in making such a marriage his father failed to exemplify in his own behavior the law of renunciation of incestuous objects. This probably made some contribution to Housman's frequently expressed sentiment that the

[11] G. B. A. Fletcher, Notes on Housman's Poetry, in Richards (1942, p. 406).
[12] *Ibid*. The source is Catullus lxi.

powers that rule the world are immoral—as when he speaks of "Whatever brute or blackguard made the world" (*LP* IX) or says of both God and man, "Their deeds I judge and much condemn" (*LP* XII). The failure of the father as an external authority led, I believe, to a defensive reinforcement of internal moral sanctions, with the result that residual positive oedipus strivings were still further repressed.

V

Returning to the tragedy of Lady Jane Grey, I should like to pursue the theme of the manner in which she died. I have mentioned before Housman's preoccupation with death being brought about by the throat being cut, or by hanging. In a similar way he speaks of strangling in "The Welsh Marches" (*ASL* XXVIII), which I have already quoted in part. Expressing the torment of his identification with both parents in the sadistic primal scene:

> None will part us, none undo
> The knot that makes one flesh of two,
> Sick with hatred, sick with pain,
> Strangling—When shall we be slain?

As I have suggested, the fantasy of an attack on the throat would seem to be related to the wish to take the passive role in relation to the father, representing castration by displacement upward. A circumstance which no doubt contributed to Housman's choice of the throat as peculiarly vulnerable was the fact that his brother Robert, who was next to him in age, suffered from severe asthma (Symons, 1937, p. 7).

In telling of the time when he wrote the greater part of *A Shropshire Lad*, Housman described the sense of almost continuous agitation which possessed him, the feeling of physical illness, and in particular the symptom of a "relaxed sore throat."[13] In later years when at a dinner party a lady asked him when more of his poems might be expected, he replied: "When next I have a relaxed sore throat" (Richards, 1942, p. 322). I shall not here go into the various other accompaniments of Housman's poetic inspiration. I only wish to connect up the sore throat which went with the writing of *A Shropshire Lad* and the theme of the execution of

---

[13] "My poetry, so far as I could make out, sprang chiefly from physical conditions, such as a relaxed sore throat during my most prolific period, the first five months of 1895" (quoted in Richards, 1942, p. 271). Cf. A. E. Housman (1950, p. 48) and Percy Withers (1940, pp. 21-22). Withers, a rare recipient of Housman's confidence, says, "He told me what *A Shropshire Lad* had cost him. . . . He told me he could never face such self-immolation again."

Lady Jane Grey. At the time of writing the song before death of Lady Jane, the adolescent Housman unconsciously longed for a love-death at his father's hands, while he also felt that he had lost his father through the father's remarriage. The one period of intense and protracted poetic inspiration in Housman's life, that in which most of the poems of *A Shropshire Lad* were written, followed almost immediately after the death of his father.[14] We may recall in this connection that a major underling fantasy in inspiration appears to be that of being possessed by the father (Kris, 1939). Housman's internalization of his dead father seems to have assumed the guise of a fulfillment of his adolescent longings, including the attack on the throat, probably associated among other things with oral impregnation. The term "relaxed" as applied to the sore throat suggests an opening up or loosening. The fantasied penetration of the throat would seem not only to have injured it but to have released something. I will only mention here in passing that Housman from his later adolescence on showed a formidable taciturnity.[15] The flow of words in the brief period of concentrated poetic production contrasted indeed with his usual condition.

The fantasy of internalization of a loved man via the throat is expressed in a later poem which is linked to that of Lady Jane Grey through repeated references to breathing (Breathe, my lute, beneath my fingers/ One regretful breath). A posthumously published poem (*More Poems* XIII) begins:

> I lay me down and slumber
> And every morn revive.
> Whose is the night-long breathing
> That keeps me man alive?

and ends by acknowledging:

> My kind and foolish comrade
> That breathes all night for me.

[14] Housman's father died at the end of November, 1894. According to Housman's own account his most intensive period of poetic activity was during the first five months of 1895 (Richards, 1942, p. 271).

[15] Symons (1937, p. 30); Withers (1940, pp. 22-25, 37-38, 50-52, 54). That Housman also had great difficulty in putting words on paper is expressed in a letter to Withers, explaining that he writes very infrequently because "I hate it. Like Miss Squeers, I am screaming out loud all the time I write, which takes off my attention rather and I hope will excuse mistakes" (Withers, p. 73). Similarly in renouncing the office of public orator, which was offered to him in Cambridge in later years, he wrote: "You none of you have any notion what a slow and barren mind I have, nor what a trouble composition is to me (in prose, I mean: poetry is either easy or impossible)" (Housman, 1938, p. 109).

Here is a fantasy of being united with the beloved man by a kind of respiratory incorporation,[16] where the meaning of having the throat penetrated has shifted from that of being slain to that of being saved. The state accompanying inspiration, with its soreness and release, would seem to combine both these meanings.[17]

VI

In the song of Lady Jane Grey, the young queen addresses her lute, with which she plays, lamenting her imminent death. Then as it becomes evening she sadly puts her lute aside, bidding it be quiet and sleep. I would suggest that Lady Jane and her lute represent the mother and her child. The mother plays with her child as evening draws near; she is sad knowing that she will soon have to part with the child and go to her love-death with the father.

Where someone is commanded to sleep or be still in Housman's later poems the predominant significance is that he should not wake to see or rage against the primal scene, or that he is exempted from trying to prevent this atrocity. So, for example, where a dead lover has been replaced in the arms of his sweetheart by his friend, he is told, "Be still, my lad, and sleep" (ASL XXVII). In a poem beginning "Wake not for the world-heard thunder," written just after his sixty-third birthday (he had then attained the age corresponding to that at which his father died, and so felt that his life had reached its end), Housman addresses himself as dead. The scene is one of carnage, an imagined invasion of England (cf. "The Welsh Marches"), but he is exempt from trying to save the mother country from the invader: "Sleep, my lad; the French are landed/ London's burning, Windsor's down"—(LP XXIX).

In a humorous variant of the theme of getting the intrusive child out of the way, called "Fragment of an English Opera," a father and mother insist with increasing impatience that their resistant daughter should go to bed. The girl appears disoriented ("Are you my mother?") and depressed ("Would I were dead!"). When she has finally gone off, father and mother exclaim together: "The coast is clear" (L. Housman, 1938, pp. 242-244). Here, in contrast to more serious treatments of this subject, the mother is no less implicated than the father in wanting to dispose of the child. We might say that in Housman's variations on this theme, the

---

16 Cf. Fenichel (1931).

17 In a recent paper, Hanna Segal (1955) stresses the interplay of destructive and restitutive tendencies in artistic activity.

degree of inculpation of the mother (as in the case of Hamlet's mother) remains uncertain. But she is not wholly free from reproach.

The child being put to sleep has also the more sinister meaning of its being put to death. In Housman's later poetry the word "sleep" is used to mean "death" in the great majority of instances (secondarily it includes death within a range of other meanings—as in "'Oh who would not sleep with the brave?" [*LP* VI]; and in only a few places, usual nocturnal sleep [Hyder, 1940]). A significant instance of someone's having been put to death before the parents come together has already been cited (*ASL* XXVIII):

> Couched upon her brother's grave
> The Saxon got me on the slave.

This is one of two instances in all of Housman's poems in which the crucial word "brother" occurs (Hyder, 1940). Since there does not seem to have been a maternal uncle who played any role in Housman's life, I would take "her brother's" to mean "my brother's." I believe this then constitutes another of Housman's basic fantasies: that of his parents putting his little brother to death before having intercourse. Perhaps the new baby used to sleep close to the mother's bed, thus replacing the older brother but at the same time being exposed to terrible danger as a potential disturber of the primal scene. I have already suggested how Housman was inclined to imagine a brother as a surrogate for himself in the oedipal situation. The brother may in this way become the killer of the father, as in "Hell Gate," or as here the father's victim. The image of the dead brother beside the parental bed appears elsewhere in more disguised form. I would take the lines "And the Nile spills his overflow/ Beside the Severn's dead" (*ASL* I) in this sense. The soldiers from his native countryside who have died to save the Queen represent brothers, while the mighty river spilling over symbolizes the father in the sexual act.

That the brothers who replaced him were not to be envied but commiserated as inheritors of his distress is one of Housman's most recurrent themes. To recall one of many instances (*ASL* LV):

> Now that other lads than I
> Strip to bathe on Severn shore,
> They, no help, for all they try,
> Tread the mill I trod before.

Repeatedly he offers whatever consolation he can to the "luckless lads" who will come after him (*ASL* LXIII). The fantasy of the grim fate of the brother who presumably replaced him in the cot close to his mother's bed is one instance of the effort to persuade himself that a brother is not to be envied. In the fantasy of a brother being killed by the father in the parental bedroom there is also a double delegation of his own motives: the brother must assume the (unsuccessful) oedipal struggle, while the father becomes the agent of his fratricidal impulses.

That brother-killing is another of the covert associations of the song of Lady Jane Grey is suggested by a further verbal analogy. There is a poem in *A Shropshire Lad* in which a rustic youth confesses having murdered his brother (*ASL* VIII); the context is one of mowing a field. The song of Lady Jane refers to reaping. These are the sole occurrences of mowing and reaping in Housman's poetry, except for one other where mowing appears as a metaphor for killing (*LP* XIII) (Hyder, 1940). In the song of Lady Jane the lute (child) is put to sleep (death):

> For the reaper stays his reaping
> On the darkened plain.

In the confession of the brother-murderer (*ASL* VIII):

> The sun burns on the half-mown hill,
> By now the blood is dried;
> And Maurice amongst the hay lies still
> And my knife is in his side.

Thus the fantasy of the parents putting his brother to death underlies Lady Jane's putting her lute to sleep. But we would suppose that on a still deeper level the child being put to death is also himself.[18] Guilt and libidinal strivings combine to impel him into the role of victim. We may recall the words in which Housman expressed the feeling he claimed to remember from when he was two and looked on at the baptism of his brother Robert: "But this is something I've seen before; only then they were doing it to me." He probably often wished for the parental ministrations which his brothers received, whether punitive or gratifying, while his passive tendencies inclined him to imagine punishment itself as pleasure. The fantasy of meeting his own death at his parents' bedside thus reveals the same motive as that of Lady Jane going to her execution: the wish for a love-death at the hands of the father.[19]

18 Cf. Sigmund Freud, "A Child is Being Beaten" (1919).

19 The later poems dealing with execution, which I mentioned previously, may now be partially interpreted. Where the poet watches through the night awaiting the execution of a friend in prison, he is anticipating the brother's being put to death in the parents' bedroom (*ASL* IX). The Carpenter's Son who "hangs for love," in a self-defeating effort to save, because he could not "leave ill alone" is the oedipal hero (brother or self) who succumbs in an effort to interrupt the primal scene (*ASL* XLVII).

VII

Lady Jane and her lute, then, represent mother and child, and the adolescent Housman in his fantasy occupied both roles. But I should like to propose a further prototype of the sad young queen and the lute with which she plays. Playing a musical instrument, like the play involved in games of chance, often symbolizes masturbation (Freud, 1928). In this sense Lady Jane and her lute may stand for the boy and his penis. I would suppose that the song of Lady Jane Grey sprang from a masturbation fantasy and perpetuates the masturbatory act under a disguise in the content of the poem. The fantasy involves love-sex-castration-death in the embrace of the father. Thus Lady Jane playing with and sadly preparing to part from her lute, the mother saying goodnight to her child before going to join the father, correspond to the boy playing with his penis with the frightening, sweet, sad, exciting thought of losing it.

Nocturnal conflicts over forbidden wishes appear in a later poem which shows a connection with the song of Lady Jane in a similar evocation of contrasting feelings of extreme heat and cold. In Lady Jane's song:

> . . . the frost has killed the rose,
> And our summer dies in snows.

The later poem (*ASL* XXX) represents desire and fear as internal sensations of fire and ice.

> Others, I am not the first,
> Have willed more mischief than they durst:
> If in the breathless night I too
> Shiver now, 'tis nothing new.
>
> . . . . . .
>
> And fire and ice within me fight
> Beneath the suffocating night.

The conflicts about masturbation and the accompanying forbidden fantasies would thus seem to be indirectly represented in the song of Lady Jane by the rapid alternations of heat and cold.

In "The Culprit" the execution of the son is again associated with the parents' act of begetting (*LP* XIV). "Eight O'Clock" anticipates in symbolic terms the victim's succumbing to the father's blow: "And then the clock collected in the tower/Its strength, and struck" (*LP* XV). These interpretations are of course summary and incomplete, and there is not space here to substantiate them adequately. I only wanted to give some indication of how they fit in with the complex of fantasies around the execution of Lady Jane Grey.

Pursuing the theme of playing a musical instrument leads to another later poem, the concluding one of *Last Poems*, "Fancy's Knell." There the poet appears as a rustic flutist to whose playing the country folk would pair off in the dance.

> There to the dances
> I fetched my flute and played.
>
> .   .   .   .   .   .
>
> The youth toward his fancy
> Would turn his brow of tan
> And Tom would pair with Nancy
> And Dick step off with Fan.

Here the recurrent wish (that was also often felt to be hopeless) to disturb the primal scene is supplanted by the fantasy of making it happen by his playing—a transformation of passivity into activity on the basis of accepting the inevitable. (Similarly he had composed his "Epithalamium" for the marriage of his best friend.) In "Fancy's Knell" as in the song of Lady Jane Grey the playing is associated with anticipations of the player's death:

> To-morrow, more's the pity,
> Away we both must hie,
> To air the ditty,
> And to earth I.

VIII

In analyzing the song of Lady Jane Grey I have considered the context of the drama for which it was intended (wherein the protagonist faces execution); the content of the poem itself (of Lady Jane playing with her lute and putting it aside); and verbal links between it and later poems of Housman's (as that between "even-star" in the early poem and "Hesper" in "Epithalamium").[20] I have tried to show the contribution

---

[20] As to the use of the kind of content analysis which gives an exact count of how often and where particular words occur, I should like to indicate what my procedure has been in the present study. When I first read the song of Lady Jane Grey I was already familiar with Housman's later poetry, and I was struck by how many echoes (if I may speak anachronistically) this juvenile poem evoked of his later work. For instance, the lines about the "even-star" immediately reminded me of the similar passage about "Hesper" in "Epithalamium." The connection thus established led to the reflection that the two poems referred to similar experiences, of regret at the marriage of a beloved man (his father, his friend). Subsequently, in tracing the fate of each word of Lady Jane's song in Housman's later work, by using Hyder's *Concordance*, I found that "even-star" occurred only in the early poem, "Hesper" uniquely in "Epithalamium." This showed that my connecting of the two passages was not arbi-

of various life experiences to the adolescent fantasies out of which this poem emerged, fantasies which were to find repeated expression in Housman's later poetry. In some cases these fantasies are very common ones, like that of the sadistic primal scene, the mutual involvement of love and death, of love and birth, and dying to save. However, such fantasies assumed peculiar intensity in Housman because of special circumstances in his life. The connection between birth and death, for instance, was confirmed for him with exceptional force by his mother's having died on his twelfth birthday. Other fantasies show a more idiosyncratic quality, as when father and mother are imagined as putting the baby brother to death before they make love. While this may be seen as a variant of "a child is being beaten," the more fatal violence and particularly the connection between the brother's fate and the love-act of the parents seem distinctive. This is related to another fairly exceptional fantasy, in which the role of oedipal hero is delegated to a brother. In the formation of these original fantasies, a major factor would seem to have been Housman's intense involvement with brothers who replaced him before and during the oedipal period. The protracted struggle to master his conflicting feelings toward his brothers is reflected in his later poetry where these lucky fellows become the "luckless lads" whom he wishes to comfort. And indeed his little brothers did also lose the mother, for whose possession he so envied them, by her early death.

IX

The last letter which, shortly before his death, Housman wrote to his brother Laurence closes with a quotation:

> Brightness falls from the air;
> Queens have died young and fair:
> Dust hath closed Helen's eyes.

There follows an indication of the source of the lines (T. Nashe, *In Time of Plague*), which Laurence had requested (L. Housman, 1938, p. 192). Over sixty years had passed since the brothers had collaborated on the

---

trary; there were no other similar passages in other contexts which I had overlooked or forgotten.

As an instance of the idiosyncratic associations which particular words may have for a poet, I should like to cite Housman's use of "sing." This word appears only twice in his poems, once in the song of Lady Jane Grey, the other time in the line " 'God save the Queen' we living sing" (*ASL* I). For Housman apparently "sing" was peculiarly connected with the life and death of a queen.

Tragedy of Lady Jane Grey. The thought of queens who died young and fair was still with them.

BIBLIOGRAPHY

Fenichel, O. (1931), Respiratory Introjection. *Collected Papers*, I. New York: Norton, 1953.

Freud, S. (1919), "A Child Is Being Beaten." *Collected Papers*, II. London: Hogarth Press, 1924.

—— (1928), Dostoevski and Parricide. *Collected Papers*, V. London: Hogarth Press, 1950.

Gow, A. S. F. (1936), *A. E. Housman: A Sketch*. Cambridge: Cambridge University Press.

Greenacre, P. (1955), *Swift and Carroll*. New York: International Universities Press.

Haber, T. B., ed. (1955), *The Manuscript Poems of A. E. Housman*. Minneapolis: University of Minnesota Press.

Housman, A. E. (1950), *The Name and Nature of Poetry*. Cambridge: Cambridge University Press.

Housman, L. (1937), *The Unexpected Years*. London: Jonathan Cape.

—— (1938), *My Brother, A. E. Housman*. New York: Scribners.

Hyder, C. K., ed. (1940), *A Concordance to the Poems of A. E. Housman*. Lawrence, Kansas; University of Kansas.

Kris, E. (1939), On Inspiration. In: *Psychoanalytic Explorations in Art*. New York: International Universities Press, 1952.

Richards, G. (1942), *Housman: 1897-1936*. New York: Oxford University Press.

Sachs, H. (1942), The Community of Daydreams. In: *The Creative Unconscious*. Cambridge, Mass.: Sci-Art Publishers.

Segal, H. (1955), A Psycho-Analytic Approach to Aesthetics. In: *New Directions in Psycho-Analysis*, ed. M. Klein et al. London: Tavistock Publications.

Symons, K. E. et al. (1937), *Alfred Edward Housman: Recollections*. New York: Henry Holt.

Withers, P. (1940), *A Buried Life: Personal Recollections of A. E. Housman*. London: Jonathan Cape.

CONTENTS OF PREVIOUS VOLUMES

VOLUME I

VOLUME II

VOLUME III/IV

VOLUME V

VOLUME VI

VOLUME VII

VOLUME VIII

VOLUME IX